Third Edition

The Leadership Experience

Richard L. Daft

Owen Graduate School of Management
Vanderbilt University

With the assistance
of Patricia G. Lane

THOMSON

SOUTH-WESTERN

Australia · Canada · Mexico · Singapore · Spain · United Kingdom · United States

THOMSON
SOUTH-WESTERN

The Leadership Experience, Third Edition
Richard L. Daft

VP/Editorial Director:
Jack W. Calhoun

VP/Editor-in-Chief:
Mike Roche

Senior Publisher:
Melissa S. Acuña

Acquisitions Editor:
Joe Sabatino

Developmental Editor:
Emma F. Guttler

Marketing Manager:
Jacquelyn Carrillo

Production Editor:
Cliff Kallemeyn

Technology Project Editor:
Kristen Meere

Media Editor:
Karen Schaffer

Senior Design Project Manager:
Michelle Kunkler

Manufacturing Coordinator:
Rhonda Utley

**Production House/
Compositor:**
DPS Associates, Inc.

Printer:
Webcom Limited, Toronto ON

Cover and Internal Design:
Beckmeyer Design
Cincinnati, OH

Cover Image:
© Corbis

For permission to use material
from this text or product, contact
us by
Tel (800) 730-2214
Fax (800) 730-2215
http://www.thomsonrights.com

For more information
contact South-Western,
5191 Natorp Boulevard,
Mason, Ohio 45040.
Or you can visit our Internet site
at http://www.swlearning.com

To the spiritual leaders who shaped my growth and development as a leader and as a human being.

Brief Contents

Contents

Part Five

About the Author

Richard L. Daft, Ph.D., is the Brownlee O. Currey, Jr., Professor of Management in the Owen Graduate School of Management at Vanderbilt University. Professor Daft specializes in the study of leadership, change management, and organization theory, and enjoys applying these ideas in his role as board member and part owner of a company called World Response Group. Dr. Daft is a Fellow of the Academy of Management and has served on the editorial boards of *Academy of Management Journal*, *Administrative Science Quarterly*, and *Journal of Management Education*. He was the Associate Editor-in-Chief of *Administrative Science Quarterly*.

Professor Daft has authored or co-authored 13 books, including *Management* (Thomson Learning/South-Western, 2003), *Organization Theory and Design* (Thomson Learning/South-Western, 2004), and *What to Study: Generating and Developing Research Questions* (Sage, 1982). He recently published *Fusion Leadership: Unlocking the Subtle Forces that Change People and Organizations* (Berrett-Koehler, 2000, with Robert Lengel). He has also published in *Administrative Science Quarterly*, *Academy of Management Journal*, *Journal of Management*, *Accounting Organizations and Society*, *Management Science*, *MIS Quarterly*, *California Management Review*, and *Organizational Behavior Teaching Review*. Professor Daft has been awarded several government research grants to pursue studies of organization design, organizational innovation and change, strategy implementation, and organizational information processing.

Dr. Daft is also an active teacher and consultant. He has taught organization design, management, leadership, change management, organizational behavior, and strategic management. He has been involved in management development and consulting for many companies and government organizations, including the American Banking Association, Bell Canada, National Transportation Research Board, USAA, Nortel, TVA, Pratt & Whitney, State Farm Insurance, Tenneco, the United States Air Force, the U.S. Army, J. C. Bradford & Co., Central Parking System, Entergy Sales and Service, Bristol-Myers Squibb, First American National Bank, and the Vanderbilt University Medical Center.

Preface

My vision for the third edition is to give students an exciting, applied, and comprehensive view of the leadership experience in today's world. The book integrates recent ideas and applications with established scholarly research in a way that makes the topic of leadership come alive. The world of leadership and organizations is undergoing a revolution, and this textbook addresses the qualities and skills leaders need in this rapidly changing world.

Recent ethical scandals, global crises, the emergence of e-commerce, learning organizations, virtual teams, globalization, knowledge work, and other ongoing transformations place new demands on leaders far beyond the topics traditionally taught in courses on management or organizational behavior. My experiences teaching leadership to students and managers, and working with leaders to change their organizations, have affirmed for me the value of traditional leadership concepts, while highlighting the importance of including new ideas and applications.

The Leadership Experience thoroughly covers the history of leadership studies and the traditional theories, but goes beyond that to incorporate valuable ideas such as leadership vision, leading a learning organization, and shaping culture and values. The book expands the treatment of leadership to capture the excitement of the subject in a way that motivates students and challenges them to develop their leadership potential.

New to the Third Edition

A primary focus for revising *The Leadership Experience*, 3rd edition, has been to offer students greater potential for self-assessment and leadership development. An important aspect of learning to be a leader involves looking inward for greater self-understanding. Each chapter of the third edition includes multiple questionnaires or exercises that relate to chapter topics and enable students to learn about their own beliefs, values, competencies, and skills. These exercises help students gauge their current standing and connect the chapter concepts and examples to ideas for expanding their own leadership abilities. A few of the topics covered in these self-assessments are: personal ethical beliefs, listening skills, visionary leadership potential, emotional intelligence, perspectives on change, approaches to motivating others, and using power and influence. In addition, each chapter of *The Leadership Experience*, 3rd edition, has been thoroughly revised and updated. Many topics have been added or expanded to address current issues that leaders face. New material has been added on emotional intelligence, adaptive learning, communication networks, leading virtual and global teams, leadership persuasion and influence, ethical issues of leadership, after-action reviews, electronic communication, leadership crisis communication, strategies for change leadership, and leading for innovation.

Organization

The organization of the book is based on first understanding basic ways in which leaders differ from managers, and the ways leaders set direction, seek alignment between organizations and followers, build relationships, and create change. Thus the organization of this book is in five parts:

1. Introduction to Leadership
2. Research Perspectives on Leadership
3. The Personal Side of Leadership
4. The Leader as Relationship Builder
5. The Leader as Social Architect.

The book integrates materials from both micro and macro approaches to leadership, from both academia and the real world, and from traditional ideas and recent thinking.

Distinguishing Features

This book has a number of special features that are designed to make the material accessible and valuable to students.

In the Lead This book is loaded with new examples of leaders in both traditional and contemporary learning organizations. Each chapter opens with a real-life example that relates to the chapter content, and several additional examples are highlighted within each chapter. These spotlight examples are drawn from a wide variety of organizations including education, the military, government agencies, businesses, and not-for-profit organizations.

Living Leadership Each chapter contains a Living Leadership box that is personal, compelling, real, and inspiring. This box may be a saying from a famous leader, or wisdom from the ages. These Living Leadership boxes provide novel and interesting material to expand the reader's thinking about the leadership experience.

Leader's Bookshelf Each chapter also includes a review of a recent book relevant to the chapter's content. The Leader's Bookshelf connects students to issues and topics being read and discussed in the worlds of academia, business, military, education, and not-for-profit.

Action Memo This margin feature helps students apply the chapter concepts in their own lives and leadership activities.

Leader's Self-Insight These boxes provide self-assessments for learners and an opportunity to experience leadership issues in a personal way. These exercises take the form of questionnaires, scenarios, and activities.

Student Development Each chapter ends with Discussion Questions and then two activities for student development. The first, **Leadership at Work**, is a practical, skill-building activity that engages the student in applying chapter concepts to real-life leadership. These exercises are designed so students can complete them on their own outside of class or in class as part of a group activity. Instructor tips are given for maximizing in-class learning with the Leadership at Work exercises. **Leadership Development: Case for Analysis**, the second end of chapter activity, provides two short, problem-oriented cases for analysis. These cases test the student's ability to apply concepts when dealing with real-life leadership issues. The cases challenge the student's cognitive understanding of leadership ideas while the Leadership at Work exercises and the feedback questionnaire assess the student's progress as a leader.

Ancillaries

This edition offers a wider range of instructor ancillaries than previous editions to fully enable instructors to bring the leadership experience into the classroom. These ancillaries include:

Instructors Manual with Test Bank and Transparency Masters
(ISBN: 0324236379)

A comprehensive Instructor's Manual and Test Bank is available to assist in lecture preparation. Included in the Instructor's Manual are chapter outlines, suggested answers to end of chapter materials, and suggestions for further study. The Test Bank includes approximately 100 questions per chapter to assist in writing examinations. Types of questions include true/false, multiple choice, essay, and matching questions. Fifty Transparency Masters, which contain prominent figures from the text, also are included in the Instructor's Manual.

NEW! Instructor's Resource CD-ROM (ISBN: 0324236387)

Key instructor ancillaries (Instructor's Manual, Test Bank, ExamView and PowerPoint slides) are provided on CD-ROM, giving instructors the ultimate tool for customizing lectures and presentations.

NEW! **ExamView**

Available on the Instructor's Resource CD, ExamView contains all of the questions in the printed test bank. This program is an easy-to-use test creation software compatible with Microsoft Windows. Instructors can add or edit questions, instructions, and answers, and select questions (randomly or numerically) by previewing them on the screen. Instructors can also create and administer quizzes online, whether over the Internet, a local area network (LAN), or a wide area network (WAN).

NEW! **PowerPoint Lecture Presentation**

An asset to any instructor, these lectures provide outlines for every chapter, graphics of the illustrations from the text, and additional examples providing instructors with a number of learning opportunities for students. The PowerPoint Lecture Presentations are available on the IRCD in Microsoft 2000 format and as downloadable files on the text support site.

NEW! **Videos** (ISBN: 0324236417)

Videos compiled specifically to accompany *The Leadership Experience*, 3rd edition, utilize real-world companies to illustrate business and leadership concepts as outlined in the text. Focusing on both small and large businesses, the video gives students an inside perspective on the situations and issues that real corporations face.

NEW! **Companion Web site**

The Leadership Experience's web site at **http://daft.swlearning.com/** provides a multitude of resources. Students can download the PowerPoint presentation slides from the web site, find links to news articles, and investigate hot marketing topics for extra student research. For instructor use only, the downloadable Instructor's Manual and Test Bank files are available in Microsoft Word 2000 format and Adobe Acrobat format. Additionally, downloadable PowerPoint presentation files are available in Microsoft PowerPoint 2000 format.

NEW! **TextChoice: Management Exercises and Cases**

TextChoice is the home of Thomson Learning's online digital content. TextChoice provides the fastest, easiest way for you to create your own learning materials. South-Western's Management Exercises and Cases database includes a variety of experiential exercises, classroom activities, management in film exercises, and cases to enhance any management course. Choose as many exercises as you like and even add your own material to create a supplement tailored to your course. Contact your South-Western/Thomson Learning sales representative for more information.

NEW! eCoursepacks

Create a custom, easy to use, and online companion for any course with eCoursepacks, from Thomson companies South-Western and Gale. eCoursepacks give educators access to content from thousands of current popular, professional, and academic periodicals, as well as NACRA and Darden cases, and business and industry information from Gale. In addition, instructors can easily add their own material with the option of even collecting a royalty. Permissions for all eCoursepack content are already secured, saving instructors the time and worry with securing rights. eCoursepacks online publishing tools also save time and energy by allowing instructors to quickly search the databases to make selections, organize all the content, and publish the final online product in a clean, uniform, and full color format. eCoursepacks are the best way to provide current information quickly and inexpensively. To learn more visit: http://ecoursepacks.swlearning.com

Acknowledgments

Textbook writing is a team enterprise. The book has integrated ideas and support from many people whom I want to acknowledge. I especially thank Bob Lengel, at the University of Texas at San Antonio. Bob's enthusiasm for leadership many years ago stimulated me to begin reading, teaching, and training in the area of leadership development. His enthusiasm also led to our collaboration on the book, *Fusion Leadership: Unlocking the Subtle Forces that Change People and Organizations*. I thank Bob for keeping our shared leadership dream alive, which in time enabled me to pursue my dream of writing this leadership textbook.

Here at Vanderbilt, in my role over the last three years as both a professor and Associate Dean at the Owen School, I want to thank my assistants, Barbara Haselton and May Woods, for the tremendous volume and quality of work they accomplish on my behalf that gives me time to write. Bill Christie, the Dean at Owen, has maintained a positive scholarly atmosphere and supported me with the time and resources needed to complete this book. I also appreciate the intellectual stimulation and support from friends and colleagues at the Owen School—Bruce Barry, Ray Friedman, Neta Moye, Rich Oliver, David Owens, and Bart Victor.

I want to acknowledge the reviewers who provided feedback and a very short turnaround. Their ideas helped me improve the book in many areas. Thanks to Thomas H. Arcy, University of Houston–Central Campus; Janey Ayres, Purdue University; Ron Franzen, Saint Luke's Hospital; Delia J. Haak, John Brown University; Ellen Jordan, Mount Olive College; Richard T. Martin, Washburn University; Chad Peterson, Baylor University; Gordon Riggles, University of Colorado; Mary L. Tucker, Ohio University; Xavier Whitaker, Baylor University; and Jean Wilson, The College of William and Mary.

Also, thanks to the reviewers from the previous two editions: Bill Bommer, Georgia State University; Nell Hartley, Robert Morris College; and Gregory Manora, Auburn University-Montgomery. Shane Spiller, University of Montevallo; Dan Sherman, University of Alabama at Huntsville; Ahmad Tootonchi, Frostburg State University; Bill Service, Samford University; and Ranjna Patel, Bethune Cookman College.

I want to extend special thanks to my editorial associate, Pat Lane. I could not have undertaken this revision without Pat's help. She skillfully drafted materials for the chapters, found original sources, and did an outstanding job with last-minute changes, the copyedited manuscript, art, and galley proofs. Pat's talent and personal enthusiasm for this text added greatly to its excellence.

The editors at South-Western also deserve special mention. Joe Sabatino, Acquisitions Editor, supported the concept for this book and obtained the resources necessary for its completion. Emma Guttler, Developmental Editor, provided terrific support for the book's writing, reviews, copyediting, and production. Cliff Kallemeyn, Production Editor, smoothly took the book through the production process.

Finally, I want to acknowledge my loving family. I received much love and support from my wife, Dorothy Marcic, and daughters, Solange and Elizabeth in college, Roxanne in London, and Amy and Danielle in Texas. I appreciate the good feelings and connections with daughters and grandchildren who live elsewhere. On occasion, we have been able to travel, ski, watch a play, or just be together—all of which reconnect me to things that really count.

Richard L. Daft

Part 1

Introduction to Leadership

What Does It Mean to Be a Leader? 1

Chapter

Your Leadership Challenge

After reading this chapter, you should be able to:

- Understand the full meaning of leadership and see the leadership potential in yourself and others.

- Recognize and facilitate the six fundamental transformations in today's organizations and leaders.

- Identify the primary reasons for leadership derailment and the new paradigm skills that can help you avoid it.

- Recognize the traditional functions of management and the fundamental differences between leadership and management.

- Appreciate the crucial importance of providing direction, alignment, relationships, personal qualities, and outcomes.

- Realize how historical leadership approaches apply to the practice of leadership today.

What Does It Mean to Be a Leader?

When Tom Freston took over as CEO of MTV Networks, Britney Spears was only 5 years old, Eminem was 13, and Sponge Bob Squarepants wasn't even a gleam in someone's creative eye. Freston has kept MTV Networks (the cable empire that includes MTV, Nickelodeon, Nick at Nite, TV Land, VH1, and CMT) consistently successful over 15 years of shifting fashions, musical tastes, entertainment interests, and economic conditions. In 2002, MTV, Nickelodeon, Nick at Nite, and TV Land had their best years ever. "[The success] can't be a coincidence," says Mel Karmazin, president of MTV Networks' parent group Viacom. "It has to be because of the leadership."

Interestingly, when asked about the success of MTV Networks, Freston gives credit to his senior leadership team and his employees rather than accepting all the applause for himself. Freston believes they're the ones who really keep MTV Networks sizzling. He has built a programming powerhouse partly by hiring talented, creative people and giving them the freedom to explore, imagine, make decisions, and become the best they can be. It is Freston, though, who provides the right environment, the vision, and the direction for what MTV Networks can be. His vision is to keep MTV on the cutting edge of popular culture without veering so far that it is perceived as radical. He's built a distinctive corporate culture that reflects shades of his antiestablishment values of the 1960s but also emphasizes keeping pace with current youth social trends and the needs of the business. When business results are less than expected, Freston's demanding side comes out. "He's tough as nails," said one executive. "If you don't perform, he's all over you."

How does Freston keep people performing at their peak and MTV Networks playing the popular-appeal game so well? He says he's just doing what he loves. "If you do something in your life that you really love . . . who wants something more?"[1]

What does it mean to be a leader? For Tom Freston, it means loving what you do and infusing others with energy and enthusiasm. It means creating an inspiring vision and building an environment where people have the ability, the freedom, and the will to accomplish amazing results. You may never have heard of Tom Freston, but almost everyone in the United States–and many other parts of the world–has watched one of the successful cable television channels built on the strength of his leadership.

When we think of leaders in today's world, we often think first of the "big names" in the news–Colin Powell or Jacques Chirac in politics, Oprah Winfrey or Rupert Murdoch in entertainment, Bill Gates in business, former president Jimmy Carter in charitable and social causes. Yet there are leaders working in every organization, large and small. In fact, leadership is all around us every day, in all facets of our lives—our families, schools, communities, churches, social clubs, and volunteer organizations, as well as in the world of business and sports. The qualities that make Tom Freston a good leader can be effective whether one is leading a school, a basketball team, a business, or a family.

The Nature of Leadership

Before we can examine what makes an effective leader, we need to know what leadership means. Leadership has been a topic of interest to historians and philosophers since ancient times, but scientific studies began only in the twentieth century. Scholars and other writers have offered more than 350 definitions of the term *leadership*, and one authority on the subject has concluded that leadership "is one of the most observed and least understood phenomena on earth."[2] Defining leadership has been a complex and elusive problem largely because the nature of leadership itself is complex. Some have even suggested that leadership is nothing more than a romantic myth, perhaps based on the false hope that someone will come along and solve our problems by sheer force of will.[3] There is some evidence that people do pin their hopes on leaders in ways that are not always realistic.For example, some struggling companies recruit well-known, charismatic CEOs and invest tremendous hopes in them, only to find that their problems actually get worse.[4] Particularly when times are tough, people may look to a larger-than-life leader to alleviate fear and uncertainty. In recent years, the romantic or heroic view of leadership has been challenged.[5] Much progress has been made in understanding the essential nature of leadership as a real and powerful influence in organizations and societies.

Definition of Leadership

Leadership studies are an emerging discipline and the concept of leadership will continue to evolve. For the purpose of this book, we will focus on a single definition that delineates the essential elements of the leadership process: Leadership is an influence relationship among leaders and followers who intend real changes and outcomes that reflect their shared purposes.[6]

The key elements in this definition are summarized in Exhibit 1.1. Leadership involves influence, it occurs among people, those people intentionally desire significant changes, and the changes reflect purposes shared by leaders and followers. *Influence* means that the relationship among people is not passive; however, also inherent in this definition is the concept that influence is multidirectional and non-coercive. The basic cultural values in North America make it easiest to think of leadership as something a leader does to a follower.[7] However, leadership is reciprocal. In most organizations, superiors influence subordinates, but subordinates also influence superiors. The people involved in the relationship want substantive *changes*— leadership involves creating change, not maintaining the status quo. In addition, the changes sought are not dictated by leaders but reflect *purposes* that leaders and followers share. Moreover, change is toward an outcome that leader and followers both want, a desired future or shared purpose that motivates them toward this more preferable outcome. An important aspect of leadership is influencing others to come together around a common vision. Thus, leadership involves the influence of people to bring about change toward a desirable future.

Also, leadership is a *people* activity and is distinct from administrative paperwork or planning activities. Leadership occurs *among* people; it is not something done *to* people. Since leadership involves people, there must be *followers*. An individual performer who achieves excellence as a scientist, musician, athlete, or woodcarver may be a leader in her field of expertise, but is not a leader as it is defined in this book unless followers are involved. Followers are an important part

Leadership

an influence relationship among leaders and followers who intend real changes and outcomes that reflect their shared purposes

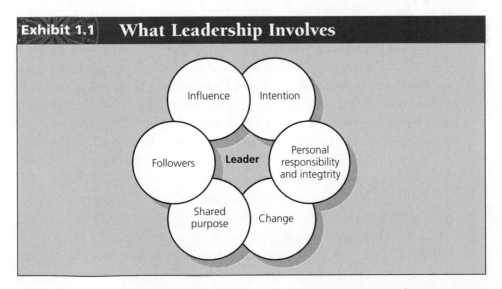

Exhibit 1.1   What Leadership Involves

of the leadership process, and leaders are sometimes followers. Good leaders know how to follow, and they set an example for others. The issue of *intention* or will means that people—leader and followers—are actively involved in the pursuit of change toward a desired future. Each person takes personal responsibility to achieve the desired future.

One stereotype is that leaders are somehow different, that they are above others; however, in reality, the qualities needed for effective leadership are the same as those needed to be an effective follower.[8] Effective followers think for themselves and carry out assignments with energy and enthusiasm. They are committed to something outside their own self-interest, and they have the courage to stand up for what they believe. Good followers are not "yes people" who blindly follow a leader. Effective leaders and effective followers may sometimes be the same people, playing different roles at different times. At its best, leadership is shared among leaders and followers, with everyone fully engaged and accepting higher levels of responsibility.

Leadership and the Business of Living

Think for a moment about someone you personally have known that you would consider a leader—a grandparent, a supervisor, a coach, or even a fellow student. Perhaps you consider yourself a leader, or know that you want to be one. If we stop equating leadership with greatness and public visibility, it becomes easier to see our own opportunities for leadership and recognize the leadership of people we interact with every day. Leaders come in all shapes and sizes, and many true leaders are working behind the scenes. Leadership that has big outcomes often starts small.

❀ Greg Mortenson had a vision that the best way to fight terrorism was by building secular schools and promoting education, especially for girls, in northern Pakistan and neighboring Afghanistan. He wrote nearly 600 letters and submitted 16 grant applications, but received only one favorable reply–a $100 check from Tom Brokaw. Undeterred, Mortenson sold all his possessions and began appealing to everyday people. Schoolchildren donated hundreds of dollars in pennies, inspiring adults to donate as well. With the $12,000 he eventually raised, Mortenson built his first school in Korphe in 1996. Today, he runs the Central Asia Institute, which has completed 28 school buildings, 15 water projects, and 4 women's vocational centers.[9]

❀ Several years ago, hundreds of unarmed residents of an Argentinean farming village stormed the local police station after officials had refused to search for a missing child who was later found by villagers, raped and strangled. The siege ended only when the provincial government agreed to replace the entire police department, with the villagers allowed to name the new chief.[10] The villagers could not have pulled off the siege without leadership, and yet no one stepped forward to claim the title of "leader," and no one was able to specifically state who had provided the leadership for this initiative.

❋ When Jeff Davis moved to Tennessee and offered to volunteer at the Nashville Humane Association, no one ever called him for help—the organization was so understaffed and overwhelmed that it didn't know how to take advantage of the many people wanting to donate their time. Davis decided to organize a truly useful volunteer program. He created a database of people willing to volunteer, redesigned forms, computerized the mailing list, developed volunteer training, and even designed a Web page. The Association now regularly uses volunteers to do everything from cleaning smelly cages to taking puppies into nursing homes for pet therapy.[11]

❋ Rosanne Haggerty founded Common Ground Community in 1990 to solve the problem of homelessness in New York City. Despite the overwhelming nature of the task and Haggerty's youth and limited experience, she believed in her vision and set about to make it a reality. She successfully partnered with major corporations such as J. P. Morgan & Co. and Clorox to purchase and renovate the run-down Times Square Hotel and turn it into a 652-unit housing facility with on-site social services. Today, Common Ground has 170 employees and provides 1,200 housing units around New York City.[12]

Action Memo

As a leader: Recognize the opportunities for leadership all around you and act like a leader to influence others and bring about changes for a better future.

There are opportunities for leadership all around us that involve influence and change toward a desired goal or outcome. Without leadership, our families and communities, as well as our organizations, would fall apart. The leaders of tomorrow's organizations will come from anywhere and everywhere, just as they always have. You can start now, wherever you are, to practice leadership in your own life. Leadership is an everyday way of acting and thinking that has little to do with a title or formal position in an organization. As we will discuss in the following section, business leaders need to understand this tenet more than ever in the world of the twenty-first century.

The New Reality for Today's Organizations

The world of organizations is changing rapidly. Globalization. Deregulation. E-business. Telecommuting. Virtual teams. Outsourcing. People in organizations around the world are feeling the impact of these and other trends, and are forced to adapt to new ways of working. Add to this the recent economic uncertainty, widespread ethical scandals, and the insecurity associated with war and terrorism, and leaders are facing a really tough job to keep people grounded, focused, and motivated toward accomplishing positive goals. It takes particularly strong leaders to guide people through the uncertainty and confusion that accompanies periods of rapid change.

Some historians and other scholars believe our world is undergoing a transformation more profound and far-reaching than any experienced since the dawn of the modern age and the Industrial Revolution some 500 years ago. Rapid environmental changes are causing fundamental shifts that have a dramatic impact on organizations and present new challenges for leaders.[13] These shifts represent a transition from a traditional to a new paradigm, as outlined in Exhibit 1.2. A **paradigm** is a shared mind-set that represents a fundamental way of thinking about, perceiving, and understanding the world.

Although many leaders are still operating from an old-paradigm mind-set, as outlined in the first column of Exhibit 1.2, they are increasingly ineffective Successful leaders in the twenty-first century will respond to the new reality outlined in the second column of the exhibit.

Paradigm
a shared mind-set that represents a fundamental way of thinking about, perceiving, and understanding the world

From Stability to Change and Crisis Management

In the past, many leaders assumed that if they could just keep things running on a steady, even keel, the organization would be successful. Yet today's world is in constant motion, and nothing seems certain anymore. If leaders still had an illusion of stability at the dawn of the twenty-first century, it is surely shattered now. Consider the following string of events that occurred over a period of less than two years:

1. After several years of fervent growth, the Internet bubble burst, leading to the failure of numerous companies and the rapid decline of technology stocks,

2. Terrorists commandeered United and American Airlines jets and crashed them into the Pentagon and the twin towers of the World Trade Center in New York City, killing thousands and virtually halting economic activity not only in the United States but around the world,

Exhibit 1.2   The New Reality for Leadership

OLD Paradigm	NEW Paradigm
Stability	Change and crisis management
Control	Empowerment
Competition	Collaboration
Uniformity	Diversity
Self-centered	Higher purpose
Hero	Humble

3. Enron Corporation, the darling of Wall Street and the poster child for enlightened management, collapsed under the pressure of a complex series of unethical and sometimes illegal partnerships and accounting machinations, creating a domino effect whereby the unethical and illegal actions of numerous corporations and executives came to light,

4. The unemployment rate in the United States soared and stocks tumbled as consumer confidence fell, the economy weakened, and companies were forced to dramatically cut costs to survive.

Most leaders, whether in the military, business, politics, education, social services, the arts, or the world of sports, recognize that maintaining stability in a world of such rapid and far-reaching change is a losing battle. The new paradigm of leadership acknowledges that, as suggested by the science of chaos theory, we live in a world characterized by randomness and uncertainty and small events often have massive and widespread consequences. For example, the ethical cloud enveloping organizations ranging from giants such as Arthur Andersen and HealthSouth to smaller companies such as King Pharmaceuticals began with some relatively innocent questions about Enron's stock valuation and business model.

Change and crisis have become the norm for many organizations.[14] Consider such events as the deaths of children due to e-coli bacteria from Jack-in-the-Box hamburgers, allegations of tainted Coca-Cola from Belgium bottling plants, charges of child labor abuse against clothing companies, or the 2003 crash of the space shuttle Columbia. Today's best leaders accept the inevitability of change and crisis and recognize them as potential sources of energy and self-renewal. Rather than being laid low, they develop effective *crisis management skills* that help their organizations weather the storm and move toward something better. This chapter's Leader's Bookshelf describes some qualities needed for effective leadership during times of crisis or uncertainty. The pervasiveness of change in the environment has taught leaders to actively embrace and create changes within the organization that can develop individual workers and move the organization forward. The best leaders know that the benefits associated with stability are a myth; that when things do not change, they die.

From Control to Empowerment

Leaders in powerful positions once thought workers should be told what to do, how to do it, when to do it, and who to do it with. They believed strict control was needed for the organization to function efficiently and effectively. Rigid organizational hierarchies, structured jobs and work processes, and detailed, inviolate procedures let everyone know that those at the top had power and those at the bottom had none.

Today, the old assumptions about the distribution of power are no longer valid. An emphasis on control and rigidity serves to squelch motivation and morale rather

LEADER'S BOOKSHELF

Leadership
By Rudolph Giuliani, with Ken Kurson

Some people probably looked to Rudy Giuliani, former mayor of New York, for inspiration even before September 11, 2001, when terrorists crashed jetliners into the twin towers of the World Trade Center. But after that horrendous event, practically the whole country recognized New York City's mayor as the epitome of what a leader should be: calm and steady in the face of crisis, strong but compassionate, honest but diplomatic. Giuliani's book, titled simply *Leadership*, shows that he has given a lot of thought, both before and after September 11, to what makes a great leader.

The Hallmarks of Great Leadership
In a clear, interesting style, Giuliani lays out his prescription for success as a leader in a complex and turbulent world. Some of his principles include:

※ *Develop and communicate strong beliefs.* Great leaders lead by ideas, so they have to know what they stand for and be able to communicate it in a compelling way. A leader "cannot simply impose his will. . . . ," Giuliani writes. "He must bring people aboard, excite them about his vision, and earn their support."

※ *Accept responsibility.* Leaders set an example for others by performing their jobs honestly and effectively and by accepting responsibility for what happens during their watches. Good leaders welcome being held accountable, and they hold others accountable for living up to high standards as well.

※ *Surround yourself with great people.* The most effective leaders are those who hire the best people they can possibly find, motivate them, provide them with challenges and opportunities to grow, and direct their energies toward positive outcomes. Giuliani recalls the September 11 aftermath: "Faced with the worst disaster New York had ever seen, it might have been understandable for some people in my administration to go through the motions. . . . Instead, without exception, my staff distinguished themselves."

※ *Study, Read, Learn Independently.* Leaders should never leave important decisions to the experts. "No matter how talented your advisors and deputies, you have to attack challenges with as much of your own knowledge as possible." Giuliani believes the best leaders are lifelong learners who "put time aside for deep study." Leaders also prepare relentlessly so they can identify potential problems before they happen.

The Making of a Leader
Giuliani makes the key point that leadership does not just happen. It can be learned and developed through practice as well as by studying the leadership ideas and behavior of great leaders. *Leadership* incorporates not only Giuliani's ideas but the thinking of numerous people—from his mother, to President Ronald Reagan, to Winston Churchill—who have shaped him as a leader. Through insights and anecdotes, Giuliani offers us a chance to learn from their wisdom as well.

Leadership, by Rudolph Giuliani with Ken Kurson, is published by Hyperion.

than produce desired results. Today's leaders share power rather than hoard it and find ways to increase an organization's brain power by getting everyone in the organization involved and committed.

One reason for this is that the financial basis of today's economy is rapidly becoming *information* rather than the tangible assets of land, buildings, and machines. Fifty years ago, tangible assets represented 73 percent of the assets of nonfinancial corporations in the United States. Today, the proportion is down to around 53 percent.[15] This means that the primary factor of production is human knowledge, which increases the power of employees. The educational and skill level of employees in the United States and other developed countries has steadily increased over the past several decades, and many people are no longer satisfied working in an organization that doesn't give them opportunities to participate and learn.

When all the organization needed was workers to run machines eight hours a day, traditional command-and-control systems generally worked quite well, but the organization received no benefit from employees' minds. Frank Ostroff, who took a summer job at a tire-making factory as a college student, recalled: "We'd spend eight hours a day doing something completely mindless. . . . And then these same people would go home and spend their evenings and weekends rebuilding entire cars from scratch or running volunteer organizations."[16] No longer can organizations afford to have workers check their minds at the door. Success depends on the intellectual capacity of all employees, and leaders have to face a hard fact: Buildings and machines can be owned; people cannot. One of the leader's most challenging jobs is to guide workers in using their power effectively and responsibly by creating and developing a climate of respect and development for all employees.[17]

From Competition to Collaboration

The move to empowerment also ties directly into new ways of working that emphasize collaboration over competition and conflict. Although some companies still encourage internal competition and aggressiveness, most of today's organizations are stressing teamwork and cooperation. Self-directed teams and other forms of horizontal collaboration are breaking down boundaries between departments and helping to spread knowledge and information throughout the organization. Compromise and sharing are recognized as signs of strength, not weakness. The concept of *knowledge management*, which relies on a culture of sharing rather than hoarding information, has taken firm hold in many companies.[18]

Some competition can be healthy for an organization, but many leaders are resisting the idea of competition as a struggle to win while someone else loses. Instead, they direct everyone's competitive energy toward being the best that they can be. There is a growing trend toward reducing boundaries and increasing collaboration with other organizations, so that companies think of themselves as teams that create value jointly rather than as autonomous entities in competition with all others.[19] A new form of global business is made up of networks of independent companies that share financial risks and leadership talents and provide access to one another's technologies and markets.[20]

The move to collaboration presents greater challenges to leaders than did the old concept of competition. Within the organization, leaders need to create an environment of teamwork and community that fosters collaboration and mutual support. The call for empowerment, combined with an understanding of organizations as part of a fluid, dynamic, interacting system, makes the use of intimidation and manipulation obsolete as a means of driving the competitive spirit.

From Uniformity to Diversity

Many of today's organizations were built on assumptions of uniformity, separation, and specialization. People who think alike, act alike, and have similar job skills are grouped into a department, such as accounting or manufacturing, separate from other departments. Homogenous groups find it easy to get along, communicate, and understand one another. The uniform thinking that arises, however, can be a disaster in a world becoming more multinational and diverse.

Two business school graduates in their twenties discovered the importance of diversity when they started a specialized advertising firm. They worked hard, and as the firm grew, they hired more people just like themselves—bright, young, intense college graduates, committed and hard working. The firm grew to about 20 employees over two and a half years, but the expected profits never materialized. The two entrepreneurs could never get a handle on what was wrong, and the firm slid into bankruptcy. Convinced the idea was still valid, they started over, but with a new philosophy. They sought employees with different ages, ethnic backgrounds, and work experience. People had different styles, yet the organization seemed to work better. People played different roles, and the diverse experiences of the group enabled the firm to respond to unique situations and handle a variety of organizational and personal needs. The advertising firm is growing again, and this time it is also making a profit.

The world is rapidly moving toward diversity at both national and international levels. In the United States, roughly 40 percent of all net additions to the labor force for the next few years will be non-white—half of these will be first-generation immigrants, mostly from Asian and Latin countries. Almost two-thirds will be female.[21] Bringing diversity into the organization is the way to attract the best human talent and to develop an organizational mind-set broad enough to thrive in a multinational world. Organizations suffer when their leaders don't respond to today's diverse environment. The reputations of well-known companies such as Coca-Cola, Texaco, and Mitsubishi have been tarnished by charges of racial or sexual discrimination.

From Self-Centered to Higher Purpose

The ethical turmoil of the early twenty-first century has prompted a determined and conscious shift in leader mind-set from a self-centered focus to emphasis on a higher purpose. Public confidence in business leaders in particular is at an all-time low, but politics, sports, and nonprofit organizations have also been affected.

Over years of business growth and success, many leaders slipped into a pattern of expecting–and getting–more. Between 1981 and 2000, the compensation of America's highest-paid CEOs, for example, increased 4,300 percent.[22] Unfortunately, the old-paradigm emphasis on individual ability, success, and prosperity sometimes pushed people to cross the line, culminating in organizational corruption on a broad scale and ugly headlines exposing leaders from companies such as Enron, WorldCom, Tyco, and Adelphia Communications as unethical and self-serving rogues. At Enron, top executives rewarded highly competitive managers who were willing to do whatever it took—whether it be hiding mistakes, fudging their reports, or backstabbing colleagues—to make the numbers and keep the stock price high. The overriding emphasis on individual ambition created an environment of vanity and greed whereby executives profited at the expense of employees, shareholders, and the community.[23] And Enron managers didn't hold a monopoly on greed. Top executives at companies including Qwest Communications, AOL Time Warner, Global Crossing, and Broadcom sold billions of dollars worth of stock at vastly inflated prices, making themselves rich even as their companies deteriorated and average investors lost as much as 90 percent of their holdings.[24]

In the new paradigm, leaders emphasize accountability, integrity, and responsibility to something larger than individual self-interest, including employees, customers, the organization, and all stakeholders.[25] These leaders reinforce the importance of doing the right thing, even if it hurts. One example is Aramark Worldwide Corp., the giant outsourcing company that provides food services for many universities and corporations. After a huge investment of time and money, CEO Joseph Neubauer walked away from a once-promising overseas merger when he discovered that the company's business practices didn't live up to Aramark's ethical standards. "It takes a lifetime to build a reputation, and only a short time to lose it all," Neubauer says.[26] Sears' chief executive, Alan Lacy, agrees. Lacy recently fired two of his top executives in the credit business for misleading him about the outlook for the business and then gave a brutally honest public account of how gloomy the outlook really was.[27] The new paradigm recognizes that honesty, integrity, and accountability to stakeholders are crucial requirements for leaders, and unbridled self-interest and arrogance have no place.

From Hero to Humble

A related shift is the move from the celebrity "leader-as-hero" to the hard-working behind-the-scenes leader who quietly builds a strong enduring company by supporting and developing others rather than touting his own abilities and successes.[28]

Action Memo

As a leader:
Respond to the
21st century
reality of change
and crisis,
empowerment,
collaboration,
diversity, and
the importance
of higher-
purpose. Move
from hero to
humble by
channeling
your ambition
toward achiev-
ing positive
organizational
goals rather
than feeding
your own ego.

During the last two decades of the twentieth century, good leadership became equated with larger-than-life personalities, strong egos, and personal ambition. The media attention helped cultivate the image.[29] In the early 1980s, Lee Iacocca was portrayed almost as a white knight riding in to save Chrysler. Over the next 20 years, corporate CEOs became superstars, featured on the covers of business and news magazines and celebrated for their charismatic or outrageous personalities as much as for their abilities. A remark made by Albert J. Dunlap, nicknamed "Chainsaw Al" for his slash-and-run tactics at companies such as Scott Paper and Sunbeam Corp. in the mid-1990s, captures the mind-set of the leader-as-hero: "Most CEOs are ridiculously overpaid, but I deserved the $100 million," Dunlap wrote in his self-congratulatory autobiography. "I'm a superstar in my field, much like Michael Jordan in basketball."[30] As we now know, Dunlap's "turnarounds" were smoke and mirrors, based mostly on short-term accounting gimickry. His efforts netted him millions but left the companies, their employees, and shareholders much worse off than they were before. Although the majority of high-profile leaders are not so self-serving, the recent ethical maelstrom in the business world has contributed to a shift in mind-set away from the individual leader as hero.

The new-paradigm leader is characterized by an almost complete lack of ego. Jim Collins, author of *Good to Great: Why Some Companies Make the Leap . . . and Others Don't,* calls this new breed Level 5 leaders.[31] In contrast to the leader as hero, Level 5 leaders often seem shy and unpretentious. Although they accept full responsibility for mistakes, poor results, or failures, they give credit for successes to other people, similar to Tom Freston at MTV Networks, described in the chapter opening. They talk about the success of their organizations almost as if they have just been sitting there while everyone else does all the work.

Yet, despite their personal humility, new-paradigm leaders are highly ambitious for their organizations, with a fierce determination to produce great and lasting results. They develop a solid corps of leaders throughout the organization and create a culture focused on high performance and integrity. Egocentric leaders often build an organization around a hero with a thousand helpers. New paradigm leaders, though, build their organizations with many strong leaders who can step forward and continue the company's success long into the future. These leaders want everyone in the organization to develop to their fullest potential. One current CEO who exemplifies the personal humility and organizational ambition of the new-paradigm leader is Reuben Mark of Colgate-Palmolive.

In the Lead   Reuben Mark, Colgate-Palmolive

When Reuben Mark was asked to comment for an article about CEOs in *BusinessWeek*, he respectfully declined, saying he couldn't see how doing so would improve his business. The CEO of Colgate-Palmolive since 1984,

Mark consistently shuns personal publicity and turns down requests for media profiles about him. Even though he has a better record of success than many high-profile leaders, Mark's brand of leadership ardently emphasizes teamwork over individual accomplishment.

By being profiled on television or in magazines, Mark believes, a leader implicitly takes credit for the efforts of his employees. "He wants his company to be the superstar, not him," says Sheila Wellington, president of Catalyst, a women's advocacy organization. And most analysts agree that Colgate qualifies as a superstar. Since Mark took over, profit margins have risen from 39 to 54 percent and earnings have grown at an annual rate of 12.8 percent. Although the stock is currently down, long-term results have been spectacular.

Mark is also known for being indifferent to executive privilege. He frequently answers his own phone and comes down from his office to personally greet visitors in the lobby. When he travels overseas he does so on a regular flight, not in a corporate jet. Although he's known to have a strong personality and a fiery temper, Mark channels all his ambition and passion to further the goals of the organization. At annual meetings, he pays tribute to employees from around the world who make even seemingly minor contributions to innovation, market increases, or business operations. One analyst who follows Colgate for USB Warburg says many of Mark's employees "would take a bullet for him."[32]

Reuben Mark has built a strong organization by creating an open, nonhierarchical culture, emphasizing continuous improvement and steady growth, suppressing his own ego and sharing credit with his employees, and staying focused on long-term success rather than the short-term profits demanded by Wall Street. Although most research regarding the new type of leader has been on corporate CEOs such as Reuben Mark, it's important to remember that new-paradigm or Level 5 leaders are in all positions and all types of organizations. Jim Collins, in discussing the growing importance of humble leaders dedicated to the greater good rather than their own personal advancement, referred to the events of September 11, 2001: "Look at the firemen who ran into those towers. There are level-fives all over the place."[33]

Comparing Management and Leadership

The shift from an old to a new paradigm, outlined in Exhibit 1.2 and discussed in the previous section, also reflects a shift from a traditional, rational management approach that emphasizes stability and control to a leadership approach that values change, empowerment, and relationships. In the old paradigm, a traditional management approach worked well, but the new paradigm requires that managers also become effective leaders. Executives like Reuben Mark have embraced the new reality and combined leadership qualities with rational management skills.

Let's begin our adventure into the study of leadership by considering what distinguishes the process of leadership from that of management. **Management** can be defined as the attainment of organizational goals in an effective and efficient manner through planning, organizing, staffing, directing, and controlling organizational resources. Much has been written in recent years about the difference between management and leadership. Unfortunately, with the current emphasis on the need for leadership, managers have gotten a bad name.[34] Managers and leaders are not inherently different types of people, and many managers already possess the abilities and qualities needed to be effective leaders. Leadership cannot replace management; it should be in addition to management. For example, at Colgate-Palmolive, Reuben Mark clearly practices good management, such as controlling costs, establishing goals and plans, providing coordination, and monitoring company operations and performance. However, he is also a consummate leader who provides vision and inspiration for employees, keeps his eye on the long-term future, creates a culture that allows others to grow and flourish, and builds an environment that fosters integrity and accountability. There are managers at all hierarchical levels in today's organizations who are also good leaders, and most people can develop the qualities needed for effective leadership. You can evaluate your own leadership potential by completing the quiz in Leader's Self-Insight 1.1.

Exhibit 1.3 compares management to leadership in five areas crucial to organizational performance—providing direction, aligning followers, building relationships, developing personal qualities, and creating leader outcomes.[35]

Providing Direction

Both leaders and managers are concerned with providing direction for the organization, but there are differences. Management focuses on establishing detailed plans and schedules for achieving specific results, then allocating resources to accomplish the plan. Leadership calls for creating a compelling vision of the future and developing farsighted strategies for producing the changes needed to achieve that vision. Whereas management calls for keeping an eye on the bottom line and short-term results, leadership means keeping an eye on the horizon and the long-term future.

A **vision** is a picture of an ambitious, desirable future for the organization or team.[36] It can be as lofty as Motorola's aim to "become the premier company in the world" or as down-to-earth as the Swedish company IKEA's simple vision "to provide affordable furniture for people with limited budgets."

To be compelling for followers, the vision has to be one they can relate to and share. In *Fortune* magazine's study of the "100 Best Companies to Work for in America," two of the recurring traits of great companies are a powerful, visionary

---

Management

the attainment of organizational goals in an effective and efficient manner through planning, organizing, staffing, directing, and controlling organizational resources

---

Vision

a picture of an ambitious, desirable future for the organization or team

LEADER'S SELF-INSIGHT 1.1

Your Leadership Potential

Questions 1–6 below are about you right now. Questions 7–22 are about how you would like to be if you were the head of a major department at a corporation. Answer yes or no to indicate whether the item describes you accurately, or whether you would strive to perform each activity.

Now

1. When I have a number of tasks or homework assignments to do, I set priorities and organize the work to meet the deadlines. _____
2. When I am involved in a serious disagreement, I hang in there and talk it out until it is completely resolved. _____
3. I would rather sit in front of my computer than spend a lot of time with people. _____
4. I reach out to include other people in activities or when there are discussions. _____
5. I know my long-term vision for career, family, and other activities. _____
6. When solving problems, I prefer analyzing things to working through them with a group of people. _____

Head of Major Department

7. I would help subordinates clarify goals and how to reach them. _____
8. I would give people a sense of mission and higher purpose. _____
9. I would make sure jobs get out on time. _____
10. I would scout for new product or service opportunities. _____
11. I would use policies and procedures as guides for problem solving. _____
12. I would promote unconventional beliefs and values. _____
13. I would give monetary rewards in exchange for high performance from subordinates. _____
14. I would inspire trust from everyone in the department. _____
15. I would work alone to accomplish important tasks. _____
16. I would suggest new and unique ways of doing things. _____
17. I would give credit to people who do their jobs well. _____
18. I would verbalize the higher values that I and the organization stand for. _____
19. I would establish procedures to help the department operate smoothly. _____
20. I would question the "why" of things to motivate others. _____
21. I would set reasonable limits on new approaches. _____
22. I would demonstrate social nonconformity as a way to facilitate change. _____

Scoring and Interpretation Count the number of yes answers to even-numbered questions. Count the number of yes answers to odd-numbered questions. Compare the two scores.

The even-numbered items represent behaviors and activities typical of leadership. Leaders are personally involved in shaping ideas, values, vision, and change. They often use an intuitive approach to develop fresh ideas and seek new directions for the department or organization. The odd-numbered items are considered more traditional management activities. Managers respond to organizational problems in an impersonal way, make rational decisions, and work for stability and efficiency.

If you answered yes to more even-numbered than odd-numbered items, you may have potential leadership qualities. If you answered yes to more odd-numbered items, you may have management qualities. Leadership qualities can be developed or improved with awareness and experience.

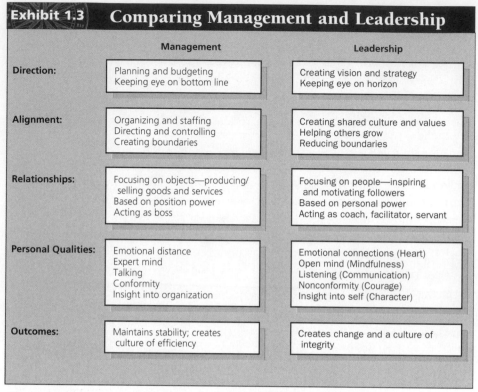

Exhibit 1.3 **Comparing Management and Leadership**

	Management	Leadership
Direction:	Planning and budgeting Keeping eye on bottom line	Creating vision and strategy Keeping eye on horizon
Alignment:	Organizing and staffing Directing and controlling Creating boundaries	Creating shared culture and values Helping others grow Reducing boundaries
Relationships:	Focusing on objects—producing/ selling goods and services Based on position power Acting as boss	Focusing on people—inspiring and motivating followers Based on personal power Acting as coach, facilitator, servant
Personal Qualities:	Emotional distance Expert mind Talking Conformity Insight into organization	Emotional connections (Heart) Open mind (Mindfulness) Listening (Communication) Nonconformity (Courage) Insight into self (Character)
Outcomes:	Maintains stability; creates culture of efficiency	Creates change and a culture of integrity

SOURCES: John P. Kotter, *Leading Change* (Boston, MA: Harvard Business School Press, 1996), 26; Joseph C. Rost, *Leadership for the Twenty-first Century* (Westport, CT; Praeger, 1993), 149; and Brian Dumaine, "The New Non-Manager Managers," *Fortune* (February 22, 1993), 80–84.

leader and a sense of purpose beyond increasing shareholder value. At Medtronic, for example, which makes pacemakers and other medical devices, company leaders stress the vision of "restoring patients to full life." Rather than concentrating on shareholders or doctors, workers at Medtronic are told to focus on the people who will actually have the company's devices implanted inside them. Workers who are inspired and motivated to help sick people get well have made the company's total return to shareholders great, too.[37]

Aligning Followers

Management entails organizing a structure to accomplish the plan; staffing the structure with employees; and developing policies, procedures, and systems to direct employees and monitor implementation of the plan. Managers are thinkers and workers are doers. Leadership is concerned instead with communicating the vision and developing a shared culture and set of core values that can lead to the desired future state. This involves others as thinkers, doers, and leaders themselves, fostering a sense of ownership in everyone.[38] Whereas the vision describes the destination, the culture and values help define the journey toward it. Leadership focuses on getting everyone lined up in the same direction. Gertrude Boyle, a housewife and mother who took charge of Columbia Sportswear after her husband's early death, created a comfortable, down-to-earth corporate culture that propelled the outdoor clothing manufacturer from sales of $800,000 to just under $300 million. She came into the company with no business experience, but says, "Running a company is like raising kids. You all have to be in the same line of thinking."[39]

Managers often organize by separating people into specialties and functions, with boundaries separating them by department and hierarchical level. Leaders break down boundaries so people know what others are doing, can coordinate easily, and feel a sense of teamwork and equalness for achieving outcomes.

Rather than simply directing and controlling employees to achieve specific results, leaders "align [people] with broader ideas of what the company should be and why."[40] Leaders encourage people to expand their minds and abilities and to assume responsibility for their own actions. Think about classes you have taken at your college or university. In some college classes, the professor tells students exactly what to do and how to do it, and many students expect this kind of direction and control. Have you ever had a class where the instructor instead inspired and encouraged you and your classmates to find innovative ways to meet goals? The difference reflects a rational management versus a leadership approach. Whereas the management communication process generally involves providing answers and solving problems, leadership entails asking questions, listening, and involving others.[41]

Building Relationships

In terms of relationships, management focuses on objects such as machines and reports, on taking the steps needed to produce the organization's goods and services. Leadership, on the other hand, focuses on motivating and inspiring people.

Whereas the management relationship is based on formal authority, leadership is a relationship based on personal influence. Formal **position power** means that there is a written, spoken, or implied contract wherein people accept either a superior or subordinate role and see the use of coercive as well as noncoercive behavior as an acceptable way to achieve desired results.[42] For example, in an authority relationship, both people accept that a manager can tell a subordinate to be at work at 7:30 A.M. or her pay will be docked. Leadership, on the other hand, relies on influence, which is less likely to use coercion. Followers are empowered to make many decisions on their own. Leadership strives to make work stimulating and challenging and involves pulling rather than pushing people toward goals. The role of leadership is to attract and energize people, motivating them through identification

Position power a written, spoken, or implied contract wherein people accept either a superior or subordinate role and see the use of coercive as well as noncoercive behavior as an acceptable way of achieving desirable results

LIVING LEADERSHIP

A Lesson for Leaders

Lesson # 2 from General Colin Powell: "The day soldiers stop bringing you their problems is the day you have stopped leading them. They have either lost confidence that you can help them or concluded that you do not care. Either case is a failure of leadership."

If this were a litmus test, the majority of CEOs would fail. One, they build so many barriers to upward communication that the very idea of someone lower in the hierarchy looking up to the leader for help is ludicrous.

Two, the corporate culture they foster often defines asking for help as weakness or failure, so people cover up their gaps, and the organization suffers accordingly. Real leaders make themselves accessible and available. They show concern for the efforts and challenges faced by [followers], even as they demand high standards. Accordingly, they are more likely to create an environment where problem analysis replaces blame.

SOURCE: Colin Powell, Secretary of State, "A Leadership Primer."

rather than rewards or punishments.[43] The formal position of authority in the organization is the source of management power, but leadership power comes from the personal character of the leader. Leadership does not require that one hold a formal position of authority, and many people holding positions of authority do not provide leadership. The differing source of power is one of the key distinctions between management and leadership. Take away a manager's formal position and will people choose to follow him? Leadership truly depends on who you are rather than on your position or title.

Developing Personal Leadership Qualities

Leadership is more than a set of skills; it relies on a number of subtle personal qualities that are hard to see but are very powerful. These include things like enthusiasm, integrity, courage, and humility. First of all, good leadership springs from a genuine passion for the work and a genuine concern for other people. Great leaders are people who love what they do and want to share that love with others. The process of management generally encourages emotional distance, but leadership means being emotionally connected to others. Where there is leadership, people become part of a community and feel that they are contributing to something worthwhile.[44] This chapter's Living Leadership emphasizes the importance of being emotionally connected to followers.

Whereas management means providing answers and solving problems, leadership requires the courage to admit mistakes and doubts, to take risks, to listen, and to trust and learn from others. Emotional connections can be uncomfortable for some managers, but they are necessary for true leadership to happen. George Sparks, a graduate of the Air Force Academy and general manager of Hewlett-Packard's measuring-equipment business, says he learned this from a Girl Scout leader.

In the Lead   Frances Hesselbein and the Girl Scout Way

"The best two days of my career" is how George Sparks describes the time he spent following Frances Hesselbein around. Hesselbein is currently chairman of the board of governors of the Leader to Leader Institute, editor-in-chief of *Leader to Leader*, and an acclaimed author and editor of several books, the most recent of which is titled *Hesselbein on Leadership*. But she began her career more than 40 years ago as a volunteer Scout leader. She eventually rose to CEO of the Girl Scouts, inheriting a troubled organization of 680,000 people, only 1 percent of whom were paid employees. By the time she retired in 1990, Hesselbein had turned around declining membership, dramatically increased participation by minorities, and replaced a brittle hierarchy with one of the most vibrant organizations in the nonprofit or business world.

Hesselbein describes how she works with others as a circle in which everyone is included. As Sparks observed her in action, the most compelling quality he noted was her ability to sense people's needs on an emotional level. He explains, "Time and again, I have seen people face two possible solutions. One is 20 percent better, but the other meets their personal needs—and that is the one they inevitably choose." He noticed that Hesselbein would listen carefully and then link people in such a way that their personal needs were met at the same time they were serving the needs of the organization. Hesselbein recognizes that the only way to achieve high performance is through the work of others, and she consistently treats people with care and respect. In her talks and writings for leaders, one of her primary lessons is that taking people for granted is contrary to the definition of what makes a leader.

Her definition of leadership, she says, was "very hard to arrive at, very painful. . . . [It] is not a basket of tricks or skills. It is the quality and character and courage of the person who is the leader. It's a matter of ethics and moral compass, the willingness to remain highly vulnerable."[45]

As Frances Hesselbein noted, developing leadership qualities can be painful. Abraham Zaleznik has referred to leaders as "twice-born personalities," who struggle to develop their sense of self through psychological and social change.[46] For leadership to happen, leaders have to know who they are and what they stand for. And they remain constant so followers know what to expect. One study revealed that people would much rather follow individuals they can count on, even when they disagree with their viewpoint, than people they agree with but who frequently shift their viewpoints or positions.[47] One employee described the kind of person she would follow as this: " . . . it's like they have a stick down through the center of them that's rooted in the ground. I can tell when someone has that. When they're not defensive, not egotistical. They're open-minded, able to joke and laugh at themselves. They can take a volatile situation and stay focused. They bring out the best in me by making me want to handle myself in the same way. I want to be part of their world."[48]

True leaders draw on a number of subtle but powerful forces within themselves. For example, leaders tend to have open minds that welcome new ideas rather than closed minds that criticize new ideas. Leaders tend to care about others and build personal connections rather than maintain emotional distance. Leaders listen and discern what people want and need more than they talk to give advice and orders. Leaders are willing to be nonconformists, to disagree and say no when it serves the larger good, and to accept nonconformity from others rather than try to squeeze everyone into the same mind-set. They and others step outside the traditional boundary and comfort zone, take risks, and make mistakes to learn and grow. Moreover, leaders are honest with themselves and others to the point of inspiring trust. They set high moral standards by doing the right thing, rather than just going along with standards set by others. Leadership causes wear and tear on the individual, because leaders are vulnerable, take risks, and initiate change, which typically encounters resistance.

Creating Outcomes

The differences between management and leadership create two differing outcomes, as illustrated at the bottom of Exhibit 1.3. Management maintains a degree of stability, predictability, and order through a *culture of efficiency*. Good management helps the organization consistently achieve short-term results and meet the expectations of various stakeholders. Leadership, on the other hand, creates change, often radical change, within a *culture of integrity* that helps the organization thrive over the long haul by promoting openness and honesty, positive relationships, and a long-term focus. Leadership facilitates the courage needed to make difficult and unconventional decisions that may sometimes hurt short-term results.

Leadership means questioning and challenging the status quo so that outdated, unproductive, or socially irresponsible norms can be replaced to meet new challenges. Good leadership can lead to extremely valuable change, such as new products or services that gain new customers or expand markets. Thus, although good management is needed to help organizations meet current commitments, good leadership is needed to move the organization into the future.

Evolving Theories of Leadership

To understand leadership as it is viewed and practiced today, it is important to recognize that the concept of leadership has evolved over time. Leadership typically reflects the larger society, and theories have evolved as norms, attitudes, and understandings in the larger world have changed.

Historical Overview of Major Approaches

The various leadership theories can be categorized into six basic approaches, each of which is briefly described below. Many of these ideas are still applicable to leadership studies today and are discussed in various chapters of this text.

Great Man Theories This is the granddaddy of leadership concepts. The earliest studies of leadership adopted the belief that leaders (who were always thought of as male) were born with certain heroic leadership traits and natural abilities of power and influence. In organizations, social movements, religions, governments, and the military, leadership was conceptualized as a single "Great Man" who put everything together and influenced others to follow along based on the strength of inherited traits, qualities, and abilities.

Trait Theories Studies of these "larger-than-life" leaders spurred research into the various traits that defined a leader. Beginning in the 1920s, researchers looked to see if leaders had particular traits or characteristics, such as intelligence, height, or energy that distinguished them from nonleaders and contributed to success. It was thought that if traits could be identified, leaders could be predicted, or perhaps even trained. Although research failed to produce a list of traits that would always guarantee leadership success, the interest in leadership characteristics has continued to the present day.

Behavior Theories The failure to identify a universal set of leadership traits led researchers in the early 1950s to begin looking at what a leader does, rather than who he or she is.[49] One line of research focused on what leaders actually do on the job, which relates to the content of managerial activities, roles, and responsibilities. These studies were soon expanded to try to determine how effective leaders differ in their behavior from ineffective ones. Researchers looked at how a leader behaved toward followers—such as whether they were autocratic or democratic in their approach, for example—and how this correlated with leadership effectiveness or ineffectiveness. Trait and behavior theories are discussed in Chapter 2.

Contingency Theories Researchers next began to consider the contextual and situational variables that influence what leadership behaviors will be effective. The idea behind contingency theories is that leaders can analyze their situation and tailor their behavior to improve leadership effectiveness. Major situational variables are the characteristics of followers, characteristics of the work environment and follower tasks, and the external environment. Contingency theories, sometimes called situational theories, emphasize that leadership cannot be understood in a vacuum separate from various elements of the group or organizational situation. Contingency theories are covered in Chapter 3.

Influence Theories These theories examine influence processes between leaders and followers. One primary topic of study is *charismatic leadership* (Chapter 4), which refers to leadership influence based not on position or formal authority but, rather, on the qualities and charismatic personality of the leader. Theories of charismatic leadership attempt to identify how charismatic leaders behave, how they differ from other people, and the conditions that typically give rise to charismatic leadership. A related area of study is *leadership vision* (Chapter 13). Leaders influence people to change by providing an inspiring vision of the future. Several chapters of this text relate to the topic of influence because it is essential to understanding leadership.

Relational Theories Since the late 1970s, many ideas of leadership have focused on the relational aspect, that is, how leaders and followers interact and influence one another. Rather than being seen as something a leader does to a follower, leadership is viewed as a relational process that meaningfully engages all participants and enables each person to contribute to achieving the vision. Interpersonal relationships are seen as the most important facet of leadership effectiveness.[50] One major relational theory is referred to as *transformational leadership* (Chapter 4). Transformational leadership develops followers into leaders and brings about significant change by elevating leaders and followers to higher levels of motivation and morality.[51] The theory of *servant leadership* (Chapter 6) means that the leader is first and foremost a person who serves others, rather than directs or controls others. The servant leader puts others' needs and interests above his or her own.[52]

Other important relational topics covered in various chapters of the text include the personal qualities that leaders need to build effective relationships, such as emotional intelligence, a leader's mind, integrity and high moral standards, and personal courage. In addition, leaders build relationships through motivation and empowerment, leadership communication, team leadership, and embracing diversity.

Emerging Leadership Theories

Elements of each of the approaches we have just discussed are still applicable to leadership today. However, with the transition to a new paradigm discussed earlier in this chapter, new ideas are emerging. The understanding of the world as "turbulent, ever-changing, risky, and always challenging"[53] is being translated into new concepts of what it means to be a leader. In this view, *facilitating change* (Chapter 16) is the key aspect of being a leader. Leading change has always been an essential part of leadership, but many of the earlier theories paid little attention to change behavior.[54] With the unpredictable environment of the early 21st century, attention has turned to how leaders create changes within followers and the organization that respond to and keep pace with change in the environment. To adapt to a chaotic world, leaders strive to create *learning organizations* (Chapter 15), in which each person is intimately involved in identifying and solving problems so the organization can grow and change to meet new challenges. Rather than directing and controlling others, leaders work with others to create a shared vision (Chapter 13) and shape the cultural values (Chapter 14) needed to attain it. Rather than relying on hierarchical control, leaders build whole organizations as communities of shared purpose and direction.

Leadership Is Not Automatic

Many leaders are caught in the transition between the practices and principles that defined the industrial era and the new reality of the twenty-first century. Attempts to achieve collaboration, empowerment, and diversity in organizations may fail because the beliefs and thought processes of leaders as well as employees are stuck in an old paradigm that values control, stability, and homogeneity. Some leaders, on the other hand, seem to have pushed individual empowerment and autonomy too far, giving employees greater freedom without maintaining appropriate controls and instilling organizational values of teamwork, integrity, and responsibility. The difficult transition between the old and the new partly explains the current crisis in organizational leadership. It is difficult for many leaders to let go of methods and practices that have made them and their organizations successful in the past.

One of the most important aspects of the new paradigm of leadership is the ability to use human skills to build a culture of performance, trust, and integrity. John Brown, who started out as a strict command-and-control manager as chief executive of Stryker Corp., learned the importance of human skills for growing his business. When Brown wanted to expand the business beyond its roots as a maker of hospital beds, he found that employee commitment, the pace of innovation, and decision making was just too slow. Brown marks his moment of transformation as the day "it became painfully obvious that the biggest problem with the company was me."[55] Brown now gives managers of the various divisions almost complete autonomy, even as he keeps a close eye on performance and provides direction and guidance. Brown created a culture of trust by leading with integrity and following through on his promises, helping Styker grow into a $2.6 billion medical equipment company.

A few clues about the importance of acquiring new leadership skills were brought to light by the Center for Creative Leadership in Greensboro, North Carolina.[56] The study compared twenty-one derailed executives with twenty executives who successfully arrived at the top of a company. The derailed managers were successful people who were expected to go far, but they reached a plateau, were fired, or were forced to retire early. They were all bright, worked hard, and excelled in a technical area such as accounting or engineering.

The striking difference between the two groups was the ability to use human skills. Only 25 percent of the derailed group were described as being good with people, whereas 75 percent of those who arrived at the top had people skills. The top seven reasons for failure are listed in Exhibit 1.4. Unsuccessful managers were insensitive to others, abrasive, cold, arrogant, untrustworthy, overly ambitious and selfish, unable to delegate or build teams, and unable to acquire appropriate staff to work for them. Leader's Self-Insight 1.2 gives you a chance to test your own people skills and see if there are areas you need to work on.

Interestingly, even people who do make it to the top of organizations sometimes fail in the role of CEO because of poor human skills, particularly the inability to select good people and help them learn and contribute. The best leaders are those who are deeply interested in others and can bring out the best in them.[57] In the new paradigm, leaders put people first. In addition, today's successful leaders value change over stability, empowerment over control, collaboration over competition, diversity over uniformity, and integrity over self-interest, as discussed earlier. A whole new industry, *executive coaching*, has emerged partly to help people through the transition to the new paradigm of leadership. Whereas management consultants generally help executives look outward, at company operations and strategic issues, executive coaches help them look inward. Coaches encourage leaders to confront their own flaws and hangups that inhibit effective leadership, then help them develop stronger emotional and interpersonal skills. One leader

---

Exhibit 1.4   Top Seven Reasons for Executive Derailment

1. Acting with an insensitive, abrasive, intimidating, bullying style
2. Being cold, aloof, arrogant
3. Betraying personal trust
4. Being overly ambitious, self-centered, thinking of next job, playing politics
5. Having specific performance problems with the business
6. Overmanaging, being unable to delegate or build a team
7. Being unable to select good subordinates

LEADER'S SELF-INSIGHT 1.2

Are You on a Fast Track to Nowhere?

Many fast-trackers find themselves suddenly derailed and don't know why. Many times, a lack of people skills is to blame. To help you determine whether you need to work on your people skills, take the following quiz using the scale below:

1 = Describes me exactly; 2 = Describes me; 3 = Somewhat describes me; 4 = Does not describe me

Think about a job or volunteer position you have now or have held in the past, and answer the following questions:

	Describes exactly			Does Not describe
People Skills				
Other people describe me as a real "people person."	1	2	3	4
I spend a part of each day making small talk with co-workers (or teammates or classmates).	1	2	3	4
I see some of my co-workers (or teammates or classmates) outside of work, and I know many of them socially.	1	2	3	4
Because I have good work relationships, I often succeed where others fail.	1	2	3	4
I do not have an inordinate need for everyone to like me.	1	2	3	4
Working with Authority				
When I have a good reason for doing so, I can express a view that differs from that of leaders in the organization.	1	2	3	4
If I see a leader making a decision that seems harmful to the organization, I speak up.	1	2	3	4
People see me as someone who can independently assess an executive decision and, when appropriate, offer an alternative perspective.	1	2	3	4
When senior people ask for my opinion, they know that I'll respond with candor.	1	2	3	4
I believe that it's more important to be honest with senior leaders than to placate them.	1	2	3	4
Networking				
I spend at least part of each week networking with colleagues.	1	2	3	4
I belong to organizations where I can make professional contacts.	1	2	3	4
A few times each month, I am invited to join key members of my team or organization for lunch.	1	2	3	4
I'm fairly well connected to the organizational grapevine.	1	2	3	4
I regularly interact with peers at other organizations.	1	2	3	4

Scoring and Interpretation: Tally your score for each set of questions.

People Skills:_____;   Working with Authority: _____;   Networking: _____

If you scored 5–8, you're right on track. Look at the areas where you scored 1 or 2 and continue to act accordingly.

If your score is 9–13, you need to fine tune your skills in that area. Review the questions where you scored a 3 or 4 and work to add those abilities to your leadership skill set.

A score of 14–17 indicates that you're dangerously close to derailment. You should take the time to do an in-depth self-assessment and find ways to expand your interpersonal skills.

If you scored 18–20, you need to act fast to get back on track. A mentor or career coach can help you do the self-examination and work that's needed to keep you from knocking out your own career.

SOURCE: Adapted from "Are You Knocking Out Your Own Career?" *Fast Company* (May 1999): 230, based on Lois P. Frankel's *Jump-Start Your Career* (New York: Three Rivers Press).

who credits an executive coach with helping him navigate the current tumultuous business environment is David Pottruck, co-CEO of Charles Schwab & Co.

In the Lead   David Pottruck, Charles Schwab & Co.

David Pottruck, now co-CEO of brokerage firm Charles Schwab & Co., spent years thinking he was a great leader, even as people around him cowered in fear. His strict, demanding, egocentric approach left hard feelings and damaged self-esteem almost everywhere he went. He issued orders and expected them to be carried out, no questions asked. He bull-dozed other people's opinions and trampled their ideas publicly. "I knew there was always a lot of glass being broken around me," Pottruck now says. "But I thought I was a great leader. I didn't understand there was a problem." One day, Pottruck's then-boss, COO Lawrence J. Stupski, called him into the office and gave it to him bluntly: "Man, you are high main-tenance—and you're painful. [People] don't like working with you—and they don't trust you."

Pottruck got the message, and he hired an executive coach to help him transform his approach to one that valued the ideas and input of oth-ers. He learned to listen, encouraged people to tell the truth about company problems without fear of reprisals, and began targeting his competitive spirit toward competitors rather than colleagues. Before long, Pottruck was preaching the message that there's more to life than work and more to work than making money. He says his new leadership approach centers on authenticity—constantly communicating with employees and being honest with them about the company's current problems and painful restructuring and layoffs. He also preaches and practices a commitment to high ethical standards. Although many exec-utives were raking in millions of dollars even as their companies strug-gled, Pottruck refused a bonus and took a 93 percent salary cut. "We overinvested with the boom," he says. "And the buck has to stop with me. I bear responsibility."

As financial and ethical scandals have rocked the corporate world, Pottruck believes leaders more than ever need to be self-aware and able to manage their own emotions so they can treat people well and do the right thing. He emphasizes to leaders that turning to a coach for help is not a sign of weakness but of strength, because it shows a willingness to improve. "It's not comfortable to have someone constantly telling you how you can be better," Pottruck says. "But it's very hard to get better on your own."[58]

Learning the Art and Science of Leadership

As we have discussed in this chapter, the concept of leadership has evolved through many perspectives and continues to change. Today's reality is that the old ways no longer work, but the new ways are just emerging. Everywhere, we hear the cry for leadership as the world around us is rocked by massive and often painful events.

How can a book or a course on leadership help you to be a better leader? It is important to remember that leadership is both an art and a science. It is an art because many leadership skills and qualities cannot be learned from a textbook. Leadership takes practice and hands-on experience, as well as intense personal exploration and development. However, leadership is also a science because a growing body of knowledge and objective facts describes the leadership process and how to use leadership skills to attain organizational goals.

Knowing about leadership research helps people analyze situations from a variety of perspectives and learn how to be more effective as leaders. By exploring leadership in both business and society, students gain an understanding of the importance of leadership to an organization's success, as well as the difficulties and challenges involved in being a leader. Studying leadership can also lead to the discovery of abilities you never knew you had. When students in a leadership seminar at Wharton were asked to pick one leader to represent the class, one woman was surprised when she outpolled all other students. Her leadership was drawn out not in the practice of leadership in student government, volunteer activities, or athletics, but in a classroom setting.[59]

Studying leadership gives you skills you can apply in the practice of leadership in your everyday life. Many people have never tried to be a leader because they have no understanding of what leaders actually do. The chapters in this book are designed to help you gain a firm knowledge of what leadership means and some of the skills and qualities that make a good leader. You can build competence in both the art and science of leadership by completing the Self-Insight exercises throughout the book, by working on the activities and cases at the end of each chapter, and by applying the concepts you learn in class, in your relationships with others, in student groups, at work, and in voluntary organizations. Although this book and your instructors can guide you in your development, only you can apply the concepts and principles of leadership in your daily life. Learning to be a leader starts now, with you. Are you up to the challenge?

Organization of the Rest of the Book

The plan for this book reflects the shift to a new paradigm summarized in Exhibit 1.2 and the discussion of management versus leadership summarized in Exhibit 1.3. The framework in Exhibit 1.5 illustrates the organization of the book. Part 1 introduces

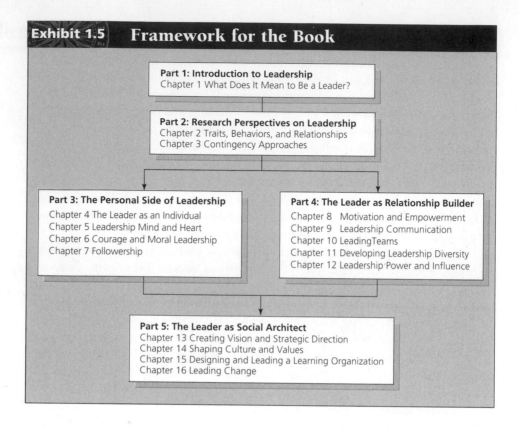

Exhibit 1.5   Framework for the Book

Part 1: Introduction to Leadership
Chapter 1 What Does It Mean to Be a Leader?

Part 2: Research Perspectives on Leadership
Chapter 2 Traits, Behaviors, and Relationships
Chapter 3 Contingency Approaches

Part 3: The Personal Side of Leadership
Chapter 4 The Leader as an Individual
Chapter 5 Leadership Mind and Heart
Chapter 6 Courage and Moral Leadership
Chapter 7 Followership

Part 4: The Leader as Relationship Builder
Chapter 8   Motivation and Empowerment
Chapter 9   Leadership Communication
Chapter 10 LeadingTeams
Chapter 11 Developing Leadership Diversity
Chapter 12 Leadership Power and Influence

Part 5: The Leader as Social Architect
Chapter 13 Creating Vision and Strategic Direction
Chapter 14 Shaping Culture and Values
Chapter 15 Designing and Leading a Learning Organization
Chapter 16 Leading Change

leadership, its importance, and the transition to a new leadership paradigm. Part 2 explores basic research perspectives that evolved during a more stable time when rational management approaches were effective. These basic perspectives, including the Great Man and trait theories, behavior theories, and contingency theories, are relevant to dealing with specific tasks and individuals and are based on a premise that leaders can predict and control various aspects of the environment to keep the organization running smoothly.

Parts 3, 4, and 5 switch to leadership perspectives that reflect the paradigm shift to the chaotic, unpredictable nature of the environment and the need for fresh leader approaches. Part 3 focuses on the personal side of leadership and looks at some of the qualities and forces that are required to be effective in the new reality. These chapters emphasize the importance of self-awareness and self-understanding, the development of one's own leadership mind and heart, moral leadership and courage, and appreciating the role of followership. Part 4 is about building effective relationships, including motivating and empowering others, communicating as a leader, leading teams, embracing the diversity of today's world, and using power and influence.

Part 5 brings together all of these ideas to examine the <u>leader as builder of a</u> <u>social architecture</u> that can help an organization create a brighter future. These chapters deal with creating vision and strategic direction, aligning culture and values to achieve the vision, and using leadership to build today's learning organizations. A final chapter focuses on leading change.

Taken together, the sections and chapters paint a complete portrait of the leadership experience as it has evolved to the present day and emphasize the new paradigm skills and qualities that are relevant from today and into the future. This book blends systematic research evidence with real-world experiences and impact.

Summary and Interpretation

This chapter introduced the concept of leadership and explained how individuals can grow as leaders. Leadership is defined as an influence relationship among leaders and followers who intend real changes and outcomes that reflect their shared purposes. Thus leadership involves people in a relationship, influence, change, a shared purpose, and taking personal responsibility to make things happen. Most of us are aware of famous leaders, but most leadership that changes the world starts small and may begin with personal frustrations about events that prompt people to initiate change and inspire others to follow them. Your leadership may be expressed in the classroom, your neighborhood, community, or volunteer organizations.

Concepts of leadership have evolved over time. Major research approaches include Great Man theories, trait theories, behavior theories, contingency theories, influence theories, and relational theories. Elements of all these approaches are still applicable to the study of leadership. In addition, emerging theories of leadership focus primarily on how leaders create change by providing vision and direction as well as the culture and values that help attain it.

The biggest challenge facing leaders today is the changing world that wants a new paradigm of leadership. The new reality involves the shift from stability to change and crisis management, from control to empowerment, from competition to collaboration, from uniformity to diversity, and from a self-centered focus to a higher purpose. In addition, the concept of leader as hero is giving way to that of the humble leader who develops others and shares credit for accomplishments. These dramatic changes suggest that a philosophy based on control and personal ambition will probably fail in the new era. The challenge for leaders is to evolve to a new mindset that relies on human skills, integrity, and teamwork.

The "soft" skills of leadership complement the "hard" skills of management, and both are needed to effectively guide organizations. Although leadership is often equated with good management, leadership and management are different processes.

Management strives to maintain stability and improve efficiency. Leadership, on the other hand, is about creating a vision for the future, designing social architecture that shapes culture and values, inspiring and motivating followers, developing personal qualities, and creating change within a culture of integrity. Leadership can be combined with management to achieve the greatest possible outcomes. Organizations need to be both managed and led, particularly in today's chaotic environment. Many managers already have the qualities needed to be effective leaders, but they may not have gone through the process needed to bring these qualities to life. It is important to remember that most people are not born with natural leadership skills and qualities, but leadership can be learned and developed.

 ## Discussion Questions

1. What do you consider your own strengths and weaknesses for leadership? Discuss your answer with another student.
2. How do you feel about changing yourself first in order to become a leader who can change an organization?
3. Of the elements in the leadership definition as illustrated in Exhibit 1.1, which is the easiest for you? Which is hardest? Explain.
4. What does the paradigm shift from control to empowerment mean for you? Discuss.
5. Describe the best leader you have known. How did this leader acquire his or her capability?
6. Why do you think there are so few people who succeed at both management and leadership? Is it reasonable to believe someone can be good at both? Discuss.
7. Discuss some recent events and societal changes that might have contributed to a shift "from hero to humble." Do you agree or disagree that humility is important for good leadership?
8. "Leadership is more concerned with people than is management." Do you agree? Discuss.
9. What personal capacities should a person develop to be a good leader versus those developed to be a good manager?
10. Why is leadership considered both an art and a science?

Leadership at Work

Leadership Right–Wrong

Leader Wrong. Think of a specific situation in which you were working with someone who was in a leadership position over you, and that person was doing something that was wrong for you. This person might have been a coach, teacher, team leader, employer, immediate boss, family member, or anyone who had a leadership position over you. "Wrong for you" means that person's behavior reduced your effectiveness, made you and/or your coworkers less productive, and was de-motivating to you and/or your colleagues. *Write a few words below that describe what the leader was doing that was wrong for you.*

_____

_____

_____

Think of a second situation in which someone in a leadership position did something wrong for you. *Write a few words below that describe what the leader was doing that was wrong for you.*

_____

_____

_____

Leader Right. Think of a specific situation in which you were working with someone who was in a leadership position over you, and that person was doing something that was *right* for you. This person might have been a coach, teacher, team leader, employer, immediate boss, family member, or anyone who had a leadership position over you. "Right for you" means that person's behavior made you and/or your coworkers more productive, highly motivated you and/or others, and removed barriers to make you more successful. *Write a few words below that describe what the leader was doing that was right for you.*

_____

_____

_____

Think of a second situation in which someone in a leadership position did something right for you. *Write a few words below that describe what the leader was doing that was right for you.*

_____

_____

_____

The previous answers are data points that can help you understand the impact of leader behaviors. Analyze your four incidents—what are the underlying qualities of leadership that enable you to be an effective performer? Discuss your answers with another student. What leadership themes are present in the eight combined incidents? What do these responses tell you about the qualities you both want and don't want in your leaders?

In Class: An interesting way to use this exercise in class is to have students write (five words maximum) their leader "rights" on one board and their leader "wrongs" on another board. The instructor can ask small groups to identify underlying themes in the collective set of leader data points on the boards to specify what makes an effective leader. After students establish four or five key themes, they can be challenged to identify the one key theme that distinguishes leaders who are effective with subordinates from those who are not.

SOURCE: Based on Melvin R. McKnight, "Organizational Behavior as a Phenomenological, Free-Will Centered Science," Working Paper, College of Business Administration, Northern Arizona University, 1997.

Leadership Development: Cases for Analysis

Sales Engineering Division

When DGL International, a manufacturer of refinery equipment, brought in John Terrill to manage its Sales Engineering division, company executives informed him of the urgent situation. Sales Engineering, with twenty engineers, was the highest-paid, best-educated, and least-productive division in the company. The instructions to Terrill: Turn it around. Terrill called a meeting of the engineers. He showed great concern for their personal welfare and asked point blank: "What's the problem? Why can't we produce? Why does this division have such turnover?"

Without hesitation, employees launched a hail of complaints. "I was hired as an engineer, not a pencil pusher." "We spend over half of our time writing asinine reports in triplicate for top management, and no one reads the reports." "We have to account for every penny, which doesn't give us time to work with customers or new developments."

After a two-hour discussion, Terrill began to envision a future in which engineers were free to work with customers and join self-directed teams for product improvement. Terrill concluded he had to get top management off the engineers' backs. He promised the engineers, "My job is to stay out of your way so you can do your work, and I'll try to keep top management off your backs too." He called for the day's reports and issued an order effective immediately that the originals be turned in daily to his office rather than mailed to headquarters. For three weeks, technical reports piled up on his desk. By month's end, the stack was nearly three feet high. During that time no one called for the reports. When other managers entered his office and saw the stack, they usually asked, "What's all this?" Terrill answered, "Technical reports." No one asked to read them.

Finally, at month's end, a secretary from finance called and asked for the monthly travel and expense report. Terrill responded, "Meet me in the president's office tomorrow morning."

The next morning the engineers cheered as Terrill walked through the department pushing a cart loaded with the enormous stack of reports. They knew the showdown had come.

Terrill entered the president's office and placed the stack of reports on his desk. The president and the other senior executives looked bewildered.

"This," Terrill announced, "is the reason for the lack of productivity in the Sales Engineering division. These are the reports your people require every month. The fact that they sat on my desk all month shows that no one reads this material. I suggest that the engineers' time could be used in a more productive manner, and that one brief monthly report from my office will satisfy the needs of the other departments."

Questions

1. Does John Terrill's leadership style fit the definition of leadership in Exhibit 1.1? Explain.
2. With respect to Exhibit 1.2, in what paradigm is Terrill? In what paradigm is headquarters?
3. What approach would you have taken in this situation?

Airstar, Inc.

Airstar, Inc. manufactures, repairs, and overhauls pistons and jet engines for smaller, often privately owned aircraft. The company had a solid niche, and most managers had been with the founder for more than twenty years. With the founder's death five years ago, Roy Morgan took over as president at Airstar. Mr. Morgan has called you in as a consultant.

Your research indicates that this industry is changing rapidly. Airstar is feeling encroachment of huge conglomerates like General Electric and

Pratt & Whitney, and its backlog of orders is the lowest in several years. The company has always been known for its superior quality, safety, and customer service. However, it has never been under threat before, and senior managers are not sure which direction to take. They have considered potential acquisitions, imports and exports, more research, and additional repair lines. The organization is becoming more chaotic, which is frustrating Morgan and his vice presidents.

Before a meeting with his team, he confides to you, "Organizing is supposed to be easy. For maximum efficiency, work should be divided into simple, logical, routine tasks. These business tasks can be grouped by similar kinds of work characteristics and arranged within an organization under a particularly suited executive. So why are we having so many problems with our executives?"

Morgan met with several of his trusted corporate officers in the executive dining room to discuss what was happening to corporate leadership at Airstar. Morgan went on to explain that he was really becoming concerned with the situation. There have been outright conflicts between the vice president of marketing and the controller over merger and acquisition opportunities. There have been many instances of duplication of work, with corporate officers trying to outmaneuver each other.

"Communications are atrocious," Morgan said to the others. "Why, I didn't even get a copy of the export finance report until my secretary made an effort to find one for me. My basis for evaluation and appraisal of corporate executive performance is fast becoming obsolete. Everyone has been working up their own job descriptions, and they all include overlapping responsibilities. Changes and decisions are being made on the basis of expediency and are perpetuating too many mistakes. We must take a good look at these organizational realities and correct the situation immediately."

Jim Robinson, vice president of manufacturing, pointed out to Morgan that Airstar is not really following the "principles of good organization." "For instance," explained Robinson, "let's review what we should be practicing as administrators." Robinson believed they should be following six principles:

1. Determine the objectives, policies, programs, and plans that will best achieve the desired results for our company.
2. Determine the various business tasks to be done.
3. Divide the business tasks into a logical and understandable organizational structure.

4. Determine the suitable personnel to occupy positions within the organizational structure.
5. Define the responsibility and authority of each supervisor clearly in writing.
6. Keep the number of kinds and levels of authority at a minimum.

Robinson proposed that the group study the corporate organizational chart, as well as the various corporate business tasks. After reviewing the corporate organizational chart, Robinson, Morgan, and the others agreed that the number and kinds of formal corporate authority were logical and not much different from other corporations. The group then listed the various corporate business tasks that went on within Airstar.

Robinson continued, "How did we ever decide who should handle mergers or acquisitions?" Morgan answered, "I guess it just occurred over time that the vice president of marketing should have the responsibility." "But," Robinson queried, "where is it written down? How would the controller know it?" "Aha!" Morgan exclaimed. "It looks like I'm part of the problem. There isn't anything in writing. Tasks were assigned superficially, as they became problems. This has all been rather informal. I'll establish a group to decide who should have responsibility for what so things can return to our previous level of efficiency."

SOURCE: Adapted from Bernard A. Deitzer and Karl A. Shilliff, *Contemporary Management Incidents* (Columbus, OH: Grid, Inc., 1977), 43–46. Copyright © 1997 by John Wiley & Sons, Inc. This material is used by permission of John Wiley & Sons, Inc.

Questions
1. What is your reaction to this conversation? What would you say to Morgan to help him lead the organization?
2. To what extent do you rate both Morgan and Robinson as a good manager versus a good leader according to the dimensions in Exhibit 1.3?
3. If you were to take over as president of Airstar, what would you do first? Second? Third?

References

1. Bill Carter, "He's Cool. He Keeps MTV Sizzling. And, Oh Yes, He's 56," *The New York Times*, June 16, 2002, Section 3, 1, 13.
2. Warren Bennis and Burt Nanus, *Leaders: The Strategies for taking Charge* (New York: Harper & Row, 2985), 4; James MacGregor Burns, *Leadership* (New York: Harper & Row, 1978), 2.
3. J. Meindl, S. Ehrlich, and J. Dukerich, "The Romance of Leadership," *Administrative Science Quarterly* 30 (1985): 78–102.

4. Rakesh Khurana, "The Curse of the Superstar CEO," *Harvard Business Review* (September 2002), 60–66.

5. Ibid.; Joseph A. Raelin, "The Myth of Charismatic Leaders," *Training and Development* (March 2003): 46.

6. Joseph C. Rost, *Leadership for the Twenty-First Century* (Westport, CT: Praeger, 1993), 102; and Joseph C. Rost and Richard A. Barker, "Leadership Education in Colleges: Toward a 21st Century Paradigm," *The Journal of Leadership Studies* 7, no. 1 (2000): 3–12.

7. Peter B. Smith and Mark F. Peterson, *Leadership, Organizations, and Culture: An Event Management Model* (London: Sage Publications, 1988), 14.

8. Robert E. Kelley, "In Praise of Followers," *Harvard Business Review*, (November–December 1988): 142–148.

9. Kevin Fedarko, "He Fights Terror with Books," *Parade Magazine*, April 6, 2003, 4–6.

10. Robin Wright and Doyle McManus, *Flashpoints: Promise and Peril in a New World* (New York: Alfred A. Knopf, 1991), 107–110.

11. Gregg Stuart, "One Person Can Make a Difference," *The Critter Chronicle: The Quarterly News Magazine of the Nashville Humane Association* (Spring 1997): 1.

12. Curtis Sittenfeld, "What Would It Take to End Homelessness?" *Fast Company* (January 2003): 42.

13. The discussion of these transformations is based in part on Daniel C. Kielson, "Leadership: Creating a New Reality," *The Journal of Leadership Studies* 3, No. 4 (1996): 104–116; and Mark A. Abramson, "Leadership for the Future: New Behaviors, New Roles, and New Attitudes," *The Public Manager* (Spring 1997). *See also* Frances Hesselbein, Marshall Goldsmith, and Richard Beckhard, eds. *The Leader of the Future: New Visions, Strategies, and Practices for the Next Era* (San Francisco: Jossey-Bass, 1996).

14. Ian Mitroff with Gus Anagnos, *Managing Crises Before They Happen* (New York: AMACOM, 2001)

15. Greg Ip, "Mind Over Matter—Disappearing Acts: The Rapid Rise and Fall of the Intangible Asset," *The Wall Street Journal*, April 4, 2002, A1, A6.

16. Thomas A. Stewart, "Brain Power: Who Owns It . . . How They Profit From It," *Fortune*, March 17, 1997, 105–110.

17. Charles Handy, *The Age of Paradox* (Boston: Harvard Business School Press, 1994), 146–147.

18. Andrew Mayo, "Memory Bankers," *People Management* (January 22, 1998), 34–38; William Miller, "Building the Ultimate Resource," *Management Review* (January 1999), 42–45; Todd Datz, "How to Speak Geek," *CIO Enterprise*, Section 2 (April 15, 1999): 46–52; and Richard McDermott, "Why Information Technology Inspired But Cannot Deliver Knowledge Management," *California Management Review* 41, No. 4 (Summer 1999): 103–117.

19. Richard L. Daft, *Organization Theory and Design*, 6th ed. (Cincinnati, OH: South-Western College Publishing, 1998), 523.

20. Cyrus F. Friedheim Jr., *The Trillion-Dollar Enterprise: How the Alliance Revolution Will Transform Global Business* (Reading, MA: Perseus Books, 1999).

21. "Keeping Your Edge: Managing a Diverse Corporate Culture," Special Advertising Section, *Fortune* (June 3, 2001): S1-S17; Steven Greenhouse, N.Y. Times News Service, "Influx of Immigrants Having Profound Impact on Economy," *Johnson City Press*, September 4, 2000, 9; Richard W. Judy and Carol D'Amico, *Workforce 2020: Work and Workers in the 21st Century* (Indianapolis, IN: Hudson Institute, 1997).

22. Jerry Useem, "Tyrants, Statesmen, and Destroyers (A Brief History of the CEO)," *Fortune*, (November 18, 2002): 82–90.

23. Bethany McLean, "Why Enron Went Bust," *Fortune* (December 24, 2001): 58–68; and John A. Byrne with Mike France and Wendy Zellner, "The Environment Was Ripe for Abuse," *BusinessWeek* (February 25, 2002): 118–120.

24. Mark Gimein, "You Bought, They Sold," *Fortune* (September 2, 2002): 64–74.

25. Patricia Sellers, "The New Breed," *Fortune* (November 18, 2002): 66–76.

26. Nanette Byrnes with John A. Byrne, Cliff Edwards, Louise Lee, Stanley Holmes, and Joann Muller, "The Good CEO," *BusinessWeek*, September 23, 2002, 80–88.

27. Sellers, "The New Breed."

28. *See* James Collins, *Good to Great: Why Some Companies Make the Leap . . . And Other Don't* (New York: HarperCollins 2001); Charles A. O'Reilly III and Jeffrey Pfeffer, *Hidden Value: How Great Companies Achieve Extraordinary Results with Ordinary People* (Boston, Mass.: Harvard Business School Press, 2000); Rakesh Khurana, *Searching for a Corporate Savior: The Irrational Quest for Charismatic CEOs* (Princeton University Press, 2002); and Joseph Badaracco, *Leading Quietly* (Boston, Mass.: Harvard Business School Press, 2002).

29. Useem, "Tyrants, Statesmen, and Destroyers."

30. Ibid.

31. Jim Collins, "Level 5 Leadership: The Triumph of Humility and Fierce Resolve," *Harvard Business Review* (January 2001): 67–76; Collins, "Good to Great," *Fast Company* (October 2001): 90–104; Edward Prewitt, "The Utility of Humility," *CIO* (December 1, 2002): 104–110; A. J. Vogl, "Onward and Upward" (an interview with Jim Collins), *Across the Board* (September–October 2001): 29–34; and Jerry Useem, "Conquering Vertical Limits," *Fortune* (February 19, 2001): 84–96.

32. James Lardner, "In Praise of the Anonymous CEO," *Business2.0* (September 2002): 104–108; and Byrnes, et al. "The Good CEO."

33. Jim Collins, interviewed in Paul Scott, "Evolution of the Successful Executive," *MBA Jungle* (February 2002): 40–45.

34. Martha H. Peak, "Anti-Manager Named Manager of the Year," *Management Review* (October 1991): 7.

35. This section is based largely on John P. Kotter, *A Force for Change: How Leadership Differs from Management* (New York: The Free Press, 1990): 3–18.

36. *Leadership, A Forum Issues Special Report* (Boston, MA: The Forum Corporation, 1990), 13.

37. Ronald B. Lieber, "Why Employees Love These Companies," *Fortune* (January 12, 1998): 72–74.

38. *Leadership: A Forum Issues Special Report* (Boston, MA: The Forum Corporation, 1990): 15.

39. James Kaplan, "Amateur's Hour," *Working Woman* (October 1997): 28–33.

40. John P. Kotter, quoted in Thomas A. Stewart, "Why Leadership Matters," *Fortune* (March 2, 1998): 71–82.

41. John P. Kotter, *Leading Change* (Boston, MA: Harvard Business School Press, 1996): 26.

42. Joseph C. Rost, *Leadership for the Twenty-First Century* (Westport, CT: Praeger, 1993): 145–146.

43. Warren Bennis, *Why Leaders Can't Lead* (San Francisco: Jossey-Bass, 1989).

44. Bennis, *Why Leaders Can't Lead*; and Stewart, "Why Leadership Matters."

45. Stratford Sherman, "How Tomorrow's Best Leaders Are Learning Their Stuff," *Fortune* (November 27, 1995): 90–102; Frances Hesselbein, "The Search for Common Ground," *Leader to Leader* no. 25 (2002), accessed at *http://www.pfdf.org*; and Frances Hesselbein, *Hesselbein on Leadership* (San Francisco, Calif.: Jossey–Bass, 2002).

46. Abraham Zaleznik, "Managers and Leaders: Are They Different?" *Harvard Business Review* (March–April 1992): 126–135.

47. Bennis, *Why Leaders Can't Lead*.

48. Sherman, "How Tomorrow's Best Leaders Are Learning Their Stuff."

49. Susan R. Komives, Nance Lucas, Timothy R. McMahon, *Exploring Leadership: For College Students Who Want to Make a Difference* (San Francisco: Jossey-Bass Publishers, 1998): 38.

50. Based on Komives, et al., *Exploring Leadership*; and Shann R. Ferch and Matthew M. Mitchell, "Intentional Forgiveness in Relational Leadership: A Technique for Enhancing Effective Leadership," *The Journal of Leadership Studies* 7, no. 4 (2001): 70–83.

51. James MacGregor Burns, *Leadership* (New York: Harper & Row, 1978); Bernard M. Bass, "Current Developments in Transformational Leadership," *The Psychologist-Manager Journal* 3, no.1 (1999): 5–21.

52. Robert K. Greenleaf, *The Servant as Leader* (Indianapolis: The Robert Greenleaf Center, 1970); and Mary Sue Polleys, "One University's Response to the Anti-Leadership Vaccine: Developing Servant Leaders," *The Journal of Leadership Studies* 8, no. 3 (2002): 117–130.

53. Komives, et al., *Exploring Leadership*, 48.

54. Gary Yukl, Angela Gordon, and Tom Taber, "A Hierarchical Taxonomy of Leadership Behavior: Integrating a Half Century of Behavior Research," *Journal of Leadership and Organizational Studies* 9, no. 1 (2002): 16–32.

55. Peter Kafka, "Diversify and Conquer," *Forbes* (May 13, 2002): 104–108.

56. Morgan W. McCall, Jr., and Michael M. Lombardo, "Off the Track: Why and How Successful Executives Get Derailed" (Technical Report No. 21, Center for Creative Leadership, Greensboro, NC: January 1983); Carol Hymowitz, "Five Main Reasons Why Managers Fail," *The Wall Street Journal*, May 2, 1988.

57. Ram Charan and Geoffrey Colvin, "Why CEOs Fail," *Fortune* (June 21, 1999): 68–78.

58. Michelle Conlin, "CEO Coaches," *BusinessWeek* (November 11, 2002): 98–104; and Joseph Nocera, "A Mug Only 20,000 Employees Could Love," *eCompany Now* (June 2000): 159–166.

59. Russell Palmer, "Can Leadership Be Learned?" *Business Today* (Fall, 1989): 100–102.

Research Perspectives on Leadership

Chapter

Your Leadership Challenge

After reading this chapter, you should be able to:

- Identify personal traits and characteristics that are associated with effective leaders.

- Recognize autocratic versus democratic leadership behavior and the impact of each.

- Know the distinction between people-oriented and task-oriented leadership behavior and when each should be used.

- Understand how the theory of individualized leadership has broadened the understanding of relationships between leaders and followers.

- Recognize how to build partnerships for greater effectiveness.

Imagine slogging through near-freezing water up to your waist, or walking for miles and then discovering you're only a hundred yards closer to your destination. That's what happened when Robert Swan led a team to the North Pole and the ice cap began to melt beneath their feet. Swan's carefully planned expedition, made up of eight people from seven countries, became a nightmare when the ice cap began to melt in April—four months earlier than usual.

The group survived—barely—because of teamwork and Swan's extraordinary leadership. Swan's honesty, as well as his ability to maintain his poise, self-confidence, and sense of purpose amid life-threatening and constantly changing conditions, helped to nourish the spirit and motivation of the team. With the completion of the journey, Swan became the first person ever to walk to both the North and the South Poles. Today, he recounts his adventures to groups around the world, including businesspeople hungry to learn what it means to be a leader in a dangerous and hostile environment.

Swan had dreamed of walking to the South Pole, tracing the route taken by Robert Falcon Scott in 1912, since he was a child. As a young adult, he spent seven years working as a taxi driver, a tree cutter, a gardener, and a hotel dishwasher to earn money, all the while selling the dream to others to help raise funds. His first expedition to Antarctica in 1986 changed his life completely. Motivated by first-hand observation of the destruction of the ozone layer and by the waste and pollution he encountered on his journey, Swan became deeply committed to environmental issues. He took on the difficult challenge of raising money for his second expedition, to the North Pole, inspired primarily by the dream of helping to save the polar regions from human destruction.

As one of today's top motivational speakers, Swan is inspiring people around the world to become involved in saving the environment. He leads young people from many countries on expeditions that focus on research and education. He offers employees of his corporate sponsors the opportunity to sail to Antarctica and participate in cleaning up the region. From an organizational viewpoint, Swan's stories of courage, adventure, determination, and risk taking are good metaphors for what many leaders feel in today's complex and uncertain environment.[1]

Robert Swan is a world-renowned explorer who is influencing young people, world leaders, businesspeople, and organizations around the globe. He works tirelessly for what he believes in and has inspired others to become more actively involved. Those who participate in his expeditions take what they learn back to their organizations, further extending Swan's influence. Several personal attributes contribute to Swan's leadership. He had the courage, self-confidence, and determination to try something that everyone told him couldn't be done. He had the drive and the commitment to work for years in menial jobs to make his dream a reality, and he continues to raise money for the causes he believes in. His poise and ability to maintain a positive attitude have helped team members survive harrowing conditions.

In considering Swan's influence, it seems evident that characteristics such as courage, self-confidence, drive, determination, and a willingness to take risks are part of the personality that make him a good leader. Indeed, personal traits are what captured the imagination of the earliest leadership researchers. Many leaders possess traits that researchers believe affect their leadership impact. For example, retired three-star general Jay Garner, who led the initial reconstruction efforts in Iraq, is recognized for his compassion, tenacity, and ability to keep a sense of humor under intense pressure. An example from the business world is Julia Stewart, whose first job was serving food at an International House of Pancakes (IHOP) in San Diego. Traits such as ambition, persistence, responsibility, and enthusiasm have helped Stewart through a series of jobs since then, eventually landing her in the CEO's chair at IHOP.[2]

Leaders display traits through patterns in their behavior. Consequently, many researchers have examined the behavior of leaders to determine what behavioral features comprise leadership style and how particular behaviors relate to effective leadership. Later research specified behavior between a leader and each distinct follower, differentiating one-on-one behavior from leader-to-group behavior.

Traits

the distinguishing personal characteristics of a leader, such as intelligence, honesty, self-confidence, and appearance

This chapter provides an overview of the initial leadership research in the twentieth century. We will examine the evolution of the trait approach and the behavior approach, and introduce the theory of individualized leadership. The path illuminated by the research into leader traits and behaviors is a foundation for the field of leadership studies and still enjoys remarkable dynamism for explaining leader success or failure.

The Trait Approach

Early efforts to understand leadership success focused on the leader's personal traits. **Traits** are the distinguishing personal characteristics of a leader, such as intelligence, honesty, self-confidence, and appearance. Research early in this century examined leaders who had achieved a level of greatness, and hence became known as the Great Man approach. Fundamental to this theory was the idea that some people are born with traits that make them natural leaders. The Great Man approach sought to identify the traits leaders possessed that distinguished them from people who were not leaders. Generally, research found only a weak relationship between personal traits and leader success.[3] Indeed, the diversity of traits that effective leaders possess indicates that leadership ability is not necessarily a genetic endowment.

Nevertheless, with the advancement of the field of psychology during the 1940s and 1950s, trait approach researchers expanded their examination of personal attributes by using aptitude and psychological tests. These early studies looked at personality traits such as creativity and self-confidence, physical traits such as age and energy level, abilities such as knowledge and fluency of speech, social characteristics such as popularity and sociability, and work-related characteristics such as the desire to excel and persistence against obstacles. Effective leaders were often identified by exceptional follower performance, or by a high status position within an organization and a salary that exceeded that of peers.[4]

In a 1948 literature review[5] Stogdill examined more than 100 studies based on the trait approach. He uncovered several traits that appeared consistent with effective leadership, including general intelligence, initiative, interpersonal skills, self-confidence, drive for responsibility, and personal integrity. Stogdill's findings also indicated, however, that the importance of a particular trait was often relative to the situation. Initiative, for example, may contribute to the success of a leader in one situation, but it may be irrelevant to a leader in another situation. Thus, possessing certain personal characteristics is no guarantee of success.

Many researchers desisted their efforts to identify leadership traits in light of Stogdill's 1948 findings and turned their attention to examining leader behavior and leadership situations. However, others continued with expanded trait lists and research projects. Stogdill's subsequent review of 163 trait studies conducted between 1948 and 1970 concluded that some personal traits do indeed seem to contribute to effective leadership.[6] The study identified many of the same traits found in the 1948 survey, along with several additional characteristics, including aggressiveness, independence, and tolerance for stress. However, Stogdill again cautioned that the value of a particular trait or set of traits varies with the organizational situation.

In recent years, there has been a resurgence of interest in examining leadership traits. A 1991 review by Kirkpatrick and Locke identified a number of personal traits that distinguish leaders from nonleaders, including some pinpointed by Stogdill.[7] Other studies have focused on followers' perceptions and indicate that certain traits are associated with individuals' perceptions of who is a leader. For example, one study found that the traits of intelligence, masculinity, and dominance were strongly related to how individuals perceived leaders.[8] More recently,

Great Man approach
a leadership perspective that sought to identify the inherited traits leaders possessed that distinguished them from people who were not leaders

the management consulting firm Accenture, with the assistance of leadership scholars, interviewed hundreds of leaders around the world and asked them to rank the importance of various characteristics. Based on these interviews and surveys, the research team developed a list of fourteen characteristics believed to be important for successful leadership in today's world.[9] Similarly, star headhunters Thomas J. Neff and James M. Citrin believe there are some traits that are shared by today's best leaders, as described in the Leader's Bookshelf.

A concern with traits is also evidenced by the recent interest in emotional intelligence, which includes characteristics such as self-awareness, the ability to manage one's emotions, the capacity to be hopeful and optimistic despite obstacles, the ability to empathize with others, and strong social and interpersonal skills.[10] Emotional intelligence will be discussed in greater detail in Chapter 5.

In summary, trait research has been an important part of leadership studies throughout the twentieth century and continues into the twenty-first. Many researchers still contend that some traits are essential to effective leadership, but only in combination with other factors.[11] Exhibit 2.1 presents some of the traits and their respective categories that have been identified through trait research over the years. Some of the traits considered essential are self-confidence, honesty and integrity, and drive.

Exhibit 2.1   Personal Characteristics of Leaders

Personal Characteristics	Social Characteristics
Energy	Sociability, interpersonal skills
Physical stamina	Cooperativeness
Intelligence and Ability	Ability to enlist cooperation
Intelligence, cognitive ability	Tact, diplomacy
Knowledge	**Work-Related Characteristics**
Judgment, decisiveness	Drive, desire to excel
Personality	Responsibility in pursuit of goals
Self-confidence	Persistence against obstacles, tenacity
Honesty and integrity	
Enthusiasm	**Social Background**
Desire to lead	Education
Independence	Mobility

SOURCES: *Bass and Stogdill's Handbook of Leadership: Theory, Research, and Management Applications,* 3rd ed. (New York: The Free Press, 1990), 80–81; and S. A. Kirkpatrick and E. A. Locke, "Leadership: Do Traits Matter?" *Academy of Management Executive* 5, no. 2 (1991), 48–60.

LEADER'S BOOKSHELF

Lessons from the Top: The Search for America's Best Business Leaders
by Thomas J. Neff and James M. Citrin

What makes a great leader? Thomas J. Neff and James M. Citrin attempt to answer that question through profiles of 50 leaders in some of America's most successful organizations, including well-known CEOs as well as lesser-known leaders. In their book, *Lessons from the Top*, Neff and Citrin (chairman and managing director respectively of Spencer Stuart, a top executive search firm) describe what they believe are the qualities and principles that define effective leadership in today's world.

The Traits and Principles of a Leader
Even though the authors found vast differences in personality among the leaders they interviewed, they also determined that there are some traits and philosophies shared by most of them. After evaluating the profiles, Neff and Citrin synthesize the qualities of effective leaders into 10 common traits: passion, intelligence, communication skill, high energy, controlled ego, inner peace, a defining background, a strong family life, a positive attitude, and a focus on "doing the right things right."

In addition, the authors distinguish six core principles that successful leaders live by:

❈ **Live with integrity; lead by example.** Integrity builds trust and confidence among followers that is necessary for high-performing organizations.

❈ **Develop a winning strategy.** Neff and Citrin point out that a successful leader has to be able to understand what the company does best and build on it.

❈ **Build a great management team.** Great leaders hire people "whose skills and experiences [complement] their own, but whose passion, attitudes, and values [are] one and the same."

❈ **Inspire employees.** To be effective, leaders communicate constantly and listen carefully. In addition they encourage risk-taking, and even failure, as a learning experience.

❈ **Create a flexible organization.** The best leaders get rid of practices and policies that stand in the way of flexibility and customer responsiveness.

❈ **Implement relevant systems.** "Compensation . . . must be consistent with and reinforce the values and strategy of the organization."

Applying the Lessons
One excellent aspect of *Lessons from the Top* is that it allows readers to spend some time getting to know 50 of today's most successful leaders. The authors also summarize the lessons from these leaders in two clear and concise chapters, "Doing the Right Things Right: A New Definition of Business Success," and "Common Traits: A Prescription for Success in Business." By taking the experiences of these 50 real-life leaders and distilling them into a framework of effective leadership, the book helps readers see how individual experiences fit into a larger picture and how to apply these lessons from the top to their own lives and leadership.

Lessons from the Top: The Search for America's Best Leaders, by Thomas J. Neff and James M. Citrin, is published by Doubleday.

Self-confidence
*assurance in
one's own judg-
ments, decision
making, ideas,
and capabilities*

Honesty
*truthfulness and
nondeception*

Integrity
*the quality of
being whole,
integrated, and
acting in accor-
dance with
solid moral
principles*

Self-Confidence   Self-confidence is assurance in one's own judgments, decision making, ideas, and capabilities. A leader with a positive self-image who displays certainty about his or her own ability fosters confidence among followers, gains respect and admiration, and meets challenges. The confidence a leader displays and develops creates motivation and commitment among followers for the mission at hand.

Active leaders need self-confidence. Leaders initiate changes and they often must make decisions without adequate information. Problems are solved continuously. Without the confidence to move forward and believe things will be okay, even if an occasional decision is wrong, leaders could be paralyzed into inaction. Setbacks have to be overcome. Risks have to be taken. Competing points of view have to be managed, with some people left unsatisfied. Self-confidence is the one trait that enables a leader to face all these challenges.[12]

Do you believe you have the self-confidence to be a strong and effective leader? Complete the questionnaire in Leader's Self-Insight 2.1 to assess your level of self-confidence.

Honesty/Integrity   Honesty refers to truthfulness and nondeception. It implies an openness that followers welcome. **Integrity** means that a leader's character is whole, integrated, and grounded in solid moral principles, and he or she acts in keeping with those principles. When leaders model their convictions through their daily actions, they command admiration, respect, and loyalty. These virtues are the foundation of trust between leaders and followers.

In the wake of widespread corporate scandals, trust is sorely lacking in many organizations. Leaders need the traits of honesty and integrity to rebuild trusting and productive relationships. People today are wary of authority and the deceptive use of power, and they are hungry for leaders who hold high standards and reinforce them through everyday actions. David Maxwell, former CEO of Fannie Mae, provides an illustration. When asked how he resisted taking actions that would drive up Fannie Mae's share price in the short term but that might ultimately hurt the company, Maxwell was truly perplexed, as if such a thought had never even occurred to him.[13]

Successful leaders have also been found to be highly consistent, doing exactly what they say they will do when they say they will do it. Successful leaders are easy to trust. They have basic principles and consistently apply them. One survey of 1,500 managers asked the values most desired in leaders. Integrity was the most important characteristic. The authors concluded:

> Honesty is absolutely essential to leadership. After all, if we are willing to follow someone, whether it be into battle or into the boardroom, we first want to assure ourselves that the

Action Memo

As a leader: Develop the personal traits of self-confidence, integrity, and drive, which are important for successful leadership in every organization and situation.

Rate Your Self-Confidence

SOURCE: This is the general self-efficacy subscale of the self-efficacy scale published in M. Sherer, J. E. Maddux, B. Mercadante, S. Prentice-Dunn, B. Jacobs, and R. W. Rogers, "The Self-Efficacy Scale: Construction and Validation," *Psychological Reports* 51 (1982): 663–671. Used with permission.

This questionnaire is designed to assess your level of self-confidence as reflected in a belief in your ability to accomplish a desired outcome. There are no right or wrong answers. Please indicate your personal feelings about each statement by circling the number that best describes your attitude or feeling, based on the following scale:

1 = Strongly disagree; 2 = Disagree; 3 = Neither agree nor disagree; 4 = Agree; 5 = Strongly agree

	Strongly disagree				Strongly agree
1. When I make plans, I am certain I can make them work.	1	2	3	4	5
2. One of my problems is that I cannot get down to work when I should.	1	2	3	4	5
3. If I can't do a job the first time, I keep trying until I can.	1	2	3	4	5
4. When I set important goals for myself, I rarely achieve them.	1	2	3	4	5
5. I give up on things before completing them.	1	2	3	4	5
6. I avoid facing difficulties.	1	2	3	4	5
7. If something looks too complicated, I will not even bother to try it.	1	2	3	4	5
8. When I have something unpleasant to do, I stick to it until I finish it.	1	2	3	4	5
9. When I decide to do something, I go right to work on it.	1	2	3	4	5
10. When trying to learn something new, I soon give up if I am not initially successful.	1	2	3	4	5
11. When unexpected problems occur, I don't handle them well.	1	2	3	4	5
12. I avoid trying to learn new things when they look too difficult for me.	1	2	3	4	5
13. Failure just makes me try harder.	1	2	3	4	5
14. I feel insecure about my ability to do things.	1	2	3	4	5
15. I am a self-reliant person.	1	2	3	4	5
16. I give up easily.	1	2	3	4	5
17. I do not seem capable of dealing with most problems that come up in life.	1	2	3	4	5

Scoring and Interpretation: Subtract each of your scores for questions 2, 4, 5, 6, 7, 10, 11, 12, 14, 16, and 17 from the number 6. Next, using your adjusted scores, sum your score for the 17 questions and then divide by 17. Enter your score here: _____ This subscale relates to one aspect of self-confidence. If your score is low, what can you do to increase your self-confidence?

person is worthy of our trust. We want to know that he or she is being truthful, ethical, and principled. We want to be fully confident in the integrity of our leaders.[14]

Drive A third characteristic considered essential for effective leadership is drive.

Drive
high motivation
that creates a
high effort level
by a leader

Drive refers to high motivation that creates a high effort level by a leader. Leaders with drive seek achievement, have energy and tenacity, and are frequently seen to have ambition and initiative to achieve their goals. Leaders rise to the top often because they actively pursue goals. Ambition enables them to set challenging goals and take initiative to achieve those goals.[15]

A strong drive is associated with high energy. Leaders work long hours over many years. They have stamina and are vigorous and full of life in order to handle the pace, the demands, and the challenges of leadership. Leaders often are responsible for initiating new projects as well as guiding projects to successful completion. The following sketch illustrates the kind of drive that predicts successful leadership.

> "I want to be able to demonstrate the things I learned in college and get to the top," said Al, "maybe even be president. I expect to work hard and be at the third level within five years, and to rise to much higher levels in the years beyond. I am specifically working on my MBA to aid in my advancement. If I am thwarted on advancement, or find the challenges lacking, I'll leave the company."[16]

Traits such as drive, self-confidence, and integrity have great value for leaders. The Living Leadership box considers the notion that personal characteristics of the leader are ultimately responsible for leadership outcomes. In Chapter 4, we will further consider individual characteristics and qualities that play a role in leadership effectiveness.

However, as indicated earlier, traits alone cannot define effective leadership. Consider, for example, how the same traits that spurred Kenneth Lay's early success also led to his downfall and contributed to one of the biggest corporate collapses in history.

In the Lead   Kenneth Lay, Enron Corporation

Many people who know Kenneth Lay, the former chairman and chief executive of Enron Corporation, consider him to be a decent, honest, hard-working man who got caught in a situation out of his control. Lay himself says he always wanted Enron to be "a highly moral and highly ethical environment." But some of Lay's personal traits may have gotten in the way.

The boy who grew up in difficult conditions in rural Missouri, once eating a Thanksgiving dinner of lunch meat and bread, clearly had self-confidence, a strong ambition, and the drive for achievement and success. He says his parents taught him that "there was really no problem too great. As long as you continued to work hard and had a lot of faith, you'd work your way through it." Lay earned a Ph.D. in economics at night school and eventually built one of the largest companies in the world. However, he will be remembered as the leader of an organization's whose demise, fueled by vast deception, wiped out billions of investor dollars and cost the jobs of thousands of employees.

It is not clear how much Kenneth Lay knew about what was going on at Enron. Some former employees believe his boundless optimism and easy trust in others led him to truly believe the company was in good shape and the complex accounting machinations were acceptable. Others think his ambition outweighed his ethics, causing him to turn a blind eye to what was going on. He was content to simply trust his senior executives as long as the stock price kept rising. In a 2002 interview with *The Wall Street Journal* after Enron's collapse, Lay consistently emphasized his personal values of "respect, integrity, and excellence." However, his reputation as a leader of integrity has been seriously—perhaps irreparably—damaged. Even so, he still has the self-confidence and optimism that he will get through this ordeal and find "something else that's going to be exciting and fun" on the other side.[17]

LIVING LEADERSHIP

Leader Qualities

The quality of the leader determines the quality of the organization.

A leader who lacks intelligence, virtue, and experience cannot hope for success.

In any conflict, the circumstances affect the outcome.

Good leaders can succeed in adverse conditions.

Bad leaders can lose in favorable conditions.

Therefore, good leaders constantly strive to perfect themselves, lest their shortcomings mar their endeavors.

When all other factors are equal, it is the character of the leader that determines the outcome.

SOURCE: Excerpt from page 66 ["Leader Qualities"] from *Everyday Tao: Living with Balance and Harmony* by Deng Ming-Dao. Copyright © 1996 by Deng Ming-Dao. Reprinted by permission of HarperCollins Publishers, Inc.

Behavior Approaches

The inability of researchers to define effective leadership based solely on personal traits led to an interest in looking at the behavior of leaders and how it might contribute to leadership success or failure. The behavior approach says that anyone who adopts the appropriate behavior can be a good leader. Diverse research programs on leadership behavior have sought to uncover the behaviors that leaders engage in rather than what traits a leader possesses. Behaviors can be learned more readily than traits, enabling leadership to be accessible to all.

Autocratic versus Democratic Leadership

Autocratic
a leader who tends to centralize authority and derive power from position, control of rewards, and coercion

Democratic
a leader who delegates authority to others, encourages participation, relies on subordinates' knowledge for completion of tasks, and depends on subordinate respect for influence

One study that served as a precursor to the behavior approach recognized autocratic and democratic leadership styles. An **autocratic** leader is one who tends to centralize authority and derive power from position, control of rewards, and coercion. A **democratic** leader delegates authority to others, encourages participation, relies on subordinates' knowledge for completion of tasks, and depends on subordinate respect for influence.

The first studies on these leadership behaviors were conducted at the University of Iowa by Kurt Lewin and his associates.[18] The research included groups of children, each with its own designated adult leader who was instructed to act in either an autocratic or democratic style. These experiments produced some interesting findings. The groups with autocratic leaders performed highly so long as the leader was present to supervise them. However, group members were displeased with the close, autocratic style of leadership, and feelings of hostility frequently arose. The performance of groups who were assigned democratic leaders was almost as good, and these groups were characterized by positive feelings rather than hostility. In addition, under the democratic style of leadership, group members performed well even when the leader was absent. The participative techniques and majority-rule decision making used by the democratic leader trained and involved the group members so that they performed well with or without the leader present. These characteristics of democratic leadership may partly explain why the empowerment of employees is a popular trend in companies today.

This early work implied that leaders were either autocratic or democratic in their approach. However, further work by Tannenbaum and Schmidt indicated that leadership behavior could exist on a continuum reflecting different amounts of employee participation.[19] Thus, one leader might be autocratic (boss-centered), another democratic (subordinate-centered), and a third a mix of the two styles. The leadership continuum is illustrated in Exhibit 2.2.

Tannenbaum and Schmidt also suggested that the extent to which leaders should be boss-centered or subordinate-centered depended on organizational circumstances, and that leaders might adjust their behaviors to fit the circumstances. For example, if

s students. To encourage students to raise their reading skills, he chal-
hem to read 25 books each. Even though parents complained that
as too high, an auditorium full of students recently received
ding 100 books each during the last school year.

achers were at first skeptical about meeting Fryer's high
n won over to his motto of "Aim High," which he
rce. One reason Fryer gained the commitment of
ved them in the process. "We finally got a
n," said Terrie Brady, president of the teach-
dinners for ten to fifteen teachers at a
ve them the training they told him they
achers also appreciate that they have
ohnson, principal of West
st schools in the county, says her
keep changing, as they have
percent of students passed
nt passed last year.

tely turn things
shift in motiva-
ole in school
hem."24

erform-
was
ty
str

Ohio State Studies

An early series of studies on leadership behavior was conducted at the Ohio
University. Researchers conducted surveys to identify specific dimensions
behavior. Narrowing a list of nearly 2,000 leader behaviors into a questi
taining 150 examples of definitive leader behaviors, they develo
Behavior Description Questionnaire (LBDQ) and administered
Hundreds of employees responded to behavior examples acc
which their leaders engaged in the various behaviors. The a
in two wide-ranging categories of leader behavior type
and initiating structure.

Consideration describes the extent to whic
nates, respects their ideas and feelings, and est
ciation, listening carefully to problems,
regarding important decisions are all ex

Initiating structure describes th
directs subordinates' work activit
behavior includes directing tas
schedules for work activitie

Although many lea
and initiating struct
another. In other
a low degree of
sideration an
ture beha
effecti
str

Consideration
the extent to
which a leader
is sensitive to
subordinates,
respects their
ideas and feel-
ings, and estab-
lishes mutual
trust

Initiating
Structure
the extent to
which a leader
is task oriented
and directs sub-
ordinates' work
activities
toward goal
achievement

create satisfied customers, which is certainly correct in her company situation.21

The findings of the original University of Iowa studies indicated that leadership behavior had a definite effect on outcomes such as follower performance and satisfaction. Equally important was the recognition that effective leadership was reflected in behavior, not simply by what personality traits a leader possessed. This recognition provided a focus for subsequent studies based on the behavior approach.

when there is
time pressure or
followers have
low skill levels
and the leader's
expertise is
needed.

What's Your Leadership Orientation?

The questions below ask about your personal leadership orientation. Each item describes a specific kind of behavior but does not ask you to judge whether the behavior is desirable or undesirable.

Read each item carefully. Think about how frequently you engage in the behavior described by the item, using a work or school group as reference. Circle one of the five numerical response codes following each question, which reflects the frequency of the behavior.

1. Put suggestions made by people in the group into operation.

Always	Often	Occasionally	Seldom	Never
1	2	3	4	5

2. Treat all people in the group as your equal.

Always	Often	Occasionally	Seldom	Never
1	2	3	4	5

3. Back up what other people in the group do.

Always	Often	Occasionally	Seldom	Never
1	2	3	4	5

4. Reject suggestions for change.

Always	Often	Occasionally	Seldom	Never
1	2	3	4	5

5. Talk about how much should be done.

A great deal	Fairly often	To some degree	Comparatively little	Not at all
1	2	3	4	5

6. Assign people in the group to particular tasks.

Always	Often	Occasionally	Seldom	Never
1	2	3	4	5

7. Offer new approaches to problems.

Often	Fairly Often	Occasionally	Once in a while	Very seldom
1	2	3	4	5

8. Emphasize meeting the deadlines.

A great deal	Fairly often	To some degree	Comparatively little	Not at all
1	2	3	4	5

Scoring and Interpretation *Consideration* behavior—Subtract your score to questions 1, 2, 3, and 4 from 6. Next, sum your adjusted response to questions 1, 2, 3, and 4 and divide by 4.

Enter your consideration score here _____.

A high score (4 and above) suggests a relatively strong orientation toward consideration-oriented behavior by you as a leader. A low score (2 and below) suggests a relatively weak consideration orientation.

Initiating structure behavior—subtract your score to questions 5, 6, 7, and 8 from 6. Next, sum your adjusted response to questions 5, 6, 7, and 8 and divide by 4.

Enter your initiating structure score here _____.

A high score (4 and above) suggests a relatively strong orientation toward initiating structure-oriented behavior by you as a leader. A low score (2 and below) suggests a relatively weak orientation toward initiating structure behavior.

SOURCE: Sample items from and reprinted with permission: Edwin A Fleishman's *Leadership Opinion Questionnaire*. (Copyright 1960, Science Research Associates, Inc., Chicago, IL.) This version is from Jon L. Pierce and John W. Newstrom, *Leaders and the Leadership Process: Readings, Self-Assessments & Applications*, 2nd edition (Boston: Irwin McGraw-Hill, 2000).

University of Michigan Studies

Studies at the University of Michigan took a different approach by directly comparing the behavior of effective and ineffective supervisors.[27] The effectiveness of leaders was determined by productivity of the subordinate group. Initial field studies and interviews at various job sites gave way to a questionnaire not unlike the LBDQ, called the Survey of Organizations.[28]

Over time, the Michigan researchers established two types of leadership behavior, each type consisting of two dimensions.[29] First, **employee-centered** leaders display a focus on the human needs of their subordinates. Leader support and interaction facilitation are the two underlying dimensions of employee-centered behavior. This means that in addition to demonstrating support for their subordinates, employee-centered leaders facilitate positive interaction among followers and seek to minimize conflict. The employee-centered style of leadership roughly corresponds to the Ohio State concept of consideration. Because relationships are so important in today's work environment, many organizations are looking for leaders who can facilitate positive interaction among others. Damark International, a general merchandise catalogue company, even has a position designed to help people get along better. Although his official title is director of leadership and team development, Mark Johansson calls himself a "relationship manager." Johansson works with managers throughout the organization to help them improve their relationship and interpersonal skills and become more employee-centered.[30]

In contrast to the employee-centered leader, the **job-centered** leader directs activities toward efficiency, cost-cutting, and scheduling. Goal emphasis and work facilitation are dimensions of this leadership behavior. By focusing on reaching task goals and facilitating the structure of tasks, job-centered behavior approximates that of initiating structure.

However, unlike the consideration and initiating structure defined by the Ohio State studies, Michigan researchers considered employee-centered leadership and job-centered leadership to be distinct styles in opposition to one another. A leader is identifiable by behavior characteristic of one or the other style, but not both. Another hallmark of later Michigan studies is the acknowledgment that often the behaviors of goal emphasis, work facilitation, support, and interaction facilitation can be meaningfully performed by a subordinate's peers, rather than only by the designated leader. Other people in the group could supply these behaviors, which enhanced performance.[31]

In addition, while leadership behavior was demonstrated to affect the performance and satisfaction of subordinates, performance was also influenced by other factors related to the situation within which leaders and subordinates worked. The situation will be explored in the next chapter.

Employee-centered
a leadership behavior that displays a focus on the human needs of subordinates

Job-centered
leadership behavior in which leaders direct activities toward efficiency, cost-cutting, and scheduling, with an emphasis on goals and work facilitation

The Leadership Grid

Blake and Mouton of the University of Texas proposed a two-dimensional leadership theory called **The Leadership Grid** that builds on the work of the Ohio State and Michigan studies.[32] Based on a week-long seminar, researchers rated leaders on a scale of one to nine according to two criteria: the concern for people and the concern for production. The scores for these criteria are plotted on a grid with an axis corresponding to each concern. The two-dimensional model and seven major leadership styles are depicted in Exhibit 2.3.

Team management (9,9) often is considered the most effective style and is recommended because organization members work together to accomplish tasks. *Country club management* (1,9) occurs when primary emphasis is given to people rather than to work outputs. *Authority-compliance management* (9,1) occurs when efficiency in operations is the dominant orientation. *Middle-of-the-road management* (5,5) reflects a moderate amount of concern for both people and production. *Impoverished management* (1,1) means the absence of a leadership philosophy; leaders exert little effort toward interpersonal relationships or work accomplishment. Consider these examples:

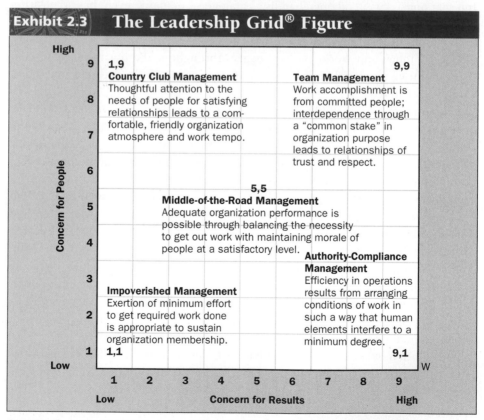

Exhibit 2.3 **The Leadership Grid® Figure**

1,9 Country Club Management Thoughtful attention to the needs of people for satisfying relationships leads to a comfortable, friendly organization atmosphere and work tempo.

9,9 Team Management Work accomplishment is from committed people; interdependence through a "common stake" in organization purpose leads to relationships of trust and respect.

5,5 Middle-of-the-Road Management Adequate organization performance is possible through balancing the necessity to get out work with maintaining morale of people at a satisfactory level.

Impoverished Management Exertion of minimum effort to get required work done is appropriate to sustain organization membership.

1,1

Authority-Compliance Management Efficiency in operations results from arranging conditions of work in such a way that human elements interfere to a minimum degree.

9,1

Concern for People — High / Low

Concern for Results — Low / High

SOURCE: The Leadership Grid figure from *Leadership Dilemma—Grid Solutions* by Robert R. Blake and Anne Adams McCanse (formerly the Managerial Grid by Robert R. Blake and Jane S. Mouton). Houston: Gulf Publishing Company, 29. Copyright 1991 by Scientific Methods, Inc. Reproduced by permission of the owners.

In the Lead TruServ and North Jackson Elementary School

When Pamela Forbes Lieberman learned that her subordinates called her *the dragon lady*, she embraced the moniker and hung a watercolor of a dragon in her office. Lieberman makes no apologies for her hard-driving management style. Her emphasis on tough goals and bottom-line results is helping to restore the health of hardware cooperative TruServ, which supplies inventory to True Value hardware stores. As soon as Lieberman became CEO, she began slashing costs and setting tough performance targets. "If [people] succeed, they will be rewarded, but if they don't, then we're going to have to look for new people sitting in their chairs," Lieberman says. Despite her hard-nosed approach, Lieberman also believes in the importance of keeping morale high. She's been known to join in karaoke nights, and she uses humor and stories to lighten up intense meetings. At the end of every meeting to outline new tasks or performance targets, she plays the song, "Nothing's Gonna Stop Us Now" to keep people motivated and focused on goals.

Compare Lieberman's approach as a new CEO at TruServ to Joyce Pully's approach as the new principal of North Jackson Elementary School in Jackson, Mississippi. Pully had a vision of transforming North Jackson into a model of creative learning. However, she didn't make any changes at all during the first year, working instead to build trust with teachers, staff, and students. She listened carefully to teachers' concerns and began involving them closely in decision making. When she presented ideas for new ways of teaching and learning, Pully assured people she'd provide them with the training they needed to succeed. When teachers realized that Pully respected them and truly valued their input, they became more involved in planning the future of the school. Today, rote teaching and rote learning are gone at North Jackson, replaced by a vibrant educational process that relies on innovation and discovery. Pully believes the change was possible only because the staff, teachers, and students played an active role in making it happen.[33]

The leadership of Pamela Forbes Lieberman is characterized by high concern for tasks and production and low-to-moderate concern for people. Joyce Pully, in contrast, is high on concern for people and moderate on concern for production. In each case, both concerns shown in the Leadership Grid are present, but they are integrated at different levels.

Theories of a "High-High" Leader

The leadership styles described by the researchers at Ohio State, University of Michigan, and University of Texas pertain to variables that roughly correspond to one another: consideration and initiating structure; employee-centered and job-centered;

concern for people and concern for production, as illustrated in Exhibit 2.4. The research into the behavior approach culminated in two predominate types of leadership behaviors—people-oriented and task-oriented.

The findings about two underlying dimensions and the possibility of leaders rated high on both dimensions raise four questions to think about. The first is whether these two dimensions are the most important behaviors of leadership. Certainly, these two behaviors are important. They capture fundamental, underlying aspects of human behavior that must be considered for organizations to succeed. One reason why these two dimensions are compelling is that the findings are based on empirical research, which means that researchers went into the field to study real leaders across a variety of settings. When independent streams of field research reach similar conclusions, they probably represent a fundamental theme in leadership behavior. One recent review of 50 years of leadership research, for example, identified task-oriented behavior and people-oriented behavior as primary categories related to effective leadership in numerous studies.[34] Concern for task and concern for people must be shown toward followers at some reasonable level, either by the leader or by other people in the system. While these are not the only important behaviors, as we will see throughout this book, they certainly require attention.

The second question is whether people orientation and task orientation exist together in the same leader, and how. The Grid theory argues that yes, both are present when people work with or through others to accomplish an activity. Although leaders may be high on either style, there is considerable belief that the best leaders are high on both behaviors. Superintendent John Fryer, described earlier, is an example of a leader who succeeds on both dimensions. How does a leader achieve both behaviors? Some researchers argue that "high-high" leaders alternate the type of behavior from one to the other, showing concern one time and task initiation another time.[35] Another approach says that effective "high-high" leaders encompass both behaviors simultaneously in a fundamentally different way than people who behave in one way or the other. For example, Fryer sets challenging goals for student performance and also works closely with teachers to provide the tools and training they feel they need to achieve those goals. A task-oriented leader might set difficult goals and simply pressure subordinates to improve quality. On the other hand, a person-oriented leader might

Action Memo

As a leader: Act as a "high-high" leader by showing concern for both tasks and people. Remember that people-oriented behavior is related to higher follower satisfaction and fewer personnel problems, and task-oriented behavior is typically associated with higher productivity. Address both the social and task dimensions to succeed as a leader in a variety of situations.

	People-Oriented	Task-Oriented
Exhibit 2.4 Themes of Leader Behavior Research		
Ohio State University	Consideration	Initiating Structure
University of Michigan	Employee-Centered	Job-Centered
University of Texas	Concern for People	Concern for Production

ignore student achievement scores and goal attainment and simply seek to improve schools by consulting with teachers and building positive relationships with them. The "high-high" leaders seem to have a knack for displaying concern for both people and production in the majority of their behaviors.[36]

The third question is whether a "high-high" leadership style is universal or situational. Universal means that the behavior will tend to be effective in every situation, while situational means the behavior succeeds only in certain settings. Research has indicated some degree of universality with respect to people-oriented and task-oriented behavior. In other words, the leader behavior of concern for people tended to be related to higher employee satisfaction and fewer personnel problems across a wide variety of situations. Likewise, task-oriented behavior was associated with higher productivity across a large number of situations.

The fourth question concerns whether people can actually change themselves into leaders high on people and/or task-orientation. In the 1950s and 1960s, when the Ohio State and Michigan studies were underway, the assumption of researchers was that the behaviors of effective leaders could be emulated by anyone wishing to become an effective leader. In general it seems that people can learn new leader behaviors, as described in Chapter 1. There is a general belief that "high-high" leadership is a desirable quality, because the leader will meet both needs simultaneously. Despite the research indicating that "high-high" leadership is not the only effective style, researchers have looked to this kind of leader as a candidate for success in a wide number of situations. However, as we will see in the next chapter, the next generation of leadership studies refined the understanding of situations to pinpoint more precisely when each type of leadership behavior is most effective.

Individualized Leadership

Traditional trait and behavior theories assume that a leader adopts a general leadership style that is used with all group members. A more recent approach to leadership behavior research, *individualized leadership*, looks instead at the specific relationship between a leader and each individual member.[37] **Individualized leadership** is based on the notion that a leader develops a unique relationship with each subordinate or group member, which determines how the leader behaves toward the member and how the member responds to the leader. In this view, leadership is a series of *dyads*, or a series of two-person interactions.

Sometimes called *dyadic theory*, individualized leadership examines why leaders have more influence over and greater impact on some members than on others. To understand leadership, then, a closer look at the specific relationship in each leader-member dyad is necessary.[38] The dyadic view focuses on the concept of *exchange*, what each party gives to and receives from the other. Leaders can meet followers' emotional

*Individualized
leadership*

*a theory based
on the notion
that a leader
develops a
unique relation-
ship with each
subordinate or
group member,
which deter-
mines how the
leader behaves
toward the
member and
how the mem-
ber responds to
the leader*

*Vertical Dyad
Linkage (VDL)
Model*

*a model of indi-
vidualized lead-
ership that
argues for the
importance of
the dyad formed
by a leader with
each member of
the group*

needs and offer a sense of support for the follower's self-worth, while followers provide leaders with commitment and high performance. Some dyads might be "rich," meaning there is a high level of both giving and receiving by both partners in the exchange, while others are "poor," reflecting little giving and receiving by dyadic partners.[39]

The first individualized leadership theory was introduced more than 25 years ago and has been steadily revised ever since. The development of this viewpoint is illustrated in Exhibit 2.5. The first stage was the awareness of a relationship between a leader and each individual, rather than between a leader and a group of subordinates. The second stage examined specific attributes of the exchange relationship. The third stage explored whether leaders could intentionally develop partnerships with each group member, and the fourth stage expanded the view of dyads to include larger systems and networks.

Vertical Dyad Linkage Model

The **Vertical Dyad Linkage (VDL) model** argues for the importance of the dyad formed by a leader with each member of the group. Initial findings indicated that

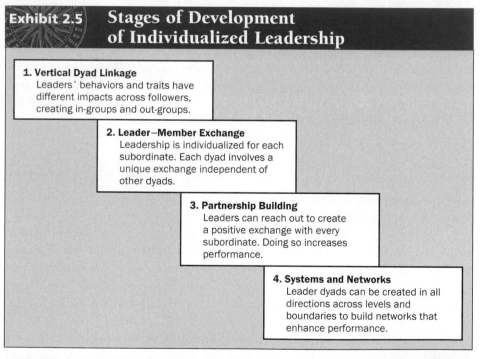

Exhibit 2.5   **Stages of Development of Individualized Leadership**

1. Vertical Dyad Linkage
Leaders' behaviors and traits have different impacts across followers, creating in-groups and out-groups.

2. Leader–Member Exchange
Leadership is individualized for each subordinate. Each dyad involves a unique exchange independent of other dyads.

3. Partnership Building
Leaders can reach out to create a positive exchange with every subordinate. Doing so increases performance.

4. Systems and Networks
Leader dyads can be created in all directions across levels and boundaries to build networks that enhance performance.

SOURCES: Based on Fred Danereau, "A Dyadic Approach to Leadership: Learning and Nurturing This Approach Under Fire," *Leadership Quarterly* 6, no. 4 (1995): 479–490, and George B. Graen and Mary Uhl-Bien, "Relationship-Based Approach to Leadership: Development of Leader-Member Exchange (LMX) Theory of Leadership Over 25 Years: Applying a Multi-level, Multi-domain Approach," *Leadership Quarterly* 6, no. 2 (1995): 219–247.

subordinates provided very different descriptions of the same leader. For example, some subordinates reported a leader, and their relationship with the leader, as having a high degree of mutual trust, respect, and obligation. These high-quality relationships might be characterized as high on both people and task orientation. Other subordinates reported a low-quality relationship with the same leader, such as having a low degree of trust, respect, and obligation. These subordinates perceived the leader as being low on important leadership behaviors.

Based on these two extreme exchange patterns, subordinates were found to exist in either an in-group or an out-group in relation to the leader. Exhibit 2.6 delineates the differences in leader behavior toward in-group versus out-group members. Most of us who have had experience with any kind of group, whether it be a college class, an athletic team, or a work group, recognize that some leaders may spend a disproportionate amount of time with certain people, and that these "insiders" are often highly trusted and may obtain special privileges. In the terminology of the VDL model, these people would be considered to participate in an *in-group exchange* relationship with the leader, while other members of the group who did not experience a sense of trust and extra consideration would participate in an *out-group exchange*.

In-group members, those who rated the leader highly, had developed close relationships with the leader and often became assistants who played key roles in the

Exhibit 2.6	**Leader Behavior toward In-Group versus Out-Group Members**

In-Group	Out-Group
• Discusses objectives; gives employee freedom to use his or her own approach in solving problems and reaching goals	• Gives employee specific directives for how to accomplish tasks and attain goals
• Listens to employee's suggestions and ideas about how work is done	• Shows little interest in employee's comments and suggestions
• Treats mistakes as learning opportunities	• Criticizes or punishes mistakes
• Gives employee interesting assignments; may allow employee to choose assignment	• Assigns primarily routine jobs and monitors employee closely
• Sometimes defers to subordinate's opinion	• Usually imposes own views
• Praises accomplishments	• Focuses on areas of poor performance

SOURCE: Based on Jean-François Manzoni and Jean-Louis Barsoux, "The Set-Up-to-Fail Syndrome," *Harvard Business Review* (March–April, 1988): 101–113.

functioning of the work unit. Out-group members were not key players in the work unit. Because of these differences, individuals often fell into subgroups, which might be considered supporters and opponents of the leader. Some subordinates were getting their needs met, while others were not. These differences were based on the dyad between the leader and each subordinate. The in-group had high access to the leader, while the out-group members tended to be passive and did not have positions of influence or access to the leader. In-group members expressed greater mutual influence and collaborative effort with the leader, and they had opportunities to receive greater rewards and perform additional duties. Out-group members tended not to experience positive leader relationships and influence, and the leader was more likely to use formal authority and coercive behavior with these subordinates. In-group members typically received more attention, more approval, and probably more status, but they were also expected to be loyal, committed, and productive.

Thus, by focusing on the relationship between a leader and each individual, the Vertical Dyad Linkage research found great variance of leader style and impact within a group of subordinates.

Leader–Member Exchange

Leader–Member Exchange (LMX)

individualized leadership model that explores how leader-member relationships develop over time and how the quality of exchange relationships impacts outcomes

Stage two in the development of the individual leadership theory explored the leader–member exchange (LMX) in more detail, discovering that the impact on outcomes depends on how the leader–member exchange process develops over time. Studies evaluating characteristics of the LMX relationship explored such things as communication frequency, value agreement, characteristics of followers, job satisfaction, performance, job climate, and commitment. Leaders typically tend to establish in-group exchange relationships with individuals who have characteristics similar to those of the leader, such as similarity in background, interests, and values, and with those who demonstrate a high level of competence and interest in the job. Overall, studies have found that the quality of the leader–member exchange relationship is substantially higher for in-group members. LMX theory proposes that this higher-quality relationship will lead to higher performance and greater job satisfaction for in-group members, and research in general supports this idea.[40] High-quality LMX relationships have been found to lead to very positive outcomes for leaders, followers, work units, and the organization. For followers, a high-quality exchange relationship may mean more interesting assignments, greater responsibility and authority, and tangible rewards such as pay increases and promotions. Leaders and organizations clearly benefit from the increased effort and initiative of in-group participants to carry out assignments and tasks successfully.

LMX theorists identified three stages dyad members go through in their working relationship. In the initial stage, the leader and follower, as strangers, test each other to identify what kinds of behaviors are comfortable. The relationship is negotiated informally between each follower and the leader. The definition of each group member's role defines what the member and leader expect the member to do. Next, as the leader and member become acquainted, they engage in shaping and refining the roles they will play together. Finally, in the third stage, as the roles reach maturity, the relationship attains a steady pattern of behavior. Leader-member exchanges are difficult to change at this point. The exchange tends to determine in-group and out-group status.

Partnership Building

In this third phase of research, the focus was on whether leaders could develop positive relationships with a large number of subordinates. Critics of early LMX theory pointed out the dangers of leaders establishing sharply differentiated in-group and out-group members, in that this may lead to feelings of resentment or even hostility among out-group participants.[41] If leaders are perceived to be granting excessive benefits and advantages to in-group members, members of the out-group may rebel, which can damage the entire organization. Moreover, some studies have found that leaders tend to categorize employees into in-groups and out-groups as early as five days into their relationship.[42]

> **Action Memo**
>
> As a leader: Build a positive, individualized relationship with each follower rather than treating people as members of an in-group or an out-group. Forge a unique, constructive partnership with each person to create an equitable work environment and provide greater benefits to yourself, followers, and the organization.

Thus, the third phase of research in this area focused on whether leaders could develop positive relationships with all subordinates, not just a few "favorites." The emphasis was not on how or why discrimination among subordinates occurred, but rather on how a leader might work with each subordinate on a one-on-one basis to develop a partnership. The idea was that leaders could develop a unique, beneficial relationship with each individual and provide all employees with access to high-quality leader-member exchanges, thereby providing a more equitable environment and greater benefits to leaders, followers, and the organization.

In this approach, the leader views each person independently, and may treat each individual in a different but positive way. Leaders strive to actively develop a positive relationship with each subordinate, although the positive relationship will have a different form for each person. For example, one person might be treated with "consideration," another with "initiating structure," depending on what followers need to feel involved and to succeed.

In cases where leaders were trained to offer the opportunity for a high-quality relationship to all group members, the followers who responded to the offer improved their performance dramatically. As these relationships matured, the entire work group became more productive, and the payoffs were tremendous. Leaders could count on followers to provide the assistance needed for high performance, and followers participated in and influenced decisions. Leaders provided support, encouragement, and training, and followers responded with high performance. In some sense, leaders were meeting both the personal and work-related needs of each subordinate, one at a time. The implications of this finding are that true performance and productivity gains can be achieved by having the leader develop positive relationships one-on-one with each subordinate.

Systems and Networks

The final stage of this work suggests that leader dyads can be expanded to larger systems. Rather than focusing on leaders and subordinates, a systems-level perspective examines how dyadic relationships can be created across traditional boundaries to embrace a larger system. This larger network for the leader may cut across work unit, functional, divisional, and even organizational boundaries. In this view, leader relationships are not limited to subordinates, but include peers, teammates, and other stakeholders relevant to the work unit. To this point, there has been little systematic research on a broader systemic view of dyadic relationships. But the theory suggests the need for leaders to build networks of one-on-one relationships and to use their traits and behaviors selectively to create positive relationships with as many people as possible. A large number of people thereby can be influenced by the leader, and these stakeholders will contribute to the success of the work unit.

One organization that is promoting the idea of creating partnerships across a larger system is University Public Schools in Stockton, California.

In the Lead University Public Schools

Education has always been a service business, with each child highly individualized and needing a specific approach. However, many schools operate on an old-fashioned factory model that treats students like pieces of equipment. University Public Schools (UPS) of Stockton, California, takes a different approach.

UPS's San Joaquin campus is a model of partnership. Teachers at San Joaquin are expected to develop partnerships with students, each other, parents, and other community members. They are given an unprecedented amount of freedom to set their own goals and develop their own curriculum. If parents want something taught that isn't being covered, they can request that it be included. "Parents can have a say about what's important to them," says Christina Cross, whose son attends UPS. "It's nice to be involved in the education that goes on here."

Teachers' pay raises are based on merit and tied to meeting both individual and team goals. Teachers sign one-year contracts and there is no notion of tenure. Despite the lack of job security, people are so willing to work at the Stockton school that some make a daily commute of nearly four hours. One reason is that teachers feel they are involved in a genuine partnership with the school system, one another, and the community. UPS is trying to build a system that empowers everyone to shape a new vision of learning and make a real difference in the lives of students and the larger world.[43]

Summary and Interpretation

The point of this chapter is to understand the importance of traits and behaviors in the development of leadership theory and research. Traits include self-confidence, honesty, and drive. A large number of personal traits and abilities distinguish successful leaders from nonleaders, but traits themselves are not sufficient to guarantee effective leadership. The behavior approach explored autocratic versus democratic leadership, consideration versus initiating structure, employee-centered versus job-centered leadership, and concern for people versus concern for production. The theme of people versus tasks runs through this research, suggesting these are fundamental behaviors through which leaders meet followers' needs. There has been some disagreement in the research about whether a specific leader is either people- or task-oriented or whether one can be both. Today, the consensus is that leaders can achieve a "high-high" leadership style.

Another approach is the dyad between a leader and each follower. Followers have different relationships with the leader, and the ability of the leader to develop a positive relationship with each subordinate contributes to team performance. The leader-member exchange theory says that high-quality relationships have a positive outcome for leaders, followers, work units, and the organization. Leaders can attempt to build individualized relationships with each subordinate as a way to meet needs for both consideration and structure.

The historical development of leadership theory presented in this chapter introduces some important ideas about leadership. While certain personal traits and abilities constitute a greater likelihood for success in a leadership role, they are not in themselves sufficient to guarantee effective leadership. Rather, behaviors are equally significant, as outlined by the research at several universities. Therefore, the style of leadership demonstrated by an individual greatly determines the outcome of the leadership endeavor. Often, a combination of styles is most effective. To understand the effects of leadership upon outcomes, the specific relationship behavior between a leader and each follower is also an important consideration.

Discussion Questions

1. Is the "Great Man" perspective on leadership still alive today? Think about some recent popular movies that stress a lone individual as hero or savior. How about some business stories? Discuss.
2. Suggest some personal traits of leaders you have known. Which traits do you believe are most valuable? Why?
3. What is the difference between trait theories and behavioral theories of leadership?
4. Would you prefer working for a leader who has a "consideration" or an "initiating-structure" leadership style? Discuss the reasons for your answer.

5. The Vertical Dyad Linkage model suggests that followers respond individually to the leader. If this is so, what advice would you give leaders about displaying people-oriented versus task-oriented behavior?

6. Does it make sense to you that a leader should develop an individualized relationship with each follower? Explain advantages and disadvantages to this approach.

7. Why would subordinates under a democratic leader perform better in the leader's absence than would subordinates under an autocratic leader?

8. Which type of leader—task-oriented or people-oriented—do you think would have an easier time becoming a "high-high" leader? Why?

Leadership at Work

Your Ideal Leader Traits

Spend some time thinking about someone you believe is an ideal leader. For the first part of the exercise, select an ideal leader you have heard about whom you don't personally know. It could be someone like Mother Teresa, Rudolph Giuliani, Martin Luther King, Abraham Lincoln, or any national or international figure that you admire. Write the person's name here: _____ . *Now, in the space below, write down three things you admire about the person, such as what he or she did or the qualities that person possesses.*

_____

_____

_____

For the second part of the exercise, select an ideal leader whom you know personally. This can be anyone from your life experiences. Write the person's name here: _____ . *Now, in the space below, write down three things you admire about the person, such as what he or she did or the qualities that person possesses.*

_____

_____

_____

The first leader you chose represents something of a projective test based on what you've heard or read. You imagine the leader has the qualities you listed. The deeds and qualities you listed say more about what you admire than about the actual traits of the leader you chose. This is something like an inkblot test, and it is important because the traits you assign to the leader are traits you are aware of, have the potential to develop, and indeed can develop as a leader. The qualities or achievements you listed are an indicator of the traits you likely will express as you develop into the leader you want to become.

The second leader you chose is someone you know, so it is less of a projective test and represents traits you have had direct experience with. You know these traits work for you and likely will become the traits you develop and express as a leader.

What is similar about the traits you listed for the two leaders? Different? Interview another student in class about traits he or she admires. What do the traits tell you about the person you are interviewing? What are the common themes in your list and the other student's list of traits? To what extent do you display the same traits as the ones on your list? Will you develop those traits even more in the future?

Leadership Development: Cases for Analysis

Consolidated Products

Consolidated Products is a medium-sized manufacturer of consumer products with nonunionized production workers. Ben Samuels was a plant manager for Consolidated Products for 10 years, and he was very well liked by the employees there. They were grateful for the fitness center he built for employees, and they enjoyed the social activities sponsored by the plant several times a year, including company picnics and holiday parties. He knew most of the workers by name, and he spent part of each day walking around the plant to visit with them and ask about their families or hobbies.

Ben believed that it was important to treat employees properly so they would have a sense of loyalty to the company. He tried to avoid any layoffs when production demand was slack, figuring that the company could not afford to lose skilled workers that are so difficult to replace. The workers knew that if they had a special problem, Ben would try to help them. For example, when someone was injured but wanted to continue working, Ben found another job in the plant that the person could do despite having a disability. Ben believed that if you treat people right, they will do a good job for you without close supervision or prodding. Ben applied the same principle to his supervisors, and he mostly left them alone to run their departments as they saw fit. He did not set objectives and standards for the plant, and he never asked the supervisors to develop plans for improving productivity and product quality.

Under Ben, the plant had the lowest turnover among the company's five plants, but the second worst record for costs and production levels. When the company was acquired by another firm, Ben was asked to take early retirement, and Phil Jones was brought in to replace him.

Phil had a growing reputation as a manager who could get things done, and he quickly began making changes. Costs were cut by trimming a number of activities such as the fitness center at the plant, company picnics and parties, and the human relations training programs for supervisors. Phil believed that human relations training was a waste of time; if employees don't want to do the work, get rid of them and find somebody else who does.

Supervisors were instructed to establish high performance standards for their departments and insist that people achieve them. A computer monitoring system was introduced so that the output of each worker could be checked closely against the standards. Phil told his supervisors to give any worker who had substandard performance one warning, and then if performance did not improve within two weeks, to fire the person. Phil believed that workers don't respect a supervisor who is weak and passive. When Phil observed a worker wasting time or making a mistake, he would reprimand the person right on the spot to set an example. Phil also checked closely on the performance of his supervisors. Demanding objectives were set for each department, and weekly meetings were held with each supervisor to review department performance. Finally, Phil insisted that supervisors check with him first before taking any significant actions that deviated from established plans and policies.

As another cost-cutting move, Phil reduced the frequency of equipment maintenance, which required machines to be idled when they could be productive. Since the machines had a good record of reliable operation, Phil believed that the current maintenance schedule was excessive and was cutting into production. Finally, when business was slow for one of the product lines, Phil laid off workers rather than finding something else for them to do.

By the end of Phil's first year as plant manager, production costs were reduced by 20 percent and production output was up by 10 percent. However, three of his seven supervisors left to take other jobs, and turnover was also high among the machine operators. Some of the turnover was due to workers who were fired, but competent machine operators were also quitting, and it was becoming increasingly difficult to find any replacements for them. Finally, there was increasing talk of unionizing among the workers.

SOURCE: Reprinted with permission from Gary Yukl, *Leadership in Organizations*, 4th ed. (Englewood Cliffs, NJ: Prentice Hall, 1998), 66–67.

Questions

1. Compare the leadership traits and behaviors of Ben Samuels and Phil Jones.
2. Which leader do you think is more effective? Why? Which leader would you prefer to work for?
3. If you were Phil Jones' boss, what would you do now?

D. L. Woodside, Sunshine Snacks

D. L. Woodside has recently accepted the position of research and development director for Sunshine Snacks, a large snack food company. Woodside has been assistant director of research at Skid's, a competing company, for several years, but it became clear to him that his chances of moving higher were slim. So, when Sunshine was looking for a new director, Woodside jumped at the chance.

At Skid's, Woodside had worked his way up from the mail room, going to school at night to obtain first a bachelor's degree and eventually a Ph.D. Management admired his drive and determination, as well as his ability to get along with just about anyone he came in contact with, and they gave him opportunities to work in various positions around the company over the years. That's when he discovered he had a love for developing new products. He had been almost single-handedly responsible for introducing four new successful product lines at Skid's. Woodside's technical knowledge and understanding of the needs of the research and development department were excellent. In addition, he was a tireless worker—when he started a project he rarely rested until it was finished, and finished well.

Despite his ambition and his hard-charging approach to work, Woodside was considered an easy-going fellow. He liked to talk and joke around, and whenever anyone had a problem they'd come to Woodside rather than go to the director. Woodside was always willing to listen to a research assistant's personal problems. Besides that, he would often stay late or come in on weekends to finish an assistant's work if the employee was having problems at home or difficulty with a particular project. Woodside knew the director was a hard taskmaster, and he didn't want anyone getting into trouble over things they couldn't help. In fact, he'd been covering the mistakes of George, an employee who had a drinking problem, ever since he'd been appointed assistant director. Well, George was on his own now. Woodside had his own career to think about, and the position at Sunshine was his chance to finally lead a department rather than play second fiddle.

At Sunshine, Woodside is replacing Henry Meade, who has been the director for almost 30 years. However, it seems clear that Meade has been slowing down over the past few years, turning more and more of his work over to his assistant, Harmon Davis. When Woodside was first introduced to the people in the research department at Sunshine, he sensed not only a loyalty to Davis, who'd been passed over for the top job because of his lack of technical knowledge, but also an undercurrent of resistance to his own selection as the new director.

Woodside knows he needs to build good relationships with the team, and especially with Davis, quickly. The company has made it clear that it wants the department to initiate several new projects as soon as possible. One reason they selected Woodside for the job was his successful track record with new product development at Skid's.

SOURCE: Based in part on "The Take Over," Incident 52 in Bernard A. Deitzer and Karl A. Shilliff, *Contemporary Management Incidents* (Columbus, OH: Grid, Inc., 1977), 161–162; and "Choosing a New Director of Research," Case 2.1 in Peter G. Northouse, *Leadership Theory and Practice*, 2nd ed. (Thousand Oaks, CA: Sage Publications, 2001), 25–26.

Questions

1. What traits does Woodside possess that might be helpful to him as he assumes his new position? What traits might be detrimental?
2. Would you consider Woodside a people-oriented or a task-oriented leader? Discuss which you think would be best for the new research director at Sunshine.
3. How might an understanding of individualized leadership theory be useful to Woodside in this situation? Discuss.

References

1. Curtis Sittenfeld, "Leader on the Edge," *Fast Company* (October 1999): 212–226.
2. Jeffrey H. Birnbaum, "Iraq's New Chief?" *Fortune*, March 31, 2003, 38; "IHOP's CEO Has Lot on Her Plate," *Fortune*, March 31, 2003, 143.
3. G. A. Yukl, *Leadership in Organizations* (Englewood Cliffs, NJ: Prentice Hall, 1981); and S. C. Kohs and K. W. Irle, "Prophesying Army Promotion," *Journal of Applied Psychology* 4 (1920), 73–87.
4. Yukl, *Leadership in Organizations*, 254.
5. R. M. Stogdill, "Personal Factors Associated with Leadership: A Survey of the Literature," *Journal of Psychology* 25 (1948), 35–71.

6. R. M. Stogdill, *Handbook of Leadership: A Survey of the Literature* (New York: Free Press, 1974); and Bernard M. Bass, *Bass & Stogdill's Handbook of Leadership: Theory, Research, and Managerial Applications,* 3rd ed. (New York: The Free Press, 1990).

7. S. A. Kirkpatrick and E. A. Locke, "Leadership: Do Traits Matter?" *The Academy of Management Executive* 5, No. 2 (1991): 48–60.

8. R. G. Lord, C. L. DeVader, and G. M. Alliger, "A Meta-Analysis of the Relation Between Personality Traits and Leadership Perceptions: An Application of Validity Generalization Procedures," *Journal of Applied Psychology* 71 (1986): 402–410.

9. Thomas A. Stewart, "Have You Got What It Takes?" *Fortune* (October 11, 1999): 318–322.

10. Daniel Goleman, *Emotional Intelligence: Why It Can Matter More Than IQ* (New York: Bantam Books, 1995), 289–290; Sharon Nelton, "Emotions in the Workplace," *Nation's Business* (February 1996), 25–30; and Lara E. Megerian and John J. Sosik, "An Affair of the Heart: Emotional Intelligence and Transformational Leadership," *The Journal of Leadership Studies* 3, No. 3 (1996): 31–48.

11. Edwin Locke and Associates, *The Essence of Leadership* (New York: Lexington Books, 1991).

12. Shelley A. Kirkpatrick and Edwin A. Locke, "Leadership: Do Traits Matter?" *Academy of Management Executive* 5, No. 2(1991): 48–60.

13. Jim Collins, "High Returns Amid Low Expectations," Manager's Journal column, *The Wall Street Journal*, February 11, 2002, A22.

14. James M. Kouzes and Barry Z. Posner, *Credibility: How Leaders Gain and Lose It, Why People Demand It* (San Francisco: Jossey-Bass Publishers, 1993), 14.

15. This discussion is based on Kirkpatrick and Locke, "Leadership: Do Traits Matter?"

16. A. Howard and D. W. Bray, *Managerial Lives in Transition: Advancing Age and Changing Times* (New York: Guilford Press, 1988).

17. Bryan Gruley and Rebecca Smith, "Anatomy of a Fall: Keys to Success Left Kenneth Lay Open to Disaster," *The Wall Street Journal*, April 26, 2002, A1, A5.

18. K. Lewin, "Field Theory and Experiment in Social Psychology: Concepts and Methods," *American Journal of Sociology* 44 (1939): 868–896; K. Lewin and R. Lippet, "An Experimental Approach to the Study of Autocracy and Democracy: A Preliminary Note," *Sociometry* 1 (1938): 292–300; and K. Lewin, R. Lippett, and R. K. White, "Patterns of Aggressive Behavior in Experimentally Created Social Climates," *Journal of Social Psychology* 10 (1939): 271–301.

19. R. Tannenbaum and W. H. Schmidt, "How to Choose a Leadership Pattern," *Harvard Business Review* 36 (1958), 95–101.

20. F. A. Heller and G. A. Yukl, "Participation, Managerial Decision-Making and Situational Variables," *Organizational Behavior and Human Performance* 4 (1969): 227–241.

21. "Jack's Recipe (Management Principles Used by Jack Hartnett, President of D. L. Rogers Corp.)," sidebar in Marc Ballon, "Equal Parts Old-Fashioned Dictator and New Age Father Figure, Jack Hartnett Breaks Nearly Every Rule of the Enlightened Manager's Code," *Inc.* (July 1998): 60; Patricia O'Toole, "How Do You Build a $44 Million Company? By Saying Please," *Working Woman* (April 1990): 88–92.

22. J. K. Hemphill and A. E. Coons, "Development of the Leader Behavior Description Questionnaire," in *Leader Behavior: Its Description and Measurement*, Eds. R. M. Stogdill and A. E. Coons (Columbus, OH: Ohio State University, Bureau of Business Research, 1957).

23. P. C. Nystrom, "Managers and the High-High Leader Myth," *Academy of Management Journal* 21 (1978): 325–331; and L. L. Larson, J. G. Hunt and Richard N. Osborn, "The Great High-High Leader Behavior Myth: A Lesson from Occam's Razor," *Academy of Management Journal* 19 (1976): 628–641.

24. Stephanie Desmon, "Schools Chief an Executive, Not an Educator," *The Palm Beach Post* (December 26, 1999): 1A, 22A.

25. E. W. Skinner, "Relationships Between Leadership Behavior Patterns and Organizational-Situational Variables," *Personnel Psychology* 22 (1969): 489–494; and E. A. Fleishman and E. F. Harris, "Patterns of Leadership Behavior Related to Employee Grievances and Turnover," *Personnel Psychology* 15 (1962): 43–56.

26. A. W. Halpin and B. J. Winer, "A Factorial Study of the Leader Behavior Descriptions," in *Leader Behavior: Its Descriptions and Measurement,* Eds. R. M. Stogdill and A. E. Coons, (Columbus, OH: Ohio State University, Bureau of Business Research, 1957); and J. K. Hemphill, "Leadership Behavior Associated with the Administrative Reputations of College Departments," *Journal of Educational Psychology* 46 (1955): 385–401.

27. R. Likert, "From Production- and Employee-Centeredness to Systems 1–4," *Journal of Management* 5 (1979): 147–156.

28. J. Taylor and D. Bowers, *The Survey of Organizations: A Machine Scored Standardized Questionnaire Instrument* (Ann Arbor, MI: Institute for Social Research, University of Michigan, 1972).

29. D. G. Bowers and S. E. Seashore, "Predicting Organizational Effectiveness with a Four-Factor Theory of Leadership," *Administrative Science Quarterly* 11 (1966): 238–263.

30. Carol Hymowitz, "Damark's Unique Post: A Manager Who Helps Work on Relationships," (In the Lead column), *The Wall Street Journal* (September 7, 1999): B1.

31. Bowers and Seashore, "Predicting Organizational Effectiveness with a Four-Factor Theory of Leadership."

32. Robert Blake and Jane S. Mouton, *The Managerial Grid III* (Houston: Gulf, 1985).

33. Jo Napolitano, "No, She Doesn't Breathe Fire," *The New York Times*, September 1, 2002, Section 3, 2; "The Transformed School," segment in Sara Terry, "Schools That Think," *Fast Company* (April 2000): 304–320.

34. Gary Yukl, Angela Gordon, and Tom Taber, "A Hierarchical Taxonomy of Leadership Behavior: Integrating a Half Century of Behavior Research," *Journal of Leadership and Organizational Studies* 9, no. 1 (2002): 15–32.

35. J. Misumi, *The Behavioral Science of Leadership: An Interdisciplinary Japanese Research Program* (Ann Arbor, MI: University of Michigan Press, 1985).

36. Fleishman and Harris, "Patterns of Leadership Behavior Related to Employee Grievances and Turnover"; and Misumi, *The Behavioral Science of Leadership: An Interdisciplinary Japanese Research Program*.

37. Francis J. Yammarino and Fred Dansereau, "Individualized Leadership," *Journal of Leadership and Organizational Studies* 9, no. 1 (2002): 90–99.

38. This discussion is based on Fred Dansereau, "A Dyadic Approach to Leadership: Creating and Nurturing This Approach Under Fire," *Leadership Quarterly* 6, No. 4 (1995): 479–490; and George B. Graen and Mary Uhl-Bien, "Relationship-Based Approach to Leadership: Development of Leader Member Exchange (LMX) Theory of Leadership Over 25 Years: Applying a Multi-Level Multi-Domain Approach," *Leadership Quarterly* 6, No. 2 (1995): 219–247.

39. Yammarino and Dansereau, "Individualized Leadership."

40. See A. J. Kinicki and R. P. Vecchio, "Influences on the Quality of Supervisor-Subordinate Relations: The Role of Time Pressure, Organizational Commitment, and Locus of Control," *Journal of Organizational Behavior,* (January 1994): 75–82; R. C. Liden, S. J. Wayne, and D. Stilwell, "A Longitudinal Study on the Early Development of Leader-Member Exchanges," *Journal of Applied Psychology* (August 1993): 662–674; Yammarino and Dansereau, "Individualized Leadership"; and Jean-François Manzoni and Jean-Louis Baraoux, "The Set-Up-to-Fail Syndrome," *Harvard Business Review* (March-April 1998): 101–113.

41. W. E. McClane, "Implications of Member Role Differentiation: Analysis of a Key Concept in the LMX Model of Leadership," *Group and Organization Studies* 16 (1991): 102–113; and Gary Yukl, *Leadership in Organizations*, 2nd ed. (New York: Prentice-Hall, 1989).

42. Manzoni and Barsoux, "The Set-Up-to-Fail Syndrome."

43. "The Service School," segment in Sara Terry, "Schools That Think," *Fast Company* (April 2000): 304–320.

Chapter

Your Leadership Challenge

After reading this chapter, you should be able to:

- Understand how leadership is often contingent on people and situations.

- Apply Fiedler's contingency model to key relationships among leader style, situational favorability, and group task performance.

- Apply Hersey and Blanchard's situational theory of leader style to the level of follower readiness.

- Explain the path–goal theory of leadership.

- Use the Vroom–Jago model to identify the correct amount of follower participation in specific decision situations.

- Know how to use the power of situational variables to substitute for or neutralize the need for leadership.

David A. Duffield, founder, chairman, and former CEO of software company PeopleSoft, was known for hugging employees (called PeoplePeople), letting people bring their dogs to work, providing free breakfasts and snacks, and signing his e-mails with the initials, D.A.D. Duffield emphasized treating people well and letting them be "whole people" who felt free to bring their emotions and outside concerns to work with them. When Duffield spoke of the PeopleSoft family, everyone knew it was in earnest. Duffield built PeopleSoft into an early enterprise software giant, and his leadership approach was successful for many years. However, as the environment and competitive conditions changed, the strong people-oriented focus and laid-back style became a liability.

In 1999, Duffield brought in a very different kind of leader to help pull PeopleSoft out of a sharp decline. Some employees doubt that Craig Conway has ever hugged anyone. Conway is a no-nonsense leader who imposed strict discipline on the company. The new CEO banned dogs and canceled the free breakfasts that were costing PeopleSoft about $1 million a year. He installed clear-cut rules and standard procedures for everything. He wore power suits and made it clear that other executives should, too. Known as hypercompetitive and relentlessly focused on results, Conway is trying to instill those same values throughout the company. He added the following mantra to the company's internal mission statement: "Competitiveness. Intensity. Accountability."

Not everyone could adapt to the new leader's style, and some left the company. However, Conway's whip-cracking has paid off in impressive sales results and a return to profitability. Duffield, who remained as PeopleSoft chairman, believes the new style of leader is just what was needed. He never even flinched as Conway demolished many of his cherished practices and priorities.[1]

Referring back to the previous chapter, Dave Duffield is strongly people-oriented—that is, characterized by high concern for people and low concern for production. Conway, in contrast, is a strong, task-oriented leader, high on concern for production and low on concern for people. Both leaders have been successful, although they display very different leadership styles. This difference points to what researchers of leader traits and behaviors eventually discovered: Many different leadership styles can be effective. What, then, determines the success of a leadership style?

In the above example, Duffield and Conway were performing leadership in very different situations. For some years during Duffield's leadership of PeopleSoft, the market for enterprise software was wide open, the economy was booming, and dot-com companies were springing up right and left. Unemployment was low, and high-tech knowledge workers could practically name their price. Duffield created a distinctive culture and organizational practices that attracted highly skilled employees who were fed up with the long hours and intensity at other software makers. He knew that if employees weren't happy at PeopleSoft, they had plenty of other jobs to choose from. Today, though, PeopleSoft is competing in a tough neighborhood against a host of competitors, including giant Oracle, which initiated a hostile takeover bid in mid-2003. The dot-com crash and the declining economy hurt sales and revenues as companies delayed their purchases of new enterprise systems. To stay competitive, PeopleSoft needed to dramatically slash costs and tighten up. With a soaring unemployment rate, employees could no longer demand high salaries and extensive perks and privileges. The differences in the organizational situation faced by these leaders helps to explain how both styles have achieved success.

This chapter explores the relationship between leadership effectiveness and the situation in which leadership activities occur. Over the years, researchers have observed that leaders frequently behave situationally—that is, they adjust their leadership style depending on a variety of factors in the situations they face. In this chapter, we will discuss the elements of leader, follower, and the situation, and the impact each has upon the others. We will examine several theories that define how leadership styles, follower attributes, and organizational characteristics fit together to enable successful leadership. The important point of this chapter is that the most effective leadership approach depends on many factors. Understanding the contingency approaches can help a leader adapt his or her approach, although it is important to recognize that leaders also develop their ability to adapt through experience and practice.

The Contingency Approach

The failure to find universal leader traits or behaviors that would always determine effective leadership led researchers in a new direction. Although leader behavior was still examined, the central focus of the new research was the situation in which leadership occurred. The basic tenet of this focus was that behavior effective in some circumstances might be ineffective under different conditions. Thus, the effectiveness of leader behavior is *contingent* upon organizational situations. Aptly called *contingency approaches*, these theories explain the relationship between leadership styles and effectiveness in specific situations.

The universalistic approach as described in Chapter 2 is compared to the contingency approach used in this chapter in Exhibit 3.1. In the previous chapter, researchers were investigating traits or behaviors that could improve performance and satisfaction in any or all situations. They sought universal leadership traits and behaviors. **Contingency** means that one thing depends on other things, and for a leader to be effective there must be an appropriate fit between the leader's behavior and style and the conditions in the situation. A leadership style that works in one situation might not work in another situation. There is no one best way of leadership. Contingency means "it depends." This chapter's Leader's Bookshelf talks about a new approach to leadership for a new kind of contingency facing today's organizations.

The contingencies most important to leadership as shown in Exhibit 3.1 are the situation and followers. Research implies that situational variables such as task, structure, context, and environment are important to leadership style, just as we saw

Contingency
a theory meaning one thing depends on other things

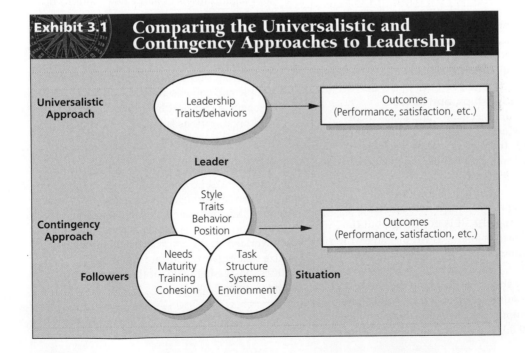

Exhibit 3.1   **Comparing the Universalistic and Contingency Approaches to Leadership**

LEADER'S BOOKSHELF

Leadership and the New Science
Margaret J. Wheatley

In searching for a better understanding of organizations and leadership, Margaret Wheatley looked to science for answers. In the world of Newtonian physics, every atom moves in a unique predictable trajectory determined by the forces exerted on it. Prediction and control are accomplished by reducing wholes into discrete parts and carefully regulating the forces that act on those parts. Applied to organizations, this view of the world led to rigid vertical hierarchies, division of labor, task description, and strict operating procedures designed to obtain predictable, controlled results.

Just as Newton's law broke down as physics explored ever-smaller elements of matter and ever-wider expanses of the universe, rigid, control-oriented leadership doesn't work well in a world of instant information, constant change, and global competition. The physical sciences responded to the failure of Newtonian physics with a new paradigm called quantum mechanics. In *Leadership and the New Science*, Wheatley explores how leaders are redesigning organizations to survive in a quantum world.

Chaos, Relationships, and Fields
From quantum mechanics and chaos theory emerge new understandings of order, disorder, and change. Individual actions, whether by atoms or people cannot be easily predicted and controlled. Here's why:

✳ Nothing exists except in relationship to everything else. It is not things, but the relationships among them that are the key determinants of a well-ordered system we perceive. Order emerges through a web of relationships that make up the whole, not as a result of controls on individual parts.

✳ The empty space between things is filled with fields, invisible material that connects elements together. In organizations, the fields that bind people include vision, shared values, culture, and information.

✳ Organizations, like all open systems, grow and change in reaction to disequilibrium, and disorder can be a source of new order.

Implications for Leadership
These new understandings provide a new way to see, understand, and lead today's organizations. The new sciences can influence leaders to:

✳ Nurture relationships and the fields between people with a clear vision, statements of values, expressions of caring, the sharing of information, and freedom from strict rules and controls.

✳ Focus on the whole, not on the parts in isolation.

✳ Reduce boundaries between departments and organizations to allow new patterns of relationships.

✳ Become comfortable with uncertainty and recognize that any solutions are only temporary, specific to the immediate context, and developed through the relationship of people and circumstances.

✳ Recognize that healthy growth of people and organizations is found in disequilibrium, not in stability.

Wheatley believes leaders can learn from the new sciences how to lead in today's fast-paced, chaotic world, suggesting that "we can forgo the despair created by such common organization events as change, chaos, information overload, and cyclical behaviors if we recognize that organizations are conscious entities, possessing many of the properties of living systems."

Leadership and The New Science, by Margaret J. Wheatley, is published by Berrett-Koehler Publishers.

in the opening examples. The nature of followers has also been identified as a key contingency. Thus, the needs, maturity, and cohesiveness of followers make a significant difference to the best style of leadership.

Several models of situational leadership have been developed. The contingency model developed by Fiedler and his associates, the situational theory of Hersey and Blanchard, path-goal theory, the Vroom–Jago model of decision participation, and the substitutes for leadership concept will all be described in this chapter. The **contingency approaches** seek to delineate the characteristics of situations and followers and examine the leadership styles that can be used effectively. Assuming that a leader can properly diagnose a situation and muster the flexibility to behave according to the appropriate style, successful outcomes are highly likely.

Two basic leadership behaviors that can be adjusted to address various contingencies are *task behavior* and *relationship behavior*, introduced in the previous chapter. Research has identified these two *metacategories*, or broadly defined behavior categories, as applicable to leadership in a variety of situations and time periods.[2] A leader can adapt his or her style to be high or low on both task and relationship behavior. Exhibit 3.2 illustrates the four possible behavior approaches—high task–low relationship, high task–high relationship, high relationship–low task, and low task–low relationship. The exhibit describes typical task and relationship behaviors. High task behaviors include planning short-term activities, clarifying tasks, objectives, and role expectations, and monitoring operations and performance. High relationship behaviors include providing support and recognition, developing followers' skills and confidence, and consulting and empowering followers when making decisions and solving problems. The questionnaire in Leader's Self-Insight 3.1 gives you a chance to assess your relative emphasis on these two important behavior categories. Both Fiedler's contingency model and Hersey and Blanchard's situational theory, discussed in the following sections, use these metacategories of leadership behavior but apply them based on different sets of contingencies.

Contingency approaches approaches that seek to delineate the characteristics of situations and followers and examine the leadership styles that can be used effectively

Fiedler's contingency model a model designed to diagnose whether a leader is task-oriented or relationship-oriented and match leader style to the situation

Fiedler's Contingency Model

An early extensive effort to link leadership style with organizational situation was made by Fiedler and his associates.[3] The basic idea is simple: Match the leader's style with the situation most favorable for his or her success. **Fiedler's contingency model** was designed to enable leaders to diagnose both leadership style and organizational situation.

Leadership Style

The cornerstone of Fiedler's theory is the extent to which the leader's style is relationship-oriented or task-oriented. A *relationship-oriented leader* is concerned with people. As

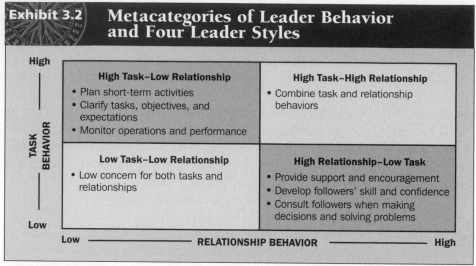

Exhibit 3.2 **Metacategories of Leader Behavior and Four Leader Styles**

High

TASK BEHAVIOR

High Task–Low Relationship
- Plan short-term activities
- Clarify tasks, objectives, and expectations
- Monitor operations and performance

High Task–High Relationship
- Combine task and relationship behaviors

Low Task–Low Relationship
- Low concern for both tasks and relationships

High Relationship–Low Task
- Provide support and encouragement
- Develop followers' skill and confidence
- Consult followers when making decisions and solving problems

Low

Low ——————— **RELATIONSHIP BEHAVIOR** ——————— High

SOURCE: Based on Gary Yukl, Angela Gordon, and Tom Taber, "A Hierarchical Taxonomy of Leadership Behavior: Integrating a Half Century of Behavior Research," *Journal of Leadership and Organizational Studies* 9, no. 1 (2002): 15–32.

with the consideration style described in Chapter 2, a relationship-oriented leader establishes mutual trust and respect, and listens to employees' needs. A *task-oriented leader* is primarily motivated by task accomplishment. Similar to the initiating structure style described earlier, a task-oriented leader provides clear directions and sets performance standards.

Leadership style was measured with a questionnaire known as the least preferred coworker (LPC) scale. The LPC scale has a set of 16 bipolar adjectives along an 8-point scale. Examples of the bipolar adjectives used by Fiedler on the LPC scale follow:

open	– – – – – – – – – – – – – – – – – –	guarded
quarrelsome	– – – – – – – – – – – – – – – – – –	harmonious
efficient	– – – – – – – – – – – – – – – – – –	inefficient
self-assured	– – – – – – – – – – – – – – – – – –	hesitant
gloomy	– – – – – – – – – – – – – – – – – –	cheerful

If the leader describes the least preferred co-worker using positive concepts, he or she is considered relationship-oriented; that is, a leader who cares about and is sensitive to other people's feelings. Conversely, if a leader uses negative concepts to describe the least preferred co-worker, he or she is considered task-oriented; that is, a leader who sees other people in negative terms and places greater value on task activities than on people.

T-P Leadership Questionnaire: An Assessment of Style

The following items describe aspects of leadership behavior. Respond to each item according to the way you would most likely act if you were a leader of a work group. Circle whether you would most likely behave in the described way: always (A), frequently (F), occasionally (O), seldom (S), or never (N).

	Always				Never
1. I would most likely act as the spokesperson of the group.	A	F	O	S	N
2. I would encourage overtime work.	A	F	O	S	N
3. I would allow members complete freedom in their work.	A	F	O	S	N
4. I would encourage the use of uniform procedures.	A	F	O	S	N
5. I would permit members to use their own judgment in solving problems.	A	F	O	S	N
6. I would stress being ahead of competing groups.	A	F	O	S	N
7. I would speak as a representative of the group.	A	F	O	S	N
8. I would needle members for greater effort.	A	F	O	S	N
9. I would try out my ideas in the group.	A	F	O	S	N
10. I would let members do their work the way they think best.	A	F	O	S	N
11. I would be working hard for a promotion.	A	F	O	S	N
12. I would tolerate postponement and uncertainty.	A	F	O	S	N
13. I would speak for the group if there were visitors present.	A	F	O	S	N
14. I would keep the work moving at a rapid pace.	A	F	O	S	N
15. I would turn the members loose on a job and let them go for it.	A	F	O	S	N
16. I would settle conflicts when they occurred in the group.	A	F	O	S	N
17. I would get swamped by details.	A	F	O	S	N
18. I would represent the group at outside meetings.	A	F	O	S	N
19. I would be reluctant to allow the members any freedom of action.	A	F	O	S	N
20. I would decide what should be done and how it should be done.	A	F	O	S	N
21. I would push for increased production.	A	F	O	S	N
22. I would let some members have authority that I could keep.	A	F	O	S	N
23. Things would usually turn out as I had predicted.	A	F	O	S	N
24. I would allow the group a high degree of initiative.	A	F	O	S	N
25. I would assign group members to particular tasks.	A	F	O	S	N
26. I would be willing to make changes.	A	F	O	S	N
27. I would ask the members to work harder.	A	F	O	S	N
28. I would trust the group members to exercise good judgment.	A	F	O	S	N
29. I would schedule the work to be done.	A	F	O	S	N
30. I would refuse to explain my actions.	A	F	O	S	N
31. I would persuade others that my ideas are to their advantage.	A	F	O	S	N
32. I would permit the group to set its own pace.	A	F	O	S	N
33. I would urge the group to beat its previous record.	A	F	O	S	N
34. I would act without consulting the group.	A	F	O	S	N
35. I would ask that group members follow standard rules and regulations.	A	F	O	S	N

T _____   P _____

Scoring and Interpretation

The T–P Leadership Questionnaire is scored as follows:
a. Circle the item number for items 8, 12, 17, 18, 19, and 35.
b. Write the number 1 in front of circled item numbers to which you responded S (seldom) or N (never).
c. Also write a number 1 in front of item numbers not circled if you responded A (always) or F (frequently).
d. Circle the number 1s that you have written in front of the following items: 3, 5, 8, 10, 15, 18, 19, 22, 24, 26, 28, 30, 32, 34, and 35.
e. Count the circled number 1s. This is your score for concern for people. Record the score in the blank following the letter P at the end of the questionnaire.
f. Count uncircled number 1s. This is your score for concern for task. Record this number in the blank following the letter T.

Some leaders deal with people needs, leaving task details to followers. Other leaders focus on specific details with the expectation that followers will carry out orders. Depending on the situation, both approaches may be effective. The important issue is the ability to identify relevant dimensions of the situation and behave accordingly. Through this questionnaire, you can identify your relative emphasis on two dimensions of leadership: task orientation (T) and people orientation (P). These are not opposite approaches, and an individual can rate high or low on either or both.

What is your leadership orientation? Compare your results from this assignment to your result from the quiz in Leader's Self-Insight 2.2 in the previous chapter. What would you consider an ideal leader situation for your style?

SOURCE: The T–P Leadership Questionnaire was adapted by J. B. Ritchie and P. Thompson in *Organization and People* (New York: West, 1984). Copyright 1969 by the American Educational Research Association. Adapted by permission of the publisher from "Toward a Particularistic Approach to Leadership Style: Some Findings" by T. J. Sergiovanni, AERA 6 (1), 1969, 62–79.

Situation

Fiedler's model presents the leadership situation in terms of three key elements that can be either favorable or unfavorable to a leader: the quality of leader–member relations, task structure, and position power.

Leader–member relations refers to group atmosphere and members' attitudes toward and acceptance of the leader. When subordinates trust, respect, and have confidence in the leader, leader–member relations are considered good. When subordinates distrust, do not respect, and have little confidence in the leader, leader–member relations are poor.

Task structure refers to the extent to which tasks performed by the group are defined, involve specific procedures, and have clear, explicit goals. Routine, well-defined tasks, such as those of assembly-line workers, have a high degree of structure. Creative, ill-defined tasks, such as research and development or strategic planning, have a low degree of task structure. When task structure is high, the situation is considered favorable to the leader; when low, the situation is less favorable.

Position power is the extent to which the leader has formal authority over subordinates. Position power is high when the leader has the power to plan and direct the work of subordinates, evaluate it, and reward or punish them. Position power is low when the leader has little authority over subordinates and cannot evaluate their work or reward them. When position power is high, the situation is considered favorable for the leader; when low, the situation is unfavorable.

Combining the three situational characteristics yields a list of eight leadership situations, which are illustrated in Exhibit 3.3. Situation I is most favorable to the leader because leader–member relations are good, task structure is high, and leader position power is strong. Situation VIII is most unfavorable to the leader because leader–member relations are poor, task structure is low, and leader position power is weak. Other octants represent intermediate degrees of favorableness for the leader.

Contingency Theory

When Fiedler examined the relationships among leadership style, situational favorability, and group task performance, he found the pattern shown at the top of Exhibit 3.3. Task-oriented leaders are more effective when the situation is either highly favorable or highly unfavorable. Relationship-oriented leaders are more effective in situations of moderate favorability.

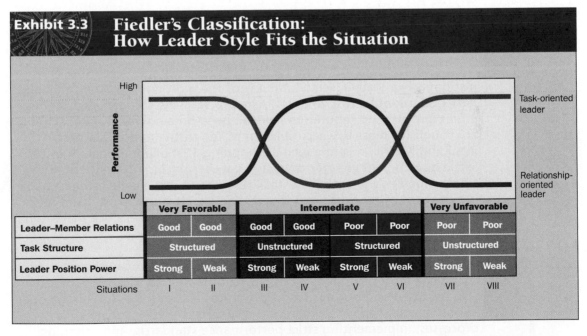

Exhibit 3.3 **Fiedler's Classification: How Leader Style Fits the Situation**

SOURCE: Based on Fred E. Fiedler, "The Effects of Leadership Training and Experience: A Contingency Model Interpretation," *Administrative Science Quarterly* 17 (1972): 455.

The task-oriented leader excels in the favorable situation because everyone gets along, the task is clear, and the leader has power; all that is needed is for someone to take charge and provide direction. Similarly, if the situation is highly unfavorable to the leader, a great deal of structure and task direction is needed. A strong leader defines task structure and can establish authority over subordinates. Because leader–member relations are poor anyway, a strong task orientation will make no difference to the leader's popularity.

The relationship-oriented leader performs better in situations of intermediate favorability because human relations skills are important in achieving high group performance. In these situations, the leader may be moderately well liked, have some power, and supervise jobs that contain some ambiguity. A leader with good interpersonal skills can create a positive group atmosphere that will improve relationships, clarify task structure, and establish position power.

A leader, then, needs to know two things in order to use Fiedler's contingency theory. First, the leader should know whether he or she has a relationship- or task-oriented style. Second, the leader should diagnose the situation and determine whether leader–member relations, task structure, and position power are favorable or unfavorable.

Consider how Stanley O'Neal's style fits his current situation as CEO of Merrill Lynch.

In the Lead   Stanley O'Neal, Merrill Lynch

A lot of employees at Merrill Lynch, the world's biggest securities firm, just don't like Stan O'Neal. But many of them grudgingly admit that the new CEO might be just what is needed to save the company, whose revenues, profits, and reputation have all been on a downhill slide. Times are tough for most U.S. securities firms. Ten of the nation's largest, including Merrill, recently paid a whopping $1.4 billion in penalties to settle government charges of investor abuses, including that they routinely issued overly optimistic stock research to win the investment banking business of big corporate clients. The loss of public trust, combined with economic uncertainty and a general decline in the stock market, has been a heavy blow.

O'Neal is on a mission to re-make Merrill into a lean, mean securities firm that is the most profitable on Wall Street. He has cut thousands of jobs, sold or closed underperforming field offices and overseas brokerage operations, and slashed costs wherever he can. He's revising management processes, implementing strict performance standards, and changing policies and procedures to improve accountability. Senior managers who disagreed with O'Neal's vision and plans for the company have been replaced with executives who believe in the O'Neal philosophy. His brash, focused style has alienated managers and employees throughout the company, but business results have been impressive.

David Komansky, the former CEO who hand-picked O'Neal as his successor, was a very different type of leader. Known as warm-hearted and friendly, he was beloved by almost everyone at Merrill. However, Komansky believed a strong task-oriented leader was needed to help Merrill through these tough times. "We need somebody who can put a management process in place, evaluate businesses, exit businesses that should be exited, ration capital—and who is effective on control of expenses," said Komansky. "I knew what I was dealing with with Stan, and I knew what to expect from him."[4]

Stan O'Neal might be characterized as using a task-oriented style in an unfavorable situation. The environment is about as challenging as any the company has ever faced. Task structure is low, and leader–member relations are poor. Many employees oppose the massive changes O'Neal is making at Merrill and believe he is destroying the company's cherished corporate culture. Although position power is high, his personal power with managers and employees is low. Overall, the situation can be characterized as very unfavorable to the leader, suggesting that O'Neal's strong task-oriented style might be the most appropriate approach. A leader using a relationship-oriented style might not be able to impose the structure and discipline needed for the organization to succeed in its current situation.

An important contribution of Fiedler's research is that it goes beyond the notion of leadership styles to try to show how styles fit the situation. Many studies have been conducted to test Fiedler's model, and the research in general seems to provide some support for the model.[5] However, Fiedler's model has also been criticized.[6] Using the LPC score as a measure of relationship- or task-oriented behavior seems simplistic to some researchers, and the weights used to determine situation favorability seem to have been determined in an arbitrary manner. In addition, some observers argue that the empirical support for the model is weak because it is based on correlational results that fail to achieve statistical significance in the majority of cases. How the model works over time is also unclear.

For instance, if a task-oriented leader is matched with an unfavorable situation and is successful, the organizational situation is likely to improve and become a situation more appropriate for a relationship-oriented leader. For example, after turning around a troubled Giddings & Lewis and spawning a steady climb in earnings and sales over a six-year period, William J. Fife, Jr. was asked to resign as director of the machine company. At Giddings, the situation improved,

Action Memo

As a leader: Use a task-oriented style when the organizational situation is highly unfavorable, such as when tasks are unstructured, leader-member relations are poor, and leader power is weak. Remember that a task-oriented style can also be effective in highly favorable situations. Use a relationship-oriented style in situations of intermediate favorability because human relations skills can create a positive atmosphere.

and the leadership needs of the organization changed. With an improved business climate, Fife's direct, quick-fix aggression became abrasive. Because the company was out of jeopardy, positive leader–member relations were more important to the organization. Creating enemies among subordinates and micromanaging every detail no longer made sense after the turnaround succeeded. Fife's extreme task-oriented leadership no longer suited the situation.[7] The Living Leadership box underscores the disadvantages of persisting in a behavior style despite the processes of change.

Finally, Fiedler's model and much of the subsequent research fails to consider *medium* LPC leaders, who some studies indicate are more effective than either high or low LPC leaders in a majority of situations.[8] Leaders who score in the mid-range on the LPC scale presumably balance the concern for relationships with a concern for task achievement more effectively than high or low LPC leaders, making them more adaptable to a variety of situations.

New research has continued to improve Fiedler's model,[9] and it is still considered an important contribution to leadership studies. However, its major impact may have been to stir other researchers to consider situational factors more seriously. A number of other situational theories have been developed in the years since Fiedler's original research.

LIVING LEADERSHIP

The phrase "too much of a good thing" is relevant in leadership. Behavior that becomes overbearing can be a disadvantage by ultimately resulting in the opposite of what the individual is hoping to achieve.

Polarities

All behavior consists of opposites or polarities. If I do anything more and more, over and over, its polarity will appear. For example, striving to be beautiful makes a person ugly, and trying too hard to be kind is a form of selfishness.

Any over-determined behavior produces its opposite:

- An obsession with living suggests worry about dying.
- True simplicity is not easy.
- Is it a long time or a short time since we last met?
- The braggart probably feels small and insecure.
- Who would be first ends up last.

Knowing how polarities work, the wise leader does not push to make things happen, but allows process to unfold on its own.

SOURCE: John Heider, *The Tao of Leadership: Leadership Strategies for a New Age* (New York: Bantam Books, 1986), 3. Copyright 1985 Humanic Ltd., Atlanta, GA. Used with permission.

Hersey and Blanchard's Situational Theory

The **situational theory** developed by Hersey and Blanchard is an interesting extension of the leadership grid outlined in Chapter 2. This approach focuses on the characteristics of followers as the important element of the situation, and consequently of determining effective leader behavior. The point of Hersey and Blanchard's theory is that subordinates vary in readiness level. People low in task readiness, because of little ability or training, or insecurity, need a different leadership style than those who are high in readiness and have good ability, skills, confidence, and willingness to work.[10]

According to this theory, a leader can adopt one of four leadership styles, based on a combination of task and relationship behaviors, as illustrated earlier in Exhibit 3.2. The four styles are telling, selling, participating, and delegating. The *telling style* reflects a high concern for tasks and a low concern for people and relationships. This is a very directive style. The leader gives explicit directions about how tasks should be accomplished. The *selling style* is based on a high concern for both relationships and tasks. The leader explains decisions and gives followers a chance to ask questions and gain clarity about work tasks. The *participating style* is characterized by high relationship and low task behavior. The leader shares ideas with followers, encourages participation, and facilitates decision making. The fourth style, the *delegating style*, reflects a low concern for both tasks and relationships. This leader provides little direction or support because responsibility for decisions and their implementation is turned over to followers.

The essence of Hersey and Blanchard's situational theory is to select a style that is appropriate for the readiness level of subordinates, such as their degree of education and skills, experience, self-confidence, and work attitudes. The relationship between leader style and follower readiness is summarized in Exhibit 3.4. Followers may be at low, moderate, high, or very high levels of readiness.

Situational theory

Hersey and Blanchard's extension of the Leadership Grid focusing on the characteristics of followers as the important element of the situation, and consequently, of determining effective leader behavior

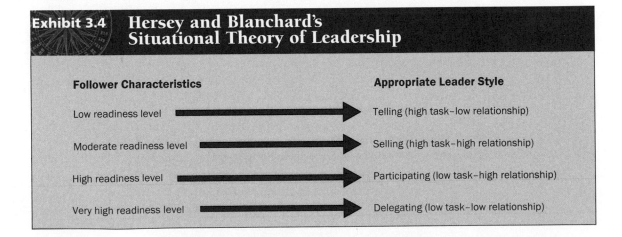

Exhibit 3.4   Hersey and Blanchard's Situational Theory of Leadership

Follower Characteristics	Appropriate Leader Style
Low readiness level	Telling (high task–low relationship)
Moderate readiness level	Selling (high task–high relationship)
High readiness level	Participating (low task–high relationship)
Very high readiness level	Delegating (low task–low relationship)

Action Memo

As a leader: Tell followers exactly what to do and how to perform their tasks if they have poor skills, little experience, and low self-confidence. Provide direction but also seek followers' input and explain your decisions when followers have a moderate degree of skill and demonstrate enthusiasm and willingness to learn.

Low Readiness Level When followers are at a low level of readiness because of poor ability and skills, little experience, insecurity, or unwillingness to take responsibility for their own task behavior, a telling style is appropriate. When one or more followers exhibit very low levels of readiness, the leader has to be very specific, telling followers exactly what to do, how to do it, and when. For example, Phil Hagans owns two McDonald's franchises in northeast Houston and gives many young workers their first job. He uses a telling style regarding everything from how to dress to the correct way to clean the grill, giving young workers the strong direction they need to develop to higher levels of skill and self-confidence.[11]

Moderate Readiness Level A selling leadership style works well when followers are at a moderate level of readiness. For example, they might lack some education and experience for the job but they demonstrate high confidence, ability, interest, and willingness to learn. With a selling style, the leader gives some direction but also seeks input from others and clarifies tasks for followers rather than merely instructing that tasks be performed. Kierstin Higgins, founder of Accommodations by Apple, a small company that handles corporate relocations, finds the selling style appropriate for her young employees, who are very energetic and enthusiastic about their jobs but have not yet gained a lot of skills and experience. By seeking their input and clarifying tasks, Higgins believes she helps her workers learn from the challenges they face rather than being frustrated by them.[12]

High Readiness Level When followers are at a high level of readiness, a participating style can be very effective. Followers might have the necessary education, skills, and experience, but they might be insecure in their abilities and need some guidance from the leader. By using a participating style, the leader can guide followers' development and act as a resource for advice and assistance. An example of the participating style is Eric Brevig, a visual-effects supervisor with Industrial Light and Magic, who maximizes the creativity of artists and animators by encouraging participation. Rather than telling people how to do their jobs, Brevig presents them with a challenge and works with them to figure out the best way to meet it.[13]

Very High Readiness Level The delegating style of leadership can be effectively used when followers have very high levels of education, experience, and readiness to accept responsibility for their own task behavior. The leader can delegate responsibility for decisions and their implementation to followers, who have the skills, abilities, and positive attitudes to follow through. The leader provides a general goal and sufficient authority to do the tasks as followers see fit. Highly educated professionals such as lawyers, college professors, and social workers would typically fall into this category. There are followers in almost every organization who demonstrate high readiness. For example, many fast-food outlets have had great success hiring retirees for part-time jobs. These older employees often have high levels of readiness because of their vast experience and positive attitudes, and leaders can effectively use a delegating style.

In summary, the telling style works best for followers who demonstrate very low levels of readiness to take responsibility for their own task behavior, the selling and participating styles are effective for followers with moderate-to-high readiness, and the delegating style is appropriate for employees with high readiness.

This contingency model is easier to understand than Fiedler's model because it focuses only on the characteristics of followers, not those of the larger situation. The leader should evaluate subordinates and adopt whichever style is needed. For example, when Jack Johnson became manager of a forklift plant, he assumed a participative style of leadership with the idea that the foreman under him was able to continue the high production levels of the past. However, production decreased, while the number of errors increased. Jack was forced to re-examine the situation and choose a new course of action. First, he determined the readiness level of the foreman. Since the foreman had not solved the problem, nor sought Jack's assistance in doing so, Jack determined a lack of commitment, thus a low level of readiness. He focused his next encounter with the foreman exclusively upon the task of decreasing errors, delineated what the foreman must do, and closely monitored the progress of the foreman. Though the transition was difficult, Jack went from a participating leadership style appropriate for a higher level of readiness, to one for a low level of readiness, telling.[14]

In this example the performance of the subordinate determined leadership style. Since the level of readiness for the foreman was low, Jack was able to gain control of the task and ensure a more effective outcome by assuming the style necessary to lead a low-readiness subordinate.

The style can be tailored to individual subordinates similar to the leader–member exchange theory described in Chapter 2. If one follower is at a low level of readiness, the leader must be very specific, telling them exactly what to do, how to do it, and when. For a follower high in readiness, the leader provides a general goal and sufficient authority to do the task as the follower sees fit. Leaders can carefully diagnose the readiness level of followers and then tell, sell, participate, or delegate. Classroom teachers face one of the toughest leadership challenges around because they usually deal with students who are at widely different levels of readiness. Consider how Carole McGraw of the Detroit, Michigan, school system met the challenge.

Action Memo

As a leader: Act as a resource to provide advice and assistance when followers have a high level of skill, experience, and responsibility. Delegate responsibility for decisions and their implementation to followers who have very high levels of skill and ability and the positive attitudes to perform well on their own.

In the Lead   Carole McGraw, Detroit Public Schools

Carole McGraw describes what she sees when she walks into a classroom for the first time: "A ubiquitous sea of easily recognizable faces. There's Jamie, whose eyes glow with enthusiasm for learning. And Terrell, who just came from the crib after having no breakfast, no supervision of his inadequate homework, and a chip on his shoulder because he needed to flip hamburgers 'til 10 o'clock at night. . . . And Matt, who slumps over his desk, fast asleep from the Ritalin he took for a learning disorder that was probably misdiagnosed to correct a behavior problem. . . . "And on and on.

McGraw diagnosed what teenagers have in common to find the best way to help students of such varying degrees of readiness learn. She realized that all teenagers are exposed to countless hours of MTV, television programs, CDs, and disc jockeys. They spend a lot of time playing sports, eating junk food, talking on the phone, playing computer games, going to the movies, reading pop magazines, hanging out with peers, and avoiding adults. After considering this, McGraw developed her teaching method focused on three concepts: painless, interesting, and enjoyable. Students in McGraw's biology class now do almost all of their work in labs or teamwork sessions. During the labs, a captain is selected to act as team leader. In teams, students select a viable problem to investigate and then split up the work and conduct research in books, on the Internet, and in laboratory experiments. Teams also spend a lot of time engaged in dialogue and brainstorming. McGraw will throw out an idea and let the students take off with it.

McGraw's teaching method combines telling and participating. Students are provided with direction about certain concepts, vocabulary words, and so forth that they must master, along with guidelines for doing so. This provides the structure and discipline some of her low-readiness level students need to succeed. However, most of her leadership focuses on supporting students as they learn and grow on their own. Does McGraw's innovative approach work? Sixty percent of the students get a grade of A and all score fairly well on objective tests McGraw gives after the teamwork is complete. Students from her classes score great on standardized tests like the SAT because they not only accumulate a lot of knowledge but also gain self-confidence and learn how to think on their feet. "All the stress my kids lived with for years disappears," McGraw says. "My classroom buzzes with new ideas and individual approaches."[15]

Path–Goal Theory

Another contingency approach to leadership is called the path–goal theory.[16] According to the **path–goal theory**, the leader's responsibility is to increase subordinates' motivation to attain personal and organizational goals. As illustrated in Exhibit 3.5, the leader increases follower motivation by either (1) clarifying the follower's path to the rewards that are available or (2) increasing the rewards that the follower values and desires. Path clarification means that the leader works with subordinates to help them identify and learn the behaviors that will lead to successful task accomplishment and organizational rewards. Increasing rewards means that the leader talks with subordinates to learn which rewards are important to them—that is, whether they desire intrinsic rewards from the work itself or extrinsic rewards

Path–goal theory

a contingency approach to leadership in which the leader's responsibility is to increase subordinates' motivation by clarifying the behaviors necessary for task accomplishment and rewards

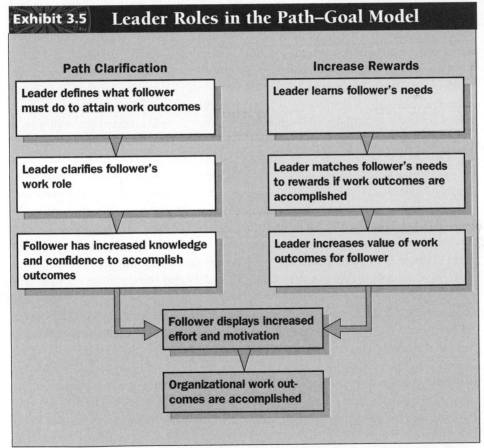

Exhibit 3.5	**Leader Roles in the Path–Goal Model**

Path Clarification

- Leader defines what follower must do to attain work outcomes
- Leader clarifies follower's work role
- Follower has increased knowledge and confidence to accomplish outcomes

Increase Rewards

- Leader learns follower's needs
- Leader matches follower's needs to rewards if work outcomes are accomplished
- Leader increases value of work outcomes for follower

- Follower displays increased effort and motivation
- Organizational work outcomes are accomplished

SOURCE: Based on and reprinted from *Organizational Dynamics* 13 (Winter 1985), Bernard M. Bass, "Leadership: Good, Better, Best," 26–40. Copyright 1985, with permission from Elsevier.

such as raises or promotions. The leader's job is to increase personal payoffs to subordinates for goal attainment and to make the paths to these payoffs clear and easy to travel.[17]

This model is called a contingency theory because it consists of three sets of contingencies—leader style, followers and situation, and the rewards to meet followers' needs.[18] Whereas the Fiedler theory made the assumption that new leaders could take over as situations change, in the path–goal theory, leaders change their behaviors to match the situation.

Leader Behavior

The path–goal theory suggests a fourfold classification of leader behaviors.[19] These classifications are the types of behavior the leader can adopt and include supportive, directive, achievement-oriented, and participative styles.

Supportive leadership shows concern for subordinates' well-being and personal needs. Leadership behavior is open, friendly, and approachable, and the leader creates a team climate and treats subordinates as equals. Supportive leadership is similar to the consideration or people-oriented leadership described earlier.

Directive leadership tells subordinates exactly what they are supposed to do. Leader behavior includes planning, making schedules, setting performance goals and behavior standards, and stressing adherence to rules and regulations. Directive leadership behavior is similar to the initiating structure or task-oriented leadership style described earlier.

Participative leadership consults with subordinates about decisions. Leader behavior includes asking for opinions and suggestions, encouraging participation in decision making, and meeting with subordinates in their workplaces. The participative leader encourages group discussion and written suggestions, similar to the selling style in the Hersey and Blanchard model.

Achievement-oriented leadership sets clear and challenging goals for subordinates. Leader behavior stresses high-quality performance and improvement over current performance. Achievement-oriented leaders also show confidence in subordinates and assist them in learning how to achieve high goals.

To illustrate achievement-oriented leadership, consider the training of army officers in the ROTC. This training goes far beyond how to command a platoon. It involves the concepts of motivation, responsibility, and the creation of a team in which decision making is expected of everyone. Fundamentally, this training will enable officers to respond to any situation, not just those outlined in the manual. Thus achievement-oriented leadership is demonstrated: The set goals are challenging, require improvement, and demonstrate confidence in the abilities of subordinates.[20]

The four types of leader behavior are not considered ingrained personality traits as in the earlier trait theories; rather, they reflect types of behavior that every leader is able to adopt, depending on the situation. For example, leader Alan Robbins shifted from a participative to a directive style at Plastic Lumber Company.

In the Lead   Alan Robbins, Plastic Lumber Company

When he started Plastic Lumber Company, which converts plastic milk, water, and soda bottles into fake lumber, Alan Robbins vowed to be both a boss and a friend to his employees. He wanted to give everyone a chance to participate and made a contribution to the organization. His approach to leadership stressed teamwork and participation, and Robbins spent a lot of time running ideas by workers on the factory floor. However, he soon learned that most of his low-skilled workers didn't really care about a chance to participate; they just wanted clear direction and consistent standards so that everyone knew what was expected of them.

The degree of freedom Robbins allowed with the participative style led to some serious problems. Workers were frequently absent or late without calling, showed up drunk or under the influence of drugs, and started fights on the factory floor. The absence of rules, guidelines, and direction weakened Robbins's authority. Workers who genuinely wanted to do a good job were frustrated by the lack of order and the fact that some workers seemed to get away with anything.

Even though Robbins's natural desire was to be a participative leader, he shifted to a directive leadership style. With a comprehensive rules and policy manual, drug testing for all workers, and clear standards of behavior, the work environment and performance at Plastic Lumber Company improved. By using a directive style and clarifying what behavior was expected and what would not be tolerated, Robbins enabled his employees to focus on meeting performance standards by following clear procedures and guidelines.[21]

Situational Contingencies

The two important situational contingencies in the path–goal theory are (1) the personal characteristics of group members and (2) the work environment. Personal characteristics of followers are similar to Hersey and Blanchard's readiness level and include such factors as ability, skills, needs, and motivations. For example, if an employee has a low level of ability or skill, the leader may need to provide additional training or coaching in order for the worker to improve performance. If a subordinate is self-centered, the leader may use monetary rewards to motivate him or her. Subordinates who want or need clear direction and authority, such as those at Plastic Lumber Company, require a directive leader to tell them exactly what to do. Craft workers and professionals, however, may want more freedom and autonomy and work best under a participative leadership style.

The work environment contingencies include the degree of task structure, the nature of the formal authority system, and the work group itself. The task structure is similar to the same concept described in Fiedler's contingency theory; it includes the extent to which tasks are defined and have explicit job descriptions and work procedures. The formal authority system includes the amount of legitimate power used by leaders and the extent to which policies and rules constrain employees' behavior. Work-group characteristics consist of the educational level of subordinates and the quality of relationships among them.

Use of Rewards

Recall that the leader's responsibility is to clarify *the path to rewards* for followers or to increase *the amount of rewards* to enhance satisfaction and job performance. In some situations, the leader works with subordinates to help them acquire the skills and confidence needed to perform tasks and achieve rewards already available. In others, the leader may develop new rewards to meet the specific needs of a subordinate.

Exhibit 3.6 illustrates four examples of how leadership behavior is tailored to the situation. In the first situation, the subordinate lacks confidence; thus, the supportive leadership style provides the social support with which to encourage the subordinate to undertake the behavior needed to do the work and receive the rewards. In the second situation, the job is ambiguous, and the employee is not performing effectively. Directive leadership behavior is used to give instructions and clarify the task so that the follower will know how to accomplish it and receive rewards. In the third situation, the subordinate is unchallenged by the task; thus, an achievement-oriented behavior is used to set higher goals. This clarifies the path to rewards for the employee. In the fourth situation, an incorrect reward is given to a subordinate, and the participative leadership style is used to change this. By discussing the subordinate's needs, the leader is able to identify the correct reward for task accomplishment. In all four cases, the outcome of fitting the leadership behavior to the situation produces greater employee effort by either clarifying how subordinates can receive rewards or changing the rewards to fit their needs.

Pat Kelly, founder and CEO of PSS World Medical, a specialty marketer and distributor of medical products, uses achievement-oriented leadership to motivate ambitious employees.

Exhibit 3.6 **Path–Goal Situations and Preferred Leader Behaviors**

Situation	Leader Behavior	Impact on Follower	Outcome
Follower lacks self-confidence	Supportive Leadership	Increases confidence to achieve work outcome	
Ambiguous job	Directive Leadership	Clarifies path to reward	Increased effort; improved satisfaction and performance
Lack of job challenge	Achievement-Oriented Leadership	Set and strive for high goals	
Incorrect reward	Participative Leadership	Clarifies followers' needs to change rewards	

In the Lead   Pat Kelly, PSS World Medical

PSS World Medical strives to hire enterprising and hard-working professionals who thrive on challenge, responsibility, and recognition. Then, Pat Kelly keeps them performing at high levels by consistently setting high financial and sales targets. Kelly realizes that what gets people's competitive juices flowing is not just reaching a new financial target, but the idea of winning. And Kelly makes sure employees have what they need to win and receive high rewards for their performance. PSS spends about 5 percent of its payroll budget each year on training, so that employees have the knowledge and skills they need to succeed. The company emphasizes promotion from within and moving people around to different divisions and different roles to give them opportunities for learning and advancement. If an employee doesn't do well in one position, PSS will help the person find another in which he can succeed.

Open communication is an important part of Kelly's leadership. To meet high goals, employees have to know how they contribute and where they stand. *Open-book management* is a cornerstone of corporate culture because Kelly believes people can succeed only when everyone knows the numbers and how they fit in. By setting high goals, providing people with the knowledge and skills to succeed, and running an open company, Kelly has created an organization full of people who think and act like business owners.[22]

Achievement-oriented leadership is just right for leading employees at PSS World Medical. By setting specific ambitious goals, Kelly keeps talented, ambitious workers challenged and motivated. Path goal theorizing can be complex, but much of the research on it has been encouraging.[23] Using the model to specify relationships and make exact predictions about employee outcomes might seem difficult at first, but the four types of leader behavior and the ideas for fitting them to situational contingencies provide a useful way for leaders to think about motivating subordinates.

The Vroom–Jago Contingency Model

Vroom–Jago contingency model

a contingency model that focuses on varying degrees of participative leadership, and how each level of participation influences quality and accountability of decisions.

The **Vroom–Jago contingency model** shares some basic principles with the previous models, yet it differs in significant ways as well. This model focuses specifically on varying degrees of participative leadership, and how each level of participation influences quality and accountability of decisions. A number of situational factors shape the likelihood that either a participative or autocratic approach will produce the best outcome.

This model starts with the idea that a leader faces a problem that requires a solution. Decisions to solve the problem might be made by a leader alone, or through inclusion of a number of followers.

The Vroom–Jago model is very applied, which means that it tells the leader precisely the correct amount of participation by subordinates to use in making a particular decision.[24] The model has three major components: leader participation styles, a set of diagnostic questions with which to analyze a decision situation, and a series of decision rules.

Leader Participation Styles

The model employs five levels of subordinate participation in decision making, ranging from highly autocratic (leader decides alone) to highly democratic (leader delegates to group), as illustrated in Exhibit 3.7.[25] The exhibit shows five decision styles, starting with the leader making the decision alone (Decide), presenting the problem to subordinates individually for their suggestions, and then making the

Exhibit 3.7   Five Leader Decision Styles

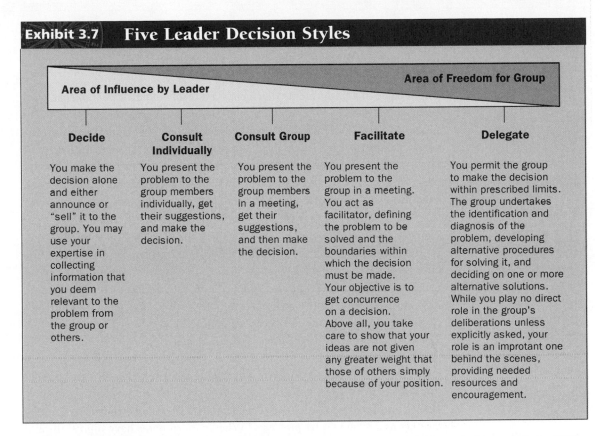

Area of Influence by Leader

Area of Freedom for Group

Decide	Consult Individually	Consult Group	Facilitate	Delegate
You make the decision alone and either announce or "sell" it to the group. You may use your expertise in collecting information that you deem relevant to the problem from the group or others.	You present the problem to group members individually, get their suggestions, and make the decision.	You present the problem to the group members in a meeting, get their suggestions, and then make the decision.	You present the problem to the group in a meeting. You act as facilitator, defining the problem to be solved and the boundaries within which the decision must be made. Your objective is to get concurrence on a decision. Above all, you take care to show that your ideas are not given any greater weight that those of others simply because of your position.	You permit the group to make the decision within prescribed limits. The group undertakes the identification and diagnosis of the problem, developing alternative procedures for solving it, and deciding on one or more alternative solutions. While you play no direct role in the group's deliberations unless explicitly asked, your role is an improtant one behind the scenes, providing needed resources and encouragement.

SOURCE: Victor H. Vroom, "Leadership and the Decision Making Process," *Organizational Dynamics* 28, no. 4 (Spring 2000): 82–94. This is Vroom's adaptation of Tannenbaum and Schmidt's Taxonomy.

decision (Consult Individually), presenting the problem to subordinates as a group, collectively obtaining their ideas and suggestions, then making the decision (Consult Group), sharing the problem with subordinates as a group and acting as a facilitator to help the group arrive at a decision (Facilitate), or delegating the problem and permitting the group to make the decision within prescribed limits (Delegate). The five styles fall along a continuum, and the leader should select one depending on the situation.

Diagnostic Questions

How does a leader decide which of the five decision styles to use? The appropriate degree of decision participation depends on a number of situational factors, such as the required level of decision quality, the level of leader or subordinate expertise, and the importance of having subordinates commit to the decision. Leaders can analyze the appropriate degree of participation by answering seven diagnostic questions.

1. **Decision significance:** *How significant is this decision for the project or organization?* If the decision is highly important and a high-quality decision is needed for the success of the project or organization, the leader has to be actively involved.

2. **Importance of commitment:** *How important is subordinate commitment to carrying out the decision?* If implementation requires a high level of commitment to the decision, leaders should involve subordinates in the decision process.

3. **Leader expertise:** *What is the level of the leader's expertise in relation to the problem?* If the leader does not have a high amount of information, knowledge, or expertise, the leader should involve subordinates to obtain it.

4. **Likelihood of commitment:** *If the leader were to make the decision alone, would subordinates have high or low commitment to the decision?* If subordinates typically go along with whatever the leader decides, their involvement in the decision-making process will be less important.

5. **Group support for goals:** *What is the degree of subordinate support for the team's or organization's objectives at stake in this decision?* If subordinates have low support for the goals of the organization, the leader should not allow the group to make the decision alone.

6. **Goal expertise:** *What is the level of group members' knowledge and expertise in relation to the problem?* If subordinates have a high level of expertise in relation to the problem, more responsibility for the decision can be delegated to them.

7. **Team competence:** *How skilled and committed are group members to working together as a team to solve problems?* When subordinates have high skills and high desire to work together cooperatively to solve problems, more responsibility for the decision making can be delegated to them.

These questions seem detailed, but considering these seven situational factors can quickly narrow the options and point to the appropriate level of group participation in decision making.

Selecting a Decision Style

Further development of the Vroom–Jago model added concern for time constraints and concern for follower development as explicit criteria for determining the level of participation. That is, a leader considers the relative importance of time versus follower development in selecting a decision style. This led to the development of two decision matrixes, *a time-based model*, to be used if time is critical, for example, if the organization is facing a crisis and a decision must be made immediately, and a *development-based model*, to be used if time and efficiency are less important criteria than the opportunity to develop the thinking and decision-making skills of followers.

Consider the example of a small auto parts manufacturer, which owns only one machine for performing welds on mufflers. If the machine has broken down and production has come to a stand-still, a decision concerning the purchase of a new machine is critical and has to be made immediately to get the production line moving again. In this case, a leader would follow the time-based model for selecting the decision style. However, if the machine is scheduled for routine replacement in three months, time is not a critical factor. The leader is then free to consider the importance of involving production workers in the decision-making to develop their skills. Thus, the leader may follow the development-based model because time is not a critical concern.

Exhibits 3.8 and 3.9 illustrate the two decision matrixes—a time-based model and a development-based model—that enables leaders to adopt a participation style by answering the diagnostic questions in sequence. Returning to the example of the welding machine, if the machine has broken down and must be replaced immediately, the leader would follow the time-based model in Exhibit 3.8. The leader enters the matrix at the left side, at Problem Statement, and considers the seven situational questions in sequence from left to right, answering high (H) or low (L) to each one and avoiding crossing any horizontal lines.

The first question would be: *How significant is this decision for the project or organization?* If the answer is High, the leader proceeds to importance of commitment: *How important is subordinate commitment to carrying out the decision?* If the answer is High, the next question pertains to leader expertise: *What is the level of the leader's expertise in relation to the problem?* If the leader's knowledge and expertise is High, the leader next considers likelihood of commitment: *If the leader were to make the decision alone, how likely is it that subordinates would be committed to the decision?* If there is a high likelihood that subordinates would be committed, the decision matrix leads directly to the Decide style of decision making, in which the leader makes the decision alone and presents it to the group.

As noted earlier, this matrix assumes that time and efficiency are the most important criteria. However, consider how the selection of a decision style would differ if the leader had several months to replace the welding machine and considered follower development of high importance and time of little concern. In this case, the leader would follow the development-driven decision matrix in Exhibit 3.9. Beginning again at the left side of the matrix: *How significant is this decision for the project or organization?* If the answer is High, proceed to importance of commitment: *How important is subordinate commitment?* If high, the next question concerns likelihood of commitment (leader expertise is not considered because the development model is focused on involving subordinates, even if the leader has knowledge and expertise): *If the leader were to make the decision alone, how likely is it that subordinates would be committed to the decision?* If there is a high likelihood, the leader next considers group support: *What is the degree of subordinate support for the team's or organization's objectives at stake in this decision?* If the degree of support for goals is low, the

Action Memo

As a leader: Apply the Vroom–Jago model to determine the appropriate amount of follower participation to use in making a decision. Follow a time-based model when time is of the essence, but use a development-based model when cultivating followers' decision-making skills is also important.

Exhibit 3.8 Time-Driven Model for Determining an Appropriate Decision-Making Style—Group Problems

Instructions: The matrix operates like a funnel. You start at the left with a specific decision problem in mind. The column headings denote situational factors which may or may not be present in that problem. You progress by selecting High or Low (H or L) for each relevant situational factor. Proceed down from the funnel, judging only those situational factors for which a judgment is called for, until you reach the recommended process.

	Decision Significance?	Importance of Commitment?	Leader Expertise?	Likelihood of Commitment?	Group Support?	Group Expertise?	Team Competence?	
PROBLEM STATEMENT	H	H	H	H	–	–	–	Decide
				L	H	H	H	Delegate
							L	Consult (Group)
						L	–	Consult (Group)
					L	–	–	Consult (Group)
			L	H	H	H	H	Facilitate
							L	Consult (Individually)
						L	–	Consult (Individually)
					L	–	–	Consult (Individually)
				L	H	H	H	Facilitate
							L	Consult (Group)
						L	–	Consult (Group)
					L	–	–	Consult (Group)
		L	H	–	–	–	–	Decide
			L	–	H	H	H	Facilitate
							L	Consult (Individually)
						L	–	Consult (Individually)
					L	–	–	Consult (Individually)
	L	H	–	H		–	–	Decide
				L	–	–	H	Delegate
							L	Facilitate
		L	–	–	–	–	–	Decide

SOURCE: Victor H. Vroom, "Leadership and the Decision Making Process," *Organizational Dynamics* 28, no. 4 (Spring 2000): 82–94.

Exhibit 3.9

Development-Driven Model for Determining an Appropriate Decision-Making Style—Group Problems

Decision Significance?	Importance of Commitment?	Leader Expertise?	Likelihood of Commitment?	Group Support?	Group Expertise?	Team Competence?	
H	H	-	H	H	H	H	Delegate
						L	Facilitate
					L	-	
				L	-	-	Consult (Group)
			L	H	H	H	Delegate
						L	Facilitate
					L	-	
				L	-	-	Consult (Group)
	L	-	-	H	H	H	Delegate
						L	Facilitate
					L	-	
				L	-	-	Consult (Group)
L	H	-	H	-	-	-	Decide
			L	-	-	-	Delegate
	L	-	-	-	-	-	Decide

SOURCE: Victor H. Vroom, "Leadership and the Decision Making Process," *Organizational Dynamics* 28, no. 4 (Spring 2000): 82–94.

leader would proceed directly to the Group Consult decision style. However, if the degree of support for goals is high, the leader would then ask: *What is the level of group members' knowledge and expertise in relation to the problem?* An answer of High would take the leader to the question: *How skilled and committed are group members to working together as a team to solve problems?* An answer of High would lead to the delegate style, in which the leader allows the group to make the decision within certain limits.

Note that the time-driven model takes the leader to the first decision style that preserves decision quality and follower acceptance, whereas the development-driven model takes other considerations into account. It takes less time to make an autocratic decision (Decide) than to involve subordinates by using a Facilitate or Delegate style. However, in many cases, time and efficiency are less important than the opportunity to further subordinate development. In many of today's organizations, where knowledge sharing and widespread participation are considered critical to organizational success, leaders are placing greater emphasis on follower development when time is not a critical issue.

Leaders can quickly learn to use the model to adapt their styles to fit the situation. However, researchers have also developed a computer-based program that allows for greater complexity and precision in the Vroom–Jago model and incorporates the value of time and value of follower development as situational factors rather than portraying them in separate decision matrixes.

The Vroom–Jago model has been criticized as being less than perfect,[26] but it is useful to decision makers, and the body of supportive research is growing.[27] Leaders can learn to use the model to make timely, high-quality decisions. Let's try applying the model to the following problem.

In the Lead   Dave Robbins, Whitlock Manufacturing

When Whitlock Manufacturing won a contract from a large auto manufacturer to produce an engine to power its flagship sports car, Dave Robbins was thrilled to be selected as a project manager. The engine, of Japanese design and extremely complex, has gotten rave reviews in the automotive press. This project has dramatically enhanced the reputation of Whitlock Manufacturing, which was previously known primarily as a producer of outboard engines for marine use.

Robbins and his team of engineers have taken great pride in their work on the project, but their excitement was dashed by a recent report of serious engine problems in cars delivered to customers. Fourteen owners of cars produced during the first month have experienced engine seizures. Taking quick action, the auto manufacturer suspended sales of the sports car, halted current production, and notified owners of the current model not to drive the car. Everyone involved knows this is a disaster. Unless the engine problem is solved quickly, Whitlock Manufacturing could be exposed to extended litigation. In addition, Whitlock's valued relationship with one of the world's largest auto manufacturers would probably be lost forever.

As the person most knowledgeable about the engine, Robbins has spent two weeks in the field inspecting the seized engines and the auto plant where they were installed. In addition, he has carefully examined the operations and practices in Whitlock's plant where the engine is manufactured. Based on this extensive research, Robbins is convinced that he knows what the problem is and the best way to solve it. However, his natural inclination is to involve other team members as much as possible in making decisions and solving problems. He not only values their input, but thinks that by encouraging greater participation he strengthens the thinking skills of team members, helping them grow and contribute more to the team and the organization. Therefore, Robbins chooses to consult with his team before making his final decision. The group meets for several hours that afternoon, discussing the problem in detail and sharing their varied perspectives, including the information Robbins has gathered during his research. Following the group session, Robbins makes his decision. He will present the decision at the team meeting the following morning, after which testing and correction of the engine problem will begin.[28]

In the Whitlock Manufacturing case, either a time-driven or a development-driven decision tree can be used to select a decision style. Although time is of importance, a leader's desire to involve subordinates can be considered equally important. Do you think Robbins used the correct leader decision style? Let's examine the problem using the development-based decision tree, since Robbins is concerned about involving other team members. Moving from left to right in Exhibit 3.9, the questions and answers are as follows: *How significant is this decision for the organization?* Definitely high. Quality of the decision is of critical importance. The company's future may be at stake. *How important is subordinate commitment to carrying out the decision?* Also high. The team members must support and implement Robbins's solution. *If Robbins makes the decision on his own, will team members have high or low commitment to it?* The answer to this question is probably also high. Team members respect Robbins, and they are likely to accept his analysis of the problem. This leads to the question, *What is the degree of subordinate support for the team's or organization's objectives at stake in this decision?* Definitely high. This leads to the question, *What is the level of group members' knowledge and expertise in relation to the problem?* The answer to this question is probably Low, which leads to the Consult Group decision style. Thus, Robbins used the style that would be recommended by the Vroom–Jago model.

Now, assume that Robbins chose to place more emphasis on time than on participant involvement and development. Using the time-based decision matrix in Exhibit 3.8, trace the questions and answers based on the information just provided and rating Robbins's level of expertise as high. Remember to avoid crossing any horizontal lines. What decision style is recommended? Is it the same or different from that recommended by the development-based tree?

Substitutes for Leadership

Substitute

a situational variable that makes leadership unnecessary or redundant

Neutralizer

a situational characteristic that counteracts the leadership style and prevents the leader from displaying certain behaviors

The contingency leadership approaches considered so far have focused on the leader's style, the follower's nature, and the situation's characteristics. The final contingency approach suggests that situational variables can be so powerful that they actually substitute for or neutralize the need for leadership.[29] This approach outlines those organizational settings in which task-oriented and people-oriented leadership styles are unimportant or unnecessary.

Exhibit 3.10 shows the situational variables that tend to substitute for or neutralize leadership characteristics. A **substitute** for leadership makes the leadership style unnecessary or redundant. For example, highly educated, professional subordinates who know how to do their tasks do not need a leader who initiates structure for them and tells them what to do. In addition, long-term education often develops autonomous, self-motivated individuals. Thus, task-oriented and people-oriented leadership is substituted by professional education and socialization.[30]

A **neutralizer** counteracts the leadership style and prevents the leader from displaying certain behaviors. For example, if a leader is physically removed from subordinates, the leader's ability to give directions to subordinates is greatly reduced. Kinko's, a nationwide copy center, includes numerous locations widely

Exhibit 3.10   Substitutes and Neutralizers for Leadership

Variable		Task-Oriented Leadership	People-Oriented Leadership
Organizational variables:	Group cohesiveness	Substitutes for	Substitutes for
	Formalization	Substitutes for	No effect on
	Inflexibility	Neutralizes	No effect on
	Low positional power	Neutralizes	Neutralizes
	Physical separation	Neutralizes	Neutralizes
Task characteristics:	Highly structured task	Substitutes for	No effect on
	Automatic feedback	Substitutes for	No effect on
	Intrinsic satisfaction	No effect on	Substitutes for
Follower characteristics:	Professionalism	Substitutes for	Substitutes for
	Training/experience	Substitutes for	No effect on
	Low value of rewards	Neutralizes	Neutralizes

scattered across regions. Regional managers enjoy very limited personal interaction due to the distances between stores. Thus, their ability to both support and direct is neutralized.

Situational variables in Exhibit 3.10 include characteristics of the followers, the task, and the organization itself. For example, when subordinates are highly professional, such as research scientists in companies like Merck or Monsanto, both leadership styles are less important. The employees do not need either direction or support. With respect to task characteristics, highly structured tasks substitute for a task-oriented style, and a satisfying task substitutes for a people-oriented style. You can measure how the task characteristics of your job or a job you've held in the past might act as substitutes for leadership by answering the questions in Leader's Self-Insight 3.2.

When a task is highly structured and routine, like auditing cash, the leader should provide personal consideration and support that is not provided by the task. Satisfied people don't need as much consideration. Likewise, with respect to the organization itself, group cohesiveness substitutes for both leader styles. For example, the relationship that develops among air traffic controllers and jet fighter pilots is characterized by high-stress interactions and continuous peer training. This cohesiveness provides support and direction that substitutes for formal leadership.[31] Formalized rules and procedures substitute for leader task orientation because the rules tell people what to do. Physical separation of leader and subordinate neutralizes both leadership styles.

The value of the situations described in Exhibit 3.10 is that they help leaders avoid leadership overkill. Leaders should adopt a style with which to complement the organizational situation. For example, the work situation for bank tellers provides a high level of formalization, little flexibility, and a highly structured task. The head teller should not adopt a task-oriented style because the organization already provides structure and direction. The head teller should concentrate on a people-oriented style. In other organizations, if group cohesiveness or previous training meets employee social needs, the leader is free to concentrate on task-oriented behaviors. The leader can adopt a style complementary to the organizational situation to ensure that both task needs and people needs of followers are met.

Recent studies examined how substitutes (the situation) can be designed to have more impact than leader behaviors on such outcomes as subordinate satisfaction.[32] The impetus behind this research is the idea that substitutes for leadership can be designed in organizations in ways to complement existing leadership, act in the absence of leadership, and otherwise provide more comprehensive leadership alternatives. For example, Paul Reeves, a foreman at Harmon Auto Parts, shared half-days with his subordinates during which they helped him perform his leader tasks. After Reeves' promotion to middle management, his group no longer required a foreman. Followers were trained to act on their own.[33] Thus, a situation

Action Memo

As a leader: Avoid leadership overkill. Adopt a style that is complementary to the organization situation to ensure that both task needs and people needs are met.

Action Memo

As a leader: Use a people-oriented style when tasks are highly structured and routine and followers are bound by formal rules and procedures. Rules and structured tasks substitute for task-oriented leadership.

LEADER'S SELF-INSIGHT 3.2

Measuring Substitutes for Leadership

Think about your current job, or a job you have held in the past, and answer each of the following questions according to this scale:

5 = Almost always true; 4 = Usually true; 3 = Sometimes true, sometimes untrue; 2 = Usually untrue; 1 = Almost always untrue

Task Structure

	Almost always untrue				Almost always true
1. Because of the nature of the tasks I perform, there is little doubt about the best way to do them.	1	2	3	4	5
2. My job duties are so simple that almost anyone could perform them well after a little instruction.	1	2	3	4	5
3. It is difficult to figure out the best way to do many of my tasks and activities.	1	2	3	4	5
4. There is really only one correct way to perform most of the tasks I do.	1	2	3	4	5

Score for Task Structure:_____

Task Feedback

5. After I've completed a task, I can tell right away from the results I get whether I have performed it correctly.	1	2	3	4	5
6. My job is the kind where you can finish a task and not know if you've made a mistake or error.	1	2	3	4	5
7. Because of the nature of the tasks I do, it is easy for me to see when I have done something exceptionally well.	1	2	3	4	5

Score for Task Feedback:_____

Intrinsic Satisfaction

8. I get lots of satisfaction from the work I do.	1	2	3	4	5
9. It is hard to imagine that anyone could enjoy performing the tasks I have performed on my job.	1	2	3	4	5
10. My job satisfaction depends primarily on the nature of the tasks and activities I perform.	1	2	3	4	5

Score for Satisfaction:_____

Scoring and Interpretation For items 3, 6, and 9, subtract your response from the number 6. Then, sum your score to items 1–4 and divide by 4. This is your score for Task Structure. Sum your score for items 5–7 and divide by 3. This is your score for task feedback. Sum your score for items 8–10 and divide by 3. This is your score for Intrinsic Satisfaction.

A high score (4 or greater) for Task Structure or Task Feedback indicates a high potential for that category to act as a substitute for *task-oriented leadership*. A high score (4 or greater) for Intrinsic Satisfaction indicates the potential to be a substitute for *people-oriented leadership*. Does your leader adopt a style that is complementary to the task situation, or is the leader guilty of *leadership overkill*? How can you apply this understanding to your own actions as a leader?

_____

SOURCE: Based on "Questionnaire Items for the Measurement of Substitutes for Leadership," Table 2 in Steven Kerr and John M. Jermier, "Substitutes for Leadership: Their Meaning and Measurement," *Organizational Behavior and Human Performance* 22 (1978): 375–403.

in which follower ability and training were highly developed created a substitute for leadership.

The ability to utilize substitutes to fill leadership "gaps" is often advantageous to organizations. Indeed, the fundamental assumption of substitutes-for-leadership researchers is that effective leadership is the ability to recognize and provide the support and direction not already provided by task, group, and organization.

Summary and Interpretation

The most important point in this chapter is that situational variables affect leadership outcomes. The contingency approaches were developed to systematically address the relationship between a leader and the organization. The contingency approaches focus on how the components of leadership style, subordinate characteristics, and situational elements impact one another. Fiedler's contingency model, Hersey and Blanchard's situational theory, the path–goal theory, the Vroom–Jago model, and the substitutes-for-leadership concept each examine how different situations call for different styles of leadership behavior.

According to Fiedler, leaders can determine whether the situation is favorable to their leadership style. Task-oriented leaders tend to do better in very easy or very difficult situations, while person-oriented leaders do best in situations of intermediate favorability. Hersey and Blanchard contend that leaders can adjust their task or relationship style to accommodate the readiness level of their subordinates. The path–goal theory states that leaders can use a style that appropriately clarifies the path to desired rewards. The Vroom–Jago model indicates that leaders can choose a participative decision style based on contingencies such as quality requirement, commitment requirement, or the leader's information. In addition, concern for time (the need for a fast decision) versus concern for follower development are taken into account. Leaders can analyze each situation and answer a series of questions that help determine the appropriate level of follower participation. Finally, the substitutes-for-leadership concept recommends that leaders adjust their style to provide resources not otherwise provided in the organizational situation.

By discerning the characteristics of tasks, subordinates, and organizations, leaders can determine the style that increases the likelihood of successful leadership outcomes. Therefore, effective leadership is about developing diagnostic skills and being flexible in your leadership behavior.

Action Memo

As a leader: Adopt a task-oriented style if group cohesiveness and followers' intrinsic satisfaction meet their social and emotional needs.

Action Memo

As a leader: Provide minimal direction and support to highly-trained employees; followers' professionalism and intrinsic satisfaction substitute for task- and people-oriented leadership.

Discussion Questions

1. Consider Fiedler's theory as illustrated in Exhibit 3.3. How often do you think very favorable, intermediate, or very unfavorable situations occur to leaders in real life? Discuss.

2. Do you think leadership style is fixed and unchangeable or flexible and adaptable? Why?

3. Consider the leadership position of the managing partner in a law firm. What task, subordinate, and organizational factors might serve as substitutes for leadership in this situation?

4. Compare Fiedler's contingency model with the path–goal theory. What are the similarities and differences? Which do you prefer?

5. Think of a situation in which you worked. At what level of readiness (very low to very high) would you rate yourself and co-workers? Did your leader use the correct style according to the Hersey and Blanchard model?

6. Think back to teachers you have had, and identify one each who fits a supportive style, directive style, participative style, and achievement-oriented style according to the path–goal theory. Which style did you find most effective? Why?

7. Do you think leaders should decide on a participative style based on the most efficient way to reach the decision? Should leaders sometimes let people participate for other reasons?

8. Consider the situational characteristics of group cohesiveness, organizational formalization, and physical separation. How might each of these substitute for or neutralize task-oriented or people-oriented leadership? Explain.

Leadership at Work

Task Versus Relationship Role Play

You are the new distribution manager for French Grains Bakery. Five drivers report to you that deliver French Grains baked goods to grocery stores in the metropolitan area. The drivers are expected to complete the Delivery Report to keep track of actual deliveries and any changes that occur. The Delivery Report is a key element in inventory control and provides the data for French Grains invoicing of grocery stores. Errors become excessive when drivers fail to complete the report each day, especially when store managers request different inventory when the driver arrives. As a result, French Grains may not be paid for several loaves of bread a day for each mistake in the Delivery Report. The result is lost revenue and poor inventory control.

One of the drivers accounts for about 60 percent of the errors in the Delivery Reports. This driver is a nice person and generally reliable, but sometimes is late for work. His major problem is that he falls behind in his paperwork. A second driver accounts for about 30 percent of the errors, and a third driver for about 10 percent of the errors. The other two drivers turn in virtually error-free Delivery Reports.

You are a high task-oriented (and low relationship-oriented) leader, and have decided to talk to the drivers about doing a more complete and accurate job with the Delivery Report. Write below exactly how you will go about correcting this problem as a task-oriented leader. Will you meet with drivers individually or in a group? When and where will you meet with them? Exactly what will you say and how will you get them to listen?

Now adopt the role of a high relationship-oriented (and low task-oriented) leader. Write below exactly what you will do and say as a relationship-oriented distribution manager. Will you meet with the drivers individually or in a group? What will you say and how will you get them to listen?

In Class: The instructor can ask students to volunteer to play the role of the Distribution Manager and the drivers. A few students can take turns role playing the Distribution Manager in front of the class to show how they would handle the drivers as task- and relationship-oriented leaders. The instructor can ask other students for feedback on the leader's effectiveness and on which approach seems more effective for this situation, and why.

SOURCE: Based on K. J. Keleman, J. E. Garcia, and K. J. Lovelace, *Management Incidents: Role Plays for Management Development* (Kendall Hunt Publishing Company, 1990), 69–72.

Leadership Development: Cases for Analysis

Alvis Corporation

Kevin McCarthy is the manager of a production department in Alvis Corporation, a firm that manufactures office equipment. After reading an article that stressed the benefits of participative management, Kevin believes that these benefits could be realized in his department if the workers are allowed to participate in making some decisions that affect them. The workers are not unionized. Kevin selected two decisions for his experiment in participative management.

The first decision involved vacation schedules. Each summer the workers were given two weeks vacation, but no more than two workers can go on vacation at the same time. In prior years, Kevin made this decision himself. He would first ask the workers to indicate their preferred dates, and he considered how the work would be affected if different people were out at the same time. It was important to plan a vacation schedule that would ensure adequate staffing for all of the essential operations performed by the department. When more than two workers wanted the same time period, and they had similar skills, he usually gave preference to the workers with the highest productivity.

The second decision involved production standards. Sales had been increasing steadily over the past few years, and the company recently installed some new equipment to increase productivity. The new equipment would allow Kevin's department to produce more with the same number of workers. The company had a pay incentive system in which workers received a piece rate for each unit produced above a standard amount. Separate standards existed for each type of product, based on an industrial engineering study conducted a few years earlier. Top management wanted to readjust the production standards to reflect the fact that the new equipment made it possible for the workers to earn more without working any harder. The savings from higher productivity were needed to help pay for the new equipment.

Kevin called a meeting of his 15 workers an hour before the end of the workday. He explained that he wanted them to discuss the two issues and make recommendations. Kevin figured that the workers might be inhibited about participating in the discussion if he were present, so he left them alone to discuss the issues. Besides, Kevin had an appointment to meet with the quality control manager. Quality problems had increased after the new equipment was installed, and the industrial engineers were studying the problem in an attempt to determine why quality had gotten worse rather than better.

When Kevin returned to his department just at quitting time, he was surprised to learn that the workers recommended keeping the standards the same. He had assumed they knew the pay incentives were no longer fair and would set a higher standard. The spokesman for the group explained that their base pay had not kept up with inflation and the higher incentive pay restored their real income to its prior level.

On the vacation issue, the group was deadlocked. Several of the workers wanted to take their vacations during the same two-week period and could not agree on who should go. Some workers argued that they should have priority because they had more seniority, while others argued that priority should be based on productivity, as in the past. Since it was quitting time, the group concluded that Kevin would have to resolve the dispute himself. After all, wasn't that what he was being paid for?

SOURCE: Reprinted with permission from Gary Yukl, *Leadership in Organizations*, Fourth Edition (Englewood Cliffs, NJ: Prentice Hall, 1998), 147–148.

Questions
1. Analyze this situation using the Hersey–Blanchard model and the Vroom–Jago model. What do these models suggest as the appropriate leadership or decision style? Explain.
2. Evaluate Kevin McCarthy's leadership style before and during his experiment in participative management.
3. If you were Kevin McCarthy, what would you do now? Why?

Finance Department

Ken Osborne stared out the window, wondering what he could do to get things back on track. When he became head of the finance department of a state government agency, Osborne inherited a group of highly trained professionals who pursued their jobs with energy and enthusiasm. Everyone seemed to genuinely love coming to work every day. The tasks were sometimes mundane, but most employees liked the structured, routine nature of the work. In addition, the lively camaraderie of the group provided an element of fun and excitement that the work itself sometimes lacked.

Ken knew he'd had an easy time of things over the last couple of years—he had been able to focus his energies on maintaining relationships with other departments and agencies and completing the complex reports he had to turn in each month. The department practically ran itself. Until now. The problem was Larry Gibson, one of the department's best employees. Well-liked by everyone in the department, Gibson had been a key contributor to developing a new online accounting system, and Ken was counting on him to help with the implementation. But everything had changed after Gibson attended a professional development seminar at a prestigious university. Ken had expected him to come back even more fired up about work, but lately Larry was spending more time on his outside professional activities than he was on his job. "If only I'd paid more attention when all this began," Ken thought, as he recalled the day Larry asked him to sign his revised individual development plan. As he'd done in the past, Ken had simply chatted with Larry for a few minutes, glanced at the changes, and initialed the modification. Larry's revised plan included taking a more active role in the state accountants' society, which he argued would enhance his value to the agency as well as improve his own skills and professional contacts.

Within a month, Ken noticed that most of Gibson's energy and enthusiasm seemed to be focused on the society rather than the finance department. On "first Thursday," the society's luncheon meeting day, Larry spent most of the morning on the phone notifying people about the monthly meeting and finalizing details with the speaker. He left around 11 A.M. to make sure things were set up for the meeting and usually didn't return until close to quitting time. Ken could live with the loss of Gibson for one day a month, but the preoccupation with society business seemed to be turning his former star employee into a part-time worker. Larry shows up late for meetings, usually doesn't participate very much, and seems to have little interest in what is going on in the department. The new accounting system is floundering because Larry isn't spending the time to train people in its effective use, so Ken is starting to get complaints from other departments. Moreover, his previously harmonious group of employees is starting to whine and bicker over minor issues and decisions. Ken has also noticed that people who used to be hard at work when he arrived in the mornings seem to be coming in later and later every day.

"Everything's gone haywire since Larry attended that seminar," Ken brooded. "I thought I was one of the best department heads in the agency. Now, I realize I haven't had to provide much leadership until now. Maybe I've had things too easy."

SOURCE: Based on David Hornestay, "Double Vision," *Government Executive* (April 2000): 41–44.

Questions

1. Why had Ken Osborne's department been so successful even though he has provided little leadership over the past two years?
2. How would you describe Osborne's current leadership style? Based on the path–goal theory, which style do you think he might most effectively use to turn things around with Larry Gibson?
3. If you were in Osborne's position, describe how you would evaluate the situation and handle the problem.

References

1. Ian Mount, "Underlings: That's *Mister* Conway to You. And I Am *Not* a PeoplePerson," *Business 2.0* (February 2002): 53–58.
2. Gary Yukl, Angela Gordon, and Tom Taber, "A Hierarchical Taxonomy of Leadership Behavior: Integrating a Half Century of Behavior Research," *Journal of Leadership and Organization Studies* 9, no.1 (2002): 15–32.
3. Fred E. Fiedler, "Assumed Similarity Measures as Predictors of Team Effectiveness," *Journal of Abnormal and Social Psychology* 49 (1954): 381–388; F. E. Fiedler, *Leader Attitudes and Group Effectiveness* (Urbana, IL: University of Illinois Press, 1958); and F. E. Fiedler, *A Theory of Leadership Effectiveness* (New York: McGraw-Hill, 1967).
4. David Rynecki, "Can Stan O'Neal Save Merrill?" *Fortune* (September 20, 2002): 76–88.
5. M. J. Strube and J. E. Garcia, "A Meta-Analytic Investigation of Fiedler's Contingency Model of Leadership Effectiveness," *Psychological Bulletin* 90 (1981): 307–321; and L. H. Peters, D. D. Hartke, and J. T. Pohlmann, "Fiedler's Contingency Theory of Leadership: An Application of the Meta-Analysis Procedures of Schmidt and Hunter," *Psychological Bulletin* 97 (1985): 274–285.
6. R. Singh, "Leadership Style and Reward Allocation: Does Least Preferred Coworker Scale Measure Tasks and Relation Orientation?" *Organizational Behavior and Human Performance* 27 (1983): 178–197; D. Hosking, "A Critical Evaluation of Fiedler's Contingency Hypotheses," *Progress in Applied Psychology* 1 (1981): 103–154; Gary Yukl, "Leader LPC Scores: Attitude Dimensions and Behavioral Correlates," *Journal of Social Psychology* 80 (1970): 207–212; G. Graen, K. M. Alvares, J. B. Orris, and J. A. Martella, "Contingency Model of Leadership Effectiveness: Antecedent and Evidential Results," *Psychological Bulletin* 74 (1970): 285–296; R. P. Vecchio, "Assessing the Validity of Fiedler's Contingency Model of Leadership Effectiveness: A Closer Look at Strube and Garcia," *Psychological Bulletin* 93 (1983): 404–408.

7. Robert L. Rose, "Sour Note," *The Wall Street Journal*, June 22, 1993.

8. J. K. Kennedy, Jr., "Middle LPC Leaders and the Contingency Model of Leadership Effectiveness," *Organizational Behavior and Human Performance* 30 (1982): 1–14; and S. C. Shiflett, "The Contingency Model of Leadership Effectiveness: Some Implications of Its Statistical and Methodological Properties," *Behavioral Science* 18, no. 6 (1973): 429–440.

9. Roya Ayman, M. M. Chemers, and F. Fiedler, "The Contingency Model of Leadership Effectiveness: Its Levels of Analysis," *Leadership Quarterly* 6, no. 2 (1995): 147–167.

10. Paul Hersey and Kenneth H. Blanchard, *Management of Organizational Behavior: Utilizing Human Resources,* 4th ed. (Englewood Cliffs, NJ: Prentice-Hall, 1982).

11. Jonathan Kaufman, "A McDonald's Owner Becomes a Role Model for Black Teenagers," *The Wall Street Journal*, August 23, 1995, A1, A6.

12. Michael Barrier, "Leadership Skills Employees Respect," *Nation's Business* (January 1999).

13. Cheryl Dahle, "Xtreme Teams," *Fast Company*, November 1999, 310–326.

14. Adapted from Oliver Niehouse, "The Strategic Nature of Leadership," *Management Solutions* (July 1987): 27–34.

15. Carole McGraw, "Teaching Teenagers? Think, Do, Learn," *Education Digest* (February 1998): 44–47.

16. M. G. Evans, "The Effects of Supervisory Behavior on the Path–Goal Relationship," *Organizational Behavior and Human Performance* 5 (1970): 277–298; M. G. Evans, "Leadership and Motivation: A Core Concept," *Academy of Management Journal* 13 (1970): 91–102; and B. S. Georgopoulos, G. M. Mahoney, and N. W. Jones, "A Path–Goal Approach to Productivity," *Journal of Applied Psychology* 41 (1957): 345–353.

17. Robert J. House, "A Path–Goal Theory of Leadership Effectiveness," *Administrative Science Quarterly* 16 (1971): 321–338.

18. M. G. Evans, "Leadership," in *Organizational Behavior*, ed. S. Kerr (Columbus, OH: Grid, 1974): 230–233.

19. Robert J. House and Terrence R. Mitchell, "Path–Goal Theory of Leadership," *Journal of Contemporary Business* (Autumn 1974): 81–97.

20. Dyan Machan, "We're Not Authoritarian Goons," *Forbes* October 24, 1994, 264–268.

21. Timothy Aeppel, "Personnel Disorders Sap a Factory Owner of His Early Idealism," *The Wall Street Journal,* January 14, 1998, A1, A14.

22. Charles A. O'Reilly III and Jeffrey Pfeffer, "Star Makers," book excerpt from *From Hidden Value: How Great Companies Achieve Extraordinary Results with Ordinary People* (Harvard Business School Press, 2000), published in *CIO* (September 15, 2000); 226–246.

23. Charles Greene, "Questions of Causation in the Path–Goal Theory of Leadership," *Academy of Management Journal* 22 (March 1979): 22–41; and C. A. Schriesheim and Mary Ann von Glinow, "The Path–Goal Theory of Leadership: A Theoretical and Empirical Analysis," *Academy of Management Journal* 20 (1977): 398–405.

24. V. H. Vroom and Arthur G. Jago, *The New Leadership: Managing Participation in Organizations* (Englewood Cliffs, NJ: Prentice-Hall, 1988).

25. The following discussion is based heavily on Victor H. Vroom, "Leadership and the Decision-Making Process," *Organizational Dynamics* 28, no. 4 (Spring 2000): 82–94.

26. R. H. G. Field, "A Test of the Vroom–Yetton Normative Model of Leadership," *Journal of Applied Psychology* (October 1982): 523–532; and R. H. G. Field, "A Critique of the Vroom–Yetton Contingency Model of Leadership Behavior," *Academy of Management Review* 4 (1979): 249–251.

27. Vroom, "Leadership and the Decision-Making Process"; Jennifer T. Ettling and Arthur G. Jago, "Participation Under Conditions of Conflict: More on the Validity of the Vroom–Yetton Model," *Journal of Management Studies* 25 (1988); 73–83; Madeline E. Heilman, Harvey A. Hornstein, Jack H. Cage, and Judith K. Herschlag, "Reactions to Prescribed Leader Behavior as a Function of Role Perspective: The Case of the Vroom–Yetton Model," *Journal of Applied Psychology* (February 1984); 50–60; and Arthur G. Jago and Victor H. Vroom, "Some Differences in the Incidence and Evaluation of Participative Leader Behavior," *Journal of Applied Psychology* (December 1982): 776–783.

28. Based on a decision problem presented in Victor H. Vroom, "Leadership and the Decision-Making Process," *Organizational Dynamics* 28, no. 4 (Spring, 2000): 82–94.

29. S. Kerr and J. M. Jermier, "Substitutes for Leadership: Their Meaning and Measurement," *Organizational Behavior and Human Performance* 22 (1978): 375–403; and Jon P. Howell and Peter W. Dorfman, "Leadership and Substitutes for Leadership Among Professional and Nonprofessional Workers," *Journal of Applied Behavioral Science* 22 (1986): 29–46.

30. J. P. Howell, D. E. Bowen, P. W. Doreman, S. Kerr, and P. M. Podsakoff, "Substitutes for Leadership: Effective Alternatives to Ineffective Leadership," *Organizational Dynamics* (Summer 1990): 21–38.

31. Howell, et al., "Substitutes for Leadership: Effective Alternatives to Ineffective Leadership."

32. P. M. Podsakoff, S. B. MacKenzie, and W. H. Bommer, "Transformational Leader Behaviors and Substitutes for Leadership as Determinants of Employee Satisfaction, Commitment, Trust, and Organizational Behaviors," *Journal of Management* 22, no. 2 (1996): 259–298.

33. Howell, et al., "Substitutes for Leadership."

The Personal Side of Leadership

Chapter

Your Leadership Challenge

After reading this chapter, you should be able to:

- Identify major personality dimensions and understand how personality influences leadership and relationships within organizations.

- Clarify your instrumental and end values, and recognize how values guide thoughts and behavior.

- Define *attitudes* and explain their relationship to leader behavior.

- Recognize individual differences in cognitive style and broaden your own thinking style to expand leadership potential.

- Practice aspects of charismatic leadership by pursuing a vision or idea that you care deeply about and want to share with others.

- Apply the concepts that distinguish transformational from transactional leadership.

Thom Keeton, an offshore oil rig manager for Transocean Sedco Forex, keeps a color chart under the glass covering his desk. When a crew member comes in, Keeton checks the color of the dot on his hard hat to help him know how to relate to the worker. The colored dots are a shorthand way to help people understand one another's personality styles. *Reds* tend to be strong-willed and decisive, whereas *Greens* are cautious and serious. *Blues* are sensitive and dislike change, and sunny *Yellows* are emotional and talkative. If Keeton, a red–green leader, sees that a worker is a blue–yellow, he knows to tone down his blunt, to-the-point style to enhance communication and understanding.

The color-coded system grew out of a training program that profiled employees' personalities based on their answers to a series of multiple-choice questions and other exercises. The program started as a way to help managers better communicate with employees, but it's now standard for Transocean's 8,300 workers worldwide. Color charts are posted not only in offices, but on the bulkheads of Transocean's rigs. Cramped living conditions, aggressive bosses, and frayed nerves can lead to volatile and dangerous conditions on an oil rig, and Transocean leaders are convinced the training has helped people get along better and relieve tensions. Jimmy Nobles, who has worked on offshore rigs for 25 years, agrees. "It's a different deal," he says. "We care about other people's feelings." Another employee, who's a laid-back blue–yellow, says he now can deal with "those high-strung red–greens" because he understands where they're coming from.

Employees aren't required to show their colors, and some don't. One employee who doesn't reveal his colors publicly is CEO J. Michael Talbert, who says he needs to be a bit of a chameleon because he has to change his own personality to suit the people he's dealing with at the time. Transocean's training instructor reveals that Talbert's really a green–blue. However, he can act like a competitive red when he needs to, the instructor says, referring to a recent merger. "Once the merger stuff settles down, he'll go back to green and blue."[1]

We all know that people differ in many ways. Some are quiet and shy while others are gregarious; some are thoughtful and serious while others are impulsive and fun-loving. All these individual differences affect the leader–follower interaction. Differences in personality, attitudes, values, and so forth influence how people interpret an assignment, whether they like to be told what to do, how they handle challenges, and how they interact with others. Leaders' personalities and attitudes, as well as their ability to understand individual differences among employees, can profoundly affect leadership effectiveness. Many of today's organizations are using personality and other psychometric tests as a way to help people better understand and relate to one another.

In Chapter 2, we examined studies of some personality traits, individual qualities, and behaviors that are thought to be consistent with effective leadership. Chapter 3 examined contingency theories of leadership, which consider the relationship between leader activities and the situation in which they occur, including followers and the environment. Clearly, organizational leadership is both an individual and an organizational phenomenon. This chapter explores the individual in more depth, looking at some individual differences that can affect leadership abilities and success. We begin by looking at personality and some leader-related personality dimensions. Then, the chapter considers how values affect leadership and the ways in which a leader's attitudes toward self and others influence behavior. We will also explore cognitive differences, including a discussion of thinking and decision-making styles and the concept of brain dominance. Finally, the chapter explores charismatic and transformational leadership, two leadership styles that are based on the personal characteristics of the leader.

Personality and Leadership

Personality

the set of unseen characteristics and processes that underlie a relatively stable pattern of behavior in response to ideas, objects, and people in the environment

Some people are consistently pleasant in a variety of situations, while others are moody or aggressive. To explain this behavior, we may say, "He has a pleasant personality," or "She has an aggressive personality." This is the most common usage of the term *personality*, and it refers to an individual's behavior patterns as well as how the person is viewed by others. However, there is also a deeper meaning to the term. **Personality** is the set of unseen characteristics and processes that underlie a relatively stable pattern of behavior in response to ideas, objects, or people in the environment. Leaders who have an understanding of how individuals' personalities differ can use this understanding to improve their leadership effectiveness.

A Model of Personality

Most people think of personality in terms of traits. As we discussed in Chapter 2, researchers have investigated whether any traits stand up to scientific scrutiny, and we looked at some traits associated with effective leadership. Although investigators have examined thousands of traits over the years, their findings have been distilled into five general dimensions that describe personality. These often are called the **Big Five personality dimensions**, as illustrated in Exhibit 4.1.[2] Each contains a wide range of specific traits—for example, all of the personality traits that you would use to describe a teacher, friend, or boss could be categorized as falling into one of the Big Five dimensions: extroversion, agreeableness, conscientiousness, emotional stability, and openness to experience. As illustrated in Exhibit 4.1, a person may have a low, moderate, or high degree of each of these general dimensions.

Big Five personality dimensions
five general dimensions that describe personality: extroversion, agreeableness, conscientiousness, emotional stability, and openness to experience

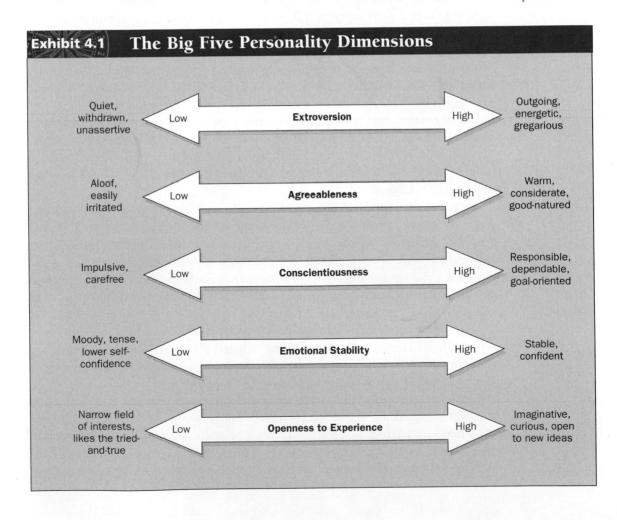

Exhibit 4.1   The Big Five Personality Dimensions

Quiet, withdrawn, unassertive	Low ← **Extroversion** → High	Outgoing, energetic, gregarious
Aloof, easily irritated	Low ← **Agreeableness** → High	Warm, considerate, good-natured
Impulsive, carefree	Low ← **Conscientiousness** → High	Responsible, dependable, goal-oriented
Moody, tense, lower self-confidence	Low ← **Emotional Stability** → High	Stable, confident
Narrow field of interests, likes the tried-and-true	Low ← **Openness to Experience** → High	Imaginative, curious, open to new ideas

Extroversion

the degree to which a person is outgoing, sociable, talkative, and comfortable meeting and talking to new people

Extroversion is made up of traits and characteristics that influence behavior in group settings. Extroversion refers to the degree to which a person is outgoing, sociable, talkative, and comfortable meeting and talking to new people. This dimension also includes the characteristic of *dominance*. A person with a high degree of dominance likes to be in control and have influence over others. These people often are quite self-confident, seek out positions of authority, and are competitive and assertive. They like to be in charge of others or have responsibility for others. Carly Fiorina, CEO of Hewlett-Packard, appears to have a high degree of both dominance and extroversion. She enjoys being "on stage," speaking before a crowd, meeting new people in HP plants around the world. Fiorina also clearly enjoys being in a position of authority and influence. In contrast, Doug Ivester, who served for a short time as CEO of Coca-Cola seems to have a low degree of both dominance and extroversion. Ivester was known to be very reserved in many situations. In addition, he did not appear to have a great desire to influence others, preferring to focus on details and strategy rather than the subtlety of interpersonal relationships. Indeed, he sometimes came off as high-handed because he made and implemented decisions without trying to persuade others to his viewpoint. Some believe Ivester's lack of self-assurance about leading others and the fact that he made little attempt to exert influence were the biggest roadblocks to his success as CEO of a major corporation.[3]

It is obvious that both dominance and extroversion could be valuable for a leader. However, not all effective leaders necessarily have a high degree of these characteristics. In addition, a high degree of dominance and extroversion could even be detrimental to effective leadership if not tempered by other qualities, such as agreeableness or emotional stability.

Agreeableness

the degree to which a person is able to get along with others by being good-natured, cooperative, forgiving, compassionate, understanding, and trusting

Agreeableness is the degree to which a person is able to get along with others by being good-natured, cooperative, forgiving, compassionate, understanding, and trusting. A leader who scores high on agreeableness seems warm and approachable, whereas one who is low on this dimension may seem cold, distant, and insensitive. People high on agreeableness tend to make friends easily and often have a large number of friends, whereas those low on agreeableness generally establish fewer close relationships.

Steve Mariucci, coach of the San Francisco 49ers, is a warm, approachable leader who is always compassionate and willing to listen. He might blow up at halftime if the team is trailing by two touchdowns, but his fairness and good-nature prevails. "I think you can be a gentleman and succeed," says Mariucci.[4]

Conscientious-ness

the degree to which a person is responsible, dependable, persistent, and achievement-oriented

The third personality dimension, **conscientiousness**, refers to the degree to which a person is responsible, dependable, persistent, and achievement-oriented. A conscientious person is focused on a few goals, which he or she pursues in a purposeful way, whereas a less conscientious person tends to be easily distracted and impulsive. This dimension of personality relates to the work itself rather than to relationships with other people. Many entrepreneurs show a high level of conscientiousness. For example, Jari Ovaskainen gave up a high-paying consultant job and sold his beloved Mercedes 300CE coupe to pursue his dream of starting a business. Ovaskainen's conscientiousness and hard work helped Iobox, the Helsinki-based company he cofounded, jump to an early lead in the market for wireless Internet service. Ovaskainen's high degree of conscientiousness is also reflected in the workplace. Unlike many Internet companies, Iobox doesn't have foosball tables or other diversions for employees: "We don't believe in mixing work life with play time," Ovaskainen says. He wants people focused on the goal of making Iobox the "next Yahoo."[5]

The dimension of **emotional stability** refers to the degree to which a person is well-adjusted, calm, and secure. A leader who is emotionally stable handles stress well, is able to handle criticism, and generally doesn't take mistakes and failures personally. In contrast, leaders who have a low degree of emotional stability are likely to become tense, anxious, or depressed. They generally have lower self-confidence and may explode in emotional outbursts when stressed or criticized. The related topic of *emotional intelligence* will be discussed in detail in the next chapter.

The final Big Five dimension, **openness to experience**, is the degree to which a person has a broad range of interests and is imaginative, creative, and willing to consider new ideas. These people are intellectually curious and often seek out new experiences through travel, the arts, movies, reading widely, or other activities. People lower in this dimension tend to have narrower interests and stick to the tried-and-true ways of doing things. Open-mindedness is important to leaders because, as we learned in Chapter 1, leadership is about change rather than stability. In a study of three nineteenth-century leaders—John Quincy Adams, Frederick Douglass, and Jane Addams—one researcher found that early travel experiences and exposure to different ideas and cultures were critical elements in developing leadership skills and qualities in these leaders.[6] Travel during the formative years helped these leaders develop a greater degree of openness to experience because it put them in situations that required adaptability.

Despite the logic of the Big Five personality dimensions, they can be difficult to measure precisely. In addition, since each dimension is made up of numerous traits, a person can be high on some of the specific traits but low on others. For example, considering the dimension of conscientiousness, it might be possible for a person to be highly responsible and dependable and yet also have a low degree of achievement-orientation. Furthermore, research has been mostly limited to subjects in the United States, so the theory is difficult to apply cross-culturally.

Although it seems logical that a high degree of each of the dimensions would generally be beneficial to leaders, few studies have carefully examined the connection between the Big Five and leadership success. One recent summary of more than seventy years of personality and leadership research did find evidence that

Emotional stability
the degree to which a person is well-adjusted, calm, and secure

Openness to experience
the degree to which a person has a broad range of interests and is imaginative, creative, and willing to consider new ideas

Action Memo

As a leader: Learn about your own basic personality dimensions and how to emphasize the positive aspects of your personality in dealing with followers.

four of the five dimensions were consistently related to successful leadership.[7] The researchers found considerable evidence that people who score high on the dimensions of extroversion, agreeableness, conscientiousness, and emotional stability are more successful leaders. Results for openness to experience were less consistent; that is, in some cases, higher scores on this dimension related to better performance, but they did not seem to make a difference in other cases. Yet, in a recent study by a team of psychologists of the personality traits of the greatest U.S. presidents (as determined by historians), openness to experience produced the highest correlation with historians' ratings of greatness. The study noted that presidents such as Abraham Lincoln and Thomas Jefferson were high on this personality dimension. Other personality dimensions the team found to be associated with great presidents were extroversion and conscientiousness, including traits such as aggressiveness, setting ambitious goals, and striving for achievement. Although agreeableness did not correlate with greatness, the ability to empathize with others and being concerned for others, which could be considered elements of emotional stability, did.[8]

It is important to note that few leaders have consistently high scores across all of the Big Five dimensions, yet there are many successful leaders. Higher scores on the Big Five dimensions are not necessarily predictive of leadership effectiveness, and persons who score toward the lower end of the scale can also be good leaders. The value of the Big Five for leaders is primarily to help them understand their own basic personality dimensions, and then learn to emphasize the positive and mitigate the negative aspects of their own natural style. Vinita Gupta provides an illustration of a leader who learned to overcome the negative aspects of her introversion.

In the Lead   Vinita Gupta, Quick Eagle Networks

Vinita Gupta, the founding CEO of Quick Eagle Networks, was facing a mystery. Sales and profits were going up, but employee morale just kept going down. Employees were quitting in droves, with annual turnover hitting 30 percent. Spirit was so low that even key executives were jumping ship, leaving profitable Quick Eagle to join profitless competitors. When Gupta tried to determine what was going on, she uncovered an unnerving possibility—could it be that her own personality was part of the problem? Introverted, soft-spoken, and highly focused on work, Gupta had always depended on other managers to be the cheerleaders and coaches in the company. But now she was hearing through the grapevine that people found her aloof and unapproachable, and that the stiff, serious atmosphere she created was making employees miserable.

Gupta began trying to learn more about herself and manage the personality characteristics and behaviors that could be contributing to decreased performance and low morale. She worked on a series of exercises to develop greater empathy and improve her social skills, including coaching employees, being more open and less defensive, and using humor to create a lighter atmosphere. Whereas before she rarely paused to speak to— or sometimes even glance at—anyone when she arrived at the office, she now makes a point of greeting people upon arrival, introducing herself to employees she's never met, and having lunch with colleagues.

Although she will never score high on extroversion, Gupta has learned to manage her behaviors to make Quick Eagle a more pleasant, comfortable place to work. Employees have noticed that the atmosphere is lighter, and people are no longer afraid to express concerns or speak up in meetings. Turnover has decreased by 20 percent from a year earlier.[9]

Exhibit 4.2 gives some tips for both introverts and extroverts to help them be better leaders. Many factors contribute to effective leadership. As we learned in the previous two chapters, situational factors play a role in determining which traits may be most important. In addition, a leader's intelligence, knowledge of the business, values and attitudes, and problem-solving styles, which are not measured by the Big Five, also play a role in leadership effectiveness. Later in this chapter, we will discuss values and attitudes, as well as examine some cognitive differences that affect leadership. First, let's look more closely at two personality attributes that have significant implications for leaders.

Personality Traits and Leader Behavior

Two specific personality attributes that have a significant impact on behavior and are thus of particular interest for leadership studies are locus of control and authoritarianism.

Locus of Control   Some people believe that their actions can strongly affect what happens to them. In other words, they believe they are "masters of their own fate." Others feel that whatever happens to them in life is a result of luck, chance, or outside people and events; they believe they have little control over their fate. A person's **locus of control** defines whether he or she places the primary responsibility within the self or on outside forces.[10] People who believe their actions determine what happens to them have a high *internal* locus of control (internals), while those who believe outside forces determine what happens to them have a high *external* locus of control (externals).

Research on locus of control has shown real differences in behavior between internals and externals across a wide range of settings.[11] Internals in general are more self-motivated, are in better control of their own behavior, participate more in

Locus of control
defines whether a person places the primary responsibility for what happens to him or her within him/herself or on outside forces

Exhibit 4.2   Maximizing Leadership Effectiveness

Tips for Extroverts	Tips for Introverts
• *Don't bask in the glow of your own personality.* Learn to hold back and listen to others when the situation calls for it.	• *Get out and about.* Resist the urge to hibernate.
• *Try to underwhelm.* Your natural exuberance can be intimidating and cause you to miss important facts and ideas.	• *Practice being friendly and outgoing in settings outside of work.* Take your new skills to the office.
• *Talk less, listen more.* Develop the discipline to let others speak first on an issue to avoid the appearance of arrogance.	• *Give yourself a script.* Come up with a few talking points you can rely on to cover silences in conversations.
• *Don't be Mr. or Ms. Personality.* Extroverts tend to agree too quickly just to be liked. These casual agreements can come back to haunt you.	• *Smile.* A frown or a soberly introspective expression can be misinterpreted. A bright countenance reflects confidence that you know where you're going and want others to follow.

SOURCE: Based on Patricia Wallington, "The Ins and Outs of Personality," *CIO* (January 15, 2003): 42, 44.

social and political activities, and more actively seek information. There is also evidence that internals are better able to handle complex information and problem solving, and that they are more achievement-oriented than externals. In addition, people with a high internal locus of control are more likely than externals to try to influence others, and thus more likely to assume or seek leadership opportunities. People with a high external locus of control typically prefer to have structured, directed work situations. They are better able than internals to handle work that requires compliance and conformity, but they are generally not as effective in situations that require initiative, creativity, and independent action. Therefore, since externals do best in situations where success depends on complying with the direction or guidance of others, they are less likely to enjoy or succeed in leadership positions.

Many top leaders of e-commerce and high-tech organizations exhibit a high internal locus of control. These managers have to cope with rapid change and uncertainty associated with Internet business and have to believe they and their employees can counter the negative impact of outside forces and events. John Chambers,

CEO of Cisco Systems, is a good example. Chambers battled a learning disability as a child and was made fun of by other kids at school, but he always believed he could overcome anything through his own hard work and determination. Later, when other high-tech executives turned up their noses at his degree from West Virginia University, Chambers's high internal locus of control again helped him believe that he alone was in control of his fate. Cisco grew to be the leading maker of Internet equipment. Despite today's tough economy and a drastically diminished stock price, Chambers hasn't lost his belief that Cisco can eventually defeat any challenge thrown its way.[12] A person with a high external locus of control would likely feel overwhelmed trying to make the rapid decisions and changes needed to keep pace with the industry, particularly in the current environment of uncertainty.

Do you believe luck, chance, or the actions of other people play a major role in your life, or do you feel in control of your own fate? To learn more about your locus of control, complete the questionnaire in Leader's Self-Insight 4.1.

Authoritarianism   The belief that power and status differences *should* exist in an organization is called **authoritarianism**.[13] Individuals who have a high degree of this personality trait tend to adhere to conventional rules and values, obey established authority, respect power and toughness, judge others critically, and disapprove of the expression of personal feelings. A leader's degree of authoritarianism will affect how the leader wields and shares power. A highly authoritarian leader is likely to rely heavily on formal authority and unlikely to want to share power with subordinates. High authoritarianism is associated with the traditional, rational approach to management described in Chapter 1. The new leadership paradigm requires that leaders be less authoritarian, although people who rate high on this personality trait can be effective leaders as well. Leaders should also understand that the degree to which followers possess authoritarianism influences how they react to the leader's use of power and authority. When leaders and followers differ in their degree of authoritarianism, effective leadership may be more difficult to achieve.

A trait that is closely related to authoritarianism is *dogmatism*, which refers to a person's receptiveness to others' ideas and opinions. A highly dogmatic person is closed-minded and not receptive to others' ideas. When in a leadership position, dogmatic individuals often make decisions quickly based on limited information, and they are unreceptive to ideas that conflict with their opinions and decisions. Effective leaders, on the other hand, generally have a lower degree of dogmatism, which means they are open-minded and receptive to others' ideas.

Understanding how personality traits and dimensions affect behavior can be a valuable asset for leaders. Knowledge of individual differences gives leaders valuable insights into their own behavior as well as that of followers. It also offers a framework that leaders can use to diagnose situations and make changes to benefit

Authoritarianism
the belief that power and status differences should exist in an organization

Action Memo

As a leader: Improve your leadership effectiveness by recognizing how personality traits such as authoritarianism and locus of control affect your relationships with followers. Tone down a strong authoritarian personality and avoid being dogmatic to succeed in today's organizations.

Measuring Locus of Control

For each of these ten questions, indicate the extent to which you agree or disagree using the following scale:

1 = Strongly disagree
2 = Disagree
3 = Slightly disagree
4 = Neither agree or disagree

5 = Slightly agree
6 = Agree
7 = Strongly agree

	Strongly disagree						Strongly agree
1. When I get what I want, it's usually because I worked hard for it.	1	2	3	4	5	6	7
2. When I make plans, I am almost certain to make them work.	1	2	3	4	5	6	7
3. I prefer games involving some luck over games requiring pure skill.	1	2	3	4	5	6	7
4. I can learn almost anything if I set my mind to it.	1	2	3	4	5	6	7
5. My major accomplishments are entirely due to my hard work and ability.	1	2	3	4	5	6	7
6. I usually don't set goals, because I have a hard time following through on them.	1	2	3	4	5	6	7
7. Competition discourages excellence.	1	2	3	4	5	6	7
8. Often people get ahead just by being lucky.	1	2	3	4	5	6	7
9. On any sort of exam or competition, I like to know how well I do relative to everyone else.	1	2	3	4	5	6	7
10. It's pointless to keep working on something that's too difficult for me.	1	2	3	4	5	6	7

Scoring and Interpretation

To determine your score, reverse the values you selected for questions 3, 6, 7, 8, and 10 (1 = 7, 2 = 6, 3 = 5, 4 = 4, 5 = 3, 6 = 2, 7 = 1). For example, if you strongly disagreed with the statement in question 3, you would have given it a value of 1. Change this value to a 7. Reverse the scores in a similar manner for questions 6, 7, 8, and 10. Now add the point values from all ten questions together.

Your score:_____

This questionnaire is designed to measure locus of control beliefs. Researchers using this questionnaire in a study of college students found a mean of 51.8 for men and 52.2 for women, with a standard deviation of 6 for each. The higher your score on this questionnaire, the more you tend to believe that you are generally responsible for what happens to you; in other words, high scores are associated with internal locus of control. Low scores are associated with external locus of control. Scoring low indicates that you tend to believe that forces beyond your control, such as powerful other people, fate, or chance, are responsible for what happens to you.

SOURCES: Adapted from J. M. Burger, Personality: Theory and Research (Belmont, CA: Wadsworth, 1986), 400–401, cited in D. Hellriegel, J. W. Slocum, Jr., and R. W. Woodman, Organizational Behavior, 6th ed. (St. Paul, Minn.: West Publishing Co., 1992), 97–100. Original Source: "Sphere-Specific Measures of Perceived Control" by D. L. Paul, Journal of Personality and Social Psychology 44, 1253–1265.

the organization. For example, when Reed Breland became a team facilitator at Hewlett-Packard's financial services center in Colorado, he noticed immediately that one team was in constant turmoil. Breland's understanding of individual differences helped him recognize that two members of the team had a severe personality clash and could not see eye-to-eye on any issue. Although Breland tried to work things out within the team, after several months he simply dissolved the group and reassigned members to other areas. The team members all did fine in other assignments; the personality conflict between the two members was just too strong to overcome and it affected the team's productivity and effectiveness.[14]

Values and Attitudes

In addition to personality differences, people differ in the values and attitudes they hold. These differences affect the behavior of leaders and followers.

Instrumental and End Values

Values are fundamental beliefs that an individual considers to be important, that are relatively stable over time, and that have an impact on attitudes and behavior.[15] Values are what cause a person to prefer that things be done one way rather than another way. Whether we recognize it or not, we are constantly valuing things, people, or ideas as good or bad, pleasant or unpleasant, ethical or unethical, and so forth.[16] When a person has strong values in certain areas, these can have a powerful influence on behavior. For example, a person who highly values honesty and integrity might lose respect and lessen his commitment and performance for a leader who tells "little white lies." The issue of moral leadership and leaders' ethical values will be considered in detail in Chapter 6.

One way to think about values is in terms of instrumental and end values.[17] Social scientist Milton Rokeach developed a list of eighteen instrumental values and eighteen end values that have been found to be more or less universal across cultures. **End values**, sometimes called *terminal values*, are beliefs about the kind of goals or outcomes that are worth trying to pursue. For example, some people value security, a comfortable life, and good health above everything else as the important goals to strive for in life. Others may place greater value on social recognition, pleasure, and an exciting life. **Instrumental values** are beliefs about the types of behavior that are appropriate for reaching goals. Instrumental values include such things as being helpful to others, being honest, or exhibiting courage.

Although everyone has both instrumental and end values, individuals differ in how they order the values into priorities, which accounts for tremendous variation among people. Part of this difference relates to culture. For example, in the United States, independence is highly valued and is reinforced by many institutions,

Values
fundamental beliefs that an individual considers to be important, that are relatively stable over time, and that have an impact on attitudes and behavior

End values
sometimes called terminal values, these are beliefs about the kind of goals or outcomes that are worth trying to pursue

Instrumental values
beliefs about the types of behavior that are appropriate for reaching goals

including schools, religious organizations, and businesses. Other cultures place less value on independence and more value on being part of a tightly knit community. A person's family background also influences his or her values. Values are learned, not inherited, but some values become incorporated into a person's thinking very early in life. Some leaders cite their parents as a primary source of their leadership abilities because they helped to shape their values.[18] For example, Thomas Charlton of Tidal Software has a strong value for ambition, achievement, and persistence. Charlton's father, who was a boxer, constantly encouraged his children to strive for excellence and never give up. The younger Charlton still brags about how, at his father's urging, he finished a high school football game with a severely broken hand.[19] William Monroe, CEO of Bertolli North America, learned values of risk-taking, responsibility, and courage from his mother. Monroe's father died when he was five years old, leaving his mother to raise two sons alone. "She picked herself up and went to work in a knitting factory," he says. She bought a house despite warnings from relatives that she wouldn't be able to make the payments. "She took the risk and never looked back," Monroe says. "She knew how to make a decision and then not worry about it."[20]

Rokeach's instrumental and end values are listed in Leader's Self-Insight 4.2. Complete the exercise to see what you can learn about your own values and how they affect your decisions and actions. Were you surprised by any of your instrumental or end values?

Our values are generally fairly well established by early adulthood, but a person's values can also change throughout life. This chapter's Living Leadership reflects on how the values that shape a leader's actions in a moment of crisis have been developed over time. Values may affect leaders and leadership in a number of ways.[21] For one thing, a leader's personal values affect his or her perception of situations and problems. By **perception**, we mean the process people use to make sense out of the environment by selecting, organizing, and interpreting information. A leader who greatly values ambition and career success may view a problem or a subordinate's mistake as an impediment to her own success, whereas a leader who values helpfulness and obedience might see it as a chance to help a subordinate improve or grow. Values also affect how leaders relate to others. A leader who values obedience, conformity, and politeness may have a difficult time understanding and appreciating a follower who is self-reliant, independent, creative, and a bit rebellious. Recognizing these value differences can help leaders better understand and work with varied followers.

Perception

the process people use to make sense out of the environment by selecting, organizing, and interpreting information

A third way in which values affect leadership is that they guide a leader's choices and actions. A leader who places high value on being courageous and standing up for what one believes in, for example, is much more likely to make decisions that may not be popular but which he believes are right. Values determine how leaders acquire and use power, how they handle conflict, and how they make decisions. A leader who values competitiveness and ambition will behave differently from one

Instrumental and End Values

In each column below, place a check mark by the five values that are most important to you. After you have checked five values in each column, rank order the checked values in each column from one to five, with 1 = Most important and 5 = Least important.

Rokeach's Instrumental and End Values

End Values		Instrumental Values	
A comfortable life	_____	Ambition	_____
Equality	_____	Broad-mindedness	_____
An exciting life	_____	Capability	_____
Family security	_____	Cheerfulness	_____
Freedom	_____	Cleanliness	_____
Health	_____	Courage	_____
Inner harmony	_____	Forgiveness	_____
Mature love	_____	Helpfulness	_____
National security	_____	Honesty	_____
Pleasure	_____	Imagination	_____
Salvation	_____	Intellectualism	_____
Self-respect	_____	Logic	_____
A sense of accomplishment	_____	Ability to love	_____
Social recognition	_____	Loyalty	_____
True friendship	_____	Obedience	_____
Wisdom	_____	Politeness	_____
A world at peace	_____	Responsibility	_____
A world of beauty	_____	Self-control	_____

NOTE: THE VALUES ARE LISTED IN ALPHABETICAL ORDER AND THERE IS NO ONE-TO-ONE RELATIONSHIP between the end and instrumental values.

Scoring and Interpretation

End values, according to Rokeach, tend to fall into two categories—personal and social. For example, mature love is a personal end value and equality is a social end value. Analyze the five end values you selected and their rank order, and determine whether your primary end values tend to be personal or social. What do your five selections together mean to you? What do they mean for how you make life decisions? Compare your end value selections with another person, with each of you explaining what you learned about your end values from this exercise.

Instrumental values also tend to fall into two categories—morality and competence. The means people use to achieve their goals might violate moral values (e.g., be dishonest) or violate one's personal sense of competence and capability (e.g., be illogical). Analyze the five instrumental values you selected, and their rank order, and determine whether your primary instrumental values tend to focus on morality or competence. What do the five selected values together mean to you? What do they mean for how you will pursue your life goals? Compare your instrumental value selections with another person and describe what you learned from this exercise.

Warning: The two columns above do *not* represent the full range of instrumental and end values. Your findings would change if a different list of values were provided. This exercise is for discussion and learning purposes only and is not intended to be an accurate assessment of your actual end and instrumental values.

SOURCES: Robert C. Benfari, *Understanding and Changing Your Management Style* (San Francisco: Jossey-Bass, 1999), 178–183; and M. Rokeach, *Understanding Human Values* (The Free Press, 1979).

LIVING LEADERSHIP

Developing Character

"The character that takes command in moments of critical choices has already been determined. It has been determined by a thousand other choices made earlier in seemingly unimportant moments. It has been determined by all those 'little' choices of years past—by all those times when the voice of conscience was at war with the voice of temptation—whispering a lie that 'it doesn't really matter.' It has been determined by all the day-to-day decisions made when life seemed easy and crises seemed far away, the decisions that piece by piece, bit by bit, developed habits of discipline or of laziness; habits of self-sacrifice or self-indulgence; habits of duty and honor and integrity—or dishonor and shame."

President Ronald Reagan, quoted in Norman R. Augustine, "Seven Fundamentals of Effective Leadership," an original essay written for the Center for the Study of American Business, Washington University in St. Louis, *CEO Series* Issue no. 27, (October 1998).

who places a high value on co-operativeness and forgiveness. Ethical values help guide choices concerning what is morally right or wrong. Values concerning end goals also help determine a leader's actions and choices in the workplace.

For many organizations today, clarifying and stating their corporate values has become an important part of defining how the organization operates. A company's values often reflect the values of the top leader, as at Frontier Airlines.

In the Lead   Jeffrey S. Potter, Frontier Airlines

Frontier Airlines, a small airline based in Denver, Colorado, has a growing reputation for doing the right thing and caring about employees and customers. As the nation's largest airlines are reeling from huge losses and passenger dissatisfaction, small carriers like Frontier have a tremendous opportunity to grow. Frontier is doing it by keeping costs low, offering cheaper fares, and easing travel restrictions.

It is also winning customers by its fair approach to doing business. "They don't gouge us when we're stuck at the last minute," says James I. Michael, president of Alliance Power Inc., who switched his company's travel business from United to Frontier. Whereas most airlines charge passengers a stiff penalty for switching their return flights, Frontier eliminated the practice after a Teamster's negotiator buttonholed the CEO and said it wasn't fair. Jeffrey S. Potter, Frontier's CEO, says, "It was the right thing to do."

Potter, a one-time aircraft cleaner and ticket agent, has always prided himself on listening to employees and trying to meet their needs. His values of openness, honesty, fairness, and cooperation are part of the culture at Frontier. Everyone, including rank-and-file employees and union representatives, gets a hearing with the top leader. Potter regularly answers phone calls from flight attendants or mechanics and listens to their ideas, complaints, or suggestions. He never makes changes without asking front-line workers how they feel about them. Potter's values have helped to build a family atmosphere among employees, who, in turn, spread that feeling to customers.[22]

Like Jeffrey Potter, leaders can be more effective when they clarify their own values and understand how values guide their actions and affect their organizations.

How Attitudes Affect Leadership

Values help determine the attitudes leaders have about themselves and about their followers. An **attitude** is an evaluation—either positive or negative—about people, events, or things. Behavioral scientists consider attitudes to have three components: cognitions (thoughts), affect (feelings), and behavior.[23] The cognitive component includes the ideas and knowledge a person has about the object of an attitude, such as a leader's knowledge and ideas about a specific employee's performance and abilities. The affective component concerns how an individual feels about the object of an attitude. Perhaps the leader resents having to routinely answer questions or help the employee perform certain tasks. The behavioral component of an attitude predisposes a person to act in a certain way. For example, the leader might avoid the employee or fail to include him or her in certain activities of the group. Although attitudes change more easily than values, they typically reflect a person's fundamental values as well as a person's background and life experiences. A leader who highly values forgiveness, compassion toward others, and helping others would have different attitudes and behave very differently toward the above-mentioned subordinate than one who highly values personal ambition and capability.

One consideration is a leader's attitudes about himself or herself. **Self-concept** refers to the collection of attitudes we have about ourselves and includes the element of self-esteem, whether a person generally has positive or negative feelings about himself. A person with an overall positive self-concept has high self-esteem, whereas one with a negative self-concept has low self-esteem. In general, leaders with positive self-concepts are more effective in all situations. Leaders who have a negative self-concept, who are insecure and have low self-esteem, often create environments that limit other people's growth and development.[24] They may also sabotage their own careers. This chapter's Leader's Bookshelf describes how certain attitudes and behavior patterns limit a leader's effectiveness and career development.

Action Memo

As a leader: Clarify your values so you know what you stand for and how your values may conflict with others in the organization. Cultivate positive attitudes toward yourself and others. Expect the best of followers rather than being cynical and looking for the worst.

Attitude

an evaluation (either positive or negative) about people, events, or things

Self-concept

the collection of attitudes we have about ourselves; includes self-esteem and whether a person generally has a positive or negative feeling about him/herself

LEADER'S BOOKSHELF

Maximum Success: Changing the 12 Behavior Patterns That Keep You From Getting Ahead
by James Waldroop and Timothy Butler

We have all known talented people who aren't as effective as they should or could be. In their book, *Maximum Success*, James Waldroop and Timothy Butler, who are directors of the MBA career development program at Harvard Business School, identify 12 behavior patterns they believe are the most common reasons some people never live up to their abilities.

Nobody's Perfect
Every person has some habits, behaviors, or attitudes that can limit his or her effectiveness. By understanding their individual "Achilles' heels," leaders can learn to change their behaviors to improve leadership effectiveness and career success. Following are a few of the weaknesses that Waldroop and Butler identify. Do you recognize any of these in your own attitudes and behaviors?

❋ **Never feeling quite "good enough."** The authors refer to this as career-related acrophobia, or fear of falling from one's position in the organization. Many people who seem quite self-confident in a lower-level position become frightened and insecure when promoted to a position of leadership because they feel they don't deserve it. These leaders hurt themselves and others. They become self-conscious and awkward, have trouble gaining respect, and don't provide the leadership strength that followers want and need. People want a leader who exudes self-assurance and certainty, not worry and fear.

❋ **Pushing too hard.** Setting high goals and working hard to achieve them isn't a bad thing for a leader. Unfortunately, some people take this too far—they relentlessly drive themselves, and others, to achieve more and more. These people work compulsively and without joy, and they cause stress and unhappiness for anyone who has to work with or for them.

❋ **Being emotionally tone-deaf.** The authors refer to a leader with this characteristic as Mr. or Ms. Spock, after the character played by Leonard Nimoy in the television series *Star Trek*. A native of the planet Vulcan, Spock is unable to feel emotions himself or understand them in others. "Spocks" don't intend to be cold or hardhearted; they simply don't recognize the role of human feelings and motivations in the organization. These leaders are usually highly rational, perceiving problems merely as objective issues to be resolved, devoid of a complex human component.

Change Is Possible
These behavior patterns are potentially fatal flaws for leaders. However, the authors emphasize that people can learn to manage their weaknesses and change their behaviors. In the first part of the book, each chapter describes one of the behavior patterns and gives tips for how to break it. The second part of the book describes four psychological patterns that, in varying combinations, underlie these weaknesses, along with exercises and tips for change.

Maximum Success: Changing the 12 Behavior Patterns that Keep You From Getting Ahead, by James Waldroop and Timothy Butler, is published by Currency/Doubleday.

The way in which the leader relates to followers also depends significantly on his or her attitudes about others.[25] A leader's style is based largely on attitudes about human nature in general—ideas and feelings about what motivates people, whether people are basically honest and trustworthy, and about the extent to which people can grow and change. One theory developed to explain differences in style was developed by Douglas McGregor, based on his experiences as a manager and consultant and his training as a psychologist.[26] McGregor identified two sets of assumptions about human nature, called **Theory X** and **Theory Y**, which represent two very different sets of attitudes about how to interact with and influence subordinates. The fundamental assumptions of Theory X and Theory Y are explained in Exhibit 4.3.

Theory X
the assumption that people are basically lazy and not motivated to work and that they have a natural tendency to avoid responsibility

Theory Y
the assumption that people do not inherently dislike work and will commit themselves willingly to work that they care about

Exhibit 4.3	**Attitudes and Assumptions of Theory X and Theory Y**

Assumptions of Theory X

- The average human being has an inherent dislike of work and will avoid it if possible.
- Because of the human characteristic of dislike for work, most people must be coerced, controlled, directed, or threatened with punishment to get them to put forth adequate effort toward the achievement of organizational objectives.
- The average human being prefers to be directed, wishes to avoid responsibility, has relatively little ambition, and wants security above all.

Assumptions of Theory Y

- The expenditure of physical and mental effort in work is as natural as play or rest. The average human being does not inherently dislike work.
- External control and the threat of punishment are not the only means for bringing about effort toward organizational objectives. A person will exercise self-direction and self-control in the service of objectives to which he or she is committed.
- The average human being learns, under proper conditions, not only to accept but to seek responsibility.
- The capacity to exercise a relatively high degree of imagination, ingenuity, and creativity in the solution of organizational problems is widely, not narrowly, distributed in the population.
- Under the conditions of modern industrial life, the intellectual potentialities of the average human being are only partially utilized.

SOURCE: Douglas McGregor, *The Human Side of Enterprise* (New York: McGraw-Hill, 1960), 33–48.

In general, Theory X reflects the assumption that people are basically lazy and not motivated to work and that they have a natural tendency to avoid responsibility. Thus, a supervisor who subscribes to the assumptions of Theory X believes people must be coerced, controlled, directed, or threatened to get them to put forth their best effort. In some circumstances, the supervisor may come across as bossy or overbearing, impatient with others, and unconcerned with people's feelings and problems. Referring back to Chapter 2, the Theory X leader would likely be task-oriented and highly concerned with production rather than people. Theory Y, on the other hand, is based on assumptions that people do not inherently dislike work and will commit themselves willingly to work that they care about. Theory Y also assumes that, under the right conditions, people will seek out greater responsibility and will exercise imagination and creativity in the pursuit of solutions to organizational problems. A leader who subscribes to the assumptions of Theory Y does not believe people have to be coerced and controlled in order to perform effectively. These leaders are more often people-oriented and concerned with relationships, although some Theory Y leaders can also be task- or production-oriented. For example, consider how Mark Schmink blended a concern for tasks with a Theory Y approach to leadership when he was a plant manager at Dana Corp.

In the Lead   Mark Schmink, Dana Corp.

Dana Corp.'s plant in Stockton, California, makes truck chassis for Toyota, a contract the company won by promising to decrease prices by 2 percent within two years, with further decreases to follow. Mark Schmink, the founding plant manager, knew that meant finding efficiencies in the production process as well as providing good wages and benefits for employees who would be asked to use their minds as well as their bodies. Schmink wanted to create a "culture of inventiveness" in which employees were constantly coming up with new and better ways of working.

He began by hiring welders with no experience and training each one to perform every job in the plant. No employee had a permanent assignment, so that everyone was constantly doing something new and bringing a fresh perspective to bear. By moving all over the plant, workers could see problems all up and down the line, not just in one particular area. Schmink also opened a library in the plant and began offering tuition reimbursement to production workers, signaling that mental work was valued. He required that each worker submit two ideas a month, and more than 80 percent of them were put into action. As workers saw their ideas implemented, they became even more excited about proposing new ways to do things, questioning every procedure and routine, right down to the sequencing of individual welds.

To keep workers motivated toward goals, Schmink provided continuous feedback both by personally responding to every suggestion and by displaying minute-by-minute productivity figures on electronic signs on the plant floor. Every significant accomplishment was celebrated with a special occasion, such as a rib-eye lunch, a day of free sodas, or a family barbecue. Schmink rarely felt the need to coerce or control his workers to do their jobs; they were so fired up by the challenge that they were always looking for improvements. In addition, employees felt that they were truly valued, so they were eager to contribute.[27]

McGregor believed Theory Y to be a more realistic and productive approach for viewing subordinates and shaping leaders' attitudes. Studies exploring the relationship between leader attitudes and leadership success in general support his idea, although this relationship has not been carefully explored.[28]

Cognitive Differences

The final area of individual differences we will explore is cognitive style. **Cognitive style** refers to how a person perceives, processes, interprets, and uses information. Thus, when we talk about cognitive differences, we are referring to varying approaches to perceiving and assimilating data, making decisions, solving problems, and relating to others.[29] Cognitive approaches are *preferences* that are not necessarily rigid, but most people tend to have only a few preferred habits of thought. One of the most widely recognized cognitive differences is between what we call left-brained versus right-brained thinking patterns.

Cognitive style
how a person perceives, processes, interprets, and uses information

Patterns of Thinking and Brain Dominance

Neurologists and psychologists have long known that the brain has two distinct hemispheres. Furthermore, science has shown that the left hemisphere controls movement on the body's right side and the right hemisphere controls movement on the left. In the 1960s and 1970s, scientists also discovered that the distinct hemispheres influence thinking, which led to an interest in what has been called left-brained versus right-brained thinking patterns. The left hemisphere is associated with logical, analytical thinking and a linear approach to problem-solving, whereas the right hemisphere is associated with creative, intuitive, values-based thought processes.[30] A recent JC Penney television commercial provides a simple illustration. The commercial shows a woman whose right brain is telling her to go out and spend money to buy fun clothes, while the left brain is telling her to be logical and save money. As another simplified example, people who are very good at verbal and written language (which involves a linear thinking process) are using the left brain, while those who prefer to interpret information through visual images are more right-brained.

Although the concept of right-brained versus left-brained thinking is not entirely accurate physiologically (not all processes associated with left-brained thinking are located in the left hemisphere and vice versa), this concept provides a powerful metaphor for two very different ways of thinking and decision making. It is also important to remember that everyone uses both left-brained and right-brained thinking, but to varying degrees.

Whole brain concept
an approach that considers not only a person's preference for right-brained versus left-brained thinking, but also conceptual versus experiential thinking; identifies four quadrants of the brain related to different thinking styles

More recently, these ideas have been broadened to what is called the **whole brain concept**.[31] Ned Herrmann began developing his concept of whole brain thinking while he was a manager at General Electric in the late 1970s and has expanded it through many years of research with thousands of individuals and organizations. The whole brain approach considers not only a person's preference for right-brained versus left-brained thinking, but also for conceptual versus experiential thinking. Herrmann's whole brain model thus identifies four quadrants of the brain that are related to different thinking styles. Again, while not entirely accurate physiologically, the whole brain model is an excellent metaphor for understanding differences in thinking patterns. Some people strongly lean toward using one quadrant in most situations, while others rely on two, three, or even all four styles of thinking.

An individual's preference for each of the four styles is determined through a survey called the *Herrmann Brain Dominance Instrument (HBDI)*, which has been administered to hundreds of thousands of individuals. A simplified exercise to help you think about your own preferences appears in Leader's Self-Insight 4.3. Before reading further, follow the instructions and complete the exercise to get an idea about your dominant thinking style according to Herrmann's whole brain model. Then, read the descriptions of each quadrant below. The whole brain model provides a useful overview of an individual's mental preferences, which in turn affect patterns of communication, behavior, and leadership.

Quadrant A
the part of the brain associated in the whole brain model with logical thinking, analysis of facts, and processing numbers

Quadrant A is associated with logical thinking, analysis of facts, and processing numbers. A person who has a quadrant A dominance is rational and realistic, thinks critically, and likes to deal with numbers and technical matters. These people like to know how things work and to follow logical procedures. A leader with a predominantly A-quadrant thinking style tends to be directive and authoritative. This leader focuses on tasks and activities and likes to deal with concrete information and facts. Opinions and feelings are generally not considered as important as facts.

What's Your Thinking Style?

The following characteristics are associated with the four quadrants identified by Herrmann's whole brain model. Think for a moment about how you approach problems and make decisions. In addition, consider how you typically approach your work or class assignments and how you interact with others. Circle ten of the terms below that you believe best describe your own cognitive style. Try to be honest and select terms that apply to you as you are, not how you might like to be. There are no right or wrong answers.

A	B	C	D
Analytical	Organized	Friendly	Holistic
Factual	Planned	Receptive	Imaginative
Directive	Controlled	Enthusiastic	Intuitive
Rigorous	Detailed	Understanding	Synthesizing
Realistic	Conservative	Expressive	Curious
Intellectual	Disciplined	Empathetic	Spontaneous
Objective	Practical	Trusting	Flexible
Knowledgeable	Industrious	Sensitive	Open-Minded
Bright	Persistent	Passionate	Conceptual
Clear	Implementer	Humanistic	Adventurous

The terms in Column A are associated with logical, analytical thinking (Quadrant A); those in Column B with organized, detail-oriented thinking (Quadrant B); those in Column C with empathetic and emotionally based thinking (Quadrant C); and those in Column D with integrative and imaginative thinking (Quadrant D). Do your preferences fall primarily in one of the four columns, or do you have a more balanced set of preferences across all four? If you have a strong preference in one particular quadrant, were you surprised by which one?

Quadrant B deals with planning, organizing facts, and careful detailed review. A person who relies heavily on quadrant B thinking is well-organized, reliable, and neat. These people like to establish plans and procedures and get things done on time. Quadrant-B leaders are typically conservative and highly traditional. They tend to avoid risks and strive for stability. Thus, they may insist on following rules and procedures, no matter what the circumstances are.

Quadrant C is associated with interpersonal relationships and affects intuitive and emotional thought processes. C-quadrant individuals are sensitive to others and enjoy interacting with and teaching others. They are typically emotional and expressive, outgoing, and supportive of others. Leaders with a predominantly quadrant-C style are friendly, trusting, and empathetic. They are concerned with people's feelings more than with tasks and procedures and may put emphasis on employee development and training.

Quadrant D is associated with conceptualizing, synthesizing, and integrating facts and patterns, with seeing the big picture rather than the details. A person with a quadrant-D preference is visionary and imaginative, likes to speculate, break the rules, and take risks, and may be impetuous. These people are curious and enjoy

Quadrant B
the part of the brain associated in the whole brain model with planning, organizing facts, and careful detailed review

Quadrant C
the part of the brain associated in the whole brain model with interpersonal relationships and intuitive and emotional thought processes

Quadrant D

the part of the brain associated in the whole brain model with conceptualizing, synthesizing, and integrating facts and patterns.

experimentation and playfulness. The D-quadrant leader is holistic, imaginative, and adventurous. This leader enjoys change, experimentation and risk taking, and generally allows followers a great deal of freedom and flexibility.

The model with its four quadrants and some of the mental processes associated with each is illustrated in Exhibit 4.4. Each style has positive and negative results for leaders and followers. There is no style that is necessarily better or worse, though any of the styles carried to an extreme can be detrimental. It is important to remember that every individual, even those with a strong preference in one quadrant, actually has a coalition of preferences from each of the four quadrants.[32] Therefore, leaders with a predominantly quadrant-A style may also have elements from one or more of the other styles, which affects their leadership effectiveness. For example, a leader with a strong A-quadrant preference might also have preferences from quadrant C, the interpersonal area, which would cause her to have concern for people's feelings even though she is primarily concerned with tasks, facts, and figures.

In addition, Herrmann believes people can learn to use their "whole brain," rather than relying only on one or two quadrants. His research indicates that very few, if any, individuals can be wholly balanced among the four quadrants, but people can be aware of their preferences and engage in activities and experiences that help develop the other quadrants. Leaders who reach the top of organizations often have well-balanced brains, according to Herrmann's research. In fact, the typical CEO has at least two, usually three, and often four strong preferences and thus has

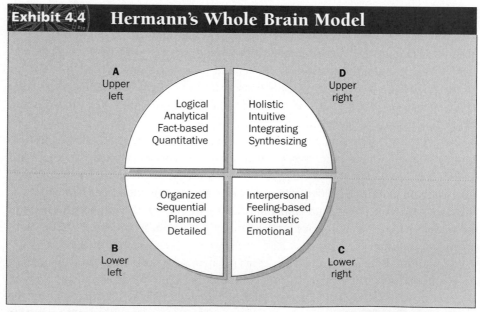

Exhibit 4.4   Hermann's Whole Brain Model

A
Upper left

Logical
Analytical
Fact-based
Quantitative

D
Upper right

Holistic
Intuitive
Integrating
Synthesizing

Organized
Sequential
Planned
Detailed

Interpersonal
Feeling-based
Kinesthetic
Emotional

B
Lower left

C
Lower right

SOURCE: Ned Hermann, *The Whole Brain Business Book*, (New York: McGraw-Hill, 1996), 15.

a wide range of thinking options available to choose from. A broad range of thinking styles is particularly important at higher levels of organizations because leaders deal with a greater variety and complexity of people and issues.[33]

Understanding that individuals have different thinking styles can also help leaders be more effective in interacting with followers. Some leaders act as if everyone responds to the same material and behavior in the same way, but this isn't true. Some people prefer facts and figures, whereas others want to know about relationships and patterns. Some followers prefer freedom and flexibility, while others crave structure and order. At Nissan Design International, Jerry Hirshberg used an understanding of cognitive differences to change how he leads.

In the Lead   Jerry Hirshberg, Nissan Design International

Jerry Hirshberg is a predominantly D-quadrant leader. He likes thinking broadly and dreaming big, deriving ideas intuitively—and he abhors tight structure and control. He once assumed that his employees would as well. Hirshberg wanted his designers to have the freedom to be creative, to take risks, and to innovate. Therefore, he was surprised when he learned that a few of his followers actually wanted and needed more structure in order to perform at their best.

Hirshberg assumed his employees would react to information and ideas the same way he did. He would throw huge amounts of information at them and expect them to respond intuitively and creatively. Some people, however, always hesitated, which Hirschberg originally interpreted as a resistance to innovation and change. However, over time, he came to realize that some of his designers simply wanted and needed time to "process" the information and to develop more logical, analytical approaches to Hirschberg's intuitively derived ideas. When they were given this time, the employees returned with significant contributions and excellent plans that moved the project forward.

It didn't take Hirshberg long to recognize that the contributions of the more logical, analytical, and detail-oriented thinkers were just as critical to the success of a project as those of the intuitive, creative thinkers. Hirshberg turned his realization into a new approach to creativity at Nissan. He now hires designers in what he calls *divergent pairs*. He believes that by putting together two spectacularly gifted people who have different cognitive styles and see the world in different ways, he builds a creative tension that keeps the organization energized and provides unlimited potential for innovation. Essentially, Hirshberg mixes styles to create a "whole brain" company at Nissan Design International.[34]

Action Memo

As a leader: Strive for "whole-brain" thinking to deal effectively with a wide variety of people and complex issues. Be aware of your natural thinking patterns and engage in activities that help you develop a wider range of thinking styles. When possible, tailor your communications and leadership approach to the thinking style of followers.

As this example illustrates, leaders can shift their styles and behaviors to more effectively communicate with followers and to help them perform up to their full potential. Leaders can also recruit people with varied cognitive styles to help achieve goals.

Problem Solving Styles: The Myers–Briggs Type Indicator

Another approach to cognitive differences grew out of the work of psychologist Carl Jung. Jung believed that differences in individual behavior resulted from preferences in how we go about gathering and evaluating information for solving problems and making decisions.[35] One of the most widely used personality tests in the United States, the **Myers-Briggs Type Indicator (MBTI)**, is one way of measuring how individuals differ in these areas.[36] The MBTI has been taken by millions of people around the world and can help individuals better understand themselves and others.

The MBTI uses four different pairs of attributes to classify people in 1 of 16 different personality types:

Myers–Briggs Type Indicator (MBTI)

personality test that measures how individuals differ in gathering and evaluating information for solving problems and making decisions

1. Introversion versus extroversion: This dimension focuses on where people gain interpersonal strength and mental energy. Extroverts (E) gain energy from being around others and interacting with others, whereas introverts (I) gain energy by focusing on personal thoughts and feelings.
2. Sensing versus intuition: This identifies how a person absorbs information. Those with a sensing preference (S) gather and absorb information through the five senses, whereas intuitive people (N) rely on less direct perceptions. Intuitives, for example, focus more on patterns, relationships, and hunches than on direct perception of facts and details.
3. Thinking versus feeling: This dimension relates to how much consideration a person gives to emotions in making a decision. Feeling types (F) tend to rely more on their values and sense of what is right and wrong, and they consider how a decision will affect other people's feelings. Thinking types (T) tend to rely more on logic and be very objective in decision making.
4. Judging versus perceiving: The judging versus perceiving dimension concerns an individual's attitudes toward ambiguity and how quickly a person makes a decision. People with a judging preference like certainty and closure. They enjoy having goals and deadlines and tend to make decisions quickly based on available data. Perceiving people, on the other hand, enjoy ambiguity, dislike deadlines, and may change their minds several times before making a final decision. Perceiving types like to gather a large amount of data and information before making a decision.

The various combinations of these preferences result in 16 unique personality types. At the end of this chapter, you will have a chance to complete an exercise that will identify your MBTI personality type. In addition, there are a number of exercises available on the Internet that can help people determine their preferences according to the MBTI. Individuals develop unique strengths and weaknesses as a result of their preferences for introversion versus extroversion, sensing versus intuition, thinking versus feeling, and judging versus perceiving. As with the whole brain approach, MBTI types should not be considered ingrained or unalterable. People's awareness of their preferences, training, and life experiences can cause them to change their preferences over time.

In addition, leaders should remember that each type can have positive and negative consequences for behavior. John Bearden, now chief executive of GMAC Home Services, became a better leader by understanding his MBTI type and learning how to maximize his strengths.

In the Lead   John Bearden, GMAC Home Services

After a long, successful career in real estate, John Bearden moved back to his home town of Nashville, Tennessee, to consider the next step in his professional life. As he thought about his future, something bothered Bearden about his past: "I was a passionate, driven and nonempathetic leader, inclined to make hasty decisions and to get to the finish line dragging people with me."

Bearden hired a personal coach to help him learn why he behaved the way he did. The coach, Anne Alexander Vincent, administered the Myers–Briggs Type Indicator, which indicated that Bearden was an ENTJ (extroverted, intuitive, thinking, and judging). ENTJ types can be dynamic, inspiring, and self-confident in making tough decisions. However, they can also be overbearing, insensitive, and hasty in their judgments. "That's me, yeah!" Bearden said when he read the profile. "Myers–Briggs can represent a quantum leap in your own personal understanding of your strengths and your potential."

As a result of his new-found self-understanding, Bearden began consciously refining his leadership style. As chief executive of GMAC Home Services, a General Motors subsidiary in Oak Brook, Illinois, he's making a determined effort to give more consideration to hard data and listen more carefully to colleagues' opinions. Bearden put himself to the test at a recent national convention. "In the past, I would have gotten very much involved interjecting my own position very early on and probably biasing the process," he said. "But here I found myself quite content to allow their positions to be articulated and argued with creative tension. All I did was sit and absorb. It was a very satisfying process."[37]

Application of the MBTI in leadership studies has rapidly increased in recent years.[38] There is no "leader type," and all 16 of the MBTI types can function effectively as leaders. As with the four quadrants of the whole brain model, leaders can learn to use their preferences and balance their approaches to best suit followers and the situation. However, research reveals some interesting, although tentative, findings. For example, although extroversion is often considered an important trait for a leader, leaders in the real world are about equally divided between extroverts and introverts. In regard to the sensing versus intuition dimension, data reveal that sensing types are in the majority in fields where the focus is on the immediate and tangible (e.g., construction, banking, manufacturing). However, in areas that involve breaking new ground or long-range planning, intuitive leaders are in the majority. Thinking (as opposed to feeling) types are more common among leaders in business and industry as well as in the realm of science. In addition, thinking types appear to be chosen more often as managers even in organizations that value "feeling," such as counseling centers. Finally, one of the most consistent findings is that judging types are in the majority among the leaders studied.

Thus, based on the limited research, the two preferences that seem to be most strongly associated with successful leadership are thinking and judging. However, this doesn't mean that people with other preferences cannot be effective leaders. Much more research needs to be done before accurate conclusions can be reached about the relationship between MBTI types and leadership. One area in which research may eventually offer insight is the relationship between cognitive styles and two types of leadership that rely heavily on the individual leader's personal characteristics: charismatic leadership and transformational leadership. Although characteristics of followers and the situation also play a significant role, these two leadership styles rely strongly on the individual leader's personal qualities and cognitive style.

Personality and Leadership Style: The Role of Charisma

Charismatic leadership has long been of great interest to researchers studying political leadership, social movements, and religious cults. In recent years, researchers have also studied the impact of charismatic leadership in organizations. Charisma is difficult to define. It has been called "a fire that ignites followers' energy and commitment, producing results above and beyond the call of duty."[39] **Charismatic leaders** have the ability to inspire and motivate people to do more than they would normally do, despite obstacles and personal sacrifice. In describing the charismatic leader, one business writer says, "He persuades people—subordinates, peers, customers, even the S.O.B. you both work for—to do things they'd rather not. People charge over the hill for him. Run through fire. Walk barefoot on broken glass. He doesn't demand attention, he commands it."[40]

Charismatic leaders have an emotional impact on people because they appeal to both the heart and the mind. They may speak emotionally about putting themselves on the line for the sake of a mission and they are perceived as people who persist in spite of great odds against them. Charismatic leaders often emerge in troubled times, whether in society or in organizations, because a strong, inspiring personality can help to reduce stress and anxiety among followers.

For example, Amr Khaled emerged as a young, charismatic Muslim religious leader in Egypt during the Mideast crisis of the early 21st century. Khaled's sermons, delivered in an emotional, impassioned manner touched people who were searching for a moderate approach to living as a good Muslim. An organizational example is Lloyd Ward, who was brought in as chief executive of the United States Olympic Committee (USOC) at a time when the organization was torn by internal strife and suffering a loss of public trust. The USOC believed Ward, known as a master motivator with the ability to unite and inspire people with a vision, could use his charisma to heal the fractures in the organization and restore the U.S. Olympics to glory.[41]

Used wisely and ethically, charisma can lift the entire organization's level of performance. Charismatic leaders can raise people's consciousness about new possibilities and motivate them to transcend their own interests for the sake of the team, department, or organization. Leader's Self-Insight 4.4 provides a short quiz to help you determine whether you have the potential to be a charismatic leader.

Charismatic leaders galvanize people to action by infusing leadership with their own passion for the work, thus tapping into followers' emotions as well as their minds. Although charisma itself cannot be learned, there are aspects of charismatic leadership that anyone can use. For one thing, charisma comes from pursuing activities that you genuinely love. Charismatic leaders are engaging their emotions in everyday work life, which makes them energetic, enthusiastic, and attractive to others. Consider Major Tony Burgess, the U.S. Army tactical officer attached on a full-time basis to Company C-2 at West Point. Burgess planned to get out of the Army after five years and become a millionaire businessman. "Then, somewhere along the way," he says, "I fell in love with leading." To Burgess, there's no better job in the world than commanding an Army company. He is so passionate about his work that he started his own Web site,

Charismatic leaders

leaders who have the ability to inspire and motivate people to do more than they would normally do, despite obstacles and personal sacrifice

LEADER'S SELF-INSIGHT 4.4

Have You Got Charisma?

This short quiz will help you determine whether you have characteristics that are associated with charismatic leaders. Circle the answer that best describes you.

1. I am most comfortable thinking in
   a. Generalities
   b. Specifics

2. I worry most about
   a. Current competition
   b. Future competition

3. I tend to focus on
   a. The opportunities I've missed
   b. The opportunities I've seized

4. I prefer to
   a. Promote traditions and procedures that have led to success in the past
   b. Suggest new and unique ways of doing things

5. I tend to ask
   a. How can we do this better?
   b. Why are we doing this?

6. I believe
   a. There's always a way to minimize risk
   b. Some risks are too high

7. I tend to persuade people by using
   a. Emotion
   b. Logic

8. I prefer to
   a. Honor traditional values and ways of thinking
   b. Promote unconventional beliefs and values

9. I would prefer to communicate via
   a. A written report
   b. A one-page chart

10. I think this quiz is
    a. Ridiculous
    b. Fascinating

Scoring and Interpretation:
The following answers are associated with charismatic leadership:
1. a; 2. b; 3. a; 4. b; 5. b; 6. a; 7. a; 8. b; 9. b; 10. b

If you responded in this way to seven or more questions, you have a high charisma quotient and may have the potential to be a charismatic leader. If you answered this way to four or fewer questions, your charisma level is considered low. Do you believe a person can develop charisma?

SOURCE: Based on "Have You Got It?" a quiz that appeared in Patricia Sellers, "What Exactly Is Charisma?" *Fortune* January 15, 1996, 68-75. The original quiz was devised with the assistance of leadership expert Jay Conger.

CompanyCommand.com, a resource for company commanders, and has written a book on the topic.[42]

What Makes a Charismatic Leader?

Understanding charismatic leadership qualities and behavior can help anyone become a stronger leader. A number of studies have identified the unique qualities of charismatic leaders, documented the impact they have on followers, and described the behaviors that help them achieve remarkable results.[43] Exhibit 4.5 compares distinguishing characteristics of charismatic and noncharismatic leaders.[44]

Charismatic leaders create an atmosphere of change and articulate an idealized vision of a future that is significantly better than what now exists. They have an ability to communicate complex ideas and goals in clear, compelling ways, so that everyone from the vice president to the janitor can understand and identify with

Exhibit 4.5	**Distinguishing Characteristics of Charismatic and Noncharismatic Leaders**	
	Noncharismatic Leaders	**Charismatic Leaders**
Likableness:	Shared perspective makes leader likable	Shared perspective and idealized vision make leader likable and an honorable hero worthy of identification and imitation
Trustworthiness:	Disinterested advocacy in persuasion attempts	Passionate advocacy by incurring great personal risk and cost
Relation to status quo:	Tries to maintain status quo	Creates atmosphere of change
Future goals:	Limited goals not too discrepant from status quo	Idealized vision that is highly discrepant from status quo
Articulation:	Weak articulation of goals and motivation to lead	Strong and inspirational articulation of vision and motivation to lead
Competence:	Uses available means to achieve goals within framework of the existing order	Uses unconventional means to transcend the existing order
Behavior:	Conventional, conforms to norms	Unconventional, counter-normative
Influence:	Primarily authority of position and rewards	Transcends position; personal power based on expertise and respect and admiration for the leader

SOURCE: Jay A. Conger and Rabindra N. Kanungo and Associates, *Charismatic Leadership: The Elusive Factor in Organizational Effectiveness* (San Francisco: Jossey-Bass, 1988), 91.

Action Memo

As a leader: Employ charismatic leadership by forcefully articulating a vision, making personal sacrifices to help achieve it, and appealing to people's emotions more than to their minds. Expand your charismatic potential by pursuing activities and jobs that you genuinely love.

their message. Charismatic leaders inspire followers with an abiding faith, even if the faith can't be stated in specific goals that are easily attained. The faith itself becomes a "reward" to followers.[45] Charismatic leaders also act in unconventional ways and use unconventional means to transcend the status quo and create change. Charismatic leaders may sometimes seem like oddballs, but this image only enhances their appeal.

Charismatic leaders earn followers' trust by being willing to incur great personal risk. Putting themselves on the line affirms charismatic leaders as passionate advocates for the vision. According to a personal friend of the King family, Martin Luther King received death threats against himself and his family almost every day during the civil rights movement.[46] By taking risks, leaders can also enhance their emotional appeal to followers. Michael Jordan is a good example of how the nerve to take great personal risks can enhance charisma and likability. Jordan temporarily left a career as a highly successful basketball player to flounder in the game of baseball, but his emotional appeal to the public never wavered. Jordan returned to basketball, retiring a second time in 1999, then met with little success as a manager for the Washington Wizards. However, companies that use him to promote products such as Gatorade and Hanes underwear recognize that Jordan's charisma is quite powerful. Many people identify more personally with him because he seems very "human."[47]

The final characteristic of charismatic leaders is that their source of influence comes from personal power as opposed to position power. People like and identify with the leader and want to be like him or her. Followers respect and admire the leader because of the leader's knowledge, experience, or personal character, not because of a title or position in the organization. Although charismatic leaders may be in formal positions of authority, charismatic leadership transcends formal organizational position because the leader's influence is based on personal qualities rather than the power and authority granted by the organization.

The Black Hat of Charisma

One characteristic of charisma noted by most researchers is that it can be a curse as well as a blessing. Leaders such as Winston Churchill, John F. Kennedy, and Mohandes Gandhi exhibited tremendous charisma. So did leaders such as Adolf Hitler, Charles Manson, and Idi Amin. Charisma isn't always used to benefit the group, organization, or society. It can also be used for self-serving purposes, which leads to deception, manipulation, and exploitation of others. Because the basis of charisma is emotional rather than logical or rational, it is risky and potentially dangerous.[48]

One explanation for the distinction between charisma that results in positive outcomes and that which results in negative outcomes relates to the difference between *personalized* leaders and *socialized* leaders.[49] Leaders who react to organizational problems in terms of their own needs rather than the needs of the whole often act in ways that can have disastrous consequences for others. Personalized charismatic leaders are characterized as self-aggrandizing, nonegalitarian, and exploitative, whereas socialized charismatic leaders are empowering, egalitarian, and supportive. Personalized behavior is based on caring about self; socialized behavior is based on valuing others. Studies have shown that personalized charismatic leaders can have a significant detrimental impact on long-term organizational performance. Leaders who have been consistently successful in improving organizational performance exhibit a pattern of socialized behavior.[50]

Transactional versus Transformational Leadership

Another type of leadership based largely on the leader's personal qualities is transformational leadership, which has a substantial impact on followers and can potentially renew an entire organization. One way to understand transformational leadership is to compare it to transactional leadership.[51]

Transactional Leadership

The basis of **transactional leadership** is a transaction or exchange process between leaders and followers. The transactional leader recognizes followers' needs and desires and then clarifies how those needs and desires will be satisfied in exchange for meeting specified objectives or performing certain duties. Thus, followers receive rewards for job performance, while leaders benefit from the completion of tasks.

Transactional leaders focus on the present and excel at keeping the organization running smoothly and efficiently. They are good at traditional management functions such as planning and budgeting and generally focus on the impersonal aspects of job performance. Transactional leadership can be quite effective. By clarifying expectations, leaders help build followers' confidence. In addition, satisfying the needs of subordinates may improve productivity and morale. However, because transactional leadership involves a commitment to "follow the rules," transactional leaders maintain stability within the organization rather than promoting change. Transactional skills are important for all leaders. However, in today's world, where organizational success often depends on continuous change, effective leaders also use a different approach.

Transformational Leadership

Transformational leadership is characterized by the ability to bring about significant change. Transformational leaders have the ability to lead changes in the organization's vision, strategy, and culture as well as promote innovation in products and technologies. Rather than analyzing and controlling specific transactions with followers using rules, directions, and incentives, transformational leadership focuses on intangible

Transactional leadership
a transaction or exchange process between leaders and followers

Transformational leadership
leadership characterized by the ability to bring about significant change in followers and the organization

qualities such as vision, shared values, and ideas in order to build relationships, give larger meaning to separate activities, and provide common ground to enlist followers in the change process. Transformational leadership is based on the personal values, beliefs, and qualities of the leader rather than on an exchange process between leaders and followers. Transformational leadership differs from transactional leadership in four significant areas.[52]

Action Memo

As a leader: Act like a transformational leader by rallying people around an inspiring vision, expressing optimism about the future, helping followers' develop their potential, and empowering people to make change happen.

1. *Transformational leadership develops followers into leaders.* Followers are given greater freedom to control their own behavior. Transformational leadership rallies people around a mission and defines the boundaries within which followers can operate in relative freedom to accomplish organizational goals. The transformational leader arouses in followers an awareness of problems and issues and helps people look at things in new ways so that productive change can happen.

2. *Transformational leadership elevates the concerns of followers from lower-level physical needs (such as for safety and security) to higher-level psychological needs (such as for self-esteem and self-actualization).* It is important that lower-level needs are met through adequate wages, safe working conditions, and other considerations. However, the transformational leader also pays attention to each individual's need for growth and development. Therefore, the leader sets examples and assigns tasks not only to meet immediate needs but also to elevate followers' needs and abilities to a higher level and link them to the organization's mission. Transformational leaders change followers so that they are empowered to change the organization.

3. *Transformational leadership inspires followers to go beyond their own self-interests for the good of the group.* Transformational leaders motivate people to do more than originally expected. They make followers aware of the importance of change goals and outcomes and, in turn, enable them to transcend their own immediate interests for the sake of the organizational mission. Followers admire these leaders, want to identify with them, and have a high degree of trust in them. However, transformational leadership motivates people not just to follow the leader personally but to believe in the need for change and be willing to make personal sacrifices for the greater purpose.

4. *Transformational leadership paints a vision of a desired future state and communicates it in a way that makes the pain of change worth the effort.*[53] The most significant role of the transformational leader may be to find a vision for the organization that is significantly better than the old one and to enlist others in sharing the dream. It is the vision that launches people into action and provides the basis for the other aspects of transformational leadership

we have just discussed. Change can occur only when people have a sense of purpose as well as a desirable picture of where the organization is going. Without vision, there can be no transformation.

Whereas transactional leaders promote stability, transformational leaders create significant change in followers as well as in organizations. Leaders can learn to be transformational as well as transactional. Completing the exercise in Leader's Self-Insight 4.5 will help you to better understand and apply transformational leadership skills. Effective leaders exhibit both transactional and transformational leadership patterns. They accentuate not only their abilities to build a vision and empower and energize others, but also the transactional skills of designing structures, control systems, and reward systems that can help people achieve the vision.[54] One leader who reflects a balance of transactional and transformational leadership is Richard Kovacevich, CEO of Wells Fargo.

In the Lead   Richard Kovacevich, Wells Fargo

Richard Kovacevich has been called one of the best bankers in America because of his careful attention to the structures and systems that keep banks stable and profitable. However, he's also a transformational leader who has steered the mid-sized Norwest Corp. through numerous acquisitions to become the fourth-largest U.S. banking company. Norwest took the name of its most recent acquisition, Wells Fargo, and Kovacevich refers to the combination as a "merger of equals."

Kovacevich is known for spouting radical notions such as "Banking is necessary, banks are not." He inspires followers with a vision of transformation—of turning Wells Fargo's nationwide network of offices (called *stores*) into a Wal-Mart-style retailing powerhouse. The company is well on its way. The average customer buys four financial products (such as checking accounts, credit cards, home equity loans, and certificates of deposit), as opposed to the industry average of two. That translates into approximately triple the amount of profit for Wells Fargo. Moreover, Kovacevich has set an ambitious goal of doubling the number of products per customer to eight, and employees are fired up to meet the target.

Kovacevich motivates with slogans such as "Mind share plus heart share equals market share." Although some people may think it sounds hokey, Kovacevich and his employees don't care. It's the substance behind the slogans that matters. Employees are rewarded for putting both their hearts and minds into their work. Kovacevich spends a lot of his time out

Identifying Transformational Leadership Qualities

Think of a situation where someone (boss, coach, teacher, group leader) was in a leadership position over you. Rate that leader on each statement below with a number 1–5 that reflects the extent of your agreement with that statement.

1 = Not at all; 2 = To a limited extent; 3 = To a moderate extent; 4 = To a considerable extent; 5 = To a very great extent

In general, the leader over me:	Not at all				To a very great extent
1. Listened carefully to my concerns.	1	2	3	4	5
2. Showed conviction in his or her values.	1	2	3	4	5
3. Helped me focus on developing my strengths.	1	2	3	4	5
4. Was enthusiastic about our mission.	1	2	3	4	5
5. Provided coaching advice for my development.	1	2	3	4	5
6. Talked optimistically about the future.	1	2	3	4	5
7. Encouraged my self development.	1	2	3	4	5
8. Fostered a clear understanding of important values and beliefs.	1	2	3	4	5
9. Provided feedback on how I was doing.	1	2	3	4	5
10. Inspired me with his or her plans for the future.	1	2	3	4	5
11. Taught me how to develop my abilities.	1	2	3	4	5
12. Gained others' commitment to his or her dream.	1	2	3	4	5

Scoring and Interpretation

The questions above represent two dimensions of transformational leadership. For the dimension of *develops followers into leaders*, sum your responses to questions 1, 3, 5, 7, 9, and 11. For the dimension of *inspires followers to go beyond their own self-interest*, sum your scores for questions 2, 4, 6, 8, 10, and 12.

The scores for my leader are:

Develops followers into leaders_____

Inspires followers to go beyond their own self-interest_____

These two scores represent how you saw your leader on two important aspects of transformational leadership. A score of 24 or above on either dimension is considered high because many leaders do not practice transformational skills in their leadership or group work. A score of 18 is about average, and a score of 12 or below would be below average. Compare your scores with other students to understand your leader's practice of transformational leadership. How do you explain your leader's score?

Remember, the important lesson from this exercise is about yourself, not your leader. Analyzing your leader is simply a way to understand the transformational leadership concepts. How would you rate on the dimensions of *developing followers into leaders* or *inspiring followers to go beyond their own self-interest*? These are difficult skills to master. Answer the 12 questions for yourself as a leader. Analyze your pattern of transformational leadership as revealed in your 12 answers. The qualities of transformational leadership are important to develop in today's fast-changing organizations.

SOURCES: These questions are based on B. Bass and B. Avolio, *Multifactor Leadership Questionnaire*, 2nd ed. (Mind Garden, Inc.); and P. M. Podsakoff, S. B. MacKenzie, R. H. Moorman, and R. Fetter, "Transformational Leader Behaviors and Their Effects on Followers' Trust in Leader, Satisfaction, and Organizational Citizenship Behaviors," *Leadership Quarterly* 1, no 2 (1990), 107–42.

in the field, meeting with team members (employees) and customers, patting backs and giving pep talks. He likes to personally remind front line employees that they are the heart of and soul of Wells Fargo, and that only through their efforts can the company succeed.[55]

Kovacevich has combined the elements of both transactional and transformational leadership to build a banking powerhouse. He focuses on keeping Wells Fargo running smoothly and efficiently even as he motivates followers to revolutionize the banking industry.

Summary and Interpretation

This chapter explores some of the individual differences that affect leaders and the leadership process. Individuals differ in many ways, including personality, values and attitudes, and styles of thinking and decision making. One model of personality, the Big Five personality dimensions, examines whether individuals score high or low on the dimensions of extroversion, agreeableness, conscientiousness, emotional stability, and openness to experience. Although there is some indication that a high degree of each of the personality dimensions is associated with successful leadership, individuals who score low on various dimensions may also be effective leaders. Two specific personality traits that have a significant impact on leader behavior are locus of control and authoritarianism.

Values are fundamental beliefs that cause a person to prefer that things be done one way rather than another. One way to think about values is in terms of instrumental and end values. End values are beliefs about the kinds of goals that are worth pursuing, while instrumental values are beliefs about the types of behavior that are appropriate for reaching goals. Values also affect an individual's attitudes. A leader's attitudes about self and others influence how the leader behaves toward and interacts with followers. Two sets of assumptions called Theory X and Theory Y represent two very different sets of attitudes leaders may hold about people in general.

Another area of individual differences is cognitive style. The whole brain concept explores a person's preferences for right-brained versus left-brained thinking and for conceptual versus experiential thinking. The model provides a powerful metaphor for understanding differences in thinking styles. Individuals can learn to use their "whole brain" rather than relying on one thinking style. Another way of looking at cognitive differences is the Myers–Briggs Type Indicator, which measures an individual's preferences for introversion versus extroversion, sensing versus intuition, thinking versus feeling, and judging versus perceiving.

Two leadership styles that rely strongly on the individual leader's personal characteristics are charismatic leadership and transformational leadership. Charismatic leaders have an emotional impact on people by appealing to both the heart and mind. They create an atmosphere of change, articulate an idealized vision of the future, communicate clearly, inspire faith and hope, and incur personal risks to influence followers. Charisma can be used to benefit organizations and society, but it can also be dangerous. Transformational leaders also create an atmosphere of change, and they inspire followers not just to follow them personally but to believe in the vision of organizational transformation. Transformational leaders inspire followers to go beyond their own self-interest for the good of the whole.

Discussion Questions

1. Extroversion is often considered a "good" quality for a leader to have. Why might introversion be considered an equally positive quality?

2. What might be some reasons the dimension of "openness to experience" correlates so strongly with historians' ratings of the greatest U.S. presidents but has been less strongly associated with business leader success? Do you think this personality dimension might be more important for business leaders of today than it was in the past? Discuss.

3. In which of the Big Five personality dimensions would you place the traits of locus of control and authoritarianism?

4. From Leader's Self-Insight 4.2, identify four or five values (either instrumental or end values) that could be a source of conflict between leaders and followers. Explain.

5. How do a person's attitudes and assumptions about human nature in general affect his or her leadership approach? How might a leader's attitudes about him or herself alter or reinforce this approach?

6. Do you believe understanding your preferences according to the whole brain model can help you be a better leader? Discuss.

7. How can a leader use an understanding of brain dominance to improve the functioning of the organization?

8. Why do you think *thinking* and *judging* are the two characteristics from the Myers-Briggs Type Indicator that seem to be most strongly associated with effective leadership?

9. What do you consider the essential traits of a charismatic leader? Why is charismatic leadership considered potentially dangerous?

10. What are the primary differences between transactional and transformational leadership?

11. What personality dimensions, values, and attitudes might be particularly useful to an individual who wants to act as a transformational leader? Do you believe anyone can develop them? Discuss.

Personality Assessment: Jung's Typology and the Myers–Briggs Type Indicator

For each item below, circle either "a" or "b." In some cases, both "a" and "b" may apply to you. You should decide which is *more* like you, even if it is only slightly more true.

1. I would rather
   a. Solve a new and complicated problem
   b. Work on something that I have done before

2. I like to
   a. Work alone in a quiet place
   b. Be where "the action" is

3. I want a boss who
   a. Establishes and applies criteria in decisions
   b. Considers individual needs and makes exceptions

4. When I work on a project, I
   a. Like to finish it and get some closure
   b. Often leave it open for possible change

5. When making a decision, the most important considerations are
   a. Rational thoughts, ideas, and data
   b. People's feelings and values

6. On a project, I tend to
   a. Think it over and over before deciding how to proceed
   b. Start working on it right away, thinking about it as I go along

7. When working on a project, I prefer to
   a. Maintain as much control as possible
   b. Explore various options

8. In my work, I prefer to
   a. Work on several projects at a time, and learn as much as possible about each one
   b. Have one project that is challenging and keeps me busy

9. I often
   a. Make lists and plans whenever I start something and may hate to seriously alter my plans
   b. Avoid plans and just let things progress as I work on them

10. When discussing a problem with colleagues, it is easy for me
    a. To see "the big picture"
    b. To grasp the specifics of the situation

11. When the phone rings in my office or at home, I usually
    a. Consider it an interruption
    b. Don't mind answering it

12. The word that describes me better is
    a. Analytical
    b. Empathetic

13. When I am working on an assignment, I tend to
    a. Work steadily and consistently
    b. Work in bursts of energy with "down time" in between

14. When I listen to someone talk on a subject, I usually try to
    a. Relate it to my own experience and see if it fits
    b. Assess and analyze the message

15. When I come up with new ideas, I generally
    a. "Go for it"
    b. Like to contemplate the ideas some more

16. When working on a project, I prefer to
    a. Narrow the scope so it is clearly defined
    b. Broaden the scope to include related aspects

17. When I read something, I usually
    a. Confine my thoughts to what is written there
    b. Read between the lines and relate the words to other ideas

18. When I have to make a decision in a hurry, I often
    a. Feel uncomfortable and wish I had more information
    b. Am able to do so with available data

19. In a meeting, I tend to
    a. Continue formulating my ideas as I talk about them
    b. Only speak out after I have carefully thought the issue through

20. In work, I prefer spending a great deal of time on issues of
    a. Ideas
    b. People

21. In meetings, I am most often annoyed with people who
    a. Come up with many sketchy ideas
    b. Lengthen the meeting with many practical details

22. I tend to be
    a. A morning person
    b. A night owl

23. My style in preparing for a meeting is
    a. To be willing to go in and be responsive
    b. To be fully prepared and sketch out an outline of the meeting

24. In meetings, I would prefer for people to
    a. Display a fuller range of emotions
    b. Be more task-oriented

25. I would rather work for an organization where
    a. My job was intellectually stimulating
    b. I was committed to its goals and mission

26. On weekends, I tend to
    a. Plan what I will do
    b. Just see what happens and decide as I go along

27. I am more
    a. Outgoing
    b. Contemplative

28. I would rather work for a boss who is
    a. Full of new ideas
    b. Practical

In the following, choose the word in each pair that appeals to you more:

29. a. Social   b. Theoretical

30. a. Ingenuity   b. Practicality

31. a. Organized   b. Adaptable

32. a. Activity   b. Concentration

Scoring

Count one point for each item listed below that you circled in the inventory.

Score For I (Introversion)	Score For E (Extroversion)	Score For S (Sensing)	Score For N (Intuition)
2a	2b	1b	1a
6a	6b	10b	10a
11a	11b	13a	13b
15b	15a	16a	16b
19b	19a	17a	17b
22a	22b	21a	21b
27b	27a	28b	28a
32b	32a	30b	30a

Totals _____   _____   _____   _____

Circle the one with more points: Circle the one with more points:

I or E   S or N

(If tied on I/E, don't count #11)   *(If tied on S/N, don't count #16)*

Score for T (Thinking)	Score for F (Feeling)	Score for J (Judging)	Score for P (Perceiving)
3a	3b	4a	4b
5a	5b	7a	7b
12a	12b	8b	8a
14b	14a	9a	9b
20a	20b	18b	18a
24b	24a	23b	23a
25a	25b	26a	26b
29b	29a	31a	31b

Totals ____   ____   ____   ____

Circle the one with more points: Circle the one with more points:

T or F   J or P

(If tied on T/F, don't count #24)   *(If tied on J/P, don't count #23)*

Your Score Is: I or E _____   S or N _____   T or F _____   J or P _____

Your MBTI type is: _____ (example: INTJ; ESFP; etc.)

_____

SOURCE: From *Organizational Behavior: Experience and Cases*, 4th edition by Marcic. © 1995. Reprinted with permission of South-Western, a division of Thomson Learning: *http://www.thomsonrights.com*. Fax 800 730-2215.

Interpretation

The Myers–Briggs Type Indicator (MBTI), based on the work of psychologist Carl Jung, is the most widely used personality assessment instrument in the world. The MBTI, which was described in the chapter text, identifies sixteen different "types," shown with their dominant characteristics in the following chart. Remember that no one is a pure type; however, each individual has preferences for introversion versus extroversion, sensing versus intuition, thinking versus feeling, and judging versus perceiving. Based on your scores on the survey, read the description of your type in the chart. Do you believe the description fits your personality?

Characteristics Frequently Associated with Each Type

Sensing Types		Intuitive Types	

Introverts

ISTJ

Quiet, serious, earn success by thoroughness and dependability. Practical, matter-of-fact, realistic, and responsible. Decide logically what should be done and work toward it steadily, regardless of distractions. Take pleasure in making everything orderly and organized—their work, their home, their life. Value traditions and loyalty.

ISFJ

Quiet, friendly, responsible, and conscientious. Committed and steady in meeting their obligations. Thorough, painstaking, and accurate. Loyal, considerate, notice and remember specifics about people who are important to them, concerned with how others feel. Strive to create an orderly and harmonious environment at work and at home.

INFJ

Seek meaning and connection in ideas, relationships, and material possessions. Want to understand what motivates people and are insightful about others. Conscientious and committed to their firm values. Develop a clear vision about how best to serve the common good. Organized and decisive in implementing their vision.

INTJ

Have original minds and great drive for implementing their ideas and achieving their goals. Quickly see patterns in external events and develop long-range explanatory perspectives. When committed, organize a job and carry it through. Skeptical and independent, have high standards of competence and performance—for themselves and others.

ISTP

Tolerant and flexible, quiet observers until a problem appears, then act quickly to find workable solutions. Analyze what makes things work and readily get through large amounts of data to isolate the core of practical problems. Interested in cause and effect, organize facts using logical principles, value efficiency.

ISFP

Quiet, friendly, sensitive, and kind. Enjoy the present moment, what's going on around them. Like to have their own space and to work within their own time frame. Loyal and committed to their values and to people who are important to them. Dislike disagreements and conflicts, do not force their opinions or values on others.

INFP

Idealistic, loyal to their values and to people who are important to them. Want an external life that is congruent with their values. Curious, quick to see possibilities, can be catalysts for implementing ideas. Seek to understand people and to help them fulfill their potential. Adaptable, flexible, and accepting unless a value is threatened.

INTP

Seek to develop logical explanations for everything that interests them. Theoretical and abstract, interested more in ideas than in social interaction. Quiet, contained, flexible, and adaptable. Have unusual ability to focus in depth to solve problems in their area of interest. Skeptical, sometimes critical, always analytical.

Extraverts

ESTP

Flexible and tolerant, they take a pragmatic approach focused on immediate results. Theories and conceptual explanations bore them—they want to act energetically to solve the problem. Focus on the here-and-now, spontaneous, enjoy each moment that they can be active with others. Enjoy material comforts and style. Learn best through doing.

ESFP

Outgoing, friendly, and accepting. Exuberant lovers of life, people, and material comforts. Enjoy working with others to make things happen. Bring common sense and a realistic approach to their work, and make work fun. Flexible and spontaneous, adapt readily to new people and environments. Learn best by trying a new skill with other people.

ENFP

Warmly enthusiastic and imaginative. See life as full of possibilities. Make connections between events and information very quickly, and confidently proceed based on the patterns they see. Want a lot of affirmation from others, and readily give appreciation and support. Spontaneous and flexible, often rely on their ability to improvise and their verbal fluency.

ENTP

Quick, ingenious, stimulating, alert, and outspoken. Resourceful in solving new and challenging problems. Adept at generating conceptual possibilities and then analyzing them strategically. Good at reading other people. Bored by routine, will seldom do the same thing the same way, apt to turn to one new interest after another.

ESTJ

Practical, realistic, matter-of-fact. Decisive, quickly move to implement decisions. Organize projects and people to get things done, focus on getting results in the most efficient way possible. Take care of routine details. Have a clear set of logical standards, systematically follow them and want others to also. Forceful in implementing their plans.

ESFJ

Warmhearted, conscientious, and cooperative. Want harmony in their environment, work with determination to establish it. Like to work with others to complete tasks accurately and on time. Loyal, follow through even in small matters. Notice what others need in their day-by-day lives and try to provide it. Want to be appreciated for who they are and for what they contribute.

ENFJ

Warm, empathetic, responsive, and responsible. Highly attuned to the emotions, needs, and motivations of others. Find potential in everyone, want to help others fulfill their potential. May act as catalysts for individual and group growth. Loyal, responsive to praise and criticism. Sociable, facilitate others in a group, and provide inspiring leadership.

ENTJ

Frank, decisive, assume leadership readily. Quickly see illogical and inefficient procedures and policies, develop and implement comprehensive systems to solve organizational problems. Enjoy long-term planning and goal setting. Usually well informed, well read, enjoy expanding their knowledge and passing it on to others. Forceful in presenting their ideas.

Leadership at Work

Past and Future

Draw a life line below that marks high and low experiences during your life. Think of key decisions, defining moments, peak experiences, and major disappointments that shaped who you are today. Draw the line from left to right, and identify each high and low point with a word or two.

Birth Year: _____   Today's Date: _____

What made these valued experiences? How did they shape who you are today?

_____

_____

_____

Now take the long view of your life. In ten-year increments, write below the leader experiences you want to have. Provide a brief past-tense description of each decade (e.g., next ten years—big starting salary, bored in first job, promoted to middle management)

Next 10 years: _____

_____

_____

Following 10 years: _____

_____

_____

Following 10 years: _____

_____

_____

Following 10 years: _____

_____

_____

What personal skills and strengths will you use to achieve the future?

_____

_____

_____

What is your core life purpose or theme as expressed in the life line and answers above?

_____

_____

What would your desired future self say to your present self?

_____

_____

How do your answers above relate to your scores on the Leader Self-Insight questionnaires you completed in this chapter?

_____

_____

_____

Leadership Development: Cases for Analysis

International Bank

Top executives and board members of a large international bank in New York are meeting to consider three finalists for a new position. The winning candidate will be in a high-profile job, taking charge of a group of top loan officers who have recently gotten the bank into some risky financial arrangements in Latin America. The bank had taken a financial bath when the Mexican peso collapsed, and the board voted to hire someone to directly oversee this group of loan officers and make sure the necessary due diligence is done on major loans before further commitments are made. Although the bank likes for decisions to be made as close to the action level as possible, they believe the loan officers have gotten out of hand and need to be reined in. The effectiveness of the person in this new position is considered to be of utmost importance for the bank's future. After carefully reviewing resumés, the board selected six candidates for the first round of interviews, after which the list of finalists was narrowed to three. All three candidates seem to have the intellect and experience to handle the job. Before the second-round interview, the board has asked their regular consulting firm to review the candidates, conduct more extensive background checks, and administer personality tests. A summary of their reports on the three candidates follows:

A.M. This candidate has a relatively poor self-concept and exhibits a fear of the unknown. She is somewhat of an introvert and is uncomfortable using power openly and conspicuously. A.M.'s beliefs about others are that all people are inherently noble, kind, and disposed to do the right thing, and that it is possible to influence and modify the behavior of anyone through logic and reason. Once a person's shortcomings are pointed out to her, A.M. will try to help the person overcome them. She believes that all employees can be happy, content, and dedicated to the goals of the organization.

J.T. J.T. is an extrovert with a strong drive for achievement and power. He likes new experiences and tends to be impulsive and adventurous. He is very self-assured and confident in his own abilities, but highly suspicious of the motives and abilities of others. J.T. believes the average person has an inherent dislike for work and will avoid responsibility when possible. He is very slow to trust others, but does have the ability over time to develop close, trusting relationships. In general, though, J.T. believes most people must be coerced, controlled, and threatened to get them to do their jobs well and to the benefit of the organization.

F.C. This candidate is also an extrovert, but, while she is competitive, F.C. does not seem to have the strong desire for dominance that many extroverts exhibit. F.C. is also highly conscientious and goal-oriented, and will do whatever she believes is necessary to achieve a goal. F.C. has a generally positive attitude toward others, believing that most people want to do their best for the organization. F.C. does, though, seem to have a problem forming close, personal attachments. Her lively, outgoing personality enables her to make many superficial acquaintances, but she seems to distrust and avoid emotions in herself and others, preventing the development of close relationships.

SOURCES: This case is based on information in "Consultant's Report" in John M. Champion and Francis J. Bridges, *Critical Incidents in Management: Decision and Policy Issues*, 6th ed. (Homewood, IL: Irwin, 1989), 55–60; and James Waldroop and Timothy Butler, "Guess What? You're Not Perfect," *Fortune*, (October 16, 2000): 415–420.

Questions

1. Based only on the consultant's summary, which of the three candidates would you select as a leader for the group of loan officers? Discuss and defend your decision.
2. The selection committee is more divided than before on who would be best for the job. What additional information do you think you would need to help you select the best candidate?
3. How much weight do you think should be given to the personality assessment? Do you believe personality tests can be useful in predicting the best person for a job? Discuss.

The Deadlocked Committee

Ned Norman tried to reconstruct, in his own mind, the series of events that had culminated in this morning's deadlocked committee meeting. Each of the members had suddenly seemed to resist any suggestions that did not exactly coincide with his or her own ideas for implementing the program under consideration. This sort of "stubbornness," as Norman considered it, was not like the normal behavior patterns of most committee participants. Of course, the comment during last week's meeting about "old fashioned seat-of-the-pants decision making" had ruffled a few feathers, but Ned didn't think that was why things had bogged down today.

Ned recalled starting this morning's session by stating that the committee had discussed several of the factors connected with the proposed expanded services program, and now it seemed about time to make a decision about which way to go. Robert Romany had immediately protested that they had barely scratched the surface of the possibilities for implementing the program. Then, both Hillary Thomas and David Huntington, who worked in the statistics department of Division B, had sided with Romany and insisted that more time was needed for in-depth research. Walter Weston had entered the fray by stating that this seemed a little uncalled for, since previous experience has clearly indicated that expansion programs such as this one should be implemented through selected area district offices. This had sparked a statement from Susan Pilcher that experience was more often than not a lousy teacher, which was followed by Todd Tooley repeating his unfortunate statement about old-fashioned decision making! Robert Romany had further heated things up by saying that it was obviously far better to go a little slower in such matters by trying any new program in one area first, rather than having the committee look "unprogressive" by just "trudging along the same old cow paths"!

At this point, Ned had intuitively exercised his prerogative as chairman to stop the trend that was developing. However, things were obviously so touchy among the members that they simply refused to either offer suggestions or support any that Ned offered for breaking the deadlock. Ned decided to approach each of the division directors for whom the various committee members worked. In each area he visited, he learned that the directors were already aware of the problems, and each one had his or her own ideas as to what should be done:

Division A: The director stated that he was not much in sympathy with people who wanted to make a big deal out of every program that came along. He recalled a similar problem years ago when the company first introduced decision support software, which was hailed as the manager's replacement in decision making. He noted that the software was still in use but that he had probably made better decisions as a result of his broad background and knowledge than any computer ever could. "When I've served as chair of a deadlocked committee," he said, "I simply made the decision and solved the problem. If you're smart, you'll do the same. You can't worry about everybody's feelings on this thing."

Division B: "I know you'll want to use the best available information in estimating any program's potential performance," the director of Division B told Ned. She sided with Hillary Thomas and David Huntington that an investigative approach was the only way to go. After all, the director said, it logically followed that a decision could be no better than the research effort behind it. She also told Ned that she had told Thomas and Huntington to go ahead and collect the data they needed. "My division will be footing the bill for this, so nobody can gripe about the cost aspects." she said. "Any price would be cheap if it awakens some of the people around here to the tremendous value of a scientific approach."

Division C: The director of Division C bluntly told Ned that he didn't really care how the decision was made. However, he thought the best course of action would be to carefully develop a plan and implement it a piece at a time. "That way," he said, "you can evaluate how it looks without committing the company to a full-scale expansion. It doesn't take a lot of figuring to figure that one out!"

Division D: "We've got a time problem here," the director of Division D said. "The committee simply can't look at all possible angles. They need to synthesize the information and understandings they have and make a decision based on two or three possible solutions."

SOURCE: This is a revised version of a case by W. D. Heier, "Ned Norman, Committee Chairman," in John E. Dittrich and Robert A. Zawacki, *People and Organizations: Cases in Management and Organizational Behavior* (Plano, TX: Business Publications, Inc., 1981), 9–11.

Questions
1. Based on the whole brain concept, what different thinking styles are represented by the committee members and division directors? Do you believe they can ever be brought together? Discuss.
2. Do you see ways in which Norman might use the ideas of transformational leadership to help resolve this dilemma and break the impasse?
3. If you were the chairman of this committee, what would you do? Discuss.

References

1. Chip Cummins, "Workers Wear Feelings on Their Hard Hats and Show True Colors: On Oil Rigs and Assembly Lines, Sensitivity Training Pays Off," *The Wall Street Journal*, November 7, 2000, A1.

2. J. M. Digman, "Personality Structure: Emergence of the Five-Factor Model," *Annual Review of Psychology* 41 (1990): 417–440; M. R. Barrick and M. K. Mount, "Autonomy as a Moderator of the Relationships Between the Big Five Personality Dimensions and Job Performance," *Journal of Applied Psychology* (February 1993): 111–118; and J. S. Wiggins and A. L. Pincus, "Personality: Structure and Assessment," *Annual Review of Psychology* 43 (1992): 473–504.

3. Quentin Hardy, "All Carly, All the Time," *Forbes* (December 13, 1999): 138–144; and Peter Burrows and Peter Elstrom, "The Boss," *BusinessWeek* (August 2, 1999): 76–84; Betsy Morris and Patricia Sellers, "What Really Happened at Coke?" *Fortune* (January 10, 2000): 114–116; and Betsy McKay, Nikhil Deogun, and Joanne Lublin, "Ivester Had All Skills of a CEO But One: Ear for Political Nuance," *The Wall Street Journal*, December 17, 1999, A1, A6.

4. Mike Freeman, "A New Breed of Coaches Relates Better to Players," *The New York Times*, Sports section, August 19, 2001, 36.

5. Jeremy Kahn, Iobox profile, in "Euro Entrepreneurs: Why Is This Man Smiling?" *Fortune* (July 24, 2000):183–196.

6. James B. Hunt, "Travel Experience in the Formation of Leadership: John Quincy Adams, Frederick Douglass, and Jane Addams," *The Journal of Leadership Studies* 7, no. 1 (2000): 92–106.

7. R. T. Hogan, G. J. Curphy, and J. Hogan, "What We Know About Leadership: Effectiveness and Personality," *American Psychologist* 49, no. 6 (1994): 493–504.

8. Randolph E. Schmid, "Psychologists Rate What Helps Make a President Great," *Johnson City Press*, August 6, 2000, 10; and "Personality and the Presidency" segment on NBC News with John Siegenthaler, Jr., August 5, 2000.

9. Julia Lawlor, "Personality 2.0," *Red Herring* (April 1, 2001): 98–103.

10. P. E. Spector, "Behavior in Organizations as a Function of Employee's Locus of Control," *Psychological Bulletin* (May 1982): 482–497; and H. M. Lefcourt, "Durability and Impact of the Locus of Control Construct," *Psychological Bulletin*, (1992), 112, 411–414.

11. Ibid.; and J. B. Miner, *Industrial-Organizational Psychology* (New York: McGraw-Hill, 1992): 151.

12. Andy Serwer, "There's Something about Cisco," *Fortune*, (May 15, 2000) 114–138; Stephanie N. Mehta, "Cisco Fractures Its Own Fairy Tale," *Fortune*, (May 14, 2001): 104–112.

13. T. W. Adorno, E. Frenkel-Brunswick, D. J. Levinson, and R. N. Sanford, *The Authoritarian Personality* (New York: Harper & Row, 1950).

14. Susan Caminiti, "What Team Leaders Need to Know," *Fortune* (February 20, 1995): 93–100.

15. E. C. Ravlin and B. M. Meglino, "Effects of Values on Perception and Decision Making: A Study of Alternative Work Value Measures," *Journal of Applied Psychology* 72 (1987): 666–673.

16. Robert C. Benfari, *Understanding and Changing Your Management Style* (San Francisco: Jossey-Bass, 1999), 172.

17. Milton Rokeach, *The Nature of Human Values* (New York: The Free Press, 1973); and M. Rokeach, *Understanding Human Values* (New York: The Free Press, 1979).

18. Carol Hymowitz, "For Many Executives, Leadership Lessons Started with Mom" (In the Lead column), *The Wall Street Journal*, May 16, 2000, B1.

19. Susan Hansen, "Stings Like a Bee," *Inc.* (November 2002): 56–64.

20. Hymowitz, "For Many Executives, Leadership Lessons Started with Mom."

21. Based on G. W. England and R. Lee, "The Relationship between Managerial Values and Managerial Success in the United States, Japan, India, and Australia," *Journal of Applied Psychology* 59 (1974): 411–419.

22. Alex Markels, "Frontier, Seeing a Chance in Denver, Elbows In," *The New York Times* September 29, 2002, Business Section, 4.

23. S. J. Breckler, "Empirical Validation of Affect, Behavior, and Cognition as Distinct Components of Attitudes," *Journal of Personality and Social Psychology* (May 1984): 1191–1205; and J. M. Olson and M. P. Zanna, "Attitudes and Attitude Change," *Annual Review of Psychology* 44 (1993): 117–154.

24. Parker J. Palmer, *Leading from Within: Reflections on Spirituality and Leadership* (Indianapolis: Indiana Office for Campus Ministries, 1990), and Diane Chapman Walsh, "Cultivating Inner Sources for Leadership," in *The Organization of the Future*, Frances Hesselbein, Marshall Goldsmith, and Richard Beckhard, eds. (San Francisco: Jossey-Bass, 1997): 295–302.

25. Based on Richard L. Hughes, Robert C. Ginnett, and Gordon J. Curphy, *Leadership: Enhancing the Lessons of Experience* (Boston: Irwin McGraw-Hill, 1999): 182–184.

26. Douglas McGregor, *The Human Side of Enterprise* (New York: McGraw-Hill, 1960).

27. Thomas J. Petzinger, Jr., "A Plant Manager Keeps Reinventing His Production Line" (The Front Lines column), *The Wall Street Journal*, September 19, 1997, B1.

28. J. Hall and S. M. Donnell, "Managerial Achievement: The Personal Side of Behavioral Theory," *Human Relations* 32 (1979): 77–101.

29. Dorothy Leonard and Susaan Straus, "Putting Your Company's Whole Brain to Work," *Harvard Business Review* (July–August 1997): 111–121.

30. Henry Mintzberg, "Planning on the Left Side and Managing on the Right," *Harvard Business Review* (July–August 1976): 49–57; Richard Restak, "The Hemispheres of the Brain Have Minds of Their Own," *The New York Times*, January 25, 1976; and Robert Ornstein, *The Psychology of Consciousness* (San Francisco: W. H. Freeman, 1975).

31. This discussion is based on Ned Herrmann, *The Whole Brain Business Book* (New York: McGraw Hill, 1996).

32. Herrmann, *The Whole Brain Business Book*, 103.

33. Herrmann, *The Whole Brain Business Book*, 179.

34. Leonard and Straus, "Putting Your Company's Whole Brain to Work"; and Katherine Mieszkowski, "Opposites Attract," *Fast Company* (December–January 1998): 42, 44.

35. Carl Jung, *Psychological Types* (London: Routledge and Kegan Paul, 1923).

36. Otto Kroeger and Janet M. Thuesen, *Type Talk* (New York: Delacorte Press, 1988); Kroeger and Thuesen, *Type Talk at Work* (New York: Dell, 1992); "Conference Proceedings," The Myers–Briggs Type Indicator and Leadership: An International Research Conference, January 12–14, 1994; and S. K. Hirsch, *MBTI Team Member's Guide* (Palo Alto, Calif.: Consulting Psychologists Press, 1992).

37. Coeli Carr, "Redesigning the Management Psyche," *The New York Times*, May 26, 2002, Business Section, 14.

38. Based on Mary H. McCaulley, "Research on the MBTI and Leadership: Taking the Critical First Step," Keynote Address, The Myers–Briggs Type Indicator and Leadership: An International Research Conference, January 12–14, 1994.

39. Katherine J. Klein and Robert J. House, "On Fire: Charismatic Leadership and Levels of Analysis," *Leadership Quarterly* 6, no. 2 (1995): 183–198.

40. Patricia Sellers, "What Exactly is Charisma?" *Fortune*, January 15, 1996, 68–75.

41. Gretel C. Kovach, "Moderate Muslim Voice Falls Silent: Charismatic Young Leader Leaves Egypt As His Popular Sermons Come Under Government Scrutiny," *The Christian Science Monitor*, November 26, 2002, 6; Selena Roberts, "U.S.O.C. Elects Former Maytag Chairman as Chief," *The New York Times*, October 21, 2001, D7.

42. Keith H. Hammonds, "You Can't Lead Without Making Sacrifices," *Fast Company*, (June 2001): 106–116.

43. Jay A. Conger, Rabindra N. Kanungo and Associates, *Charismatic Leadership: The Elusive Factor in Organizational Effectiveness* (San Francisco: Jossey-Bass, 1988); Robert J. House and Jane M. Howell, "Personality and Charismatic Leadership," *Leadership Quarterly* 3, no. 2 (1992): 81–108; Klein and House, "On Fire: Charismatic Leadership and Levels of Analysis"; and Harold B. Jones, "Magic, Meaning, and Leadership: Weber's Model and the Empirical Literature," *Human Relations* 54, no. 6 (June 2001): 753–771.

44. The following discussion is based primarily on Conger, et. al., *Charismatic Leadership.*

45. Boas Shamir, Michael B. Arthur, and Robert J. House, "The Rhetoric of Charismatic Leadership: A Theoretical Extension, A Case Study, and Implications for Future Research," *Leadership Quarterly* 5, no. 1 (1994): 25–42.

46. Richard L. Daft and Robert H. Lengel, *Fusion Leadership: Unlocking the Subtle Forces that Change People and Organizations* (San Francisco: Berrett-Koehler, 1998), 169.

47. Sellers, "What Exactly Is Charisma?"

48. Rakesh Khurana, "The Curse of the Superstar CEO," *Harvard Business Review*, (September 2002): 60–66; Joseph A. Raelin, "The Myth of Charismatic Leaders," *T & D* 57, no. 3 (March 2003): 46; and Janice M. Beyer, "Taming and Promoting Charisma to Change Organizations," *The Leadership Quarterly* 10, no. 2 (1999): 307–330.

49. Robert J. House and Jane M. Howell, "Personality and Charismatic Leadership," *Leadership Quarterly* 3, no. 2 (1992): 81–108; and Jennifer O'Connor, Michael D. Mumford, Timothy C. Clifton, Theodore L. Gessner, and Mary Shane Connelly, "Charismatic Leaders and Destructiveness: An Historiometric Study," *Leadership Quarterly* 6, no. 4 (1995): 529–555.

50. O'Connor et. al. "Charismatic Leaders and Destructiveness."

51. The terms transactional and transformational leadership are from James MacGregor Burns, *Leadership* (New York: Harper & Row, 1978), and Bernard M. Bass, "Leadership: Good, Better, Best," *Organizational Dynamics* 13 (Winter 1985): 26–40.

52. Based on Bernard M. Bass, "Theory of Transformational Leadership Redux," *Leadership Quarterly* 6, no. 4 (Winter 1995): 463–478, and "From Transactional to Transformational Leadership: Learning to Share the Vision," *Organizational Dynamics* 18, no. 3 (Winter 1990): 19–31; Francis J. Yammarino, William D. Spangler, and Bernard M. Bass, "Transformational Leadership and Performance: A Longitudinal Investigation," *Leadership Quarterly* 4, no. 1 (Spring 1993): 81–102; and B. M. Bass, "Current Developments in Transformational Leadership," *The Psychologist-Manager Journal* 3, no. 1 (1999), 5–21.

53. Noel M. Tichy and Mary Anne Devanna, *The Transformational Leader* (New York: John Wiley & Sons, 1986), 265–266.

54. Manfred F. R. Kets De Vries, "Charisma in Action: The Transformational Abilities of Virgin's Richard Branson and ABB's Percy Barnevik," *Organizational Dynamics*, (Winter 1998): 7–21.

55. Bethany McLean, "Is This Guy the Best Banker in America?" *Fortune* (July 6, 1998): 126–128; and John R. Enger, "Cross-Sell Campaign," *Banking Strategies* 77, no. 6 (November–December 2001); 34; Jacqueline S. Gold, "Bank to the Future," *Institutional Investor* 35, no. 9 (September 2001): 54–63.

Chapter

Your Leadership Challenge

After reading this chapter, you should be able to:

- Recognize how mental models guide your behavior and relationships.

- Engage in independent thinking by staying mentally alert, thinking critically, and being mindful rather than mindless.

- Break out of categorized thinking patterns and open your mind to new ideas and multiple perspectives.

- Begin to apply systems thinking and personal mastery to your activities at school or work.

- Exercise emotional intelligence, including being self-aware, managing your emotions, motivating yourself, displaying empathy, and managing relationships.

- Apply the difference between motivating others based on fear and motivating others based on love.

When Rear Admiral Albert H. Konetzni took command of the U.S. Navy's Pacific submarine fleet, the Navy was facing a serious personnel crisis. Despite a large pay increase, recruitment was dismal and sailors were jumping ship as soon as possible. Keeping a full crew on many ships and subs was a constant struggle. Some Navy officials blamed a strong economy or poor recruiting strategies, but Admiral Konetzni thought the problem was more basic. The assumptions, perceptions, and mindsets of top officers, he believed, were creating an environment that simply ran people off.

Adm. Konetzni wanted to try a new approach. He reasoned that the best way to keep his sailors was to make sure they had time for a life outside the Navy between their grueling six-month-long deployments. The old model was that submarine commanders expected hard work, long hours, and near-perfection. A long-standing joke is that SSN, the acronym the Navy uses to designate its attack submarines, stands for "Saturdays, Sundays, and Nights," a reference to the long hours sailors spend working in port. Within weeks of taking command, Konetzni ordered that crews should work from 8 A.M. to 4 P.M. in port. He used $500,000 from his spare-parts budget to hire civilians to paint subs and fix the galleys, and spent an additional $12,000 on a conveyor belt to load boxes onto ships (rather than using a line of sailors to do the work). He declared that some subs, even though they had high certification scores or got a lot of praise from top officials, were "unsuccessful" because sailors were miserable and just waiting for their tour to be over so they could leave the Navy.

Adm. Konetzni made a number of other changes, some of them controversial. However, despite criticisms, there's no doubt that Konetzni's approach that considers the needs and feelings of sailors had positive results. Within two years, the percentage of Pacific fleet sailors who signed up for a second tour of duty doubled, morale dramatically improved, and there has been no indication that the fleet's ability to execute its mission has been diminished. Discussing the changes, Commander Dick Pusateri, the Pacific fleet's lead chaplain, said, "The admiral was telling us that taking care of people means something, even if we've been pretending it does not.[1]

Rear Admiral Albert Konetzni created a new model for the U.S. Navy's Pacific submarine fleet, one that puts a priority on people and relationships. Throughout the world of organizations, leaders are beginning to talk about building work relationships based on trust, caring, and respect. Peter Drucker, a writer who is widely read by practicing managers, has been stressing the importance of people and relationships for years. Wayne Calloway, former CEO of PepsiCo, when asked the secret to his company's success, once said, "The three Ps: people, people, people."[2] And at West Point, where future Army leaders are trained, cadets are taught that the great leaders are those who genuinely care about their soldiers and never ask others to do anything they aren't willing to do themselves.[3] Many leaders have a growing appreciation for the fact that the strength and quality of relationships with employees, customers, suppliers, and competitors is just as important as formal rules, contracts, plans, and even profits. In a time of uncertainty, leaders focus on personal relationships as a way to bind people together.

Making relationships rather than rules and schedules a priority is not easy for traditional managers who have been accustomed to thinking emotions should be left outside the company gate. However, smart leaders are increasingly aware that human emotion is the most basic force in organizations and that acknowledging and respecting employees as whole people can enhance organizational performance. People cannot be separated from their emotions, and it is through emotion that leaders generate employee commitment to shared vision and mission, values and culture, and caring for the work and each other.

This chapter and the next explore current thinking about the importance of leaders becoming whole people by exploring the full capacities of their minds and spirits. By doing so, they help others reach their full potential and contribute fully to the organization. We will first examine what we mean by leader capacity. Then we will expand on some of the ideas introduced in the previous chapter to consider how the capacity to shift our thinking and feeling can help leaders alter their behavior, influence others, and be more effective. We will discuss perception and the concept of mental models, and look at how qualities such as independent thinking, an open mind, and systems thinking are important for leaders. Then we take a closer look at human emotion as illustrated in the concept of emotional intelligence and the emotions of love versus fear in leader-follower relationships. The next chapter will turn to spirit as reflected in moral leadership and courage.

Leader Capacity versus Competence

Traditionally, effective leadership, like good management, has been thought of as competence in a set of skills; once these specific skills are acquired, all one has to do to succeed is put them into action. However, as we all know from personal experience, working effectively with other people requires much more than practicing specific, rational skills; it often means drawing on subtle aspects of ourselves—our thoughts, beliefs, or feelings—and appealing to those aspects in others. Anyone who has participated on an athletic team knows how powerfully thoughts and emotions can affect performance. Some players are not as highly skilled from a technical standpoint, but put forth amazing performances by playing with heart. Players who can help others draw on these positive emotions and thoughts usually emerge as team leaders.

In today's organizations, just like on the playing field, skills competence is important, but it is not enough. Although leaders have to attend to organizational issues such as production schedules, structure, finances, costs, profits, and so forth, they also tend to human issues, particularly in times of uncertainty and rapid change. Key issues include how to give people a sense of meaning and purpose when major shifts occur almost daily; how to make employees feel valued and respected in an age of downsizing and job uncertainty; and how to keep morale and motivation high in the face of uncertainty and the stress it creates.

In this chapter, rather than discussing competence, we will explore a person's *capacity* for mind and heart. Whereas competence is limited and quantifiable, capacity is unlimited and defined by the potential for expansion and growth.[4] As discussed in the Leader's Bookshelf, a person's ability to learn and grow from life's experiences is an important sign of leadership potential. **Capacity** means the potential each of us has to do more and be more than we are now. The U.S. Army's leadership expression "Be, Know, Do," coined more than 25 years ago, puts *Be* first because who a leader is as a person—his or her character, values, spirit, and ethical center—colors everything else.

Developing leadership capacity goes beyond learning the skills for organizing, planning, or controlling others. It also involves something deeper and more subtle than the leadership traits and styles we discussed in Chapters 2 and 3. Living, working, and leading based on our capacity means using our whole selves, including intellectual, emotional, and spiritual abilities and understandings. A broad literature has emphasized that being a whole person means operating from mind, heart, spirit, and body.[5] Although we can't "learn" capacity the way we learn a set of skills, we can expand and develop leadership capacity. Just as the physical capacity of our lungs is increased through regular aerobic exercise, the capacities of the mind, heart, and spirit can be expanded through conscious development and regular use. In the previous chapter, we introduced some ideas about how individuals think, make decisions, and solve problems based on values, attitudes, and patterns of thinking. This chapter builds on some of those ideas to provide a broader view of the leadership capacities of mind and heart.

Action Memo

As a leader: Expand the capacity of your mind, heart, and spirit by consciously engaging in activities and exercises that use and develop aspects of the whole self. Reflect on your experiences to learn and grow from them.

Capacity
the potential each of us has to do more and be more than we are now

LEADER'S BOOKSHELF

Geeks and Geezers: How Era, Values and Defining Moments Shape Leaders
By Warren G. Bennis, and Robert J. Thomas

Noted leadership scholar Warren G. Bennis and consultant Robert J. Thomas, authors of *Geeks and Geezers: How Era, Values and Defining Moments Shape Leaders*, set out to evaluate the effect of generational era on leader values and success. They conducted extensive interviews with 43 successful leaders they categorized as being either "geeks" (aged 21-34) or "geezers" (aged 70-80).

The most interesting thing Bennis and Thomas discovered from their research, however, wasn't generational differences, but rather what successful leaders from the two eras had in common. Each leader, no matter which generation they belonged to, had experienced at least one life-changing event that enabled his or her leadership ability to emerge. These life changing events (which the authors call "crucibles"), challenged the individual's ability to examine values, identity, and experience and emerge reshaped, improved, and strengthened.

The Four Leadership Competencies
In both generations, successful leaders possess certain attributes that contribute to success.

* *Adaptive capacity.* First and foremost is the capacity to successfully navigate through and grow from a crucible. In each case, the leader was able to respond constructively to life-changing events, grow stronger, and create positive meaning from them.
* *The ability to engage others in shared meaning.* Effective leaders engage others by articulating their own hopes and dreams and involving followers in such a way that a shared vision emerges. As Teach for America founder Wendy Kopp puts it, "the essence of leadership is mobilizing people to achieve great things."
* *Character and a distinctive voice.* "Leadership is always about character," the authors write. People respond to leaders who have "conviction, [a] powerful sense of justice, and [a] passionate desire to do the right thing." Leaders communicate largely through their actions.
* *Integrity and strong values.* Bennis and Thomas suggest that the integrity of a leader is made up of three elements that have to be kept in balance: ambition (having a strong desire to achieve something), competence (mastery of particular skills), and moral compass (strong moral values that acknowledge the leader's role in the larger human community and distinguish between right and wrong). "Let's not mince words," the authors write. "Ambition, absent a moral compass, is naked destructiveness."

A Shared Path to Success
The authors of *Geeks and Geezers* acknowledge that there are genuine generational differences: "Our era determines choices both mundane and profound, from the music we prefer to the things that we long for, the things we take for granted, and much of the emotional coloration of our lives." While we all come of age in a particular environment that shapes us, the core essentials of successful leadership have remained constant across generations.

Geeks and Geezers, by Warren G. Bennis and Robert J. Thomas, is published by Harvard Business School Press.

Mental Models

A mental model can be thought of as an internal picture that affects a leader's actions and relationships with others. Mental models are theories people hold about specific systems in the world and their expected behavior.[6] A system means any set of elements that interact to form a whole and produce a specified outcome. An organization is a system, as is a football team, a sorority pledge drive, a marriage, the registration system at a university, or the claims process at an insurance company. Leaders have many mental models that tend to govern how they interpret experiences and how they act in response to people and situations. For example, one mental model about what makes an effective team is that members share a sense of team ownership and feel that they have authority and responsibility for team actions and outcomes.[7] A leader with this mental model would likely push power, authority, and decision making down to the team level and strive to build norms that create a strong group identity and trust among members. However, a leader with a mental model that every group needs a strong leader who takes control and makes the decisions is less likely to encourage norms that lead to effective teamwork. Exhibit 5.1 shows leader Lynn Mercer's mental model of how her Lucent Technologies factory in Mount Olive, New Jersey, should operate. Mercer shifted the traditional machine-based assembly line to a system based on teamwork, empowerment, and shared information.[8] Mercer's leadership is discussed in more detail in Chapter 15.

Leaders should be aware of how their own and others' mental models affect thinking and may cause blind spots that limit understanding and effectiveness. Indeed, in today's world of rapid and discontinuous change, the greatest factor determining the success of leaders and organizations may be the ability to shift

Mental models
theories people hold about specific systems in the world and their expected behavior

Action Memo

As a leader: Become aware of your mental models and how they affect your thinking and behavior. Don't get trapped by limited assumptions and perceptual distortions. Learn to regard your assumptions as temporary ideas and strive to expand your mind-set.

Exhibit 5.1   **One Leader's Mental Model for the Factory System: Lucent Technologies, Mount Olive, New Jersey**

- Hire attitude over aptitude.
- Create mission from above, methods from below.
- Foster feedback.
- Unite inside and outside.
- Reward teamwork.

SOURCE: Based on Thomas Petzinger, Jr., "How Lynn Mercer Manages a Factory that Manages Itself," *The Wall Street Journal*, March 7, 1997, B1.

one's mental model.[9] Leaders strive to create mental models that are aligned with organizational needs, goals, and values. Consider the administrative assistant at a hospital that emphasized "life-saving" as a core value. While on break chatting with a new employee, the administrative assistant grabbed her cell phone and said she'd be back after making a personal call. Upon her return, the new employee asked if the hospital would "bust you for making personal calls on company phones." She answered, "No, but we're in the business to save lives, and my call wasn't going to save a life."[10] In this case, the employee had a strong mental model that was consistent with the values and goals of the organization. However, personal values, attitudes, beliefs, biases, and prejudices can all affect one's mental models. Two important components of mental models are assumptions and perception.[11]

Assumptions

In the previous chapter, we discussed two very different sets of attitudes and assumptions that leaders may have about subordinates, called Theory X and Theory Y, and how these assumptions affect leader behavior. A leader's assumptions naturally are part of his or her mental model. Someone who assumes that people can't be trusted will act very differently in a situation than someone who has the assumption that people are basically trustworthy. Leaders also have assumptions about events, situations, and circumstances as well as about people. For example, leaders at National Grange Mutual (NGM), a property/casualty insurance company, used to assume that the best way to provide the personalized claims service customers wanted was to have all claims handled on the local level. However, a team of employees explored assumptions about how to provide the greatest value to customers and recommended that NGM establish a national claims adjuster center. Routine calls are now handled at the centralized center, while claims that truly need more personal attention or specialized expertise are referred to regional offices. The result is that claims are turned around 55 percent faster than under the old claims system. Customers are happier, too, because they get paid faster and with less hassle. NGM's customer satisfaction rates continue to climb because leaders acted on new assumptions about the claims system.[12]

This example illustrates how important it is for leaders to regard their assumptions as temporary ideas rather than fixed truths. The more aware a leader is of his or her assumptions, the more the leader understands how assumptions guide behavior. In addition, the leader can begin to question whether long-held assumptions fit the reality of the situation. Questioning assumptions can lead to successful new approaches, as it did at National Grange Mutual. As another example, consider how some charitable foundations have revised their assumptions based on changes in the economic and social environment.

In the Lead   Charles F. Feeney, Atlantic Philanthropies

Charles Feeney recently convinced the board of his Atlantic Philanthropies foundation to do what some once considered unthinkable: *Give it all away*. The foundation adopted a plan to exhaust its $4 billion endowment over a period of about 15 years. Charitable foundations have long functioned on the assumption that they should sustain their endowments and their grant making forever, but Feeney began acting on a different idea—that urgent problems need solving right now and long-term economic growth will take care of the future.

With the stock market slump taking a huge bite out of endowments, the goal of self-perpetuation has put a crimp in charitable giving, and foundations have cut back spending at a time grants are needed even more. Legally, foundations are obligated to distribute only 5 percent of their assets, and many stick close to that limit. It's hard for foundations to break out of this mental model because donors often see a permanent endowment as a permanent legacy. "As I go talk to living donors, I can't offend their desire for immortality," says Mark Kramer, managing director of the Foundation Strategy Group. "But it makes it hard to move the field forward."

Many long-established foundations, such as the John D. and Catherine T. MacArthur Foundation and the Pew Charitable Trust, continue to manage their assets for perpetuity. But a few agree with Feeney that new assumptions are needed to enable foundations to focus on bold problem solving. They believe the returns on "social" investments—improvements in global public health or better opportunities for disadvantaged youth, for example—will be higher than long-term financial returns.

Under the new assumptions, delaying social investment through conservative granting policies to perpetuate the foundation helps no one and harms society. It also means these foundations have a new goal, essentially to put themselves out of business by granting large amounts of money targeted toward major social problems. As Richard Goldman, president of the Richard and Rhoda Goldman Fund in San Francisco puts it, "I think there's too much money accumulating in foundations that should be put to use. The needs are out there, so give it away."[13]

Leaders can become prisoners of their own assumptions. They find themselves simply going along with the traditional way of doing things—whether it be managing a foundation, handling insurance claims, selling cosmetics, or coaching a basketball team—without even realizing they are making decisions and acting within the limited frame of their own mind-sets.[14] For example, successful global managers have learned to expand their mind-sets by questioning assumptions about the "right" way to conduct business. They learn to appreciate and respect other values and methods, yet also look for ways to push beyond the limits of cultural assumptions and find opportunities to innovate.[15] Consider how acting based on limited assumptions hurt Swedish furniture maker Ikea when it first entered the U.S. market. Leaders duplicated traditional Swedish concepts such as no home delivery, a Swedish cafeteria, and beds made the way they were in Sweden (which conformed to Swedish rather than U.S. standards). They seemed almost blind to any other way to conduct business. The company's disappointing performance, however, quickly led leaders to reevaluate their ideas and assumptions and consider how acting from a "Swedish mind-set" was posing a barrier to success in foreign markets.[16]

Perception: How Leaders Interpret Experience

As described in the previous chapter, perception is the process people use to make sense out of the environment by selecting, organizing, and interpreting information from the environment. There are many different ways of processing and interpreting information, which means that perception can vary widely from individual to individual. In terms of the Myers–Briggs psychological types described in the previous chapter, for example, people with a sensing preference base their perceptions largely on what they consider the facts and details of a situation, while intuitive types may rely more on impressions. Perceptions become part of a person's mental model, determining how a leader views people, situations, and events.

Perception occurs so naturally and spontaneously that we rarely think about it. However, perception can be broken down into a step-by-step process, as illustrated in Exhibit 5.2. First, we observe information (sensory data) from the environment through our senses. Next, our mind screens the data and selects only certain items to process further. Third, we organize the selected data into meaningful patterns for interpretation and response. We are all aware of the environment, but not everything in it is equally important to our perception. We tune in to some data (such as a familiar voice off in the distance) and tune out other data (such as paper shuffling next to us). What a person selects to pay attention to depends on a number of factors, including characteristics of the individual as well as characteristics of the stimuli. For example, a leader's values, attitudes, personality, and past experiences all affect the selection of stimuli or sensory data. In addition, characteristics of the data itself affect selection. People tend to notice something that stands out from surrounding stimuli, such as a loud noise in a quiet room. Something that is different from what we're accustomed to also gets noticed more. Thus, a leader might notice an employee who dresses in brightly colored ethnic clothing when everyone else in the office wears dark suits. Furthermore, depending on the leader's values, beliefs, and

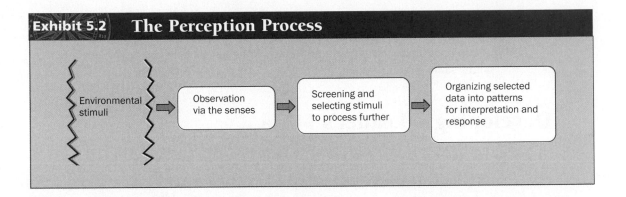

Exhibit 5.2   The Perception Process

Environmental stimuli → Observation via the senses → Screening and selecting stimuli to process further → Organizing selected data into patterns for interpretation and response

assumptions, this perception can lead to either a positive or negative impression of the employee.

By being aware of various factors that affect perception and influence thinking, leaders can avoid some perceptual distortions that are detrimental to the leadership process. One such distortion is **stereotyping**, which is the tendency to assign a person to a group or broad category and then to attribute widely held generalizations about the group to the individual. Stereotypes prevent leaders from getting to know people as individuals and often prevent the individual from contributing fully to the organization. Joe Booker learned all about the power of stereotypes, but his own values and mental model enabled him to build a highly successful leadership career. As the only African American at an Air Force school in Mississippi, Booker was routinely ignored by instructors who held negative stereotypes about minorities. Rather than giving up, Booker only worked harder and ended up scoring tops in his class. He faced similar prejudices at his first assignment at Keeler Air Force Base. Booker overcame stereotypes by taking on the most difficult assignments and becoming an expert, which brought him positive attention. He always focused on where he wanted to go in his career and what jobs could take him there. Since those early days, he has served as CEO of two successful Silicon Valley companies.[17]

Becoming aware of assumptions and perceptions and understanding how they influence emotions and actions is the first step toward being able to shift mental models and see the world in new ways. Leaders can break free from outdated mental models. They can recognize that what worked yesterday may not work today. Following conventional wisdom about "how things have always been done" may be the surest route to failure in a fast-changing environment. Leaders can learn to continually question their own beliefs, assumptions, and perceptions in order to see things in unconventional ways and meet the challenge of the future head on.[18]

Stereotyping
the tendency to assign a person to a group or broad category and then to attribute widely held generalizations about the group to the individual

Leaders like Admiral Albert Konetzni, described in the chapter opening, are constantly questioning the status quo, looking for new ideas, and encouraging novel solutions to problems. They question their own mental models and encourage others to do the same. Issues of the mind are more critical to effective leadership than ever.

Developing a Leader's Mind

How do leaders make the shift to a new mental model? The leader's mind can be developed beyond the nonleader's in four critical areas: independent thinking, open-mindedness, systems thinking, and personal mastery. Taken together, these four disciplines provide a foundation that can help leaders examine their mental models and overcome blind spots that may limit their leadership effectiveness and the success of their organizations.

Independent Thinking

Independent thinking

questioning assumptions and interpreting data and events according to one's own beliefs, ideas, and thinking, rather than pre-established rules or categories defined by others

Mindfulness

the process of continuously reevaluating previously learned ways of doing things in the context of evolving information and shifting circumstances

Independent thinking means questioning assumptions and interpreting data and events according to one's own beliefs, ideas, and thinking, not according to pre-established rules, routines, or categories defined by others. People who think independently are willing to stand apart, to have opinions, to say what they think, and to determine a course of action based on what they personally believe rather than on what other people think. To think independently means staying mentally alert, and thinking critically. Independent thinking is one part of what is called leader mindfulness.[19] **Mindfulness** can be defined as continuously reevaluating previously learned ways of doing things in the context of evolving information and shifting circumstances. Mindfulness involves independent thinking, and also involves leader curiosity and learning. Mindful leaders are open minded and stimulate the thinking of others through their curiosity and questions. Mindfulness is the opposite of *mindlessness*, which means blindly accepting rules and labels created by others. Mindless people let others do the thinking for them, but mindful leaders are always looking for new ideas and approaches.

In the world of organizations, everything is constantly changing. What worked in one situation may not work the next time. In these conditions, mental laziness and accepting others' answers can hurt the organization and all its members. Leaders apply critical thinking to explore a situation, problem, or question from multiple perspectives and integrate all the available information into a possible solution. When leaders think critically, they question all assumptions, vigorously seek divergent opinions, and try to give balanced consideration to all alternatives.[20] Leaders at today's best-performing organizations, for example, deliberately seek board members who can think independently and are willing to challenge senior management or other board members. Consider the board member at Medtronic who stood his ground against the CEO and 11 other members concerning an acquisition. The

board approved the acquisition, but CEO Bill George was so persuaded by the dis-
senter's concerns that he reconvened the board by conference call. After hearing the
dissenting board member's cogent argument that the deal would take Medtronic into
an area it knew nothing about and divert attention from the core business, the board
decided against the deal.[21]

Thinking independently and critically is hard work, and most of us can easily
relax into temporary mindlessness, accepting black-and-white answers and relying
on standard ways of doing things. Companies that have gotten into ethical and legal
trouble in recent years often had executives and board members who failed to question enough or to challenge the status quo.

Leaders also encourage others to be mindful rather than mindless. Bernard Bass,
who has studied charismatic and transformational leadership, talks about the value
of *intellectual stimulation*—arousing followers' thoughts and imaginations as well as
stimulating their ability to identify and solve problems creatively.[22] People admire
leaders who awaken their curiosity, challenge them to think and learn, and encourage openness to new, inspiring ideas and alternatives. You can evaluate your skill in
three dimensions of mindfulness, including intellectual stimulation, by completing
the exercise in Leader's Self-Insight 5.1.

Open-Mindedness

One approach to independent thinking is to try to break out of the mental boxes, the
categorized thinking patterns we have been conditioned to accept as correct. Leaders
have to "keep their mental muscle loose."[23] John Keating, the private school teacher
portrayed in the movie, *Dead Poets Society*, urged his students to stand on their desks
to get a new perspective on the world: "I stand on my desk to remind myself we must
constantly look at things a different way. The world looks different from here."

The power of the conditioning that guides our thinking and behavior is illustrated by what has been called the Pike Syndrome. In an experiment, a northern pike
is placed in one half of a large glass-divided aquarium, with numerous minnows
placed in the other half. The hungry pike makes repeated attempts to get the minnows, but succeeds only in battering itself against the glass, finally learning that trying to reach the minnows is futile. The glass divider is then removed, but the pike
makes no attempt to attack the minnows because it has been conditioned to believe
that reaching them is impossible. When people assume they have complete knowledge of a situation because of past experiences, they exhibit the Pike Syndrome, a
trained incapacity that comes from rigid commitment to what was true in the past
and a refusal to consider alternatives and different perspectives.[24]

Leaders have to forget many of their conditioned ideas to be open to new ones.
This openness—putting aside preconceptions and suspending beliefs and opinions—can be referred to as "beginner's mind." Whereas the expert's mind rejects
new ideas based on past experience and knowledge, the beginner's mind reflects

Action Memo

As a leader:
Think inde-
pendently. Don't
let others do
your thinking
for you. Be
curious, keep an
open mind, look
at a problem or
situation from
multiple per-
spectives before
reaching your
conclusions.
Challenge pre-
established
rules and
routines if they
are detrimental
to the
organization.

LEADER'S SELF-INSIGHT 5.1

Mindfulness

Think back to how you behaved toward others at work or in a group when you were in a formal or informal leadership position. Please answer the following questions based on how frequently you did each behavior.

1 = Not at all; 2 = Once in a while; 3 = Sometimes; 4 = Fairly often; 5 = Frequently

	Not at all			Frequently	
1. Enjoyed hearing new ideas.	1	2	3	4	5
2. Challenged someone to think about an old problem in a new way.	1	2	3	4	5
3. Tried to carry the conversation to a higher level.	1	2	3	4	5
4. Appreciated the viewpoints of others.	1	2	3	4	5
5. Would ask someone about the assumptions underlying his or her suggestions.	1	2	3	4	5
6. Came to my own conclusion despite what others thought.	1	2	3	4	5
7. Was open about myself to others.	1	2	3	4	5
8. Encouraged others to express opposing ideas and arguments.	1	2	3	4	5
9. Did not probe deeply into a subject.	1	2	3	4	5
10. Fought for my own ideas.	1	2	3	4	5
11. Asked "dumb" questions.	1	2	3	4	5
12. Offered insightful comments on the meaning of data or issues.	1	2	3	4	5
13. Experienced a sense of wonder.	1	2	3	4	5
14. Asked questions to prompt others to think more about an issue.	1	2	3	4	5
15. Expressed a controversial opinion.	1	2	3	4	5
16. Welcomed opposite points of view.	1	2	3	4	5
17. Suggested ways of improving my and others' ways of doing things.	1	2	3	4	5

Scoring and Interpretation

Reverse score questions 9 and 10 (1 = 5, 2 = 4, 4 = 2, 5 = 1). There are three subscale scores that represent three dimensions of leader mindfulness. For the dimension of *open* or *beginner's mind*, sum your responses to questions 1, 4, 7, 10, 13, and 16, and divide by 6. For the dimension of *independent thinking*, sum your scores for questions 3, 6, 9, 12, 15, and 17, and divide by 6. For the dimension of *intellectual stimulation*, sum your scores for questions 2, 5, 8, 11, and 14, and divide by 5.

My average scores are:

Open or beginner's mind   _____

Independent Thinking   _____

Intellectual Stimulation   _____

These scores represent three aspects of leader mindfulness—what is called open mind or beginner's mind, independent thinking, and intellectual stimulation. An average score of 4.0 or above on any of these dimensions is considered high because many people do not practice mindfulness in their leadership or group work. A score of 2.5 is about average, and below 2.0 is below average. Compare your three scores to understand your own practice of mindfulness. Analyze the specific questions on which you scored higher or lower to see more deeply into your pattern of mindfulness strengths or weaknesses. Open mind, independent thinking, and intellectual stimulation are important qualities to develop for effective leadership.

SOURCES: The questions above are based on ideas from R. L. Daft and R. M. Lengel, *Fusion Leadership*, Chapter 4, (Berrett Koehler, 2000); B. Bass and B. Avolio, *Multifactor Leadership Questionnaire*, 2nd ed. (Mind Garden, Inc.); and P. M. Podsakoff, S. B. MacKenzie, R. H. Moorman, and R. Fetter, "Transformational Leader Behaviors and Their Effects on Followers' Trust in Leader, Satisfaction, and Organizational Citizenship Behaviors," *Leadership Quarterly* 1, no. 2 (1990), 107–42.

the openness and innocence of a young child just learning about the world. The value of a beginner's mind is captured in the story told in this chapter's Living Leadership box.

Nobel prize-winning physicist Richard Feynman, one of the most original scientific minds of the twentieth century, illustrates the power of the beginner's mind. Feynman's IQ was an unremarkable 125. The heart of his genius was a childlike curiosity and a belief that doubt was the essence of learning and knowing. Feynman was always questioning, always uncertain, always starting over, always resisting any authority that prevented him from doing his own thinking and exploring.[25]

Effective leaders strive to keep open minds and cultivate an organizational environment that encourages curiosity. They understand the limitations of past experience and reach out for diverse perspectives. Rather than seeing any questioning of their ideas as a threat, these leaders encourage everyone throughout the organization to openly debate assumptions, confront paradoxes, question perceptions, and express feelings.[26]

Some companies, such as Microsoft, Southwest Airlines, and Manco, make curiosity and interest in learning a more important hiring criterion than experience or expertise. Leaders can also support and reward people who are willing to ask questions, stretch boundaries, experiment, and keep learning. At Manco, employees can enroll in any outside course they choose, whether it's business management or basketweaving, and be reimbursed as long as they pass the course. CEO Jack Krahl's rationale is that "It lets people know . . . that one of the highest values at Manco is to be curious and to allow curiosity to take place."[27]

Leaders can use a variety of approaches to help themselves and others keep an open mind. At McKinsey & Co., worldwide managing director Rajat Gupta reads poetry at the end of the partners' regular meetings. Poetry and literature, he says, "help us think in more well-rounded ways. . . . Poetry helps us reflect on the important questions: What is the purpose of our business? What are our values? Poetry helps us recognize that we face tough questions and that we seldom have perfect answers."[28]

Systems Thinking

Systems thinking

the ability to see the synergy of the whole rather than just the separate elements of a system and to learn to reinforce or change whole system patterns

Systems thinking means the ability to see the synergy of the whole rather than just the separate elements of a system and to learn to reinforce or change whole system patterns.[29] Many people have been trained to solve problems by breaking a complex system, such as an organization, into discrete parts and working to make each part perform as well as possible. However, the success of each piece does not add up to the success of the whole. In fact, sometimes changing one part to make it better actually makes the whole system function less effectively. New drugs have been a lifesaver for people living with HIV, for example, but the drop in mortality rates has led to a reduction in perceived risk and therefore more incidences of risky behavior. After years of decline, HIV infection rates are once again rising, indicating that the system of HIV treatment is not well understood. California's partial deregulation of the electricity market was designed to lower costs to consumers, but poor understanding of the overall system contributed to rolling blackouts, record rates, and political and economic turmoil. Or consider a small city that embarked on a road building program to solve traffic congestion without whole-systems thinking. With new roads available, more people began moving to the suburbs. The solution actually increased traffic congestion, delays, and pollution by enabling suburban sprawl.[30]

It is the *relationship* among the parts that form a whole system—whether it be a community, an automobile, a nonprofit agency, a human being, or a business organization—that matters. Systems thinking enables leaders to look for patterns of movement over time and focus on the qualities of rhythm, flow, direction, shape, and networks of relationships that accomplish the performance of the whole. Systems thinking is a mental discipline and framework for seeing patterns and interrelationships.

It is important to see organizational systems as a whole because of their complexity. Complexity can overwhelm leaders, undermining confidence. When leaders can see the structures that underlie complex situations, they can facilitate improvement. But it requires a focus on the big picture. Leaders can develop what David McCamus, former Chairman and CEO of Xerox Canada, calls "peripheral vision"—the ability to view the organization through a wide-angle lens, rather than a telephoto lens—so that they perceive how their decisions and actions affect the whole.[31]

An important element of systems thinking is to discern circles of causality. Peter Senge, author of *The Fifth Discipline*, argues that reality is made up of circles rather than straight lines. For example, Exhibit 5.3 shows circles of influence for producing new products. In the circle on the left, a high-tech firm grows rapidly by pumping out new products quickly. New products increase revenues, which enable the further increase of the R&D budget to add more new products.

But another circle of causality is being influenced as well. As the R&D budget grows, the engineering and research staff increases. The burgeoning technical staff becomes increasingly hard to manage. The management burden falls on senior engineers, who provide less of their time for developing new products, which slows product development time. The slowing of product development time has a negative impact on new products, the very thing that created organizational success. Maintaining product development time in the face of increasing management complexity depends upon senior engineers' management ability. Thus, understanding the circle of causality enables leaders to allocate resources to the training and development of engineering leadership as well as directly to new products. Without an understanding of the system, top leaders would fail to understand why increasing R&D budgets can actually increase product development time and reduce the number of new products coming to market.

Action Memo

As a leader: Cultivate an ability to see whole systems rather than collections of separate parts. Analyze and understand the relationships among parts of a team, organization, family, or other system to avoid making changes that have unintended negative consequences.

Exhibit 5.3   Two Circles of Causality in an Organization

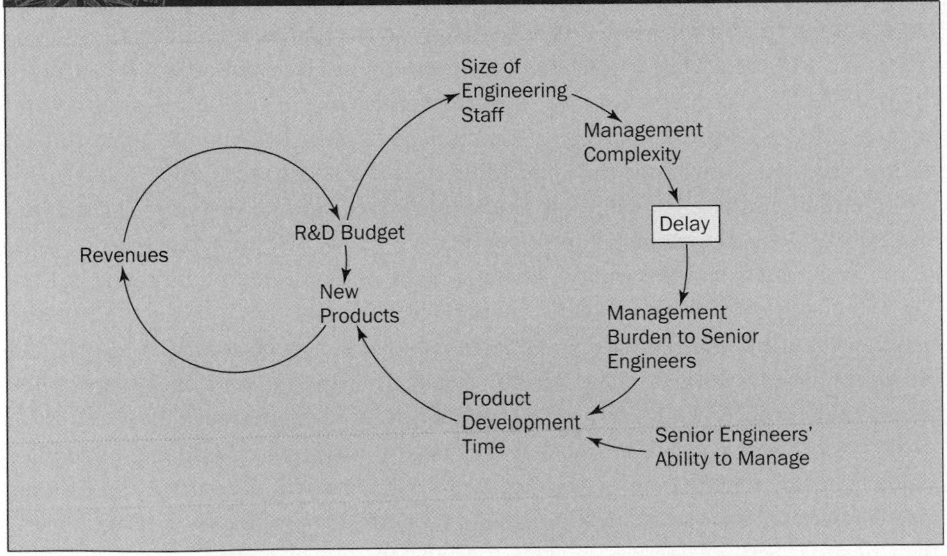

SOURCE: From *The Fifth Discipline: The Art and Practice of the Learning Organization* by Peter M. Senge, 97. Copyright © 1990 by Peter M. Senge. Used by permission of Doubleday, a division of Bantam Doubleday Dell Publishing Group, Inc.

The other element of systems thinking is learning to influence the system with reinforcing feedback as an engine for growth or decline. In the example of new products, after managers see how the system works, they can allocate revenues to speed new products to market, either by hiring more engineers, or by training senior engineers in management and leadership skills. They can guide the system when they understand it conceptually. Without this kind of understanding, managers will hit blockages in the form of seeming limits to growth and resistance to change because the large complex system will appear impossible to manage. Systems thinking is a significant solution.

Personal Mastery

Another concept introduced by Senge is *personal mastery*, a term he uses to describe the discipline of personal growth and learning, of mastering yourself in a way that facilitates your leadership and achieves desired results.[32]

Personal mastery embodies three qualities—personal vision, facing reality, and holding creative tension. First, leaders engaged in personal mastery know and clarify what is important to them. They focus on the end result, the vision or dream that motivates them and their organization. They have a clear vision of a desired future, and their purpose is to achieve that future. One element of personal mastery, then, is the discipline of continually focusing and defining what one wants as their desired future and vision.

Second, facing reality means a commitment to the truth. Leaders are relentless in uncovering the mental models that limit and deceive them and are willing to challenge assumptions and ways of doing things. These leaders are committed to the truth, and will break through denial of reality in themselves and others. Their quest for truth leads to a deeper awareness of themselves and of the larger systems and events within which they operate. Commitment to the truth enables them to deal with reality, which increases the opportunity to achieve desired results.

Third, often there is a large gap between one's vision and the current situation. The gap between the desired future and today's reality, say between the dream of starting a business and the reality of having no capital, can be discouraging. But the gap is the source of creative energy. Acknowledging and living with the disparity between the truth and the vision, and facing it squarely, is the source of resolve and creativity to move forward. The effective leader resolves the tension by letting the vision pull reality toward it, in other words, by reorganizing current activities to work toward the vision. The leader works in a way that moves things toward the vision. The less effective way is to let reality pull the vision downward toward it. This means lowering the vision, such as walking away from a problem or settling for less than desired. Settling for less releases the tension, but also engenders mediocrity. Leaders with personal mastery learn to accept both the dream and the reality simultaneously, and to close the gap by moving toward the dream.

Personal mastery

the discipline of personal growth and learning and of mastering yourself; it embodies personal visions, facing reality, and holding creative tension

All five elements of mind are interrelated. Independent thinking and open-mindedness improve systems thinking and enable personal mastery, helping leaders shift and expand their mental models. Since they are all interdependent, leaders working to improve even one element of their mental approach can move forward in a significant way toward mastering their minds and becoming more effective.

Emotional Intelligence— Leading with Heart and Mind

Psychologists and other researchers, as well as leaders in all walks of life, are increasingly recognizing the critical importance of emotional intelligence. Some have suggested that emotion, more than intellectual ability, drives our thinking and decision making, as well as our interpersonal relationships.[33] Emotional intelligence refers to a person's abilities to perceive, identify, understand, and successfully manage emotions in self and others. Being emotionally intelligent means being able to effectively manage ourselves and our relationships.[34]

Emotional intelligence
a person's abilities to perceive, identify, understand, and successfully manage emotions in self and others

Emotional understanding and skills impact our success and happiness in our work as well as our personal lives. Leaders can harness and direct the power of emotions to improve follower satisfaction, morale, and motivation, as well as to enhance overall organizational effectiveness. Moreover, in a study of entrepreneurs, researchers at Rensselaer Polytechnic Institute found that those who are more expressive of their own emotions and in tune with the emotions of others make more money, as illustrated in Exhibit 5.4.

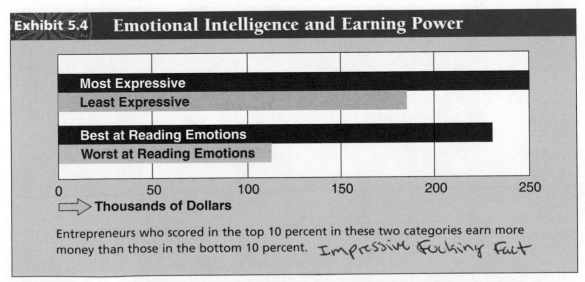

Exhibit 5.4 | Emotional Intelligence and Earning Power

Most Expressive
Least Expressive

Best at Reading Emotions
Worst at Reading Emotions

0   50   100   150   200   250
⇨ Thousands of Dollars

Entrepreneurs who scored in the top 10 percent in these two categories earn more money than those in the bottom 10 percent. *Impressive fucking fact*

SOURCE: Rensselaer Polytechnic Institute, Lally School of Management and Technology, as reported in *BusinessWeek Frontier* (February 5, 2001): F4.

Action Memo

As a leader: Develop emotional intelligence to enhance your personal and work life. Remember that emotions can be contagious, so act as a positive role model by being optimistic and enthusiastic. Don't leave your emotions at home or expect your followers to do so.

Some leaders act as if people leave their emotions at home when they come to work, but we all know this isn't true. "There are companies that don't want people to talk about their personal lives," says Paula Lawlor of MediHealth Outsourcing. "But I say, 'Bring it on.' If people can get something off their chests for an hour, then I've got them for the next 10."[35]

What Are Emotions?

There are hundreds of emotions and more subtleties of emotion than there are words to explain them. One important ability for leaders is to understand the range of emotions people have and how these emotions may manifest themselves. Many researchers accept eight categories or "families" of emotions, as illustrated in Exhibit 5.5.[36] These categories do not resolve every question about how to categorize emotions, and scientific debate continues. The argument for there being a set of core emotions is based partly on the discovery that specific facial expressions for four of them (fear, anger, sadness, and enjoyment) are universally recognized. People in cultures around the world have been found to recognize these same basic emotions when shown photographs of facial expressions. The primary emotions and some of their variations follow.

* *Anger:* fury, outrage, resentment, exasperation, indignation, animosity, annoyance, irritability, hostility, violence.
* *Sadness:* grief, sorrow, gloom, melancholy, self-pity, loneliness, dejection, despair, depression.

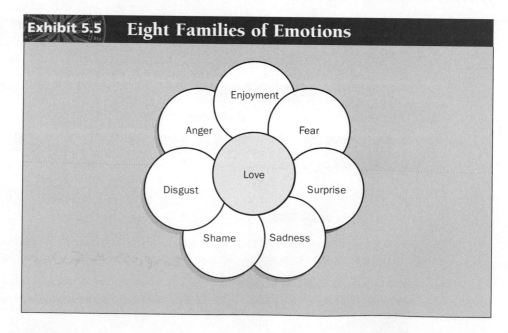

Exhibit 5.5   Eight Families of Emotions

❋ *Fear:* anxiety, apprehension, nervousness, concern, consternation, wariness, edginess, dread, fright, terror, panic.

❋ *Enjoyment:* happiness, joy, relief, contentment, delight, amusement, pride, sensual pleasure, thrill, rapture, gratification, satisfaction, euphoria.

❋ *Love:* acceptance, respect, friendliness, trust, kindness, affinity, devotion, adoration, infatuation.

❋ *Surprise:* shock, astonishment, amazement, wonder.

❋ *Disgust:* contempt, disdain, scorn, abhorrence, aversion, distaste, revulsion.

❋ *Shame:* guilt, embarrassment, chagrin, remorse, humiliation, regret, mortification, contrition.

Leaders who are attuned to their own feelings and the feelings of others can use their understanding to enhance the organization.

The Components of Emotional Intelligence

The competencies and abilities of emotional intelligence are grouped into four fundamental categories, as illustrated in Exhibit 5.6.[37] It is important to remember that emotional intelligence can be learned and developed. Anyone can strengthen his or her abilities in these four categories.

Exhibit 5.6	The Components of Emotional Intelligence

	SELF	OTHERS
AWARENESS	**Self-Awareness** • Emotional self-awareness • Accurate self-assessment • Self-confidence	**Social Awareness** • Empathy • Organizational awareness • Service orientation
BEHAVIOR	**Self-Management** • Emotional self-control • Trustworthiness • Conscientiousness • Adaptability • Optimism • Achievement-orientation • Initiative	**Relationship Management** • Development of others • Inspirational leadership • Influence • Communication • Change catalyst • Conflict management • Bond building • Teamwork and collaboration

SOURCE: Adapted from Richard E. Boyatzis and Daniel Goleman, *The Emotional Competence Inventory—University Edition* (Boston, Mass: The Hay Group, 2001).

Self-awareness might be considered the basis of all the other competencies. It includes the ability to recognize and understand your own emotions and how they affect your life and work. People who are in touch with their emotions are better able to guide their own lives. Leaders with a high level of self-awareness learn to trust their "gut feelings" and realize that these feelings can provide useful information about difficult decisions. Answers are not always clear as to whether to propose a major deal, let an employee go, reorganize a business, or revise job responsibilities. When the answers are not available from external sources, leaders have to rely on their own feelings. This component also includes the ability to accurately assess your own strengths and limitations, along with a healthy sense of self-confidence.

Self-management, the second key component, includes the ability to control disruptive or harmful emotions. Leaders learn to balance their own emotions so that worry, anxiety, fear, or anger do not get in the way, thus enabling them to think clearly and be more effective. Managing emotions does not mean suppressing or denying them but understanding them and using that understanding to deal with situations productively.[38]

Other characteristics in this category include *trustworthiness*, which means consistently displaying honesty and integrity, *conscientiousness*, which means managing and honoring your responsibilities, and *adaptability*, the ability to adjust to changing situations and overcome obstacles. Showing initiative to seize opportunities and achieve high internal standards is also a part of self-management. Leaders skilled at self-management remain hopeful and optimistic despite obstacles, setbacks, or even outright failures.

Martin Seligman, a professor of psychology at the University of Pennsylvania, once advised the MetLife insurance company to hire a special group of job applicants who tested high on optimism but failed the normal sales aptitude test. Compared to salespeople who passed the regular aptitude test but scored high on pessimism, the "optimistic" group made 21 percent more sales in their first year and 57 percent more in the second.[39]

Social awareness relates to one's ability to understand others. Socially aware leaders practice **empathy**, which means being able to put yourself in other people's shoes, sense their emotions, and understand their perspective. These leaders are capable of understanding divergent points of view and interacting effectively with many different types of people and emotions. The characteristic of *organizational awareness* refers to the ability to navigate the currents of organizational life, build networks, and effectively use political behavior to accomplish positive results. This component also includes a *service orientation*, which refers to the ability to recognize and serve the needs of employees, customers, or clients.

Relationship management refers to the ability to connect with others and build positive relationships. Leaders with high emotional intelligence treat others with compassion, sensitivity, and kindness.[40] This aspect of EQ encompasses developing others, inspiring others with a powerful vision, learning to listen and communicate clearly and convincingly, and using emotional understanding to influence others in positive ways. Leaders use their understanding of emotions to inspire change and lead people toward something better, to build teamwork and collaboration, and to resolve conflicts that inevitably arise. These leaders cultivate and maintain a web of relationships both within and outside the organization.

Taken together, these four components build a strong base of emotional intelligence that leaders can use to more effectively guide teams and organizations. Recent research by the consulting firm Hay/McBer identified six effective leadership styles, all arising from different components of emotional intelligence.[41] The best leaders use all of the components to combine styles or vary their styles, depending on the situation or problem at hand. By being sensitive to their own and others' emotions, these leaders can recognize what effect they are having on followers and seamlessly adjust their approach to create a positive result. Consider how Joe Torre uses his emotional intelligence to bring out the best in his players.

> **Action Memo**
>
> As a leader: Recognize and manage your own emotions so that negative feelings don't cloud your mind, distort your judgment, or cripple your ability to lead.

In the Lead   Joe Torre, New York Yankees

Joe Torre, coach of the New York Yankees, believes success means "playing—or working—to the best of your abilities." For Torre, a leader's job is to help people fulfill their potential as individuals and as members of a team—an approach that requires putting the needs and feelings of followers first.

Torre's leadership is based on knowing his team members as individuals and treating everyone with fairness, trust, and respect, the three elements he considers essential for productive relationships. Torre doesn't give a lot of big, motivational speeches. Instead, he relies mostly on one-on-one communication. He watches, listens, and tries to understand the needs, motivations, and problems of each player, recognizing that what's going on in a player's personal life affects performance on the field. If he has to sort out a problem with a player, he does so in private, never using fear, manipulation, or public humiliation to motivate or control people. On the other hand, praise is lavished in public. During the 1999 World Series, Torre made a special point to publicly praise Scott Brosius, whose father had died during the season, for staying committed to the team even as he mourned the loss of his father. During the victory celebration after the final game, he heaped praise on other players for their unique contributions.

> Torre never treats a player differently just because he isn't playing well. He makes his goals and standards clear and lets everyone know how they're contributing to the team, but he knows that everyone sometimes hits a slump. By standing by the player and maintaining confidence in him, Torre helps the player regain confidence in himself. His emphasis on people and relationships has created a high-performance organization where mistakes and failure are accepted as part of being human. Emotions are channeled toward creating a positive rather than a negative impact.[42]

Joe Torre has created the kind of workplace that many of today's organizations need. In an environment where relationships with employees and customers are becoming more important than technology and material resources, interest in developing leaders' emotional intelligence continues to grow. You can evaluate your level of emotional intelligence by completing the questionnaire in Leader's Self-Insight 5.2. All leaders have to pay attention to the emotional climate in their organizations. Recent world events have thrust emotions to the forefront for both individuals and organizations.

Implications for Leadership

How is emotional intelligence related to effective leadership? For one thing, a leader's emotional abilities and understandings play a key role in charismatic and transformational leadership behavior, as described in the previous chapter.[43] Charismatic leaders generally hold strong emotional convictions and appeal to followers on an emotional basis. Transformational leaders project an inspiring vision for change and motivate followers to achieve it, which requires using all the components of emotional intelligence. Charismatic and transformational leaders typically exhibit self-confidence, determination, and persistence in the face of adversity.

A high level of self-awareness, combined with the ability to manage one's own emotions, enables a leader to display self-confidence and earn the respect and trust of followers. In addition, the ability to manage or temporarily restrain one's emotions can enable a leader to objectively consider the needs of others over his or her own immediate feelings. Giving in to strong feelings of anger or depression, for example, may intensify a self-centered focus on one's own needs and limit the ability of the leader to understand the needs of others or see things from other perspectives.

The emotional state of the leader impacts the entire group, department, or organization. Most of us recognize that we can "catch" emotions from others. If we're around someone who is smiling and enthusiastic, the positive emotions rub off on us. Conversely, someone in a bad mood can bring us down. This *emotional contagion*[44] means that leaders who are able to maintain balance and keep themselves motivated are positive role models to help motivate and inspire those around them.

Action Memo

As a leader: Empathize with others so you can interact effectively with different people and emotions. Treat people with compassion and sensitivity, build teamwork, and learn to listen, interpret emotions, and resolve interpersonal conflicts. Cultivate and maintain a web of emotional relationships at work and in your personal life.

Emotional Intelligence

For each item below, rate how well you are able to display the ability described. Before responding, try to think of actual situations in which you have had the opportunity to use the ability.

	Very slight ability	Moderate ability			Very much ability
1. Associate different internal physiological cues with different emotions.	1	2	③	4	5
2. Relax when under pressure in situations.	1	2	3	④	5
3. Know the impact that your behavior has on others.	1	2	3	④	5
4. Initiate successful resolution of conflict with others.	1	②	3	4	5
5. Calm yourself quickly when angry.	1	2	3	④	5
6. Know when you are becoming angry.	1	2	3	④	5
7. Recognize when others are distressed.	1	2	③	4	5
8. Build consensus with others.	1	2	3	4	5
9. Know what senses you are currently using.	1	2	3	4	5
10. Produce motivation when doing uninteresting work.	1	2	3	4	5
11. Help others manage their emotions.	1	2	3	4	5
12. Make others feel good.	1	2	3	4	5
13. Identify when you experience mood shifts.	1	2	3	4	5
14. Stay calm when you are the target of anger from others.	1	2	3	4	5
15. Show empathy to others.	1	2	3	4	5
16. Provide advice and emotional support to others as needed.	1	2	3	4	5
17. Know when you become defensive.	1	2	3	4	5
18. Follow your words with actions.	1	2	3	4	5
19. Engage in intimate conversations with others.	1	2	3	4	5
20. Accurately reflect people's feelings back to them.	1	2	3	4	5

Scoring

Sum your responses to the twenty questions to obtain your overall emotional intelligence score. Your score for self-awareness is the total of questions 1, 6, 9, 13, and 17. Your score for self-management is the total of questions 2, 5, 10, 14, and 18. Your score for social awareness is the sum of questions 3, 7, 11, 15, and 19. Your score for relationship management is the sum of questions 4, 8, 12, 16, and 20.

Interpretation

This questionnaire provides some indication of your emotional intelligence. If you received a total score of 80 or more, you are certainly considered a person with high emotional intelligence. A score from 50 to 80 means you have a good platform of emotional intelligence from which to develop your leadership capability. A score below 50 indicates that you realize that you are probably below average in emotional intelligence. For each of the four components of emotional intelligence—self-awareness, self-management, social awareness, and relationship management—a score above 20 is considered high, while a score below 10 would be considered low. Review the discussion earlier in this chapter of the four components of emotional intelligence and think about what you might do to develop those areas where you scored low. Compare your scores to those of other students. What will you do to improve your scores?

SOURCE: Adapted from Hendrie Weisinger, *Emotional Intelligence at Work* (San Francisco: Jossey-Bass, 1998), 214–215.

The energy level of the entire organization increases when leaders are optimistic and hopeful. The ability to empathize with others and to manage interpersonal relationships also contributes to motivation and inspiration because it helps leaders create feelings of unity and team spirit.

Perhaps most importantly, emotional intelligence enables leaders to recognize and respect followers as whole human beings with feelings, opinions, and ideas of their own. Leaders treat followers as individuals with unique needs, abilities, and dreams. They can use their emotional intelligence to help followers grow and develop, see and enhance their self-image and feelings of self-worth, and help meet their needs and achieve their personal goals.

Emotionally intelligent leaders can have a positive impact on organizations by helping employees grow, learn, and develop; creating a sense of purpose and meaning; instilling unity and team spirit; and building relationships of trust and respect that allow each employee to take risks and fully contribute to the organization.

The Emotional Intelligence of Teams

Much of the work in today's organizations, even at top management levels, is done in teams rather than by individuals. Although most studies of emotional intelligence have focused on individuals, research is beginning to emerge concerning how emotional intelligence relates to teams. For example, one study found that untrained teams made up of members with high emotional intelligence performed as well as trained teams made up of members who rated low on emotional intelligence.[45] The high emotional intelligence of the untrained team members enabled them to assess and adapt to the requirements of teamwork and the tasks at hand.

Moreover, research has suggested that emotional intelligence can be developed as a *team* competency and not just an individual competency.[46] That is, teams themselves—not just their individual members—can become emotionally intelligent Leaders build the emotional intelligence of teams by creating norms that support emotional development and influence emotions in constructive ways. Emotionally intelligent team norms are those that (1) create a strong group identity, (2) build trust among members, and (3) instill a belief among members that they can be effective and succeed as a team.

Leaders "tune in" to the team's emotional state and look for unhealthy or unproductive norms that inhibit cooperation and team harmony.[47] Building the emotional intelligence of the team means exploring unhealthy norms, deliberately bringing emotions to the surface, and understanding how they affect the team's work. Raising these issues can be uncomfortable, and a leader needs both courage and individual emotional intelligence to guide a team through the process. Only by getting emotions into the open can the team build new norms and move to a higher level of group satisfaction and performance. Leaders continue to build emotional intelligence by encouraging and enabling the team to explore and use emotion in its everyday work.

Leading with Love versus Leading with Fear

You wouldn't expect a high-ranking military officer to go around spouting talk about love, but that's exactly what Rear Admiral Albert Konetzni, described in the chapter opening, does. One of his favorite phrases, is, "I love you guys." He repeats variations of it dozens of times a day—to fellow admirals, sailors, and others he comes in contact with. Konetzni's leadership approach, of course, reflects his own personality and style—not all leaders would feel comfortable with such an open approach. However, many leaders are learning that an environment that reflects care and respect for people is much more effective than one in which people are fearful. Love in the workplace means genuinely caring for others and sharing one's knowledge, understanding, and compassion to enable others to grow and succeed.

Traditionally, leadership in many organizations has been based on fear. An unspoken notion among many senior-level executives is that fear is a good thing and benefits the organization.[48] Indeed, fear can be a powerful motivator. When organizational success depended primarily on people mindlessly following orders, leading with fear often met the organization's needs. Today, however, success depends on the knowledge, mind-power, commitment, and enthusiasm of everyone in the organization. A fear-based organization loses its best people, and the knowledge they take with them, to other firms. In addition, even if people stay with the organization, they typically don't perform up to their real capabilities.

One major drawback of leading with fear is that it creates avoidance behavior, because no one wants to make a mistake, and this inhibits growth and change. Leaders can learn to bind people together for a shared purpose through more positive forces such as caring and compassion, listening, and connecting to others on a personal level. The emotion that attracts people to take risks, learn, grow, and move the organization forward comes from love, not fear.

Showing respect and trust not only enables people to perform better; it also allows them to feel emotionally connected with their work so that their lives are richer and more balanced. Leaders can rely on negative emotions such as fear to fuel productive work, but by doing so they may slowly destroy people's spirits, which ultimately is bad for employees and the organization.[49]

Fear in Organizations

The workplace can hold many kinds of fear, including fear of failure, fear of change, fear of personal loss, and fear of the boss. All of these fears can prevent people from doing their best, from taking risks, and from challenging and changing the status quo. Fear gets in the way of people feeling good about their work, themselves, and the organization. It creates an atmosphere in which people feel powerless, so that their confidence, commitment, enthusiasm, imagination, and motivation are diminished.[50]

Aspects of Fear A particularly damaging aspect of fear in the workplace is that it can weaken trust and communication. Employees feel threatened by repercussions if they speak up about work-related concerns. A survey of employees in 22 organizations around the country found that 70 percent of them "bit their tongues" at work because they feared repercussions. Twenty-seven percent reported that they feared losing their credibility or reputation if they spoke up. Other fears reported were lack of career advancement, possible damage to the relationship with their supervisor, demotion or losing their job, and being embarrassed or humiliated in front of others.[51] When people are afraid to speak up, important issues are suppressed and problems hidden. Employees are afraid to talk about a wide range of issues. These "undiscussables" can range from the poor performance of a co-worker to concerns over benefits to suggestions for organizational improvement. However, by far the largest category of undiscussables is the behavior of executives, particularly their interpersonal and relationship skills. When fear is high, managers destroy the opportunity for feedback, blinding them to reality and denying them the chance to correct damaging decisions and behaviors.

Relationship with Leaders Leaders control the fear level in the organization. We all know from personal experience that it is easier to report bad news to some people than to others. A boss or teacher who is understanding and compassionate is much easier to approach than one who is likely to blow up and scream at us. The relationship between an employee and supervisor is the primary factor determining the level of fear experienced at work. The legacy of fear and mistrust associated with traditional hierarchies in which bosses gave orders and employees jumped to obey "or else" still colors organizational life. Leaders are responsible for creating a new environment that enables people to feel safe speaking their minds. Leaders can act from love rather than fear to free employees and the organization from the chains of the past.

Bringing Love to Work

When leaders act from their own fear, they create fear in others. Organizations have traditionally rewarded people for strong qualities such as rational thinking, ambition, and competitiveness. These qualities are important, but their overemphasis has left many organizational leaders out of touch with their softer, caring, creative capabilities, unable to make emotional connections with others and afraid to risk showing any sign of "weakness." A leader's fear can manifest itself in arrogance, selfishness, deception, unfairness, and disrespect for others.[52]

Leaders can learn to develop their capacity for the positive emotions of love and caring. Former General Electric chairman and CEO Jack Welch was known as something of a hard-nosed manager, but he was also a master at leading with love, and followers responded, contributing to growth and success for the organization. Jeffrey Immelt, who succeeded Welch as CEO, recalls the comment Welch made to him once when he'd had a terrible year: "I love you and I know you can do better."[53] Another leader who discovered within himself the capacity to lead with love rather than fear is Andy Pearson, founding chairman and former CEO of Tricon Global Restaurants.

In the Lead   Andy Pearson, Tricon Global Restaurants

When he was CEO of PepsiCo Inc., Andy Pearson was named one of the ten toughest bosses in the United States by *Fortune* magazine. He was notorious for his brutal management style and the extreme, relentless demands he put on his subordinates. Twenty years later, as founding chairman and former CEO of Tricon Global Restaurants, Pearson is still tough, but he's learned that demanding high standards doesn't have to mean inflicting pain. Today, he leads not with fear, surprise, and intimidation but with humility, respect, and genuine caring.

Pearson began his transformation when he started asking himself what it would take to unleash the power of everyone in the organization. He had noticed how his co-leader David Novak (now Tricon's CEO) inspired people with his warmth, energy, and personal attention. He saw employees actually weep with gratitude in reaction to little more than a few words of praise from Novak. And gradually, he began to see how tapping into positive human emotions was the key driver of success at Tricon, which owns 30,000 KFC, Taco Bell, and Pizza Hut restaurants around the world.

Pearson's new approach to leadership is not to issue orders but to seek answers from others. He talks and listens to people throughout the company and makes an enormous effort to let people know their individual contribution is vital to the organization's success. If he disagrees with something, rather than beating people down and belittling their ideas, as the "old" Andy Pearson would have done, he will challenge them to think about the problem in a different light.

Most significantly, Pearson now considers caring about others and giving people recognition and approval a sign of leadership strength rather than weakness. "There's a human yearning for a certain amount of toughness," Pearson says. "But it can't be unmitigated toughness." What's his advice for successful leadership in today's workplace? "Ultimately, it's all about having more genuine concern for the other person," Pearson says. "There's an important aspect [of leadership] that has to do with humility."[54]

Most of us have experienced the power of love at some time in our lives. There are many different kinds of love—for example, the love of a mother for her child, romantic love, brotherly love, or the love of country, as well as the love some people feel for certain sports, hobbies, or recreational pursuits.

Despite its power, the "L" word is often looked upon with suspicion in the business world.[55] However, there are a number of aspects of love that are directly relevant to work relationships and organizational performance.

Love as motivation is the force within that enables people to feel alive, connected, energized, and "in love" with life and work. Western cultures place great emphasis on the mind and the rational approach. However, it is the heart rather than the mind that powers people forward. Recall a time when you wanted to do something with all your heart, and how your energy and motivation flowed freely. Also recall a time when your head said you had to do a task, but your heart was not in it. Motivation is reduced, perhaps to the point of procrastination. There's a growing interest in helping people feel a genuine passion for their work.[56] People who are engaged rather than alienated from their work are typically more satisfied, productive, and successful. The best leaders are those who love what they do, because they infect others with their enthusiasm and passion.

Love as feelings involves attraction, fascination, and caring for people, work, or other things. This is what people most often think of as love, particularly in relation to romantic love between two people. However, love as feelings is also relevant in work situations. Feelings of compassion and caring for others are a manifestation of love, as are forgiveness, sincerity, respect, and loyalty, all of which are important for healthy working relationships. One personal feeling is *bliss*, best articulated for the general public by Joseph Campbell in his PBS television series and companion book with Bill Moyers, *The Power of Myth*.[57] Finding your bliss means doing things that make you light up inside, things you do for the sheer joy of doing rather than for the material rewards. Most of us experience moments of this bliss when we become so absorbed in enjoyable work activities that we lose track of time. This type of feeling and caring about work is a major source of charisma. Everyone becomes more charismatic to others when they pursue an activity they truly care about.

Love as action means more than feelings; it is translated into behavior. Stephen Covey points out that in all the great literature, love is a verb rather than a noun.[58] Love is something you do, the sacrifices you make and the giving of yourself to others. The feelings of compassion, respect, and loyalty, for example, are translated into acts of friendliness, teamwork, cooperation, listening, and serving others. Feelings of unity and cooperation in organizations by leaders or followers translate into acts of helping, sharing, and understanding. Sentiments emerge as action.

Why Followers Respond to Love

Most people yearn for more than a paycheck from their jobs. Leaders who lead with love have extraordinary influence because they meet five unspoken employee needs:

1. Hear and understand me.
2. Even if you disagree with me, please don't make me wrong.

3. Acknowledge the greatness within me.
4. Remember to look for my loving intentions.
5. Tell me the truth with compassion.[59]

When leaders address these subtle emotional needs directly, people typically respond by loving their work and becoming emotionally engaged in solving problems and serving customers. Enthusiasm for work and the organization increases. People want to believe that their leaders genuinely care. From the followers' point of view, love versus fear has different motivational potential.

❋ **Fear-based motivation:** I need a job to pay for my basic needs (fulfilling lower needs of the body). You give me a job, and I will give you just enough to keep my job.

❋ **Love-based motivation:** If the job and the leader make me feel valued as a person and provide a sense of meaning and contribution to the community at large (fulfilling higher needs of heart, mind, and body), then I will give you all I have to offer.[60]

A good example comes from Southwest Airlines, the only major airline to remain profitable through the recent turmoil in the airline industry. Founder and former CEO Herb Kelleher built the organization based on love, and employees responded with amazing performance and acts of selflessness. After the terrorist attacks on the United States in September 2001, most airlines asked their employees to donate portions of their pay back to the company, leading to strained union–management relations. At Southwest, which is also highly unionized, the employees themselves organized the give-back effort because of their positive feelings for the organization.[61] Many examples throughout this book illustrate what happens when positive emotion is used. One management consultant went so far as to advise that finding creative ways to love could solve every imaginable leadership problem.[62] Rational thinking is important, but leading with love can build trust, stimulate creativity, inspire commitment, and create boundless energy.

Fear-based motivation
motivation based on fear of losing a job

Love-based motivation
motivation based on feeling valued in the job

Summary and Interpretation

Leaders use intellectual as well as emotional capabilities and understandings to guide organizations through a turbulent environment and help employees feel energized, motivated, and cared for in the face of rapid change, uncertainty, and job insecurity. Leaders can expand the capacities of their minds and hearts through conscious development and practice.

Leaders should be aware of how their mental models affect their thinking and may cause "blind spots" that limit understanding. Two components of mental models are assumptions and perceptions. Becoming aware of mental models is a first step toward being able to see the world in new and different ways. Four key issues important to expanding and developing a leader's mind are independent thinking, open-mindedness, systems thinking, and personal mastery.

Leaders should also understand the importance of emotional intelligence. Four basic components of emotional intelligence are self-awareness, self-management, social awareness, and relationship management. Emotionally intelligent leaders can have a positive impact on organizations by helping employees grow, learn, and develop; creating a sense of purpose and meaning; instilling unity and team spirit; and basing relationships on trust and respect, which allows employees to take risks and fully contribute to the organization. Most work in organizations is done in teams, and emotional intelligence applies to teams as well as to individuals. Leaders develop a team's emotional intelligence by creating norms that foster a strong group identity, build trust among members, and instill a belief among members that they can be effective and succeed as a team.

Traditional organizations have relied on fear as a motivator. While fear does motivate people, it prevents people from feeling good about their work and often causes avoidance behavior. Fear can reduce trust and communication so that important problems and issues are hidden or suppressed. Leaders can choose to lead with love instead of fear. Love can be thought of as a motivational force that enables people to feel alive, connected, and energized; as feelings of liking, caring, and bliss; and as actions of helping, listening, and cooperating. Each of these aspects of love has relevance for organizational relationships. People respond to love because it meets unspoken needs for respect and affirmation. Rational thinking is important to leadership, but it takes love to build trust, creativity, and enthusiasm.

 ## Discussion Questions

1. How do you feel about developing the emotional qualities of yourself and other people in the organization as a way to be an effective leader? Discuss.
2. Do you agree that people have a capacity for developing their minds and hearts beyond current competency? Can you give an example? Discuss.
3. What are some specific reasons leaders need to be aware of their mental models?
4. Discuss the similarities and differences between mental models and open-mindedness.
5. What is the concept of personal mastery? How important is it to a leader?
6. Which of the four elements of emotional intelligence do you consider most essential to an effective leader? Why?
7. Consider fear and love as potential motivators. Which is the best source of motivation for soldiers during a war? For members of a new product development team? For top executives at a media conglomerate? Why?
8. Have you ever experienced love and/or fear from leaders at work? How did you respond?

9. Do you think it is appropriate for a leader to spend time developing a team's emotional intelligence? Why or why not?

10. Think about the class for which you are reading this text as a system. How might making changes without whole-systems thinking cause problems for students?

Leadership at Work

Mentors

Think of a time when someone reached out to you as a mentor or coach. This might have been a time when you were having some difficulty, and the person who reached out would have done so out of concern for you rather than for their own self interest.

Briefly describe below the situation, who the mentor was, and what the mentor did for you.

Mentoring comes from the heart, is a generous act, and is usually deeply appreciated by the recipient. How does it feel to recall the situation in which a mentor assisted you?

Share your experience with one or more students. What are the common characteristics that mentors possess based on your combined experiences?

In Class: A discussion of experiences with mentors is excellent for small groups. The instructor can ask each group to identify the common characteristics that their mentors displayed, and each group's conclusions can be written on the board. From these lists of mentor characteristics, common themes associated with mentors can be defined. The instructor can ask the class the following key questions: What are the key characteristics of mentors? Based on the key mentor characteristics, is effective mentoring based more on a person's heart or mind? Will you (the student) reach out as a mentor to others in life, and how will you do it? What factors might prevent you from doing so?

Leadership Development: Cases for Analysis

The New Boss

Sam Nolan clicked the mouse for one more round of solitaire on the computer in his den. He'd been at it for more than an hour, and his wife had long ago given up trying to persuade him to join her for a movie or a rare Saturday night on the town. The mind-numbing game seemed to be all that calmed Sam down enough to stop agonizing about work and how his job seemed to get worse every day.

Nolan was Chief Information Officer at Century Medical, a large medical products company based in Connecticut. He had joined the company four years ago, and since that time Century had made great progress integrating technology into its systems and processes. Nolan had already led projects to design and build two highly successful systems for Century. One was a benefits-administration system for the company's human resources department. The other was a complex Web-based purchasing system that streamlined the process of purchasing supplies and capital goods. Although the system had been up and running for only a few months, modest projections were that it would save Century nearly $2 million annually. The new Web-based system dramatically cut the time needed for processing requests and placing orders. Purchasing managers now had more time to work collaboratively with key stakeholders to identify and select the best suppliers and negotiate better deals.

Nolan thought wearily of all the hours he had put in developing trust with people throughout the company and showing them how technology could not only save time and money but also support team-based work, encourage open information sharing, and give people more control over their own jobs. He smiled briefly as he recalled one long-term HR employee, 61-year-old Ethel Moore. She had been terrified when Nolan first began showing her the company's intranet, but she was now one of his biggest supporters. In fact, it had been Ethel who had first approached him with an idea about a Web-based job posting system. The two had pulled together a team and developed an idea for linking Century managers, internal recruiters, and job applicants using artificial intelligence software on top of an integrated Web-based system. When Nolan had presented the idea to his boss, executive vice-president Sandra Ivey, she had enthusiastically endorsed it. Within a few weeks the team had authorization to proceed with the project.

But everything began to change when Ivey resigned her position six months later to take a plum job in New York. Ivey's successor, Tom Carr, seemed to have little interest in the project. During their first meeting, Carr had openly referred to the project as a waste of time and money. He immediately disapproved several new features suggested by the company's internal recruiters, even though the project team argued that the features could double internal hiring and save millions in training costs. "Just stick to the original plan and get it done. All this stuff needs to be handled on a personal basis anyway," Carr countered. "You can't learn more from a computer than you can talking to real people—and as for internal recruiting, it shouldn't be so hard to talk to people if they're already working right here in the company." Carr seemed to have no understanding of how and why technology was being used. He became irritated when Ethel Moore referred to the system as "Web-based." He boasted that he had never visited Century's intranet site and suggested that "this Internet fad" would blow over in a year or so anyway. Even Ethel's enthusiasm couldn't get through to him. "Technology is for those people in the IS department. My job is people, and yours should be too." Near the end of the meeting, Carr even jokingly suggested that the project team should just buy a couple of good filing cabinets and save everyone some time and money.

Nolan sighed and leaned back in his chair. The whole project had begun to feel like a joke. The vibrant and innovative human resources department his team had imagined now seemed like nothing more than a pipe dream. But despite his frustration, a new thought entered Nolan's mind: "Is Carr just stubborn and narrow-minded or does he have a point that HR is a people business that doesn't need a high-tech job posting system?"

SOURCES: Based on Carol Hildebrand, "New Boss Blues," *CIO Enterprise*, Section 2, (November 15, 1998): 53–58; and Megan Santosus, "Advanced Micro Devices' Web-Based Purchasing System," *CIO*, Section 1 (May 15, 1998), 84. A version of this case originally appeared in Richard L. Daft, *Organization Theory and Design*, 7th ed. (Cincinnati, OH: South-Western, 2001), 270–271.

Questions
1. Describe the two different mental models represented in this story.
2. What are some of the assumptions and perceptions that shape the mind-set of Sam Nolan? Of Tom Carr?

3. Do you think it is possible for Carr to shift to a new mental model? If you were Sam Nolan, what would you do?

The USS Florida

The atmosphere in a Trident nuclear submarine is generally calm and quiet. Even pipe joints are cushioned to prevent noise that might tip off a pursuer. The Trident ranks among the world's most dangerous weapons—swift, silent, armed with 24 long-range missiles carrying 192 nuclear warheads. Trident crews are the cream of the Navy crop, and even the sailors who fix the plumbing exhibit a white-collar decorum. The culture aboard ship is a low-key, collegial one in which sailors learn to speak softly and share close quarters with an ever-changing roster of shipmates. Being subject to strict security restrictions enhances a sense of elitism and pride. To move up and take charge of a Trident submarine is an extraordinary feat in the Navy—fewer than half the officers qualified for such commands ever get them. When Michael Alfonso took charge of the USS *Florida*, the crew welcomed his arrival. They knew he was one of them—a career Navy man who joined up as a teenager and moved up through the ranks. Past shipmates remembered him as basically a loner, who could be brusque but generally pleasant enough. Neighbors on shore found Alfonso to be an unfailingly polite man who kept mostly to himself.

The crew's delight in their new captain was short-lived. Commander Alfonso moved swiftly to assume command, admonishing his sailors that he would push them hard. He wasn't joking—soon after the *Florida* slipped into deep waters to begin a postoverhaul shakedown cruise, the new captain loudly and publicly reprimanded those whose performance he considered lacking. Chief Petty Officer Donald MacArthur, chief of the navigation division, was only one of those who suffered Alfonso's anger personally. During training exercises, MacArthur was having trouble keeping the boat at periscope depth because of rough seas. Alfonso announced loudly, "You're disqualified." He then precipitously relieved him of his diving duty until he could be recertified by extra practice. Word of the incident spread quickly. The crew, accustomed to the Navy's adage of "praise in public, penalize in private," were shocked. It didn't take long for this type of behavior to have an impact on the crew, according to Petty Officer Aaron Carmody: "People didn't tell him when something was wrong. You're not supposed to be afraid of your captain, to tell him stuff. But nobody wanted to."

The captain's outbursts weren't always connected with job performance. He bawled out the supply officer, the executive officer, and the chief of the boat because the soda dispenser he used to pour himself a glass of Coke one day contained Mr. Pibb instead. He exploded when he arrived unexpected at a late-night meal and found the fork at his place setting missing. Soon, a newsletter titled *The Underground* was being circulated by the boat's plumbers, who used sophomoric humor to spread the word about the captain's outbursts over such petty matters. By the time the sub reached Hawaii for its "Tactical Readiness Evaluation," an intense week-long series of inspections by staff officers, the crew was almost completely alienated. Although the ship tested well, inspectors sent word to Rear Admiral Paul Sullivan that something seemed to be wrong on board, with severely strained relations between captain and crew. On the Trident's last evening of patrol, much of the crew celebrated with a film night—they chose *The Caine Mutiny* and *Crimson Tide*, both movies about Navy skippers who face mutinies and are relieved of command at sea. When Humphrey Bogart, playing the captain of the fictional USS *Caine*, exploded over a missing quart of strawberries, someone shouted, "Hey, sound familiar?"

When they reached home port, the sailors slumped ashore. "Physically and mentally, we were just beat into the ground," recalls one. Concerned about reports that the crew seemed "despondent," Admiral Sullivan launched an informal inquiry that eventually led him to relieve Alfonso of his command. It was the first-ever firing of a Trident submarine commander. "He had the chance of a lifetime to experience the magic of command, and he squandered it," Sullivan said. "Fear and intimidation lead to certain ruin." Alfonso himself seemed dumbfounded by Admiral Sullivan's actions, pointing out that the USS *Florida* under his command posted "the best-ever grades assigned for certifications and inspections for a postoverhaul Trident submarine."

SOURCE: Thomas E. Ricks, "A Skipper's Chance to Run a Trident Sub Hits Stormy Waters," *The Wall Street Journal*, November 20, 1997, A1, A6.

Questions

1. Analyze Alfonso's impact on the crew in terms of love versus fear. What might account for the fact that he behaved so strongly as captain of the USS *Florida*?
2. Which do you think a leader should be more concerned about aboard a nuclear submarine—high certification grades or high-quality interpersonal relationships? Do you agree with Admiral Sullivan's decision to fire Alfonso? Discuss.
3. Discuss Commander Alfonso's level of emotional intelligence in terms of the four components listed in the chapter. What advice would you give him?

References

1. Greg Jaffe, "How Admiral Konetzni Intends to Mend Navy's Staff Woes," *The Wall Street Journal*, July 6, 2000, A1, A6.

2. Lester C. Thurow, "Peter's Principles," *Boston Magazine*, January 1998, 89–90; Michele Morris, "The New Breed of Leaders: Taking Charge in a Different Way," *Working Woman*, (March 1990): 73–75.

3. Keith H. Hammonds, "'You Can't Lead Without Making Sacrifices,'" *Fast Company* (June 2001): 106–116.

4. Robert B. French, "The Teacher as Container of Anxiety: Psychoanalysis and the Role of Teacher," *Journal of Management Education* 21, no. 4 (November 1997): 483–495.

5. This basic idea is found in a number of sources, among them: Jack Hawley, *Reawakening the Spirit in Work* (San Francisco: Berrett-Koehler, 1993); Aristotle, *The Nicomachean Ethics*, trans. by the Brothers of the English Dominican Province, rev. by Daniel J. Sullivan (Chicago: Encyclopedia Britannica, 1952); Alasdair MacIntyre, *After Virtue: A Study in Moral Theory* (Notre Dame, IN: University of Notre Dame Press, 1984); and Stephen Covey, *The Seven Habits of Highly Effective People: Powerful Lessons in Personal Change* (New York: Fireside Books/Simon & Schuster, 1990).

6. Vanessa Urch Druskat and Anthony T. Pescosolido, "The Content of Effective Teamwork Mental Models in Self-Managing Teams: Ownership, Learning, and Heedful Interrelating," *Human Relations* 55, no. 3 (2002): 283–314; and Peter M. Senge, *The Fifth Discipline: The Art and Practice of the Learning Organization* (New York: Doubleday, 1990).

7. Druskat and Pescosolido, "The Content of Effective Teamwork Mental Models."

8. Thomas Petzinger, Jr., "How Lynn Mercer Manages a Factory That Manages Itself," *The Wall Street Journal*, March 7, 1997, B1.

9. Geoffrey Colvin, "The Most Valuable Quality in a Manager," *Fortune* (December 29, 1997): 279–280; and Marlene Piturro, "Mindshift," *Management Review* (May 1999): 46–51.

10. Dave Logan, Laree Kiely, and Jennifer Greer, "Getting Your People to Think," *Across the Board* (January–February 2003): 25–29.

11. This discussion is based partly on Robert C. Benfari, *Understanding and Changing Your Management Style* (San Francisco: Jossey-Bass, 1999): 66–93.

12. John Guaspari, "A Shining Example," *Across the Board* (May–June 2002): 67–68.

13. David Bank, "Giving While Living: Socked by Stocks, Some Foundations Spend What's Left," *The Wall Street Journal*, September 10, 2002, A1, A8.

What makes a leader.

14. Gary Hamel, "Why... It's Better to Question Answers Than to Answer Questions," *Across the Board* (November–December 2000): 42–46; Jane C. Linder and Susan Cantrell, "It's All in the Mind(set)," *Across the Board* (May–June 2002): 39–42.

15. Anil K. Gupta and Vijay Govindarajan, "Cultivating a Global Mindset," *Academy of Management Executive* 16, no. 1 (2002): 116–126.

16. Ibid.

17. Hal Lancaster, "Take on Tough Jobs, Assess Your Own Work, and Other Life Lessons" (Managing Your Career column), *The Wall Street Journal*, December 7, 1999, B1.

18. Hamel, "Why... It's Better to Question Answers Than to Answer Questions."

19. Ellen Langer and John Sviokla, "An Evaluation of Charisma from the Mindfulness Perspective," unpublished manuscript, Harvard University. Part of this discussion is also drawn from Richard L. Daft and Robert H. Lengel, *Fusion Leadership: Unlocking the Subtle Forces that Change People and Organizations* (San Francisco: Berrett-Koehler, 1998).

20. T. K. Das, "Educating Tomorrow's Managers: The Role of Critical Thinking," *The International Journal of Organizational Analysis* 2, no. 4 (October 1994): 333–360.

21. Carol Hymowitz, "Building a Board That's Independent, Strong, and Effective," (In the Lead column), *The Wall Street Journal*, November 19, 2002, B1.

22. Bernard M. Bass, *Leadership and Performance Beyond Expectations* (New York: The Free Press, 1985); and *New Paradigm Leadership: An Inquiry into Transformational Leadership* (Alexandria, VA: U.S. Army Research Institute for the Behavioral and Social Sciences, 1996).

23. Leslie Wexner, quoted in Rebecca Quick, "A Makeover That Began at the Top," *The Wall Street Journal*, May 25, 2000, B1, B4.

24. The Pike Syndrome has been discussed in multiple sources.

25. James Gleick, *Genius: The Life and Science of Richard Feynman* (New York: Pantheon Books, 1992).

26. Chris Argyris, *Flawed Advice and the Management Trap* (New York: Oxford University Press, 2000); and Eileen C. Shapiro, "Managing in the Cappuccino Economy" (review of *Flawed Advice*), *Harvard Business Review* (March–April 2000): 177–183.

27. Oren Harari, "Mind Matters," *Management Review*, (January 1996): 47–49.

28. Quoted in *Fast Company* (September 1999): 120.

29. This section is based on Peter M. Senge, *The Fifth Discipline: The Art and Practice of the Learning Organization* (New York: Doubleday, 1990); and John D. Sterman, System Dynamics Modeling: Tools for Learning in a Complex World," *California Management Review* 43, no. 4 (Summer, 2001): 8–25; and Ron Zemke, "Systems Thinking," *Training* (February 2001): 40–46.

30. These examples are cited in Sterman, "Systems Dynamics Modeling."

31. Peter M. Senge, Charlotte Roberts, Richard B. Ross, Bryan J. Smith, and Art Kleiner, *The Fifth Discipline Fieldbook* (New York: Currency/Doubleday, 1994), 87.

32. Senge, *The Fifth Discipline.*

33. Daniel Goleman, *Emotional Intelligence: Why It Can Matter More Than IQ* (New York: Bantam Books, 1995); Pamela Kruger, "A Leader's Journey," *Fast Company* (June 1999): 116–129; Hendrie Weisinger, *Emotional Intelligence at Work* (San Francisco: Jossey-Bass, 1998).

34. Based on Goleman, *Emotional Intelligence*; Goleman, "Leadership That Gets Results," *Harvard Business Review* (March–April 2000): 79–90; J. D. Mayer, D. R. Caruso, and P. Salovey, "Emotional Intelligence Meets Traditional Standards for an Intelligence," *Intelligence* 27, no. 4 (1999): 266–298; Neal M. Ashkanasy and Catherine S. Daus, "Emotion in the Workplace: The New Challenge for Managers," *Academy of Management Executive* 16, no.1 (2002): 76–86; Weisinger, *Emotional Intelligence at Work.*

35. Donna Fenn, "Personnel Best," *Inc.* (February 2000): 75–83.

36. This section is based largely on Daniel Goleman, *Emotional Intelligence: Why It Can Matter More Than IQ* (New York: Bantam Books, 1995), 289–290.

37. Goleman, "Leadership that Gets Results"; and Richard E. Boyatzis and Daniel Goleman, *The Emotional Competence Inventory—University Edition*, The Hay Group, 2001.

38. Hendrie Weisinger, *Emotional Intelligence at Work* (San Francisco: Jossey-Bass, 1998).

39. Alan Farnham, "Are You Smart Enough to Keep Your Job?" *Fortune* (January 15, 1996): 34–47.

40. Rolf W. Habbel, "The Human[e] Factor: Nurturing a Leadership Culture," *Strategy & Business* 26 (First Quarter 2002), 83–89.

41. Goleman, "Leadership that Gets Results."

42. Joe Torre with Henry Dreher, *Joe Torre's Ground Rules for Winners* (New York: Hyperion, 1999); Jerry Useem, "A Manager for All Seasons," *Fortune* (April 30, 2001): 66–72; Malcolm Moran, "Conflict Resolution the Joe Torre Way," *The New York Times*, July 14, 1997, C5; and Goleman, "Leadership that Gets Results."

43. Lara E. Megerian and John J. Sosik, "An Affair of the Heart: Emotional Intelligence and Transformational Leadership," *The Journal of Leadership Studies* 3, no. 3 (1996): 31–48; and Ashkanasy and Daus, "Emotion in the Workplace."

44. E. Hatfield, J. T. Cacioppo, and R. L. Rapson, *Emotional Contagion* (New York: Cambridge University Press, 1994).

45. P. J. Jordan, N. M. Ashkanasy, C. E. J. Härtel, and G. S. Hooper, "Workgroup Emotional Intelligence: Scale Development and Relationship to Team Process Effectiveness and Goal Focus," *Human Resource Management Review* 12, no.2 (Summer 2002): 195–214.

46. This discussion is based on Vanessa Urch Druskat and Steven B. Wolf, "Building the Emotional Intelligence of Groups," *Harvard Business Review* (March 2001), 81–90.

47. Daniel Goleman, Richard Boyatzis, and Annie McKee, "The Emotional Reality of Teams," *Journal of Organizational Excellence* (Spring 2002): 55–65.

48. Kathleen D. Ryan and Daniel K. Oestreich, *Driving Fear Out of the Workplace: How to Overcome the Invisible Barriers to Quality, Productivity, and Innovation* (San Francisco: Jossey-Bass, 1991).

49. David E. Dorsey, "Escape from the Red Zone," *Fast Company*, (April/May 1997): 116–127.

50. This section is based on Ryan and Oestreich, *Driving Fear Out of the Workplace*; and Therese R. Welter, "Reducing Employee Fear: Get Workers and Managers to Speak Their Minds," *Small Business Reports* (April 1991): 15–18.

51. Ryan and Oestreich, *Driving Fear Out of the Workplace*, 43.

52. Donald G. Zauderer, "Integrity: An Essential Executive Quality," *Business Forum* (Fall 1992): 12–16.

53. Geoffrey Colvin, "What's Love Got to Do with It?" *Fortune* (November 12, 2001): 60.

54. David Dorsey, "Andy Pearson Finds Love," *Fast Company* (August 2001): 78–86.

55. Jack Hawley, *Reawakening the Spirit at Work* (San Francisco: Berrett-Koehler, 1993): 55; and Rodney Ferris, "How Organizational Love Can Improve Leadership," *Organizational Dynamics*, 16, no. 4 (Spring 1988): 40–52.

56. Barbara Moses, "It's All About Passion," *Across the Board* (May–June 2001): 55–58.

57. Joseph Campbell with Bill Moyers, *The Power of Myth* (New York: Doubleday, 1988).

58. Stephen R. Covey, *The Seven Habits of Highly Effective People: Powerful Lessons in Personal Change* (New York: Fireside/Simon & Schuster, 1990): 80.

59. Hyler Bracey, Jack Rosenblum, Aubrey Sanford, and Roy Trueblood, *Managing from the Heart* (New York: Dell Publishing, 1993): 192.

60. Madan Birla with Cecilia Miller Marshall, *Balanced Life and Leadership Excellence* (Memphis, TN: The Balance Group, 1997): 76–77.

61. Colvin, "What's Love Got to Do with It?"

62. Ferris, "How Organizational Love Can Improve Leadership."

Chapter

Your Leadership Challenge

After reading this chapter, you should be able to:

- Combine a rational approach to leadership with a concern for people and ethics.

- Recognize your own stage of moral development and ways to accelerate your moral maturation.

- Apply the principles of stewardship and servant leadership.

- Know and use mechanisms that enhance an ethical organizational culture.

- Recognize courage in others and unlock your own potential to live and act courageously.

During the waning months of World War II, a young man climbed atop the roof of a train ready to start for Auschwitz. Ignoring shouts—and later bullets—from Nazis and soldiers of the Hungarian Arrow Cross, he began handing fake Swedish passports to the astonished Jews inside and ordering them to walk to a caravan of cars marked in Swedish colors. By the time the cars were loaded, the soldiers were so dumbfounded by the young man's actions that they simply stood by and let the cars pass, carrying to safety dozens of Jews who had been headed for the death camps.

Virtually alone in Hungary, one of the most perilous places in Europe in 1944, Raoul Wallenberg worked such miracles on a daily basis, using as his weapons courage, self-confidence, and his deep, unwavering belief in the rightness of his mission. His deeds inspired hope, courage, and action in many people who otherwise felt powerless. No one knows how many people he directly or indirectly saved from certain death, though it is estimated at more than 100,000.

Wallenberg was 32 years old in 1944, a wealthy, politically connected, upper-class Swede from a prominent, well-respected family. When asked by the U.S. War Refugee Board to enter Hungary and help stop Hitler's slaughter of innocent civilians, Wallenberg had everything to lose and nothing to gain. Yet he left his life of safety and comfort to enter Hungary under cover as a diplomat, with the mission of saving as many of Hungary's Jews as possible. Wallenberg boldly demanded—and was granted—a great deal of latitude in the methods he would use. He personally conceived the plan to use false Swedish passports and designed them himself as masterpieces of the formal, official-looking pomp that so impressed the Nazis. Later, as Wallenberg plunged into the midst of the struggle to free Jews from the trains and death marches, he convinced his enemies to accept such things as library cards and laundry tickets as Swedish passports. The Nazi and Hungarian Arrow Cross soldiers, accustomed to yielding unquestioningly to authority, yielded to Wallenberg on the strength of his character, personal authority, and courage.

Wallenberg never returned from Hungary, but apparently was captured as a suspected anti-Soviet spy, and died in a Soviet prison. He gave up his life fighting for a cause he believed in, and his actions made a real difference in the world.[1]

Raoul Wallenberg emerged from a dismal period in human history as a courageous leader who made the ultimate sacrifice for what he believed. Most leaders never have the opportunity to save lives, and few leaders help as many people as Wallenberg did, but the principles of leadership he demonstrated are valuable to anyone who aspires to make a positive difference in the world.

One of the primary lessons from Wallenberg's life is that being a real leader means learning who you are and what you stand for, and then having the courage to act. Leaders demonstrate confidence and commitment in what they believe and what they do. A deep devotion to a cause or a purpose larger than one's self sparks the courage to act. In addition, Wallenberg's story demonstrates that leadership has less to do with using other people than with *serving* other people. Placing others ahead of oneself is a key to successful leadership, whether in politics, war, education, sports, social services, or business.

This chapter explores ideas related to courage and moral leadership. In the previous chapter, we discussed mind and heart, two of the three elements that come together for successful leadership. This chapter focuses on the third element, spirit—on the ability to look within, to contemplate the human condition, to think about what is right and wrong, to see what really matters in the world, and to have the courage to stand up for what is worthy and right. We will begin by examining the situation in which most organizations currently operate, the dilemma leaders face in the modern world, and the kinds of behaviors that often contribute to an unethical organizational climate. Next we will explore how leaders can act in a moral way, examine a model of personal moral development, and look at the importance of stewardship and servant leadership. The final sections of the chapter will explore what courage means and how leaders develop the courage for moral leadership to flourish.

 ## Moral Leadership Today

Every decade sees its share of political, social, and corporate villains, but the pervasiveness of ethical lapses in recent years has been astounding. The corporate world, in particular, has reeled from scandals—the names of once-revered companies have become synonymous with greed, deceit, and financial chicanery: Enron, Adelphia, Arthur Andersen, HealthSouth, WorldCom, Tyco. No wonder a CBS poll taken in the fall of 2002 found that 79 percent of respondents believe questionable business practices are widespread. Fewer than one-third think most CEOs are honest.[2] Harvard Business School professor and author Shoshana Zuboff describes the impact of these public sentiments: "The chasm between individuals and organizations is marked by frustration, mistrust, disappointment, and even rage."[3]

The Ethical Climate in U.S. Business

Ethical lapses occur at all levels of organizations, but top leaders have really been on the hot seat lately as unethical and illegal actions have come to light. At Tyco International, former CEO Dennis Kozlowski was accused of tax evasion and using company funds for personal use. Domestic style maven Martha Stewart came under investigation for alleged insider trading.[4] And years after the Enron fairy tale first began to unravel, evidence that top leaders intentionally misled investors in order to pump up the stock price and cash in their options continues to surface. An example in the world of politics comes from New Haven, Connecticut, where Mayor Joseph P. Ganim was convicted of racketeering and other charges for accepting more than $500,000 in bribes.[5]

What's going on at the top trickles down through organizations and society. When leaders fail to set and live up to high ethical standards, organizations, employees, shareholders, and the general public suffer. Unethical and illegal behavior can lead to serious consequences for organizations. For one thing, companies have a hard time attracting good employees. Evidence shows that the current wave of scandals has prompted job seekers to go to great lengths to check out companies' ethical standards.[6] When current employees lose trust in leaders, morale, commitment, and performance suffer. Customers who lose trust in the organization will bolt, as evidenced by the mass desertion of Arthur Andersen after the firm was found guilty of obstruction of justice for destroying tons of documents related to Enron. Investors may also withdraw their support from the company—or even file suit if they believe they've been lied to and cheated.

Leaders at all levels carry a tremendous responsibility for setting the ethical climate. At the same time, they face many pressures that challenge their ability to do the right thing. Pressures to cut costs, increase profits, meet the demands of vendors or business partners, and look successful can all contribute to ethical lapses. During the stock market bubble, many leaders simply got caught up in the overriding emphasis on fast profit and ever-growing stock prices. The practice of rewarding managers with stock options, originally intended to align the interests of managers with those of shareholders, caused basic human greed to get out of hand during this period.[7] At *The New York Times*, where reporter Jayson Blair was discovered to be fabricating research on top stories such as the Jessica Lynch rescue, there are indications that top executives knew something was wrong long before the scandal broke. They ignored the signs because they didn't want to either believe or admit that a newspaper of the *Times'* reputation could be associated with that kind of dishonesty and irresponsibility.[8] Most people want to be liked, and they want their organizations to appear successful. Leaders sometimes do the wrong thing just so they will look good to others. The question for leaders is whether they can summon the fortitude to do the right thing despite

Action Memo

As a leader: Set the example you want followers to live by. Establish an ethical climate by putting moral values into action. Resist pressures to act unethically just to avoid criticism or achieve short-term gains. Be honest and straightforward, fulfill your commitments, and treat everyone with respect and fairness.

outside pressures. "Life is lived on a slippery slope," says Harvard Business School's Richard Tedlow. "It takes a person of character to know what lines you don't cross."[9]

What Leaders Do to Make Things Go Wrong

What actions of leaders contribute to a dearth of integrity within the organization? Recall from Chapter 2 that integrity means adhering to moral principles and acting based on those beliefs. Leaders signal what matters through their behavior, and when leaders operate from principles of selfishness and greed, many employees come to see unethical behavior as okay. At Enron, for example, senior executives were openly arrogant and ambitious for personal successes, and they blatantly flouted the rules and basic standards of fairness and honor to achieve personal gain. As one young Enron employee said, "It was easy to get into, 'Well, everybody else is doing it, so maybe it isn't so bad.'"[10]

Exhibit 6.1 compares unethical and ethical leadership by looking at 10 things leaders do that make things go wrong for the organization from a moral standpoint. The behaviors listed in column 1 contribute to an organizational climate ripe for ethical and legal abuses. Column 2 lists the opposite behaviors, which contribute to a climate of trust, fairness, and doing the right thing.[11]

As we discussed in Chapter 1, the leader as hero is an outdated notion, but some executives are preoccupied with their own importance and take every opportunity to feed their greed or nourish their own egos. They focus on having a huge salary, a big office, and other symbols of status rather than on what is good for the organization. These leaders typically pay more attention to gaining benefits for themselves than for the organization or larger society. For example, top executives who expect big salaries and perks at the same time the company is struggling and laying off thousands of workers are not likely to create an environment of trust and integrity.[12]

Unethical leaders are dishonest with employees, partners, customers, vendors, and shareholders, and they regularly fail to honor their agreements or commitments to others. In a *USA Today* survey, 82 percent of CEOs said they lied about their golf scores. It seems like a small thing, but little by little, dishonesty can become a way of life and business.[13] Unethical leaders also frequently treat people unfairly, perhaps by giving special favors or privileges to followers who flatter their egos or by promoting people based on favoritism rather than concrete business results.

Unethical leaders tend to take all the credit for successes, but they blame others when things go wrong. By taking credit for followers' accomplishments, failing to allow others to have meaningful participation in decision making, and generally treating people with discourtesy and disrespect, they diminish the dignity of others. They see followers as a means to an end, and they show little concern for treating people as individuals or helping followers develop their own potential. Whereas ethical leaders serve others, unethical leaders focus on their own personal needs and goals.

Exhibit 6.1	Comparing Unethical Versus Ethical Leadership	
The Unethical Leader	**The Ethical Leader**	
Is arrogant and self-serving	Possesses humility	
Excessively promotes self-interest	Maintains concern for the greater good	
Practices deception	Is honest and straightforward	
Breaches agreements	Fulfills commitments	
Deals unfairly	Strives for fairness	
Shifts blame to others	Takes responsibility	
Diminishes others' dignity	Shows respect for each individual	
Neglects follower development	Encourages and develops others	
Withholds help and support	Serves others	
Lacks courage to confront unjust acts	Shows courage to stand up for what is right	

SOURCE: Based on Donald G. Zanderer, "Integrity: An Essential Executive Quality," *Business Forum* (Fall 1992): 12–16.

Finally, one of the primary ways leaders contribute to an unethical and potentially corrupt organization is by failing to speak up against acts they believe are wrong. A leader who holds his tongue in order to "fit in with the guys" when colleagues are telling sexually offensive jokes is essentially giving his support for that type of behavior. If a leader knows someone is being treated unfairly by a colleague and does nothing, the leader is setting a precedent for others to behave unfairly as well. Peers and subordinates with lax ethical standards feel free to act as they choose. It is often hard to stand up for what is right, but this is a primary way in which leaders create an environment of integrity.

Acting Like a Moral Leader

Many leaders forget that business is about values, not just economic performance. Moral leadership doesn't mean ignoring profit and loss, stock price, production costs, and other hard measurable facts. But it does require recognizing the importance of moral values, human meaning, quality, and higher purpose.[14] Henry Ford's century-old comment seems tailor-made for today's poor ethical climate: "For a long time people believed that the only purpose of industry was to make a profit. They are wrong. Its purpose is to serve the general welfare."[15]

Despite the corporate realities of greed, competition, and the drive to achieve goals and profits, leaders can act from moral values and encourage others to develop and use moral values in the workplace. The single most important factor in ethical decision making in organizations is whether leaders show commitment to ethics in their talk and especially their behavior. Employees learn about the values that are important in the organization by watching leaders. Consider the example of Alfred P. West of SEI Investments Company.

In the Lead   Alfred P. West, SEI Investments Co.

"The CEO sets the tone for an organization's [values]." says Alfred P. West, the founder and CEO of SEI Investments, a financial services firm that operates the back office services for mutual funds and bank trust departments. West is careful to espouse and model values that build integrity, accountability, and trustworthiness into the organization's culture.

West doesn't have a spacious corner office with an executive assistant. Instead, he answers his own phone and has the same open-plan office space as everyone else at SEI's headquarters. He doesn't take stock options, and he pays himself a modest $660,000. Compare that to the $2 million Dennis Kozlowski earned in total compensation as CEO of Tyco in 2002, or the $136 million Tyco's former CFO, Mark Swartz, pulled in. At SEI, West also shuns the perks that are typically demanded by today's top executives. He believes if you separate yourself from employees with corporate jets, enormous stock options, and other special benefits, it sends the wrong message.

West spends a lot of time banging home his vision for the company to employees and making sure they have complete information about the company—good and bad. He believes an open culture not only improves performance, but makes it easier for employees to report ethical lapses or unfair practices.[16]

Leaders like Alfred West put values into action. Exhibit 6.2 lists some specific ways leaders act to build an environment that allows and encourages people to behave ethically and morally. Leaders create organizational systems and policies that support ethical behavior, such as creating open-door policies that encourage employees to talk about anything without fear, establishing clear ethics codes, rewarding ethical conduct, and showing zero tolerance for violations. Exhibit 6.3 shows the clear, concise, personal honor code used by NASA's Jet Propulsion Laboratory. Most importantly, leaders articulate and uphold high moral standards, and they do the right thing even if they think no one is looking. Leaders who cut corners or bend the rules when they think they won't get caught will ultimately suffer the consequences. Moreover, leaders realize that what they do in their personal lives carries over to the professional arena. Leaders are a model for the organization twenty-four hours a day,

---

Exhibit 6.2	**How to Act Like a Moral Leader**

1. Develop, articulate, and uphold high moral principles.
2. Focus on what is right for the organization as well as all the people involved.
3. Set the example you want others to live by.
4. Be honest with yourself and others.
5. Drive out fear and eliminate undiscussables.
6. Establish and communicate ethics policies.
7. Develop a backbone—show zero tolerance for ethical violations.
8. Reward ethical conduct.
9. Treat everyone with fairness, dignity, and respect, from the lowest to the highest level of the organization.
10. Do the right thing in both your private and professional life—even if no one is looking.

Character

SOURCES: Based on Linda Klebe Treviño, Laura Pincus Hartman, and Michael Brown, "Moral Person and Moral Manager: How Executives Develop a Reputation for Ethical Leadership," *California Management Review* 42, no. 4 (Summer 2000): 128–142; Christopher Hoenig, "Brave Hearts," *CIO* (November 1, 2000): 72–74; and Patricia Wallington, "Honestly?!" *CIO* (March 15, 2003): 41–42.

seven days a week. Consider Mike Price, who was fired as the University of Alabama's football coach before he ever coached a game. While in Florida participating in a golf tournament, Price spent hundreds of dollars on drinks and tips for exotic dancers and spent the night with a woman other than his wife, who ran up a $1,000 room-service bill. The university administration fired Price as a clear signal that the "boys-will-be-boys" mind-set in the athletic department would no longer be tolerated. A visible leadership position entails the responsibility for conducting both one's personal and professional life in an ethical manner.

Leaders build ethical organizations by demonstrating the importance of serving people and society, as well as winning football games or increasing business profits. Tony Burns, former CEO of Ryder Systems, provides an excellent example of a leader

---

Exhibit 6.3	**Personal Ethics Code for Jet Propulsion Laboratory**

Ethics Honor Code

I will conduct all business dealings with fairness, honesty, and integrity.

I will protect all information and resources available to me from loss, theft, and misuse.

I will avoid even the appearance of conflict of interest or any other impropriety.

I will treat my fellow employees fairly and with dignity and respect.

I will help create and sustain an atmosphere conducive to the spirit of this code.

SOURCE: Jet Propulsion Laboratory, http://eis.jpl.nasa.gov/ethics/code.html accessed on December 11, 2003.

who serves both business and society. Burns has had a long-standing commitment to public service, which earned him the Humanitarian of the Year award from the Greater Miami chapter of the American Red Cross. As CEO of Ryder, he also created an atmosphere for service within the company. Burns' commitment to helping others may have come from his grandfather, who "always thought the best thing you could do was giving service to other people."[17]

Leaders like Tony Burns illustrate that leaders can run successful organizations based on moral principles. There is some evidence that doing right by shareholders, employees, customers, and the community is good business. A recent study by Governance Metrics International, an independent corporate governance ratings agency in New York, found that the stocks of companies that are run on more selfless principles perform better than those run in a self-serving manner. Top-ranked companies such as Pfizer, Johnson Controls, and Sunoco also outperformed lower-ranking companies in measures like return on assets, return on investment, and return on capital.[18]

Becoming a Moral Leader

Leadership is not merely a set of practices with no association with right or wrong. All leadership practices can be used for good or evil and thus have a moral dimension. Leaders choose whether to act from selfishness and greed to diminish others or in ways that serve and motivate others to develop to their full potential as employees and as human beings.[19] Moral leadership is about distinguishing right from wrong and doing right, seeking the just, the honest, the good, and the right conduct in its practice. Leaders have great influence over others, and moral leadership gives life to others and enhances the lives of others. Immoral leadership takes away from others in order to enhance oneself.[20] Leaders who would do evil toward others, such as Hitler, Stalin, or Cambodia's Pol Pot, are immoral, while Raoul Wallenberg, described in the chapter opening, typifies the height of moral leadership. Moral leadership uplifts people, enabling them to be better than they were without the leader. This chapter's Leader's Bookshelf argues that work, just like life and personal relationships, can be enriched by a spiritual foundation. Leaders are responsible for building a foundation that strengthens and enriches the lives of organization members.

Specific personality characteristics such as ego strength, self-confidence, and a sense of independence may enable leaders to behave morally in the face of opposition. Moreover, leaders can develop these characteristics through their own hard work.

Viktor Frankl was in one of the death camps in Nazi Germany, and he learned that people have choices about whether to behave morally.

> We who lived in concentration camps can remember the men who walked through the huts comforting the others, giving away their last piece of bread. They may have been few

Moral leadership

distinguishing right from wrong and doing right; seeking the just, honest, and good in the practice of leadership

LEADER'S BOOKSHELF

Managing with the Wisdom of Love: Uncovering Virtue in People and Organizations
Dorothy Marcic

The changes and challenges faced by today's organizations have spurred a new leadership paradigm based on concepts such as vision, commitment, empowerment, and accountability. All of these concepts, argues Dorothy Marcic, can become more than just words when leaders recognize that work—like life and personal relationships—is enriched by a spiritual foundation. Quoting extensively from major religious texts, Marcic illustrates the similar messages in a variety of religions and demonstrates the application of this spiritual wisdom to organizations. By citing figures of faith such as Buddha, Jesus Christ, and Baháulláh, (the founder of the Baha'i tradition), Marcic distills five "new management virtues" that can provide a necessary balance among the physical, intellectual, emotional, volitional (willingness to change for the better), and spiritual dimensions of work.

New Management Virtues
These five virtues form a philosophical and spiritual foundation for the issues leaders struggle with every day and for the relationships between a leader and others.

* **Trustworthiness** This virtue corresponds to the organizational issue of accountability or stewardship. It means being honest, behaving ethically, and building relationships with customers and employees based on integrity.
* **Unity** Unity is the foundation for shared vision, commitment, and reciprocity. Unity in action means seeking unanimity in important decisions, satisfying customers, and going from controlling to coaching.
* **Respect and Dignity** An attitude of respect and dignity is the basis for true empowerment. Leaders listen, act as coaches and mentors, create self-determining teams, and reward and appreciate workers for their contributions.
* **Justice** The virtue of justice corresponds to equal opportunity and profit sharing in organizations. Leading with justice means treating everyone fairly, eliminating barriers to equal opportunity, and providing equitable compensation and profit sharing.
* **Service and Humility** In organizations, service corresponds to the emphasis on quality and customer satisfaction. Truly serving others means being a servant to employees and customers. Leaders who embrace the virtue of service and humility share power, admit mistakes, and trust others.

Virtues at Work
When leaders go about their work and relate to others according to a spiritual foundation, they cultivate virtue in others by creating a balance in the work lives of organizational members. Marcic emphasizes that spirituality is not a quick fix but a process that takes time, commitment, and effort. Leaders can make a commitment to long-term organizational health and base their behavior on these five virtues to develop happier, more committed employees and stronger organizations.

Managing with the Wisdom of Love, by Dorothy Marcic, is published by Jossey-Bass.

Preconventional level the level of personal moral development in which individuals are egocentric and concerned with receiving external rewards and avoiding punishments

Conventional level *Norming* the level of personal moral development in which people learn to conform to the expectations of good behavior as defined by colleagues, family, friends, and society

Principled level the level of personal moral development in which leaders are guided by an internalized set of principles universally recognized as right or wrong

in number, but they offer sufficient proof that everything can be taken from a man but one thing: the last of the human freedoms—to choose one's attitude in any given set of circumstances. To choose one's own way.

And there were always choices to make. Every day, every hour, offered the opportunity to make a decision, a decision which determined whether you would or would not submit to those powers which threatened to rob you of your very self, your inner freedom. . . . [21]

A leader's capacity to make moral choices is related to the individual's level of moral development.[22] Exhibit 6.4 shows a simplified illustration of one model of personal moral development. At the **preconventional level**, individuals are egocentric and concerned with receiving external rewards and avoiding punishments. They obey authority and follow rules to avoid detrimental personal consequences or satisfy immediate self-interests. The basic orientation toward the world is one of taking what one can get. Someone with this orientation in a leadership position would tend to be autocratic toward others and use the position for personal advancement.

At level two, the **conventional level**, people learn to conform to the expectations of good behavior as defined by colleagues, family, friends, and society. People at this level follow the rules, norms, and values in the corporate culture. If the rules are to not steal, cheat, make false promises, or violate regulatory laws, a person at the conventional level will attempt to obey. They adhere to the norms of the larger social system. However, if the social system says it is okay to inflate bills to the government, or make achieving the bottom line more important than integrity, people at the conventional level will often go along with that norm also. Often, when organizations do something illegal, many managers and employees are simply going along with the system.[23]

At the postconventional or **principled level**, leaders are guided by an internalized set of principles universally recognized as right or wrong. People at this level may even disobey rules or laws that violate these principles. These internalized values become more important than the expectations of other people in the organization or community. A leader at this level is visionary, empowering, and committed to serving others and a higher cause. Consider how Roy Vagelos of Merck broke the rules to honor higher principles.

In the Lead   Roy Vagelos, Merck & Co.

"We are in the business of preserving and improving human life," Merck's mission statement reads. However, when, in the late 1970s Roy Vagelos (then Merck's senior vice president of research) and his colleagues found a potential cure for river blindness, they faced a dilemma. The drug

| Exhibit 6.4 | **Three Levels of Personal Moral Development** |

Level 3: Postconventional
Follows internalized universal principles of justice and right. Balances concern for self with concern for others and the common good. Acts in an independent and ethical manner regardless of expectations of others.

Level 2: Conventional
Lives up to expectations of others. Fulfills duties and obligations of social system. Upholds laws.

Level 1: Preconventional
Follows rules to avoid punishment. Acts in own interest. Blind obedience to authority for its own sake.

SOURCES: Based on Lawrence Kohlberg, "Moral Stages and Moralization: The Cognitive-Developmental Approach," in *Moral Development and Behavior: Theory, Research, and Social Issues*, ed. Thomas Likona (Austin, TX: Holt, Rinehart and Winston, 1976), 31–53; and Jill W. Graham, "Leadership, Moral Development, and Citizenship Behavior," *Business Ethics Quarterly* 5, No. 1 (January 1995), 43–54.

would cost more than $200 million to develop, and it was needed only by people who couldn't afford to pay for it—poor villagers in West Africa and other developing countries. One of the world's most dreaded diseases, river blindness had long frustrated public health agencies trying to control its spread. When a scientist in Merck's laboratories hit upon a possible solution, many people in the company argued that proceeding with the drug's development was a costly mistake. However, Vagelos (who was promoted to CEO during this period) held firmly to the company's stated axiom that "health precedes wealth" and authorized the continuation.

His decision to authorize a drug that would likely never make money and would cost more than $3 a tablet to produce and distribute was not an easy one, but Vagelos stood by his beliefs and those espoused by his organization. When Merck couldn't get the governments of developing nations to buy the new drug, Mectizan, the company announced that they would give the drug away. Some people argued that the decision was irresponsible and violated the fiduciary trust placed in Vagelos by Merck's stockholders. But Vagelos believed that focusing on the company's guiding mission was the best way to create shareholder value in the long run, and he stuck by these principles. According to Vagelos, "I thought that the company couldn't have done otherwise." By showing the entire world the integrity and consistency of Merck's organizational leadership, the decision ultimately served the company well. The development of Mectizan is considered one of the twentieth century's greatest medical triumphs, and river blindness has nearly been eradicated as a public health threat in many areas. Merck's reputation soared, helping the company attract some of the best scientific researchers in the world. However, even without this benefit, Roy Vagelos says he would still make the same decision, indicating that he really had no choice. "My whole life has been dedicated to helping people."[24]

Vagelos broke unspoken corporate rules by putting the lives of poor children in developing countries above the short-term interests of shareholders. Despite opposition, he believed doing so was the only moral choice.

Most adults operate at level two of moral development, and some have not advanced beyond level one. Only about 20 percent of American adults reach the third, postconventional level of moral development, although most of us have the capacity to do so. People at level three are able to act in an independent, ethical manner regardless of expectations from others inside or outside the organization. Impartially applying universal standards to resolve moral conflicts balances self-interest with a concern for others and for the common good. Research has consistently found a direct relationship between higher levels of moral development and more ethical behavior on the job, including less cheating, a tendency toward helpfulness to others, and the reporting of unethical or illegal acts, known as whistleblowing.[25] Leaders can use an understanding of these stages to enhance their own and followers' moral development and to initiate ethics training programs to move people to higher levels of moral reasoning. When leaders operate at level three of moral development, they focus on higher principles and encourage others to think for themselves and expand their understanding of moral issues.

Leadership Control versus Service

Assumptions about the relationship between leaders and followers are changing dramatically, and the concept of leadership is expanding. What is a leader's moral responsibility toward followers? Is it to limit and control them to meet the needs of the organization? Is it to pay them a fair wage? Or is it to enable them to grow and create and expand themselves as human beings?

Much of the thinking about leadership today implies that moral leadership encourages change toward developing followers into leaders, thereby developing their potential rather than using a leadership position to control or limit followers. Exhibit 6.5 illustrates a continuum of leadership thinking and practice. Traditional organizations were based on the idea that the leader is in charge of subordinates and the success of the organization depends on leader control over followers. In the first stage, subordinates are passive—not expected to think for themselves but simply to

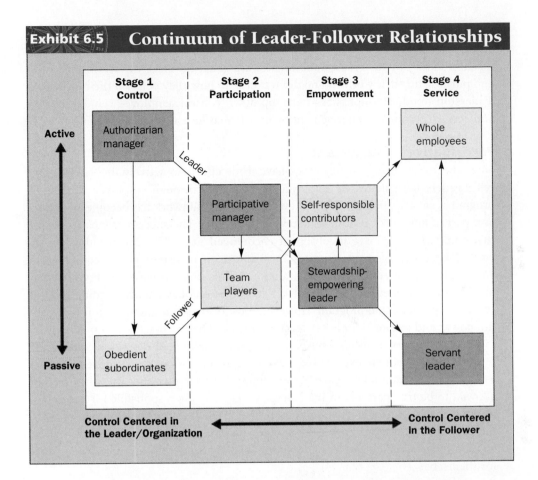

Exhibit 6.5 **Continuum of Leader-Follower Relationships**

do as they are told. Stage two in the continuum involves subordinates more actively in their own work. Stage three is stewardship, which represents a significant shift in mind-set by moving responsibility and authority from leaders to followers. Servant leadership represents a stage beyond stewardship, where leaders give up control and make a choice to serve employees. In the following sections, we will discuss each stage of this leadership continuum.

Authoritarian Management

The traditional understanding of leadership is that leaders are good managers who direct and control their people. Followers are obedient subordinates who follow orders. In Chapter 2, we discussed the autocratic leader, who makes the decisions and announces them to subordinates. Power, purpose, and privilege reside with those at the top of the organization. At this stage, leaders set the strategy and goals, as well as the methods and rewards for attaining them. Organizational stability and efficiency are paramount, and followers are routinized and controlled along with machines and raw materials. Subordinates are given no voice in creating meaning and purpose for their work and no discretion as to how they perform their jobs. This leadership mind-set emphasizes tight top-down control, employee standardization and specialization, and management by impersonal measurement and analysis.

Participative Management

Since the 1980s, many organizations have made efforts to actively involve employees. Leaders have increased employee participation through employee suggestion programs, participation groups, and quality circles. Teamwork has become an important part of how work is done in many organizations. The success of Japanese firms that emphasize employee involvement encouraged many U.S. organizations to try participatory management practices in response to increased global competition. One study, sponsored by the Association for Quality and Participation, revealed that more than 70 percent of the largest U.S. corporations have adopted some kind of employee participation program. However, most of these programs do not redistribute power and authority to lower-level workers.[26] The mind-set is still paternalistic in that top leaders determine purpose and goals, make final decisions, and decide rewards. Employees are expected to make suggestions for quality improvements, act as team players, and take greater responsibility for their own jobs, but they are not allowed to be true partners in the enterprise. Leaders are responsible for outcomes, but they may act as mentors and coaches. They have given up some of their control, but they are still responsible for the morale, emotional well-being, and performance of subordinates, which can lead to treating followers as if they are not able to think for themselves.[27]

Stewardship

Stewardship
a belief that leaders are deeply accountable to others as well as to the organization, without trying to control others, define meaning and purpose for others, or take care of others

Stewardship is a pivotal shift in leadership thinking. Followers are empowered to make decisions and they have control over how they do their own jobs. Leaders give followers the power to influence goals, systems, and structures and become leaders themselves. **Stewardship** supports the belief that leaders are deeply accountable to others as well as to the organization, without trying to control others, define meaning and purpose for others, or take care of others.[28] In fact, stewardship has been called an alternative to leadership because the spotlight is on the people actually doing the work, making the product, providing the service, or working directly with the customer. Four principles provide the framework for stewardship.

1. *Reorient toward a partnership assumption.* Partnership can happen only when power and control shift away from formal leaders to core workers. Partners have a right to say "no" to one another. They are totally honest with one

another, neither hiding information nor protecting the other from bad news. In addition, partners (leaders and followers) are jointly responsible for defining vision and purpose and jointly accountable for outcomes.

2. *Localize decisions and power* to those closest to the work and the customer. Decision-making power and the authority to act should reside right at the point where the work gets done. This means reintegrating the "managing" and the "doing" of work, so that everyone is doing some of the core work of the organization part of the time. Nobody gets paid simply to plan and manage the work of others.

3. *Recognize and reward the value of labor.* The reward systems tie everyone's fortunes to the success of the enterprise. Stewardship involves redistributing wealth by designing compensation so that core workers can make significant gains when they make exceptional contributions. Everyone earns his or her pay by delivering real value, and the organization pays everyone as much as possible.

4. *Expect core work teams to build the organization.* Teams of workers who make up the core of the organization or division define goals, maintain controls, create a nurturing environment, and organize and reorganize themselves to respond to a changing environment and the marketplace they serve.

Stewardship leaders guide the organization without dominating it and facilitate followers without controlling them. Stewardship allows for a relationship between leaders and followers in which each makes significant, self-responsible contributions to organizational success. In addition, it gives followers a chance to use their minds, bodies, and spirits on the job, thereby allowing them to be whole human beings.

Stewardship leaders can help organizations thrive in today's complex environment because they tap into the energy and commitment of followers. Although the ideas we have discussed may sound new, an early management thinker, Mary Parker Follett, captured the spirit of stewardship 80 years ago when she described the type of leader who motivated her.

> The skillful leader, then, does not rely on personal force; he controls his group not by dominating but by expressing it. He stimulates what is best in us; he unifies and concentrates what we feel only gropingly and scatteringly, but he never gets away from the current of which we and he are both an integral part. He is a leader who gives form to the inchoate energy in every man. The person who influences me most is not he who does great deeds but he who makes me feel I can do great deeds.[29]

Servant Leadership

Servant leadership takes stewardship assumptions about leaders and followers one step further. Robert Wood Johnson, who built Johnson & Johnson from a small private company into one of the world's greatest corporations, summarized his ideas

Action Memo

As a leader: Apply the principles of stewardship to enhance your leadership effectiveness. Treat followers as true partners by sharing power and authority for setting goals, making decisions, and maintaining control over their own work and performance. Enable followers to achieve substantial personal gains when they make outstanding contributions to the enterprise.

about management in the expression "to serve." In a statement called "Our Management Philosophy," Johnson went on to say, "It is the duty of the leader to be a servant to those responsible to him."[30] Johnson died more than thirty years ago, but his beliefs about the moral responsibility of a leader are as fresh and compelling (and perhaps as controversial) today as they were when he wrote them.

Servant leadership

leadership in which the leader transcends self-interest to serve the needs of others, help others grow, and provide opportunities for others to gain materially and emotionally

Servant leadership is leadership upside-down. Servant leaders transcend self-interest to serve the needs of others, help others grow and develop, and provide opportunity for others to gain materially and emotionally. In organizations, these leaders' top priority is service to employees, customers, shareholders, and the general public. In their minds, the purpose of their existence is to serve; leadership flows out of the act of service because it enables other people to grow and become all they are capable of being.[31] There has been an explosion of interest in the concept of leader as servant in recent years because of the emphasis in organizations on empowerment, participation, shared authority, and building a community of trust.[32] The questionnaire in Leader's Self-Insight 6.1 enables you to evaluate your own leadership approach along the dimensions of authoritarian leadership, participative leadership, stewardship, and servant leadership, as illustrated in Exhibit 6.5.

Servant leadership was first described by Robert Greenleaf in his book, *Servant Leadership*. Greenleaf began developing his ideas after reading Hermann Hesse's novel, *Journey to the East*. The central character of the story is Leo, who appears as a servant to a group of men on a journey. Leo performs the lowliest, most menial tasks to serve the group, and he also cheers them with his good spirits and his singing. All goes well until Leo disappears, and then the journey falls into disarray. Years later, when the narrator is taken to the headquarters of the Order that had sponsored the original journey, he encounters Leo again. There, he discovers that Leo is in fact the titular head of the Order, a great leader.[33] Hesse's fictional character is the epitome of the servant leader, and some doubt whether real human beings functioning in the real world of organizations can ever achieve Leo's level of selflessness in service to others. However, many organizational leaders have shown that it is possible to operate from the principles of servant leadership, even in the business world. When Robert Townsend took over as head of the investment department at American Express, he made it his mission to stay out of his employees' way and invest his time and energy in getting them the pay, titles, and recognition they deserved from the organization.[34] Bob Thompson of the road-building company Thompson-McCully distributed $128 million to his 550 employees when he sold the company 40 years after he founded it. Thompson also made sure he chose a buyer who agreed not to break up the company or fire workers. He believed it just wasn't fair not to share the proceeds of the sale with the workers who had made the business a success.[35]

Action Memo

As a leader: Act like a servant leader by putting the needs, interests, and goals of others above your own. Use your personal gifts to help others grow and achieve their highest potential. Give followers power, responsibility, control, information, recognition, and rewards so they can flourish.

LEADER'S SELF-INSIGHT 6.1

Your Servant Leadership Orientation

Think about situations in which you were in a formal or informal leadership role in a group or organization. Imagine using your personal approach as a leader. To what extent does each of the following statements characterize your leadership?

1 = Very little; 2 = Somewhat; 3 = A moderate amount; 4 = A great deal; 5 = Very much

	Very little				Very much
1. My actions meet the needs of others before my own.	1	2	3	4	5
2. I enable others to feel ownership for their work.	1	2	3	4	5
3. I follow up after delegating.	1	2	3	4	5
4. I'm a perfectionist.	1	2	3	4	5
5. I work to create a sense of community.	1	2	3	4	5
6. I appreciate the needs and perspectives of others.	1	2	3	4	5
7. I utilize the skills and talents of others.	1	2	3	4	5
8. I am assertive about how to do things.	1	2	3	4	5
9. I give away credit and recognition to others.	1	2	3	4	5
10. I trust what people say.	1	2	3	4	5
11. I inform others of developments that affect their work.	1	2	3	4	5
12. I automatically take charge.	1	2	3	4	5
13. I encourage the growth of others, expecting nothing in return.	1	2	3	4	5
14. I value cooperation over competition.	1	2	3	4	5
15. I involve others in planning and goal setting.	1	2	3	4	5
16. I talk others into doing things my way.	1	2	3	4	5
17. I like to be of service to others.	1	2	3	4	5
18. I believe that others have good intentions.	1	2	3	4	5
19. I consult with people.	1	2	3	4	5
20. I put people under pressure.	1	2	3	4	5

Scoring and Interpretation: There are four subscale scores that represent four dimensions of leadership. For the dimension of *authoritarian leadership*, sum your responses to questions 4, 8, 12, 16, and 20. For the dimension of *participative leadership*, sum your scores for questions 2, 6, 10, 14, 18. For the dimension of *stewardship*, sum your scores for questions 3, 7, 11, 15, and 19. For the dimension of *servant leadership*, sum your scores for questions 1, 5, 9, 13, and 17.

My leadership scores are:

Authoritarian   _____.
Participative   _____.
Stewardship   _____.
Servant   _____.

These scores represent the four aspects of leadership called authoritarian, participative, stewardship, and servant as described in the text and illustrated in Exhibit 6.5. A score of 20 or above on any of these dimensions is above average, and a score below 10 is below average. A score of 15 is about average. Compare your four scores to one other to understand your own approach to stewardship and servant leadership. On which of the four dimensions would you like to score highest? Lowest? Study the specific questions on which you scored higher or lower to analyze your pattern of strengths and weaknesses. It is not possible to display all four dimensions of leadership simultaneously, so you should think about the type of leader you are and the type you wish to become.

There are four basic precepts in Greenleaf's servant leadership model:[36]

1. *Put service before self-interest.* Servant leaders make a conscious choice to use their gifts in the cause of change and growth for other individuals and for the organization. The desire to help others takes precedence over the desire to achieve a formal leadership position or to attain power and control over others. The servant leader calls for doing what is good and right for others, even if it does not "pay off" financially. In this view, the organization exists as much to provide meaningful work to the person as the person exists to perform work for the organization.

2. *Listen first to affirm others.* The servant leader doesn't have answers; he asks questions. One of the servant leader's greatest gifts to others is listening, fully understanding the problems others face, and affirming his confidence in others. The servant leader tries to figure out the will of the group and then further it however he can. The leader doesn't impose his or her will on others. By understanding others, the leader can contribute to the best course of action.

3. *Inspire trust by being trustworthy.* Servant leaders build trust by doing what they say they will do, being totally honest with others, giving up control, and focusing on the well-being of others. They share all information, good and bad, and they make decisions to further the good of the group rather than their own interests. In addition, trust grows from trusting others to make their own decisions. Servant leaders gain trust because they give everything away—power, control, rewards, information, and recognition. Trust allows others to flourish.

4. *Nourish others and help them become whole.* Servant leaders care about followers' spirits as well as their minds and bodies, and they believe in the unique potential of each person to have a positive impact on the world. Servant leaders help others find the power of the human spirit and accept their responsibilities. This requires an openness and willingness to share in the pain and difficulties of others. Being close to people also means leaders make themselves vulnerable to others and are willing to show their own pain and humanity.

Servant leadership can mean something as simple as encouraging others in their personal development and helping them understand the larger purpose in their work. When Linda Burzynski became president of Molly Maid International, she learned about servant leadership from one of her cleaners. Posing as a new member of the cleaning crew, Burzynski entered a home with her partner, Dawn, to find dishes piled high, food spilled on countertops, clothes and magazines strewn about, and pet hair everywhere. Surveying the mess, Burzynski was ready to walk out, but

Dawn explained that the woman who owned the house was going through a divorce and dealing with three rebellious teenage sons. "She's barely hanging on," said Dawn, and having a clean house gave her a sense of order and control. Burzynski noticed that Dawn seemed to take extra care because she knew she was helping the woman with more than just her household chores. Burzynski says she learned that day about the power of being a servant to her employees and helping them find larger meaning in their difficult jobs.[37] Another example of a leader who puts service to workers first is William Pollard, chairman of ServiceMaster.

In the Lead   C. William Pollard, ServiceMaster

ServiceMaster is a successful, dynamic company that cleans and maintains hospitals, schools, and other buildings. It's not a glamorous industry, and many of the jobs are menial—cleaning toilets, scrubbing floors, killing bugs. But ServiceMaster has instilled its employees with a sense of dignity, responsibility, and meaningfulness, thanks largely to the servant leadership of chairman C. William Pollard.

Pollard believes it is immoral to take away an employee's right to make decisions and take action. He sees leaders as having a moral responsibility to help employees grow and develop to their full potential, which means giving them the skills, information, tools, and authority they need to act independently. Pollard describes himself as a "leader who leads with a servant's heart," and he encourages others to lead in the same manner. Leaders throughout the organization don't see their jobs as just getting people to perform at work. Instead, their role is to help employees become well rounded people—enabling them to grow as individuals who contribute not only at work but also at home and in their communities. They care how employees feel about themselves, about their work, and about the people they interact with. ServiceMaster also insists that leaders keep an open-door policy and make themselves available to listen to any concern.

To Pollard, the real leader is not the "person with the most distinguished title, the highest pay, or the longest tenure . . . but the role model, the risk taker, the servant; not the person who promotes himself or herself, but the promoter of others."[38]

For leaders like William Pollard, Bob Thompson, and Robert Townsend, leadership contains a strong moral component. Servant leaders truly value and respect others as human beings, not as objects of labor. To fully trust others relies on an assumption that we all have a moral duty to one another.[39] To make the choice for service requires a belief in a purpose higher than acquiring more material goods for oneself. Raoul Wallenberg, described at the beginning of the chapter, made the choice for service when he exchanged a comfortable life of privilege for war-torn Hungary. Organizational leaders can act from moral values rather than from greed, selfishness, and fear. Indeed, Greenleaf believed that many people have the capacity for servant leadership. He said the greatest enemy to organizations and to society is fuzzy thinking on the part of good, intelligent, vital people who "have the potential to lead but do not lead, or who choose to follow a nonservant."[40]

Leadership Courage

Throughout this chapter, you have probably noticed words like *backbone*, *guts*, *fortitude*, and *fearlessness*. No doubt about it, doing the right thing requires courage. Leaders sometimes have to reach deep within themselves to find the strength and courage to resist temptations or to stand up for moral principles when others may ridicule them.

Some would say that without courage, leadership can't exist. However, for many leaders, particularly those working in large organizations, the importance of courage is easily obscured—the main thing is to get along, fit in, and do whatever brings promotions and pay raises. In a world of stability and abundance, it was easy to forget even the *meaning* of courage, so how can leaders know where to find it when they need it? In the following sections, we will examine the nature of leadership courage and discuss some ways courage is expressed in organizations. The final section of the chapter will explore the sources of leadership courage.

What Is Courage?

Many people know intuitively that courage can carry you through deprivation, ridicule, and rejection and enable you to achieve something about which you care deeply. Courage is both a moral and a practical matter for leaders. Years of stability and abundance misled American businesses into thinking that courage isn't needed in the business world. The lesson executives learned to advance in their careers was "Don't fail. Let someone else take the risk. Be careful. Don't make mistakes." Such a philosophy is no longer beneficial. Indeed, the courage to take risks has always been important for living a full, rewarding life, as discussed in the Living Leadership box. For today's organizations, things are constantly changing, and leaders thrive by solving problems through trial and error. They create the future by moving forward in the face of uncertainty, by taking chances, by acting with courage.[41] The defining characteristic of courage is the ability to step forward through fear. Courage doesn't mean the absence of doubt or fear, but the ability to act in spite of them.

Courage
the ability to step forward through fear

LIVING LEADERSHIP

Is It Worth the Risk?

To *laugh* . . . is to risk appearing the fool.

To *weep* . . . is to risk appearing sentimental.

To *reach out* . . . is to risk involvement.

To *expose feelings* . . . is to risk exposing your true self.

To *place your ideas and dreams before a crowd* . . . is to risk rejection.

To *love* . . . is to risk not being loved in return.

To *live* . . . is to risk dying.

To *hope* . . . is to risk despair.

To *try* . . . is to risk failure.

But risks must be taken, because the greatest hazard in life is to risk nothing.

Those who risk nothing do nothing and have nothing.

They may avoid suffering and sorrow,

But they cannot learn, feel, change, grow, or love.

Chained by their certitude, they are slaves; they have forfeited their freedom.

Only one who risks is free.

© Janet Rand

In fact, if there were no fear or doubt, courage would not be needed. People experience all kinds of fears, including fear of death, mistakes, failure, embarrassment, change, loss of control, loneliness, pain, uncertainty, abuse, rejection, success, and public speaking. It is natural and right for people to feel fear when real risk is involved, whether the risk be losing your life, losing your job, losing the acceptance of peers, or losing your reputation. But many fears are learned and prevent people from doing what they want. True leaders step through these learned fears to accept responsibility, take risks, make changes, speak their minds, and fight for what they believe.

Courage means accepting responsibility. Leaders make a real difference in the world when they are willing to step up and take personal responsibility. Some people just let life happen to them; leaders make things happen. Courageous leaders create opportunities to make a difference in their organizations and communities. One societal example is Robert Hicks, an ordinary man who made an extraordinary difference during the Civil Rights movement in the South. Hicks was a union representative at the local paper mill in Bogalusa, Louisiana, when the movement began heating up. Even though it spurred daily death threats to him and his family, Hicks stepped forward as a leader, organizing sit-ins, marches, and protests to help bring an end to institutionalized discrimination.[42]

By having the courage to speak up and accept responsibility, leaders in organizations can make a real difference as well. However, leaders sometimes fail in their efforts. They also demonstrate courage by openly taking responsibility for their failures and mistakes, rather than avoiding blame or shifting it to others. The acceptance of responsibility in many of today's large, bureaucratic organizations seems nonexistent. In one large agency of the federal government, for example, the slightest mistake created a whirlwind of blaming, finger pointing, and extra effort to avoid responsibility. The absence of courage froze the agency to the point that many employees were afraid to even do their routine tasks.[43]

Courage often means nonconformity. Leadership courage means going against the grain, breaking traditions, reducing boundaries, and initiating change. Leaders are willing to take risks for a higher purpose, and they encourage others to do so, as Georg Bauer did at Mercedes-Benz Credit Corporation (MBCC).

In the Lead   Georg Bauer, Mercedes-Benz Credit Corporation

From all outward appearances, nothing needed fixing at MBCC when Georg Bauer took over as president of the division. But Bauer saw a need to become a faster, leaner, and more customer-focused organization to keep pace with changes in the environment, and he encouraged employees to rebuild the organization from the bottom up. Bauer's "no fear" principle assured people that they could take risks and make mistakes without fear of recrimination or job loss.

"The future is all about risk-taking," Bauer says. "It's not enough to say, 'We encourage risk.' Leaders throughout the organization have to support people who take risks and make mistakes. . . . You have to have a fear-free environment." Employees worked in cross-functional teams to draft a new mission statement, attack waste, and redesign operational processes. During the reorganization, some employees actually came up with ideas that eliminated their own jobs, but the no-fear rule assured them that they would be reassigned to other areas.

By the time the new organization began to take shape, four of the company's eight layers of management had been stripped out. Assigned executive parking spots became a thing of the past, and every employee, from the lowest to the highest, became eligible for a leased Mercedes-Benz. New bonus programs compensated people not just for individual performance but for teamwork and organizational success. Bauer's courage to take risks enabled MBCC to cut costs, diversify into new financing arenas, improve customer service and employee satisfaction, and continue to change to keep pace with shifting market conditions.[44]

Going against the status quo is difficult. It's often easier to stay with what is familiar, even if it will lead to certain failure, than to initiate bold change. A naval aviator once said that many pilots die because they choose to stay with disabled aircraft, preferring the familiarity of the cockpit to the unfamiliarity of the parachute.[45] Similarly, many leaders hurt their organizations and their own careers by sticking with the status quo rather than facing the difficulty of change. Most leaders initiating change find some cooperation and support, but they also encounter resistance, rejection, loneliness, and even ridicule. Taking chances means making mistakes, enduring mockery or scorn, being outvoted by others, and sometimes failing miserably.

Courage means pushing beyond the comfort zone. To take a chance and improve things means leaders have to push beyond their comfort zone. According to Barry Diller, the former chairman of Paramount Pictures, Fox, Inc., and QVC, Inc., his secret to success is to "plunge into the uncomfortable; push, or be lucky enough to have someone push you, beyond your fears and your sense of limitations. That's what I've been doing . . . overcoming my discomfort as I go along."[46] When people go beyond the comfort zone, they encounter an invisible "wall of fear." They may encounter it when about to ask someone for a date, confront the boss, break off a relationship, launch an expensive project, or change careers. Facing the invisible wall of fear is when courage is needed most.

Courage means asking for what you want and saying what you think. Leaders have to speak out to influence others. However, the desire to please others—especially the boss—can sometimes block the truth. Everyone wants approval, so it is difficult to say things when you think others will disagree or disapprove. Author and scholar Jerry Harvey tells a story of how members of his extended family in Texas decided to drive 40 miles to Abilene for dinner on a hot day when the car air conditioning did not work. They were all miserable. Talking about it afterward, each person admitted they had not wanted to go but went along to please the others. The *Abilene Paradox* is the name Harvey uses to describe the tendency of people to not voice their true thoughts because they want to please others.[47] A top executive at Pepsi-Cola once said: "One of the things we look for when we are assessing people on their way up is, 'Do they have a point of view? Do they have the guts to recommend what might be unpopular solutions to things?'"[48] Courage means speaking your mind even when you know others may disagree with you and may even deride you. Courage also means asking for what you want and setting boundaries. It is the ability to say no to unreasonable demands from others, as well as the ability to ask for what you want to help achieve the vision.

Courage means fighting for what you believe. Courage means fighting for valued outcomes that benefit the whole. Leaders take risks, but they do so for a higher purpose. Kailash Satyarthi, head of the South Asian Coalition on Child Servitude, receives regular threats and two of his co-workers have been killed, but Satyarthi

> **Action Memo**
>
> As a leader: Develop the backbone to accept personal responsibility for achieving desired outcomes, go against the status quo, and stand up for what you believe. Push beyond your comfort zone and break through the wall of fear that limits you.

continues striving to free India's millions of children forced to work in bonded labor.[49] He doesn't risk his life just for the thrill of it. He does so for a cause he deeply believes in—the dignity of all human beings. Taking risks that do not offer the possibility of valuable and ethical outcomes is at best foolish and at worst evil. Leaders at Enron, for example, pushed risk to the limits, but they did so for selfish and unethical reasons. Courage doesn't mean doing battle to destroy the weak, feed one's own ego, or harm others. It means doing what you believe is right, even when this goes against the status quo and possibly opens you to failure and personal sacrifice. Complete the exercise in Leader's Self-Insight 6.2 to assess your level of leadership courage.

How Does Courage Apply to Moral Leadership?

There are many people working in organizations who have the courage to be unconventional, to do what they think is right, to dare to treat employees and customers as whole human beings who deserve respect. Balancing profit with people, selfishness with service, and control with stewardship requires individual moral courage.

One good example of the application of courage to moral leadership in the business world is Lawrence Fish, chairman, president, and CEO of Citizen's Bank.

In The Lead   Lawrence Fish, Citizens Bank

Lawrence Fish, chairman, president, and CEO of Citizens Bank, is a man who has known both success and failure as a result of his unconventional approaches and ethical beliefs. His effort to rescue the Bank of New England ended in defeat with the bank's sale to Fleet Financial Group. However, Fish's unconventional ideas have led to success at Citizens. Under his leadership, Citizens has grown more than seven-fold to become the second largest commercial banking company in New England and one of the thirty-five largest in the United States. According to Cornelius Hurley, a banking consultant in Boston, Fish has "put together a powerhouse." Yet when he talks about the company, Fish says, "If we just make money, we'll fail."

Fish is widely known for his volunteer efforts and commitment to the community. He once donated half of his salary to Drake University in Iowa, his alma mater. When he was offered the job at Citizens, he postponed taking it for three months so he could work in a shelter for abused kids—washing walls, feeding children, reading stories. He also serves as founding chairman of the Rhode Island Commission for National and Community Service, which is recognized as one of the most creative and successful Americorps programs in the country.

LEADER'S SELF-INSIGHT 6.2

Assess Your Moral Courage

Think about situations in which you either assumed or were given a leadership role in a group or organization. Imagine using your own courage as a leader. To what extent does each of the following statements characterize your leadership?

1 = Very little; 2 = Somewhat; 3= A moderate amount; 4 = A great deal; 5 = Very much

	Very little				Very much
1. I risk substantial personal loss to achieve the vision.	1	2	3	4	5
2. I take personal risks to defend my beliefs.	1	2	3	4	5
3. I say no even if I have a lot to lose.	1	2	3	4	5
4. My actions are linked to higher values.	1	2	3	4	5
5. I often act against the opinions and approval of others.	1	2	3	4	5
6. I quickly tell people the truth, even when it is negative.	1	2	3	4	5
7. I am relaxed most of the time.	1	2	3	4	5
8. I speak out against organizational injustice.	1	2	3	4	5
9. I stand up to offensive people.	1	2	3	4	5
10. I act according to my conscience even if it means I lose stature.	1	2	3	4	5

Scoring and Interpretation

Each question above pertains to some aspect of displaying courage in a leadership situation. Add up your scores to the 10 questions: _____. If you received a score of 40 or higher, you would be considered a courageous leader. A score below 20 indicates that you avoid difficult issues or have not been in situations that challenge your moral leadership. Is your score consistent with your understanding of your own courage? Look at the individual questions for which you scored highest and lowest to learn more about your specific strengths and weaknesses. Compare your score to that of other students. How might you increase your courage as a leader?

Fish's approach at Citizens is to turn the conventional wisdom of banking on its head. Unlike most big banks, Citizens courts working-class customers and specializes in the human touch rather than promoting fancy electronic devices and new technology. Although the bank has all the modern conveniences, including online banking, Fish believes banking the old-fashioned way—with a human touch—is the best way to long-term profitability. He gives local bank executives the freedom to decide how to make loans rather than insisting on approval from the home office. He makes a point of writing a thank-you note to at least one employee a day, and he encourages his staff to spend part of their time doing volunteer work. He is sometimes derided for "having too much heart" or "being too soft." However, Anat Bird, a banking consultant in New York, says Citizens' success shows there is still room for banks that operate efficiently but with a heart.

Fish believes there's more to life than material success. It's a belief that goes back to 1968, when he graduated from Harvard Business School. Rather than heading for Wall Street, the nonconformist Fish ended up at a remote ashram in northern India, where he lived as an ascetic for a year. "There are forces that brought me to India that are still with me," he says. "Ultimately, what matters is the good that we do."[50]

Acting like a moral leader requires personal courage. To practice moral leadership, leaders have to know themselves, understand their strengths and weaknesses, know what they stand for, and often be nonconformists. Honest self-analysis can be painful, and acknowledging one's limitations in order to recognize the superior abilities of others takes personal strength of character. In addition, moral leadership means building relationships, which requires sharing yourself, listening, having significant personal experiences with others, and making yourself vulnerable—qualities that frighten many people. The quest for emotional strength requires people to overcome their deepest fears and to accept emotions as a source of strength rather than weakness. True power lies in the emotions that connect people. By getting close and doing what is best for others—sharing the good and the bad, the pain and anger as well as the success and the joy—leaders bring out the best qualities in others.[51]

One example of this in practice is when William Peace had to initiate a layoff as general manager of the Synthetic Fuels Division of Westinghouse. To make the division attractive to buyers, executives made a painful decision to cut any jobs not considered essential. Peace had the courage to deliver the news about layoffs personally. He took some painful blows in the face-to-face meetings he held with the workers to be laid off, but he believed that allowing them to vent their grief and anger at him and the situation was the moral thing to do. His action sent a message to the remaining workers that, even though layoffs were necessary, leaders valued each of them as individuals. Because the workers recognized that layoffs were a last resort and the executive team was doing everything they could to save as many jobs as possible, they rededicated themselves to helping save the division. A buyer was found and the company had the opportunity to rehire half of those who had been laid off. Everyone contacted agreed to come back because the humane way they had been treated overcame negative feelings about the layoff.[52] For Peace, the courage to practice moral leadership gained respect, renewed commitment, and higher performance, even though he suffered personal rejection in the short run. Standing up for one's beliefs often entails great risk and tremendous courage. Nowhere is this more evident than in the case of ethical whistleblowing.

Opposing unethical conduct requires courage. **Whistleblowing** means employee disclosure of illegal, immoral, or unethical practices in the organization.[53] One recent example of courage in this area is Colleen Rowley, the Minneapolis FBI staff

Whistleblowing employee disclosure of illegal, immoral, or unethical practices in the organization

attorney whose whistleblowing letter called attention to agency shortcomings that may have contributed to the September 11, 2001, terrorist tragedy. A colleague of Rowley's said, "She always does what is right, even when no one is watching."[54]

Whistleblowing has become widespread in recent years, but it is still highly risky for employees, who may lose their jobs, be ostracized by co-workers, or be transferred to undesirable positions. Consider Mark Graf, a Wackenhut Services security specialist stationed at Rocky Flats nuclear facility outside Denver, Colorado. Graf was alarmed when the company temporarily removed 450 kilograms of plutonium oxide from a vault-like room to a less secure location. After speaking to company officials and getting no response, Graf blew the whistle to outsiders. In the years that followed, Graf was ordered to consult a psychologist, was consistently given unfavorable assignments, was eventually placed on administrative leave, and nearly lost his wife and family because of the stress caused by this situation.[55]

Although some whistleblowers believe nothing bad will happen to them because they are doing the right thing, most realize they may suffer financially and emotionally from their willingness to report unethical conduct on the part of bosses or coworkers.[56] They step forward to tell the truth despite a jumble of contradictory emotions and fears. As one professor put it, "Depending upon the circumstances, including our own courage, we can choose to act and be ethical both as individuals and as leaders."[57] Choosing to act courageously means conflicting emotions— whistleblowers may feel an ethical obligation to report the wrongdoing but may also feel disloyal to their bosses and co-workers. Some may do battle within themselves about where their responsibility lies. Robert A. Bugai, who challenged college marketers on unethical business practices in the early 1980s, warns that there are considerable costs involved—"mentally, financially, physically, emotionally, and spiritually." However, when asked if he'd do it again, he says, "You bet."[58]

Finding Personal Courage

How does a leader find the courage to step through fear and confusion, to act despite the risks involved? All of us have the potential to live and act courageously, if we can push through our own fears. Most of us have learned fears that limit our comfort zones and stand in the way of being our best and accomplishing our goals. We have been conditioned to follow the rules, not rock the boat, to go along with things we feel are wrong so others will like and accept us. There are a number of ways people can unlock the courage within themselves, including committing to causes they believe in, connecting with others, welcoming failure as a natural and beneficial part of life, and harnessing anger.

Believe in a Higher Purpose   Courage comes easily when we fight for something we really believe in. Service to a larger vision or purpose gives people the courage to step through fear. For someone to risk his life as Raoul Wallenberg did

Action Memo

As a leader: Find your personal courage by committing to something you deeply believe in. Welcome potential failure as a means of growth and development. Build bonds of caring and mutual support with family, friends, and colleagues to reduce fear. Harness anger and frustration as a source of courage.

requires a profound conviction that there is a greater good than the self. In organizations, too, courage depends on belief in a higher vision. A leader who is concerned only with his own career advancement would not be willing to report wrongdoing for fear of losing his position. Colleen Rowley blew the whistle at the FBI after September 11 because she believed people's lives were at stake. When she was a young girl, Rowley had the courage to tell teachers after class if they were wrong or unclear because she wanted to help classmates learn the material.[59] These higher purposes overshadowed concerns about her own self-interests.

Draw Strength from Others Caring about others and having support from others is a potent source of courage in a topsy-turvy world. Consider a caring parent who will risk his or her own life to save a child. Leaders who genuinely care about the people they work with will take risks to help those people grow and succeed. Having the support of others is also a source of courage, and the best leaders aren't afraid to lean on others when they need to. People who feel alone in the world take fewer risks because they have more to lose.[60] Being part of an organizational team that is supportive and caring, or having a loving and supportive family at home, can reduce the fear of failure and help people take risks they otherwise wouldn't take.

Welcome Failure Walt Disney, who had a business venture go bankrupt before he went on to achieve major success, once said, "It's important to have a good hard failure when you're young."[61] Today, many people want success to come without difficulties, problems, or struggles. However, accepting—even welcoming—failure enables courage. Failure can play a creative role in work and in life. Success and failure are two sides of the same coin; one cannot exist without the other.

When people accept failure and are at peace with the worst possible outcome, they find they have the fortitude to move forward. Leaders know that failure can lead to success and that the pain of learning strengthens individuals and the organization. Sharon McCollick was hired for a top sales and planning position at a hot software startup partly because she had started a business and failed. Company leaders liked the fact that she had been willing to take the risks associated with starting a designer apparel business and then move forward after the failure. Even people who invested in her business and lost money say they'd do it again. "She tried and failed and so what?" said one backer. "The next time, my bet's on her."[62] McCollick believes that having hit rock bottom and survived has given her greater courage. In addition, she radiates self-confidence because she is no longer terrified of failure. There is evidence that with repeated practice, people can overcome fears such as a fear of flying or fear of heights. Practice also enables people to overcome fear of risk-taking in their work. Every time you push beyond your comfort zone, every time you fail and try again, you build psychological strength and courage.

Harness Frustration and Anger If you have ever been really angry about something, you know that it can cause you to forget about fear of embarrassment or fear that others won't like you. In organizations, we can also see the power of frustration and anger. Glenn McIntyre used his anger and frustration to start a new life and a new business. After he was paralyzed in a motorcycle accident, McIntyre first used his anger to overcome thoughts of suicide and begin intensive physical therapy. Later, frustration over how poorly hotels served handicapped guests led him to start a consulting firm, Access Designs. The firm helps hotels such as Quality Suites and Renaissance Ramada redesign their space to be more usable for disabled travelers.[63] People in organizations can harness their anger to deal with difficult situations. When someone has to be fired for just cause, a supervisor may put if off until some incident makes her angry enough to step through the fear and act. Sometimes, outrage over a perceived injustice can give a mild-mannered person the courage to confront the boss head on.[64] In addition, getting mad at yourself may be the motivation to change. Anger, in moderate amounts, is a healthy emotion that provides energy to move forward. The challenge is to harness anger and use it appropriately.

Summary and Interpretation

This chapter has explored a number of ideas concerning moral leadership and leadership courage. People want honest and trustworthy leaders. However, the ethical climate in many organizations is at a low point. Leaders face pressures that challenge their ability to do the right thing—pressures to cut costs, increase profits, meet the demands of various stakeholders, and look successful. Creating an ethical organization requires that leaders act based on moral principles. Leaders cause things to go wrong in the organization when they excessively promote self-interest, practice deception and breach agreements, and lack the courage to confront unjust acts. Ethical leaders are humble, honest, and straightforward. They maintain a concern for the greater good, strive for fairness, and demonstrate the courage to stand up for what is right. Acting as a moral leader means demonstrating the importance of serving people and society as well as increasing profits or personal gain.

One personal consideration for leaders is the level of moral development. Leaders use an understanding of the stages of moral development to enhance their own as well as followers' moral growth. Leaders who operate at higher stages of moral development focus on the needs of followers and universal moral principles.

Ideas about control versus service between leaders and followers are changing and expanding, reflected in a continuum of leader-follower relationships. The continuum varies from authoritarian managers to participative managers to stewardship to servant leadership. Leaders who operate from the principles of stewardship and servant leadership can help build ethical organizations.

The final sections of the chapter discussed leadership courage and how leaders can find their own courage. Courage means the ability to step forward through fear, to accept responsibility, to take risks and make changes, to speak your mind, and to fight for what you believe. Two expressions of courage in organizations are moral leadership and ethical whistleblowing. Sources of courage include belief in a higher purpose, connection with others, experience with failure, and harnessing anger.

Discussion Questions

1. If you were in a position similar to Raoul Wallenberg, what do you think you would do? Why?
2. What are some pressures you face as a student that challenge your ability to do the right thing? Do you expect to face more or fewer pressures as a leader? Discuss what some of these pressure might be.
3. If most adults are at a conventional level of moral development, what does this mean for their potential for moral leadership?
4. Do you feel that the difference between authoritarian leadership and stewardship should be interpreted as a moral difference? Discuss.
5. Should serving others be placed at a higher moral level than serving oneself? Discuss.
6. If you find yourself avoiding a situation or activity, what can you do to find the courage to move forward? Explain.
7. If it is immoral to prevent those around you from growing to their fullest potential, are you being moral?
8. Do you have the courage to take a moral stand that your peers and even authority figures will disagree with? Why?
9. Do you agree that it is important for leaders to do the right thing even if no one will ever know about it? Why or why not?

Leadership at Work

Scary Person

Think of a person in your life right now who is something of a scary person for you. Scary people are those you don't really know but who are scary to you because you anticipate that you won't like them, perhaps because you don't like the way they act or look from a distance, and hence you avoid building relationships with them. A scary person might be a student at school, someone at work, a neighbor, or someone you are aware of in your social circle.

Scary people trigger a small amount of fear in us—that is why we avoid them and don't really get to know them. A test of courage is whether you can step through your fear. You will experience fear many times as a leader.

For this exercise, your assignment is to reach out to one or more scary persons in your life. Invite the person for lunch or just walk up and introduce yourself and start a conversation. Perhaps you can volunteer to work with the person on an assignment. The key thing is to step through your fear and get to know this person well enough to know what he or she is really like.

After you have completed your assignment, share what happened with another person. Were you able to reach out to the scary person? What did you discover about the scary person? What did you discover about yourself by doing this activity? If you found the exercise silly and refused to do it, you may have let fear get the better of you by rationalizing that the assignment has little value.

In Class: The instructor can give this assignment to be done prior to a specific class. During class it is a good exercise for students to discuss their scary person experiences among themselves in small groups. The instructor can ask students to report to their groups about the scary person, revealing as many details as they are comfortable with, explaining how they summoned the courage to reach out, and the result. After the groups have finished their exchange, the instructor can ask a couple of student volunteers to report their experiences to the entire class. Then students can be asked questions such as: Looking back on this experience, what is courage? How was it expressed (or not) in this exercise? How will fear and courage be part of organizational leadership?

Leadership Development: Cases for Analysis

Young Leaders Council

Gehan Rasinghe was thrilled to be appointed to the Young Leaders Council at Werner & Burns, a large consulting and financial management firm located in Boston. When Rasinghe had first joined the firm he'd had a hard time fitting in, with his accented English and quiet manner. However, through hard work and persistence, he had overcome many obstacles, made many friends, and worked his way up in the organization. He had been in a leadership position as an account manager for two years, and he particularly loved working with new employees and helping them find their niches in the company and develop greater skills and confidence. His employee evaluations by both superiors and subordinates had been exceptional, and Rasinghe himself was pleased with his success as a leader.

Now, this! The purpose of the Young Leaders Council was to provide a training ground for young executives at Werner & Burns and help them continue to improve their leadership skills. In addition, top executives and the Board used the Council as a way to evaluate the potential of young managers for higher-level positions. Everyone knew that a good showing on the Council often resulted in a promotion. Typically, an appointment to the Council was for a one-year period, with new members added every six months on a rotating basis. Occasionally, some members would stay an additional six months, based on the results of an appraisal process personally introduced by the CEO. The process involved each member of the Council being rated by each of the other members on four criteria: (1) general intelligence and knowledge of the business; (2) creativity and innovativeness; (3) cooperation and team spirit; and (4) adherence to company values.

Rasinghe was attending his fifth monthly meeting when several members of the Council raised a concern about the rating system. They felt that it was being forced on the group, was controlled by top management, and was not used as a fair and accurate rating of each member's abilities but just as a way "to pat your buddies on the back," as his colleague Cathy Patton put it. Most of the other members seemed to agree with their arguments, at least to some degree. Rasinghe agreed that the system was flawed, but he was surprised by their suggestion for a solution. One member made an informal motion that in the next appraisal every member of the Council should simply give every other member the highest rating in each category.

Rasinghe quickly considered what to do as the chairman called for a show of hands from those in favor of the motion. His gut feeling is that such a "solution" to the problem of the rating system would be dishonest and unethical, but he remembers what it felt like to be an "outsider," and he doesn't want to be there again.

SOURCE: Based on "Junior Board," in John M. Champion and Francis J. Bridges, *Critical Incidents in Management*, rev. ed., (Homewood, IL: Irwin, 1969), 106–107.

Questions

1. What personal and organizational factors might influence Rasinghe's decision?

2.   Do you believe it would take courage for Rasinghe to vote against the motion? What sources of courage might he call upon to help him vote his conscience?
3.   What do you think about the current rating system? If you were in Rasinghe's position, what would you do? Discuss.

The Boy, the Girl, the Ferryboat Captain, and the Hermits

There was an island, and on this island there lived a girl. A short distance away there was another island, and on this island there lived a boy. The boy and the girl were very much in love with each other.

The boy had to leave his island and go on a long journey, and he would be gone for a very long time. The girl felt that she must see the boy one more time before he went away. There was only one way to get from the island where the girl lived to the boy's island, and that was on a ferryboat that was run by a ferryboat captain. And so the girl went down to the dock and asked the ferryboat captain to take her to the island where the boy lived. The ferryboat captain agreed and asked her for the fare. The girl told the ferryboat captain that she did not have any money. The ferryboat captain told her that money was not necessary: "I will take you to the other island if you will stay with me tonight."

The girl did not know what to do, so she went up into the hills on her island until she came to a hut where a hermit lived. We will call him the first hermit. She related the whole story to the hermit and asked for his advice. The hermit listened carefully to her story, and then told her, "I cannot tell you what to do. You must weigh the alternatives and the sacrifices that are involved and come to a decision within your own heart."

And so the girl went back down to the dock and accepted the ferryboat captain's offer.

The next day, when the girl arrived on the other island, the boy was waiting at the dock to greet her. They embraced, and then the boy asked her how she got over to his island, for he knew she did not have any money. The girl explained the ferryboat captain's offer and what she did. The boy pushed her away from him and said, "We're through. That's the end. Go away from me. I never want to see you again," and he left her.

The girl was desolate and confused. She went up into the hills of the boy's island to a hut where a second hermit lived. She told the whole story to the second hermit and asked him what she should do. The hermit told her that there was nothing she could do, that she was welcome to stay in his hut, to partake of his food, and to rest on his bed while he went down into the town and begged for enough money to pay the girl's fare back to her own island.

When the second hermit returned with the money for her, the girl asked him how she could repay him. The hermit answered, "You owe me nothing. We owe this to each other. I am only too happy to be of help." And so the girl went back down to the dock and returned to her own island.

Questions

1. List in order the characters in this story that you like, from most to least. What values governed your choices?
2. Rate the characters on their level of moral development. Explain.
3. Evaluate each character's level of courage. Discuss.

References

1. John C. Kunich and Richard I. Lester, "Profile of a Leader: The Wallenberg Effect," *The Journal of Leadership Studies* 4, no. 3 (Summer 1997): 5–19.
2. Patricia Wallington,"Honestly?!" *CIO* (March 15, 2003): 41–42.
3. Brian Cronin, "After Enron: The Ideal Corporation," *BusinessWeek* (August 26, 2002), 68–74.
4. "High Profiles in Hot Water," *The Wall Street Journal*, June 28, 2002, B1.
5. Rebecca Smith, "New Charges Added Against Fastow," *The Wall Street Journal*, May 2, 2003, A3, A8; "Mayor Convicted of 16 of 21 Charges," *Johnson City Press*, March 20, 2003, 9.
6. Kris Maher, "Wanted: Ethical Employer," *The Wall Street Journal*, July 9, 2002, B1, B8.
7. David Wessel, "Venal Sins: Why the Bad Guys of the Boardroom Emerged en Masse," *The Wall Street Journal*, June 20, 2002, A1, A6.
8. Sydney Finkelstein, "Jayson Blair, Meet Nicholas Leeson," (Manager's Journal column), *The Wall Street Journal*, May 20, 2003, B2.
9. Wessel, "Venal Sins."
10. John A. Byrne with Mike France and Wendy Zellner, "The Environment Was Ripe for Abuse," *BusinessWeek* (February 25, 2002): 118–120.
11. This section is based on Donald G. Zauderer, "Integrity: An Essential Executive Quality," *Business Forum* (Fall, 1992): 12–16.
12. Jerry Useem, "Have They No Shame?" *Fortune* (April 28, 2003): 56–64.
13. Wallington, "Honestly?!"

14. Al Gini, "Moral Leadership and Business Ethics," *The Journal of Leadership Studies* 4, no. 4 (Fall 1997): 64–81.

15. Henry Ford, Sr., quoted by Thomas Donaldson, *Corporations and Morality* (Prentice Hall, Inc., 1982), 57 in Al Gini, "Moral Leadership and Business Ethics," 64–81.

16. John A. Bryne, "After Enron: The Ideal Corporation," *BusinessWeek*, August 26, 2002, 68–74; and Nancy D. Holt, "Alfred P. West Jr., SEI Investments," (Workspaces column), *The Wall Street Journal*, February 19, 2003 , B10

17. John Grossmann, "A Whirlwind of Humanity," *Sky*, January 1997, 96–101.

18. Gretchen Morgenson, "Shares of Corporate Nice Guys Can Finish First," *New York Times*, April 27, 2003, 1.

19. Donald G. Zauderer, "Integrity: An Essential Executive Quality," *Business Forum* (Fall 1992): 12–16; and LaBarre, "Do You Have the Will to Lead?"

20. James M. Kouzes and Barry Z. Posner, *Credibility: How Leaders Gain and Lose It, Why People Demand It* (San Francisco: Jossey-Bass, 1993), 255.

21. Viktor E. Frankl, *Man's Search for Meaning* (New York: Pocket Books, 1959), 104.

22. Lawrence Kolhberg, "Moral Stages and Moralization: The Cognitive Developmental Approach," in Thomas Likona, ed. *Moral Development and Behavior: Theory, Research, and Social Issues* (Austin, TX: Holt, Rinehart and Winston, 1976), 31–53; Jill W. Graham, "Leadership, Moral Development, and Citizenship Behavior," *Business Ethics Quarterly* 5, no. 1 (January 1995): 43–54; James Weber, "Exploring the Relationship between Personal Values and Moral Reasoning," *Human Relations* 46, no. 4 (April 1993): 435–463; and Duane M. Covrig, "The Organizational Context of Moral Dilemmas: The Role of Moral Leadership in Administration in Making and Breaking Dilemmas," *The Journal of Leadership Studies* 7, no. 1 (2000): 40–59.

23. Tom Morris, *If Aristotle Ran General Motors* (New York: Henry Holt, 1997).

24. "Roy Vagelos Attacks River Blindness," in Michael Useem, *The Leadership Moment: Nine Stories of Triumph and Disaster and Their Lessons for Us All,* (New York: Times Business, 1998), 10–42.

25. James Weber, "Exploring the Relationship Between Personal Values and Moral Reasoning," *Human Relations* 46, no. 4 (April 1993): 435–463.

26. Peter Block, "Reassigning Responsibility," *Sky* (February 1994): 26–31; and David P. McCaffrey, Sue R. Faerman, and David W. Hart, "The Appeal and Difficulty of Participative Systems," *Organization Science* 6, no. 6 (November–December 1995): 603–627.

27. Block, "Reassigning Responsibility."

28. This discussion of stewardship is based on Peter Block, *Stewardship: Choosing Service Over Self-Interest* (San Francisco: Berrett-Koehler Publishers, 1993), 29–31; and Block, "Reassigning Responsibility."

29. Mary Parker Follett, from *The New State* (1918), as quoted in David K. Hurst, "Thoroughly Modern—Mary Parker Follett," *Business Quarterly* 56, no. 4 (Spring 1992): 55–58.

30. Lawrence G. Foster, *Robert Wood Johnson—The Gentleman Rebel* (Lemont, PA: Lillian Press, 1999); and John Cunniff, "Businessman's Honesty, Integrity Lesson for Today," *Johnson City Press*, May 28, 2000.

31. Sen Sendjaya and James C. Sarros, "Servant Leadership: Its Origin, Development, and Application in Organizations," *Journal of Leadership and Organizational Studies* 9, no. 2 (2002): 57–64.

32. Ibid.; examples include B. M. Bass, "The Future of Leadership in Learning Organizations," *The Journal of Leadership Studies* 7, no. 3 (2000): 18–40; I. H. Buchen, "Servant Leadership: A Model for Future Faculty and Future Institutions," *The Journal of Leadership Studies* 5, no. 1 (1998): 125; Y. Choi and R. R. Mai-Dalton, "On the Leadership Function of Self-Sacrifice," *Leadership Quarterly* 9, no. 4 (1998): 475–501; R. F. Russel, "The Role of Values in Servant Leadership," *Leadership and Organizational Development Journal* 22, no. 2 (2001): 76–83.

33. Robert K. Greenleaf, *Servant Leadership: A Journey into the Nature of Legitimate Power and Greatness* (Mahwah, N.J.: Paulist Press, 1977), 7.

34. Robert Townsend, "Leader at Work," *Across the Board* (January 2001): 13–14.

35. Sharon Cohen, "Boss Treats His Workers Like a Million Bucks—By Giving It To Them," *Johnson City Press*, September 12, 1999, 28; and Michelle Singletary, "Saluting a Generous Spirit, *The Washington Post*, August 1, 1999, H1.

36. The following is based on Greenleaf, *Servant Leadership*, and Walter Kiechel III, "The Leader as Servant," *Fortune* (May 4, 1992): 121–122; and Mary Sue Polleys, "One University's Response to the Anti-Leadership Vaccine: Developing Servant Leaders," *The Journal of Leadership Studies* 8, no. 3 (2002): 117–130.

37. Marcia Heroux Pounds, "Execs Should Head For Trenches to Find Out How Business Works," *The Tennessean*, May 9, 1999, 2H.

38. C. William Pollard, "The Leader Who Serves," in *The Leader of the Future*, Frances Hesselbein, Marshall Goldsmith, and Richard Beckhard, eds. (San Francisco: Jossey-Bass, 1996), 241–248; and C. W. Pollard, "The Leader Who Serves," *Strategy and Leadership* (September–October 1997): 49–51.

39. LaRue Tone Hosmer, "Trust: The Connecting Link between Organizational Theory and Philosophical Ethics," *Academy of Management Review* 20, no. 2 (April 1995): 379–403.

40. Greenleaf, *Servant Leadership*, 45.
41. Richard L. Daft and Robert H. Lengel, *Fusion Leadership: Unlocking the Subtle Forces that Change People and Organizations* (San Francisco: Berrett-Koehler, 1998).
42. Lisa Frazier Page, "Ordinary People, Extraordinary Acts," *The Washington Post* (February 22, 2001), T02.
43. Daft and Lengel, *Fusion Leadership*, 155.
44. "Credit Where Credit Is Due," segment in Thomas Petzinger Jr., "In Search of the New World (of Work)," *Fast Company* (April 1999): 214–227.
45. Reported in Nido R. Qubein, *Stairway to Success: The Complete Blueprint for Personal and Professional Achievement* (New York: John Wiley & Sons, 1997).
46. Barry Diller, "The Discomfort Zone," *Inc.* (November 1995): 19–20.
47. Jerry B. Harvey, *The Abilene Paradox and Other Meditations on Management* (Lexington, MA: Lexington Books, 1988), 13–15.
48. Lester Korn, *The Success Profile: A Leading Headhunter Tells You How to Get to the Top* (New York: Simon & Schuster, 1988).
49. Kerry Kennedy Cuomo, "'Courage Begins with One Voice,'" *Parade Magazine* (September 24, 2000), 6–8.
50. Joseph Rebello, "Radical Ways of Its CEO Are a Boon to Bank," *The Wall Street Journal*, March 20,1995, B1, B2; and Profile of Lawrence W. Fish, *http://www.citizensbank.com*, accessed on August 11, 2000.
51. A. J. Vogl, "Risky Work," an interview with Max DePree, *Across the Board* (July/August 1993): 27–31.
52. William H. Peace, "The Hard Work of Being a Soft Manager," *Harvard Business Review*, (November–December 1991): 40–47.
53. Janet P. Near and Marcia P. Miceli, "Effective Whistle-Blowing," *Academy of Management Review* 20, no. 3 (1995), 679–708.
54. Wallington, "Honestly?!"
55. Susan Orenstein, "Exposing Your Superiors: A Practical Guide," *Business 2.0* (April 2002): 112–113.
56. Hal Lancaster, "Workers Who Blow the Whistle on Bosses Often Pay a High Price," *The Wall Street Journal* (July 18, 1995), B1.
57. Richard P. Nielsen, "Changing Unethical Organizational Behavior," *The Executive* (May 1989): 123–130.
58. Barbara Ettorre, "Whistleblowers: Who's the Real Bad Guy?" *Management Review* (May 1994): 18–23.
59. Curtis C. Verschoor, "Are 'Whistle-Blowers' Heroes or Just Doing Their Job?" *Strategic Finance* (March 2003): 18–19.
60. James M. Kouzes and Barry Z. Posner, *The Leadership Challenge: How to Get Extraordinary Things Done in Organizations* (San Francisco: Jossey-Bass, 1988).

61. Quoted by Michael Eisner, interviewed by Laura Rich in "Talk About Failure," *The Industry Standard* (July 30, 2001): 41–47.

62. Thomas Petzinger Jr. "She Failed. So What? An Entrepreneur Finds Her Prestige Rising" (The Front Lines column), *The Wall Street Journal*, October 31, 1997, B1.

63. Michael Warshaw, ed., "Great Comebacks," *Success* (July/August 1995): 33–46.

64. Ira Cheleff, *The Courageous Follower: Standing Up To and For Our Leaders* (San Francisco: Berrett-Koehler, 1995).

Chapter

Your Leadership Challenge

After reading this chapter, you should be able to:

- Recognize your followership style and take steps to become a more effective follower.

- Understand the leader's role in developing effective followers.

- Apply the principles of effective followership, including responsibility, service, challenging authority, participating in change, and knowing when to leave.

- Implement the strategies for effective followership at school or work.

- Know what followers want and contribute to building a community among followers.

Five hours into her shift, four harried customers line up at Dawn Marshall's cash register at the Pathmark supermarket in Upper Derby, Pennsylvania. Eight minutes and 27 bags later, they're all out the door with smiles on their faces. Few people would think Marshall has a glamourous or influential job—but she treats it like the most significant job in the world.

In a society that is rapidly going self-service, Marshall specializes in giving people a little bit of luxury in the mundane chore of grocery shopping. She's a good cashier, but her forte is bagging. Marshall knows how to pack the flimsy plastic bags so that eggs don't get broken, bread doesn't get squashed, and ground beef doesn't leak all over the cereal boxes. In 2002, she won a National Grocers Association contest as the best bagger in America, based on speed, bag-building technique, style, and attitude. "I believe it's an art that should be taken seriously," Marshall says of her work. Many Pathmark customers agree. They're tired of cashiers and baggers who simply throw the stuff in bags without giving a care for the customer's convenience or needs. One customer admits that she shops at Pathmark rather than a store closer to her home because of Marshall. "I like her attitude," says the customer. "She bags it so I can carry my groceries without a real strain. Clone her."

Even though Marshall works on her feet all day and often has to put up with rude or insensitive customers, she handles whatever comes her way with a positive attitude. For Marshall, her job is not bagging groceries, but making people's lives easier. Thus, she approaches her work with energy and enthusiasm, striving to do her best in every encounter. She doesn't need close supervision or someone pushing her to work harder. The busier it is, the better she likes it.[1]

At Pathmark, Dawn Marshall has taken what some would consider a boring, low-paying job and imbued it with meaning and value. She accepts responsibility for her own personal fulfillment and finds ways to expand her potential and use her capacities to serve the needs of others and the organization. These are the hallmarks of not only good followers, but good leaders as well.

Leadership and followership are closely intertwined. As a Pathmark cashier, Dawn Marshall is a follower, but she acts as a leader by setting an example for others and using her positive attitude to inspire and uplift other people. She is capable of self-management rather than needing someone else to tell her how to approach her work, and she strives to create a positive impact rather than dwelling on the negative aspects of her job. Effective followers like Dawn Marshall are essential to the success of any endeavor, whether it be running a supermarket, winning a basketball game, completing a class assignment, or organizing a United Way fund drive.

In this chapter, we will examine the important role of followership, including the nature of the follower's role, the different styles of followership that individuals express, and how effective followers behave. The chapter also explores sources of power available to followers and how followers develop their personal potential to be more effective. Finally, we will look at the leader's role in developing effective followers and how followers can work with leaders to build a sense of community within their organizations.

The Role of Followers

Followership is important in the discussion of leadership for several reasons. First, leadership and followership are fundamental roles that individuals shift into and out of under various conditions. Everyone—leaders included—is a follower at one time or another. Indeed, most individuals, even those in a position of authority, have some kind of boss or supervisor. Individuals are more often followers than leaders.[2]

Second, recall that the definition of a leader from Chapter 1 referred to an influence relationship among leaders and followers. This means that in a position of leadership, an individual is influenced by the actions and the attitudes of followers. In fact, the contingency theories introduced in Chapter 3 are based on how leaders adjust their behavior to fit situations, especially their followers. Thus, the nature of leader-follower relationships involves reciprocity, the mutual exchange of influence.[3] The followers' influence upon a leader can enhance the leader or underscore the leader's shortcomings.[4]

Third, many of the qualities that are desirable in a leader are the same qualities possessed by an effective follower. In addition to demonstrating initiative, independence, commitment to common goals, and courage, a follower can provide enthusiastic support of a leader, but not to the extent that the follower fails to challenge the leader who threatens the values or objectives of the organization.[5] This is not very different from the role of leader. Both leader and follower roles are proactive; together they can achieve a shared vision. The military often provides insight into the interaction of leadership and followership. A performance study of U.S. Navy personnel found that the outstanding ships were those staffed by followers who supported their leaders but also took initiative and did not avoid raising issues or concerns with their superiors. D. Michael Abrashoff, former commander of the USS *Benfold*, recognized as one of the best ships in the Navy, always encouraged his followers to speak up. To Abrashoff, the highest boss should be the sailor who does the work—the follower—not the person with the most stripes on his or her uniform.[6] You will learn more about Abrashoff's leadership in the next chapter. In any organization, leaders can help develop effective followers, just as effective followers develop better leaders. The performance of followers, leaders, and the organization are variables that depend on one another.

Styles of Followership

Despite the importance of followership and the critical role followers play in the success of any endeavor, research on the topic is limited. One theory of followership was proposed by Robert E. Kelley, who conducted extensive interviews with leaders and followers and came up with five styles of followership.[7] These followership styles are categorized according to two dimensions, as illustrated in Exhibit 7.1. The first dimension is the quality of independent, **critical thinking** versus dependent, **uncritical thinking**. Independent thinking recalls our discussion of mindfulness in Chapter 5; independent critical thinkers are mindful of the effects of people's behavior on achieving organizational goals. They are aware of the significance of their own actions and the actions of others. They can weigh the impact of decisions on the vision set forth by a leader and offer constructive criticism, creativity, and innovation. Conversely, a dependent, uncritical thinker does not consider possibilities beyond what he or she is told, does not contribute to the cultivation of the organization, and accepts the leader's ideas without thinking.

According to Kelley, the second dimension of followership style is active versus passive behavior. An active individual participates fully in an organization, engages in behavior that is beyond the limits of the job, demonstrates a sense of ownership, and initiates problem solving and decision making. A passive individual is characterized by a need for constant supervision and prodding by superiors. Passivity is often regarded as laziness; a passive person does nothing that is not required and avoids added responsibility.

The extent to which one is active or passive and is a critical, independent thinker or a dependent, uncritical thinker determines whether he or she is an alienated follower, a passive follower, a conformist, a pragmatic survivor, or an effective follower, as shown in Exhibit 7.1.

Critical thinking

thinking independently and being mindful of the effects of one's own and other people's behavior on achieving the organization's vision

Uncritical thinking

failing to consider possibilities beyond what one is told; accepting the leader's ideas without thinking

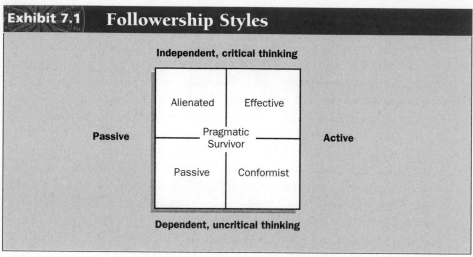

Exhibit 7.1   Followership Styles

SOURCE: Adapted from *The Power of Followership* by Robert E. Kelley, 97. Copyright © 1992 by Consultants to Executives and Organizations, Ltd. Used by permission of Doubleday, a division of Random House, Inc.

Alienated follower

a person in the organization who is a passive, yet independent, critical thinker

The alienated follower is a passive, yet independent, critical thinker. Alienated followers are often effective followers who have experienced setbacks and obstacles, perhaps promises broken by superiors. Thus, they are capable, but they focus exclusively on the shortcomings of the organization and other people. Often cynical, alienated followers are able to think independently, but they do not participate in developing solutions to the problems or deficiencies they see. For example, Barry Paris spent more than 10 years writing on and off for the *Pittsburgh Post-Gazette*, where he was known for his bad attitude and lack of enthusiasm and teamwork. Eventually Paris realized that he wasted that time ruminating over what he perceived as the hypocrisy of journalistic objectivity. "I could never resign myself to it," says Paris. Thus, rather than doing his best and trying to help others maintain standards of integrity, he allowed hostility and cynicism to permeate his work.[8]

Conformist

a follower who participates actively in the organization but does not utilize critical thinking skills in his or her task behavior

The conformist participates actively in the organization but does not utilize critical thinking skills in his or her task behavior. In other words, a conformist typically carries out any and all orders regardless of the nature of those tasks. The conformist participates willingly, but without considering the consequences of what he or she is being asked to do—even at the risk of contributing to a harmful endeavor. A conformist is concerned only with avoiding conflict. Indeed, this style often results from rigid rules and authoritarian environments in which leaders perceive subordinate recommendations as a challenge or threat. When Kelley, the author who developed the two dimensions of followership, was consulted about how to improve employee creativity and innovation for an oil company, he discovered that each office was virtually identical, owing to strict company policies that prohibited individual expression. This is specifically the kind of environment that suppresses effective followership and creates conformists.[9]

The **pragmatic survivor** has qualities of all four extremes—depending on which style fits with the prevalent situation. This type of follower uses whatever style best benefits his or her own position and minimizes risk. Pragmatic survivors often emerge when an organization is going through desperate times, and followers find themselves doing whatever is needed to get themselves through the difficulty. Within any given company, some 25 to 35 percent of followers tend to be pragmatic survivors, avoiding risks and fostering the status quo, often for political reasons. Government appointees often demonstrate this followership style because they have their own agendas and a short period of time in which to implement them. They may appeal to the necessary individuals, who themselves have a limited time to accomplish goals, and are therefore willing to do whatever is necessary to survive in the short run.[10]

The **passive follower** exhibits neither critical, independent thinking nor active participation. Being passive and uncritical, these followers display neither initiative nor a sense of responsibility. Their activity is limited to what they are told to do, and they accomplish things only with a great deal of supervision. Passive followers leave the thinking to their leaders. Often, however, this style is the result of a leader who expects and encourages passive behavior. Followers learn that to show initiative, accept responsibility, or think creatively is not rewarded, and may even be punished by the leader, so they grow increasingly passive. Passive followers are often the result of leaders who are overcontrolling of others and who punish mistakes.[11]

The **effective follower** is both a critical, independent thinker and active in the organization. Effective followers behave the same toward everyone, regardless of their positions in the organization. They do not try to avoid risk or conflict. Rather, effective followers have the courage to initiate change and put themselves at risk or in conflict with others, even their leaders, to serve the best interest of the organization.

Characterized by both mindfulness and a willingness to act, effective followers are essential for an organization to be effective. They are capable of self-management, they discern strengths and weaknesses in themselves and in the organization, they are committed to something bigger than themselves, and they work toward competency, solutions, and positive impact. Effective followers are far from powerless—and they know it. Therefore, they do not despair in their positions, nor do they resent or manipulate others. The Living Leadership box provides highlights from a speech given by Nelson Mandela that underscores his meaning of effective followership. You can evaluate how well you carry out a followership role by completing the questionnaire in Leader's Self-Insight 7.1.

Pragmatic survivor

a follower who has qualities of all four extremes (alienated, effective, passive, conformist), depending on which style fits with the prevalent situation

Passive follower

a person in an organization who exhibits neither critical, independent thinking nor active participation

Effective follower

a critical, independent thinker who actively participates in the organization

LIVING LEADERSHIP

Our Deepest Fear

Our deepest fear is not that we are inadequate, Our deepest fear is that we are powerful beyond measure.

It is our light, not our darkness, that most-frightens us.

We ask ourselves, who am I to be brilliant, gorgeous, talented and fabulous?

Actually, who are you NOT to be? You are a child of God.

Your playing small doesn't serve the world.

There's nothing enlightened about shrinking so that other people won't feel insecure around you.

We were born to make manifest the glory . . . that is within us.

It's not just in some of us; it's in everyone.

And as we let our own light shine, we unconsciously give other people permission to do the same.

As we are liberated from our own fear, our presence automatically liberates others.

SOURCE: From the 1994 Inaugural Speech of Nelson Mandela.

Action Memo

As a leader: Be an effective follower. Think independently and critically instead of blindly accepting what your leader tells you. Actively participate in the organization and look for solutions rather than dwelling on the shortcomings of leaders or the organization.

Demands on the Effective Follower

Effective followership is not always easy. The discussion of courage and integrity in Chapter 6 applies to followers as well as leaders. Indeed, followers sometimes experience an even greater need for these qualities because of their subordinate position. To be effective, followers have to know what they stand for and be willing to express their own ideas and opinions to their leaders, even though this might mean risking their jobs, being demeaned, or feeling inadequate.[12] Effective followers are willing to accept responsibility, serve the needs of the organization, challenge authority, participate in change, and leave the organization when necessary.[13]

The Will to Assume Responsibility The effective follower feels a sense of personal responsibility and ownership in the organization and its mission. Thus, the follower assumes responsibility for his or her own behavior and its impact on the organization. Effective followers do not presume that a leader or an organization will provide them with security, permission to act, or personal growth. Instead, they initiate the opportunities through which they can achieve personal fulfillment, exercise their potential, and provide the organization with the fullest extent of their capabilities. Consider the In the Lead example for Chuck Lucier.

The Power of Followership

For each statement below, please use the six-point scale to indicate the extent to which the statement describes you. Think of a specific but typical followership situation and how you acted.

	Rarely		Occasionally		Almost always	
1. Does your work help you fulfill some societal goal or personal dream that is important to you?	0 1	2	3	4	5	6
2. Are your personal work goals aligned with the organization's priority goals?	0 1	2	3	4	5	6
3. Are you highly committed to and energized by your work and organization, giving them your best ideas and performance?	0 1	2	3	4	5	6
4. Does your enthusiasm also spread to and energize your co-workers?	0 1	2	3	4	5	6
5. Instead of waiting for or merely accepting what the leader tells you, do you personally identify which organizational activities are most critical for achieving the organization's priority goals?	0 1	2	3	4	5	6
6. Do you actively develop a distinctive competence in those critical activities so that you become more valuable to the leader and the organization?	0 1	2	3	4	5	6
7. When starting a new job or assignment, do you promptly build a record of successes in tasks that are important to the leader?	0 1	2	3	4	5	6
8. Can the leader give you a difficult assignment without the benefit of much supervision, knowing that you will meet your deadline with highest-quality work and that you will "fill in the cracks" if need be?	0 1	2	3	4	5	6
9. Do you take the initiative to seek out and successfully complete assignments that go above and beyond your job?	0 1	2	3	4	5	6
10. When you are not the leader of a group project, do you still contribute at a high level, often doing more than your share?	0 1	2	3	4	5	6
11. Do you independently think up and champion new ideas that will contribute significantly to the leader's or the organization's goals?	0 1	2	3	4	5	6
12. Do you try to solve the tough problems (technical or organizational), rather than look to the leader to do it for you?	0 1	2	3	4	5	6
13. Do you help out other co-workers, making them look good, even when you do not get any credit?	0 1	2	3	4	5	6
14. Do you help the leader or group see both the upside potential and downside risks of ideas or plans, playing the devil's advocate if need be?	0 1	2	3	4	5	6

	Rarely	Occasionally	Almost always

15. Do you understand the leader's needs, goals, and constraints, and work hard to meet them?   0 1 2 3 4 5 6

16. Do you actively and honestly own up to your strengths and weaknesses rather than put off evaluation?   0 1 2 3 4 5 6

17. Do you make a habit of internally questioning the wisdom of the leader's decision rather than just doing what you are told?   0 1 2 3 4 5 6

18. When the leader asks you to do something that runs contrary to your professional or personal preferences, do you say no rather than yes?   0 1 2 3 4 5 6

19. Do you act on your own ethical standards rather than the leader's or the group's standards?   0 1 2 3 4 5 6

20. Do you assert your views on important issues, even though it might mean conflict with your group or reprisals from the leader?   0 1 2 3 4 5 6

Scoring and Interpretation

Questions 1, 5, 11, 12, 14, 16, 17, 18, 19, and 20 measure "independent thinking." Sum your answers and write your score below.

Questions 2, 3, 4, 6, 7, 8, 9, 10, 13, and 15 measure "active engagement." Sum your answers and write your score below.

Independent Thinking Total Score = _____

Active Engagement Total Score = _____

These two scores indicate how you carry out your followership role. A score of 20 or below is considered low. A score of 40 or higher is considered high. A score between 20 and 40 is in the middle. Based on whether your score is high, middle, or low, assess your followership style.

Followership Style	Independent Thinking Score	Active Engagement Score
Effective	High	High
Alienated	High	Low
Conformist	Low	High
Pragmatist	Middling	Middling
Passive	Low	Low

How do you feel about your followership style? Compare your style to others. What might you do to be more effective as a follower?

_____

In the Lead   Chuck Lucier, Booz, Allen & Hamilton

Chuck Lucier of Booz, Allen & Hamilton believes effective followers are the linchpins of their organizations. By understanding the needs of the organization and their boss's objectives, he believes, followers can expand their own potential and move the organization forward.

Lucier recalls his will to assume responsibility as a junior partner more than a decade ago. "I took a career risk by standing up and saying, 'This firm isn't perfect; there are big opportunities we're missing and I want to be part of the solution.'" His willingness to step forward led his bosses to put Lucier in charge of a company strategy study. Even though one of his superiors warned him that no one who had ever been put in charge of such a study "was still around three years later," Lucier threw his whole energies into the task with the belief that he could make a real difference. He and his team recommended that Booz, Allen take a different approach to working with clients. Rather than courting numerous clients and working on many small projects, why not do more and bigger projects for a small number of major clients? The strategy was a success. Booz Allen cut its client base and more than doubled its revenue.

Lucier survived the "three-year" period warned of by his boss. He's now a 19-year veteran and senior vice-president of Booz, Allen & Hamilton.[14]

The Will to Serve An effective follower discerns the needs of the organization and actively seeks to serve those needs. Just as leaders can serve others, as discussed in the previous chapter, so can followers. A follower can provide strength to the leader by supporting the leader's decisions and by contributing to the organization in areas that complement the leader's position. By displaying the will to serve others over themselves, followers act for the common mission of the organization with a passion that equals that of a leader. As vice president under Ronald Reagan, George Bush was recognized as an exceptional follower. Even though he had his own opinions and sometimes disagreed with the president, Bush suppressed these in public and supported Reagan for the good of the country.[15]

The Will to Challenge Although effective followers serve and support others, they don't sacrifice their personal integrity or the good of the organization in order to maintain harmony. If a leader's actions and decisions contradict the best interests of the organization, effective followers take a stand. The U.S. Army teaches soldiers that they have a duty to disobey an order if the order is illegal or unethical.[16] Good leaders want followers who are willing to challenge them. When he was CEO of IBM,

Action Memo

As a leader: Assume responsibility for your own personal development, behavior, and work performance. Look for opportunities where you can make a difference in the organization. Actively seek to meet organizational needs, serve others, and work toward the common good.

Action Memo

As a leader:
Support leaders
through diffi-
cult times.
Bravely
confront the
difficult
changes
involved in
organizational
transformation.
Have the
courage to
challenge your
superiors when
their behavior
or decisions
contradict the
best interests
of the
organization.

Lou Gerstner hired Larry Ricciardi as senior vice president and corporate counsel even though he knew Ricciardi would challenge his thinking and decisions.[17] Leaders are human and make mistakes. Effective leaders depend on followers who have the will to challenge.

The Will to Participate in Transformation Effective followers view the struggle of corporate change and transformation as a mutual experience shared by all members of the organization. When an organization undergoes a difficult transformation, effective followers support the leader and the organization. They are not afraid to confront the changes and work toward reshaping the organization. David Chislett, of Imperial Oil's Dartmouth, Nova Scotia refinery, was faced with this test of courage. The refinery was the least efficient in the industry and the Board of Directors gave management nine months to turn things around. Chislett's bosses asked him to give up his management position and return to the duties of a wage earner as part of an overall transformation strategy. He agreed to the request, thereby contributing to the success of the refinery's transformation.[18]

The Will to Leave Sometimes organizational or personal changes create a situation in which a follower must withdraw from a particular leader–follower relationship. If followers are faced with a leader or an organization unwilling to make necessary changes, it is time to take their support elsewhere. For example, Dianne Martz had the courage to leave her sales job at a pharmaceutical company when she learned about the company's practice of withholding information, which helped sales but not the customer. She discovered that HIV was present in a clotting factor for hemophilia patients, and that doctors and the pharmaceuticals industry had known about it for two years before they told anyone. As the mother of a hemophiliac son, Martz could not justify her participation in the company.[19] Another reason for leaving is a person's desire to move on to another phase of his or her life. Sometimes people know they need new challenges, but they have a hard time leaving a comfortable job where they might be quite happy and have many friends and valued colleagues.

Developing Personal Potential

How do followers expand their potential to be critical, independent thinkers who make active contributions to their organizations? Later in this chapter, we'll discuss the crucial role of leaders in developing effective followers. However, followers can expand their own capabilities by developing and applying personal leadership qualities in both their private and work lives. One well-known and widely acclaimed approach to helping people deal courageously with life's changes and challenges is Stephen Covey's *The*

7 Habits of Highly Effective People.[20] Covey defines a habit as the intersection of knowledge, skill, and desire. His approach to personal and interpersonal effectiveness includes seven habits arranged along a maturity continuum, from dependence to independence to interdependence, as illustrated in Exhibit 7.2. Each habit builds on the previous one so that individuals grow further along the maturity continuum as they develop these personal effectiveness habits.

In organizations, many people fall into a mind-set of dependency, expecting someone else to take care of everything and make all the decisions. The *dependent* person is comparable to the passive follower we described earlier, displaying neither initiative nor a sense of personal responsibility. Dependent people expect someone else to take care of them and blame others when things go wrong. An *independent* person, on the other hand, has developed a sense of self-worth and an attitude of self-reliance. Independent people accept personal responsibility and get what they want through their own actions. To be a truly effective follower—or leader—requires

Exhibit 7.2	**The Maturity Continuum®**

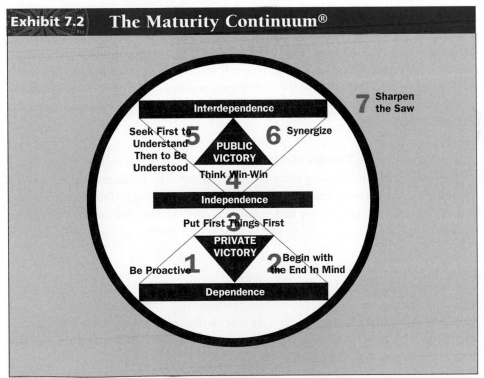

a further step to *interdependence*, the realization that the best things happen by working cooperatively with others, that life and work are better when one experiences the richness of close interpersonal relationships.

From Dependence to Independence

Covey's first three habits deal with self-reliance and self-mastery. Covey calls these *private victories* because they involve only the individual follower growing from dependence to independence, not the follower in relationship with others.[21]

Habit 1: Be Proactive® Being proactive means more than merely taking initiative; it means being responsible for your own life. Proactive people recognize that they have the ability to choose and to act with integrity. They don't blame others or life's circumstances for their outcomes. Eleanor Roosevelt was talking about being proactive when she observed that, "No one can make you feel inferior without your consent."[22] Proactive people know that it is not what happens to them but how they respond to it that ultimately matters.

Habit 2: Begin with the End in Mind® This means to start with a clear mental image of your destination. For each individual, beginning with the end in mind means knowing what you want, what is deeply important to you, so that you can live each day in a way that contributes to your personal vision. In addition to clarifying goals and plans, this habit entails establishing guiding principles and values for achieving them.

Habit 3: Put First Things First® This habit encourages people to gain control of time and events by relating them to their goals and by managing themselves. It means that, rather than getting tangled up dealing with things, time, and activities, we should focus on preserving and enhancing *relationships* and on accomplishing *results*.

Effective Interdependence

The first three habits build a foundation of independence, from which one can move to interdependence—caring, productive relationships with others—which Covey calls *public victories*. Moving to effective interdependence involves open communication, effective teamwork, and building positive relationships based on trust, caring, and respect, topics that are discussed throughout this book. No matter what position you hold in the organization, when you move to interdependence, you step into a leadership role.

Action Memo

As a leader: Expand your followership potential by consciously developing and applying leadership qualities in your personal and work life. Move from dependence and passivity toward greater independence and self-reliance. Build a foundation for interdependence so you will have positive, productive relationships with others.

Habit 4: Think Win–Win® To think win–win means understanding that without cooperation, the organization cannot succeed. When followers understand this, they cooperate in ways that ensure their mutual success and allow everyone to come out a winner. Win–win is a frame of mind and heart that seeks agreements or solutions that are mutually beneficial and satisfying.

Habit 5: Seek First to Understand, Then to Be Understood® This principle is the key to effective communication. Many people don't listen with the intent to understand; they are too busy thinking about what they want to say. Seeking first to understand requires being nonjudgmental and able to empathize with the other person's situation. *Empathetic listening* gets inside another person's frame of reference so that you can better understand how that person feels. Communication will be discussed in detail in Chapter 9.

Habit 6: Synergize® Synergy is the combined action that occurs when people work together to create new alternatives and solutions. In addition, the greatest opportunity for synergy occurs when people have different viewpoints, because the differences present new opportunities. The essence of synergy is to value and respect differences and take advantage of them to build on strengths and compensate for weaknesses.

Habit 7: Sharpen the Saw® This habit encompasses the previous six—it is the habit that makes all the others possible. "Sharpening the saw" is a process of using and continuously renewing the physical, mental, spiritual, and social aspects of your life. To be an effective follower or an effective leader requires living a balanced life. For example, Larry Ricciardi of IBM, introduced earlier, is an avid traveler and voracious reader who likes to study art, literature, and history. He once spent 18 months learning everything he could about the Ottoman Empire just because he "realized he knew nothing about the Ottoman Empire." He also likes to read tabloids in addition to his daily fare of *The Wall Street Journal*. On business trips, he scouts out side trips to exotic or interesting sites, and he likes to take adventurous vacations with his family and friends. Ricciardi loves his job, but he also loves exploring other aspects of life.[23]

Sources of Follower Power

Another issue of concern is how followers gain and use power in organizations. Formal leaders typically have more power than followers do. Nevertheless, effective followers participate fully in organizations by culling power from the available sources. Even the lowest-level follower has personal and position-based sources of power that can be used to generate upward influence, thereby impacting the organization and establishing a mutually beneficial relationship with leaders.[24] Personal sources of power include knowledge, expertise, effort, and persuasion. Position sources of power include location, information, and access.

Personal Sources

A knowledgeable follower has skills and talents that are a valuable resource to the leader and to the organization. Such a follower is of real value, and his or her departure would be a loss. *Knowledge* is a source of upward influence. In addition, a follower who has a demonstrated record of performance often develops *expertise* and in this way can influence decisions. A record of successes and a history of contributions can garner expert status for followers, from which followers can derive the power to influence operations and establish themselves as a resource to the leader. The power to influence is also associated with the *effort* put forth by a follower. By demonstrating a willingness to learn, to accept difficult or undesirable projects, and to initiate activities beyond the scope of expected effort, a follower can gain power in an organization.[25] Tim Chapman was hired by Spartan Motors during his senior year of high school. By age 20, he was the head electrical engineer, troubleshooting and consorting with key vendors. "I guess I'm willing to learn," says Chapman.[26]

Followers can also use persuasion as a source of personal power. *Persuasion* refers to the direct appeal to leaders in an organization for desired outcomes.[27] In addition to being direct, speaking truthfully to a leader can be a source of power for effective followers.[28] Rob Hummel, head of international post-production at Dreamworks SKG, once promoted an employee who was known for being "difficult" because he always challenged his superiors. The fact that this follower was willing to speak truthfully to higher-ups based on his own knowledge and creative brilliance gave him increased power.[29] Power doesn't always come from titles or seniority in the organization; sometimes it comes from one's knowledge and contributions.

Position Sources

Often the formal position of a follower in an organization can provide sources of power. For example, the location of a follower can render him or her *visible* to numerous individuals. A *central location* provides influence to a follower, because the follower is known to many and contributes to the work of many. Similarly, a position that is key to the *flow of information* can establish that position and the follower in it as critical—thus, influential—to those who seek the information. Access to people and information in an organization provides the follower in the position a means to establish relationships with others. With a *network of relationships*, a follower has greater opportunity to persuade others and to make contributions to numerous organizational processes.

Strategies for Managing Up

There is growing recognition that how followers manage their leaders is just as important as how their leaders manage them.[30] Most followers at some point complain about the leader's deficiencies, such as the leader's failure to listen, to encourage, or to recognize followers' efforts.[31] Effective followers, however, transform the leader–follower relationship by striving to improve their leaders rather than just criticize them. To be effective, followers develop a meaningful, task-related relationship with their bosses that enables them to add value to the organization even when their ideas disagree with those of the bosses.[32] You might have experienced this with a special teacher or coach. For example, students who are especially interested in a class sometimes challenge the teacher on a topic as a way to expand the teacher's thinking and enhance the learning experience for everyone.

Followers should also be aware of behaviors that can annoy leaders and interfere with building a quality relationship. A business magazine recently interviewed powerful people about their pet peeves and identified 30 misdemeanors that followers often commit without being aware of it. Leader's Self-Insight 7.2 gives you a chance to see if you're guilty of being an annoying follower.

Most relationships between leaders and followers are characterized by some emotion and behavior based on authority and submission. Leaders are authority figures and may play a disproportionately large role in the mind of a follower. Followers may find themselves being overcritical of their leaders, or rebellious, or passive. Irvin D. Yalom, a professor of psychiatry and author of the novels *Lying on the Couch* and *When Nietzsche Wept*, once had a patient in group therapy who ranted at great length about her boss who never listened and refused to pay her any respect. Interestingly, this woman's complaints persisted through three different jobs and three different bosses.[33] The relationships between leaders and followers are not unlike those between parents and children, and individuals may engage old family patterns when entering into leader–follower relationships.[34] Effective followers, conversely, typically perceive themselves as the equals of their leaders, not inherently subordinate.[35] Exhibit 7.3 illustrates the strategies that enable followers to overcome the authority-based relationship and develop an effective, respectful relationship with their leaders.

Be a Resource for the Leader

Effective followers align themselves to the purpose and the vision of the organization. They ask the leader about vision and goals and help achieve them. They understand their impact on the organization's achievement. In this way, followers are a resource of strength and support for the leader. This alignment involves understanding the leader's position, that is, his or her goals, needs, and constraints. Thus, an effective follower can complement the leader's weaknesses with the follower's own

Action Memo

As a leader: Use strategies for managing up to create an equitable and respectful relationship with your superiors. Be a resource for the leader. Help the leader be the best he or she can be. Get beyond submissive feelings and behaviors. Recognize that leaders are fallible. View your leader realistically.

LEADER'S SELF-INSIGHT 7.2

Are You an Annoying Follower?

1. If you think there might be a mistake in something you've done, what do you do?
   A.   Fess up. It's better to share your concerns up front so your boss can see if there is a problem and get it corrected before it makes him look bad.
   B.   Try to hide it. Maybe there isn't really a problem, so there's no use in making yourself look incompetent.

2. How do you handle a criticism from your boss?
   A.   Poke your head in her door or corner her in the cafeteria multiple times to make sure everything is okay between the two of you.
   B.   Take the constructive criticism, make sure you understand what the boss wants from you, and get on with your job.

3. You're in a crowded elevator with your boss after an important meeting where you've just landed a million-dollar deal. You:
   A.   Celebrate the victory by talking to your boss about the accomplishment and the details of the meeting.
   B.   Keep your mouth shut or talk about non–business-related matters.

4. Your boss has an open-door policy and wants people to feel free to drop by her office any time to talk about anything. You pop in just in after lunch and find her on the phone. What do you do?
   A.   Leave and come back later.
   B.   Wait. you know most of her phone calls are quick, so she'll be free in a few minutes.

5. You've been called to the boss's office and have no idea what he wants to talk about.
   A.   You show up on time, empty-handed, and ask the boss what you need to bring with you.
   B.   You show up on time with a pen, paper, and your calendar or PDA.

6. You've been trying to get some face time with your boss for weeks and luckily catch him or her in the bathroom. You:
   A.   Take care of personal business and get out of there.
   B.   Grab your chance to schmooze with the boss. You might not get another any time soon.

Here are the appropriate follower behaviors:

1. **A.** Honest self-assessment and fessing up to the boss builds mutual confidence and respect. Nothing destroys trust faster than incompetence exposed after the fact.

2. **B.** David Snow, former president and COO of Empire Blue Cross and Blue Shield, refers to insecure, thin-skinned people who have to check in frequently after a criticism as *door swingers*. Door swingers are annoying in both our personal and work lives. Just get on with things.

3. **B.** You have no idea who else is in the elevator. Keep your mouth shut. You can crow about the new deal later in private.

4. **A.** There's nothing worse than having someone hovering while you're trying to carry on a phone conversation. Leave a note with your boss's assistant or come back later.

5. **B.** You can usually be safe in assuming your boss hasn't called you in for idle chit-chat. Never show up without a pen and paper to make notes.

6. **A.** At best, to use the bathroom as a place to try to impress the boss makes you look desperate. It also shows a lack of tact and judgment.

Most of these seem obvious, but based on interviews with leaders, subordinates commit these sins over and over in the workplace. Keep these missteps in mind so you don't become an annoying follower.

SOURCE: Based on William Speed Weed, Alex Lash, and Constance Loizos, "30 Ways to Annoy Your Boss," *MBA Jungle* (March–April 2003): 51–55.

Exhibit 7.3	**Ways to Influence Your Leader**

Be a Resource for the Leader	**Help the Leader Be a Good Leader**
Determine the leader's needs.	Ask for advice.
Zig where leader zags.	Tell leader what you think.
Tell leader about you.	Find things to thank leader for.
Align self to team purpose/vision.	
Build a Relationship	**View the Leader Realistically**
Ask about leader at your level/position.	Give up idealized leader images.
Welcome feedback and criticism, such as "What experience led you to that opinion?"	Don't hide anything.
	Don't criticize leader to others.
Ask leader to tell you company stories.	Disagree occasionally.

strengths.[36] Similarly, effective followers indicate their personal goals and the resources they bring to the organization. Effective followers inform their leaders about their own ideas, beliefs, needs, and constraints. The more leaders and followers can know the day-to-day activities and problems of one another, the better resources they can be for each other. For example, one group of handicapped workers took advantage of a board meeting to issue rented wheelchairs to the members, who then tried to move around the factory in them. Realizing what the workers faced, the board got the factory's ramps improved, and the handicapped workers became a better resource for the organization.[37]

Help the Leader Be a Good Leader

Good followers seek the leader's counsel and look for ways the leader can help them improve their skills, abilities, and value to the organization. They help their leaders be good leaders by simply saying what they need in order to be good followers. If a leader believes a follower values his or her advice, the leader is more likely to give constructive guidance rather than unsympathetic criticism.

A leader can also become a better leader when followers compliment the leader and thank him or her for behavior that followers appreciate, such as listening, rewarding followers' contributions, and sharing credit for accomplishments.[38] If a leader knows what followers appreciate, the leader is more likely to repeat that behavior. Similarly, effective followers find diplomatic ways to let leaders know when their behavior is counterproductive. At Alliance Funding, a mortgage-lending division of Superior Bank FSB, Lee Burnley and Stephen Lynch found an online assessment tool that enabled them and their co-workers to rate their boss's performance in an array of important leadership behaviors. The boss, vice-president Sonia Russomanno, appreciated the chance to improve in areas where employees found her behavior weak or ineffective. After years of asking for honest feedback and getting only glowing reviews, the online forum gave her some specific weak points to work on.[39]

Asking for advice, thanking the leader for helpful behaviors, and being honest about areas that need improvement are important ways followers can affect the conduct of leaders and help them be better leaders.

Build a Relationship with the Leader

Effective followers work toward a genuine relationship with their leaders, which includes developing trust and speaking honestly on the basis of that trust.[40] By building a relationship with a leader, a follower makes every interaction more meaningful to the organization. Furthermore, the relationship is imbued with mutual respect rather than authority and submission. Wes Walsh used mindful initiatives to create a relationship with his boss that maximized his own upward influence.

In the Lead   Wes Walsh

When Wes Walsh came under an autocratic manager, his position predecessor warned him to either stay away from the infamously autocratic boss, or else be prepared to give up any influence over the unit operations. Walsh decided to ignore this advice. Instead, he started dropping by his boss's office on a regular basis to discuss production progress. Walsh also sought approval on very small matters because they were virtually impossible for his boss to oppose. Walsh continued these frequent, informal interactions over a lengthy period of time before moving on to more consequential matters.

Eventually, major projects had to be addressed. For example, an increase in the volume of materials processed had rendered Walsh's unit too slow and too limited to adequately serve the increased production. In response, Walsh first requested his boss to devote a couple of hours to him at some designated point in the near future. When the appointed time arrived, Walsh took his boss on a lengthy tour of the plant, pointing out the volume of material scattered about waiting to be processed. He supplemented this visual evidence with facts and figures.

The boss was compelled to acknowledge the problem. Thus, he asked for Walsh's proposal, which Walsh had carefully prepared beforehand. Although the boss had rejected identical proposals from Walsh's predecessor, this time the boss almost immediately approved the sum of $150,000 for updating the unit equipment.[41]

Walsh's conscious effort to interact and get his boss comfortable saying yes on small matters set a precedent for a pattern of respect that was not lost even on his autocratic superior.

Followers can generate respect by asking their leaders questions, such as about the leader's experiences in the follower's position and what the source was for specific feedback and criticism. Followers can also ply the leader for company stories.[42] By doing so, followers are getting beyond submissive behavior by asking leaders to be accountable for their criticism, to have empathy for the followers' position, and to share history about something both parties have in common—the organization.

View the Leader Realistically

To view leaders realistically means to give up idealized images of them. Understanding that leaders are fallible and will make many mistakes leads to acceptance and the potential for an equitable relationship. The way in which a follower perceives his or her boss is the foundation of their relationship. It helps to view leaders as they really are, not as followers think they should be.[43]

Similarly, effective followers present realistic images of themselves. Followers do not try to hide their weaknesses or cover their mistakes, nor do they criticize their leaders to others.[44] Hiding things is symptomatic of conforming and passive followers. Criticizing leaders to others merely bolsters alienation, and reinforces the mindset of an alienated follower. These kinds of alienated and passive behaviors can have negative—and sometimes disastrous—consequences for leaders, followers, and the organization, as illustrated by the stories in this chapter's Leader's Bookshelf. Only positive things about a leader should be shared with others. It is an alienated follower who complains without engaging in constructive action. Instead of criticizing a leader to others, it is far more constructive to directly disagree with a leader on matters relevant to the department's or organization's work.

What Followers Want

Throughout much of this chapter, we've been talking about demands on followers and how followers can become more effective and powerful in the organization. However, the full responsibility doesn't fall on the follower. To have good followers,

LEADER'S BOOKSHELF

Leading Up: How to Lead Your Boss So You Both Win
By Michael Useem

Michael Useem, professor of management and director of the Center for Leadership and Change Management at the Wharton School of the University of Pennsylvania, puts a new twist on leadership advice by stressing that leadership has to come from below as well as from above. "We have all known a supervisor or president, a coach or minister, an officer or director who should have made a difference but did not," Useem writes. "We privately complained, we may even have quit, but we rarely stepped forward to help them transcend their limitations and be the best boss they could be." In *Leading Up: How to Lead Your Boss So You Both Win*, Useem offers lessons in leading up by examining both positive and negative real-life examples.

Examples of Leading Up
Here are a few real life successes and failures that bring the concept of upward leadership to life:

* Civil War commanders on both the Union and Confederate sides openly disrespected and often misinformed their commanders-in-chief, which contributed to tragic consequences for both sides. For example, Union General George McClellan didn't even try to disguise his contempt for President Abraham Lincoln and eventually alienated every member of Lincoln's cabinet. Two days before the Peninsula Campaign in mid-spring 1862, Lincoln relieved McClellan from his position. Lesson: Disdain and contempt for your superior will be returned in kind. To build your superior's confidence in you, give your confidence to the leader.
* U.S. Marine Corps general Peter Pace had to report to six bosses with varying agen-

das, but he successfully brought together conflicting priorities by keeping everyone informed of what he was recommending to all the others. In addition, Pace was willing to challenge his superiors when their proposals or policies were at odds with his own informed judgment. Lesson: Total honesty and frequent face-to-face discussions are a must for communicating what the boss needs to know and maintaining the trust that is essential to good leader-follower relationships.

* Eight climbers died on Mount Everest in May of 1996 partly because the mountaineers failed to question their guides' flawed and inconsistent instructions and decisions. The surviving climbers admit they might have protected themselves and others from harm if they had been willing to rise up when their leaders were faltering. Lesson: While respect for and confidence in your superior is vital, good followers know that nobody is invincible or faultless. "Biding your time and deferring to authority serves no one well when it's clear that the boss would fare far better with your upward help."

Answering the Call to Upward Leadership
Useem uses heroic accounts and moments of crisis as examples because he believes they are the best teachers. However, he points out that opportunities for leading up come to all of us in many different situations. Without effective followers who act as upward leaders to offer information, guidance, insight, and initiative—and to challenge their superiors when necessary—leadership is an incomplete and impotent exercise.

Leading Up: How To Lead Your Boss So You Both Win, by Michael Useem, is published by Crown Business.

the requirements and obligations of those in a leadership role should be reexamined as well.[45] Leaders have a duty to create a leader–follower relationship that engages whole people rather than treats followers as passive sheep who should blindly follow orders and support the boss.

Research indicates that followers have expectations about what constitutes a desirable leader.[46] Exhibit 7.4 shows the top four choices in rank order based on surveys of followers about what they desire in leaders and colleagues.

Followers want their leaders to be honest, forward-thinking, inspiring, and competent. A leader must be worthy of trust, envision the future of the organization, inspire others to contribute, and be capable and effective in matters that will affect the organization. In terms of competence, leadership roles may shift from the formal leader to the person with particular expertise in a given area.

Followers want their fellow followers to be honest and competent, but also dependable and cooperative. Thus, desired qualities of colleagues share two qualities with leaders—honesty and competence. However, followers themselves want followers to be dependable and cooperative, rather than forward-thinking and inspiring. The hallmark that distinguishes the role of leadership from the role of followership, then, is not authority, knowledge, power, or other conventional notions of what a follower is not. Rather, the distinction lies in the clearly defined leadership activities of fostering a vision and inspiring others to achieve that vision. Vision will be discussed in detail in Chapter 13. Organizations that can boast of effective followers tend to have leaders who deal primarily with change and progress.[47] The results in Exhibit 7.4 also underscore the idea that behaviors of effective leaders and followers often overlap. Followers do not want to be subjected to leader behavior that denies them the opportunity to make valued contributions. Leaders have a responsibility to enable followers to fully contribute their ideas and abilities.

Action Memo

As a leader: Learn to give and receive feedback that contributes to growth and improvement rather than fear and hard feelings. Practice empathy so you can understand what the other person may be feeling.

Exhibit 7.4	Rank Order of Desirable Characteristics

Desirable Leaders Are	Desirable Colleagues (Followers) Are
Honest	Honest
Forward thinking	Cooperative
Inspiring	Dependable
Competent	Competent

SOURCE: Adapted from James M. Kouzes and Barry Z. Posner, *Credibility: How Leaders Gain and Lose It, Why People Demand It* (San Francisco, CA: Jossey-Bass Publishers, 1993), 255.

Using Feedback to Develop Followers

Feedback

using evaluation and communication to help individuals and the organization learn and improve

Giving and receiving feedback is often difficult for both leaders and followers. At annual review time in many organizations, for example, bosses worry that even the slightest criticism will provoke anger or tears, while employees are terrified that they'll hear nothing but complaints.[48] Thus, people often say as little as possible, and both followers and leaders lose a valuable opportunity. Feedback should be seen as a route to improvement and development, not as something to dread or fear.

Observations

visible occurrences, such as a follower's behavior on a job

Feedback occurs when a leader uses evaluation and communication to help individuals and the organization learn and improve.[49] The feedback process involves four elements, as illustrated in Exhibit 7.5. **Observations** are visible occurrences, such as a follower's behavior on the job. An **assessment** is the interpretation of observed behaviors, an evaluation of the results in terms of vision and goals. A **consequence** refers to the outcome of what was observed, and can include both actual consequences and the consequences possible if no change takes place. **Development** refers to the sustainment or improvement of behaviors. Leaders communicate what they observe, how they assess it, what consequences it has, and how to effectively address the observed behavior and consequence. Each element is communicated from the leader to the individual or organization.[50]

Assessment

the interpretation of observed behaviors; an evaluation of the results in terms of vision and goals

Furthermore, the development becomes an observation in the next feedback loop. For example, a leader who observes development and assesses it positively may consequently promote the responsible follower. Leaders use these elements to provide feedback that facilitates growth for followers and organizations.

Consequence

the outcome of what was observed; can include both actual consequences and the consequences possible if no change takes place

There are several ways leaders can optimize the use of feedback and minimize the conflict and fear that often accompanies it. *Empathy*, as described in Chapter 5, is one of the leader's most powerful tools during the feedback process. The leader must be able to put him or herself in the follower's shoes and understand what the follower might be feeling. Empathy helps the leader approach feedback in a way that reflects a genuine concern for the follower. Here are some other tips for using feedback to develop effective followers:

✳   *Make regular feedback a habit.* Leaders should not save everything up for an annual performance review. In addition, by tying feedback to specific goals and objectives, leaders make criticisms and suggestions for improvement concrete to the follower.

Development

the sustainment or improvement of follower behaviors

✳   *Use elements of storytelling.* Followers as well as leaders usually learn a lot more from examining the *story* of how and why something happened than they do from conventional evaluations that might seem like a "chewing out from the boss."[51] Examining the story of what happened and why typically puts the leader and follower on an equal footing, with both trying to examine their roles and responsibilities in the problem. Communication and using metaphor and story will be discussed in detail in the next chapter.

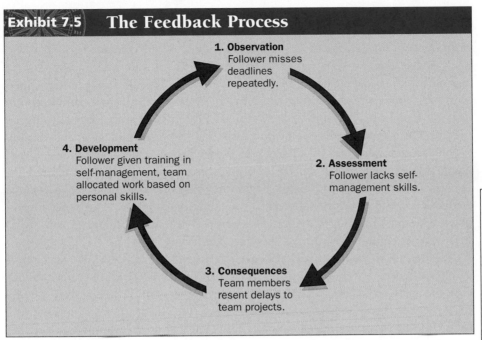

Exhibit 7.5   **The Feedback Process**

1. Observation
Follower misses deadlines repeatedly.

2. Assessment
Follower lacks self-management skills.

3. Consequences
Team members resent delays to team projects.

4. Development
Follower given training in self-management, team allocated work based on personal skills.

SOURCE: Adapted from Mary Mavis, "Painless Performance Evaluations," *Training and Development* (October 1994): 42–22.

❋ *Be generous with positive feedback.* Too many leaders offer feedback only when something goes wrong. They should remember to congratulate behaviors that support the organization's vision and goals, while working to improve the behaviors that do not. When feedback is limited to moments of shortcoming, followers can become discouraged and demoralized. The best leaders look for opportunities to provide positive feedback to even the weakest performers.

❋ *Train followers to view feedback as an opportunity for development.* Followers can learn to think of feedback as a positive rather than a negative process. When people recognize and acknowledge their emotions in response to criticisms, they can then "reframe" the feedback to their own advantage. That is, followers can see feedback as a way to advance their own interests. One follower who practiced the technique of reframing feedback discovered that he wasn't really happy doing the tasks that were required of him. After requesting a transfer to another department, he became much more satisfied and successful.[52]

Leading Others to Lead Themselves

One of the most important steps a leader can take to develop effective followers is to accept and acknowledge his or her own limitations and, indeed, his or her inability

Action Memo

As a leader: Make feedback a regular habit and remember to include positive comments and praise. Apply the process of observation, assessment, consequence and development to facilitate effective feedback. As a follower: view feedback as a chance to improve yourself. Reframe negative feedback in a way that helps you take positive action toward what you want out of your work and life.

to accomplish anything without the help of followers.[53] The leader who tries to do it all alone never gets very far. By acknowledging imperfections and limits, leaders open the door for followers to contribute their own unique competencies.

Good leaders strive toward a collaborative relationship with followers. One approach proposed by Charles Manz and Henry Sims is **self-management leadership**, which means leading others to lead themselves.[54] Self-management leadership calls for leaders to share power and responsibility in such a way that anyone can become a leader, depending on the circumstances of the situation. The organization becomes a community where anyone who is capable and willing can assume a leadership role. Formal leaders act as coaches and mentors, show trust in others, remove barriers to learning, offer encouragement and support, and provide constructive feedback. Leaders develop followers by providing them with opportunities to gain new experience and understandings. However, followers and leaders are active partners who are continually learning, growing, and changing.[55]

Leaders who practice self-management leadership do not try to control employee behavior in traditional ways, but coach employees to think critically about their own performance and judge how well they are accomplishing tasks and achieving goals. Leaders also make sure employees have the information they need to perform effectively and an understanding of how their jobs are relevant to attaining the organization's vision. By linking individual jobs with larger organizational goals, employees have a framework within which to act. Self-management leadership hinges on providing employees with this directed autonomy.[56]

Empowerment of frontline employees, participative management, and other forms of democratic practice are growing trends in organizations. Thus, there are more situations that call for self-management leadership. However, there has been little research to test the effectiveness of this new approach. As with other styles of leadership, it is likely that self-management leadership is effective for some, but not all, situations. Yet all leaders can act in ways that encourage followers to think independently and be willing to take risks, challenge unproductive or unethical norms, and initiate change for the benefit of the organization. Consider how West Point trains future military leaders by emphasizing the importance of followership.

Self-management leadership

leading others to lead themselves

In the Lead   U. S. Military Academy, West Point

At West Point, everyone leads and everyone follows. It's a 24-hour leadership laboratory where people learn that leadership and followership are two sides of the same whole. An important lesson is that leaders are nothing without followers. "You learn from the beginning that you're not in a position of leadership because you're smarter or better," says cadet Joe Bagaglio. "As soon as you think you know it all, you get burned."

Each spring, West Point graduates 900 some men and women who leave with a bachelor's degree and a commission as second lieutenant in the U. S. Army. After a six-week leave, these new graduates take their first jobs as military officers in places like Kosovo, Germany, Guam, Afghanistan, or Iraq. Most of us think of West Point as a place of rules, rigidity, structure, and conformity, and to a great extent, it is. Cadets have to learn to subordinate their self-interest for the good of the whole, because that's what they'll be called upon to do when they graduate. However, there's another side to the story, one that instills creativity and flexibility into students who might someday have to make rapid decisions in the chaos of a battlefield. Cadets learn to rely on the competencies of followers and their own judgment. They learn that everyone is part of the team and no one individual—no matter his or her rank—is more important than the mission of the whole. The entire community relies on this interdependence.

At West Point, everyone is evaluated all the time, and every action is an opportunity to learn, to gain new experience, and to grow in understanding. Formal leaders are continually pushing people—including themselves—to get out of their comfort zone so that they expand their capacity for leadership. "Everyone's a teacher," says cadet Chris Kane, a platoon leader in Company C-2 at West Point. "That's what I love about this place. We're all teachers."[57]

Building a Community of Followers

Together, followers and leaders provide the dependability, cooperation, and commitment to build a sense of community and interdependence in the organization. When there is a sense of community, as at West Point, people feel a strong commitment to the whole and feel that they are important to others in the group. You may have felt this in your personal life as a member of a social club, a religious organization, or a sports team. Community provides a spirit of connection that sustains effective relationships and commitment to purpose. People in a community know that only through trust and teamwork can they accomplish shared goals.[58] The learning organization, which will be described in detail in Chapter 15, depends on community, wherein all people feel encouraged, respected, and dedicated to a common purpose. In a community, people are able to communicate openly with one another, maintain their uniqueness, and be firmly committed to something larger than selfish interests. In short, a group of effective followers provides the basis for community. It is not by coincidence that effective followers and effective community members share certain characteristics. Historically, communities of all sorts were based on service, informed participation, and individual contributions.[59]

Characteristics of Community

Successful communities share a number of important characteristics. In effective communities, members practice inclusivity, a positive culture, conversation, caring and trust, and shared leadership.[60]

Inclusivity In a community, everyone is welcome and feels a sense of belonging. Diversity, divergent ideas, and different points of view are encouraged, as a true community cannot exist without diversity.[61] However, community focuses on the whole rather than the parts, and people emphasize what binds them together. People can speak honestly when their convictions differ from others. This courage often stems from the belief in the inherent equality between themselves, other followers, and their leaders—that is, wholeness.

Positive Culture Leaders and followers perceive the organization as a community with shared norms and values. Members care about newcomers and work to socialize them into the culture. In addition, effective communities are not insular. They encourage adaptive values that help the group or organization interact effectively with a dynamic environment.

Conversation Conversation is how people make and share the meanings that are the basis of community. One special type of communication, **dialogue**, means that each person suspends his attachment to a particular viewpoint so that a deeper level of listening, synthesis, and meaning evolves from the whole community. Individual differences are acknowledged and respected, but the group searches for an expanded collective perspective.[62] Dialogue will be explained more thoroughly in Chapter 9. Only through conversation can people build collaboration and collective action so they move together on a common path.

Caring and Trust Members of a community genuinely care about one another. People consider how their actions affect others and the community as a whole. In addition, members accept others and help them grow without trying to control them, strive to understand others' viewpoints and problems, and have empathy for others. Trust is developed from caring relationships and an emphasis on ethical behavior that serves the interests of the whole.

Shared Leadership In a community, a leader is one among many equals. People do not try to control others, and anyone can step forward as a leader. There is a spirit of equality, and everyone has an opportunity to make a valued contribution. Like plugs of zoysia grass planted far apart that eventually meld together into a beautiful carpet of lawn, leaders and followers who join in a true community meld together to make good things happen.[63]

Action Memo

As a leader: Work cooperatively with others to build a sense of community, interdependence, and common purpose. Practice inclusivity and respect, and contribute to a positive culture and a spirit of equality. Initiate a community of practice by making friendships across organizational boundaries.

Dialogue

a type of communication in which each person suspends his attachment to a particular viewpoint so that a deeper level of listening, synthesis, and meaning evolves from the whole community

Communities of Practice

One way in which people can build a sense of community in organizations is by enabling and supporting communities of practice. Communities of practice often form spontaneously in organizations as people gravitate toward others who share their interests and face similar problems.

Communities of practice are made up of individuals who are informally bound to one another through exposure to a similar set of problems and a common pursuit of solutions.[64] For example, a community of practice might be customer service technicians at Dell Computer who share tips around the water cooler, a district sales office that has a goal of being the top district office in the country, or people located in various departments of a social services agency who share an interest in computer games. Communities of practice are similar to professional societies—people join them and stay in them *by choice*, because they think they have something to learn and something to contribute. Communities of practice are, by their nature, informal and voluntary. However, anyone can spur the creation of a community of practice simply by purposefully developing personal relationships and facilitating relationships among others throughout the organization who share common interests or goals.

Both leaders and followers can encourage and support these groups to help people find meaning and purpose and build the relationships needed to move the whole organization forward. However, followers are typically in a better position than formal leaders to enable communities of practice. If a formal leader tries to establish such a group, it might be perceived by others as obligatory, which destroys the voluntary nature of the community. Followers who are willing to assume responsibility and serve others can be highly effective in pulling together communities of practice based on common interests, problems, needs, and objectives. By facilitating relationships across boundaries, communities of practice move both leadership and followership to new levels.

Communities of practice made up of individuals who are informally bound to one another through exposure to a similar set of problems and a common pursuit of solutions

Summary and Interpretation

Leadership doesn't happen without followers, and the important role of followership in organizations is increasingly recognized. People are followers more often than leaders, and effective leaders and followers share similar characteristics. An effective follower is both independent and active in the organization. Being an effective follower depends on not becoming alienated, conforming, passive, nor a pragmatic survivor.

Effective followership is not always easy. Effective followers display the will to assume responsibility, to serve, to challenge, to participate in transformation, and to leave when necessary. Followers also are aware of their own power and its sources, which include personal and position sources. Strategies for being an effective follower include being a resource, helping the leader be a good leader, building a relationship with the leader, and viewing the leader realistically.

Followers want both their leaders and their colleagues to be honest and competent. However, they want their leaders also to be forward-thinking and inspirational. The two latter traits distinguish the role of leader from follower. Followers want to be led, not controlled. Leaders play an important role by creating an environment that enables people to contribute their best. Leaders can use feedback to develop effective followers by making regular feedback a habit, using elements of storytelling, being generous with positive feedback, and helping followers see feedback as an opportunity. They further expand followers' potential and contributions through self-management leadership, which calls for leaders to share power and responsibility in such a way that anyone can become a leader.

Together, leaders and followers forge a sense of interdependence and community in the organization. Community is characterized by inclusivity, a positive culture, conversation, caring, trust, and shared leadership. Communities of practice are an important tool for building community in the organization. Because they are voluntary by nature, communities of practice are created and sustained primarily by followers rather than leaders.

 ## Discussion Questions

1. Discuss the role of a follower. Why do you think so little emphasis is given to followership compared to leadership in organizations?
2. Compare the alienated follower with the passive follower. Can you give an example of each? How would you respond to each if you were a leader?
3. Do you think self-management leadership should be considered a leadership style? Why or why not?
4. Which of the five demands on effective followers do you feel is most important? Least important? How does a follower derive the courage and power to be effective? Discuss.
5. Do you think you would respond better to feedback that is presented using elements of storytelling rather than with a traditional performance review format? Discuss. How might using story and metaphor help followers reframe negative feedback?
6. Describe the strategy for managing up that you most prefer. Explain.
7. What do the traits followers want in leaders and in other followers tell us about the roles of each? Discuss.
8. How might the characteristics of effective followership contribute to building community? Discuss.
9. Is the will to leave the ultimate courage of a follower, compared to the will to participate in transformation? Which would be hardest for you?

Leadership at Work

Follower Role Play

You are a production supervisor at Hyperlink Systems. Your plant produces circuit boards that are used in Nokia cell phones and IBM computers. Hyperlink is caught in a competitive pricing squeeze, so senior management hired a consultant to study the production department. The plant manager, Sue Harris, asked that the consultant's recommendations be implemented immediately. She thought that total production would increase right away. Weekly production goals were set higher than ever. You don't think she took into account the time required to learn new procedures, and plant workers are under great pressure. A handful of workers have resisted the new work methods because they can produce more circuit boards using the old methods. Most workers have changed to the new methods, but their productivity has not increased. Even after a month, many workers think the old ways are more efficient, faster, and more productive.

You have a couple of other concerns with Harris. She asked you to attend an operations conference, and at the last minute sent another supervisor instead, without any explanation. She has made other promises of supplies and equipment to your section, and then has not followed through. You think she acts too quickly without adequate implementation and follow up.

You report directly to Harris and are thinking about your responsibility as a follower. Write below specifically how you would handle this situation. Will you confront her with the knowledge you have? When and where will you meet with her? What will you say? How will you get her to hear you?

_____

_____

_____

What style—Effective, Conformist, Passive, Alienated—best describes your response to this situation? Referring to Exhibit 7.3, which strategy would you like to use to assist Harris?

_____

_____

_____

In Class: The instructor can ask students to volunteer to play the role of the plant manager and the production supervisor. A few students can take turns role-playing the production supervisor in front of the class to show different approaches to being a follower. Other students can be asked to provide feedback on each production supervisor's effectiveness and on which approach seems more effective for this situation.

SOURCE: Based on K. J. Keleman, J. E. Garcia, and K. J. Lovelace, *Management Incidents: Role Plays for Management Development*, (Kendall Hunt Publishing Company, 1990), 73–75, 83.

Leadership Development: Cases for Analysis

General Products Britain

Carl Mitchell was delighted to accept a job in the British branch office of General Products, Inc., a multinational consumer products corporation. Two months later, Mitchell was miserable. The problem was George Garrow, the general manager in charge of the British branch, to whom Mitchell reported.

Garrow had worked his way to the general manager position by "keeping his nose clean" and not making mistakes, which he accomplished by avoiding controversial and risky decisions.

As Mitchell complained to his wife, "Any time I ask him to make a decision, he just wants us to dig deeper and provide 30 more pages of data, most of which are irrelevant. I can't get any improvements started."

For example, Mitchell believed that the line of frozen breakfasts and dinners he was in charge of would be more successful if prices were lowered. He and his four product managers spent weeks preparing graphs and charts to justify a lower price. Garrow reviewed the data but kept waffling, asking for more information. His latest request for weather patterns that might affect shopping habits seemed absurd.

Garrow seemed terrified of departing from the status quo. The frozen breakfast and dinner lines still had 1970s-style packaging, even though they had been reformulated for microwave ovens. Garrow would not approve a coupon program in March because in previous years coupons had been run in April. Garrow measured progress not by new ideas or sales results but by hours spent in the office. He arrived early and shuffled memos and charts until late in the evening and expected the same from everyone else.

After four months on the job, Mitchell made a final effort to reason with Garrow. He argued that the branch was taking a big risk by avoiding decisions to improve things. Market share was slipping. New pricing and promotion strategies were essential. But Garrow just urged more patience and told Mitchell that he and his product managers would have to build a more solid case. Soon after, Mitchell's two best product managers quit, burned out by the marathon sessions analyzing pointless data without results.

Questions

1. How would you evaluate Mitchell as a follower? Evaluate his courage and style.
2. If you were Mitchell, what would you do now?
3. If you were Garrow's boss and Mitchell came to see you, what would you say?

Trams Discount Store

"Things are different around here" were the first words Jill heard from her new manager. Mr. Tyler was welcoming Jill back to another summer of working at Trams, a nationwide discount store. Jill was not at all thrilled with the prospect of another summer at Trams, but jobs were hard to find.

Reluctantly, Jill had returned to work the 6:00 P.M. to 10:00 P.M. shift at Trams, where she worked in the ladies' and children's apparel department. Her job consisted of folding clothes, straightening up the racks, and going to the registers for "price checks." Jill's stomach tied in knots as she remembered her previous work experience at Trams. She was originally hired because management had found that college students work hard, and work hard Jill did. Her first boss at Trams was Ms. Williams, who had strict rules that were to be adhered to or else you were fired. There was to be no talking between employees, or to friends and family who entered the store. Each of the four clerks who worked the night shift was assigned a section of the department and was held responsible for it. With the clientele and the number of price checks, it was almost impossible to finish the work, but each night Jill would race against the clock to finish her section. Ms. Williams was always watching through a one-way mirror, so everyone was alert at all times. It seemed there wasn't a minute to breathe—her 20-minute break (and not a minute more!) was hardly enough to recover from the stress of trying to beat the clock.

As Jill talked to Mr. Tyler, she sensed that things really were different. She was introduced to the other employees she'd be working with and, to her surprise, they all seemed to know one another well and enjoy working at Trams. Mr. Tyler then left a little after 6 P.M., leaving the night shift with no supervision! One of the girls explained that they all worked as a team to get the work done. There was constant chatter, and her co-workers seemed eager to get to know her and hear about her experiences at college. It was hard for Jill at first, but she gradually became used to talking and working. The others teased her a bit for working so hard and fast and rushing back to the department at the end of her allotted 20 minutes of break time.

At first, Jill was appalled by the amount of goofing off the clerks did, but as time passed she began to enjoy it and participate. After all, the work got done with time to spare. Maybe things weren't quite as neat as before—and the store manager had alerted the department that sales were down—but no one had asked the workers to change their behavior. Everyone, including Jill, began taking longer and longer breaks. Some of the clerks even snacked on the sales floor, and they were becoming sloppier and sloppier in their work. Jill liked the relaxed atmosphere, but her work ethic and previous training made it hard for her to accept this. She felt responsible for the decline in sales, and she hated seeing the department so untidy. She began to make a few suggestions, but the other workers ignored her and began excluding her from their bantering. She even talked to Mr. Tyler, who agreed that her suggestions were excellent, but he never said anything to the others. Their behavior grew more and more lax. None of the clerks did their job completely, and breaks often stretched to an hour long. Jill knew the quality of her own work went down as well, but she tried hard to keep up with her own job and the jobs of the others. Again, Trams became a nightmare.

The final straw came when her co-worker Tara approached Jill and asked her to change the price tag on a fashionable tank top to $2 and then "back her up" at the register. Jill replied that the tag said $20, not $2. Tara explained that she worked hard, did her job, and never received any reward. The store owed her this "discount." Jill adamantly refused. Tara changed the price tag herself, went to the register to ring it up, and called Jill a college snob. Jill knew it was time for her to act.

SOURCE: Adapted from "Things Are Different Around Here," prepared by Ann Marie Calacci, with the assistance of Frank Yeandel, in John E. Dittrich and Robert A. Zawacki, *People and Organizations: Cases in Management and Organizational Behavior* (Plano, TX: Business Publications, Inc., 1981), 72–75.

Questions

1. What types of "follower will" does Jill need in this situation?
2. If you were Jill, what actions would you take first? If that didn't produce results, what would you do second? Third?
3. How might Jill use this experience to develop her personal potential?

References

1. Melanie Trottman, "Baggers Get the Sack, But Dawn Marshall Still Excels as One," *The Wall Street Journal* (May 2, 2003): A1, A6.
2. Robert E. Kelley, "In Praise of Followers," *Harvard Business Review* (November/December 1988): 142–148.
3. Bernard M. Bass, *Bass & Stodgill's Handbook of Leadership*, 3rd ed. (New York: Free Press, 1990).
4. Ira Chaleff, *The Courageous Follower: Standing Up To and For Our Leaders* (San Francisco, CA: Berrett-Koehler, 1995).
5. Ira Chaleff, "Learn the Art of Followership," *Government Executive* (February 1997): 51.
6. D. E. Whiteside, *Command Excellence: What It Takes to Be the Best!*, Department of the Navy, Washington, DC: Naval Military Personnel Command, 1985; Polly LaBarre, "'The Most Important Thing a Captain Can Do Is to See the Ship From the Eyes of the Crew,'" *Fast Company* (April 1999): 115–126.
7. Robert E. Kelley, *The Power of Followership* (New York: Doubleday, 1992).
8. Ibid., 101.
9. Ibid., 111–112.
10. Ibid., 117–118.
11. Ibid., 123.
12. David N. Berg, "Resurrecting the Muse: Followership in Organizations," presented at the 1996 International Society for the Psychoanalytic Study of Organizations (ISPSO) Symposium, New York, N.Y., June 14–16, 1996.
13. Chaleff, *The Courageous Follower: Standing Up To and For Our Leaders*.
14. Carol Hymowitz, "Being an Effective Boss Means Knowing How to 'Manage Up,' Too" (In the Lead column), *The Wall Street Journal*, February 20, 2001, B1.
15. Berg, "Resurrecting the Muse."
16. "The Leader and Leadership: What the Leader Must Be, Know, and Do," FM22-100, Chapter 2, http://www.adtdl.army.mil/cgi-bin/atdl.dll/fm/22-100/ch2.htm

17. Ira Sager with Diane Brady, "Big Blue's Blunt Bohemian," *BusinessWeek* (June 14, 1999): 107–112.

18. Merle MacIsaac, "Born Again Basket Case," *Canadian Business* (May 1993): 38–44.

19. Dianne Martz, "Hard Lessons, Well Learned," *Inc.* (December 1993): 29–30.

20. Stephen R. Covey, *The 7 Habits of Highly Effective People: Powerful Lessons in Personal Change* (New York: Simon & Schuster 1989).

21. This discussion of the seven habits is based on Covey, *The 7 Habits of Highly Effective People*; and Don Hellriegel, John W. Slocum, Jr., and Richard Woodman, *Organizational Behavior*, 8th ed. (Cincinnati, OH: South-Western College Publishing, 1998), 350–352.

22. Stephen R. Covey, *The 7 Habits of Highly Effective People* (New York: Fireside edition/Simon & Schuster, 1990), 72.

23. Sager with Brady, "Big Blue's Blunt Bohemian."

24. David C. Wilson and Graham K. Kenny, "Managerially Perceived Influence Over Interdepartmental Decisions," *Journal of Management Studies* 22 (1985): 155–173; Warren Keith Schilit, "An Examination of Individual Differences as Moderators of Upward Influence Activity in Strategic Decisions," *Human Relations* 39 (1986): 933–953; David Mechanic, "Sources of Power of Lower Participants in Complex Organizations," *Administrative Science Quarterly* 7 (1962): 349–364.

25. Peter Moroz and Brian H. Kleiner, "Playing Hardball in Business Organizations," *IM* (January/February 1994): 9–11.

26. Edward O. Welles, "The Shape of Things to Come," *Inc.* (February 1992): 66–74.

27. Warren Keith Schilit and Edwin A. Locke, "A Study of Upward Influence in Organizations," *Administrative Science Quarterly* 27 (1982): 304–316.

28. Chaleff, *The Courageous Follower: Standing Up To and For Our Leaders.*

29. "Open Mouth, Open Career," sidebar in Michael Warshaw, "Open Mouth, Close Career?" *Fast Company* (December 1998): 240ff.

30. David K. Hurst, "How to Manage Your Boss," *Strategy & Business*, Issue 28 (Third Quarter 2002): 99–103; Joseph L. Badaracco, Jr., *Leading Quietly: An Unorthodox Guide to Doing the Right Thing* (Boston: Harvard Business School Press, 2002); Michael Useem, *Leading Up: How to Lead Your Boss So You Both Win* (New York: Crown Business, 2001).

31. Len Schlesinger, "It Doesn't Take a Wizard to Build a Better Boss," *Fast Company* (June/July 1996): 102–107.

32. Hurst, "How to Manage Your Boss."

33. Irvin D. Yalom, M.D., with Ben Yalom, "Mad About Me," *Inc.* (December 1998): 37–38.

34. Frank Pittman, "How to Manage Mom and Dad," *Psychology Today* (November/December 1994): 44–74.

35. Kelley, "In Praise of Followers."

36. Chaleff, *The Courageous Follower: Standing Up To and For Our Leaders.*

37. Christopher Hegarty, *How to Manage Your Boss* (New York: Ballantine 1985), 147.

38. Ibid.

39. Ann Harrington, "Workers of the World, Rate Your Boss!" *Fortune* (September 18, 2000): 340–342.

40. Chaleff, *The Courageous Follower: Standing Up To and For Our Leaders.*

41. Peter B. Smith and Mark F. Peterson, *Leadership, Organizations and Culture* (London: Sage Publications, 1988), 144–145.

42. Pittman, "How to Manage Mom and Dad."

43. Hegarty, *How to Manage Your Boss.*

44. Pittman, "How to Manage Mom and Dad."

45. Berg, "Resurrecting the Muse."

46. James M. Kouzes and Barry Z. Posner, *Credibility: How Leaders Gain and Lose It, Why People Demand It* (San Francisco: Jossey-Bass, 1993).

47. Kelley, "In Praise of Followers."

48. Jay M. Jackman and Myra H. Strober, "Fear of Feedback," *Harvard Business Review* (April 2003): 101–108.

49. John C. Kunich and Richard I. Lester, "Leadership and the Art of Feedback: Feeding the Hands That Back Us," *The Journal of Leadership Studies* 3, no. 4 (1996): 3–22.

50. Mary Mavis, "Painless Performance Evaluations," *Training & Development* (October 1994): 40–44.

51 Thomas A. Stewart, "The Cunning Plots of Leadership," *Fortune* (September 7, 1998): 165–166.

52. Jackman and Strober, "Fear of Feedback."

53. Berg, "Resurrecting the Muse."

54. Charles C. Manz and Henry P. Sims, Jr., "Leading Workers to Lead Themselves: The External Leadership of Self-Managing Work Teams," *Administrative Science Quarterly* (March 1987): 106–129; and Charles C. Manz, *Mastering Self-Leadership: Empowering Yourself for Personal Excellence* (Englewood Cliffs, NJ: Prentice Hall, 1992).

55. Iain L. Densten and Judy H. Gray, "The Links Between Followership and the Experiential Learning Model: Followership Coming of Age," *The Journal of Leadership Studies* 8, no. 1 (2001): 70–76.

56. Robert C. Ford and Myron D. Fottler, "Empowerment: A Matter of Degree," *Academy of Management Executive* 9 (1995): 21–31.

57. Keith H. Hammonds, "You Can't Lead Without Making Sacrifices," *Fast Company* (June 2001): 106–116.

58. Susan Komives, Nance Lucas, and Timothy R. McMahon, *Exploring Leadership* (San Francisco: Jossey-Bass, 1998): 229.

59. Juanita Brown and David Isaacs, "Building Corporations as Communities: The Best of Both Worlds," in *Community Building: Renewing Spirit & Learning in Business*, Kazimierz Gozdz, ed. (San Francisco: Sterling & Stone, Inc., 1995): 69–83.

60. These are based on M. Scott Peck, *The Different Drum: Community Making and Peace* (New York: Touchstone, 1987); J. W. Gardner, *On Leadership* (New York: The Free Press): 116–118; and Komives, et al., *Exploring Leadership*.

61. W. B. Gudykunst, *Bridging Differences: Effective Intergroup Communication* (Newbury Park, Calif.: Sage, 1991): 146.

62. Brown and Isaacs, "Building Corporations as Communities"; Glenna Gerard and Linda Teurfs, "Dialogue and Organizational Transformation," in Kazimierz Gozdz, ed., *Community Building* (San Francisco: Sterling & Stone, Inc., 1995): 142–153; and Edgar G. Schein, "On Dialogue, Culture, and Organizational Learning," *Organizational Dynamics* (Autumn 1993): 40–51.

63. Brown and Isaacs, "Building Corporations as Communities."

64. Verna Allee, *The Knowledge Evolution* (Oxford: Butterworth-Heinemann, 1997): 218–219; Thomas A. Stewart, *Intellectual Capital* (New York: Bantam Books, 1998), 96–100; and W. H. Drath and C. J. Palus, *Making Common Sense: Leadership as Meaning-Making in a Community of Practice* (Greensboro, N.C.: Center for Creative Leadership, 1994).

The Leader as Relationship Builder

Chapter

Your Leadership Challenge

After reading this chapter, you should be able to:

- Recognize and apply the difference between intrinsic and extrinsic rewards.

- Motivate others by meeting their higher-level needs.

- Apply needs-based theories of motivation.

- Implement individual and systemwide rewards.

- Avoid the disadvantages of "carrot-and-stick" motivation.

- Implement empowerment by providing the five elements of information, knowledge, discretion, meaning, and rewards.

Motivation and Empowerment

When D. Michael Abrashoff took command of the U.S. Navy destroyer USS *Benfold*, he came face to face with the biggest leadership challenge of his Navy career. Despite the fact that the *Benfold* was a technological marvel, most of its sailors couldn't wait to leave. People were so deeply unhappy and demoralized that walking aboard ship felt like entering a deep well of despair. Abrashoff vowed that he would create an environment where sailors were so engaged with their work that they would perform at peak levels, willingly stick around for their entire tours, and maybe even happily reenlist.

Previous commanders of the *Benfold* had pursued command-and-control leadership to the max, but Abrashoff knew he needed to be a different kind of leader to turn things around. He believed the best way to tap into the energy, enthusiasm, and creativity of his sailors was by empowering them to contribute all their skills and brainpower. Rather than issuing orders from the top, Abrashoff started listening to ideas from below, meeting individually in his cabin with every one of the *Benfold*'s 310 sailors. He admits that listening doesn't come easily for him, but he made a commitment that he would treat every encounter with every sailor as the most important thing in the world at that particular moment. When sailors saw that Abrashoff sincerely wanted and valued their ideas and input, they responded with energy, enthusiasm, and commitment. Abrashoff set clear boundaries and guidelines and then gave his sailors the ship to run. Any member of the crew was free to question or criticize any other, including the captain, as long as it was done respectfully and with an aim of helping to fulfill the mission.

Under Abrashoff's empowering leadership, the *Benfold* set all-time records for performance and retention. Even though Abrashoff eventually moved on to a top post at the Space and Naval Warfare Systems Command, the motivation he sparked at the *Benfold* continued. "This crew . . . [knows] what results they get when they play an active role," Abrashoff says. "And they now have the courage to raise their hands and get heard. That's almost irreversible."[1]

D. Michael Abrashoff improved motivation as captain of the USS *Benfold* by creating an environment of trust and empowerment. By giving sailors a strong voice in how things were done aboard the *Benfold*, Abrashoff revived morale and improved satisfaction and commitment. Moreover, his emphasis on helping people contribute and grow changed many crew members' personal as well as work lives. Empowerment of lower-level employees is a powerful trend in today's organizations, and one reason for this is the favorable impact that true empowerment can have on employee motivation.

This chapter will explore motivation in organizations and examine how leaders can bring out the best in organizational followers. We will examine the difference between intrinsic and extrinsic rewards and how they meet the needs of followers. Individuals have both lower and higher needs, and there are different methods of motivation to meet those needs. The chapter presents several theories of motivation, with particular attention to the differences between leadership and conventional management methods for creating a motivated workforce. The final sections of the chapter explore empowerment and other recent motivational tools that do not rely on traditional reward and punishment methods.

Leadership and Motivation

Most of us get up in the morning, go to school or work, and behave in ways that are predictably our own. We usually respond to our environment and the people in it with little thought as to why we work hard, enjoy certain classes, or find some recreational activities so much fun. Yet all these behaviors are motivated by something. **Motivation** refers to the forces either internal or external to a person that arouse enthusiasm and persistence to pursue a certain course of action. Employee motivation affects productivity, and so part of a leader's job is to channel followers' motivation toward the accomplishment of the organization's vision and goals.[2] The study of motivation helps leaders understand what prompts people to initiate action, what influences their choice of action, and why they persist in that action over time.

Exhibit 8.1 illustrates a simple model of human motivation. People have basic needs, such as for food, recognition, or monetary gain, that translate into an internal tension that motivates specific behaviors with which to fulfill the need. To the extent that the behavior is successful, the person is rewarded when the need is satisfied. The reward also informs the person that the behavior was appropriate and can be used again in the future.

The importance of motivation, as illustrated in Exhibit 8.1, is that it can lead to behaviors that reflect high performance within organizations. Studies have found that high employee motivation and high organizational performance and profits go

Motivation

the forces either internal or external to a person that arouse enthusiasm and persistence to pursue a certain course of action

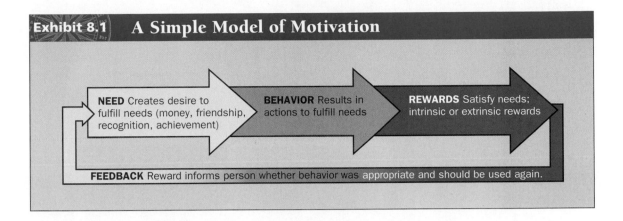

Exhibit 8.1   A Simple Model of Motivation

NEED Creates desire to fulfill needs (money, friendship, recognition, achievement)

BEHAVIOR Results in actions to fulfill needs

REWARDS Satisfy needs; intrinsic or extrinsic rewards

FEEDBACK Reward informs person whether behavior was appropriate and should be used again.

hand in hand.[3] The Gallup organization recently completed an extensive survey and found that when all of an organization's employees are highly motivated and performing at their peak, customers are 70 percent more loyal, turnover drops by 70 percent, and profits jump 40 percent.[4] Leaders can use motivation theory to help satisfy followers' needs and simultaneously encourage high work performance. When workers are not motivated to achieve organizational goals, the fault is often the leader's.

Intrinsic and Extrinsic Rewards

Rewards can be either intrinsic or extrinsic, systemwide or individual. Exhibit 8.2 illustrates the categories of rewards, combining intrinsic and extrinsic rewards with those that are applied systemwide or individually.[5] **Intrinsic rewards** are the internal satisfactions a person receives in the process of performing a particular action. Solving a problem to benefit others may fulfill a personal mission, or the completion of a complex task may bestow a pleasant feeling of accomplishment. An intrinsic reward is internal and under the control of the individual, such as to engage in task behavior to satisfy a need for competency and self-determination.

Conversely, **extrinsic rewards** are given by another person, typically a supervisor, and include promotions and pay increases. Because they originate externally as a result of pleasing others, extrinsic rewards compel individuals to engage in a task behavior for an outside source that provides what they need, such as money to survive in modern society. Consider, for example, the difference in motivation for polishing a car if it belongs to you versus if you work at a car wash. Your good feelings from making your own car shine would be intrinsic. However, buffing a car that is but one of many in a day's work requires the extrinsic reward of a paycheck.[6]

Rewards can be given systemwide or on an individual basis. **Systemwide rewards** apply the same to all people within an organization or within a specific

Intrinsic rewards
internal satisfactions a person receives in the process of performing a particular action

Extrinsic rewards
rewards given by another person, typically a supervisor, such as pay increases and promotions

Systemwide rewards
rewards that apply the same to all people within an organization or within a specific category or department

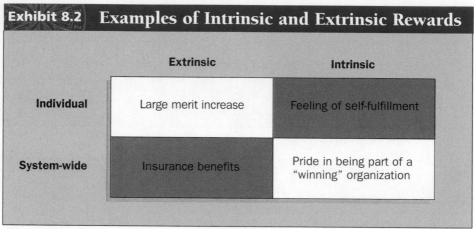

Exhibit 8.2   **Examples of Intrinsic and Extrinsic Rewards**

	Extrinsic	Intrinsic
Individual	Large merit increase	Feeling of self-fulfillment
System-wide	Insurance benefits	Pride in being part of a "winning" organization

SOURCE: Adapted from Richard M. Steers, Lyman W. Porter, and Gregory A. Bigley, *Motivation and Leadership at Work*, 6th ed. (New York: McGraw-Hill, 1996), 498. Reprinted with permission of the McGraw-Hill Companies.

Individual
rewards

*rewards that
differ among
individuals
within the same
organization or
department*

category or department. **Individual rewards** may differ among people within the same organization or department. An extrinsic, systemwide reward could be insurance benefits or vacation time available to an entire organization or category of people, such as those who have been with the organization for two years or more. An intrinsic, systemwide reward would be the sense of pride that comes from within by virtue of contributing to a "winning" organization. An extrinsic, individual reward is a promotion or a bonus check. An intrinsic, individual reward would be a sense of self-fulfillment that an individual derives from his or her work.

Although extrinsic rewards are important, leaders work especially hard to enable followers to achieve intrinsic rewards—both individually and systemwide. Employees who get intrinsic satisfaction from their jobs often put forth increased effort. In addition, as we described in Chapter 1, leaders genuinely care about others and want them to feel good about their work. Leaders create an environment that brings out the best in people. We all know that people voluntarily invest time and energy in activities they enjoy, such as hobbies, charitable causes, or community projects.

On the job, employees may always have to perform some activities they don't particularly like, but leaders try to match followers with jobs and tasks that provide individual intrinsic rewards. They also strive to create an environment where people feel valued and feel that they are contributing to something worthwhile, helping followers achieve systemwide intrinsic rewards. On the USS *Benfold*, for example, one systemwide intrinsic reward was the joy and satisfaction crew members got from transforming the ship into the pride of the Pacific fleet, with sailors from other ships clamoring to join its crew. In *Fortune* magazine's annual list of "100 Best Companies to Work For," companies that rank high are typically ones that show genuine caring for employees, enabling them to feel like important members of a community. These companies feel like more than just a place to work. As one employee of number four-ranked Xilinx put it, "There's a sense that we sink or swim as one big family."[7]

Higher versus Lower Needs

Intrinsic rewards appeal to the "higher" needs of individuals, such as accomplishment, competence, fulfillment, and self-determination. Extrinsic rewards appeal to the "lower" needs of individuals, such as material comfort and basic safety and security. Exhibit 8.3 outlines the distinction between conventional management and leadership approaches to motivation based on people's needs. Conventional management approaches often appeal to an individual's lower, basic needs and rely on extrinsic rewards and punishments—carrot-and-stick methods—to motivate subordinates to behave in desired ways. These approaches are effective, but they are based on controlling the behavior of people by manipulating their decisions about how to act. The higher needs of people may be unmet in favor of utilizing their labor in exchange for external rewards. Under conventional management, people perform adequately to receive the "carrot," or avoid the "stick," since they will not necessarily derive intrinsic satisfaction from their work.

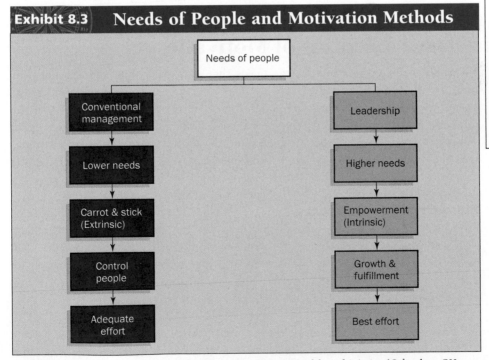

Exhibit 8.3   **Needs of People and Motivation Methods**

Needs of people

Conventional management → Lower needs → Carrot & stick (Extrinsic) → Control people → Adequate effort

Leadership → Higher needs → Empowerment (Intrinsic) → Growth & fulfillment → Best effort

SOURCE: Adapted from William D. Hitt, *The Leader-Manager: Guidelines for Action* (Columbus, OH: Battelle Press, 1988), 153.

Action Memo

As a leader: Use the right motivational tools to meet followers' needs and spur high organizational performance. Provide adequate extrinsic rewards such as promotions, pay raises, and praise. Give special attention to helping followers achieve intrinsic rewards and meet their higher-level needs for accomplishment, growth, and fulfillment.

Leaders often try to motivate others by providing them with the opportunity to satisfy higher needs and become intrinsically rewarded. For example, employees in companies infused with a social mission or that find ways to enrich the lives of others are typically more highly motivated because of the intrinsic rewards they get from helping other people.[8] J. M. Smucker, the 105-year-old company that makes jams, jellies, and Jif peanut butter, offers employees paid time off for volunteer activities, contributing to high employee satisfaction and motivation and low turnover.[9] Remember, though, that the source of an intrinsic reward is internal to the follower. Thus, what is intrinsically rewarding to one individual may not be so to another. One way in which leaders try to enable all followers to achieve intrinsic rewards is by giving them more control over their own work and the power to affect outcomes. When leaders empower others, allowing them the freedom to determine their own actions, subordinates reward themselves intrinsically for good performance. They may become creative, innovative, and develop a greater commitment to their objectives. So motivated, they often achieve their best possible performance.

Ideally, work behaviors should satisfy both lower and higher needs, as well as serve the mission of the organization. Unfortunately, this is often not the case. The leader's motivational role, then, is to create a situation that integrates the needs of people—especially higher needs—and the fundamental objectives of the organization.

Needs-Based Theories of Motivation

Needs-based theories emphasize the needs that motivate people. At any point in time, people have basic needs such as those for food, achievement, or monetary reward. These needs are the source of an internal drive that motivates behavior to fulfill the needs. An individual's needs are like a hidden catalog of the things he or she wants and will work to get. To the extent that leaders understand worker needs, they can design the reward system to reinforce employees for directing energies and priorities toward attainment of shared goals.

Hierarchy of Needs Theory

Hierarchy of needs theory
Maslow's theory that proposes that humans are motivated by multiple needs and those needs exist in a hierarchical order

Probably the most famous needs-based theory is the one developed by Abraham Maslow.[10] Maslow's **hierarchy of needs theory** proposes that humans are motivated by multiple needs and those needs exist in a hierarchical order, as illustrated in Exhibit 8.4, wherein the higher needs cannot be satisfied until the lower needs are met. Maslow identified five general levels of motivating needs.

* **Physiological** The most basic human physiological needs include food, water, and oxygen. In the organizational setting, these are reflected in the needs for adequate heat, air, and base salary to ensure survival.

Exhibit 8.4 | **Maslow's Hierarchy of Needs**

Need Hierarchy	Fulfillment on the Job
Self-actualization Needs	Opportunities for advancement, autonomy, growth, creativity
Esteem Needs	Recognition, approval, high status, increased responsibilities
Belongingness Needs	Work groups, clients, coworkers, supervisors
Safety Needs	Safe work, fringe benefits, job security
Physiological Needs	Heat, air, base salary

❋ **Safety** Next is the need for a safe and secure physical and emotional environment and freedom from threats—that is, for freedom from violence and for an orderly society. In an organizational workplace, safety needs reflect the needs for safe jobs, fringe benefits, and job security.

❋ **Belongingness** People have a desire to be accepted by their peers, have friendships, be part of a group, and be loved. In the organization, these needs influence the desire for good relationships with coworkers, participation in a work team, and a positive relationship with supervisors.

❋ **Esteem** The need for esteem relates to the desires for a positive self-image and for attention, recognition, and appreciation from others. Within organizations, esteem needs reflect a motivation for recognition, an increase in responsibility, high status, and credit for contributions to the organization.

❋ **Self-actualization** The highest need category, self-actualization, represents the need for self-fulfillment: developing one's full potential, increasing one's competence, and becoming a better person. Self-actualization needs can be met in the organization by providing people with opportunities to grow, be empowered and creative, and acquire training for challenging assignments and advancement.

According to Maslow's theory, physiology, safety, and belonging are deficiency needs. These low-order needs take priority—they must be satisfied before higher-order, or growth needs, are activated. The needs are satisfied in sequence: Physiological needs are satisfied before safety needs, safety needs are satisfied before social needs, and so on. A person desiring physical safety will devote his or her efforts to securing a safer environment and will not be concerned with esteem or self-actualization. Once a need is satisfied, it declines in importance and the next higher need is activated. When a union wins good pay and working conditions for its members, basic needs will be met; union members may then want to have social and esteem needs met in the workplace.

Two-Factor Theory

Frederick Herzberg developed another popular theory of motivation called the *two-factor theory*.[11] Herzberg interviewed hundreds of workers about times when they were highly motivated to work and other times when they were dissatisfied and unmotivated to work. His findings suggested that the work characteristics associated with dissatisfaction were quite different from those pertaining to satisfaction, which prompted the notion that two factors influence work motivation.

The two-factor theory is illustrated in Exhibit 8.5. The center of the scale is neutral, meaning that workers are neither satisfied nor dissatisfied. Herzberg believed that two entirely separate dimensions contribute to an employee's behavior at work. The first dimension, called **hygiene factors**, involves the presence or absence of job dissatisfiers, such as working conditions, pay, company policies, and interpersonal relationships. When hygiene factors are poor, work is dissatisfying. This is similar to the concept of deficiency needs described by Maslow. Good hygiene factors remove the dissatisfaction, but they do not in themselves cause people to become highly satisfied and motivated in their work.

The second set of factors does influence job satisfaction. **Motivators** fulfill high-level needs and include achievement, recognition, responsibility, and opportunity for growth. Herzberg believed that when motivators are present, workers are highly motivated and satisfied. Thus, hygiene factors and motivators represent two distinct factors that influence motivation. Hygiene factors work in the area of lower-level needs, and their absence causes dissatisfaction. Unsafe working conditions or a noisy working environment will cause people to be dissatisfied; but their correction will not cause a high level of work enthusiasm and satisfaction. Higher-level motivators such as challenge, responsibility, and recognition must be in place before employees will be highly motivated to excel at their work.

The implication of the two-factor theory for leaders is clear. The leader's role is to go beyond the removal of dissatisfiers to the use of motivators to meet higher-level needs and propel employees toward greater achievement and satisfaction. You can evaluate your current or a previous job according to Maslow's needs theory and Herzberg's two-factor theory by answering the questions in Leader's Self-Insight 8.1. The following example illustrates how Ann Price strives to meet employees' higher as well as lower-level needs at Motek, a company that makes software for tracking the movement of goods in warehouses.

Hygiene factors
the first dimension of Herzberg's two-factor theory; involves working conditions, pay, company policies, and interpersonal relationships

Motivators
the second dimension of Herzberg's two-factor theory; involves job satisfaction and meeting higher-level needs such as achievement, recognition, and opportunity for growth

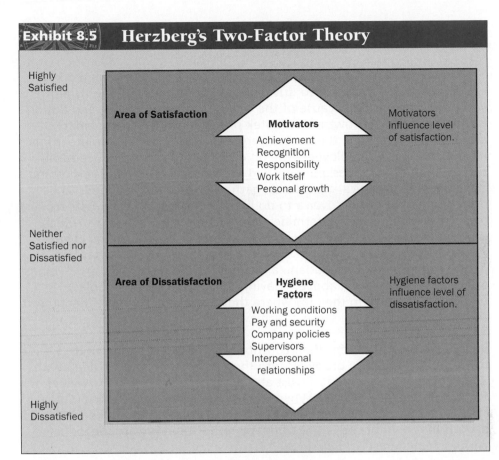

Exhibit 8.5   Herzberg's Two-Factor Theory

Highly
Satisfied

Area of Satisfaction

Motivators
Achievement
Recognition
Responsibility
Work itself
Personal growth

Motivators
influence level
of satisfaction.

Neither
Satisfied nor
Dissatisfied

Area of Dissatisfaction

**Hygiene
Factors**
Working conditions
Pay and security
Company policies
Supervisors
Interpersonal
  relationships

Hygiene factors
influence level of
dissatisfaction.

Highly
Dissatisfied

In the Lead Ann Price, Motek

When Ann Price founded Motek, she wanted to create a company whose primary mission was to improve the lives of its employees and customers rather than to reward shareholders or investors. She decided early on to take a long-term approach to business, rather that drive for rapid growth, so that employees could "have a life along the way."

Price incorporates both low-level hygiene factors and high-level motivators at Motek. Pay is satisfactory, but the benefits are amazing. All employees get five weeks of paid vacation and 10 paid holidays, and no one is permitted to work past 5 P.M. or on weekends. After 10 years with the company, workers are given a leased Lexus, or whatever car they choose within a $6,000 annual limit. The working environment at Motek is calm, almost serene. Employees are serious about their work, but relationships are marked by an easy camaraderie. Shop talk during lunch hour is forbidden as part of Price's mission to promote a balanced life.

Yet , what really motivates employees at Motek is not the calm working environment or the chance to drive a Lexus. Employees are highly motivated and committed because of the challenge, responsibility, and opportunity for personal growth that Motek provides. Price believes smart employees can manage themselves very well if they have complete information. At Motek, employees vote on everything from the office furniture to their own job assignments and pay raises. Every Monday morning, the company's technical consultants gather to discuss what needs to be done that week, poring over a to-do list of hundreds of tasks. Rather than having a manager determine which people should perform which jobs, individuals volunteer for various chores and decide among themselves the best way to accomplish all the work. "We decide what happens," explains Ran Ever-Hadani, a member of the technical staff. "Things are rarely decreed from above." Having this level of input enables employees to perform the jobs where they feel they can make the biggest contribution,enabling a sense of achievement and accomplishment.

People are recognized for their contributions to the company and rewarded for bringing problems into the open so they can be dealt with appropriately. The degree of trust and autonomy at Motek also makes employees feel like owners. When workers vote on decisions about pay raises and bonuses, they often decide to pay down debt or take other actions that benefit the entire company rather than reward individuals with increased pay.[12]

At Motek, Ann Price has successfully applied the two-factor theory to provide both low-level hygiene factors and incorporate high-level motivators. By meeting employees' higher as well as lower-level needs, Price has created happy employees and a successful organization.

Acquired Needs Theory

Another needs-based theory was developed by David McClelland. The **acquired needs theory** proposes that certain types of needs are acquired during an individual's lifetime. In other words, people are not born with these needs but may learn them through their life experiences.[13] Three needs are most frequently studied.

* *Need for achievement*—the desire to accomplish something difficult, attain a high standard of success, master complex tasks, and surpass others.
* *Need for affiliation*—the desire to form close personal relationships, avoid conflict, and establish warm friendships.

Acquired needs theory

McClelland's theory that proposes that certain types of needs (achievement, affiliation, power) are acquired during an individual's lifetime

LEADER'S SELF-INSIGHT 8.1

Are Your Needs Met?

Think of a specific job (current or previous) you have held. If you are a full-time student, think of your classes and study activities as your job. Please answer the questions below about those work activities. Please answer the 12 questions on the 1–5 scale based on the extent to which you agree with each statement.

	Strongly disagree				Strongly agree
1. I feel physically safe at work.	1	2	3	4	5
2. I have good health benefits.	1	2	3	4	5
3. I am satisfied with what I'm getting paid for my work.	1	2	3	4	5
4. I feel that my job is secure as long as I want it.	1	2	3	4	5
5. I have good friends at work.	1	2	3	4	5
6. I have enough time away from my work to enjoy other things in life.	1	2	3	4	5
7. I feel appreciated at work.	1	2	3	4	5
8. People at my workplace respect me as a professional and expert in my field.	1	2	3	4	5
9. I feel that my job allows me to realize my full potential.	1	2	3	4	5
10. I feel that I am realizing my potential as an expert in my line of work.	1	2	3	4	5
11. I feel I'm always learning new things that help me to do my work better.	1	2	3	4	5
12. There is a lot of creativity involved in my work.	1	2	3	4	5

Scoring and Interpretation

Compute the *average* scores for the questions that represent each level of Maslow's hierarchy, as indicated below, and write your average score where indicated:

Questions 1-2: Physiological and health needs. Average = _____

Questions 3-4: Economic and safety needs. Average = _____

Questions 5-6: Belonging and social needs. Average = _____

Questions 7-8: Esteem needs. Average = _____

Questions 9-12: Self-actualization needs. Average = _____

These five scores represent how you see your needs being met in the work situation. An average score for overall need satisfaction (all 12 questions) is typically 3 or slightly above 3, and the average for lower level needs tends to be higher than for higher level needs. Is that true for you? What do your five scores say about the need satisfaction in your job? Which needs are less filled for you? How would that affect your choice of a new job? In developed countries, lower needs are often taken for granted, and work motivation is based on the opportunity to meet higher needs. Compare your scores to those of another student. How does that person's array of five scores differ from yours? Ask questions about the student's job to help explain the difference in scores.

Reread the 12 questions above. Which questions would you say are about the *motivators* in Herzberg's Two-Factor Theory? Which questions are about *hygiene factors*? Calculate the average score for the motivator questions and the average score for the hygiene factor questions. What do you interpret from your scores on these two factors compared to the five levels of needs in Maslow's hierarchy?

SOURCE: The questions above are taken from *Social Indicators Research* 55 (2001), 241–302, "A New Measure of Quality of Work Life (QWL) based on Need Satisfaction and Spillover Theories," M. Joseph Sirgy, David Efraty, Phillip Siegel and Dong-Jin Lee. Copyright © and reprinted with kind permission of Kluwer Academic Publishers.

Reinforcement theory

a motivational theory that looks at the relationship between behavior and its consequences by changing or modifying followers' on-the-job behavior through the appropriate use of immediate rewards or punishments

✻   *Need for power*—the desire to influence or control others, be responsible for others, and have authority over others.

For more than 20 years, McClelland studied human needs and their implications for management. People with a high need for achievement tend to enjoy work that is entrepreneurial and innovative. People who have a high need for affiliation are successful "integrators," whose job is to coordinate the work of people and departments.[14] Integrators include brand managers and project managers, positions that require excellent people skills. A high need for power is often associated with successful attainment of top levels in the organizational hierarchy. For example, McClelland studied managers at AT&T for 16 years and found that those with a high need for power were more likely to pursue a path of continued promotion over time.

Needs-based theories focus on underlying needs that motivate how people behave. The hierarchy of needs theory, the two-factor theory, and the acquired needs theory all identify the specific needs that motivate people. Leaders can work to meet followers' needs and hence elicit appropriate and successful work behaviors.

Other Motivational Theories

Three additional motivation theories, the reinforcement perspective, expectancy theory, and equity theory, focus primarily on extrinsic rewards and punishments. Relying on extrinsic rewards and punishments is sometimes referred to as the "carrot-and-stick" approach.[15] The behavior that produces a desired outcome is rewarded with "carrots," such as a pay raise or a promotion. Conversely, undesirable or unproductive behavior brings the "stick," such as a demotion or withholding a pay raise. Carrot-and-stick approaches tend to focus on lower needs, although higher needs can sometimes also be met.

Behavior modification

the set of techniques by which reinforcement theory is used to modify behavior

Law of effect

states that positively reinforced behavior tends to be repeated and behavior that is not reinforced tends not to be repeated

Reinforcement Perspective on Motivation

The reinforcement approach to employee motivation sidesteps the deeper issue of employee needs described in the needs-based theories. **Reinforcement theory** simply looks at the relationship between behavior and its consequences by changing or modifying followers' on-the-job behavior through the appropriate use of immediate rewards or punishments.

Behavior modification is the name given to the set of techniques by which reinforcement theory is used to modify behavior.[16] The basic assumption underlying behavior modification is the **law of effect**, which states that positively reinforced behavior tends to be repeated, and behavior that is not reinforced tends not to be repeated. **Reinforcement** is defined as anything that causes a certain behavior to be repeated or inhibited. Four ways in which leaders use reinforcement to modify or shape employee behavior are: positive reinforcement, negative reinforcement, punishment, and extinction.

Positive reinforcement is the administration of a pleasant and rewarding consequence following a behavior. A good example of positive reinforcement is immediate praise for an employee who arrives on time or does a little extra in his or her work. The pleasant consequence will increase the likelihood of the excellent work behavior occurring again.

Negative reinforcement is the withdrawal of an unpleasant consequence once a behavior is improved. Sometimes referred to as *avoidance learning*, negative reinforcement means people learn to perform the desired behavior by avoiding unpleasant situations. A simple example would be when a supervisor stops reprimanding an employee for tardiness once the employee starts getting to work on time.

Punishment is the imposition of unpleasant outcomes on an employee. Punishment typically occurs following undesirable behavior. For example, a supervisor may berate an employee for performing a task incorrectly. The supervisor expects that the negative outcome will serve as a punishment and reduce the likelihood of the behavior recurring. The use of punishment in organizations is controversial and often criticized because it fails to indicate the correct behavior.

Extinction is the withdrawal of a positive reward, meaning that behavior is no longer reinforced and hence is less likely to occur in the future. If a perpetually tardy employee fails to receive praise and pay raises, he or she will begin to realize that the behavior is not producing desired outcomes. The behavior will gradually disappear if it is continually not reinforced.

Leaders can reinforce behavior after each and every occurrence, which is referred to as *continuous reinforcement*, or they can choose to reinforce behavior intermittently, which is referred to as *partial reinforcement*. With partial reinforcement, the desired behavior is reinforced often enough to make the employee believe the behavior is worth repeating, but not every time it is demonstrated. Continuous reinforcement can be very effective for establishing new behaviors, but research has found that partial reinforcement is more effective for maintaining behavior over extended time periods.[17]

Some leaders have applied reinforcement theory very effectively to shape followers' behavior. At TNT UK, managing director Alan Jones motivates van drivers with personal calls or notes to congratulate them for outstanding service or particular achievements.[18] Studies have found that positive reinforcement can help to improve performance. Moreover, nonfinancial reinforcements, such as positive feedback, social recognition, and attention, are just as effective as financial incentives.[19] UPS sends all supervisors at its distribution centers through training that helps them learn how to better communicate and demonstrate interest in their workers as individuals.[20] Another company where leaders have successfully applied reinforcement theory is Emerald Packaging in Union City, California.

Reinforcement *anything that causes a certain behavior to be repeated or inhibited*

Positive reinforcement *the administration of a pleasant and rewarding consequence following a behavior*

Negative reinforcement *the withdrawal of an unpleasant consequence once a behavior is improved*

Punishment *the imposition of unpleasant outcomes on an employee following undesirable behavior*

Extinction *the withdrawal of a positive reward, meaning that behavior is no longer reinforced and hence is less likely to occur in the future*

In the Lead   Kevin Kelly, Emerald Packaging Inc.

Emerald Packaging is a family-owned business that prints plastic bags for prepackaged salads and other vegetables. The company employs about 100 people and is the tenth largest manufacturer in Union City, California, located about 30 miles southeast of San Francisco.

Kevin Kelly, vice president of operations for Emerald, and other leaders wanted to fire up employees by developing a positive reinforcement scheme that would motivate and reward workers. The plan at Emerald includes the following:

1. *Monthly Quality Award.* Each month, managers pick the best print job in the plant from samples submitted by printing press employees. The winning press operator gets $100 and the operator's helper wins $50.
2. *Safety Program.* When the company has three or fewer minor accidents and no lost-time accidents in one quarter, leaders raffle off $1,000, provide workers with company shirts and jackets, and buy lunch for everyone. If employees make it through the entire year with only 12 minor accidents and no lost-time injuries, the company raffles a total of $10,000 to three winners and throws a party for all employees.
3. *Profit-Sharing Plan.* A certain percentage of operating profit is set aside into a bonus pool, which is shared among employees.

Has Emerald's plan for reinforcing correct behaviors worked? Kelly reports that customer returns for poor quality are down 75 percent over last year. The quality rewards of $50–100 are substantial enough to get employees' attention and make it worth their while to put increased effort into producing a high-quality print job. So far, safety results are also impressive. During the first five months of the program, the company had only one minor accident. Employees are much more careful about how they conduct themselves on the job because no one wants to derail the raffle.[21]

Expectancy theory

a theory that suggests that motivation depends on individuals' mental expectations about their ability to perform tasks and receive desired rewards

Expectancy Theory

Expectancy theory suggests that motivation depends on individuals' mental expectations about their ability to perform tasks and receive desired rewards. Expectancy theory is associated with the work of Victor Vroom, although a number of scholars have made contributions in this area.[22] Expectancy theory is concerned not with understanding types of needs but with the thinking process that individuals use to achieve rewards. Consider Holly Mason, a university student with a strong desire for an A on her accounting exam. Holly's motivation to study for the exam will be influenced by her expectation that hard study will truly lead to an A on the exam. If Holly believes she cannot get an A on the exam, she will not be motivated to study exceptionally hard.

Expectancy theory is based on the relationship among the individual's effort, the possibility of high performance, and the desirability of outcomes following high performance. These elements and the relationships among them are illustrated in Exhibit 8.6. The $E > P$ expectancy is the probability that putting effort into a task will lead to high performance. For this expectancy to be high, the individual must have the ability, previous experience, and necessary tools, information, and opportunity to perform. The $P > O$ expectancy involves whether successful performance will lead to the desired outcome. If this expectancy is high, the individual will be more highly motivated. Valence refers to the value of outcomes to the individual. If the outcomes that are available from high effort and good performance are not valued by an employee, motivation will be low. Likewise, if outcomes have a high value, motivation will be higher. A simple example to illustrate the relationships in Exhibit 8.6 is Alfredo Torres, a salesperson at Diamond Gift Shop. If Alfredo believes that increased selling effort will lead to higher personal sales, his $E > P$ expectancy would be considered high. Moreover, if he also believes that higher personal sales will lead to a promotion or pay raise, the $P > O$ expectancy is also high. Finally, if Alfredo places a high value on the promotion or pay raise, valence is high and he will be highly motivated. For an

Action Memo

As a leader: Change follower behavior through the appropriate use of rewards and punishments. To establish new behaviors quickly, reinforce the desired behavior after each and every occurrence. To sustain the behaviors over a long time period, reinforce the behaviors intermittently.

Exhibit 8.6   **Key Elements of Expectancy Theory**

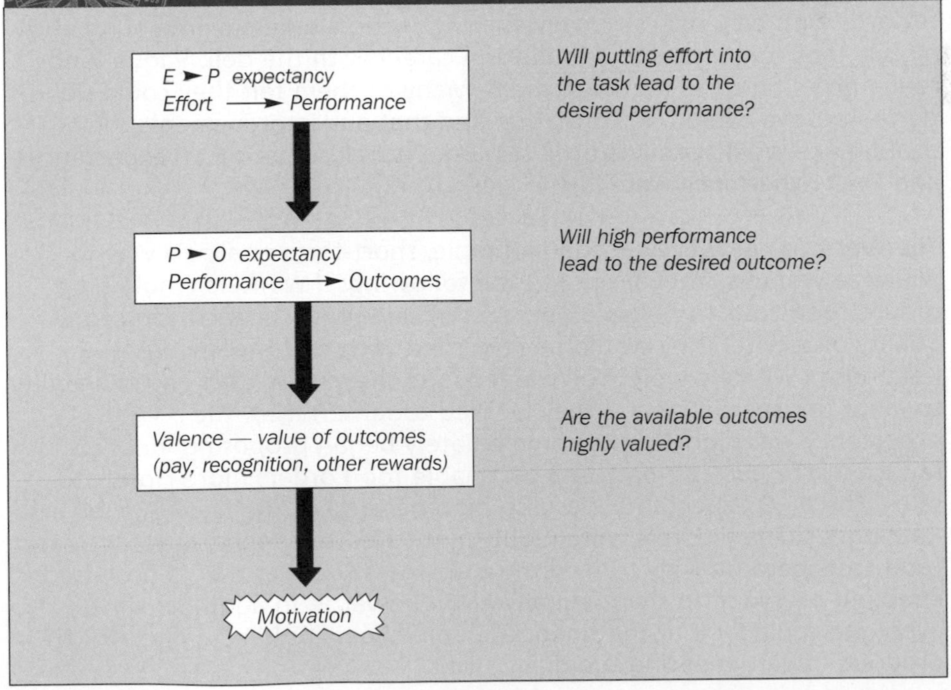

$E \blacktriangleright P$ expectancy
Effort ⟶ Performance

Will putting effort into the task lead to the desired performance?

$P \blacktriangleright O$ expectancy
Performance ⟶ Outcomes

Will high performance lead to the desired outcome?

Valence — value of outcomes
(pay, recognition, other rewards)

Are the available outcomes highly valued?

Motivation

employee to be highly motivated, all three factors in the expectancy model must be high.[23]

Like the path–goal theory of leadership described in Chapter 3, expectancy theory is personalized to subordinates' needs and goals. A leader's responsibility is to help followers meet their needs while attaining organizational goals. One employee may want to be promoted to a position of increased responsibility, and another may want a good relationship with peers. To increase motivation, leaders can increase followers' expectancy by clarifying individual needs, providing the desired outcomes, and ensuring that individuals have the ability and support needed to perform well and attain their desired outcomes.

Some companies use expectancy theory principles by designing incentive systems that identify desired organizationwide outcomes and give everyone a shot at getting the rewards. The trick is designing a system that fits with employees' abilities and needs. Consider the following example from Katzinger's Delicatessen.

In the Lead   Steve and Diane Warren, Katzinger's Delicatessen

When Steve and Diane Warren implemented open book management, they taught employees how to read the financial statements and told them if financial performance improved, the owners would share the rewards with employees. However, most of the workers were young and mobile, not committed to a long-term career with the deli. Vague long-range goals failed to motivate them. Many of them felt they could do little to improve overall performance, and that any improvements they could make would provide little reward. Therefore both $E{\rightarrow}P$ expectancy and $P{\rightarrow}O$ expectancy were low.

The Warrens knew they needed a simple, short-term goal as a way to energize workers. They proposed the following: If workers would help reduce food costs to below 35 percent of sales without sacrificing food quality or service, they would be rewarded with half the savings. Katzinger's workers were well trained, and they knew they had the ability to meet this specific goal if they worked together; thus, the $E{\rightarrow}P$ expectancy was high. Workers immediately began proposing ideas to reduce waste, such as matching perishable food orders more closely to sales. The $P{\rightarrow}O$ expectancy was also high because of the level of trust at Katzinger's. The workers were highly motivated to cooperate to decrease food costs because they trusted the co-owners to do as they'd promised, enabling everyone to share equally in the rewards. In addition, since everyone could look at the financials, employees could actually track their progress toward meeting the goal.

At the end of the first month, food costs had fallen nearly 2 percent and employees took home about $40 each from the savings. Later monthly payouts were as high as $95 per employee. By the end of the year, food quality and service had actually improved, while Katzinger's had reduced its food costs to below 35 percent of total sales, saving the company $30,000. The Warrens gladly distributed $15,000 of that amount to their workers for helping to meet the goal.[24]

> **Action Memo**
>
> As a leader: Manage followers' expectations. Clarify the rewards a follower desires and ensure that he or she has the knowledge, skills, resources, and support to perform and obtain desired rewards. Remember that perceived equity or inequity in rewards also influence motivation.

Expectancy theory and reinforcement theory, discussed earlier, are widely used in all types of organizations and leadership situations. The questionnaire in Leader's Self-Insight 8.2 gives you the opportunity to see how effectively you apply these motivational ideas in your own leadership.

Equity Theory

Sometimes employees' motivation is affected not only by their expectancies and the rewards they receive, but also by their perceptions of how fairly they are treated in relation to others. **Equity theory** proposes that people are motivated to seek social equity in the rewards they receive for performance.[25] According to the theory, if people perceive their rewards as equal to what others receive for similar contributions, they will believe they are treated fairly and will be more highly motivated. When they believe they are not being treated fairly and equitably, motivation will decline.

> *Equity theory*
> *a theory that proposes that people are motivated to seek social equity in the rewards they expect for performance*

People evaluate equity by a ratio of inputs to outcomes. That is, employees make comparisons of what they put into a job and the rewards they receive relative to those of other people in the organization. Inputs include such things as education, experience, effort, and ability. Outcomes include pay, recognition, promotions, and other rewards. A state of equity exists whenever the ratio of one person's outcomes to inputs equals the ratio of others' in the work group. Inequity occurs when the input/outcome ratios are out of balance, such as when an employee with a high level of experience and ability receives the same salary as a new, less educated employee. One example is from the J. Peterman Company. John Peterman had created a comfortable, creative culture where employees were highly motivated to work together toward common goals. However, when the company began to grow rapidly, Peterman found himself having to hire people very quickly—and he often had to offer them higher salaries than those of his current employees to match what they were making elsewhere. In addition, when making important decisions, leaders tended to pay more attention to the ideas and thoughts of the new staff than they did the "old timers." Long-time employees felt slighted, and motivation declined significantly. Employees were no longer willing to put in the extra effort they once had because of a perceived state of inequity.[26]

LEADER'S SELF-INSIGHT 8.2

Your Approach to Motivating Others

Think about situations in which you were in a formal or informal leadership role in a group or organization. Imagine using your personal approach as a leader. Please rate each of the following statements on the 1–5 scale according to how well it characterizes your leadership. 1 = Very little; 2 = Somewhat; 3 = A moderate amount; 4 = A great deal; 5 = Very much

	Very little				Very much
1. I ask the other person what rewards they value for high performance.	1	2	3	4	5
2. I determine if the person has the ability to do what needs to be done.	1	2	3	4	5
3. I explain exactly what needs to be done to the person I'm trying to motivate.	1	2	3	4	5
4. Before giving somebody a reward, I attempt to find out what would appeal to that person.	1	2	3	4	5
5. I negotiate what people will receive if they accomplish the goal.	1	2	3	4	5
6. I make sure people have the ability to achieve performance targets.	1	2	3	4	5
7. I give special recognition when others' work is very good.	1	2	3	4	5
8. I typically only reward people if their performance is up to standard.	1	2	3	4	5
9. I use a variety of rewards to reinforce exceptional performance.	1	2	3	4	5
10. I generously praise people who perform well.	1	2	3	4	5
11. I promptly commend others when they do a better-than-average job.	1	2	3	4	5
12. I publically compliment others when they do outstanding work.	1	2	3	4	5

Scoring and Interpretation

The questions above represent two related aspects of motivation theory. For the aspect of *expectancy theory*, sum your responses to questions 1–6. For the aspect of *reinforcement theory*, sum your scores for questions 6–12.

The scores for my approach to motivation are:

My use of expectancy theory _____

My use of reinforcement theory _____

These two scores represent how you see yourself applying the motivational concepts of expectancy and reinforcement in your own leadership style. A score of 24 or above on *expectancy theory* means you motivate people by managing expectations—which means understanding how a person's effort leads to performance and making sure that high performance leads to valued rewards. A score of 18 is about average, and a score of 12 or below would be below average on your use of expectancy theory. A score of 24 or above for *reinforcement theory* means that you attempt to modify people's behavior in a positive direction with frequent and prompt positive reinforcement. Exchange information about your scores with other students to understand how your application of these two motivation theories compares to other students. Remember, leaders are expected to master the use of these two motivation theories. If you didn't receive an average score or higher, you can consciously do more with expectations and reinforcement when you are in a leadership position.

SOURCES: The questions above are based on D. Whetten and K. Cameron, *Developing Management Skills*, 5th ed. (Prentice-Hall, 2002), 302–303; and P.M. Podsakoff, S.B. Mackenzie, R.H. Moorman, and R. Fetter, "Transformational Leader Behaviors and Their Effects on Followers' Trust in Leader, Satisfaction, and Organizational Citizenship Behaviors," *Leadership Quarterly* 1, no. 2 (1990): 107–142.

This discussion provides only a brief overview of equity theory. The theory's practical use has been criticized because a number of key issues are unclear. However, the important point of equity theory is that, for many people, motivation is influenced significantly by relative as well as absolute rewards. The concept reminds leaders that they should be cognizant of the possible effects of perceived inequity on follower motivation and performance.

The Carrot-and-Stick Controversy

Reward and punishment motivation practices dominate organizations; as many as 94 percent of companies in the United States engage in practices that reward performance or merit with pay.[27] In addition, many companies regard their incentive programs as successful. For example, U.S. Healthcare, a health maintenance organization (HMO), pays physicians who meet performance goals up to an additional 28 percent of their regular monthly premium. This HMO earned the highest quality care rating of any in the United States.[28]

Financial incentives can be quite effective. For one thing, giving employees pay raises or bonuses can signal that leaders value their contributions to the organization. Some researchers argue that using money as a motivator almost always leads to higher performance.[29] However, despite the testimonies of numerous organizations that enjoy successful incentive programs, the arguments against the efficacy of carrot-and-stick methods are growing. Critics argue that extrinsic rewards are neither adequate nor productive motivators and may even work against the best interests of organizations. Reasons for this criticism include the following.

Action Memo

As a leader: Avoid total reliance on carrot-and-stick motivational techniques. Acknowledge the positive but limited effects of extrinsic motivators. Appeal to people's higher needs for intrinsic satisfaction.

1. *Extrinsic rewards diminish intrinsic rewards.* The motivation to seek an extrinsic reward, whether a bonus or approval, leads people to focus on the reward, rather than on the work they do to achieve it.[30] Reward seeking of this type necessarily diminishes the intrinsic satisfaction people receive from the process of working. Numerous studies have found that giving people extrinsic rewards undermines their interest in the work itself.[31] When people lack intrinsic rewards in their work, their performance levels out; it stays just adequate to reach the reward. In the worst case, people perform hazardously, such as covering up an on-the-job accident to get a bonus based on a safety target. In addition, with extrinsic rewards, individuals tend to attribute their behavior to extrinsic rather than intrinsic factors, diminishing their own contributions.[32]

2. *Extrinsic rewards are temporary.* Bestowing outside incentives on people might ensure short-term success, but not long-term quality.[33] The success of reaching immediate goals is quickly followed by the development of

unintended consequences. Because people are focusing on the reward, the work they do holds no interest for them, and without interest in their work, the potential for exploration, innovation, and creativity disappears.[34] The current deadline may be met, but better ways of working will not be discovered.

3. *Extrinsic rewards assume people are driven by lower needs.* The perfunctory rewards of praise and pay increases tied only to performance presumes that the primary reason people initiate and persist in actions is to satisfy lower needs. However, behavior is also based on yearning for self-expression, and on self-esteem, self-worth, feelings, and attitudes. A survey of employees at *Fortune* magazine's "100 Best Companies to Work for in America" found that the majority mentioned intrinsic rather than extrinsic rewards as their motivation. Although many of these workers had been offered higher salaries elsewhere, they stayed where they were because of such motivators as a fun, challenging work environment; flexibility that provided a balance between work and personal life; and the potential to learn, grow, and be creative.[35] Offers of an extrinsic reward do not encourage the myriad behaviors that are motivated by people's need to express elements of their identities. Extrinsic rewards focus on the specific goals and deadlines delineated by incentive plans rather than enabling people to facilitate their vision for a desired future, that is, to realize their possible higher need for growth and fulfillment.[36]

4. *Organizations are too complex for carrot-and-stick approaches.* The current organizational climate is marked by uncertainty and high interdependence among departments and with other organizations. In short, the relationships and the accompanying actions that are part of organizations are overwhelmingly complex.[37] By contrast, the carrot-and-stick plans are quite simple, and the application of an overly simplified incentive plan to a highly complex operation usually creates a misdirected system.[38] It is difficult for leaders to interpret and reward all the behaviors that employees need to demonstrate to keep complex organizations successful over the long term. Thus, extrinsic motivators often wind up rewarding behaviors that are the opposite of what the organization wants and needs. Although managers may espouse long-term growth, for example, they reward quarterly earnings; thus, workers are motivated to act for quick returns for themselves. In recent years, numerous scandals have erupted because the practice of rewarding executives with stock options unintentionally encouraged managers to push accounting rules to the limits in order to make their financial statements look good and push up the stock prices.[39] This chapter's Living Leadership box further examines how incentives can end up motivating the wrong behaviors.

5. *Carrot-and-stick approaches destroy people's motivation to work as a group.*
    Extrinsic rewards and punishments create a culture of competition versus a
    culture of co-operation.[40] In a competitive environment, people see their
    goal as individual victory, as making others appear inferior. Thus, one per-
    son's success is a threat to another's goals. Furthermore, sharing problems
    and solutions is out of the question when co-workers may use your weak-
    ness to undermine you, or when a supervisor might view the need for assis-
    tance as a disqualifier for rewards. The organization is less likely to achieve
    excellent performance from employees who are mistrustful and threatened
    by one another. In contrast, replacing the carrot-and-stick with methods
    based on meeting higher *as well as* lower needs enables a culture of collab-
    oration marked by compatible goals; all the members of the organization are
    trying to achieve a shared vision. Without the effort to control behavior
    individually through rigid rewards, people can see co-workers as part of
    their success. Each person's success is mutually enjoyed because every suc-
    cess benefits the organization. When leaders focus on higher needs, they
    can make everyone feel valued, which facilitates excellent performance.

Managers' difficulty getting people to cooperate and share knowledge at
Blackmer/Dover Resources Inc. illustrates some of the problems associated with
carrot-and-stick approaches.

In the Lead   Blackmer/Dover Inc.

Bill Fowler is one of the fastest and most accurate workers at the
Blackmer/Dover factory in Grand Rapids, Michigan, where the 24-year
plant veteran cuts metal shafts for heavy-duty industrial pumps. It's a precision task that requires a high level of skill, and managers would love to
know Fowler's secrets so they could improve other workers and the manufacturing process. But Fowler refuses to share his tricks of the trade,
even with his closest fellow workers. According to another employee,
machinist Steve Guikema, Fowler "has hardly ever made a suggestion for
an improvement" in the plant.

One reason is that Fowler believes managers could use his ideas and
shortcuts to speed production and ultimately make his job harder.
Another is that his knowledge has given him power, increased status, and
a bigger paycheck. Until recently, workers could earn a premium on top of
their hourly wage based on the number of pumps or pump parts they produced. That practice gave people a strong incentive to keep their output-
enhancing tricks secret from fellow workers. A revised compensation

LIVING LEADERSHIP

On the Folly of Rewarding A While Hoping for B

Managers who complain about the lack of motivation in workers might do well to examine whether the reward system encourages behavior different from what they are seeking. People usually determine which activities are rewarded and then seek to do those things, to the virtual exclusion of activities not rewarded. Nevertheless, there are numerous examples of fouled-up systems that reward unwanted behaviors, while the desired actions are not being rewarded at all.

In sports, for example, most coaches stress teamwork, proper attitude, and one-for-all spirit. However, rewards are usually distributed according to individual performance. The college basketball player who passes the ball to teammates instead of shooting will not compile impressive scoring statistics and will be less likely to be drafted by the pros. The big-league baseball player who hits to advance the runner rather than to score a home run is less likely to win the titles that guarantee big salaries. In universities, a primary goal is the transfer of knowledge from professors to students; yet professors are rewarded primarily for research and publication, not for their commitment to good teaching. Students are rewarded for making

good grades, not necessarily for acquiring knowledge, and may resort to cheating rather than risk a low grade on their college transcript.

In business, there are often similar discrepancies between the desired behaviors and those rewarded. For example, see the table below.

What do a majority of managers see as the major obstacles to dealing with fouled-up reward systems?

1. The inability to break out of old ways of thinking about reward and recognition. This includes entitlement mentality in workers and resistance by management to revamp performance review and reward systems.
2. Lack of an overall systems view of performance and results. This is particularly true of systems that promote subunit results at the expense of the total organization.
3. Continuing focus on short-term results by management and shareholders.

Motivation theories must be sound because people do what they are rewarded for. But when will organizations learn to reward what they say they want?

SOURCES: Steven Kerr, "An Academy Classic: On the Folly of Rewarding A, While Hoping for B," and "More on the Folly," *Academy of Management Executive* 9, no. 1 (1995): 7–16.

Managers Hope For	But They Reward
Teamwork and collaboration	The best individual performers
Innovative thinking and risk taking	Proven methods and not making mistakes
Development of people skills	Technical achievements and accomplishment
Employee involvement and empowerment	Tight control over operations and resources
High achievement	Another year's routine effort
Commitment to quality	Shipping on time, even with defects
Long-term growth	Quarterly earnings

system has done away with such incentives, but a long tradition of hoarding knowledge means there are still an estimated 10 to 20 percent of workers who refuse to cooperate with either managers or fellow employees. The culture of competition and hoarding knowledge is too entrenched.

These workers, like Fowler, see their expertise and accumulated experience as their only source of power. If other workers gained the same knowledge, they would no longer enjoy a superior status. New leaders at Blackmer/Dover Resources are looking for motivational tools that will encourage another kind of behavior: greater cooperation, knowledge sharing, and collaboration between workers and management to improve the plant and help it weather the economic slump. Revising compensation is the first step in establishing a system that will focus on meeting higher as well as lower-level needs.[41]

Incentive programs can be successful, especially when people are actually motivated by money and lower needs. However, individual incentives are rarely enough to motivate behaviors that benefit the organization as a whole. One way for leaders to address the carrot-and-stick controversy is to understand a program's strengths and weaknesses and acknowledge the positive but limited effects of extrinsic motivators. A leader also appeals to people's higher needs, and no subordinate should have work that does not offer some self-satisfaction as well as a yearly pay raise. Furthermore, rewards can be directly linked to behavior promoting the higher needs of both individuals and the organization, such as rewarding quality, long-term growth, or a collaborative culture.[42]

Empowering People to Meet Higher Needs

A significant way in which leaders can meet the higher motivational needs of subordinates is to shift power down from the top of the organizational hierarchy and share it with subordinates. They can decrease the emphasis on incentives designed to affect and control subordinate behavior and instead attempt to share power with organizational members to achieve shared goals. One of the problems at the Blackmer/Dover factory, for example, is that workers are accustomed to hoarding knowledge and expertise because they feel powerless otherwise. They have no motivation to help others because they don't feel a sense of responsibility and commitment toward shared goals.

Empowerment refers to power sharing, the delegation of power or authority to subordinates in the organization.[43] Leaders are shifting from efforts to control behavior through carrot-and-stick approaches to providing employees with the power, information, and authority that enables them to find greater intrinsic satisfaction with

Empowerment
power sharing;
the delegation
of power or
authority to
subordinates in
the organization

their work. Leaders provide their followers with an understanding of how their jobs are important to the organization's mission and performance, thereby giving them a direction within which to act freely.[44] Consider the effect empowerment has on motivation at General Electric's aircraft engine factory in Durham, North Carolina.

In the Lead   GE/Durham

At General Electric's aircraft engine factory in Durham, North Carolina, nine teams of workers build some of the world's most powerful jet engines, including the ones that keep Air Force One running. The plant manager is the only supervisor in the factory, and teams are given only one directive—the deadline for when their next engine is due to be shipped. The teams themselves make all other decisions. For example, they decide who does what job each day, how to make the manufacturing process more efficient, and what to do about slackers. It is the teams on the shop floor, not bosses in the front office, who write the assembly process, figure out the schedule, order tools and parts, and perform any other jobs necessary, including keeping the plant clean and the machinery and tools in good order. Each team "owns" an engine from beginning to end. The team is responsible for every step of the process from the time when parts are unpacked to the moment a completed engine is loaded on a truck for shipment.

Obviously, to work in such an environment means employees have to be highly skilled. GE/Durham is the only one of the company's engine plants that requires job candidates to be FAA-certified mechanics, for example. Then, everyone learns to assemble different parts of the engine. Employees have a high level of responsibility and strive every day to produce perfect jet engines. The philosophy of continuous improvement permeates the plant—employees don't think their job is to make jet engines but to make jet engines *better*.

Some of the factory's workers remember what it was like to work in a place where they were expected to check their minds at the door and follow strict rules and procedures. The difference at GE/Durham is reflected in the words of mechanic Duane Williams, talking about his first six months on the job: "I was never valued that much as an employee in my life. I had never been at the point where I couldn't wait to get to work. But here, I couldn't wait to get to work every day."[45]

As at GE/Durham, the autonomy of empowered employees can create flexibility and motivation that is an enormous advantage for a company.[46] Empowering workers enables leaders to create a unique organization with superior performance capabilities.[47]

For one thing, empowerment provides strong motivation because it meets the higher needs of individuals. Research indicates that individuals have a need for *self-efficacy*, which is the capacity to produce results or outcomes, to feel they are effective.[48] Most people come into an organization with the desire to do a good job, and empowerment enables leaders to release the motivation already there. Increased responsibility motivates most people to strive to do their best, as we saw in the opening example of the USS *Benfold*. The sailors felt like an important part of the process and wanted to prove that they could come through on their own without the traditional, strong top-down control.

In addition, leaders greatly benefit from the expanded capabilities that employee participation brings to the organization. This enables them to devote more attention to vision and the big picture. It also takes the pressure off of leaders when subordinates are able to respond better and more quickly to the markets they serve.[49] Frontline workers often have a better understanding than do leaders of how to improve a work process, satisfy a customer, or solve a production problem.

Elements of Empowerment

Typically, increased power and responsibility leads to greater motivation, increased employee satisfaction, and decreased turnover and absenteeism. In one survey, for example, empowerment of workers, including increased job responsibility, authority to define their work, and power to make decisions, was found to be the most dramatic indicator of workplace satisfaction.[50]

The first step toward effective empowerment is effective hiring and training. Leaders look for people who have the ability as well as the desire to make a genuine contribution to the organization and then provide them with the training they need to excel. For example, at GE/Durham, described earlier, there is a significant emphasis on selection and training because the organization needs people who can perform complex tasks. However, having a team of competent employees isn't enough. Five elements must be in place before employees can be truly empowered to perform their jobs successfully: information, knowledge, discretion, meaning, and rewards.[51]

1. *Employees receive information about company performance.* In companies where employees are fully empowered, no information is secret. Meritor, a components manufacturer, goes to great lengths to help employees understand companywide business measures and gives them regular information about the performance of individual businesses and plants.[52]

2. *Employees receive knowledge and skills to contribute to company goals.* Companies train employees to have the knowledge and skills they need to personally contribute to company performance. Knowledge and skills lead to competency—the belief that one is capable of accomplishing one's job successfully.[53] For example, when DMC, which makes pet supplies,

Action Memo

As a leader:
Give employees greater power and authority as a good way to meet higher motivational needs. Implement empowerment by providing the five elements of information, knowledge, discretion, significance, and rewards.

gave employee teams the authority and responsibility for assembly-line shut downs, it provided extensive training on how to diagnose and interpret line malfunctions, as well as the costs related to shut-down and start-up. Employees worked through case studies to practice line shut-downs so they would feel they had the skills to make good decisions in real-life situations.[54]

3. *Employees have the power to make substantive decisions.* Many of today's most competitive companies are giving workers the power to influence work procedures and organizational direction through quality circles and self-directed work teams. Teams of tank house workers at BHP Copper Metals in San Manuel, Arizona, identify and solve production problems and determine how best to organize themselves to get the job done. In addition, they can even determine the specific hours they need to handle their own workloads. For example, an employee could opt to work for four hours, leave, and come back to do the next four.[55]

4. *Employees understand the meaning and impact of their jobs.* Empowered employees consider their jobs important and meaningful, see themselves as capable and influential, and recognize the impact their work has on customers, other stakeholders, and the organization's success.[56] At AES Corporation, an electricity producer with facilities all over the world, empowerment means that employees know they have the power to make a difference every day for themselves, their customers, and the company.[57] Understanding the connection between one's day-to-day activities and the overall vision for the organization gives people a sense of direction, an idea of what their jobs mean. It enables employees to fit their actions to the vision and have an active influence on the outcome of their work.[58]

5. *Employees are rewarded based on company performance.* Studies have revealed the important role of fair reward and recognition systems in supporting empowerment. By affirming that employees are progressing toward goals, rewards help to keep motivation high.[59] Leaders are careful to examine and redesign reward systems to support empowerment and teamwork. Two ways in which organizations can financially reward employees based on company performance are through profit sharing and employee stock ownership plans (ESOPs). At W. L. Gore and Associates, makers of Gore-Tex, compensation takes three forms—salary, profit sharing, and an associates stock ownership program.[60] Unlike traditional carrot-and-stick approaches, these rewards focus on the performance of the group rather than individuals. Joe Cabral, CEO of Chatsworth Products Inc., a small company that makes support gear for computer networks, uses an ESOP because it "gets everyone pulling in the same direction. Everybody wants the company to do the best

it possibly can."[61] Furthermore, rewards are just one component of empowerment rather than the sole basis of motivation.

Empowerment Applications

Many of today's organizations are implementing empowerment programs, but they are empowering workers to varying degrees. At some companies, empowerment means encouraging employee ideas while managers retain final authority for decisions; at others it means giving frontline workers almost complete power to make decisions and exercise initiative and imagination.[62] Have you felt empowered in a job you have held? Take the quiz in Leader's Self-Insight 8.3 to evaluate your empowerment experience and compare it to the experience of other students.

Current methods of empowering workers fall along a continuum as shown in Exhibit 8.7. The continuum runs from a situation where frontline workers have no discretion (such as on a traditional assembly line) to full empowerment where workers even participate in formulating organizational strategy. An example of full empowerment is when self-directed teams are given the power to hire, discipline, and dismiss team members and to set compensation rates. Few organizations have moved to this level of empowerment. One that has is Semco, a $160 million South American company involved in manufacturing, services, and e-business. Majority owner Ricardo Semler believes that people will act in their own, and by extension, the organization's best interests if they're given complete freedom. Semco allows its 1,300 employees to choose what they do, where and when they do it, and even how they get paid for it. Semco has remained highly successful and profitable under a system of complete empowerment for more than twenty years.[63]

Empowerment programs can be difficult to implement in established organizations because they destroy hierarchies and upset the familiar balance of power. A study of *Fortune* 1000 companies found that the empowerment practices that have diffused most widely are those that redistribute power and authority the least, for example, quality circles or job enrichment. Managers can keep decision authority and there is less chance that workers will resist because of the added responsibilities that full empowerment brings.[64]

Organizationwide Motivational Programs

Leaders can motivate organizational members using other recent ideas that are more than the carrot-and-stick approaches described earlier in this chapter, but may be less than full empowerment.

One approach is to foster an organizational environment that helps people find true value and meaning in their work. A second approach is to implement organizationwide programs such as employee ownership, job enrichment, or new types of incentive plans.

LEADER'S SELF-INSIGHT 8.3

Are You Empowered?

Think of a job—either current or previous job—that was important to you, and then answer the questions below with respect to the managers above you in that job. Please answer each question with a number 1–5 that reflects the extent of your agreement.

1 = Not at all; 2 = To a limited extent; 3 = To a moderate extent; 4 = To a considerable extent; 5 = To a very great extent

In general, my supervisor/manager:	Not at all		To a very great extent		
1. Gave me the support I needed to do my job well.	1	2	3	4	5
2. Gave me the performance information I needed to do my job well.	1	2	3	4	5
3. Explained top management's strategy and vision for the organization.	1	2	3	4	5
4. Gave me many responsibilities.	1	2	3	4	5
5. Trusted me.	1	2	3	4	5
6. Allowed me to set my own goals.	1	2	3	4	5
7. Encouraged me to take control of my own work.	1	2	3	4	5
8. Used my ideas and suggestions when making decisions.	1	2	3	4	5
9. Made me responsible for what I did.	1	2	3	4	5
10. Encouraged me to figure out the causes and solutions to problems.	1	2	3	4	5

Scoring and Interpretation

Add up your responses to the 10 questions to obtain your total score. The questions represent aspects of empowerment that an employee may experience in a job. If your score was 40 or above, you probably felt empowered in the job for which you answered the questions. If your score was 20 or below, you probably did not feel empowered. How motivated did you feel in that job, and how was your motivation related to your empowerment? What factors explained the level of empowerment you felt? Was empowerment mostly based on your supervisor's leadership style or personality? The leadership style of higher management? Was the level of empowerment based on other factors such as company history or type of work? Compare your scores with another student. Take turns describing the job, the level of empowerment you experienced, and the reasons for the empowerment. Do you want a job in which you are fully empowered? Why or why not?

SOURCES: These questions were adapted from Bradley L. Kirkman and Benson Rosen, "Beyond Self-management: Antecedents and Consequences of Team Empowerment," *Academy of Management Journal* 42, no. 1 (February 1999): 58–74; and Gretchen M. Spreitzer, "Psychological Empowerment in the Workplace: Dimensions, Measurements, and Validation," *Academy of Management Journal* 38, no. 5 (October 1995): 1442–1465.

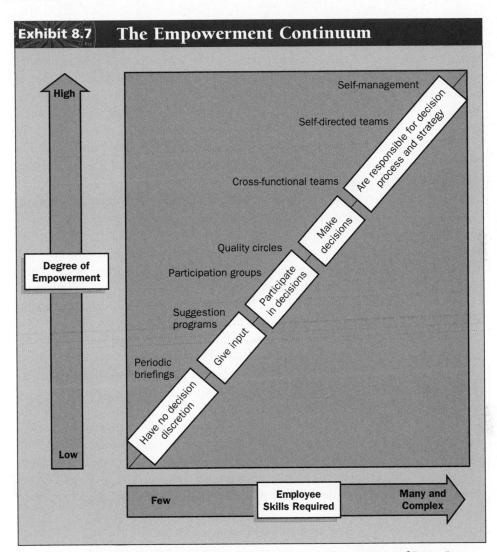

Exhibit 8.7 | **The Empowerment Continuum**

Degree of Empowerment — High / Low

- Self-management
- Self-directed teams
- Cross-functional teams
- Quality circles
- Participation groups
- Suggestion programs
- Periodic briefings

Are responsible for decision process and strategy

Make decisions

Participate in decisions

Give input

Have no decision discretion

Employee Skills Required — Few / Many and Complex

SOURCES: Based on Robert C. Ford and Myron D. Fottler, "Empowerment: A Matter of Degree," *Academy of Management Executive* 9, no. 3 (1995): 21–31; Lawrence Holpp, "Applied Empowerment," *Training* (February 1994): 39–44; and David P. McCaffrey, Sue R. Faerman, and David W. Hart, "The Appeal and Difficulties of Participative Systems," *Organization Science* 6, no. 6 (November–December 1995): 603–627.

Giving Meaning to Work

Throughout this chapter, we have talked about the importance of intrinsic rewards to high motivation. One way people get intrinsic rewards at work is when they feel a deep sense of importance and meaningfulness, such as people who work for a social cause or mission. However, people can find a sense of meaning and importance no matter what type of organization they work in if leaders build an environment in which people can flourish. Researchers have found that highly successful factories in less-developed countries such as Morocco or Mexico, for example, have leaders who treat people with care and respect, engender a culture of mutual trust, and build on local values to create a community of meaning. Employees who feel that they're a part of something special are highly motivated and committed to the success of the organization and all its members.[65]

> **Action Memo**
>
> As a leader: Use organizationwide motivational approaches as a middle ground between carrot-and-stick approaches and full empowerment. Build an environment that allows people to find meaning in their work. Implement employee ownership, job enrichment, and new types of incentive pay plans to motivate employees toward greater cooperation and teamwork.

A Gallup Organization study conducted over 25 years found that the single most important variable in whether employees feel good about their work is the relationship between employees and their direct supervisor, as discussed in this chapter's Leader's Bookshelf.[66] A leader's role is not to control others but to organize the workplace in such a way that each person can learn, contribute, and grow. Good leaders channel employee motivation toward the accomplishment of goals by tapping into each individual's unique set of talents, skills, interests, attitudes, and needs. The Gallup researchers developed a metric called the Q12, a list of 12 questions that provides a way to evaluate how leaders are doing in creating an environment that provides intrinsic rewards by meeting higher-level needs. The Q12 evaluates characteristics such as whether employees know what is expected of them, whether they have opportunities to learn and grow, and whether they feel that their opinions are important. The full list of questions on the Q12 survey can be found in the book, *First Break All the Rules*, which is profiled in the Leader's Bookshelf. When a majority of employees can answer the Q12 questions positively, the organization enjoys a highly motivated, engaged, and productive workforce.

Results of the Gallup study show that organizations where employees give high marks on the Q12 have less turnover, are more productive and profitable, and enjoy greater employee and customer loyalty. For example, among 400 Best Buy retail outlets, the store that scored the highest on the Q12 ranks in the top 10 percent on financial performance, while the store with the lowest score ranks in the bottom 10 percent.[67]

One organization that used the Q12 to spark a transformation is St. Lucie Medical Center.

In the Lead   St. Lucie Medical Center

In the late 1990s, St. Lucie Medical Center, a for-profit hospital in St. Lucie County, Florida, was serving more patients more profitably than ever before. But leaders knew there was a serious problem brewing just under the surface. Annual turnover of nurses, clinicians, and support staff was a troubling 35 percent. Even more alarming was the growing talk of patients and physicians being put off by the hospital staff's pervasive discontentment. St. Lucie couldn't expect to remain competitive over the long-term unless something was done to revive the energy, motivation, and enthusiasm of the workforce.

To determine where things stood and provide a measure for improvement efforts, St. Lucie employees took the Gallup's Q12 survey to measure their engagement with their jobs. The results were expected, but still disheartening. St. Lucie ranked in the 24th percentile in Gallup's worldwide database. There was an encouraging note, however. The survey also revealed pockets of some highly motivated work units, and St. Lucie leaders set about trying to replicate the dynamics of those units across the organization. A series of assessments identified the talents, shortcomings, and feelings of "role model" employees. Leaders also underwent an in-depth assessment of their own strengths and weaknesses and considered how they could do a better job of articulating a vision that employees would be drawn by. Armed with knowledge about their own strengths and the strengths of their employees, leaders of various departments began building work units around the complementary talents of individual workers. They discovered that nurses who were more empathetic for example, often struggled with time-management issues. Creating the work unit so nurses could work with their strengths rather than struggling to develop traits they didn't have improved both empathetic care and operational excellence.

The results of the revitalization process were astounding. The attrition rate dropped significantly, and nurse turnover in particular decreased 50 percent. When Gallup measured employee engagement two years later, St. Lucie soared to the 99th percentile in Gallup's database. The satisfaction rates of employees, patients, and physicians have all zoomed.[68]

Other Approaches

There are a number of other approaches to improving organizationwide motivation. Some of the most common are job enrichment programs, employee ownership, gain-sharing, paying for knowledge, and paying for performance. Variable compensation and various forms of "at risk" pay are key motivational tools today and are becoming more common than fixed salaries at many companies

Employee ownership occurs on two levels. First, empowerment can result in a psychological commitment to the mission of an organization whereby members act as "owners" rather than employees. Second, by owning stock in the companies for which they work, individuals are motivated to give their best performances.

At Manco, a private company that supplies a broad line of consumer products for retail outlets such as Wal-Mart, employees (called *partners*) own 30 percent of the company.[69] Giving all employees ownership is a powerful way to motivate people to

Employee ownership
giving employees real and psychological ownership in the organization; as owners, people are motivated to give their best performance

LEADER'S BOOKSHELF

First, Break All the Rules: What the World's Greatest Managers Do Differently
Marcus Buckingham and Curt Coffman

Money can't buy employee commitment and motivation, increased performance, or greater profits. That's the conclusion Gallup researchers reached following two mammoth studies carried out over the last 25 years. During the studies, researchers talked to more than 80,000 managers and a million employees in 400 companies. The results are reported by Marcus Buckingham and Curt Coffman in their book, *First, Break All the Rules.* The strength of a workplace, they say, depends on factors such as whether employees know what is expected of them, have the right tools and information to do their jobs, get to do what they do best, have their opinions heard and considered, and feel that someone at work truly cares about them. That is, it depends largely on leadership.

Great Leaders Create Great Companies
Based on results of the second phase of the Gallup studies, Buckingham and Coffman offer some guidelines for how leaders build strong workplaces by creating environments that allow people to flourish.

❋ **Recognize that you have no control.** The first step is for leaders to understand that they actually have less control than their subordinates. It is only through other people that leaders can accomplish anything in the organization. "Each individual employee can decide what to do and what not to do. He can decide the hows, the whens, and the with whoms. For good or for ill, he can make things happen." The leader's job is to channel each employee's motivation toward the accomplishment of organizational goals.

❋ **Build on the talents of employees.** Each employee arrives at an organization with a unique set of needs, motivations, and talents. Great leaders "try to draw out what was left in, not put in what was left out." Rather than trying to get people to do things they aren't suited for and don't enjoy, leaders spend loads of time trying to recognize the unique qualities and talents each person brings to the workplace and how those qualities can benefit the organization. By treating each employee as an individual, leaders can put people in the right positions, which provides intrinsic rewards to every employee every day.

❋ **Focus people on performance.** Organizations achieve their purpose and goals only when employees perform well. Great leaders clearly define performance outcomes and then let each person find his or her own route toward those outcomes. The authors argue that the most efficient way to turn each individual's talents into high performance is to help employees find their own "path of least resistance" by doing things in a way that works for them.

The Bottom Line
By putting people in the right jobs, clearly defining outcomes, and then getting out of the way, the leader "creates a hero in every role." But does all this have a real impact on performance and profitability? The authors offer compelling statistical evidence that it does. Companies where employees gave high marks to the company on the survey qualities consistently showed higher profits and better financial performance. When employees are more engaged and motivated, they—and their organizations—thrive.

First, Break All the Rules, by Marcus Buckingham and Curt Coffman, is published by Simon & Schuster.

work for the good of the entire company. Achieving organizational goals is celebrated with much fun and fanfare at Manco, because employees know they will reap rewards from the success. Employee ownership also signals that leaders acknowledge each person's role in reaching corporate goals. Employee ownership programs are usually supported by *open book management*, which enables all employees to see and understand how the company is doing financially and how their actions contribute to the bottom line.[70]

Gainsharing is another approach that motivates people to work together rather than focus on individual achievements and rewards. Gainsharing refers to an employee involvement program that ties additional pay to improvements in total employee performance.[71] Employees are asked to actively search for ways to make process improvements, with any resulting financial gains divided among employees. A gainsharing program at Meritor that rewards employees for improvements in their own unit as well as companywide has proven to be a powerful incentive for teamwork.[72]

Pay for knowledge programs base an employee's salary on the number of task skills he or she possesses. If employees increase their skills, they get paid more. A workforce in which individuals skillfully perform numerous tasks is more flexible and efficient. At BHP Copper Metals, for example, leaders devised a pay-for-skills program that supported the move to teamwork. Employees can rotate through various jobs to build their skills and earn a higher pay rate. Rates range from entry-level workers to lead operators. Lead operators are those who have demonstrated a mastery of skills, the ability to teach and lead others, and effective self-directed behavior.[73]

Pay for performance, which links at least a portion of employees' monetary rewards to results or accomplishments, is a significant trend in today's organizations.[74] Gainsharing is one type of pay for performance. Other examples include profit sharing, bonuses, and merit pay. In addition to the potential for greater income, pay for performance can give employees a greater sense of control over the outcome of their efforts. At Semco, described earlier, employees choose how they are paid based on 11 compensation options, which can be combined in various ways. Exhibit 8.8 lists Semco's 11 ways to pay. Semco leaders indicate that the flexible pay plan encourages innovation and risk-taking and motivates employees to perform in the best interest of the company as well as themselves.

Job enrichment incorporates high-level motivators into the work, including job responsibility, recognition, and opportunities for growth, learning, and achievement. In an enriched job, the employee controls resources needed to perform well and makes decisions on how to do the work. One way to enrich an oversimplified job is to enlarge it, that is, to extend the responsibility to cover several tasks instead of only one.

Leaders at Ralcorp's cereal manufacturing plant in Sparks, Nevada, enriched jobs by combining several packing positions into a single job and cross-training employees to operate all of the packing line's equipment. Employees were given

Gainsharing *motivational approach that encourages people to work together rather than focus on individual achievements and rewards; ties additional pay to improvements in overall employee performance*

Pay for knowledge *programs that base an employee's pay on the number of skills he or she possesses*

Pay for performance *a program that links at least a portion of employees' monetary rewards to results or accomplishments*

Exhibit 8.8	Semco's 11 Ways to Pay

Semco, a South American company involved in manufacturing, services, and e-business, lets employees choose how they are paid based on 11 compensation options:

1. Fixed salary

2. Bonuses

3. Profit sharing

4. Commission

5. Royalties on sales

6. Royalties on profits

7. Commission on gross margin

8. Stock or stock options

9. IPO/sale warrants that an executive cashes in when a business unit goes public or is sold

10. Self-determined annual review compensation in which an executive is paid for meeting self-set goals

11. Commission on difference between actual and three-year value of the company

SOURCE: Ricardo Semler, "How We Went Digital Without a Strategy," *Harvard Business Review*, (September–October 2000): 51–58.

Job enrichment

a motivational approach that incorporates high-level motivators into the work, including job responsibility, recognition, and opportunities for growth, learning, and achievement

both the ability and the responsibility to perform all the various functions in their department, not just a single task. In addition, line employees are responsible for all screening and interviewing of new hires as well as training and advising one another. They also manage the production flow to and from their upstream and downstream partners—they understand the entire production process so they can see how their work affects the quality and productivity of employees in other departments. Ralcorp invests heavily in training to be sure employees have the needed operational skills as well as the ability to make decisions, solve problems, manage quality, and contribute to continuous improvement. Enriched jobs have improved employee motivation and satisfaction, and the company has benefited from higher long-term productivity, reduced costs, and happier employees.[75]

Summary and Interpretation

This chapter introduced a number of important ideas about motivating people in organizations. Individuals are motivated to act to satisfy a range of needs. The leadership approach to motivation tends to focus on the higher needs of employees. The role of the leader is to create a situation in which followers' higher needs and the needs of the organization can be met simultaneously.

Needs-based theories focus on the underlying needs that motivate how people behave. Maslow's hierarchy of needs proposes that individuals satisfy lower needs before they move on to higher needs. Herzberg's two-factor theory holds that dissatisfiers must be removed and motivators then added to satisfy employees. McClelland asserted that people are motivated differently depending on which needs they have acquired. Other motivation theories, including the reinforcement perspective, expectancy theory, and equity theory, focus primarily on extrinsic rewards and punishments, sometimes called *carrot-and-stick* methods of motivation. The reinforcement perspective proposes that behavior can be modified by the use of rewards and punishments. Expectancy theory is based on the idea that a person's motivation is contingent upon his or her expectations that a given behavior will result in desired rewards. Equity theory proposes that individuals' motivation is affected not only by the rewards they receive but also by their perceptions of how fairly they are treated in relation to others. People are motivated to seek social equity in the rewards they expect for performance.

Although carrot-and-stick methods of motivation are pervasive in North American organizations, many critics argue that extrinsic rewards undermine intrinsic rewards, bring about unintended consequences, are too simple to capture organizational realities, and replace workplace cooperation with unhealthy competition.

An alternative approach to carrot-and-stick motivation is that of empowerment, by which subordinates know the direction of the organization and have the autonomy to act as they see fit to go in that direction. Leaders provide employees with the knowledge to contribute to the organization, the power to make consequential decisions, and the necessary resources to do their jobs. Empowerment typically meets the higher needs of individuals. Empowerment is tied to the trend toward helping employees find value and meaning in their jobs and creating an environment where people can flourish. When people are fully engaged with their work, satisfaction, performance, and profits increase. Leaders create the environment that determines employee motivation and satisfaction. One way to measure how engaged people are with their work is the Q12, a list of 12 questions about the day-to-day realities of a person's job. Other current organizationwide motivational programs include employee ownership, gainsharing, pay for knowledge, pay for performance, and job enrichment.

Discussion Questions

1. Describe the kinds of needs that people bring to an organization. How might a person's values and attitudes, as described in Chapter 4, influence the needs he or she brings to work?
2. What is the relationship among needs, rewards, and motivation?
3. What do you see as the leader's role in motivating others in an organization?
4. What is the carrot-and-stick approach? Do you think that it should be minimized in organizations? Why?
5. What are the features of the reinforcement and expectancy theories that make them seem like carrot-and-stick methods for motivation? Why do they often work in organizations?
6. Why is it important for leaders to have a basic understanding of equity theory? Can you see ways in which some of today's popular compensation trends, such as gainsharing or pay for performance, might contribute to perceived inequity among employees? Discuss.
7. What are the advantages of an organization with empowered employees? Why might some individuals *not* want to be empowered?
8. Do you agree that hygiene factors, as defined in Herzberg's two-factor theory, cannot provide increased satisfaction and motivation? Discuss.
9. Discuss whether you believe it is a leader's responsibility to help people find meaning in their work? How might leaders do this for employees at a fast-food restaurant? How about for employees who clean restrooms at airports?
10. If you were a leader at a company like Blackmer/Dover, discussed on page 313 of the chapter, what motivational techniques might you use to improve cooperation and teamwork?

Leadership at Work

Should, Need, Like, Love

Think of a school or work task that you feel an obligation or commitment to complete, but you don't really want to do it. Write the task here:

_____

_____

_____

Think of a school or work task you do because you need to, perhaps to get the benefit, such as money or credit. Write the task here:

_____

_____

_____

Think of a school or work task you like to do because it is enjoyable or fun. Write the task here:

_____

_____

_____

Think of a task you love to do—one in which you become completely absorbed and from which you feel a deep satisfaction when finished. Write the task here:

_____

_____

_____

Now reflect on those four tasks and what they mean to you. How motivated (high, medium, low) are you to accomplish each of these four tasks? How much mental effort (high, medium, low) is required from you to complete each task?

_____

_____

_____

Now estimate the percentage of your weekly tasks that you would rate as *should, need, like, love*. The combined estimates should total 100%.

Should _____%

Need _____%

Like _____%

Love _____%

If your *should* and *need* percentages are substantially higher than your *like* and *love* categories, what does that mean for you? Does it mean that you are forcing yourself to do tasks you find unpleasant? Why? Why not include more *like* and *love* tasks in your life? Might you grow weary of the *should* and *need* tasks at some point and select a new focus or job in your life? Think about this and discuss your percentages with another student in the class.

Tasks you *love* connect you with the creative spirit of life. People who do something they love have a certain charisma, and others want to follow their lead. Tasks you *like* typically are those that fit your gifts and talents and are tasks for which you can make a contribution. Tasks you do because of *need* are typically practical in the sense that they produce an outcome you want, and these tasks often do not provide as much satisfaction as the *like* and *love* tasks. Tasks you do strictly because you *should*, and which contain no *love*, *like*, or *need*, may be difficult and distasteful and require great effort to complete. You are unlikely to become a leader for completing *should* tasks.

What does the amount of each type of task in your life mean to you? How do these tasks relate to your passion and life satisfaction? Why don't you have more *like* and *love* tasks? As a leader, how would you increase the *like* and *love* tasks for people who report to you? Be specific.

_____

_____

_____

In Class: The instructor can have students talk in small groups about their percentages and what the percentages mean to them. Students can be asked how the categories of *should*, *need*, *like*, and *love* relate to the theories of motivation in the chapter. Do leaders have an obligation to guide employees toward tasks they like and love, or is it sufficient at work for people to perform need and should tasks?

The instructor can write student percentages on the board so students can see where they stand compared to the class. Students can be asked to interpret the results in terms of the amount of satisfaction they receive from various tasks. Also, are the percentages related to the students' stage of life?

Leadership Development: Cases for Analysis

The Parlor

The Parlor, a local franchise operation located in San Francisco, serves sandwiches and small dinners in an atmosphere reminiscent of the "roaring twenties." Period fixtures accent the atmosphere and tunes from a mechanically driven, old-time player piano greet one's ears upon entering. Its major attraction, however, is a high-quality, old-fashioned soda fountain that specializes in superior ice cream sundaes and sodas. Fresh, quality sandwiches are also a popular item. Business has grown steadily during the seven years of operation.

The business has been so successful that Richard Purvis, owner and manager, decided to hire a parlor manager so that he could devote more time to other business interests. After a month of quiet recruitment and interviewing, he selected Paul McCarthy, whose prior experience included the supervision of the refreshment stand at one of the town's leading burlesque houses.

The current employees were unaware of McCarthy's employment until his first day on the job, when he walked in unescorted (Purvis was out of town) and introduced himself.

During the first few weeks, he evidenced sincere attempts at supervision and seemed to perform his work efficiently. According to his agreement with Purvis, he is paid a straight salary plus a percentage of the amount he saves the business monthly, based on the previous month's operating expenses. All other employees are on a straight hourly rate.

After a month on the job, McCarthy single-mindedly decided to initiate an economy program designed to increase his earnings. He changed the wholesale meat supplier and lowered both his cost and product quality in the process. Arbitrarily, he reduced the size and portion of everything on the menu, including those fabulous sundaes and sodas. He increased the working hours of those on minimum wage and reduced the time of those employed at a higher rate. Moreover, he eliminated the fringe benefit of a one-dollar meal credit for employees who work longer than a five-hour stretch, and he cut out the usual 20 percent discount on anything purchased by the employees.

When questioned by the owner about the impact of his new practices, McCarthy swore up and down that there would be no negative effect on the business. Customers, though, have begun to complain about the indifferent service of the female waitresses and the sloppy appearance of the male soda fountain clerks—"Their hair keeps getting in the ice cream." And there has been almost a complete turnover among the four short-order cooks who work two to a shift.

Ron Sharp, an accounting major at the nearby university, had been a short-order cook on the night shift for five months prior to McCarthy's arrival. Conscientious and ambitious, Ron enjoys a fine work record, and even his new boss recognizes Ron's superiority over the other cooks—"The best we got."

Heavy customer traffic at the Parlor has always required two short-order cooks working in tandem on each shift. The work requires a high degree of interpersonal cooperation in completing the food orders. An unwritten and informal policy is that each cook would clean up his specific work area at closing time.

One especially busy night, Ron's fellow cook became involved in a shouting match with McCarthy after the cook returned five minutes late from his shift break. McCarthy fired him right on the spot and commanded him to turn in his apron. This meant that Ron was required to stay over an extra half-hour to wash the other fellow's utensils. He did not get to bed until 3 A.M. But McCarthy wanted him back at the store at 9 A.M. to substitute for a daytime cook whose wife reported him ill. Ron was normally scheduled to begin at 4 P.M. However, when Ron arrived somewhat sleepily at 10 A.M. (and after an 8 A.M. accounting class), McCarthy was furious. He thereupon warned Ron, "Once more and you can look for another job. If you work for me, you do things my way or you don't work here at all." "Fine with me," fired back Ron as he slammed his apron into the sink. "You know what you can do with this job!"

The next day, McCarthy discussed his problems with the owner. Purvis was actually very upset. "I can't understand what went wrong. All of a sudden, things have gone to hell."

SOURCE: Bernard A. Deitzer and Karl A. Schillif, *Contemporary Incidents in Management* (Columbus, OH: Grid, Inc., 1977), 167–168. Reprinted by permission of John Wiley & Sons, Inc.

Questions

1. Contrast the beliefs about motivation held by Purvis and McCarthy.
2. Do you consider either Purvis or McCarthy a leader? Discuss.
3. What would you do now if you were in Purvis's position? Why?

Cub Scout Pack 81

Things certainly have changed over the past six years for Cub Scout Pack 81. Six years ago, the pack was on the verge of disbanding. There were barely enough boys for an effective den, and they had been losing membership for as long as anyone could remember. The cub master was trying to pass his job onto any parent foolish enough to take the helm of a sinking ship, and the volunteer fire department that sponsored the pack was openly considering dropping it.

But that was six years ago. Today the pack has one of the largest memberships of any in the Lancaster/Lebanon Council. It has started its own Boy Scout troop, into which the Webelos can graduate, and it has received a presidential citation for its antidrug program. The pack consistently wins competitions with other packs in the Council, and the fire department is very happy about its sponsorship. Membership in the pack is now around 60 cubs at all levels, and they have a new cub master.

"Parents want their boys to be in a successful program," says Cub Master Mike Murphy. "Look, I can't do everything. We depend on the parents and the boys to get things done. Everybody understands that we want to have a successful program, and that means we all have to participate to achieve that success. I can't do it all, but if we can unleash the energy these boys have, there isn't anything in the Cub Scout Program we can't do!"

It was not always like that. "About five years ago we placed fourth for our booth in the Scout Expo at the mall," says Mike. "Everybody was surprised! Who was Pack 81? We were all elated! It was one of the best things to happen to this pack in years. Now, if we don't win at least something, we're disappointed. Our kids expect to win, and so do their parents."

Fourth place at the Scout Expo eventually led to several first places. Success leads to success, and the community around Pack 81 knows it.

"Last year, we made our annual presentation to the boys and their parents at the elementary school. We were with several other packs, each one trying to drum up interest in their program. When everyone was finished, the boys and their parents went over to the table of the pack that most interested them. We must have had well over half of the people at our table. I was embarrassed! They were standing six or seven deep in front of our table, and there was virtually nobody in front of the others."

SOURCE: "Case IV: Cub Scout Pack 81," in *2001–02 Annual Editions: Management*, Fred H. Maidment, ed. (Guilford, CT: McGraw-Hill/Dushkin, 2001), 130.

Questions

1. What are some of Mike Murphy's basic assumptions about motivation?
2. Why do you think he has been so successful in turning the organization around?
3. How would you motivate people in a volunteer organization such as the Cub Scouts?

References

1. D. Michael Abroashoff, "Retention Through Redemption," *Harvard Business Review* (February 2001): 136–141; and Polly LaBarre, "The Most Important Thing a Captain Can Do Is to See the Ship from the Eyes of the Crew," *Fast Company* (April 1999): 114–126.

2. Michael West and Malcolm Patterson, "Profitable Personnel," *People Management* (January 8, 1998): 28–31; Richard M. Steers and Lyman W. Porter, eds. *Motivation and Work Behavior*, 3rd ed. (New York: McGraw-Hill, 1983); Don Hellriegel, John W. Slocum, Jr., and Richard W. Woodman, *Organizational Behavior*, 7th ed. (St. Paul, MN: West Publishing Co., 1995), 170; and Jerry L. Gray and Frederick A. Starke, *Organizational Behavior: Concepts and Applications,* 4th ed. (New York: Macmillan, 1988), 104–105.

3. Linda Grant, "Happy Workers, High Returns," *Fortune* (January 12, 1998): 81; Elizabeth J. Hawk and Garrett J. Sheridan, "The Right Staff," *Management Review,* (June 1999): 43–48; and West and Patterson, "Profitable Personnel."

4. Anne Fisher, "Why Passion Pays," *FSB* (September 2002): 58; and Curt Coffman and Gabriel Gonzalez-Molina, *Follow This Path: How the World's Greatest Organizations Drive Growth by Unleashing Human Potential* (New York: Warner Books, 2002.)

5. Richard M. Steers, Lyman W. Porter, and Gregory A. Bigley, *Motivation and Leadership at Work*, 6th ed. (New York: McGraw-Hill, 1996), 496–498.

6. Steven Bergals, "When Money Talks, People Walk," *Inc.* (May 1996): 25–26.

7. Robert Levering and Milton Moskowitz, "100 Best Companies to Work For," *Fortune* (January 20, 2003): 127–152.

8. Rosabeth Moss Kanter, "How to Fire Up Employees Without Cash or Prizes," *Business 2.0* (June 2002): 134–152.

9. Levering and Moskowitz, "100 Best Companies to Work For."

10. Abraham F. Maslow, "A Theory of Human Motivation," *Psychological Review* 50 (1943): 370–396.

11. Frederick Herzberg, "One More Time: How Do You Motivate Employees?" *Harvard Business Review* (January–February 1968): 53–62.

12. Ellyn Spragins, "Is This the Best Company to Work for Anywhere?" *FSB* (November 2002): 66–70.

13. David C. McClelland, *Human Motivation* (Glenview, IL: Scott Foresman, 1985).

14. David C. McClelland, "The Two Faces of Power," in *Organizational Psychology*, D. A. Colb, I. M. Rubin, and J. M. McIntyre, eds. (Englewood Cliffs, NJ: Prentice-Hall, 1971); 73–86.

15. Alfie Kohn, "Why Incentive Plans Cannot Work," *Harvard Business Review* (September-October 1993): 54–63; A. J. Vogl, "Carrots, Sticks, and Self-Deception," (an interview with Alfie Kohn), *Across the Board*, (January 1994), 39–44; and Alfie Kohn, "Challenging Behaviorist Dogma: Myths about Money and Motivation," *Compensation and Benefits Review* (March-April 1998), 27, 33–37.

16. H. Richlin, *Modern Behaviorism* (San Francisco: Freeman, 1970); B. F. Skinner, *Science and Human Behavior* (New York: Macmillan, 1953); Alexander D. Stajkovic and Fred Luthans, "A Meta-Analysis of the Effects of Organizational Behavior Modification on Task Performance 1975–1995," *Academy of Management Journal* (October 1997): 1122–1149; F. Luthans and R. Kreitner, *Organizational Behavior Modification and Beyond*, 2nd ed. (Glenview, IL: Scott Foresman, 1985).

17. Luthans and Kreitner, *Organizational Behavior Modification and Beyond*; L. M. Saari and G. P. Latham, "Employee Reaction to Continuous and Variable Ratio Reinforcement Schedules Involving a Monetary Incentive," *Journal of Applied Psychology* 67 (1982): 506–508; and R. D. Pritchard, J. Hollenback, and P. J. DeLeo, "The Effects of Continuous and Partial Schedules of Reinforcement on Effort, Performance, and Satisfaction," *Organizational Behavior and Human Performance* 25 (1980): 336–353.

18. Trevor Merriden, "Measured for Success," *Management Review* (April 1999): 27–32.

19. Alexander D. Stajkivic, and Fred Luthans, "A Meta-Analysis of the Effects of Organizational Behavior Modification on Task Performance, 1975–95," *Academy of Management Journal* (October 1997): 1122–1149; and Fred Luthans and Alexander D. Stajkovic, "Reinforce for Performance: The Need to Go Beyond Pay and Even Rewards" *Academy of Management Executive* 13, no. 2 (1999): 49–57.

20. Keith H. Hammonds, "Handle with Care," *Fast Company* (August 2002): 103–107.

21. Kevin Kelly, "Firing Up the Team," *BusinessWeek Frontier* (May 24, 1999): 32.

22. Victor H. Vroom, *Work and Motivation* (New York: Wiley, 1969); B. S. Gorgopoulos, G. M. Mahoney, and N. Jones, "A Path–Goal Approach to Productivity," *Journal of Applied Psychology* 41 (1957): 345–353; and E. E. Lawler III, P*ay and Organizational Effectiveness: A Psychological View* (New York: McGraw-Hill, 1981).

23. Richard M. Daft and Richard M. Steers, *Organizations: A Micro/Macro Approach* (Glenview, IL: Scott, Foresman, 1986).

24. Mike Hofman, "Everyone's a Cost Cutter," *Inc.* (July 1998): 117; and Abby Livingston, "Gain Sharing Encourages Productivity," *Nation's Business* (January 1998): 21–22

25. J. Stacy Adams, "Injustice in Social Exchange," in *Advances in Experimental Social Psychology*, 2nd ed., L. Berkowitz, ed. (New York: Academic Press, 1965); and J. Stacy Adams, "Toward an Understanding of Inequity," *Journal of Abnormal and Social Psychology* (November 1963): 422–436.

26. John Peterman, "The Rise and Fall of the J. Peterman Company," *Harvard Business Review* (September–October 1999): 59–66.

27. Vogl, "Carrots, Sticks, and Self-Deception."

28. James M. Kouzes and Barry Z. Posner, *The Leadership Challenge* (San Francisco, CA: Jossey-Bass, 1995).

29. Nina Gupta and Jason D. Shaw, "Let the Evidence Speak: Financial Incentives *Are* Effective!!" *Compensation and Benefits Review* (March/April 1998): 26, 28–32.

30. Vogl, "Carrots, Sticks, and Self-Deception," 40; and Alfie Kohn, "Incentives Can Be Bad for Business," *Inc.*, (January 1998): 93–94.

31. Kohn, "Challenging Behaviorist Dogma."

32. Jerry L. Gray and Frederick A. Starke, *Organizational Behavior: Concepts and Applications*, 4th ed. (New York, NY: Merrill, 1988).

33. Richard M. Steers, Lyman W. Porter, and Gregory A. Bigley, *Motivation and Leadership at Work*, 6th ed. (New York: McGraw-Hill, 1996), 512.

34. Steers, Porter, and Bigley, *Motivation and Leadership at Work*, 517; Vogl, "Carrots, Sticks, and Self-Deception," 40.

35. Steers, Porter, and Bigley, *Motivation and Leadership at Work*, 154–157; Anne Fisher, "The 100 Best Companies to Work for in America," *Fortune* (January 12, 1998): 69–70.

36. William D. Hitt, *The Leader-Manager: Guidelines for Action* (Columbus, OH: Battelle Press, 1988), 153.

37. Steers, Porter, and Bigley, *Motivation and Leadership at Work*, 520–525.

38. Vogl, "Carrots, Sticks, and Self-Deception," 43.

39. Greg Hitt and Jacob M. Schlesinger, "Perk Police: Stock Options Come Under Fire in Wake of Enron's Collapse," *The Wall Street Journal* (March 26, 2002): A1, A8.

40. Kouzes and Posner, *The Leadership Challenge*, 153.
41. Timothy Aeppel, "Tricks of the Trade: On Factory Floors, Top Workers Hide Secrets to Success," *The Wall Street Journal* (July 1, 2002): A1, A10.
42. Kouzes and Posner, *The Leadership Challenge*, 282.
43. Edwin P. Hollander and Lynn R. Offerman, "Power and Leadership in Organizations," *American Psychology* 45 (February 1990): 179–189.
44. Robert C. Ford and Myron D. Fottler, "Empowerment: A Matter of Degree," *Academy of Management Executive* 9 (1995): 21–31.
45. Charles Fishman, "Engines of Democracy," *Fast Company* (October 1999): 174–202.
46. David P. McCaffrey, Sue R. Faerman, and David W. Hart, "The Appeal and Difficulties of Participative Systems," *Organization Science* 6, no. 6 (November–December 1995): 603–627.
47. David E. Bowen and Edward E. Lawler III, "Empowering Service Employees," *Sloan Management Review* (Summer 1995): 73–84.
48. Jay A. Conger and Rabindra N. Kanungo, "The Empowerment Process: Integrating Theory and Practice," *Academy of Management Review* 13 (1988): 471–482.
49. McCaffrey, Faerman and Hart, "The Appeal and Difficulties of Participative Systems."
50. "Great Expectations?" *Fast Company* (November 1999): 212–224.
51. Bowen and Lawler, "Empowering Service Employees."
52. Hawk and Sheridan, "The Right Staff."
53. Gretchen Spreitzer, "Social Structural Characteristics of Psychological Empowerment," *Academy of Management Journal* 39, no. 2 (April 1996): 483–504.
54. Russ Forrester, "Empowerment: Rejuvenating a Potent Idea," *Academy of Management Executive* 14, no. 3 (2000): 67–80.
55. Glenn L. Dalton, "The Collective Stretch," *Management Review* (December 1998): 54–59.
56. Bradley L. Kirkman and Benson Rosen, "Powering Up Teams," *Organizational Dynamics* (Winter 2000): 48–66; and Gretchen M. Spreitzer, "Psychological Empowerment in the Workplace: Dimensions, Measurement, and Validation," *Academy of Management Journal* 38, no. 5 (October 1995): 1442.
57. Kirkman and Rosen, "Powering Up Teams."
58. Spreitzer, "Social Structural Characteristics of Psychological Empowerment."
59. Roy C. Herrenkohl, G. Thomas Judson, and Judith A. Heffner, "Defining and Measuring Employee Empowerment," *The Journal of Applied Behavioral Science* 35, no. 3 (September 1999): 373–389.

60. Frank Shipper and Charles C. Manz, "Employee Self-Management Without Formally Designated Teams: An Alternative Road to Empowerment," *Organizational Dynamics* (Winter 1992), 48–61.

61. Steve Kaufman, "ESOPs' Appeal on the Increase," *Nation's Business* (June 1997): 43–44.

62. Ford and Fottler, "Empowerment: A Matter of Degree."

63. Ricardo Semler, "How We Went Digital Without a Strategy," *Harvard Business Review* (September–October 2000): 51–58.

64. McCaffrey, Faerman, and Hart, "The Appeal and Difficulties of Participative Systems."

65. Philippe d'Iribarne, "Motivating Workers in Emerging Countries: Universal Tools and Local Adaptations," *Journal of Organizational Behavior* 23 (2002): 243–256.

66. This discussion is based on Tony Schwartz, "The Greatest Sources of Satisfaction in the Workplace are Internal and Emotional," *Fast Company* (November 2000): 398–402; and Marcus Buckingham and Curt Coffman, *First, Break All the Rules: What the World's Greatest Managers Do Differently* (New York: Simon & Schuster, 1999).

67. Polly LaBarre, "Marcus Buckingham Thinks Your Boss Has an Attitude Problem" *Fast Company* (August 2001), 88–98.

68. Brad Black, "The Road to Recovery," *Gallup Management Journal* (Winter 2000), 10–12.

69. Raj Aggarwal and Betty J. Simkins, "Open Book Management—Optimizing Human Capital," *Business Horizons* (September–October 2001): 5–13.

70. Ibid.

71. Michael J. Gaudioso, "How a Successful Gainsharing Program Arose from an Old One's Ashes at Bell Atlantic (Now Verizon) Directory Graphics," *Journal of Organizational Excellence* (Winter 2000): 11–18.

72. Hawk and Sheridan, "The Right Staff."

73. Dalton, "The Collective Stretch."

74. Christopher Caggiano, "The Right Way to Pay," Inc. (November 2002): 84–92.

75. Dalton, "The Collective Stretch."

Chapter

Your Leadership Challenge

After reading this chapter, you should be able to:

- Act as a communication champion rather than just as an information processor.

- Use key elements of effective listening and understand why listening is important to leader communication.

- Recognize and apply the difference between dialogue and discussion.

- Select an appropriate communication channel for your leadership message.

- Use communication to influence and persuade others.

- Effectively communicate during times of stress or crisis.

In December of 1955, Martin Luther King, Jr., became president of the new Montgomery Improvement Association. That same evening, he was called upon to address a crowd of thousands about the bus boycott that had begun only days earlier. In his impromptu speech, King referred to his audience as people "tired of being pushed out of the glittering sunlight of life's July and left standing amidst the chill of an alpine November." He reminded the audience of Rosa Parks' arrest and conviction for refusing to give up her bus seat to a white person. He commended her integrity; her action was a move toward justice and reflected a belief that all Americans are entitled to basic rights and privileges. King pointed out that the bus boycott was a means of protest with similar integrity. The boycott was nonviolent, it required patience, and it rested on the expectation of equal treatment of all people—values King had preached in his sermons as a minister.

The audience rallied in agreement, and under King's guidance 50,000 citizens of Montgomery, Alabama, participated in the boycott for the duration of the protest, despite the fact that most of those same citizens needed to ride the buses to get to and from work.

King's actions over the next several months were a witness of his sincerity to the protesters. He was the first to be arrested for participating in the boycott. His home was bombed the same day as his arrest. Despite these tribulations, he declared his determination inviolate. The boycott continued.

After nearly a year of protest, the U.S. Supreme Court ruled that Alabama's segregation laws were indeed unconstitutional. The boycott ended in victory, and King declared the verdict a leap of progress for the entire American population.[1]

What made King's first public role in a political drama so powerful that it ignited the support of thousands? How did King manage to maintain the support of so many people over a long period of hardship? Much of King's impact occurred the moment he gave his first speech. With his initial words, King created the parameters of a social movement. He discerned that the audience was tired of injustice. His metaphor contrasting summer sunshine with winter winds made the experience of racism tangible, felt upon the skin of each person in the crowd. King stood before the crowd and directed their collective attention to the immediate situation—Parks' action and the decision to boycott. Then he defined the significance of the boycott by comparing it to the incident on the bus—in effect, every boycotter was Rosa Parks.

King was thrust into a position of leadership where others looked to him for direction and inspiration. As he endured arrest and violence against his family without changing course, he symbolized his message of determination in the face of hardship. He communicated with both words and actions a vision and possibility of equality. King's followers wanted a future based on basic religious values and American ideals, a future King motivated them to work for and helped them see. For thousands, Martin Luther King, Jr., created a purpose and an identity that had not existed before.

In the previous chapter, we discussed motivation and reviewed some of the ways in which leaders motivate followers toward the accomplishment of the organization's goals. As this story of Martin Luther King, Jr., clearly illustrates, motivation depends greatly on a leader's ability to communicate effectively. We have all had both positive and negative experiences with communication in our personal as well as our work lives. Have you ever had a supervisor or instructor whose communication skills were so poor that you didn't have any idea what was expected of you or how to accomplish the job you were asked to do? On the other hand, have you experienced the communication flair of a teacher, boss, or coach who "painted a picture in words" that both inspired you and clarified how to achieve an objective?

Leadership cannot happen without effective communication. The styles of leadership we have discussed in earlier chapters of this book, particularly charismatic and transformational leadership, depend on powerful communication. Recall that leadership means influencing people to bring about change toward a vision, or desirable future for the organization. Leaders communicate to share the vision with others, inspire and motivate them to strive toward the vision, and build the values and trust that enable effective working relationships and goal accomplishment.

Successful leader communication also includes deceptively simple components, such as actively listening to others. Today's fast-paced environment does not always provide time for the listening and reflection that good communication requires.[2] Surveys of executives typically reveal that they consider communication their most important skill and one of their top responsibilities. However, one study found that fewer than half bother to tailor their messages to employees, customers, or suppliers, and even fewer seek feedback from those constituencies. Furthermore, investors appear to have a better idea of the vision and mission of companies than do employees.[3]

This chapter will describe the tools and skills that overcome the communication deficit pervading today's organizations and the broader social world. We will also examine how leaders can use communication skills to make a difference in their organizations and the lives of followers.

How Leaders Communicate

Leadership means communicating with others in such a way that they are influenced and motivated to perform actions that further common goals and lead toward desired outcomes. **Communication** is a process by which information and understanding are transferred between a sender and a receiver, such as between a leader and an employee, an instructor and a student, or a coach and a football player. The key elements of the communication process are shown in Exhibit 9.1. The leader initiates a communication by *encoding* a thought or idea, that is, by selecting symbols (such as words) with which to compose and transmit a message. The message is the tangible formulation of the thought or idea sent to the receiver, and the *channel* is the medium by which the message is sent. The channel could be a formal report, a telephone call, an e-mail message, or a face-to-face conversation. The receiver *decodes* the symbols to

Communication
a process by which information and understanding are transferred between a sender and a receiver

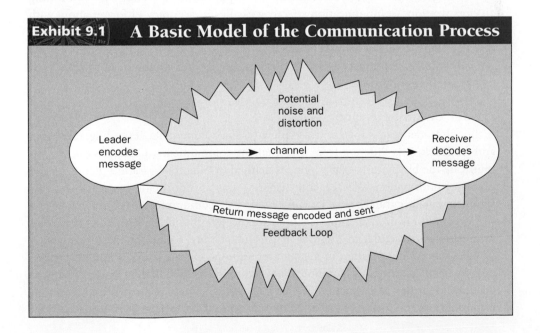

Exhibit 9.1   A Basic Model of the Communication Process

Potential noise and distortion

Leader encodes message → channel → Receiver decodes message

Return message encoded and sent

Feedback Loop

interpret the meaning of the message. Encoding and decoding can sometimes cause communication errors because individual differences, knowledge, values, attitudes, and background act as filters and may create "noise" when translating from symbols to meaning. Employees and supervisors, husbands and wives, parents and children, friends and strangers all have communication breakdowns because people can easily misinterpret messages. *Feedback* is the element of the communication process that enables someone to determine whether the receiver correctly interpreted the message. Feedback occurs when a receiver responds to a leader's communication with a return message. Without feedback, the communication cycle is incomplete. Effective communication involves both the transference and the mutual understanding of information.[4] The process of sending, receiving, and feedback to test understanding underlies both management and leadership communication.

Management Communication

A manager's primary role is that of "information processor." Managers spend some 80 percent of each working day in communication with others.[5] In other words, 48 minutes of every hour are spent in meetings, on the telephone, or talking informally with others. Managers scan their environments for important written and personal information, gathering facts, data, and ideas, which in turn are sent to subordinates and others who can use them. A manager then receives subordinate messages and feedback to see if "noise" interfered with translation, and determines whether to modify messages for accuracy.

Managers have a huge communication responsibility directing and controlling an organization. Communication effectiveness lies in accuracy of formulation, with less "noise" as one determinant of success. Managers communicate facts, statistics, and decisions. Effective managers establish themselves at the center of information networks to facilitate the completion of tasks. Leadership communication, however, serves a different purpose.

Leader Communication

Communication champion

a person who is philosophically grounded in the belief that communication is essential to building trust and gaining commitment to a vision

Although leader communication also includes the components of sending, receiving, and feedback, it is different from management communication. Leaders often communicate the big picture—the vision, as defined in Chapter 1—rather than facts and pieces of information. Whereas a manager acts as an information processor to disseminate data accurately, a leader can be seen as a communication champion.[6]

A communication champion is philosophically grounded in the belief that communication is essential to building trust and gaining commitment to the vision. Leaders use communication to inspire and unite people around a common sense of purpose and identity. A communication champion enables followers to "live" the vision in their day-to-day activities.[7] This chapter's Living Leadership highlights the importance of this aspect of leader communication. People need a vision to motivate

LIVING LEADERSHIP

Opening a Window to a Brighter World

A blind man was brought to the hospital. He was both depressed and seriously ill. He shared a room with another man, and one day asked, "What is going on outside?" The man in the other bed explained in some detail about the sunshine, the gusty winds, and the people walking along the sidewalk. The next day, the blind man again asked, "Please tell me what is going on outside today." The roommate responded with a story about the activities in a park across the way, the ducks on the pond, and the people feeding them. The third day and each day thereafter for two weeks, the blind man asked about the world outside and the other man answered, describing a different scene. The blind man enjoyed these talks, and he grew happier learning about the world seen through the window.

Then the blind man's roommate was discharged from the hospital. A new roommate was wheeled in—a tough-minded businessman who felt terrible but wanted to get work done. The next morning, the blind man said, "Will you please tell me what is going on outside?" The businessman didn't feel well, and he didn't want to be bothered to tell stories to a blind man. So he responded assertively, "What do you mean? I can't see outside. There is no window here. It's only a wall."

The blind man again became depressed, and a few days later he took a turn for the worse and was moved to intensive care.

SOURCE: Based on a story the author heard at a spiritual service in Santa Fe, New Mexico.

Action Memo

As a leader: Be a communication champion. Use verbal, nonverbal, and symbolic communication to unite people around a common vision. Actively communicate with people on a regular basis to facilitate strategic conversations and build trust.

them toward the future. Learning, problem solving, decision making, and strategizing are all oriented around and stem from the vision. Furthermore, communication champions visibly and symbolically engage in communication-based activities. Whether they walk around asking and answering questions or thoughtfully listen to a subordinate's problem, the actions of champions convey a commitment to communication. Communication isn't just about occasional meetings, formal speeches, or presentations. Leaders actively communicate through both words and actions every day. Regular communication is essential for building personal relationships with followers.

Exhibit 9.2 shows the leader-as-communication-champion model. By establishing an open communication climate, actively listening to others, learning to discern underlying messages, and applying the practice of dialogue, leaders facilitate and support *strategic conversations* that help move the organization forward. Leader communication is *purpose-directed* in that it directs everyone's attention toward the vision, values, and desired outcomes of the group or organization and persuades people to act in a way to help achieve the vision.

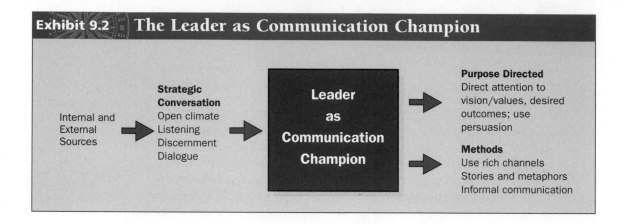

Exhibit 9.2   The Leader as Communication Champion

Internal and External Sources →

Strategic Conversation
Open climate
Listening
Discernment
Dialogue

→ **Leader as Communication Champion** →

Purpose Directed
Direct attention to vision/values, desired outcomes; use persuasion

Methods
Use rich channels
Stories and metaphors
Informal communication

Leaders can use many communication methods, including selecting rich channels of communication, stories, metaphors, and informal communication. For example, in communicating his message about the federal budget, President Ronald Reagan spoke of a trillion dollars in terms of stacking it next to the Empire State Building. Framed this way, the message redefined the meaning of a trillion dollars, and took on a new reality for the audience. Historical and contemporary leaders as diverse as Reagan, Martin Luther King, Jr., Aung San Suu Kyi, Bill Gates, and Carly Fiorina all share the ability to powerfully communicate their messages to followers and others.

Leading Strategic Conversations

Strategic conversation
communication that takes place across boundaries and hierarchical levels about the group or organization's vision, critical strategic themes, and values that can help achieve desired outcomes

Strategic conversation refers to people talking across boundaries and hierarchical levels about the group or organization's vision, critical strategic themes, and the values that can help achieve desired outcomes. Leaders facilitate strategic conversations by (1) actively listening to others to understand their attitudes and values, needs, personal goals, and desires; (2) setting the agenda for conversation by underscoring the key strategic themes that are linked to organizational success; and (3) selecting the right communication channels and facilitating dialogue.[8] For example, at Royal Philips Electronics, Europe's largest electronics outfit, president Gerard Kleisterlee has defined four key technology themes that he believes should define Philips' future in the industry: display, storage, connectivity, and digital video processing. These themes intentionally cross technology boundaries, requiring people to communicate and collaborate across departments and divisions. A strategic conversation for each theme begins with a one-day summit that brings together everyone who has relevant information to contribute—regardless of rank or job position—so that people can together gain a clear sense of goals and establish cooperative working relationships.[9]

Four key components necessary for strategic conversations are an open communication climate, active listening, discernment, and dialogue.

Creating an Open Communication Climate

Open communication means sharing all types of information throughout the company, especially across functional and hierarchical levels. Open communication runs counter to the traditional flow of selective information downward from supervisors to subordinates. But leaders want communication to flow in all directions. People throughout the organization need a clear direction and an understanding of how they can contribute.[10] Leaders break down conventional hierarchical and departmental boundaries that may be barriers to communication, enabling them to convey a stronger awareness of and commitment to organizational vision, goals, and values. In an open climate, a leader's communication of the vision "cascades" through an organization, as explained in Exhibit 9.3. Consistent and frequent communication brings follower acceptance and understanding. Open communication also builds trust, which is an essential element in effective leader-follower relationships because it inspires collaboration and commitment to common goals.[11] In a recent survey, more than 50 percent of executives reported that open communication is essential for building trust.[12]

Leaders also want an open communication climate because it helps employees understand how their actions interact with and affect others in the organization, which makes them more effective followers. Open communication encompasses the recent trend toward *open-book management*, which means sharing financial information with all employees to engender an attitude of employee ownership. Recall from

Open communication leaders sharing all types of information throughout the company and across all levels

---

Exhibit 9.3	**Why Open the Communication Climate?**

An open climate is essential for cascading vision, and cascading is essential because:

Natural Law 1: You Get What You Talk About
A vision must have ample 'air time' in an organization. A vision must be shared and practiced by leaders at every opportunity.

Natural Law 2: The Climate of an Organization Is a Reflection of the Leader
A leader who doesn't embody the vision and values doesn't have an organization that does.

Natural Law 3: You Can't Walk Faster Than One Step at a Time
A vision is neither understood nor accepted overnight. Communicating must be built into continuous, daily interaction so that over time followers will internalize it.

SOURCE: Based on Bob Wall, Robert S. Slocum, and Mark R. Sobol, *Visionary Leader* (Rocklin, CA: Prima Publishing, 1992), 87–89.

the previous chapter that when employees feel a sense of ownership in the company, they are more highly motivated to achieve goals. In addition, when employees have access to complete information, they make decisions that are good for the company. For example, leaders at Tampa-based AmeriSteel say opening the books and training all employees to understand the numbers helped cut the cost of converting a ton of scrap steel into a ton of finished steel from $145 to $127.[13] The open-book management program helped workers understand how every decision and action affects organizational success.

Communication across traditional boundaries enables leaders to hear what followers have to say, which means the organization gains the benefit of all employees' minds. The same perspectives batted back and forth between top executives don't lead to effective change, the creation of a powerful shared vision, or the network of personal relationships that keep organizations thriving. New voices and continuous conversation involving a broad spectrum of people revitalize and enhance communication.[14] At Advanced Cardiovascular Systems (now Guidant Corporation), Ginger Graham created an open communication climate in order to build a culture of trust that could help the company change and improve to meet new competitive conditions.

In the Lead   Ginger Graham, Advanced Cardiovascular Systems

Advanced Cardiovascular Systems (now Guidant Corporation) was the darling of the medical devices industry. The company, owned by pharmaceutical giant Eli Lilly, reached $100 million in sales within five years of launching its first product and revolutionized the field of angioplasty by producing one innovation after another. But when Ginger Graham took over as president and CEO of the medical device manufacturer, she realized that something was terribly wrong. Even though top managers were still touting ACS's strong internal and external relationships as key to the company's success, the reality was that these relationships were increasingly marked by conflict and discord rather than harmony and cooperation. The internal strife was already beginning to affect the company's competitiveness.

When Graham gave her first address to the company, she decided to tell the truth: "I've always heard about what a wonderful company ACS is," she began, "but frankly, that's not what I see. What I see is deteriorating morale, disillusioned customers, and finger-pointing. . . . We're all so busy blaming each other that nothing gets done." The response of employees—standing and cheering their approval—confirmed Graham's suspicions. People just wanted to hear that someone at the top knew the truth and was willing to admit it. From that moment, Graham began building a culture at ACS where everyone feels free to tell the truth without fear of negative consequences.

Graham established a number of practices to foster open and honest communications. To start, she reversed the top-down communication structure in an immediately visible way. Each top manager was assigned a "coach" from lower ranks of the organization. The coaches were trained to ask questions and gather very specific information from everyone throughout the company about the manager's openness and honest communication skills. Managers met with their coaches once a quarter. Because it had support from the top, the coaching program worked to close the communication gap. Managers also began sharing all financial and operational information with employees—good and bad—and asking for their help in solving company problems. Employees who went above and beyond the call of duty to meet organizational goals were recognized and rewarded.[15]

> **Action Memo**
>
> As a leader: Break down communication barriers. Create an open communication climate by sharing both good and bad information throughout your organization. Encourage and support communication across groups, departments, and divisions, as well as across hierarchical levels.

Creating an open communication climate helped alleviate much of the tension and conflict between departments at ACS, reaffirm employee commitment to a shared vision, and make the company more competitive. With open communications, ACS regularly launched innovative new products every year, could produce enough to supply the entire market in a matter of weeks, completed clinical studies in record-setting time, and improved quality while cutting costs.

Listening

One of the most important tools in a leader's communication tool kit is listening, both to followers and customers. Many leaders now believe that important information flows from the bottom up, not top down, and that a crucial component of leadership is to listen effectively.[16] It is only by listening that leaders can identify strategic themes and understand how to influence others to achieve desired outcomes. Listening also helps to build trust and create an open communication climate, because people are willing to share their ideas, suggestions, and problems when they think someone is listening and genuinely values what they have to say.

Listening involves the skill of grasping and interpreting a message's genuine meaning. Remember that message reception is a vital link in the communication process. However, many people do not listen effectively. They concentrate on formulating what they are going to say next rather than on what is being said to them. Our listening efficiency, as measured by the amount of material understood and remembered by subjects 48 hours after listening to a 10-minute message, is, on average, no better than 25 percent.[17]

What constitutes good listening? Exhibit 9.4 gives 10 keys to effective listening and illustrates a number of ways to distinguish a bad listener from a good one. A key to effective listening is focus. A good listener's total attention is focused on the message; he

Listening
the skill of grasping and interpreting a message's genuine meaning

Exhibit 9.4   Ten Keys to Effective Listening

Keys	Poor Listener	Good Listener
1. Listen actively	Is passive, laid back	Asks questions; paraphrases what is said
2. Find areas of interest	Tunes out dry subjects	Looks for opportunities, new learning
3. Resist distractions	Is easily distracted	Fights distractions; tolerates bad habits; knows how to concentrate
4. Capitalize on the fact that thought is faster than speech	Tends to daydream with slow speakers	Challenges, anticipates, summarizes; listens between lines to tone of voice
5. Be responsive	Is minimally involved	Nods; shows interest, positive feedback
6. Judge content, not delivery	Tunes out if delivery is poor	Judges content; skips over delivery errors
7. Hold one's fire	Has preconceptions; argues	Does not judge until comprehension is complete
8. Listen for ideas	Listens for facts	Listens to central themes
9. Work at listening	No energy output; faked attention	Works hard; exhibits active body state, eye contact
10. Exercise one's mind	Resists difficult material in favor of light, recreational material	Uses heavier material as exercise for the mind

SOURCES: Adapted from Sherman K. Okum, "How to Be a Better Listener," *Nation's Business* (August 1975), 62; and Philip Morgan and Kent Baker, "Building a Professional Image: Improving Listening Behavior," *Supervisory Management* (November 1985), 34–38.

isn't thinking about an unrelated problem in the purchasing department, how much work is piled up on his desk, or what to have for lunch. A good listener also listens actively, finds areas of interest, is flexible, works hard at listening, and uses thought speed to mentally summarize, weigh, and anticipate what the speaker says. You can evaluate your listening skills by answering the questions in Leader's Self-Insight 9.1.

Effective listening is engaged listening. Good leaders ask lots of questions, force themselves to get out of their office and mingle with others, set up listening forums where people can say whatever is on their minds, and provide feedback to let people know they have been heard.[18]

LEADER'S SELF-INSIGHT 9.1

Listening Self-Inventory

Go through the following questions, answering yes or no next to each question. Mark each as truthfully as you can in light of your behavior in the last few meetings or gatherings you attended.

	Yes	No
1. I frequently attempt to listen to several conversations at the same time.	___	___
2. I like people to give me only the facts and then let me make my own interpretation.	___	___
3. I sometimes pretend to pay attention to people.	___	___
4. I consider myself a good judge of nonverbal communications.	___	___
5. I usually know what another person is going to say before he or she says it.	___	___
6. I usually end conversations that don't interest me by diverting my attention from the speaker.	___	___
7. I frequently nod, frown, or whatever to let the speaker know how I feel about what he or she is saying.	___	___
8. I usually respond immediately when someone has finished talking.	___	___
9. I evaluate what is being said while it is being said.	___	___
10. I usually formulate a response while the other person is still talking.	___	___
11. The speaker's "delivery" style frequently distracts me from the content.	___	___
12. I usually ask people to clarify what they have said rather than guess at the meaning.	___	___
13. I make a concerted effort to understand other people's points of view.	___	___
14. I frequently hear what I expect to hear rather than what is actually said.	___	___
15. Most people feel that I have understood their point of view even when we disagree.	___	___

Scoring and Interpretation

The correct answers according to communication theory are as follows: No for questions 1, 2, 3, 5, 6, 7, 8, 9, 10, 11, 14. Yes for questions 4, 12, 13, 15.

If you missed only one or two questions, you strongly approve of your own listening habits and you are on the right track to becoming an effective listener in your role as a leader. If you missed three or four questions, you have uncovered some doubts about your listening effectiveness, and your knowledge of how to listen has some gaps. If you missed five or more questions, you probably are not satisfied with the way you listen, and your followers and co-workers might not feel you are a good listener either. Work on improving your active listening skills.

Being a good listener expands a leader's role in the eyes of others and enhances the leader's influence. A new CEO at Griffin Hospital in Derby, Connecticut, started actively listening to employees and patients when it became clear that the community hospital would have to change to survive against larger, more aggressive competitors. CEO Patrick Charmel implemented virtually every requested change, including installing wooden rather than steel handrails in hallways, banning fluorescent bulbs in favor of soft, indirect lighting, and adding cozy, home-style kitchens within easy access of all patient

Action Memo

As a leader:
Listen! Focus
your total
attention on
what the other
person is
saying. Work
hard to listen—
use eye contact;
ask questions
and paraphrase
the message;
and offer posi-
tive feedback.
Pay attention to
body language,
patterns of
interaction, and
other clues to
discern what
followers really
think, feel, or
want.

rooms. In addition, every patient now takes part in a detailed "case conference" with doctors, nurses, and other caregivers. They're encouraged to look at their medical charts and given detailed literature about their condition. Employees throughout the hospital are authorized to make decisions and take actions within their area of expertise based on the best interest of the patient.[19] By listening to the needs of patients and employees, and subsequently responding to those needs, Charmel transformed Griffin Hospital—as well as the relationships between leaders and employees and between employees and patients. This kind of transformation is what leader listening—indeed, communication—is all about.

Active listening is a daily, ongoing part of a leader's communication. The connection between personal satisfaction and being listened to, whether one is a customer or an employee, is not a mystery. When people sense that they have been heard, they simply feel better. Dr. Robert Buckman, a cancer specialist who teaches other doctors, as well as businesspeople, how to break bad news, says you have to start by listening. "The trust that you build just by letting people say what they feel is incredible," Buckman says.[20] Few things are as maddening to people as not being listened to by doctors or other professionals. In the business world, customers are often infuriated when their requests are ignored or they are told they can't be accommodated, signals that nobody is listening to their needs. Furthermore, when leaders fail to listen to employees, it sends the signal, "you don't matter," which decreases employee commitment and motivation.

Discernment

One of the most rewarding kinds of listening involves discernment. By this kind of listening, a leader detects the unarticulated messages hidden below the surface of spoken interaction, complaints, behavior, and actions. A discerning leader pays attention to patterns and relationships underlying the organization and those it serves.

Companies such as Kimberly-Clark and Procter & Gamble that live or die on new products have discovered the importance of discernment. Customers are frequently unable to articulate to market researchers exactly what they want, but good leaders can discern unspoken desires, as they did at Kimberly-Clark to create Huggies Pull-Ups. Through interacting with parents in focus groups and in their own homes, leaders tried to discern what customers valued rather than asking them what they wanted. They found that customers didn't want to use diapers anymore but also didn't want their toddlers to wet the bed. The innovative solution of a pull-up diaper resolved these two contradictory needs.[21]

Effective communication with followers also depends on discernment. One leader dealing with a problem employee in the kitchen at an upscale restaurant got nowhere by asking outright why her sous chef had gone from consistently good performance to frequently being tardy or absent. After several days working almost full-time in the kitchen and keeping her eyes and ears open, the restaurant manager

Discernment

*listening in
which a leader
detects unarticu-
lated messages
hidden below the
surface of spo-
ken interaction*

discerned that the quiet, introverted employee felt insecure and inadequate since a new head chef with a flamboyant personality had been hired. With this understanding, she got the two employees together and was able to solve the problem. As another example, leaders who are trying to implement major changes frequently have to use discernment to detect deep-seated reasons for employee resistance.

A leader hears the undercurrents that have yet to emerge.[22] Remember how Martin Luther King, Jr., discerned a readiness to fight injustice in his audience, a frustration just beginning to surface to which he subsequently gave definition and organization? Discernment is a critical skill for leaders because it enables them to tap into the unarticulated, often deep-seated needs, desires, and hopes of followers and customers.

Dialogue

When a group of people are actively listening to one another and paying attention to unspoken undercurrents, an amazing type of communication, referred to as dialogue, occurs. The "roots of dialogue" are *dia* and *logos*, which can be thought of as *stream of meaning*. In **dialogue**, people together create a stream of shared meaning that enables them to understand each other and share a view of the world.[23] People may start out as polar opposites, but by actively listening and talking authentically to one another, they discover their common ground, common issues, and common dreams on which they can build a better future.

Most of us have a tendency to infuse everything we hear with our own opinions rather than being genuinely open to what others are saying. In addition, traditional business values in the United States and most other Western countries reward people for forcefully asserting their own ideas and opinions and trying to discredit or contradict others.[24] But people can engage in dialogue only when they come to a conversation free of prejudgments, personal agendas, and "right" answers. Participants in a dialogue do not presume to know the outcome, nor do they sell their convictions.

One way to understand the distinctive quality of dialogue is to contrast it with discussion.[25] Exhibit 9.5 illustrates the differences between a dialogue and a discussion. Typically, the intent of a discussion is to present one's own point of view and persuade others in the group to adopt it. A discussion is often resolved by logic or by "beating down" opposing viewpoints. Dialogue, on the other hand, requires that participants suspend their attachments to a particular point of view so that a deeper level of listening, synthesis, and meaning can emerge from the group. A dialogue's focus is to reveal feelings and build common ground, with the emphasis on inquiry rather than advocacy. As discussed in the Leader's Bookshelf, dialogue is particularly useful for conversations about difficult and emotionally charged issues. Consider how Henry Bertolon, cofounder and CEO of NECX, introduced dialogue into the company to improve communication.

Dialogue
active sharing and listening in which people explore common ground and grow to understand each other and share a world view

Action Memo

As a leader: Use dialogue to help people create a shared sense of meaning and purpose. Create a communication environment where people feel free to express their hopes and fears, will suspend their convictions and explore assumptions, and are motivated to search for common ground.

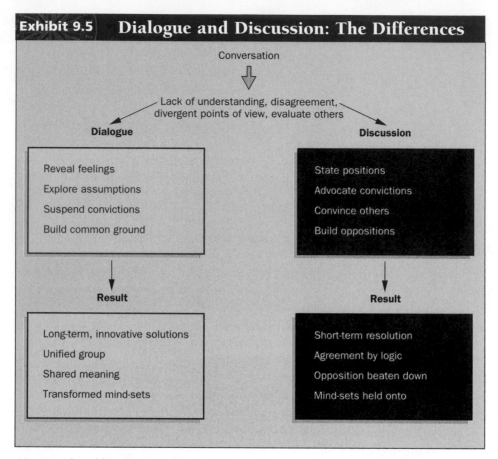

Exhibit 9.5   Dialogue and Discussion: The Differences

Conversation

⇓

Lack of understanding, disagreement, divergent points of view, evaluate others

Dialogue

Reveal feelings

Explore assumptions

Suspend convictions

Build common ground

Result

Long-term, innovative solutions

Unified group

Shared meaning

Transformed mind-sets

Discussion

State positions

Advocate convictions

Convince others

Build oppositions

Result

Short-term resolution

Agreement by logic

Opposition beaten down

Mind-sets held onto

SOURCE: Adapted from Edgar Schein, "On Dialogue, Culture, and Organizational Learning," *Organizational Dynamics* (Autumn 1993), 46.

In the Lead   Henry Bertolon, NECX

From the outside, everything looked rosy at NECX, a leading independent distributor of semiconductors and other computer products. However, CEO Henry Bertolon could see that the company was suffering from the strain of rapid growth and beginning to come apart at the seams. "We'd have meetings that just melted down," he says. "Everyone would scream at each other and then leave."

Bertolon hired Wil Calmas, a psychologist with an MBA, to help solve NECX's communication problems. Calmas set up a one-day-a-week program to get people talking—and listening—to one another on a

LEADER'S BOOKSHELF

Crucial Conversations: Tools for Talking When Stakes Are High
By Kerry Patterson, Joseph Grenny, Ron McMillan, and Al Switzler

Almost all of us have experienced the discomfort of a *crucial conversation*, which refers to a discussion where emotions run strong, opinions vary, and the stakes are high. Crucial conversations are conversations about tough issues that may cause conflict. Some examples that occur in the workplace include: (1) Confronting a co-worker who makes suggestive comments or behaves offensively; (2) Approaching a boss who is breaking his own safety rules; or (3) Talking to a team member who isn't keeping commitments. For most of us, the more crucial the conversation, the less likely we are to handle it well. The authors of *Crucial Conversations: Tools for Talking When Stakes Are High* take a step-by-step approach to explore tools leaders can use to help create the conditions, within themselves and others, for effectively dealing with difficult issues.

The Leader's Role in Crucial Conversations
Leaders use the technique of dialogue to keep themselves and others calm and focused when discussions turn into crucial conversations. Here are a few guidelines:

❊ *Encourage a free flow of information.* When it comes to controversial, risky, and emotional conversations, effective leaders find a way to get all relevant information from themselves and others into the open. At the core of every successful crucial conversation is the free flow of information and ideas, with people feeling safe enough to openly and honestly express their opinions, feelings, and theories.

❊ *Start with heart.* A key principle of dialogue is that the leader starts with getting his or her own heart right. In a high-risk conversation, the leader has to start with the right motives and stay calm and focused no matter what happens. To stay focused, leaders have to know what they want for themselves, for others, and for the relationship.

❊ *When people are at cross purposes, think CRIB.* Commit to seek a mutual purpose; Recognize the purpose behind the strategy; Invent a mutual purpose; Brainstorm new strategies. When people are poles apart on what they want, leaders can use this tool to bring people back to dialogue. They first get people to commit to finding some agreement, strive to discern the true purpose behind one another's words; find broader goals that can serve as a basis for mutual purpose; and, with a mutual purpose as a grounding, brainstorm ideas for meeting each person's individual needs.

Communicating When It Matters Most
When we're angry, upset, frustrated, anxious, or otherwise influenced by strong emotions, conversation often deteriorates into *silence* or *violence*, verbally attacking the other person or verbally withdrawing. These are the times when dialogue is most important. *Crucial Conversations* offers ideas for thinking about and preparing for difficult conversations, along with specific tips and tools that can help leaders say and do the right thing.

Crucial Conversations: Tools for Talking When Stakes Are High, by Kerry Patterson, Joseph Grenny, Ron McMillan, and Al Switzler, is published by McGraw-Hill.

deeper, authentic level. The day begins with a 90-minute meeting of top leaders. There's never a formal agenda—people are encouraged to express fear, hostility, frustration, secret wishes, whatever feelings are affecting their lives and work. The early morning meeting is just the beginning of a day-long series of dialogues among NECX employees from all ranks and departments. The sales department became so adept at dialogue that they quickly began meeting on their own, without Calmas's guidance.

Bertolon is convinced that the sessions have had a positive impact on communication, interpersonal relationships, and the bottom line. In a fast-growing business, he believes that getting people communicating in a way that builds shared understanding and meaning is critical to success. The dialogue sessions created a safe environment for people to reveal their feelings, explore ideas, and build common ground. It also keeps them loose, flexible, and open to new ideas—ready to respond to the rapid changes taking place all around them.[26]

Both forms of communication, dialogue and discussion, can result in organizational change. However, the result of a discussion is limited to a specific topic being deliberated, whereas the result of dialogue is characterized by group unity, shared meaning, and transformed mindsets. This kind of result is far-reaching. A new, common mindset is not the same thing as agreement, because it creates a reference point from which subsequent communication can start. As new and deeper solutions are developed, a trusting relationship is built among communicators, as occurred at NECX, and this is important to all communication episodes that follow. Dialogue thus transforms communication and, by extension, the organization.

The Leader as Communication Champion

To act as a communication champion, as described earlier in this chapter, leaders don't communicate just to convey information, but to persuade and influence others. They use communication skills to sell others on the vision and influence them to behave in ways that achieve goals and help accomplish the vision.

The ability to persuade others is more critical today than ever before. The command-and-control mindset of managers telling workers what to do and how to do it is gone. Employees don't just want to know *what* they should do but *why* they should do it. Leaders can follow four steps to practice the art of persuasion:[27]

1. *Establish credibility.* A leader's credibility is based on the leader's knowledge and expertise as well as his or her relationships with others. When leaders

have demonstrated that they make well-informed, sound decisions, followers have confidence in their expertise. Leaders also build credibility by establishing good relationships with others and showing that they have others' best interests at heart.

2. *Build goals on common ground.* To be persuasive, leaders describe how what they're requesting will benefit others as well as the leader. For example, to get fast food franchisees to support new pricing discounts desired by headquarters, one leader cited research showing that the new pricing policies improved franchisees' profits. When people see how they will personally benefit from doing something, they're usually eager to do it. When leaders can't find common advantages, it's a good signal that they need to adjust their goals and plans.

3. *Make your position compelling to others.* Leaders appeal to others on an emotional level by using symbols, metaphors, and stories to express their messages, rather than relying on facts and figures alone. By tapping into the imaginations of their followers, leaders can inspire people to accomplish amazing results.

4. *Connect emotionally.* Recall the discussion of emotional intelligence from Chapter 5. Good leaders sense others' emotions and adjust their approach to match the audience's ability to receive their message. Leaders use their emotional understanding to influence others in positive ways. In addition, by looking at how people have interpreted and responded to past events in the organization, leaders can get a better grasp on how followers may react to their ideas and proposals.

Action Memo

As a leader: Be persuasive. Build your credibility as a leader by becoming knowledgeable and establishing positive relationships with others. Show people how your plans will benefit them. Tap into followers' imaginations and emotions to inspire their support.

Persuasion is a valuable communication process that individuals can use to lead others to a shared solution or commitment. To effectively persuade and influence others, leaders pay attention to the channels of communication they use, employ aspects of storytelling and metaphor to enrich their communications, and use informal as well as formal communication techniques.

Acting as a communication champion requires that leaders communicate frequently and easily with others in the organization. Yet for some individuals, communication experiences are unrewarding, so they may consciously or unconsciously avoid situations where communication is required.[28] The term *communication apprehension* describes this avoidance behavior, and is defined as "an individual's level of fear or anxiety associated with either real or anticipated communication with another person or persons."[29] Complete the questions in Leader's Self-Insight 9.2 to learn your level of communication apprehension.

Personal Assessment of Communication Apprehension

The questions below are about your feelings toward communication with other people. Indicate the degree to which each statement applies to you by marking (5) Strongly agree, (4) Agree, (3) Are undecided, (2) Disagree, or (1) Strongly disagree with each statement. There are no right or wrong answers. Many of the statements are similar to other statements. Do not be concerned about this. Work quickly and just record your first impressions.

	Strongly disagree				Strongly agree
1. When talking in a small group of acquaintances, I am tense and nervous.	1	2	3	4	5
2. When presenting a talk to a group of strangers, I am tense and nervous.	1	2	3	4	5
3. When conversing with a friend or colleague, I am calm and relaxed.	1	2	3	4	5
4. When talking in a large meeting of acquaintances, I am calm and relaxed.	1	2	3	4	5
5. When presenting a talk to a group of friends or colleagues, I am tense and nervous.	1	2	3	4	5
6. When conversing with an acquaintance or colleague, I am calm and relaxed.	1	2	3	4	5
7. When talking in a large meeting of strangers, I am tense and nervous.	1	2	3	4	5
8. When talking in a small group of strangers, I am tense and nervous.	1	2	3	4	5
9. When talking in a small group of friends or colleagues, I am calm and relaxed.	1	2	3	4	5
10. When presenting a talk to a group of acquaintances, I am calm and relaxed.	1	2	3	4	5
11. When I am conversing with a stranger, I am calm and relaxed.	1	2	3	4	5
12. When talking in a large meeting of friends, I am tense and nervous.	1	2	3	4	5
13. When presenting a talk to a group of strangers, I am calm and relaxed.	1	2	3	4	5
14. When conversing with a friend or colleague, I am tense and nervous.	1	2	3	4	5
15. When talking in a large meeting of acquaintances, I am tense and nervous.	1	2	3	4	5
16. When talking in a small group of acquaintances, I am calm and relaxed.	1	2	3	4	5
17. When talking in a small group of strangers, I am calm and relaxed.	1	2	3	4	5
18. When presenting a talk to a group of friends, I am calm and relaxed.	1	2	3	4	5
19. When conversing with an acquaintance or colleague, I am tense and nervous.	1	2	3	4	5
20. When talking in a large meeting of strangers, I am calm and relaxed.	1	2	3	4	5
21. When presenting a talk to a group of acquaintances, I am tense and nervous.	1	2	3	4	5
22. When conversing with a stranger, I am tense and nervous.	1	2	3	4	5
23. When talking in a large meeting of friends or colleagues, I am calm and relaxed.	1	2	3	4	5
24. When talking in a small group of friends or colleagues, I am tense and nervous.	1	2	3	4	5

Scoring:

This questionnaire permits computation of four subscores and one total score. Sub-scores relate to communication apprehension in four common situations—public speaking, meetings, group discussions, and interpersonal conversations. To compute your scores, add or subtract your scores for each item as indicated below.

Subscore/Scoring Formula

For each subscore, start with 18 points. Then add the scores for the plus (+) items and subtract the scores for the minus (–) items.

Public Speaking

18 + scores for items 2, 5, and 21; – scores for items 10, 13, and 18. Score = _____

Meetings

18 + scores for items 7, 12, and 15; – scores for items 4, 20, and 23. Score = _____

Group Discussions

18 + scores for items 1, 8, and 24; – scores for items 9, 16, and 17. Score = _____

Interpersonal Conversations

18 + scores for items 14, 19, and 22; – scores for items 3, 6, and 11. Score = _____

Total Score

Sum the four scores above for the Total Score _____

Interpretation:

This personal assessment provides an indication of how much apprehension (fear or anxiety) you feel in a variety of communication settings. Total scores may range from 24 to 120. Scores above 72 indicate that you are more apprehensive about communication than the average person. Scores above 85 indicate a very high level of communication apprehension. Scores below 59 indicate a very low level of apprehension. These extreme scores (below 59 and above 85) are generally outside the norm. They suggest that the degree of apprehension you may experience in any given situation may not be associated with a realistic response to that communication situation.

Scores on the subscales can range from a low of 6 to a high of 30. Any score above 18 indicates some degree of apprehension. For example, if you score above 18 for the public speaking context, you are like the overwhelming majority of people.

To be an effective communication champion, you should work to overcome communication anxiety. The interpersonal conversations create the least apprehension for most people, followed by group discussions, larger meetings, and then public speaking. Compare your scores with another student. What aspect of communication creates the most apprehension for you? How do you plan to improve it?

SOURCE: J. C. McCroskey, "Measures of Communication-Bound Anxiety," *Speech Monographs* 37 (1970): 269–277; J. C. McCroskey and V. P. Richmond, "Validity of the PRCA as an Index of Oral Communication Apprehension," *Communication Monographs* 45 (1978): 192–203; J. C. McCroskey and V. P. Richmond, "The Impact of Communication Apprehension on Individuals in Organizations," *Communication Quarterly* 27 (1979): 55–61; J. C. McCroskey, *An Introduction to Rhetorical Communication*, Prentice Hall, Englewood Cliffs, NJ: Prentice Hall, 1982.

Selecting Rich Communication Channels

Channel

a medium by which a communication message is carried from sender to receiver

A **channel** is a medium by which a communication message is carried from sender to receiver. Leaders have a choice of many channels through which to communicate to subordinates. A leader may discuss a problem face-to-face, use the telephone, write a memo or letter, use e-mail, send an instant message, or put an item in a newsletter, depending on the nature of the message. New communication media such as Web pages, intranets, and extranets have expanded leaders' options for communicating to followers as well as the organization's customers, clients, or shareholders.

Channel richness

the amount of information that can be transmitted during a communication episode

The Continuum of Channel Richness

Recent research has attempted to explain how leaders select communication channels to enhance communication effectiveness.[30] The research has found that channels differ in their capacity to convey information. Just as a pipeline's physical characteristics limit the kind and amount of liquid that can be pumped through it, a communication channel's physical characteristics limit the kind and amount of information that can be conveyed among people. The channels available to leaders can be classified into a hierarchy based on information richness. Channel richness is the amount of information that can be transmitted during a communication episode. The hierarchy of channel richness is illustrated in Exhibit 9.6.

The richness of an information channel is influenced by three characteristics: (1) the ability to handle multiple cues simultaneously; (2) the ability to facilitate rapid, two-way feedback; and (3) the ability to establish a personal focus for the communication. Face-to-face discussion is the richest medium, because it permits direct experience, multiple information cues, immediate feedback, and personal focus. Face-to-face discussions facilitate the assimilation of broad cues and deep, emotional understanding of the situation. For example, Tony Burns, former CEO of Ryder System, Inc., likes to handle things face-to-face: "You can look someone in the eyes. You can tell by the look in his eyes or the inflection of his voice what the real problem or question or answer is."[31]

Telephone conversations are next in the richness hierarchy. Eye contact, gaze, posture, and other body language cues are missing, but the human voice still carries a tremendous amount of emotional information. Electronic messaging, or e-mail, which lacks both visual and verbal cues, is increasingly being used for communications that were once handled over the telephone. E-mail has improved the speed and reduced the cost of long-distance communication in particular. Rather than playing "phone tag," a leader or employee can send an e-mail message to communicate necessary information. A recent survey by Ohio State University researchers found that about half of the respondents reported making fewer telephone calls since they began using e-mail. However, respondents also said they preferred the telephone or face-to-face conversations for expressing affection, giving advice, or communicating difficult

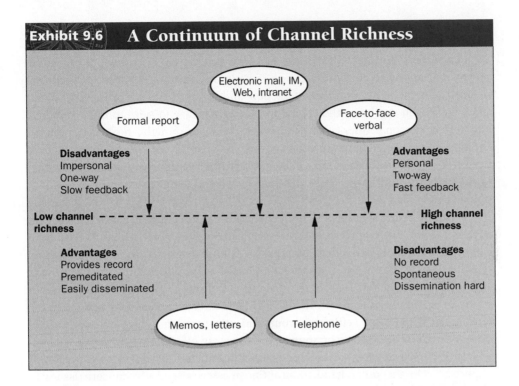

Exhibit 9.6   A Continuum of Channel Richness

Electronic mail, IM, Web, intranet

Formal report

Face-to-face verbal

Disadvantages
Impersonal
One-way
Slow feedback

Advantages
Personal
Two-way
Fast feedback

Low channel richness

High channel richness

Advantages
Provides record
Premeditated
Easily disseminated

Disadvantages
No record
Spontaneous
Dissemination hard

Memos, letters

Telephone

news.³² Some studies have found that e-mail, instant messaging, and other forms of electronic communication can enable reasonably rich communication if the technology is used appropriately.³³ However, the proliferation of electronic media has contributed to *poorer* communication in many organizations. Employees who work in offices down the hall from one another will often send e-mail rather than communicating face to face. One employee reported that he was fired via e-mail—by a manager who sat five feet away in the same office.³⁴

Other forms of electronic communication, such as video conferencing, recognize the need for channel richness, allowing for voice as well as body language cues. A lower level of richness is offered by the World Wide Web and company intranets, but these have opened new avenues for keeping in touch with employees and customers. An intranet enables leaders to disseminate certain types of information to a huge number of employees simultaneously, such as a traditional company newsletter might. Company Web pages are increasingly being used to keep in closer touch with customers, suppliers, or partners, and unlike print media, the Web allows for rapid feedback.

Written media that are personalized, such as notes and letters, can be personally focused, but they convey only the cues written on paper and are slow to provide feedback. Impersonal written media, including fliers, bulletins, and standard

Action Memo

As a leader: Use a rich form of communication, such as face to face or the telephone, when an issue is complex, emotionally charged, or especially important. Handle the most difficult issues face to face. For a routine, straightforward message, use a written or electronic form of communication for efficiency.

computer reports, are the lowest in richness. The channels are not focused on a single receiver, use limited information cues, and do not permit feedback. Paul Stevenson, president and CEO of ATI Medical, Inc., banned the practice of writing memos to encourage employees to use rich communication channels. He felt that memos substituted for human interaction and wasted valuable decision-making time. Stevenson attributes the company's yearly increase in sales to the productive and timely personal interactions that have resulted from the no-memo policy.[35] Lacking memos as a communication channel, ATI employees must communicate in person to get their ideas out, and they build strong relationships with one another in the process. Leaders recognize that innovation and teamwork are the byproducts of using rich channels.

It is important for leaders to understand that each communication channel has advantages and disadvantages, and that each can be an effective means of communication in the appropriate circumstances.[36] Channel selection depends on whether the message is routine or nonroutine. Routine communications are simple and straightforward, such as a product price change. Routine messages convey data or statistics or simply put into words what people already understand and agree on. Routine messages can be efficiently communicated through a channel lower in richness. Written or electronic communications also are effective when the audience is widely dispersed or when the communication is "official" and a permanent record is required.[37] On the other hand, nonroutine messages typically concern issues of change, conflict, or complexity that have great potential for misunderstanding. Nonroutine messages often are characterized by time pressure and surprise. Leaders can communicate nonroutine messages effectively only by selecting a rich channel.

Consider a CEO trying to work out a press release with public relations people about a plant explosion that injured 15 employees. If the press release must be ready in three hours, the communication is truly nonroutine and forces a rich information exchange. The group will meet face-to-face, brainstorm ideas, and provide rapid feedback to resolve disagreement and convey the correct information. If the CEO has three days to prepare the release, less information capacity is needed. The CEO and public relations people might begin developing the press release with an exchange of telephone calls and e-mail messages.

The leadership key is to select a channel to fit the message. During a major acquisition, one firm elected to send senior executives to all major work sites, where 75 percent of the acquired workforce met the officials in person. The results were well worth the time and expense of the personal appearances. Participating leaders claimed that the workers saw them as understanding and willing to listen—people they would not mind working for.[38] On the other hand, consider the executive who addressed a letter "Dear Team" to inform employees in his department that they would be required to make significant changes to achieve a new corporate quality goal of zero defects. Although the letter indicated that the supervisor realized this would "not be welcome news," it directs employees to renew their commitment to quality and pull together as a team. The letter concludes with a P.S.: "As of tomorrow, I will be on vacation in Hawaii for the next four weeks and out of reach." If you were a member of this supervisor's team, how would you feel about such a communication? Most leader communication by its very nature is comprised of nonroutine messages. Although leaders maximize the use of all channels, they don't let anything substitute for the rich face-to-face channel when important issues are at stake.

Effectively Using Electronic Communication Channels

Virtual communication through voice mail, e-mail, video conferencing, and instant messaging has become a fact of life in today's organizations. The U.S. Army uses electronic technology to rapidly transmit communications about weather conditions, the latest intelligence on the enemy, and so forth to lieutenants on the battlefield. Companies such as Celanese Chemicals use wireless text messaging to keep in touch with salespeople in the field and help them close deals faster.[39] These new tools provide highly efficient ways of communicating, and can be particularly useful for routine messages. Instant messaging (IM), which allows people to tell who is connected to a network and share short-hand messages or documents with them instantly, is rapidly growing in use and may be more common than e-mail within a few years.[40] In March 2003, 84 percent of companies surveyed in North America reported using instant messaging.[41] Many leaders find that IM helps them get responses faster and collaborate with people more smoothly. "It's just like having my office next to any of [my employees] and being able to stick my head in and ask a question," says Jim McCain, president of sales consulting firm McCain and Associates, which has employees scattered from Tallahassee, Florida, to Hyderabad, India.[42]

Electronic communication has many advantages, but there are disadvantages as well. For one thing, electronic methods increase the potential for communication errors. People often come across as sounding cold, arrogant, or insensitive when they attempt to discuss delicate issues via e-mail, for example. Things that might be handled smoothly in a face-to-face conversation or over the phone turn into massive problems by fostering resentment, bitterness, and hard feelings.[43]

Another equally disturbing concern, one psychiatrist argues, is that the growing use of technology for communicating has created hidden problems for both individuals and organizations by depriving people of the "human moments" that are needed to energize people, inspire creativity, and support emotional well-being.[44] People need to interact with others in physical space to build the connections that create great organizations. Electronic communication is here to stay, and has brought wonderful advantages. The key for leaders is to benefit from the tremendous efficiencies of new technologies while preventing their unintended problems. Here are some tips for effectively using electronic communication:

❊ *Combine high-tech and high-touch.* Never allow electronic communication to take the place of human connections. People who work together should meet face to face on a regular basis. Many companies that use virtual workers, for example, require that they come into the office at least once a month for unstructured face time.[45] Leaders should meet and get to know their followers in real as well as virtual space. A real-estate developer in Boston set up a free-pizza day once a week when widely scattered workers could come by the office, sit around the table in his office, and just talk.[46]

❊ *Consider the circumstances.* People who know one another well and have worked together a long time can typically communicate about more complex issues via e-mail or instant messaging than can people who have a new working relationship.[47] When people have a long-term working relationship, there is less potential for misunderstandings and hard feelings. In addition, when all parties involved have a good grasp of the issues being discussed, e-mail can be used effectively. A leader of a long-standing, well-functioning team could thus use e-mail more extensively than the leader of a team that has just been formed.

❊ *Read twice before you hid the "Send" button.* Never send an e-mail or instant message without reading it at least twice. You wouldn't send a letter without reading it over to make sure it says what you meant to say and checking the grammar and spelling. Give the same attention to your electronic messages. Make sure you use the niceties, like saying please and thank you, and signing your name. Be as courteous to the receiver as if you were delivering the message in person. Another important point is to never send an electronic message when you are angry or upset. This is a situation that definitely calls for richer communication channels.

❊ *Know what's off limits.* Select richer channels of communication as well for important, complex, or sensitive messages. Layoffs, firings, and reprimands should always be given face-to-face, or at least via telephone. In addition, never use e-mail to complain about or ridicule your boss or colleagues. A human resources employee at CNN tells of writing an e-mail calling her boss all sorts of evil names, intending to send it to a friend in another department. Only too late did she realize she'd sent the e-mail to the boss instead.[48] It's easy to do. Be careful what you write. Exhibit 9.7 lists some further dos and don'ts concerning subjects appropriate for electronic mail.

Stories and Metaphors

The Ute Indians of Utah, as well as other native tribes, made the best storytellers their tribal leaders.[49] Why? Because storytelling is a powerful means of persuasion

Exhibit 9.7	**Dos and Don'ts of Electronic Mail**

Do

* Use e-mail to set up meetings, to recap spoken conversations, or to follow up on information already discussed face to face.

* Keep e-mail messages short and to-the-point. Many people read e-mail on handheld devices, which have small screens.

* Use e-mail to prepare a group of people for a meeting. For example, it is convenient to send the same documents to a number of people and ask them to review the materials before the meeting.

* Use e-mail to transmit standard reports.

* Act like a newspaper reporter. Use the subject line to quickly grab the reader's attention, much like a newspaper headline. Put the most important information in the first paragraph. Answer any questions–who, what, when, where, why, and how—that are pertinent.

Don't

* Use e-mail to discuss something with a colleague who sits across the aisle or down the hall from you. Take the old-fashioned approach of speaking to each other.

* Lambaste a friend or colleague via e-mail—and especially don't copy others on the message.

* Use e-mail to start or perpetuate a feud. If you get an e-mail that tempts you to respond in a scathing manner, stop yourself. You may be misinterpreting the message. Even if you're not, take the high road.

* Write anything in an e-mail you wouldn't want published in a newspaper. E-mail with sensitive or potentially embarrassing information has an uncanny way of leaking out.

SOURCES: Based on "15 Dos and Don'ts" box in Andrea C. Poe, "Don't Touch that 'Send' Button," *HR Magazine* (July 2001): 74–80; and Michael Goldberg, "The Essential Elements of E-Mail," *CIO* (June 1, 2003): 24.

and influence. Stories enable leaders to connect with people on an emotional as well as an intellectual level. In addition, telling stories helps people make sense of complex situations, inspires action, and brings about change in ways that other forms of communication cannot.

Leaders have to be conscious of the language they use in all situations. Just being aware of the terminology they choose and the definitions and context they create is one way leaders enhance communications with others. Even simple language choices make a tremendous difference for leadership. However, it is by using language rich in metaphor and storytelling that leaders can create a deep and lasting effect on others. For example, at National Grange Mutual, a property-casualty insurance company, leaders in the claims unit picked up on a statement made by one of the company's independent agents. When discussing how the claims unit should relate to customers, the agent said, "I want my customers to feel your arm go around them when they have a claim." Leaders used this evocative image to focus employees on reengineering the claims process to provide better, faster, more caring service.[50]

A study of the speeches of U.S. presidents found that those who used imagery to convey their messages were rated higher in both personal charisma and historical greatness, suggesting that a leader's ability to achieve a vision is related to the ability to paint followers a verbal picture of what can be accomplished if everyone pulls together.[51] A leader is responsible for directing followers' attention to a vision and the values that can help attain it, for defining the meaning of situations and objectives, and for presenting messages in ways that make them palpable and meaningful to organizational members. People seek meaning in their daily work and want to understand their role in the larger context of the organization. It is up to leaders to provide that context for followers, to frame activity with discrete meaning.[52] By using language rich in metaphor and storytelling, leaders can make sense of situations in ways that will be understood similarly throughout the organization.

Stories need not be long, complex, or carefully constructed. A story can be a joke, an analogy, or a verbal snapshot of something from the leader's past experience.[53] One company president believed the best way for his company to compete was to channel most of its research dollars into current products rather than aiming for cutting-edge innovation. To get everyone committed to that view, he pointed out that although the early bird gets the worm, "something that is just as true—and people don't talk about as much—is that the second mouse gets the cheese. The first mouse gets his head squished. I don't want to be the first mouse. I want to be the second. I want our company to be smart about where we put our money. Let someone else be first; second is where the money is."[54]

Perhaps the true impact of a leader depends primarily on the stories he or she tells and how followers receive them.[55] Telling stories is a powerful way to relay a message because a story evokes both visual imagery and emotion, which helps employees connect with the message and the key values. People are almost always able to apply some aspect of the story to themselves, and a story is often much more convincing and more likely to be remembered than a simple directive or a batch of facts and figures.[56]

Stories can bind people together and create a shared sense of purpose and meaning.[57] Almost everyone can learn to be an effective storyteller. Companies such as IBM, Coca-Cola, and Royal Dutch/Shell have sent managers to workshops to learn about the advantages of stories as a way to transmit cultural values and promote change.[58] Rolf Jensen, director of the Copenhagen Institute for Futures Studies, asserts that in the twenty-first century, people will place increasing importance on the "language of emotion," and that companies will thrive on the basis of

Action Memo

As a leader: Employ stories and metaphors to help people connect emotionally with your message and the key values you want to instill. Symbolize important messages through your appearance, body language, facial expressions, and daily actions.

their stories and myths. One leader who agrees is Anita Ward, vice president of Cambridge Technology Partners. An anthropologist by training, Ward uses stories to help employees cope with dramatic change. "Campfire stories," she says, "turn experience into narratives, people into heroes, and new ideas into enduring traditions."[59]

Evidence for the compatibility of stories with human thinking was demonstrated by a study at the Stanford Business School.[60] The point was to convince MBA students that a company practiced a policy of avoiding layoffs. For some students, only a story was used. For others, statistical data were provided that showed little turnover compared to competitors. For other students, statistics and stories were combined, and yet other students were shown the company's policy statement. Of all these approaches, students presented with the story alone were most convinced about the avoiding layoffs policy.

Nonverbal communication messages transmitted through action and behavior

Informal Communication

Leaders don't just communicate stories in words. They also *embody* the stories in the way that they live their lives and what they seek to inspire in others.[61] Leaders are watched, and their appearance, behavior, actions, and attitudes are symbolic to others. Even the selection of a communication channel, as described earlier, can convey a symbolic message. In other words, members of an organization attach meaning to the channel itself. Reports and memos typically convey formality and legitimize a message. Personal visits from a leader are interpreted as a sign of teamwork and caring.[62] The very modes of communication are symbolic, such as when students gauge the importance of a topic by the amount of time a professor spends talking about it, or when an individual experiences indignation at receiving a "Dear John" letter instead of having a relationship terminated in person.

Symbols are a powerful informal tool for communicating what is important. Many people don't realize that they are communicating all the time, without saying a word, by their facial expressions, body language, and actions.[63] Leaders strive to be aware of what they signal to others in addition to verbal messages. Indeed, nonverbal communication, that is, messages transmitted through action and behavior, accounts for over one half of the entire message received in a personal encounter.[64] People interpret leader actions as symbols, just as they attach meaning to words.

In interpreting a leader's nonverbal cues, followers determine the extent to which a leader's actions correspond with his or her verbal messages. If a leader talks about customer service but spends no time with customers, followers would likely place little value on service. Research suggests that if there is a discrepancy between a person's verbal and nonverbal communication, the nonverbal is granted more weight by the interpreter.[65] Consider how a plant manager symbolized the

Action Memo

As a leader: Use informal communication and *management by wandering around.* Get out and mingle with followers and clients or customers. Learn about their ideas, problems, and needs through informal observation and conversations.

importance of cost-cutting when he took over at a struggling factory. He noticed that when most of the management team had to travel, they flew first-class. Rather than issuing a directive that first-class travel was not allowed, the plant manager always flew coach. Soon, everyone throughout the company was flying coach.[66] Leaders use actions to symbolize their vision and draw attention to specific values and ideas.

Informal communication is built into an open communication climate and includes interactions that go beyond formal, authorized channels. Informal communication is important not only because it can be symbolic of leader vision, but also because it has great impact on participants. One example of informal communication is "management by wandering around (MBWA)."[67] MBWA means that leaders leave their offices and speak directly to employees as they work. These impromptu encounters send positive messages to followers. In addition, the communication is richer, and therefore likely to make a lasting impression in both directions. When E. Grady Bogue became interim chancellor at Louisiana State University, one of the first things he did was walk through the departments on campus. He wound up in the biology building, where he enjoyed an extended tour of the facility by a faculty member he ran across. Bogue remarked that he learned an enormous amount about the university operations and the strengths and weaknesses of the biology program that was "more direct, personal and meaningful than any written communication might have conveyed."[68] Thus, both leaders and followers benefit from informal channels.

Communicating in a Crisis

A leader's skill at communicating becomes even more crucial during times of rapid change and crisis. Over the past few years, the sheer number and scope of crises—everything from terrorist attacks, the space shuttle explosion, and the SARS epidemic to corporate accounting scandals, massive downsizing, and plant closings—have made communication a more demanding role for leaders. Organizations face small crises every day, such as the loss of computer data, charges of racial discrimination, a factory fire, or a flu epidemic. Moreover, incidents of intentional evil acts such as bombings and kidnappings continue to increase, with the impact on people and organizations rivaling that of major natural disasters.[69]

Communicating in a crisis has always been part of a leader's job, but the world has become so fast, interconnected, and complex that unexpected events happen more frequently and often with greater and more painful consequences. As the former governor of California put it in referring to California's 2000–2001 energy crisis, ". . . extraordinary times . . . require extraordinary leadership."[70] To be prepared, leaders can develop four skills for communicating in a crisis.[71]

1. *Stay calm; listen harder.* A leader's emotions are contagious, so leaders have to stay calm and focused. Perhaps the most important part of a leader's job in a crisis situation is to absorb people's fears and uncertainties, which means listening is more important than ever. Leaders also tailor their messages to reflect hope and optimism at the same time they acknowledge the danger and difficulties, thus giving comfort, inspiration, and hope to others. "You do not pass uncertainty down to your team members," said Eugene Kranz, the NASA flight director charged with returning the crippled *Apollo 13* spacecraft safely to earth in 1970. "No matter what is going on around you, you have to be cooler than cool."[72]

2. *Be visible.* When people's worlds have become ambiguous and uncertain, they need to feel that someone is in control. Many leaders underestimate just how important their presence is during a crisis.[73] Whether it be the crash of an American Airlines flight or charges of Third World exploitation against Nike, leaders have a tendency to want to hide, gather information, think things through, deal with their own emotions, and develop a strategy for tackling the problem. However, being a leader means stepping out immediately, both to reassure followers and respond to public concerns. Face-to-face communication with followers during difficult times is crucial for good leadership. People want to know that their leaders care about them and what they're going through.

3. *Tell the truth.* Leaders gather as much information from as many diverse sources as they can, do their best to determine the facts, and then "get the awful truth out" to employees and the public as soon as possible.[74] Rumor control is critical. Consider what happened at Duke University Hospital after doctors there made one of the worst mistakes in modern medical history—transplanting the wrong heart and lungs into 17-year-old Jesica Santillan, who later died. Although the story was already out, it took nine days for Duke leaders to fully admit the hospital's mistake. By that time, the organization's image was severely damaged, and rumors of unauthorized medical experiments and doctors pulling the plug against the family's wishes were rampant. To counteract the damage, Duke's health chief and the surgeons involved in the transplant went on CBS's *60 Minutes* to tell the whole story and offer a mournful public apology.[75]

4. *Communicate a vision for the future.* Although leaders should first deal with the physical and emotional needs of people, they also need to get back to work as soon as possible. The group, organization, or community has to keep going, and most people want to be a part of the rebuilding process, to feel that they have something to look forward to. Moments of crisis present excellent opportunities for leaders to communicate a vision for the future that taps into people's emotions and desires for something better.

Action Memo

As a leader: Stay calm and focused during times of rapid change, uncertainty, or crisis. Step forward to acknowledge people's concerns and fears. Provide accurate and up-to-date information. Help people deal with emotional and physical needs, and help them see a better tomorrow.

The following example illustrates how leaders at Agilent Technologies handled communication when the economy slumped, sales plummeted, and the company had to lay off thousands of employees.

In the Lead   Ned Barnholt, Agilent Technologies

Agilent Technologies, an $8.3 billion technology spinoff of Hewlett-Packard, has been battered not only by the slumping economy but also by the downfall of telecom giants that were once big buyers of its chips, electronic components, and testing devices. Over the past few years, Agilent has had to lay off a large percentage of its workforce. Yet, *Fortune* magazine writers interviewing dozens of former and current staff members for a story on the "100 Best Companies to Work For" could find almost no one with a bad word to say about Agilent. Part of the reason is leaders' communication strategy.

During the boom years, Agilent leaders had worked extremely hard to build a climate of trust and open communication. CEO Ned Barnholt considers Agilent the true keeper of the "HP Way," the management philosophy espoused by Hewlett-Packard's founders. The key tenet of the HP Way is that workers will give their best if they are treated honestly and listened to, which at Agilent means keeping a strict open-door policy and practicing *management by wandering around* (MBWA). The climate of trust became extremely valuable when the technology bubble burst. Barnholt held a series of meeting with top managers in early 2001, who then met with others throughout the organization. Everyone was asked to cut costs, including some salary cuts, with leaders explaining why the cuts were necessary and how employees could help save the company. People pitched in enthusiastically, but times just got worse after the September 11, 2001 terrorist attacks in the United States.

As soon as it became clear that job cuts were unavoidable, Barnholt asked his management team to find a way to eliminate people division by division, looking at each program and each employee. No across-the-board cuts would be acceptable, and Barnholt insisted that employees be told they were being laid off in person by their direct manager. The day before Agilent would publicly report its first-ever quarterly loss, Barnholt himself got on the PA system and told employees about the bad financial state of the company, thanked them for their commitment to cutting costs, and let them know that downsizing was inevitable. He wanted people to hear it from him rather than from the evening news. Next, he sent 3,000 managers to a series of daylong training sessions where they did role-plays, learned how to stay calm and focused, and learned about the wrong way and the right way to let people go. Barnholt knew it would be hard on managers to bear the brunt of employee pain, but he insisted they be as honest as possible, keep their doors even more open than usual, and field every question or challenge sent their way.[76]

When they realized their company was in trouble, Agilent's leaders didn't hide in their offices and send out pink slips. They emphasized face-to-face communication and keeping employees up to date on the company's problems. By being visible and honest, listening to employees, and helping people focus on the hope for a better future, leaders made the downsizing process smoother and less traumatic for everyone. Many employees—even those who knew they would soon be out of a job—worked longer, harder, and with a greater intensity than before. They felt a genuine commitment to the company and a belief that things could be better in the future. "We were brutally honest with them about what we're doing—what drove the decision, what the timing is, what's going to happen," explains Agilent's Dave Allen. "That honesty and integrity up front is critical. If you don't have it, you lose their hearts and minds. . . ."[77]

Summary and Interpretation

Effective communication is an essential element of leadership. Leaders are communication champions who inspire and unite people around a common sense of purpose and identity. They lead strategic conversations that get people talking across boundaries about the vision, key strategic themes, and the values that can help the group or organization achieve desired outcomes. Four elements necessary for strategic conversations are an open communication climate, active listening, discernment, and dialogue. Open communication is essential for building trust, and it paves the way for more opportunities to communicate with followers, thus enabling the organization to gain the benefits of all employees' minds. However, leaders must be active listeners and must learn to discern the hidden undercurrents that have yet to emerge. It is through listening and discernment, both with followers and customers, that leaders identify strategic issues and build productive relationships that help the organization succeed. When active listening spreads throughout a group, a type of communication referred to as dialogue occurs. Through dialogue, people discover common ground and together create a shared meaning that enables them to understand each other and share a view of the world.

Leader communication is purpose-directed, and an important element is persuading others to act in ways that achieve goals and accomplish the vision. Four steps for practicing the art of persuasion are to establish credibility, build goals on common ground, make your position compelling, and connect with others on an emotional level. Leaders use rich communication channels, communicate through stories and metaphors, and rely on informal as well as formal communication. Electronic communication channels present new challenges for leader communication. Electronic channels can be very advantageous if used appropriately, but their use increases the potential for communication errors, and these channels are not effective for complex or sensitive messages. The final point emphasized in this chapter is that effective communication becomes even more crucial during times of rapid change and crisis. Four critical skills for communicating in a crises are to remain calm, be visible, "get the awful truth out," and communicate a vision for the future.

 Discussion Questions

1. How do you think leadership communication differs from conventional management communication?

2. If you were to evaluate an organization based on the degree of open communication climate, what things would you look for? Discuss.

3. A manager in a communication class remarked, "Listening seems like minimal intrusion of oneself into the conversation, yet it also seems like more work." Do you agree or disagree? Discuss.

4. How does dialogue differ from discussion? Give an example of each from your experience.

5. Some senior executives believe they should rely on written information and computer reports because these yield more accurate data than face-to-face communications do. Do you agree? Discuss.

6. Why is *management by wandering around* considered effective communication?

7. If you were to communicate symbolically with your team to create a sense of trust and team work, what would you do?

8. How do leaders use communication to influence and persuade others? Think of someone you have known who is skilled in the art of persuasion. What makes this person an effective communicator?

9. Why is storytelling such a powerful means of communication for a leader? Can you give examples from your own experience of leaders who have used metaphor and story? What was the effect on followers?

Leadership at Work

Listen Like a Professional

The fastest way to become a great listener is to act like a professional listener, such as a clinical psychologist who uses listening to heal another person. Therapists drop their own point of view to concentrate on the patient's point of view. The therapist listens totally, drawing out more information rather than thinking about a response.

The next time you are in a conversation in which the other person talks about some problem or concern, practice professional listening by doing the following: (1) Hold a steady gaze on the person's left eye (not the nose or face, but the left eye)—use a soft gaze, not a hard stare. (2) Remove your thoughts and opinions from the conversation—quell your mind chatter and your desire to say something in response. (3) Suspend judgment—rather than critically analyzing what is being said, feel empathy as if you are walking in the other person's shoes. (4) Draw out the other person's thoughts with brief questions and paraphrasing. Repeat the professional listening approach at least three times with different people to get comfortable with it.

List your thoughts on how the other people responded to your listening, and what it felt like to you.

Other person responded:

1. _____
_____
_____

2. _____
_____
_____

3. _____
_____
_____

What I felt:

1. _____

_____

_____

2. _____

_____

_____

3. _____

_____

_____

In Class: The instructor can divide students into pairs—listener and speaker—in class to practice this exercise. The "speaking" students can be asked to talk about some small problem or annoyance they encountered in the previous day or two. The "listening" students can be given instructions to not speak during the first trial, and instead just maintain a soft gaze into the speaker's left eye and respond only with body language (facial expressions and nods). The speaking student should continue until they have no more to say or until they feel an emotional shift and the problem seems to have disappeared. After students switch roles and play both speaker and listener, the instructor can ask the class for perceptions of what happened and what they were feeling during the conversation.

It works well to have the students choose a second pairing, and re-do the exercise with a new problem. The only difference the second time is that the "listener" role is given fewer restrictions, so the listener can make brief comments such as to paraphrase or ask a short question. The listeners, however, should keep spoken comments to a minimum and definitely should not offer their own ideas or point of view. After the students finish, the instructor can gather opinions about what the experience was like for both the speaker and the listener. Key questions include the following: What did it feel like to listen rather than respond verbally to what another person said? What is the value of this professional listening approach? In what situations is professional listening likely to be more or less effective? If the instructor desires, the exercise can be done a third time to help students get more comfortable with a true listening role.

SOURCE: Adapted from Michael Ray and Rochelle Myers, *Creativity in Business* (Broadway Books, 2000), 82–83.

Leadership Development: Cases for Analysis

The Superintendent's Directive

Educational administrators are bombarded by possible innovations at all educational levels. Programs to upgrade math, science, and social science education, state accountability plans, new approaches to administration, and other ideas are initiated by teachers, administrators, interest groups, reformers, and state regulators. In a school district, the superintendent is the key leader; in an individual school, the principal is the key leader.

In the Carville City School District, Superintendent Porter has responsibility for 11 schools—eight elementary, two junior high, and one high school. After attending a management summer course, Porter sent an e-mail directive to principals stating that every teacher in their building was required to develop a set of performance objectives for each class they taught. These objectives were to be submitted one month after the school opened, and copies were to be forwarded to the superintendent's office. Porter also wrote that he had hired the consultant who taught the summer management course to help teachers write objectives during their annual opening in-service day of orientation work.

Mr. Weigand, Principal of Earsworth Elementary School, sent his teachers the following memo: "Friends, Superintendent Porter has asked me to inform you that written performance objectives for your courses must be handed in one month from today. This afternoon at the in-service meeting, you will receive instruction in composing these objectives."

In response, one teacher sent a note asking, "Is anything wrong with our teaching? Is this the reason we have to spend hours writing objectives?"

Another teacher saw Weigand in the hall and said, "I don't see how all this objectives business will improve my classroom. It sounds like an empty exercise. In fact, because of the time it will take me to write objectives, it may hurt my teaching. I should be reading on new developments and working on lesson plans."

In response to these and other inquiries, Principal Weigand announced to the teachers with a follow-up memo, "I was told to inform all of you to write performance objectives. If you want to talk about it, contact Dr. Porter."

SOURCE: Based on Robert C. Mills, Alan F. Quick, and Michael P. Wolfe, *Critical Incidents in School Administration* (Midland, MI: Pendell Publishing Co., 1976).

Questions

1. Evaluate the communications of Porter and Weigand. To what extent do they communicate as leaders? Explain.
2. How would you have handled this if you were Superintendent Porter?
3. How would you have handled the communication if you were the principal of Earsworth Elementary School? Why?

Imperial Metal Products

Imperial Metal Products, a mid-sized manufacturing company located in the Southeast, makes wheel rims for automobiles. With 42 furnaces on the production floor, the temperature often reaches well over 100 degrees Fahrenheit. Even employees who work in the lab complain of the heat because they have to venture onto the production floor numerous times a day to take metal samples from the furnaces.

A year ago, the top executive team recommended to the Board that the employee lounge, located at the far end of the production floor near the plant manager's office, be air-conditioned. Company profits had been good, and the managers wanted to do something to show appreciation for employees' good work. The Board enthusiastically approved the proposal and the work was completed within a month.

At the end of the fiscal year, the top management team met to review the company's operations for the past year. Profits were higher than ever, and productivity for the past year had been excellent. The team unanimously agreed that the employees deserved additional recognition for their work, and they considered ways to show management's appreciation. Robb Vaughn suggested that it might be interesting to see what workers thought about the action managers took last year to have the lounge air-conditioned. Everyone agreed, and the human resources director, Amy Simpkins, was instructed to send a questionnaire to a sample of employees to get their reaction to the air-conditioned lounge. The team agreed to meet in six weeks and review the results.

Simpkins mailed a simple form to 100 randomly selected employees with the following request: "Please state your feelings about the recently air-conditioned employee lounge." The response rate was excellent, with 96 forms being returned. Simpkins classified the responses into the following categories and presented her report to the top management team:

1. I thought only managers could use the lounge.   25
2. I didn't know it was air-conditioned.   21

3. If management can spend that kind of money, they
   should pay us more.   21
4. The whole plant should be air-conditioned.   10
5. I never use the lounge anyway.   8
6. OK   8
7. Miscellaneous comments   3

Top managers were shocked by the responses. They had expected a majority of the employees to be grateful for the air conditioning. One of the
managers suggested that it was useless to do anything else for employees,
since it wouldn't be appreciated anyway. Another argued, however, that
top managers just needed to communicate better with plant workers. She
suggested posting flyers on the bulletin boards announcing that the
lounge was now air-conditioned, and perhaps putting a memo in with
employees' next paycheck. "They slave away eight or nine hours a day in
that heat; at least we need to let them know they have a cool place to
take a break or eat lunch!" she pointed out. "And if we plan to do
another 'employee appreciation' project this year, maybe we should send
out another questionnaire and ask people what they want."

SOURCE: Based on "The Air Conditioned Cafeteria," in John M. Champion and John H. James, *Critical
Incidents in Management: Decision and Policy Issues*, 6th ed. (Homewood, IL: Irwin, 1989), 280–281.

Questions
1. How would you rate the communication climate at Imperial Metal
   Products?
2. What channels do you think top managers should use to improve
   communications and both keep employees informed as well as
   learn about what they are thinking?
3. If you were a top manager at Imperial, what is the first step you
   would take? Why?

References

1. Howard Gardner, *Leading Minds: An Anatomy of Leadership* (New York: Basic
   Books, 1995), 204–208.
2. Cynthia Crossen, "Blah, Blah, Blah," *The Wall Street Journal*, July 10, 1997;
   Paul Roberts, "Live! From Your Office! It's . . . " *Fast Company*, (October
   1999): 151–170; and Cathy Olofson, "Can We Talk? Put Another Log on the
   Fire," *Fast Company*, (October 1999): 86.
3. Eric Berkman, "Skills," *CIO*, (March 1, 2002): 78–82; Peter Lowry and Byron
   Reimus, "Ready, Aim, Communicate," *Management Review* (July 1996).

4. Bernard M. Bass, *Bass & Stogdill's Handbook of Leadership*, 3rd ed. (New York: The Free Press, 1990).

5. Henry Mintzberg, *The Nature of Managerial Work* (New York: Harper & Row, 1973).

6. Mary Young and James E. Post, "Managing to Communicate, Communicating to Manage: How Leading Companies Communicate with Employees," *Organizational Dynamics* (Summer 1993): 31–43; and Warren Bennis and Burt Nanus, *Leaders: The Strategies for Taking Charge* (New York: Harper & Row, 1985).

7. Colin Mitchell, "Selling the Brand Inside," *Harvard Business Review* (January 2002): 99–105.

8. Phillip G. Clampitt, Laurey Berk, and M. Lee Williams, "Leaders as Strategic Communicators," *Ivey Business Journal* (May–June 2002): 51–55.

9. Ian Wylie, "Can Philips Learn to Walk the Talk?" *Fast Company* (January 2003): 44–45.

10. John Luthy, "New Keys to Employee Performance and Productivity," *Public Management* (March 1998): 4–8.

11. Mirta M. Martin, "Trust Leadership," *The Journal of Leadership Studies* 5, no. 3 (1998): 41–49.

12. "What Is Trust," results of a survey by Manchester Consulting, reported in Jenny C. McCune, "That Elusive Thing Called Trust," *Management Review* (July–August 1998): 10–16.

13. Julie Carrick Dalton, "Between the Lines: The Hard Truth About Open-Book Management," *CFO* (March 1999): 58–64.

14. Gary Hamel, "Killer Strategies That Make Shareholders Rich," *Fortune* (June 23, 1997): 70–84.

15. Ginger L. Graham, "If You Want Honesty, Break Some Rules," *Harvard Business Review* (April 2002): 42–47.

16. C. Glenn Pearce, "Doing Something About Your Listening Ability," *Supervisory Management* (March 1989): 29–34; and Tom Peters, "Learning to Listen," *Hyatt Magazine* (Spring 1988): 16–21.

17. Gerald M. Goldhaber, *Organizational Communication*, 4th ed. (Dubuque, IA: Wm. C. Brown, 1980), 189.

18. Tom Peters, "Learning to Listen."

19. David H. Freedman, "Intensive Care," *Inc.* (February 1999): 72–80.

20. Curtis Sittenfeld, "Good Ways to Deliver Bad News," *Fast Company* (April 1999): 58, 60.

21. Dorothy Leonard, "The Limitations of Listening," box in Anthony W. Ulwick, "Turn Customer Input Into Innovation," *Harvard Business Review* (January 2002): 91–97.

22. Joseph Jaworski, *Synchronicity: the Inner Path of Leadership* (San Francisco, CA.: Berrett-Koehler, 1996).

23. David Bohm, *On Dialogue* (Ojai, CA: David Bohm Seminars, 1989).

24. Bill Isaacs, *Dialogue and the Art of Thinking Together* (New York: Doubleday, 1999); and "The Art of Dialogue," column in Roberts, "Live! From Your Office!"

25. Based on Glenna Gerard and Linda Teurfs, "Dialogue and Organizational Transformation," in *Community Building: Renewing Spirit and Learning in Business*, Kazimierz Gozdz, ed. (New Leaders Press, 1995).

26. Scott Kirsner, "Want to Grow? Hire a Shrink!" *Fast Company* (December–January 1998): 68, 70.

27. This section is based heavily on Jay A. Conger, "The Necessary Art of Persuasion," *Harvard Business Review* (May–June 1998): 84–95.

28. J. C. McCroskey and V. P. Richmond, "The Impact of Communication Apprehension on Individuals in Organizations, *Communication Quarterly*, 27 (1979): 55–61.

29. J. C. McCroskey, "The Communication Apprehension Perspective," in J. C. McCroskey & J. A. Daly, eds. *Avoiding Communication: Shyness, Reticence, and Communication Apprehension* (London: Sage Publications Inc., 1984): 13–38.

30. Robert H. Lengel and Richard L. Daft, "The Selection of Communication Media as an Executive Skill," *Academy of Management Executive* 2 (August 1988), 225–232; and Richard L. Daft and Robert Lengel, "Organizational Information Requirements, Media Richness and Structural Design," *Managerial Science* 32 (May 1986): 554–572.

31. Ford S. Worthy, "How CEOs Manage Their Time," *Fortune* (January 18, 1988): 88–97.

32. "E-mail Can't Mimic Phone Calls," *Johnson City Press* (September 17, 2000): 31.

33. John R. Carlson and Robert W. Zmud, "Channel Expansion Theory and the Experiential Nature of Media Richness Perceptions, *Academy of Management Journal* 42, no. 2 (1999), 153–170; R. Rice and G. Love, "Electronic Emotion," *Communication Research* 14 (1987), 85–108.

34. Anne Fisher, "Readers Weigh in on Rudeness and Speechmaking" (Ask Annie column), *Fortune* (January 10, 2000): 194.

35. "Enforcing a No-Memo Policy," *Small Business Report* (July 1988): 26–27.

36. Ronald E. Rice, "Task Analyzability, Use of New Media, and Effectiveness: A Multi-Site Exploration of Media Richness," *Organizational Science* 3, no. 4 (November 1994): 502–527.

37. Richard L. Daft, Robert H. Lengel, and Linda Klebe Treviño, "Message Equivocality, Media Selection and Manager Performance: Implications for Information Systems," *MIS Quarterly* 11 (1987): 355–368.

38. Young and Post, "Managing to Communicate, Communicating to Manage."
39. Greg Jaffe, "Tug of War: In the New Military, Technology May Alter Chain of Command," *The Wall Street Journal* (March 30, 2001), A3, A6; Susanna Patton, "The Wisdom of Starting Small," *CIO* (March 15, 2001): 80–86.
40. Scott Kirsner, "IM Is Here. RU Prepared?" *Darwin Magazine* (February 2002): 22–24.
41. Daniel Nasaw, "Instant Messages Are Popping Up All Over," *The Wall Street Journal* (June 12, 2003): B4.
42. Kirsner, "IM Is Here."
43. Edward M. Hallowell, "The Human Moment at Work" *Harvard Business Review* (January–February 1999): 58–66; Andrea C. Poe, "Don't Touch That 'Send' Button!" *HR Magazine* (July 2003): 74–80.
44. Hallowell,"The Human Moment at Work."
45. Hallowell, "The Human Moment at Work"; Deborah L. Duarte and Nancy Tennant Snyder, *Mastering Virtual Teams: Strategies, Tools, and Techniques That Succeed* (San Francisco: Jossey-Bass, 2000).
46. Hallowell, "The Human Moment."
47. Carlson and Zmud, "Channel Expansion Theory and the Experiential Nature of Media Richness Perceptions."
48. Jared Sandberg, "Workplace E-Mail Can Turn Radioactive in Clumsy Hands," *The Wall Street Journal* (February 12, 2003): B1.
49. David M. Boje, "Learning Storytelling: Storytelling to Learn Management Skills," *Journal of Management Education* 15, no. 3 (August 1991): 279–294.
50. John Guaspari, "A Shining Example," *Across the Board* (May–June 2002): 67–68.
51. Cynthia G. Emrich, Holly H. Brower, Jack M. Feldman, and Howard Garland, "Images in Words: Presidential Rhetoric, Charisma, and Greatness," *Administrative Science Quarterly* 46 (2001): 527–557.
52. Linda Smircich and Gareth Morgan, "Leadership: The Management of Meaning," *Journal of Applied Behavioral Science* 18 (November 3, 1982): 257–273.
53. Bill Birchard, "Once Upon a Time," *Strategy & Business*, Issue 27 (Second Quarter 2002): 99–104.
54. Ibid.
55. Gardner, *Leading Minds*.
56. Robert F. Dennehy, "The Executive as Storyteller," *Management Review* (March 1999): 40–43.
57. Beverly Kaye and Betsy Jacobson, "True Tales and Tall Tales: The Power of Organizational Storytelling," *Training and Development* (March 1999), 45–50.

58. Dennehy, "The Executive as Storyteller;" and Elizabeth Weil, "Every Leader Tells a Story," *Fast Company* (June–July 1998): 38–39.

59. Cathy Olofson, "To Transform Culture, Tap Emotion," *Fast Company* (April 1999): 54.

60. J. Martin and M. Powers, "Organizational Stories: More Vivid and Persuasive than Quantitative Data," in B. M. Staw, ed., *Psychological Foundations of Organizational Behavior* (Glenview, IL: Scott Foresman, 1982), 161–168.

61. Gardner, *Leading Minds.*

62. Jane Webster and Linda Klebe Treviño, "Rational and Social Theories as Complementary Explanations of Communication Media Choices: Two Policy Capturing Studies," *Academy of Management Journal* (December 1995): 1544–1572.

63. Mac Fulfer, "Nonverbal Communication: How To Read What's Plain As the Nose . . . or Eyelid . . . or Chin . . . On Their Faces," *Journal of Organizational Excellence* (Spring, 2001): 19–27.

64. Albert Mehrabian, *Silent Messages* (Belmont, CA: Wadsworth, 1971); and Albert Mehrabian, "Communicating Without Words," *Psychology Today* (September 1968): 53–55.

65. I. Thomas Sheppard, "Silent Signals," *Supervisory Management* (March 1986): 31–33.

66. Linda Klebe Treviño, Laura Pincus Hartman, and Michael Brown, "Moral Person and Moral Manager: How Executives Develop a Reputation for Ethical Leadership," *California Management Review* 42, no. 4 (Summer 2000): 128–142.

67. Thomas H. Peters and Robert J. Waterman, Jr., *In Search of Excellence* (New York: Harper & Row, 1982); and Tom Peters and Nancy Austin, *A Passion for Excellence: The Leadership Difference* (New York: Random House, 1985).

68. Grady Bogue, *Leadership by Design: Strengthening Integrity in Higher Education* (San Francisco, CA: Jossey-Bass, Inc., 1994), 81.

69. Ian I. Mitroff and Murat C. Alpaslan, "Preparing for Evil," *Harvard Business Review* (April 2003): 109–115.

70. Quoted in James Sterngold, "Power Crisis Abates, But It Hounds Gov. Davis," *The New York Times* (October 5, 2001): A16.

71. This section is based on Leslie Wayne and Leslie Kaufman, "Leadership, Put to a New Test," *The New York Times* (September 16, 2001): Section 3, 1, 4; Jerry Useem, "What It Takes," *Fortune* (November 12, 2001): 126–132; Andy Bowen, "Crisis Procedures That Stand the Test of Time," *Public Relations Tactics* (August 2001): 16; and Matthew Boyle, "Nothing Really Matters," *Fortune* (October 15, 2001): 261–264.

72. Useem, "What It Takes."

73. Stephen Bernhut, "Leadership, with Michael Useem," (Leader's Edge interview), *Ivey Business Journal* (January–February 2002): 42–43.

74. Ian I. Mitroff, "Crisis Leadership," *Executive Excellence* (August 2001), 19.

75. Allison Fass, "Duking It Out," *Forbes* (June 9, 2003): 74–76.

76. Robert Levering and Milton Moskowitz, "The 100 Best Companies to Work For: The Best in the Worst of Times," *Fortune* (February 4, 2002): 60–68.

77. Ibid.

Chapter

Your Leadership Challenge

After reading this chapter, you should be able to:

- Turn a group of individuals into a collaborative team that achieves high performance through shared mission and collective responsibility.

- Develop and apply the personal qualities of effective team leadership for traditional, virtual, and global teams.

- Understand and handle the stages of team development, and design an effective team in terms of size, diversity, and levels of interdependence.

- Handle conflicts that inevitably arise among members of a team.

Leading Teams

The battle lines were drawn: On one side, the Los Angeles Lakers, looking for their first National Basketball Association championship since 1988; on the other, the Indiana Pacers, playing in the finals for the first time in the team's history. In the end, the Lakers prevailed, clinching the title in Game 6. But almost everyone recognized that both teams played with a spirit and heart that made them winners. Both teams struggled for years to reach this point, and they made it largely because, as one half-time commentator put it, "These players believe in their coaches."

The coach of the winning Lakers, Phil Jackson, had previously led the Chicago Bulls to six NBA championships, but many critics dismissed his coaching ability. Anyone could win, they said, with basketball's greatest player, Michael Jordan, on the team. Now people were taking a second look as Jackson smoothly guided the Lakers to their first NBA championship in 12 years. Jackson bases his leadership approach on Native American and Eastern spiritual principles, stressing awareness, compassion, and the importance of selfless team play to achieve victory. His greatest strength is an ability to get wealthy, pampered, and sometimes conceited young players to pull together mentally and spiritually to achieve a common goal.

The coach on the other side of the court, Larry Bird (now president of basketball operations for the Pacers), showed the same passionate team leadership in his final coaching season as he had shown in his first, when he took a struggling group of players and turned them into one of the NBA's finest teams. The Pacers might have lost the championship, but they never lost their team spirit. Bird instilled players with a vision of being the best, established clear goals and standards of performance, worked players hard on the practice court, and then let them do their jobs rather than micromanaging from the sidelines. "My whole thing is preparedness," Bird says. "But I feel that once the game starts, let the players play the game."

Both Jackson and Bird expected each player to bring his own sense of commitment and personal responsibility to the game. In addition, both insisted on open and honest communication as the only way everyone could come together around a shared purpose. By focusing on the spirit of teamwork, the coaches cultivated the leadership abilities of everyone on the team. Phil Jackson and Larry Bird offer lessons in leadership not only in the world of pro basketball but also in today's high-pressure, team-based workplace.[1]

Coaching a pro basketball team might seem very different from leading a group of people in an organization, but both require similar leadership skills and qualities. Particularly in today's changing organizations, the ability to inspire and support teamwork is critical to effective leadership. From the classroom to the battlefield, from the assembly line to the executive suite, and from giant corporations such as Cisco and Boeing to small companies like plantscaping firm Growing Green and nonprofit organizations like Parkland Memorial Hospital, teams are becoming the basic building block of organizations.

The use of teams has increased dramatically in response to new competitive pressures, the need for greater flexibility and speed, and a desire to give people more opportunities for involvement and decision making. Many organizations have reported great success with teams, including increased productivity, quality improvements, greater innovation, and higher employee satisfaction. At Xerox, for example, production plants using teams reported a 30 percent increase in productivity. Federal Express cut service problems such as incorrect bills or lost packages by 13 percent by using teams.[2] A recent study of team-based organizations in Australia supports the idea that teams provide benefits for both organizations and employees through higher labor productivity, a flatter management structure, and lower employee turnover.[3]

However, teams present greater leadership challenges than does the traditional hierarchical organization. Every team member has to develop some leadership capability. This chapter explores team leadership in today's organizations. We will define various types of teams, look at how teams develop, and examine characteristics such as size, interdependence, and diversity that can influence team effectiveness. The chapter will then explore topics such as cohesiveness and performance, task and socioemotional roles of team members, and the leader's personal impact on building effective teams. The new challenge of leading virtual and global teams will also be discussed. The final part of the chapter will look at how leaders manage team conflict.

Teams in Organizations

The concept of teamwork is a fundamental change in the way work is organized. More and more companies are recognizing that the best way to meet the challenges of higher quality, faster service, and total customer satisfaction is through an aligned, coordinated, and committed effort by all employees.[4] At the Frito-Lay plant in Lubbock, Texas, team members handle everything from potato processing to equipment maintenance. Each team has authority to select new hires, determine crew scheduling, and discipline team members who are not pulling their load. The four owners of Crescent Manufacturing in Fremont, Ohio, run their company as a team, switching jobs among themselves as the company's needs change. At Massachusetts

General Hospital, the emergency trauma team performs so smoothly that the team switches leaders seamlessly, depending on the crisis at hand. With each new emergency, direction may come from a doctor, intern, nurse, or technician—whoever is particularly experienced with the problem.[5]

Yet, teams are not right for every organizational situation. Some tasks by their very nature, such as creative writing, are better performed by individuals. In addition, organizations frequently fail to realize the benefits of teams because they have a hard time balancing authority between leaders and teams, fail to provide adequate training or support for teamwork, or continue to manage people as a collection of individuals rather than on a team level.[6] Effective teams have leaders who consciously build a team identity, actively involve all members, act as coaches and facilitators rather than managers, and invest time and resources for team learning.[7]

What Is a Team?

A team is a unit of two or more people who interact and coordinate their work to accomplish a shared goal or purpose.[8] This definition has three components. First, teams are made up of two or more people. Teams can be large, but most have fewer than 15 people. Second, people in a team work together regularly. People who do not interact regularly, such as those waiting in line at the company cafeteria or riding together in the elevator, do not comprise a team. Third, people in a team share a goal, whether it be to build a car, place mentally challenged clients in job training, or write a textbook. Today's students are frequently assigned to complete assignments in teams. In this case, the shared goal is to complete the task and receive an acceptable grade. However, in many cases, student teams are provided with a great deal of structure in terms of team roles and responsibilities, time frame, activities, and so forth. In a work setting, these elements are often much more ambiguous and have to be worked out within the team.

A team is a group of people, but the two are not equal. A professor, coach, or employer can put together a *group* of people and never build a *team*. The sports world is full of stories of underdog teams that have won championships against a group of players who were better individually but did not make up a better team.[9] Only when people sublimate their individual needs and desires and synthesize their knowledge, skills, and efforts toward accomplishment of a communal goal do they become a team. This chapter's Living Leadership illustrates the spirit and power of teamwork.

The team concept implies a sense of shared mission and collective responsibility. Exhibit 10.1 lists the primary differences between groups and teams. A team achieves high levels of performance through shared leadership, purpose, and responsibility by all members working toward a common goal. Teams are characterized by equality; in the best teams, there are no individual "stars" and everyone sublimates individual ego to the good of the whole.

Team

a unit of two or more people who interact and coordinate their work to accomplish a shared goal or purpose

LIVING LEADERSHIP

Lessons from Geese

Fact 1: As each goose flaps its wings, it creates an "uplift" for the birds that follow. By flying in a "V" formation, the whole flock adds 71 percent greater flying range than if each bird flew alone.

Lesson: People who share a common direction and sense of community can get where they are going quicker and easier because they are traveling on the thrust of one another.

Fact 2: When a goose falls out of formation, it suddenly feels the drag and resistance of flying alone. It quickly moves back into formation to take advantage of the lifting power of the bird immediately in front of it.

Lesson: If we have as much sense as a goose, we stay in formation with those headed where we want to go. We are willing to accept their help and give our help to others.

Fact 3: When the lead goose tires, it rotates back into the formation and another goose flies to the point position.

Lesson: It pays to take turns doing the hard tasks and sharing leadership. Like geese, people are interdependent on each other's

skills, capabilities, and unique arrangements of gifts, talents, or resources.

Fact 4: The geese flying in formation honk to encourage those up front to keep up their speed.

Lesson: We need to make sure our honking is encouraging. In groups where there is encouragement, the production is much greater. The power of encouragement (to stand by one's heart or core values and encourage the heart and core of others) is the quality of honking we seek.

Fact 5: When a goose gets sick, wounded, or shot down, two geese drop out of the formation and follow it down to help and protect it. They stay until it dies or is able to fly again. Then, they launch out with another formation or catch up with the flock.

Lesson: If we have as much sense as geese, we will stand by each other in difficult times as well as when we are strong.

SOURCE: 1991 Organizational Development Network. Original author unknown

---

Action Memo

Action Memo

As a leader: Guide your team through its stages of development. Help members know one another during the *forming stage*. Encourage participation and lead members to find a common purpose and values during the *storming stage*. Focus on clarifying goals and expectations during the *norming stage*. Concentrate on helping the team achieve high performance during the *performing stage*.

All organizations are made up of groups of people who work together to accomplish specific goals. Not all organizations use teams as they are defined in Exhibit 10.1, but many of the leadership ideas presented in this chapter can also be applied in leading other types of groups.

How Teams Develop

Smoothly functioning teams don't just happen. They are built by leaders who take specific actions to help people come together as a team. One important point is for leaders to understand that teams go through distinct stages of team development.[10]

Exhibit 10.1 Differences Between Groups and Teams

Group	Team
Has a designated, strong leader	Shares or rotates leadership roles
Individual accountability	Mutual and individual accountability (accountable to each other)
Identical purpose for group and organization	Specific team vision or purpose
Performance goals set by others	Performance goals set by team
Works within organizational boundaries	Not inhibited by organizational boundaries
Individual work products	Collective work products
Organized meetings, delegation	Mutual feedback, open-ended discussion, active problem-solving

SOURCES: Based on Jon R. Katzenbach and Douglas K. Smith, "The Discipline of Teams," *Harvard Business Review* (March–April 1995), 111–120; and Milan Moravec, Odd Jan Johannessen, and Thor A. Hjelmas, "Thumbs Up for Self-Managed Teams," *Management Review* (July–August 1997), 42–47 (chart on 46).

New teams are different from mature teams. If you have participated in teams to do class assignments, you probably noticed that the team changed over time. In the beginning, members have to get to know one another, establish some order, divide responsibilities, and clarify tasks. These activities help members become part of a smoothly functioning team. The challenge for leaders is to recognize the stages of development and help teams move through them successfully.

Research suggests that teams develop over several stages. One model describing these stages is shown in Exhibit 10.2. These four stages typically occur in sequence, although there can be overlap. Each stage presents team members and leaders with unique problems and challenges.

Forming The forming stage of development is a period of orientation and getting acquainted. Team members find out what behavior is acceptable to others, explore friendship possibilities, and determine task orientation. Uncertainty is high because no one knows what the ground rules are or what is expected of them. Members will usually accept whatever power or authority is offered by either formal or informal leaders. The leader's challenge at this stage of development is to facilitate communication and interaction among team members to help them get acquainted and establish guidelines for how the team will work together. It is important at this stage that the leader try to make everyone feel comfortable and like a part of the team. Leaders can draw out shy or quiet team members to help them establish relationships with others.

Forming

stage of team development that includes orientation and getting acquainted

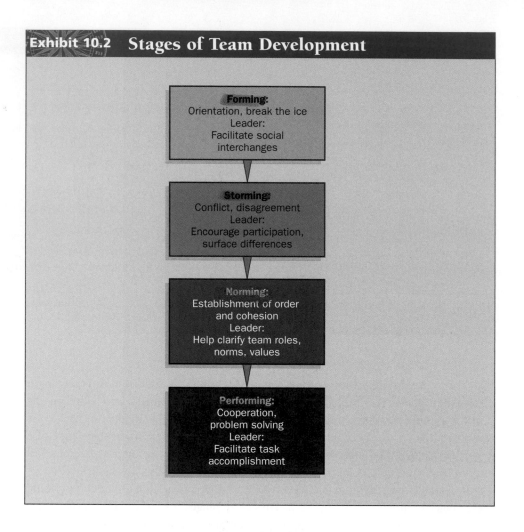

Exhibit 10.2   Stages of Team Development

Forming:
Orientation, break the ice
Leader:
Facilitate social
interchanges

Storming:
Conflict, disagreement
Leader:
Encourage participation,
surface differences

Norming:
Establishment of order
and cohesion
Leader:
Help clarify team roles,
norms, values

Performing:
Cooperation,
problem solving
Leader:
Facilitate task
accomplishment

Storming

stage of team development in which individual personalities and conflicts emerge

Storming During the storming stage, individual personalities emerge more clearly. People become more assertive in clarifying their roles. This stage is marked by conflict and disagreement. Team members may disagree over their perceptions of the team's mission or goals. They may jockey for position or form subgroups based on common interests. The team is characterized by a general lack of unity and cohesiveness. It is essential that teams move beyond this stage or they will never achieve high performance. The leader's role is to encourage participation by each team member and help them find their common vision and values. Members need to debate ideas, surface conflicts, disagree with one another, and work through the uncertainties and conflicting perceptions about team tasks and goals.

Norming At the norming stage, conflict has been resolved and team unity and harmony emerge. Consensus develops as to who the natural team leaders are, and members' roles are clear. Team members come to understand and accept one another. Differences are resolved and members develop a sense of cohesiveness. This stage typically is of short duration and moves quickly into the next stage. The team leader should emphasize openness within the team and continue to facilitate communication and clarify team roles, values, and expectations.

Performing During the performing stage, the major emphasis is on accomplishing the team's goals. Members are committed to the team's mission. They interact frequently, coordinate their actions, and handle disagreements in a mature, productive manner. Team members confront and resolve problems in the interest of task accomplishment. At this stage, the team leader should concentrate on facilitating high task performance and helping the team self-manage to reach its goals.

Leaders at McDevitt Street Bovis, one of the country's largest construction management firms, strive to accelerate the stages of team development to help put teams on a solid foundation.

Norming stage of team development in which conflicts have been resolved and team unity emerges

Performing stage of team development in which the major emphasis is on accomplishing the team's goals

In the Lead   McDevitt Street Bovis

McDevitt Street Bovis credits its team-building process for quickly and effectively unifying teams, circumventing damaging and time-consuming conflicts, and preventing lawsuits related to major construction projects. The goal is to take the team to the performing stage as quickly as possible by giving everyone an opportunity to get to know one another, explore the ground rules, and clarify roles, responsibilities and expectations.

Rather than the typical construction project characterized by conflicts, frantic scheduling, and poor communications, Bovis wants its collection of contractors, designers, suppliers, and other partners to function like a true team—putting the success of the project ahead of their own individual interests. The team is first divided into separate groups that may have competing objectives—such as the clients in one group, suppliers in another, engineers and architects in a third, and so forth—and asked to come up with a list of their goals for the project. Although interests sometimes vary widely in purely accounting terms, there are almost always common themes. By talking about conflicting goals and interests, as well as what all the groups share, facilitators help the team gradually come together around a common purpose and begin to develop shared values that will guide the project. After jointly writing a mission statement for the team, each party says what it expects from the others, so that roles and responsibilities can be clarified. The intensive team-building session helps take members quickly through the forming and storming stages of development, but meetings continue all the way through the project to keep relationships strong and to keep people on target toward achieving the team mission. "We prevent conflicts from happening," says facilitator Monica Bennett. Leaders at McDevitt Street Bovis believe building better teams builds better buildings.[11]

Team Types and Characteristics

In the following sections, we will look at various types of teams that have traditionally been used in organizations and examine some characteristics that are important to team dynamics and performance. Later in the chapter, we will discuss the new challenge of leading virtual and global teams.

Traditional Types of Teams

There are three fundamental types of teams used in today's organizations: functional teams, cross-functional teams, and self-directed teams. The types of teams are illustrated in Exhibit 10.3.

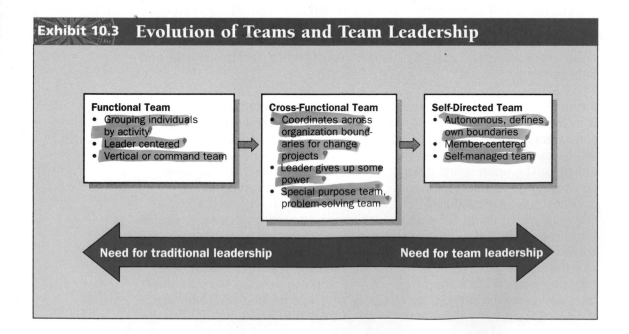

Exhibit 10.3   Evolution of Teams and Team Leadership

Functional Team
- Grouping individuals by activity
- Leader centered
- Vertical or command team

Cross-Functional Team
- Coordinates across organization boundaries for change projects
- Leader gives up some power
- Special purpose team, problem-solving team

Self-Directed Team
- Autonomous, defines own boundaries
- Member-centered
- Self-managed team

Need for traditional leadership ⟷ Need for team leadership

Functional Teams A functional team is part of the traditional vertical hierarchy. This type of team is made up of a supervisor and his or her subordinates in the formal chain of command. Sometimes called a *vertical team* or a *command team*, the functional team can include three or four levels of hierarchy within a department. Typically, a functional team makes up a single department in the organization. For example, the quality control department at Blue Bell Creameries in Brenham, Texas, is a functional team that tests all incoming ingredients to make sure only the best products go into the company's ice cream. A financial analysis department, a human resources department, and a sales department are all functional or vertical teams. Each is created by the organization within the vertical hierarchy to attain specific goals through members' joint activities.

Cross-Functional Teams As the name implies, cross-functional teams are made up of members from different functional departments within the organization. Employees are generally from about the same hierarchical level in the organization, although cross-functional teams sometimes cross vertical as well as horizontal boundaries. Cross-functional teams typically have a specific team leader and coordinate across boundaries to lead change projects, such as creating a new product in a manufacturing organization or developing an interdisciplinary curriculum in a middle school. Cross-functional teams are generally involved in projects that affect several departments and therefore require that many views be considered.

Cross-functional teams facilitate information sharing across functional boundaries, generate suggestions for coordinating the departments represented, develop new ideas and solutions for existing organizational problems, and assist in developing new practices or policies. The members of one type of cross-functional team, the *problem-solving* or *process-improvement* team, meet voluntarily to discuss ways to improve quality, efficiency, and the work environment. Their recommendations are proposed to top executives for approval. A frequent application of cross-functional teams is for change projects, especially new product innovation, because effectively developing new products and services requires coordination across many departments. For example, US Airways set up a cross-functional team made up of mechanics, flight attendants, reservations agents, ramp workers, luggage attendants, aircraft cleaners, and others to plan and design a low-fare airline to compete with the expansion of Southwest Airlines into the east.[12] Cross-functional teams may gradually evolve into self-directed teams, which represent a fundamental change in how work is organized.

Evolution to Self-Directed Teams Exhibit 10.3 illustrates the evolution of teams and team leadership. The functional team represents grouping individuals by common skill and activity within the traditional structure. Leadership is based on

Functional team

team made up of a supervisor and subordinates in the formal chain of command

Cross-functional team

team made up of members from different functional departments within an organization

Action Memo

As a leader: Create a cross-functional team to handle a change project, such as product innovation, that requires coordination across organizational boundaries. Use a problem-solving or process-improvement team to initiate ideas for improving quality and efficiency.

the vertical hierarchy. In cross-functional teams, members have more freedom from the hierarchy, but the team typically is still leader-centered and leader-directed. The leader is most often assigned by the organization and is usually a supervisor or manager from one of the departments represented on the team. Leaders do, however, have to give up some of their control and power at this stage in order for the team to function effectively.

In the highest stage of evolution, team members work together without the direction of managers, supervisors, or assigned team leaders.[13] Self-directed teams are member- rather than leader-centered and directed. Hundreds of companies, including Consolidated Diesel, Industrial Light and Magic, the Mayo Clinic, and Edy's Grand Ice Cream, are using self-directed teams, which can enable workers to feel challenged, find their work meaningful, and develop a strong sense of identity with the organization.[14]

Self-directed teams typically consist of 5 to 20 members who rotate jobs to produce an entire product or service or at least one complete aspect or portion of a product or service (for example, engine assembly or insurance claim processing).[15] Self-directed teams often are long-term or permanent in nature, although many of today's fast-moving companies also use temporary self-directed teams that come together to work on a specific project and then disband when their work is done. Self-directed teams typically include three elements:

1. The team includes workers with varied skills and functions, and the combined skills are sufficient to perform a major organizational task, thereby eliminating barriers among departments and enabling excellent coordination.

2. The team is given access to resources such as information, financial resources, equipment, machinery, and supplies needed to perform the complete task.

3. The team is empowered with decision-making authority, which means that members have the freedom to select new members, solve problems, spend money, monitor results, and plan for the future.

Action Memo

As a leader: Use a self-directed team when members are capable of working without active supervision. Give the team access to the financial resources, equipment, supplies, and information needed to perform its project or task. Empower the team with decision-making authority.

In self-directed teams, members take over duties such as scheduling work or vacations, ordering materials, and evaluating performance. Teams work with minimum supervision, and members are jointly responsible for conflict resolution and decision making. Many self-directed teams elect one of their own to serve as team leader, and the leader may change each year. Some teams function without a designated leader, so anyone may play a leadership role, depending on the situation. In either case, equality and empowerment are key values in organizations based on self-directed teams.

Understanding Team Characteristics

One of a leader's most important jobs is to get the team designed right by considering such characteristics as size, diversity, and interdependence. The quality of team design has a significant impact on the success of teams.[16]

Size The ideal size of work teams is thought to be 7, although variations from 5 to 12 are associated with high performance. These teams are large enough to take advantage of diverse skills, yet small enough to permit members to feel an intimate part of a community. In general, as a team increases in size it becomes harder for each member to interact with and influence the others. A recent Gallup poll in the United States found that 82 percent of employees reported believing that small teams are more productive, compared to 16 percent who preferred big teams.[17]

A summary of research on size suggests that small teams show more agreement, ask more questions, and exchange more opinions. Members want to get along with one another. Small teams report more satisfaction and enter into more personal discussions, and members feel a greater sense of cohesiveness and belonging. Large teams (generally defined as 12 or more members) tend to have more disagreements and differences of opinion. Subgroups often form and conflicts among them may occur. Demands on leaders are greater in large teams because there is less member participation. Large teams also tend to be less friendly and members do not feel that they are part of a cohesive community.[18] As a general rule, it is more difficult to satisfy members' needs in large teams, forcing leaders to work harder to keep members focused and committed to team goals.

Diversity Since teams require a variety of skills, knowledge, and experience, it seems likely that heterogeneous teams would be more effective because members bring diverse abilities and information to bear on a project or problem. In general, research supports this idea, showing that heterogeneous teams produce more innovative solutions to problems than do homogeneous teams.[19] Diversity within a team can be a source of creativity. In addition, diversity can contribute to a healthy level of conflict that leads to better decision making. Some conflict helps to prevent "groupthink," in which people are so committed to a cohesive team that they are reluctant to express contrary opinions. Among top management teams, for example, low levels of conflict are associated with poor decision making. Furthermore, many of these low-conflict teams reflect little diversity among members.[20]

However, despite the value of some conflict, conflict that is too strong or is not handled appropriately can limit team members' satisfaction and performance. Diversity provides fertile ground for disagreements and disputes that may be based on personal rather than team issues.[21] Racial and national differences can interfere with team interaction and performance, particularly in the short term.[22] Teams made up of racially and culturally diverse members tend to have more difficulty learning to work well together, but, with effective leadership and conflict resolution, the problems seem to dissipate over a period of time. The benefits and challenges of diversity will be discussed in detail in the next chapter.

Interdependence Interdependence means the extent to which team members depend on each other for information, resources, or ideas to accomplish their tasks. Tasks such as performing surgery or directing military operations, for example, require a high degree of interaction and exchange, whereas tasks such as assembly-line manufacturing require very little.[23]

Three types of interdependence can affect teams: pooled, sequential, and reciprocal.[24]

In pooled interdependence, the lowest form of interdependence, members are fairly independent of one another in completing their work, participating on a team, but not *as* a team.[25] They may share a machine or a common secretary, but most of their work is done independently. An example might be a sales team, with each salesperson responsible for his or her own sales area and customers, but sharing the same appointment secretary. Salespersons need not interact to accomplish their work and little day-to-day coordination is needed.[26]

Sequential interdependence is a serial form wherein the output of one team member becomes the input to another team member. One member must perform well in order for the next member to perform well, and so on. Because team members have to exchange information and resources and rely upon one another, this is a higher level of interdependence. An example might be an engine assembly team in an automobile plant. Each team member performs a separate task, but his work depends on the satisfactory completion of work by other team members. Regular communication and coordination is required to keep work running smoothly.

The highest level of interdependence, reciprocal interdependence, exists when team members influence and affect one another in reciprocal fashion. The output of team member A is the input to team member B, and the output of team member B is the input back again to team member A. Reciprocal interdependence characterizes most teams performing knowledge-based work. Writing a technical manual, for example, rarely moves forward in a logical, step-by-step fashion. It is more like "an open-ended series of to-and-fro collaborations, iterations, and reiterations" among team members.[27] On reciprocal teams, each individual member makes a contribution, but only the team as a whole "performs."

The Labor and Delivery unit at Parkland Memorial Hospital provides an excellent example of reciprocal interdependence.

Interdependence *the extent to which team members depend on each other for information, resources, or ideas to accomplish their tasks*

Pooled interdependence *the lowest form of team interdependence; members are relatively independent of one another in completing their work*

Sequential interdependence *serial form of interdependence in which the output of one team member becomes the input to another team member*

Reciprocal interdependence *highest form of team interdependence; members influence and affect one another in reciprocal fashion*

In the Lead   Parkland Memorial Hospital

Parkland Memorial Hospital in Dallas, Texas, delivered 16,597 babies in 2001—four out of every thousand born in the United States, 40 or 50 babies a day. The hospital's stillbirth and neonatal death rates are lower than the national average despite the fact that 95 percent of the women who come into the labor and delivery unit (L & D) are indigent and many have drug or alcohol problems. As the county hospital, Parkland takes everyone—from private patients to illegal immigrants—and manages to deliver high-quality care on a shoestring. "We don't have fancy birthing rooms, hardwood floors, and pretty wallpaper," says RN Reina Duerinckx. "But we have the important stuff."

Part of the important stuff that helps Parkland achieve such phenomenal results with limited staff and money is superb teamwork that provides the intense coordination needed to meet any demand. Although L & D operates within an established hierarchy and a set of carefully codified protocols regarding medical care, the rules are applied in a relaxed, informal, and flexible way. A structure is needed to give people a sense of order among the chaos, but flexibility and teamwork by L & D's highly trained professionals are needed to translate the rules into appropriate action. Decision making is decentralized so that employees can respond on their own initiative based on problems that arise. Clerks, midwives, nurses, technicians, and doctors smoothly coordinate their activities to provide a variety of services as they are needed, adjusting to each team member's strengths and weaknesses and to the changing demands of the problem at hand. It's sometimes hard for an outsider to tell the most senior doctor from a nurse in training. It isn't unusual to see a doctor mopping out a delivery room to get ready for the next mother, for example. When a stat-C section (emergency Caesarian) is called, people drop whatever they're doing and fall right into place when and where they're needed. "Then the baby's out, the baby's fine. And the doors open again and everybody's gone," says Idella Williams, the RN in charge of L & D, who was herself born at the hospital. "Those are my proudest moments here."

Although Parkland's leaders believe it is important to have defined roles, they make clear that there should be no boundaries. Communication is frequent, face-to-face, and flowing in all directions. It has to be when as many as 14 babies are delivered in a single hour and the next crisis may be right around the corner.[28]

Action Memo

As a leader: Pay attention to the size, diversity, and interdependence of your team. When interdependence among members is high, empower the team to make decisions and take action on its own.

Leaders are responsible for facilitating the degree of coordination and communication needed among team members, depending on the level of team interdependence.

True team leadership, which involves empowering the team to make decisions and take action, is especially important to high performance when team interdependence is high. However, for teams with low interdependence, traditional leadership, individual rewards, and granting authority and power to individuals rather than the team may be appropriate.[29]

Leading Effective Teams

Team effectiveness
the extent to which a team achieves four performance outcomes: innovation/adaptation, efficiency, quality, and employee satisfaction

Team effectiveness can be defined as achieving four performance outcomes—innovation/adaptation, efficiency, quality, and employee satisfaction.[30] *Innovation/ adaptation* means the degree to which teams affect the organization's ability to rapidly respond to environmental needs and changes. *Efficiency* pertains to whether the team helps the organization attain goals using fewer resources. *Quality* refers to achieving fewer defects and exceeding customer expectations. *Satisfaction* pertains to the team's ability to maintain employee commitment and enthusiasm by meeting the personal needs of its members. Three areas related to understanding team effectiveness are team cohesiveness and performance; team task and socioemotional roles; and the personal impact of the team leader.

Team Cohesiveness and Effectiveness

Team cohesiveness
the extent to which members stick together and remain united in the pursuit of a common goal

Team cohesiveness is defined as the extent to which members stick together and remain united in the pursuit of a common goal.[31] Members of highly cohesive teams are committed to team goals and activities, feel that they are involved in something significant, and are happy when the team succeeds. Members of less cohesive teams are less concerned about the team's welfare. Cohesiveness is generally considered an attractive feature of teams. Leader's Self-Insight 10.1 gives you a chance to measure the cohesiveness of a team you have been involved in at school or work.

Determinants of Cohesiveness Leaders can use several factors to influence team cohesiveness. One is team *interaction*. The greater the amount of contact between team members and the more time they spend together, the more cohesive the team. Through frequent interaction, members get to know one another and become more devoted to the team. Another factor is *shared mission and goals*. When team members agree on purpose and direction, they will be more cohesive. The most cohesive teams are those that feel they are involved in something immensely relevant and important—that they are embarking on a journey together that will make the world better in some way. An aerospace executive, recalling his participation in an advanced design team, put it this way: "We even walked differently than anybody else. We felt we were way out there, ahead of the whole world."[32] A third factor is *personal attraction* to the team, meaning members find their common ground and have similar attitudes and values and enjoy being together. Members like and respect one another.

LEADER'S SELF-INSIGHT 10.1

Is Your Team Cohesive?

Think of a team of which you are or were recently a part, either at work or school, and answer the following questions about your perception of the team. Please answer the questions on the 1–5 scale based on the extent to which you agree with each statement.

1 = Strongly disagree; 2 = Disagree; 3 = Neutral; 4 = Agree 5 = Strongly agree

	Strongly disagree				Strongly agree
1. Members are proud to tell others they are part of the team.	1	2	3	4	5
2. Members are willing to put a great deal of effort into their work for the team to be successful.	1	2	3	4	5
3. Members seem as though they are trying to make other team members look bad.	1	2	3	4	5
4. Members are willing to "talk up" the team's work with other employees as being good for the organization.	1	2	3	4	5
5. Members seem to take advantage of each other's mistakes.	1	2	3	4	5
6. Members really care about the success of the team.	1	2	3	4	5
7. Members feel there is not much to be gained by sticking with this team's project.	1	2	3	4	5
8. Members of this team really like spending time together.	1	2	3	4	5

Scoring and Interpretation

Subtract each of your scores for questions 3, 5, and 7 from the number 6. Next, using your adjusted scores, sum your score for the 8 questions: _____. These questions pertain to team cohesion—the extent to which team members like, trust, and respect one another and are united toward a common goal. These questions were originally designed to assess the commitment of hospital upper management teams to joint strategic decisions. If your score is 32 or higher, your team would be considered high in cohesion and members are committed to one another and the team's goal. A score of 16 or less indicates below-average team cohesion.

SOURCE: Adapted from Robert S. Dooley and Gerald E. Fryxell, "Attaining Decision Quality and Commitment from Dissent: The Moderating Effects of Loyalty and Competence in Strategic Decision-Making Teams," *Academy of Management Journal* 42, no. 4 (1999): 389–402.

The organizational context can also affect team cohesiveness. When a team is in moderate *competition* with other teams, its cohesiveness increases as it strives to win. Finally, *team success* and the favorable evaluation of the team's work by outsiders add to cohesiveness. When a team succeeds and others in the organization recognize this success, members feel good and their commitment to the team will be higher.

Consequences of Team Cohesiveness The consequences of team cohesiveness can be examined according to two categories: morale and performance. As a general rule, employee *morale* is much higher in cohesive teams because of increased communication,

Action Memo

As a leader: Facilitate team cohesiveness. Make sure members can interact and know one another. Use friendly competition with other teams to increase cohesion. Develop high performance norms with the support of top leaders.

a friendly atmosphere, loyalty, and member participation in decisions and activities. High team cohesiveness has almost uniformly positive effects on the satisfaction and morale of team members.[33]

With respect to team *performance*, it seems that cohesiveness and performance are generally positively related, although research results are mixed. Cohesive teams can sometimes unleash enormous amounts of employee energy and creativity. One explanation for this is the research finding that working in a team increases individual motivation and performance. *Social facilitation* refers to the tendency for the presence of other people to enhance an individual's motivation and performance. Simply interacting with others has an energizing effect.[34] In relation to this, one study found that cohesiveness is more closely related to high performance when team interdependence is high, requiring frequent interaction, coordination, and communication, as discussed earlier in this chapter.[35]

Another factor influencing performance is the relationship between teams and top leadership. One study surveyed more than 200 work teams and correlated job performance with cohesiveness.[36] Highly cohesive teams were more productive when team members felt supported by organizational leaders and less productive when they sensed hostility and negativism from leaders. The support of leaders contributes to the development of high performance norms, whereas hostility leads to team norms and goals of low performance. Consider the performance norms and effectiveness of teams at the Ralston Foods plant in Sparks, Nevada.

In the Lead   Ralston Foods, Sparks, Nevada

The Ralston Foods Sparks, Nevada, plant is a small segment of Ralcorp Holdings, the largest store-brand manufacturer in the United States. The plant previously produced pet food, but that operation was shut down in 1990 and the factory was retrofitted into a cereal plant. Plant manager Daniel Kibbe knew from the beginning that he wanted to start the new cereal plant as a team-based organization, and he got full support from the division manager and higher corporate executives, who never interfered with the project.

Kibbe began by assembling a small team of leaders who believed in participative management and were eager to give up some of their authority to plant workers. Then, before the plant ever made a pound of cereal, it spent millions of dollars training people how to work in a team environment. For example, Ralston spent $1.5 million just training employees how to hire, counsel, and discipline because leaders knew those areas could be difficult for teams to handle. In addition, the leadership team created a culture of trust, credibility, and openness. Most employees believed that they, not managers, were the ones who could make the cereal operation a success.

The plant's 150 or so workers are divided into six operating work groups, most of which are, in turn, divided into small, semi-autonomous or self-directed teams. Leaders believe smaller teams of around 10 or fewer people are more cohesive and can manage themselves more easily. Small teams in the warehouse and mill areas function entirely without designated leaders and handle all issues and problems that arise in their areas, including hiring and firing, scheduling, quality, budget management, and disciplinary problems. These teams have learned to function so well through shared leadership that they consistently have a better and more dependable performance record than teams in other areas with assigned leaders. In all cases, team members function quite independently and have developed strong bonds that motivate them to perform well for the sake of the team.

Thanks to a combination of team cohesiveness and top leadership support that created high performance norms from the beginning, the Ralston Foods plant has produced record-breaking output levels and generated significant cost reductions.[37]

Meeting Task and Socio-Emotional Needs

Another important factor in team effectiveness is ensuring that the needs for both task accomplishment and team members' socio-emotional well-being are met. Recall from Chapter 2 the discussion of task-oriented and people-oriented leadership behaviors. Task-oriented behavior places primary concern on tasks and production and is generally associated with higher productivity, while people-oriented behavior emphasizes concern for followers and relationships and is associated with higher employee satisfaction.

For a team to be successful over the long term, it must both maintain its members' satisfaction and accomplish its task. These requirements are met through two types of team leadership roles, as illustrated in Exhibit 10.4. A *role* might be thought of as a set of behaviors expected of a person occupying a certain position, such as that of team leader. The **task-specialist role** is associated with behaviors such as initiating new ideas or different ways of considering problems; evaluating the team's effectiveness by questioning the logic, facts, or practicality of proposed solutions; seeking information to clarify tasks, responsibilities, and suggestions; summarizing facts and ideas for others; and stimulating others to action when energy and interest wane. The **socio-emotional role** includes behaviors such as facilitating the participation of others and being receptive to others' ideas; smoothing

Task-specialist role *team leadership role associated with initiating new ideas, evaluating the team's effectiveness, seeking to clarify tasks and responsibilities, summarizing facts and ideas for others, and stimulating others to action*

Socio-emotional role *team leadership role associated with facilitating others' participation, smoothing conflicts, showing concern for team members' needs and feelings, serving as a role model, and reminding others of standards for team interaction*

Exhibit 10.4   Two Types of Team Leadership Roles

Task-Specialist Behavior	Socio-Emotional Behavior
Propose solutions and initiate new ideas	Encourage contributions by others; draw out others' ideas by showing warmth and acceptance
Evaluate effectiveness of task solutions; offer feedback on others' suggestions	Smooth over conflicts between members; reduce tension and help resolve differences
Seek information to clarify tasks, responsibilities, and suggestions	Be friendly and supportive of others; show concern for members' needs and feelings
Summarize ideas and facts related to the problem at hand	Maintain standards of behavior and remind others of agreed-upon norms and standards for interaction
Energize others and stimulate the team to action	Seek to identify problems with team interactions or dysfunctional member behavior; ask for others' perceptions

SOURCES: Based on Robert A. Baron, *Behavior in Organizations*, 2nd ed. (Boston: Allyn & Bacon, 1986); Don Hellriegel, John W. Slocum, Jr., and Richard W. Woodman, *Organizational Behavior*, 8th ed. (Cincinnati, OH: South-Western, 1998), 244; and Gary A. Yukl, *Leadership in Organizations*, 4th ed. (Upper Saddle River, NJ: Prentice Hall, 1998): 384–387.

Action Memo

As a leader: Make sure that both the task and socio-emotional needs of team members are met. Enable a task-specialist role that initiates and evaluates new ideas and focuses the team on high performance. Encourage a socio-emotional role that provides friendship and support to team members, resolves conflicts, and encourages everyone's participation.

over conflicts between team members and striving to reduce tensions; showing concern for team members' needs and feelings; serving as a role model and reminding others of agreed-upon standards for interaction and cooperation; and seeking to identify problems with team interactions or dysfunctional member behaviors.[38]

Ideally, a team leader plays both task-specialist and socio-emotional roles. By satisfying both types of needs, the leader gains the respect and admiration of others. However, a leader might find it necessary to put more emphasis on one role over another. For example, if many members of the team are highly task-oriented, the leader might put more emphasis on meeting socio-emotional needs. On the other hand, when most members seem to emphasize relationships, the leader will need to be more task-oriented to ensure that the team performs its tasks and meets its goals. It is the leader's responsibility to make sure both types of needs are met, whether through the leader's own behaviors or through the actions and behaviors of other team members. A well-balanced team does best over the long term because it is personally satisfying for members and also promotes the successful accomplishment of team tasks and goals.

The Team Leader's Personal Role

Successful teams begin with confident and effective team leaders. Harvard Business School professors studying cardiac surgery teams found the attitude and actions of the team leader to be the most important factor determining team effectiveness.[39] However, leading a team requires a shift in mind-set and behavior for those who are accustomed to working in traditional organizations where managers make the decisions. Complete the exercise in Leader's Self-Insight 10.2 to evaluate your capacity for team leadership.

Most people can learn the new skills and qualities needed for team leadership, but it is not always easy. To be effective team leaders, people have to be willing to change themselves, to step outside their comfort zone and let go of many of the assumptions that have guided their behavior in the past. Here we will discuss three specific changes leaders can make to develop a foundation for effective team leadership.[40]

Recognize the Importance of Shared Purpose and Values   Team leaders have to articulate a clear and compelling vision so that everyone is moving in the same direction. Moreover, good leaders help people feel that their work is meaningful and important. A study of cross-functional teams at Hewlett–Packard's Medical Products Group, for example, found that the most successful teams were those that had a clear sense of their mission and goals and believed their work was essential to the success of the company.[41] At heart, building a team means creating a community united by shared values and commitment. Leaders may use ritual, stories, ceremonies and other symbolism to create a sense of community, shared purpose, and meaning for team members.

Admit Your Mistakes   The best team leaders are willing to make themselves vulnerable by admitting they don't know everything. Being an effective team leader means enabling everyone to contribute their unique skills, talents, and ideas. Leaders can serve as a *fallibility model* by admitting their ignorance and mistakes and asking for help, which lets people know that problems, errors, and concerns can be discussed openly without fear of appearing incompetent.[42] When Bruce Moravec was asked to lead a team to design a new fuselage for the Boeing 757, he had to gain the respect and confidence of people who worked in areas he knew little about. "You don't want to pretend you're more knowledgeable about subjects other people know more about," Moravec says. "That dooms you to failure. . . . They're the experts."[43]

LEADER'S SELF-INSIGHT 10.2

Assess Your Team Leadership Skills

Answer the following questions based on what you have done, or think you would do, related to the team situations and attitudes described. Check either mostly true or mostly false for each question.

	Mostly true	Mostly false
1. I am more likely to handle a high-priority task than to assign it to the team.	_____	_____
2. An important part of leading a team is to keep members informed almost daily of information that could affect their work.	_____	_____
3. I love communicating online to work on tasks with team members.	_____	_____
4. Generally, I feel tense while interacting with team members from different cultures.	_____	_____
5. I nearly always prefer face-to-face communications with team members over e-mail.	_____	_____
6. Building trust is very important for building a team.	_____	_____
7. I enjoy doing things in my own way and in my own time.	_____	_____
8. If a new member were hired, I would expect the entire team to interview the person.	_____	_____
9. I become impatient when working with a team member from another culture.	_____	_____
10. I suggest ways each team member can make a contribution to the project.	_____	_____
11. I am uneasy interacting with people from different ethnic or racial groups.	_____	_____
12. If I were out of the office for a week, most of the important work of the team would get accomplished anyway.	_____	_____
13. Delegation is hard for me when an important task has to be done right.	_____	_____
14. I enjoy working with people with different accents.	_____	_____
15. I am confident about leading team members from different cultures.	_____	_____

Scoring and Interpretation

The answers for effective team leadership are as follows:

1. Mostly false	6. Mostly true	11. Mostly false
2. Mostly true	7. Mostly false	12. Mostly true
3. Mostly true	8. Mostly true	13. Mostly false
4. Mostly false	9. Mostly false	14. Mostly true
5. Mostly false	10. Mostly true	15. Mostly true

If your score is 12 or higher, you understand the ingredients to be a highly effective team leader. If your score is 6 or lower, you might have an authoritarian approach to leadership, or are not comfortable with culturally diverse team membership or virtual team communications, such as e-mail. Questions 1, 2, 6, 7, 8, 10, 12, and 13 pertain to authoritarian versus participative team leadership. Questions 4, 9, 11, 14, and 15 pertain to cultural differences. Questions 3 and 5 pertain to virtual team communications. Which aspects of team leadership reflect your leader strengths? Your leader weaknesses? Team leadership requires that the leader learn to share power, information, and responsibility, be inclusive of diverse members, and be comfortable with electronic communications.

SOURCE: Adapted from "What Style of Leader Are You or Would You Be?" in Andrew J. DuBrin, *Leadership: Research Findings, Practice, and Skills*, 3rd ed. (Boston: Houghton Mifflin Company, 2001), 126–127, and James W. Neuliep and James C. McCroskey, "The Development of Intercultural and Interethnic Communication Apprehension Scales," *Communication Research Reports*, 14, no. 2 (1997), 145–156.

Provide Support and Coaching to Team Members Good team leaders make sure people get the training, development opportunities, and resources they need and that they are adequately rewarded for their contributions to the organization.

Rather than always thinking about oneself and how to get the next promotion or salary increase, effective team leaders spend their time taking care of team members. Most team members share the critically important needs for recognition and support. Leaders frequently overlook how important it is for people to feel that their contribution is valued, and they may especially forget to acknowledge the contributions of lower-level support staff. One woman who has held the same secretarial position for many years attributes her high enthusiasm to her team leader: "For the last several years, our team of four has reported to him. At the end of each day—no matter how hectic or trying things have been—he comes by each of our desks and says, 'Thank you for another good day.'"[44]

The Leader's New Challenge: Virtual and Global Teams

Being a team leader is even more challenging when people are scattered in different geographical locations and may be separated by language and cultural differences as well. Virtual and global teams are a reality for many of today's leaders. Exhibit 10.5 illustrates the primary differences between conventional types of teams and today's virtual and global teams. Conventional types of teams discussed earlier in this chapter meet and conduct their interactions face to face in the same physical space. Team members typically share similar cultural backgrounds and characteristics. The key characteristics of virtual and global teams, on the other hand, are (1) spatial distance limits face-to-face interaction, and (2) the use of technological communication is the primary means of connecting team members.[45] Virtual and global teams are scattered in different locations, whether it be different offices and business locations around the country or around the world. Most communication is handled via telephone, fax, e-mail, instant messaging, virtual document sharing, videoconferencing, and other media. In some virtual teams, members share the same dominant culture, but global teams are often made up of members whose cultural values vary widely. The leadership challenge is thus highest for global teams because of the increased potential for misunderstandings and conflicts.

Virtual team
a team made up
of geographi-
cally or organi-
zationally
dispersed mem-
bers who share
a common pur-
pose and are
linked prima-
rily through
advanced
information
technologies

Virtual Teams

Economist William Knoke, author of *Bold New World*, refers to the "technology of placelessness," which characterizes the technological advances that have made virtual teamwork a reality. A virtual team is made up of geographically or organizationally dispersed members who share a common purpose and are linked primarily through

Exhibit 10.5 Differences Between Conventional, Virtual, and Global Teams

Type of Team	Spatial Distance	Communications	Member Cultures	Leader Challenge
Conventional	Colocated	Face to face	Same	High
Virtual	Scattered	Mediated	Same	Higher
Global	Widely scattered	Mediated	Different	Very High

advanced information and telecommunications technologies.[46] Team members use e-mail, voice mail, videoconferencing, Internet and intranet technologies, and various forms of collaboration software to perform their work rather than meeting face to face.

Uses of Virtual Teams Virtual teams, sometimes called distributed teams, may be temporary cross-functional teams that work on specific projects, or they may be long-term, self-directed teams. Virtual teams sometimes include customers, suppliers, and even competitors to pull together the best minds to complete a project. For example, three of the top men's magazines—*Esquire, Men's Health,* and *Rolling Stone*—are fierce competitors, and leaders from the three organizations once barely spoke to one another. Several years ago, however, the three put together a virtual team to develop a successful joint proposal for a major Haggar advertising campaign. Without this collaboration, it is unlikely that either organization could have competed against *Sports Illustrated,* a magazine with a circulation equal to that of the other three combined.[47]

Using virtual teams allows organizations to use the best people for a particular job, no matter where they are located, thus enabling a fast response to competitive pressures. When IBM needs to staff a project, it gives a list of skills needed to the human resources department, which provides a pool of people who are qualified. The team leader then puts together the best combination of people for the project, which often means pulling people from many different locations. IBM estimates that about a third of its employees participate in virtual teams.[48]

Leading the Virtual Team Despite their potential benefits, virtual teams also bring a number of leadership challenges.[49] Leaders of conventional teams can monitor how team members are doing and if everything is on track, but virtual team leaders can't see when or how well people are working. Virtual team leaders have to trust people to do their jobs without constant supervision, and they learn to focus more on results than on the process of accomplishing them. Too much control can kill a virtual team, so leaders have to give up most of their control and yet at the same time provide encouragement, support, and development. The ideas presented earlier regarding the team leader's personal role are applicable to virtual teams as well. In addition, to be successful, virtual team leaders can master the following skills:

❋ *Select the right team members.* Effective virtual team leaders put a lot of thought into getting the right mix of people on the team. Team members need to have the technical knowledge, skills, and personalities to work effectively in a virtual environment. When people are highly skilled and professional, they don't need to be monitored or supervised in a traditional way. As with other types of teams, small virtual teams tend to be more cohesive and work together more effectively. However, diversity of views and experiences is also important to the success of a virtual team. Diversity is usually built into virtual teams because when leaders can pick the right people for the job, no matter where they are located, members usually reflect diverse backgrounds and viewpoints.[50]

❋ *Build trust by building connections.* No matter how effective team members are as individuals, unless they can come together as a team, virtual teamwork will fail. Virtual team leaders work hard to establish connections among people, from which trust can grow. There simply is no substitute for initial face-to-face interaction for building trust quickly. At Mobil Corp., leaders bring virtual team members together in one location at the beginning of a project so they can begin to build personal relationships and gain an understanding of their goals and responsibilities.[51] These intense meetings allow the team to rapidly go through the *forming* and *storming* stages of development, as discussed earlier in this chapter. Studies of virtual teams suggest these processes are best accomplished at the same time and in the same place.[52] ➔ I important

❋ *Agree on ground rules.* Teams should work together to choose the collaboration software and other communications technologies they will use and then immediately practice using the new technology together.[53] At the beginning of the team's work, all team members need to explicitly understand both team and individual goals, deadlines, and expectations for participation and performance. This enables people to monitor their own performance and regulate their behavior to meet the needs of teammates. Agreeing on communications etiquette is also essential. The team has to agree on issues such as whether good-natured flaming is okay or off limits, whether there are time limits on responding to voice mail or e-mail, and so forth.

❋ *Effectively use technology.* Communication can be a tremendous problem for virtual teams, and the ideas for using electronic communication channels in Chapter 9 can help virtual team leaders be more effective. When possible, leaders

Action Memo

As a leader: Create a virtual team that can perform effectively with limited control and supervision. Select members who can perform in a virtual environment. Arrange opportunities for both face-to-face and online interaction. Ensure that members understand the goals and agree on ground rules and performance standards.

Global teams

teams made up of culturally diverse members who live and work in different countries and coordinate some part of their activities on a global basis

should use face-to-face communication sessions when rich communication is needed, such as for problem solving or whenever misunderstandings and frustration threaten the team's work.[54] Leaders can also schedule regular times for people to interact online and be sure all team members are trained in how to effectively use electronic communications. For example, leaders find that they need to give much more support and positive feedback in a virtual environment than in person. Everything needs to be made more explicit online. Experienced virtual workers have learned how to "verbalize" to colleagues online when they're shifting mental gears or need more feedback.

Global Teams

Virtual teams are frequently also global teams, which means people are working together not only across spatial distances but across time barriers and cultural and language differences as well. The use of global teams is rapidly increasing. A recent survey of 103 firms found that nearly half now use global teams for new product development. Moreover, one out of every five teams in these companies is likely to be global.[55] Global teams are work teams made up of culturally diverse members who live and work in different countries and coordinate some part of their activities on a global basis.[56] For example, American Express Technology (AET) uses a virtual human resources team whose members span the globe and coordinate their work to help AET's technology experts partner with business leaders around the world.[57] When NCR was spun off from AT&T, it used global virtual teams to design its WorldMark enterprise computer server. Teams involved more than 1,000 people working in five U.S. states, Ireland, India, China, and six other locations. During the project, most teams worked together on a daily basis even though they were spread around the world.[58]

Why Global Teams Often Fail All of the challenges of virtual teamwork are magnified in the case of global teams because of the added problem of language and cultural barriers.[59] Building trust is an even greater challenge when people bring different norms, values, attitudes and patterns of behavior to the team For example, members from different cultures often have different beliefs about such things as authority, time orientation, decision making, and even teamwork itself. In Mexico, U.S. companies trying to use teams have run into trouble because the concept of shared leadership conflicts with traditional values that there should be status and power differences in organizations.[60]

Communication barriers can be formidable. Not only do global teams have to cope with different time zones and conflicting schedules, but members often speak different languages. Even when members can communicate in the same language, differences such as accent, tone of voice, dialect, and semantics can present problems. A survey found that senior leaders consider building trust and overcoming communication barriers as the two most important—but also the two most difficult—leader tasks related to the success of global teams.[61]

Leading the Global Team If managed correctly, global teams have many advantages. Increasingly, the expertise and knowledge needed to complete a project is scattered around the world. In addition, as discussed earlier, diversity can be a powerful stimulus for creativity and the development of better alternatives for problem solving. All of the guidelines for leading traditional and virtual teams apply to global teams as well. For example, a strong sense of shared purpose can help bridge language and culture gaps. In addition, global team leaders can improve success by incorporating the following ideas:[62]

❋   *Manage language and culture.* Organizations using global teams can't skimp on training. Language and cross-cultural education can help overcome linguistic and cultural hurdles. Language training encourages more direct and spontaneous communication by limiting the need for translators. Understanding one another's cultures can also enrich communications and interpersonal relationships. For the team to succeed, all team members have to gain an appreciation of cultural values and attitudes that are different from their own.

❋   *Stretch minds and behavior.* As team members learn to expand their thinking and embrace cultural differences, they also learn to develop a shared team culture. In global teams, all members have to be willing to deviate somewhat from their own values and norms and establish new norms for the team.[63] Leaders can work with team members to set norms and guidelines for acceptable behavior. These guidelines can serve as a powerful self-regulating mechanism, enhance communications, enrich team interactions, and help the team function as an integrated whole.

One company that has made successful use of global teams is STMicroelectronics, the world's third largest computer chip maker.

In the Lead   STMicroelectronics

Leaders at STMicroelectronics (STM) faced a problem when the company won a coveted order for microchips to power the brains for a navigational mapping system to be installed in new Fiats and Peugeots. Winning the order was a major coup, but filling it wasn't going to be easy. Car makers needed the chips in a hurry—if they couldn't get the new navigational systems installed fast, they would lose sales.

STM leaders knew the chip project would require collaboration among a wide range of disciplines, including chip design, engineering, fabrication, systems integration, quality control, packaging, marketing, and sales. Moreover, the people with the expertise to complete the project lived in five different countries, spanned 14 time zones, and spoke six different native languages. Time constraints on the project, as well as personal and cost factors, made it impossible to get everyone together in one location, so a virtual global team was formed to collaborate on the project using electronic communications technologies.

Thanks to extensive training and excellent team leadership, STM's global team was a success. One reason the team worked so well is that everyone united around a common purpose and members subordinated their individual viewpoints and egos to the shared goal. When there were disagreements, team members worked hard to understand different points of view rather than letting their own values and attitudes get in the way. As the team's work progressed, people came to care about each other as well as the project. Openly discussing things and sharing different viewpoints led to substantial operational insights and personal development. At the end of the project, one of the team members said, "This was the best experience of my life. I learned so much."[64]

The use of global and virtual teams is likely to grow as companies look for ways to harness knowledge and respond faster to increased global competition. Some researchers have suggested that within a few years, organizations might come to resemble amoebas—collections of people connected electronically who are divided into ever-changing teams that can best exploit the organization's unique resources, capabilities, and core competencies.[65]

Handling Team Conflict

As one would expect, there is an increased potential for conflict among members of global and virtual teams because of the greater chances for miscommunication and misunderstandings. Also, one study found that in global virtual teams people show a greater propensity for shirking their duties or giving less than their full effort, which can also lead to team conflicts.[66] Cultural value differences, little face-to-face interaction, and lack of on-site monitoring make it harder to build team identity and commitment. Teams that develop a strong team identity are less likely to have members who withhold their full effort. For all team leaders, though, no skill is more important than managing the conflicts that will inevitably arise.

Conflict refers to hostile or antagonistic interaction in which one party attempts to thwart the intentions or goals of another. Conflict is natural and occurs in all

Conflict

antagonistic interaction in which one party attempts to thwart the intentions or goals of another teams and organizations. It can arise between members of a team or between teams. Too much conflict can be destructive, tear relationships apart, and interfere with the healthy exchange of ideas and information needed for team development and cohesiveness.[67] High-performing teams typically have lower levels of conflict, and the conflict is more often associated with tasks than with interpersonal relationships. In addition, teams that reflect healthy patterns of conflict are usually characterized by high levels of trust and mutual respect.[68]

Causes of Conflict

Leaders can be aware of several factors that cause conflict among individuals or teams. Whenever teams compete for scarce resources, such as money, information, or supplies, conflict is almost inevitable. Conflicts also emerge when task responsibilities are unclear. People might disagree about who has responsibility for specific tasks or who has a claim on resources, and leaders help members reach agreement. Truly sharing responsibility can be a major challenge for teams, as discussed in this chapter's Leader's Bookshelf. Another reason for conflict is simply because individuals or teams are pursuing conflicting goals. For example, individual salespeople's targets may put them in conflict with one another and with the sales manager. Finally, it sometimes happens that two people simply do not get along with one another and will never see eye to eye on any issue. Personality clashes are caused by basic differences in personality, values, and attitudes, as described in Chapter 4, and can be particularly difficult to deal with. Sometimes, the only solution is to separate the parties and reassign them to other teams where they can be more productive.

Styles to Handle Conflict

Teams as well as individuals develop specific styles for dealing with conflict, based on the desire to satisfy their own concerns versus the other party's concerns. Exhibit 10.6 describes five styles of handling conflict. How an individual approaches conflict is measured along two dimensions: *assertiveness* and *cooperation*. Effective leaders and team members vary their style to fit a specific situation, as each style is appropriate in certain cases.[69]

1. The *competing style*, which reflects assertiveness to get one's own way, should be used when quick, decisive action is vital on important issues or unpopular actions, such as during emergencies or urgent cost cutting.
2. The *avoiding style*, which reflects neither assertiveness nor cooperativeness, is appropriate when an issue is trivial, when there is no chance of winning, when a delay to gather more information is needed, or when a disruption would be costly.
3. The *compromising style* reflects a moderate amount of both assertiveness and cooperativeness. It is appropriate when the goals on both sides are

> **Action Memo**
>
> As a leader: Adopt the best approach for handling a team conflict. Choose among the competing, avoiding, compromising, accommodating, or collaborating styles based on the degree of assertiveness and cooperativeness needed to effectively manage the situation.

LEADER'S BOOKSHELF

The Responsibility Virus: How Control Freaks, Shrinking Violets—And the Rest of Us—Can Harness the Power of True Partnership
By Roger Martin

According to Roger Martin, author of *The Responsibility Virus*, we are all highly susceptible to either wanting to take charge when something goes wrong or to shirk responsibility. This pervasive infection is a major barrier to teamwork because it causes some people to take on more than they should (the hero) while others shirk their duties and make sure the responsibility falls on someone else (the passive team member). The hero typically grows increasingly frustrated with those who aren't doing their share, while the passive member may harbor anger and resentment at those who seem to hog the power and control. Martin contends that the reason behind both behaviors is ego and fear of failure. With *The Responsibility Virus*, he paves the way toward truly shared responsibility and collaborative solutions.

Taming the Responsibility Virus
For teams to learn and perform well, they need good communication, shared decision making, and effective collaboration skills. Martin introduces a set of four tools that, when used together, can help eradicate both the hero and the passive team member.

❊ *The choice-structuring process:* This seven-step decision-making process uses group dynamics to encourage teamwork and reduce the likelihood that anyone will seize or surrender control of the decision. Group decision making can lead to better and more inspired decisions than any one person could make alone.

❊ *The frame experiment:* This is a remedial behavioral tool for individuals trapped in a cycle of over- or under-performance. The frame experiment encourages constructive conversation by helping people "re-frame" their own and others' roles. By helping one member think about the situation from another's point of view, the exercise can spur productive talk and lead to the beginnings of collaboration.

❊ *The responsibility ladder:* This procedure helps a team divide responsibilities in such a way that everyone plays an important role. By using the ladder, tasks are divided so that responsibilities are assigned to match each person's capabilities and interests.

❊ *The redefinition of leadership and followership:* This redefines outdated and unproductive notions of what it means to be a team leader or a follower. The old idea is that a leader takes control and responsibility, while followers do as they are told. In the redefinition, team leaders and followers essentially have the same job and are mutually responsible for outcomes.

Toward Genuine Partnership
Martin, who is currently dean of the Roman School of Management at the University of Toronto, draws numerous examples from actual situations he faced during his years as a consultant. The tools described in *The Responsibility Virus* can help people transcend the desire to maintain control or abdicate responsibility, engage in true dialogue, and exchange ideas based on the logic and reasoning of all team members.

The Responsibility Virus: How Control Freaks, Shrinking Violets—And the Rest of Us—Can Harness the Power of True Partnership, by Roger Martin, is published by Basic Books.

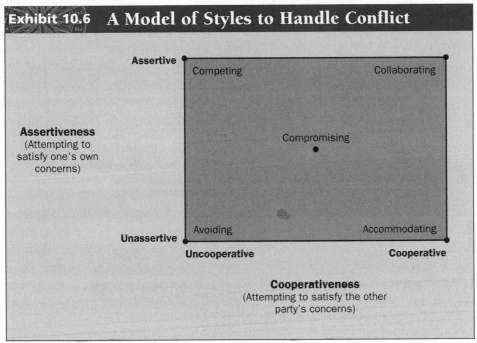

Exhibit 10.6   A Model of Styles to Handle Conflict

SOURCE: Adapted from Kenneth Thomas, "Conflict and Conflict Management," in *Handbook of Industrial and Organizational Behavior*, ed. M.D. Dunnette (New York: John Wiley, 1976), 900. Used by permission of Marvin D. Dunnette.

equally important, when opponents have equal power and both sides want to split the difference, or when people need to arrive at temporary or expedient solutions under time pressure.

4. The *accommodating style* reflects a high degree of cooperativeness, which works best when people realize that they are wrong, when an issue is more important to others than to oneself, when building social credits for use in later discussions, or when maintaining cohesiveness is especially important.

5. The *collaborating style* reflects both a high degree of assertiveness and of cooperativeness. This style enables both parties to win, although it may require substantial dialogue and negotiation. The collaborating style is important when both sets of concerns are too important to be compromised, when insights from different people need to be merged into an overall solution, or when the commitment of both sides is needed for a consensus.

Each approach can be successful, depending on the people involved and the situation. Answer the questions in Leader's Self-Insight 10.3 to see which conflict-handling style you tend to use most frequently. Also, try to think of conflict situations you've been involved in where each of the styles might be appropriate.

In a study of conflict in virtual teams, researchers found that the competing and collaborating styles had a positive effect on team performance.[70] The effectiveness of the competing style might be related to the use of electronic communication, in that team members don't interpret the individual's approach as being aggressive and are more willing to accept a quick resolution.

Other Approaches

The various styles of handling conflict illustrated in Exhibit 10.6 are especially effective for an individual to use when he or she disagrees with another. But what can a team leader do when conflict erupts among others? Research suggests several techniques that help resolve conflicts among people or teams.

Vision A compelling vision can pull people together. A vision is for the whole team and cannot be attained by one person. Its achievement requires the cooperation of conflicting parties. To the extent that leaders can focus on a larger team or organizational vision, conflict will decrease because the people involved see the big picture and realize they must work together to achieve it.

Bargaining/Negotiating Bargaining and negotiating mean that the parties engage one another in an attempt to systematically reach a solution. They attempt logical problem solving to identify and correct the conflict. This approach works well if the individuals can set aside personal animosities and deal with conflict in a businesslike way.

Mediation Using a third party to settle a dispute involves mediation. A mediator could be a supervisor, another team leader, or someone from the human resources department. The mediator can discuss the conflict with each party and work toward a solution. If a solution satisfactory to all parties cannot be reached, the parties may be willing to turn the conflict over to the mediator and abide by his or her solution.

Facilitating Communication One of the most effective ways to reduce conflict is to help conflicting parties communicate openly and honestly. As conflicting parties exchange information and learn more about one another, suspicions diminish and teamwork becomes possible. A particularly promising avenue for reducing conflict is through dialogue, as discussed in Chapter 9. Dialogue asks that participants suspend their attachments to their own viewpoint so that a deeper level of listening, synthesis, and meaning can evolve from the interaction. Individual differences are acknowledged and respected, but rather than trying to figure out who is right or wrong, the parties search for a joint perspective.

Each of these approaches can be helpful in resolving conflicts between individuals or teams. Effective leaders use a combination of these on a regular basis—such as articulating a larger vision and continuously facilitating communication—to keep conflict at a minimum while the team moves forward.

LEADER'S SELF-INSIGHT 10.3

How Do You Handle Team Conflict?

Think of some disagreements you have had with a team member, a student group, manager, friend, or co-worker. Then answer the questions below based on how frequently you engage in each behavior. There are no right or wrong answers. Respond to all items using the 1–5 scale.

1 = Not at all; 2 = Once in a while; 3 = Sometimes; 4 = Fairly often; 5 = Frequently

	Not at all				Frequently
1. I shy away from topics that might cause a dispute.	1	2	3	4	5
2. I strongly assert my opinion in a disagreement.	1	2	3	4	5
3. I suggest solutions that combine others' points of view.	1	2	3	4	5
4. I give in a little when other people do the same.	1	2	3	4	5
5. I avoid a person who wants to discuss a topic of disagreement.	1	2	3	4	5
6. I combine arguments into a new solution from the ideas raised in a dispute.	1	2	3	4	5
7. I will split the difference to reach a settlement.	1	2	3	4	5
8. I am quick to agree when someone I am arguing with makes a good point.	1	2	3	4	5
9. I keep my views to myself rather than argue.	1	2	3	4	5
10. I try to include other people's ideas to create a solution they will accept.	1	2	3	4	5
11. I offer trade-offs to reach solutions in a disagreement.	1	2	3	4	5
12. I try to smooth over disagreements by making them seem less serious.	1	2	3	4	5
13. I hold my tongue rather than argue with another person.	1	2	3	4	5
14. I raise my voice to get other people to accept my position.	1	2	3	4	5
15. I stand firm in expressing my viewpoints during a disagreement.	1	2	3	4	5

Scoring and Interpretation

Five categories of conflict-handling strategies are measured in this instrument: competing, avoiding, compromising, accommodating, and collaborating. By comparing your scores on the following five scales, you can see which is your preferred conflict-handling strategy.

To calculate your five scores, add the individual scores for the three items indicated and divide by three.

Competing: Items 2, 14, 15: _____
Avoiding: Items 1, 5, 9: _____
Compromising: Items 4, 7, 11: _____
Accommodating: Items 8, 12, 13: _____
Collaborating: Items 3, 6, 10: _____

Briefly review the text material (pages 411 and 413) about these five strategies for handling conflict. The average score across all 15 items is typically about three. Which of the five strategies do you use the most? Which strategy do you find the most difficult to use? How would your strategy differ if the other person was a family member rather than a team member? Are there some situations where a strategy in which you are weak might be more effective? Explain your scores to another student and listen to the explanation for his or her scores. How are your conflict-handling strategies similar or different?

SOURCE: Adapted from "How Do You Handle Conflict?" in Robert E. Quinn et al., *Becoming a Master Manager* (New York: Wiley, 1990), 221–223.

Summary and Interpretation

Teams are a reality in most organizations, and leaders are called upon to facilitate teams rather than manage direct-report subordinates. Functional teams typically are part of the traditional organization structure. Cross-functional teams, including problem-solving teams, process-improvement teams, and change teams, often represent an organization's first move toward greater team participation. Cross-functional teams may evolve into self-directed teams, which are member- rather than leader-centered and directed. Two recent types of teams, virtual teams and global teams, have resulted from advances in technology, changing employee expectations, and the globalization of business. New technology both supports teamwork and increases the pressures on organizations to expand opportunities for employee participation and the widespread sharing of information.

Teams go through stages of development and change over time. Guiding a team through these stages is an important part of team leadership. In addition, leaders have to get the team designed right by considering such factors as size, diversity, and interdependence and ensuring that task and socio-emotional roles are filled. These considerations help to determine team effectiveness. The leader's personal role is also crucial. People typically have to change themselves to become good team leaders. Three principles that provide a foundation for team leadership are to recognize the importance of shared purpose and values, admit your mistakes, and provide support and coaching to team members.

These principles apply to virtual and global teams as well. However, being a team leader is even more challenging when people are scattered in different geographic locations and may be separated by language and cultural differences. To create effective, smoothly functioning virtual teams, leaders build trust by building connections in both physical and virtual space, select team members who have the skills and temperaments to work virtually, agree on ground rules for the team, and ensure that all team members effectively use technology. For global teams, leaders also have to manage language and cultural differences and guide people to stretch their minds and behavior to establish a shared culture for the team.

Virtual and global teams increase the potential for misunderstanding, disagreements, and conflicts. However, all teams experience some conflict because of scarce resources, faulty communication, goal conflicts, power and status differences, or personality clashes. Leaders use varied styles to handle conflict. In addition, they employ the following techniques to help resolve conflicts: unite people around a shared vision, use bargaining and negotiation, bring in a mediator, and help conflicting parties communicate openly and honestly, particularly through dialogue.

Discussion Questions

1. What is the difference between a "team" and a "group"? Describe your personal experience with each.
2. Discuss the differences between a cross-functional team and a self-directed team.
3. Why do you think organizations are increasingly using virtual and global teams? Would you like to be a member or leader of a virtual global team? Why or why not?
4. Why might a person need to go through significant personal changes to be an effective team leader? What are some of the changes required?
5. Describe the three levels of interdependence and explain how they affect team leadership.
6. Which is more important to team effectiveness—the task-specialist role or the socio-emotional role? Discuss.
7. What are the stages of team development? How can a team leader best facilitate the team at each stage?
8. Discuss the relationship between team cohesiveness and performance.
9. What style of handling conflict do you typically use? Can you think of instances where a different style might have been more productive?

Leadership at Work

Team Feedback

Think back to your most recent experience working in a team, either at work or school. Write down your answers to the following questions about your role in the team.

What did the team members appreciate about you?

_____

_____

_____

What did the team members learn from you?

_____

_____

_____

What could the team members count on you for?

_____

_____

_____

How could you have improved your contribution to the team?

_____
_____
_____

Evaluate your answers. What is the overall meaning of your answers? What are the implications for your role as a team member? As a team leader?

_____
_____
_____

In Class: Team Feedback is an excellent exercise to use for student feedback to one another after a specific team class project or other activities done together during the class. If there were no assigned team activities, but students have gotten to know each other in class, they can be divided into groups and provide the information below with respect to their participation in the class instead of in the student team.

The instructor can ask the student groups to sit in a circle facing one another. Then one person will volunteer to be the focal person, and each of the other team members will tell that team member the following:

• What I appreciate about you

• What I learned from you

• What I could count on you for

• My one suggestion for improvement as a team leader/member

When the team members have given feedback to the focal person, another team member volunteers to hear feedback, and the process continues until each person has heard the four elements of feedback from every other team member.

The key questions for student learning are: "Are you developing the skills and behaviors to be a team leader?" If not, what does that mean for you? If you are now providing team leadership, how can you continue to grow and improve as a team leader?

SOURCE: Thanks to William Miller for suggesting the questions for this exercise.

Leadership Development: Cases for Analysis

Valena Scientific Corporation

Valena Scientific Corporation (VSC) is a large manufacturer of health care products. The health care market includes hospitals, clinical laboratories, universities, and industries. Clinical laboratories represent 52 percent of VSC's sales. Laboratories are located in hospitals and diagnostic centers where blood tests and urine analyses are performed for physicians. Equipment sold to laboratories can range from a five-cent test tube to a $195,000 blood analyzer.

By 1980, the industry experienced a move into genetic engineering. Companies such as Genentech Corporation and Cetus Scientific Laboratories were created and staffed with university microbiologists. These companies were designed to exploit the commercial potential for gene splicing.

Senior executives at VSC saw the trend developing and decided to create a Biotech Research Program. Skilled microbiologists were scarce, so the program was staffed with only nine scientists. Three scientists were skilled in gene splicing, three in recombination, and three in fermentation. The specialties reflected the larger departments to which they were assigned. However, they were expected to work as a team on this program. Twenty technicians were also assigned to the program to help the scientists.

Senior management believed that the biotech research program could be self-managed. For the first 18 months of operation, everything went well. Informal leaders emerged among the scientists in gene splicing, recombination, and fermentation. These three informal leaders coordinated the work of the three groups, which tended to stay separate. For example, the work typically started in the gene-splicing group, followed by work in recombination, and then in fermentation. Fermentation was used to breed the bacteria created by the other two groups in sufficient numbers to enable mass production.

During the summer of 1983, the biotech research program was given a special project. Hoffman-LaRoche was developing leukocyte interferon to use as a treatment against cancer. VSC contracted with Hoffman-LaRoche to develop a technique for large-scale interferon production. VSC had only six months to come up with a production technology. Scientists in each of the subgroups remained in their own geographical confines and began immediately to test ideas relevant to their specialty. In September, the informal group leaders met and discovered that each group had taken a different research direction. Each of the subgroups believed their direction was best and the informal leaders argued vehemently for their positions, rather than change to another direction. Future meetings were conflict-laden and did not resolve the issues. When managers became aware of the crisis, they decided to appoint a formal leader to the program.

On November 15, a Stanford professor with extensive research experience in recombinant DNA technology was hired. His title was chief biologist for the Biotech Research Program, and all project members reported to him for the duration of the interferon project.

The chief biologist immediately took the nine scientists on a two-day retreat. He assigned them to three tables for discussions, with a member from each subgroup at each table, so they had to talk across their traditional boundaries. He led the discussion of their common ground as scientists, and of their hopes and vision for this project. After they developed a shared vision, the group turned to scientific issues and in mixed groups discussed the ideas that the VSC subgroups had developed. Gradually, one approach seemed to have more likelihood of success than the others. A consensus emerged, and the chief biologist adopted the basic approach that would be taken in the interferon project. Upon their return to VSC, the technicians were brought in and the scientists explained the approach to them. At this point, each subgroup was assigned a set of instructions within the overall research plan. Firm deadlines were established based on group interdependence. Weekly progress reports to the chief biologist were required from each group leader.

Dramatic changes in the behavior of the scientists were observed after the two-day retreat. Communication among groups became more common. Problems discovered by one group were communicated to other groups so that effort was not expended needlessly. Subgroup leaders coordinated many solutions among themselves. Lunch and coffee gatherings that included several members of the subgroups began to appear. Group leaders and members often had daily discussions and cooperated on research requirements. Enthusiasm for the department and the interferon project was high, and cohesion seemed especially strong.

SOURCE: From *Organization Theory and Design*, 5th edition, by Daft © 1995. Reprinted with permission of South-Western, a division of Thomson Learning: http://www.thomsonrights.com Fax 800 730-2215.

Questions

1. Was the research program a group or a team? If a team, what type of team was it (functional, cross-functional, self-directed)? Explain.

2. Did the interdependence among the subgroups change with the interferon project? What were the group norms before and after the retreat?
3. What factors account for the change in cohesiveness after the chief biologist took over?

Burgess Industries

Managers at Burgess Industries, one of the few remaining garment manufacturing companies in eastern North Carolina, are struggling to improve productivity and profits. If things don't get better, they and their 650 employees will be out of work. Top executives have been evaluating whether to close the plant, which makes pants for several different clothing companies, and move production to Mexico. However, everyone hopes to keep the North Carolina factory going. The latest effort to turn things around is a shift to teamwork.

Top executives directed managers to abandon the traditional assembly system, where workers performed a single task, such as sewing zippers or attaching belt loops. In the new team system, teams of 30 to 35 workers coordinate their activities to assemble complete garments. People were given training to help master new machinery and also attended a brief team-building and problem-solving seminar prior to the shift to teamwork. Approximately 50 workers at a time were taken off the production floor for an afternoon to attend the seminars, which were spread over a month's time. As an introduction to the seminar, employees were told that the new team system would improve their work lives by giving them more autonomy, eliminating the monotony of the old assembly system and reducing the number of injuries people received from repeating the same task over and over.

The pay system was also revised. Previously, workers were paid based on their total output. A skilled worker could frequently exceed his or her quota of belt loops or fly stitching by 20 percent or more, which amounted to a hefty increase in pay. In the new system, people are paid based on the total output of the team. In many cases, this meant that the pay of top performers went down dramatically because the productivity of the team was adversely affected by slower, inexperienced, or inefficient team members. Skilled workers were frustrated having to wait for slower colleagues to complete their part of the garment, and they resented having to pitch in and help out the less-skilled workers to speed things up. Supervisors, unaccustomed to the team system, provided little direction beyond telling people they needed to resolve work flow and personality issues among themselves. The idea was to empower employees to have more control over their own work.

So far, the experiment in teamwork has been a dismal failure. The quantity of garments produced per hour has actually declined 25 percent from pre-team levels. Labor costs have gone down, but morale is terrible. Threats and insults are commonly heard on the factory floor. One seamstress even had to restrain a co-worker who was about to throw a chair at a team member who constantly griped about "having to do everyone else's work."

SOURCE: Based on information reported in N. Munk, "How Levi's Trashed a Great American Brand," *Fortune* (April 12, 1999), 83–90; and R. King, "Levi's Factory Workers Are Assigned to Teams, and Morale Takes a Hit," *The Wall Street Journal*, (May 20, 1998), A1, A6.

Questions

1. Why do you think the experiment in teamwork at Burgess Industries has been unsuccessful? Consider the definition of teams, team characteristics and team dynamics, and issues of leadership.
2. If you were a consultant to Burgess, what would you recommend managers do to promote more effective teamwork?
3. How would you alleviate the conflicts that have developed among employees?

 References

1. Dennis McCafferty, "Managing to Win," *USA Weekend*, April 24–26, 1998, 4–6; "Bird Leaves Pacers with Head Held High," Associated Press report, *Johnson City Press*, June 20, 2000, 20; "Coach Bio: Phil Jackson," *http://www.nba.com/lakers/ bios/coach.html* accessed on May 19, 2000; Paul Buker, "The Man with the Jewelry," *OregonLive*, Monday, May 22, 2000, *http://www.oregonlive.com* accessed on May 22, 2000; Brian S. Moskal, "Running with the Bulls," *IW*, (January 8, 1996): 26–34; Charley Rosen, "No More Bull," *Cigar Aficionado*, (September–October 1998): *http://www. cigaraficionado.com/Cigar/Aficionado/people/fe1098.html*; "The NBA at 50: Phil Jackson," *http://nba.com/history/Jackson_50.html*.

2. J. D. Osburn, L. Moran, E. Musselwhite, and J. H. Zenger, *Self-Directed Work Teams: The New American Challenge* (Homewood, IL.: Business One Irwin, 1990).

3. Linda I. Glassop, "The Organizational Benefit of Teams," *Human Relations* 55, no. 2 (2002), 225–249.

4. Jeffrey Pfeffer, "Producing Sustainable Competitive Advantage through the Effective Management of People," *Academy of Management Executive* 9, no. 1 (1995): 55–72.

5. Wendy Zellner, "No More Same Ol'-Same Ol'," *BusinessWeek* (October 17, 1994), 95–96; Michael Barrier, "However You Slice It," *Nation's Business* (June 1996): 16; Kenneth Labich, "Elite Teams Get the Job Done," *Fortune* (February 19): 1996, 90–99.

6. J. Richard Hackman, "Why Teams Don't Work," in *Theory and Research on Small Groups*, R. Scott Tindale, et al., eds. (New York: Plenum Press, 1998).

7. Avan R. Jassawalla and Hemant C. Sashittal, "Strategies of Effective New Product Team Leaders," *California Management Review* 42, no. 2 (Winter 2000): 34–51.

8. Carl E. Larson and Frank M. J. LaFasto, *Team Work* (Newbury Park, CA: Sage, 1989); and C. P. Aldefer, "Group and Intergroup Relations," in *Improving Life at Work*, J. R. Hackman and J. S. Suttle, eds., (Santa Monica, Calif.: Goodyear, 1977).

9. Lee G. Bolman and Terrence E. Deal, "What Makes a Team Work?" *Organizational Dynamics* (August 1992): 34–44.

10. Kenneth G. Koehler, "Effective Team Management," *Small Business Report* (July 19, 1989), 14–16; Connie J. G. Gersick, "Time and Transition in Work Teams: Toward a New Model of Group Development," *Academy of Management Journal* 31 (1988), 9–41; and John Beck and Neil Yeager, "Moving Beyond Myths," *Training & Development* (March 1996): 51–55.

11. Thomas Petzinger Jr., "Bovis Team Helps Builders Construct a Solid Foundation" (The Front Lines column), *The Wall Street Journal* (March 21, 1997), B1.

12. Susan Carey, "US Air 'Peon' Team Pilots Start-Up of Low-Fare Airline," *The Wall Street Journal*, March 24, 1998, B1.

13. Pierre van Amelsvoort and Jos Benders, "Team Time: A Model for Developing Self-Directed Work Teams," *International Journal of Operations and Production Management* 16, no. 2 (1996): 159–170.

14. Jeanne M. Wilson, Jill George, and Richard S. Wellins, with William C. Byham, *Leadership Trapeze: Strategies for Leadership in Team-Based Organizations* (San Francisco: Jossey-Bass, 1994).

15. Patricia Booth, "Embracing the Team Concept," *Canadian Business Review* (Autumn 1994), 10–13.

16. Ruth Wageman, "Critical Success Factors for Creating Superb Self-Managing Teams," *Organizational Dynamics* (Summer 1997): 49–61.

17. "Vive La Difference," box in Julie Connelly, "All Together Now," *Gallup Management Journal* (Spring 2002): 13–18.

18. For research findings on group size, see M. E. Shaw, *Group Dynamics*, 3rd ed. (New York: McGraw-Hill, 1981); G. Manners, "Another Look at Group Size, Group Problem-Solving and Member Consensus," *Academy of Management Journal* 18 (1975): 715–724; and Albert V. Carron and Kevin S. Spink, "The Group Size-Cohesion Relationship in Minimal Groups," *Small Group Research* 26, no. 1 (February 1995): 86–105.

19. Warren E. Watson, Kamalesh Kumar, and Larry K. Michaelsen, "Cultural Diversity's Impact on Interaction Process and Performance: Comparing Homogeneous and Diverse Task Groups," *Academy of Management Journal* 36 (1993): 590–602; Gail Robinson and Kathleen Dechant, "Building a Business Case for Diversity," *Academy of Management Executive* 11, no. 3 (1997): 21–31; R. A. Guzzo and G. P. Shea, "Group Performance and Intergroup Relations in Organizations," in M. D. Dunnette and L. M. Hough, eds., *Handbook of Industrial & Organizational Psychology*, 2nd ed., vol. 3 (Palo Alto, CA: Consulting Psychologists Press, 1992): 288–290; and David A. Thomas and Robin J. Ely, "Making Differences Matter: A New Paradigm for Managing Diversity," *Harvard Business Review* (September–October 1996): 79–90.

20. Kathleen M. Eisenhardt, Jean L. Kahwajy, and L. J. Bourgeois III, "Conflict and Strategic Choice: How Top Management Teams Disagree," *California Management Review* 39, no. 2 (Winter 1997): 42–62.

21. Dora C. Lau and J. Keith Murnighan, "Demographic Diversity and Faultlines: The Compositional Dynamics of Organizational Groups," *Academy of Management Review* 23, no. 2 (1998): 325–340; and K. A. Jehn, "A Multimethod Examination of the Benefits and Detriments of Intragroup Conflict," *Administrative Science Quarterly* 40 (1995): 256–282.

22. Watson, Kumar, and Michaelsen, "Cultural Diversity's Impact on Interaction Process and Performance."

23. Stanley M. Gully, Dennis J. Devine, and David J. Whitney, "A Meta-Analysis of Cohesion and Performance: Effects of Level of Analysis and Task Interdependence," *Small Group Research* 26, no. 4 (November 1995): 497–520.

24. James Thompson, *Organizations in Action* (New York: McGraw-Hill, 1967).

25. Peter F. Drucker, *Managing in a Time of Great Change* (New York: Truman Talley Books/Dutton, 1995), 98.

26. Ibid.

27. Thomas A. Stewart, "The Great Conundrum—You vs. the Team," *Fortune* (November 25, 1996): 165–166.

28. Charles Fishman, "Miracle of Birth," *Fast Company* (October 2002): 106–116.

29. Robert C. Liden, Sandy J. Wayne, and Lisa Bradway, "Connections Make the Difference," *HR Magazine* (February 1996): 73.

30. Dexter Dunphy and Ben Bryant, "Teams: Panaceas or Prescriptions for Improved Performance," *Human Relations* 49, no. 5 (1996): 677–699; Susan G. Cohen, Gerald E. Ledford, and Gretchen M. Spreitzer, "A Predictive Model of Self-Managing Work Team Effectiveness," *Human Relations* 49, no. 5 (1996): 643–676; Martin Hoegl and Hans Georg Gemuenden, "Teamwork Quality and the Success of Innovative Projects: A Theoretical Concept and Empirical Evidence," *Organization Science* 12, no. 4 (July–August 2001): 435–449.

31. Carron and Spink, "The Group Size-Cohesion Relationship in Minimal Groups."

32. Harold J. Leavitt and Jean Lipman-Blumen, "Hot Groups," *Harvard Business Review* (July–August 1995): 109–116.

33. Dorwin Cartwright and Alvin Zander, *Group Dynamics: Research and Theory*, 3rd ed. (New York: Harper & Row, 1968); Eliot Aronson, *The Social Animal* (San Francisco: W. H. Freeman, 1976); and Thomas Li-Ping Tang and Amy Beth Crofford, "Self-Managing Work Teams," *Employment Relations Today* (Winter 1995/96): 29–39.

34. Tang and Crofford, "Self-Managing Work Teams."

35. Gully, Devine, and Whitney, "A Meta-Analysis of Cohesion and Performance: Effects of Level of Analysis and Task Interdependence."

36. Stanley E. Seashore, *Group Cohesiveness in the Industrial Work Group* (Ann Arbor, MI: Institute for Social Research, 1954).

37. Daniel R. Kibbe and Jill Casner-Lotto, "Ralston Foods: From Greenfield to Maturity in a Team-Based Plant," *Journal of Organizational Excellence* (Summer 2002): 57–67.

38. Based on Robert A. Baron, *Behavior in Organizations*, 2nd ed. (Boston: Allyn & Bacon, 1986); Don Hellriegel, John W. Slocum, Jr., and Richard W. Woodman, *Organizational Behavior*, 8th ed. (Cincinnati: South-Western, 1998), 244; and Gary A. Yukl, *Leadership in Organizations*, 4th ed. (Upper Saddle River, NJ: Prentice Hall, 1998), 384–387.

39. Amy Edmondson, Richard Bohmer, and Gary Pisano, "Speeding Up Team Learning," *Harvard Business Review* (October 2001): 125–132.

40. This section is based on Mark Sanborn, *Team Built: Making Teamwork Pay* (New York: MasterMedia Limited, 1992); Wilson, et al. *Leadership Trapeze*; J. Richard Hackman and R. E. Walton, "Leading Groups in Organizations," in *Designing Effective Work Groups*, P.S. Goodman and Associateds, eds. (San Fransicso: Jossey-Bass, 1986); and Bolman and Deal, "What Makes a Team Work?"

41. Thomas L. Legare, "How Hewlett-Packard Used Virtual Cross-Functional Teams to Deliver Healthcare Industry Solutions," *Journal of Organizational Excellence* (Autumn 2001): 29–38.

42. Edmondson, Bohmer, and Pisano, "Speeding Up Team Learning."

43. Eric Matson, "Congratulations, You're Promoted. (Now What?)," *Fast Company* (June–July 1997): 116–130.

44. Mark Sanborn, *TeamBuilt: Making Teamwork Pay* (New York: MasterMedia Limited, 1992): 100.

45. Bradford W. Bell and Steve W. J. Kozlowski, "A Typology of Virtual Teams: Implications for Effective Leadership," *Group and Organization Management* 27, no. 1 (March 2002): 14–49.

46. The discussion of virtual teams is based on Anthony M. Townsend, Samuel M. DeMarie, and Anthony R. Hendrickson, "Virtual Teams: Technology and the Workplace of the Future," *Academy of Management Executive* 12, no. 3 (August 1998): 17–29; Deborah L. Duarte and Nancy Tennant Snyder, *Mastering Virtual Teams* (San Francisco: Jossey-Bass, 1999); and Jessica Lipnack and Jeffrey Stamps, "Virtual Teams: The New Way to Work," *Strategy & Leadership* (January–February 1999): 14–18.

47. Lipnack and Stamps, "Virtual Teams."

48. Carla Joinson, "Managing Virtual Teams," *HR Magazine* (June 2002): 69–73.

49. This section is based on Bradford S. Bell and Steve W. J. Kozlowski, "A Typology of Virtual Teams: Implications for Effective Leadership," *Group & Organization Management* 27, no. 1 (March 2002): 14–49; Lipnack and Stamps, "Virtual Teams: A New Way to Work"; Joinson, "Managing Virtual Teams"; and Jon R. Katzenbach and Douglas K. Smith, "The Discipline of Virtual Teams," *Leader to Leader* (Fall 2001): 16–25.

50. Terri L. Griffith and Margaret A. Neale, "Information Processing in Traditional, Hybrid, and Virtual Teams: From Nascent Knowledge to Transactive Memory," *Research in Organizational Behavior* 23 (2001): 379–421.

51. Solomon, "Building Teams Across Borders."

52. Ron Young, "The Wide-Awake Club," *People Management* (February 5, 1998): 46–49.

53. Katzenbach and Smith, "The Discipline of Virtual Teams."

54. Griffith and Neale, "Information Processing in Traditional, Hybrid, and Virtual Teams."

55. Edward F. McDonough III, Kenneth B. Kahn, and Gloria Barczak, "An Investigation of the Use of Global, Virtual, and Colocated New Product Development Teams," *The Journal of Product Innovation Management* 18 (2001): 110–120.

56. Mary O'Hara-Devereaux and Robert Johansen, *Globalwork: Bridging Distance, Culture, and Time* (San Francisco: Jossey-Bass, 1994); Charles C. Snow, Scott A. Snell, Sue Canney Davison, and Donald C. Hambrick, "Use Transnational Teams to Globalize Your Company," *Organizational Dynamics* 24, no. 4 (Spring 1996), 50–67; Vijay Govindarajan and Anil K. Gupta,

"Building an Effective Global Business Team," *MIT Sloan Management Review* (Summer, 2001): 63–71; and McDonough, et al., "An Investigation of the Use of Global, Virtual, and Colocated New Product Development Teams."

57. Jon Katzenbach and Douglas Smith, "Virtual Teaming." *Forbes* (May 21, 2001): 48–51.

58. Lipnack and Stamps, "Virtual Teams."

59. This section is based on Govindarajan and Gupta, "Building an Effective Global Business Team."

60. Chantell E. Nicholls, Henry W. Lane, and Mauricio Brehm Brechu, "Taking Self-Managed Teams to Mexico," *Academy of Management Executive* 13, no. 2 (1999): 15–27.

61. Govindarajan and Gupta, "Building an Effective Global Business Team."

62. Govindarajan and Gupta, "Building an Effective Global Business Team."

63. Sylvia Odenwald, "Global Work Teams," *Training and Development* (February 1996): 54–57; and Debby Young, "Team Heat," *CIO*, Section 1 (September 1, 1998): 43–51.

64. Katzenbach and Smith, "Virtual Teaming."

65. R. Duane Ireland and Michael A. Hitt, "Achieving and Maintaining Strategic Competitiveness in the 21st Century: The Role of Strategic Leadership," *Academy of Management Executive* 13, no. 1 (1999): 43–57.

66. Debra L. Shapiro, Stacie A. Furst, Gretchen M. Spreitzer, and Mary Ann Von Glinow, "Transnational Teams in the Electronic Age: Are Team Identity and High Performance at Risk?" *Journal of Organizational Behavior* 23 (2002): 455–467.

67. Koehler, "Effective Team Management"; and Dean Tjosvold, "Making Conflict Productive," *Personnel Administrator* 29 (June 1984): 121

68. Karen A. Jehn and Elizabeth A. Mannix, "The Dynamic Nature of Conflict: A Longitudinal Study of Intragroup Conflict and Group Performance," *Academy of Management Journal* 44, no. 2 (2001): 238–251.

69. This discussion is based on K. W. Thomas, "Towards Multidimensional Values in Teaching: The Example of Conflict Behaviors," *Academy of Management Review* 2 (1977): 487.

70. Mitzi M. Montoya-Weiss, Anne P. Massey, and Michael Song, "Getting It Together: Temporal Coordination and Conflict Management in Global Virtual Teams," *Academy of Management Journal* 44, no. 6 (2001): 1251–1262.

Chapter

Your Leadership Challenge

After reading this chapter, you should be able to:

- Apply an awareness of the dimensions of diversity and multicultural issues in your everyday life.

- Encourage and support diversity to meet organizational needs.

- Consider the role of cultural values and attitudes in determining how to deal with employees from different cultures or ethnic backgrounds.

- Reduce the difficulties faced by minorities in organizations.

- Break down your personal barriers that may stand in the way of enhancing your level of diversity awareness and appreciation.

Myrtle Potter still remembers what it felt like to arrive for her first day of college at the University of Chicago. She was an outsider from the start, Potter recalls: "rural, African American, and female." One of six children from a family of modest means, Potter was able to attend the university only because her father mortgaged the house. Today, Potter is chief operating officer of biotechnology firm Genentech, but her goal is to be a CEO. "It is important to me not only as an African American or a woman but as an African-American woman," she says. Potter thinks she'll make it to the top one day, and experts agree that she has a pretty good shot. But the road hasn't been an easy one.

Potter began her career in the sales department at Merck, where she constantly pressed for greater responsibilities. She had a hard time moving up the corporate hierarchy, but she continued to make lateral moves just so she could keep learning, broadening her skills, and building a network of contacts. During the mid-1980s, Potter had one manager tell her that black women lacked the "intellectual ability" for analytical managerial work, suggesting that she should stick with her sales job. Potter proved him wrong by accomplishing every challenge set before her. Moving on from Merck to Bristol-Myers Squibb (BMS), she eventually achieved the position of president of the company's U.S. cardiovascular/metabolic sales division. Her energy, operational savvy, leadership skills, and commitment to a diverse culture contributed to significant sales growth and doubled the number of women in senior field management positions.

Although Potter is highly ambitious for her own advancement, she is perhaps even more committed to helping others break through barriers. "One of my goals is to keep my mentoring circle as wide as I possibly can handle," Potter says, and she mentors men as well as women and people of any race or ethnicity. At Genentech, as at BMS, she has an uncanny knack for cultivating and inspiring people from all backgrounds to achieve beyond their expectations. She believes diversity is a key to successful organizations. "My view is that there is already one Myrtle," Potter says. "I don't need five more Myrtles to reinforce me. I need people who can look at a problem in a way that I might not have viewed it and yet can still come together to work toward a common vision and be committed to a common purpose." It's that kind of attitude that could land Potter in the CEO's chair.[1]

The face of organizations in America is beginning to change, with women and minorities slowly moving into upper-level leadership positions. However, there are still many challenges for creating diverse organizations. One of the most important roles for leaders in the coming years will be developing a solid base of diverse leadership talent. "In any organization in America, you will see diversity at the bottom of the house," says Roberta (Bobbi) Gutman, vice president and director of global diversity at Motorola. "But to get it higher up takes the clout and the wingspan of company leadership."[2]

Diversity in terms of race, gender, religion, ethnicity, age, nationality, sexual orientation, physical and mental ability, and so forth, is a fact of life for today's organizations. In the United States, the population, the workforce, and the customer base are changing dramatically. According to U.S. Department of Labor statistics, the workforce will soon be dominated by female and minority workers. In addition, there has been a slow but emphatic shift in our attitudes toward racial, ethnic, cultural, or other "differences." In the past, the United States was seen as a melting pot where people of different national origins, races, ethnicity, and religions came together and blended to resemble one another. Opportunities for advancement in society and in organizations favored people who fit easily into the mainstream culture. Many times, immigrants chose desperate measures, such as changing their last names, abandoning their native languages, and sacrificing their own cultures. People were willing to assimilate in order to get ahead.

Today, however, the burden of adaptation rests more on the organization than on the individual. People of different races, nationalities, genders, sexual orientations, religions, and ethnic backgrounds, are no longer willing to give up or hide their own values, beliefs, and ways of doing things in order to fit in. Carlton Yearwood, director of diversity management at Allstate, points out that whereas diversity programs in the past were usually aimed at assimilating cultural differences, the focus today is on accepting differences and finding a way to bring workforce differences together to benefit the organization.[3]

In addition to the increasing heterogeneity of the U.S. population, organizations are increasingly operating on a global playing field, which means that people of different races and nationalities are working and living together at an unprecedented level. Talented, educated knowledge workers seek opportunities all over the world, just as organizations search the world for the best minds to help them compete in a global economy. Radha Basu, for example, leads teams of Hewlett-Packard software writers who work in the United States, Australia, England, Germany, India, Japan, and Switzerland. Schering AG, the German pharmaceuticals company, employs 56 percent of its 22,000 workers outside its home country. Even the smallest organizations today are often enmeshed with suppliers, competitors, and customers from all over the world.[4]

Successful leaders in an increasingly diverse world have a responsibility to acknowledge and value cultural differences and understand how diversity affects organizational operations and outcomes.[5] This chapter explores the topic of diversity and multiculturalism. We will first define diversity and explore the need for diversity in today's organizations. Then we will look at new styles of leadership and the multicultural challenges brought about by globalization. We will also examine some of the specific challenges facing minority employees and leadership initiatives for supporting and valuing diversity in the workplace.

Diversity Today

At 3Com Corporation's modem factory in Morton Grove, Illinois, 65 different national flags are displayed, each representing the origin of at least one person who has worked at the plant. The factory's 1,200 workers speak more than 20 languages, including Tagalog, Chinese, and Gujarati. On the plant floor, employees must learn to mingle and cooperate, but in the company lunchroom, they often cluster into ethnic and linguistic groups. Semifreddi's, a $7.1 million artisan-bread bakery in Emeryville, California, has only 100 employees, but most of them come from Mexico, Laos, China, Peru, Cambodia, Yemen, and Vietnam. CEO Tom Frainier had to hire translators to help him communicate with workers.[6] In Silicon Valley, where at least one third of scientists and engineers are immigrants from Europe, Latin America, the Middle East, and Asia, Jesse Jackson has criticized organizations for the low participation of blacks and Hispanics.[7] Although diversity brings many advantages to organizations, these examples illustrate that it also brings many challenges.

Definition of Diversity

Workforce diversity means a workforce made up of people with different human qualities or who belong to various cultural groups. From the perspective of individuals, **diversity** refers to differences among people in terms of dimensions such as age, ethnicity, gender, or race. It is important to remember that diversity includes everyone, not just racial or ethnic minorities.

Several important dimensions of diversity are illustrated in Exhibit 11.1. This *diversity wheel* shows the myriad combinations of traits that make up diversity. The inside wheel represents primary dimensions of diversity, which include inborn differences or differences that have an impact throughout one's life.[8] Primary dimensions are core elements through which people shape their self-image and world view. These dimensions are age, race, ethnicity, gender, mental or physical abilities, and sexual orientation. Turn the wheel and these primary characteristics match up with various secondary dimensions of diversity.

Workforce diversity
a workforce made up of people with different human qualities or who belong to various cultural groups

Diversity
differences among people in terms of age, ethnicity, gender, race, or other dimensions

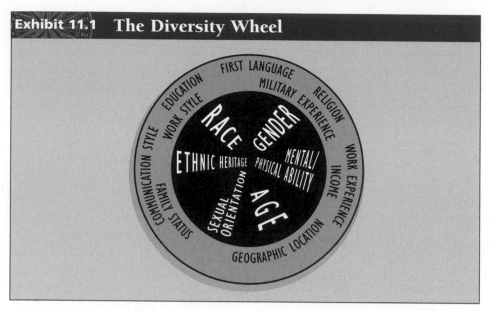

Exhibit 11.1 The Diversity Wheel

SOURCE: Marilyn Loden, *Implementing Diversity* (Homewood, IL: Irwin, 1996). Used with permission.

Secondary dimensions can be acquired or changed throughout one's lifetime. These dimensions tend to have less impact than those of the core but nevertheless affect a person's self-definition and worldview and have an impact on how the person is viewed by others. For example, veterans of the war in Iraq may have been profoundly affected by their military experience and may be perceived differently from other people. An employee living in a public housing project will be perceived differently from one who lives in an affluent part of town. Secondary dimensions such as work style, communication style, and educational or skill level are particularly relevant in the organizational setting.[9] One challenge for organizational leaders is to recognize that each person can bring value and strengths to the workplace based on his or her own combination of diversity characteristics. Organizations establish workforce diversity programs to promote the hiring, inclusion, and promotion of diverse employees and to ensure that differences are accepted and respected in the workplace.

The Reality of Diversity

Attitudes toward diversity are changing partly because they have to—organizations are recognizing and welcoming cultural differences as a result of significant changes in our society, including globalization and the changing workforce.[10] The average worker is older now, and many more women, people of color, and immigrants are entering the workforce. Immigration accounted for nearly half of the increase in the labor force in the 1990s, and immigrants likely will constitute an increasing share of workers in the coming decades.[11] Figures from the Bureau of Labor Statistics indicate that the number of immigrant workers continues to grow.[12] In addition, minorities are expected to make up about 40 percent of people entering the workforce during the first decade of this century—many, first-generation immigrants, and almost two-thirds female. Men's participation in the U.S. labor force has been on a slow but steady decline since 1953, while the participation of women has dramatically increased over the same time period.[13] By 2020, it is estimated that women will make up fully half of the total full-time U.S. workforce. White males, the majority of workers in the past, already make up less than half the U.S. workforce.[14]

The other factor contributing to increased acceptance of diversity is globalization. In today's world, ideas, capital investments, products, services, and people flow freely and rapidly around the world. Some large multinational corporations, including Canada's Northern Telecom, U.S.-based Coca-Cola, Switzerland's Nestlé, and France's Carrefour, all get a large percentage of their sales from outside their home countries. Companies like Starbucks and MTV Networks are finding that the only potential for growth lies overseas. These organizations need diversity of leadership and sometimes find that U.S. managers don't have the broad experience needed to succeed in a global environment. An unprecedented number of foreign-born CEOs now run major companies in the United States, Britain, and several other countries.[15] Employees with global experience and cultural sensitivity are in high demand in many industries, and almost every employee is dealing with a wider range of cultures than ever before. The Leader's Bookshelf further examines the need for global literacy.

The Need for Organizational Diversity

Top leaders of organizations are responding to diversity and new attitudes for a number of reasons beyond the simple fact that shifting demographics make it necessary to do so. There is no question that the workforce is changing and organizations have to change to reflect the new workforce composition. However, there are a number of other reasons leaders need to incorporate and support diversity.

Recent research supports the idea that diversity adds value to organizations and can contribute to a firm's competitive advantage.[16] There are a number of ways in which diversity is beneficial to organizations. For one thing, they can use internal diversity to meet the needs of diverse customers. Culture plays an important part in determining the goods, entertainment, social services, and household products that people use and buy. A Glass Ceiling Commission study noted that two out of every three people in the United States are minority-group members or females or both, so organizations are recruiting minority employees who can understand how diverse people live and what they want and need.[17] The

LEADER'S BOOKSHELF

Global Literacies: Lessons on Business Leadership and National Cultures
By Robert Rosen, with Patricia Digh, Marshall Singer, and Carl Phillips

Companies with globally illiterate leaders can get into trouble. Consider KFC's slogan, "Finger-lickin' good," which was translated into Chinese as an unappetizing, "Eat your fingers off." Another U.S. company sent an impressive pigskin-bound business proposal to Saudi Arabia, but it was never opened because the Muslim recipients consider pigs unclean.

Robert Rosen, author of *Global Literacies: Lessons on Business Leadership and National Cultures,* and his colleagues found that globally literate American leaders are in short supply. Only 28 percent of surveyed U.S. executives think multicultural experience is important. Rosen warns that all business is now global business, and ethnocentric leaders will have to overcome their provincial mind-sets if they hope to succeed.

Leadership Competencies
In *Global Literacies,* Rosen draws on lessons he learned through interviews with CEOs in 28 countries and surveys of senior leaders around the world. He identifies four literacies that every leader must practice to succeed in today's global, multicultural world:

1. *Personal literacy* involves understanding and valuing yourself. Global leaders must first commit to self-understanding, personal growth, and continuous learning.
2. *Social literacy* is about involving and engaging others from diverse backgrounds and experiences. The technological revolution has produced a world of complexity and speed that requires collaborative leaders. These leaders focus on assembling the best people, focusing them on important goals, and connecting their knowledge and insights to achieve great things.
3. *Business literacy* refers to focusing and mobilizing your organization. Constant change forces companies to be fast and flexible, which requires a culture of openness, learning, and change.
4. *Cultural literacy* means knowing about and leveraging cultural differences. Leaders need an understanding of national cultures to interact with and influence people of different cultures and backgrounds. Additionally, they should apply their cultural understanding to strengthen their organization's competitive advantage.

The Global-Centric Leader
To be successful today requires being globally literate—thinking, seeing, acting, and moving in a culturally conscious manner. The four global literacies help leaders expand their perception of themselves and the world, think and act with global-centric leadership, and mobilize and inspire people across national cultures to accomplish the organization's goals. "Competition comes from everywhere; we're all each other's customers, suppliers, and labor markets," Rosen writes. "The challenge is, how do we grow and thrive in this borderless marketplace?"

Global Literacies: Lessons on Business Leadership and National Cultures, by Robert Rosen, with Patricia Digh, Marshall Singer, and Carl Phillips, is published by Simon and Schuster.

marketing of goods and services is perhaps the area in which leaders' response to a changing customer base is most evident. After years of simply translating American advertisements into foreign languages, U.S. organizations like McDonald's, Taco Bell, Revlon, and Anheuser Busch are developing targeted marketing campaigns that tap into the cultural norms and colloquialisms of different groups.[18] One McDonald's ad shows a father trying in vain to get his toddler to say "daddy." Only when he shakes a bag of McDonald's fries before the child does the little girl cheerfully utter "papa." Hispanics got the joke—in Spanish, the word for dad and fries is the same.

Diverse employees can also help an organization build better relationships with customers by making them feel connected to the organization. When customers see and interact with people like themselves, they feel better about doing business with the company. One company that has built its success on the principle that the organization should be inclusive rather than exclusive is Allstate Insurance Company, which launched its first diversity program in 1969 and today ties 25 percent of managers' bonus pay to diversity performance.

In the Lead   Allstate Insurance Company

"Being in a relationship business, how can you not look like and sound like your clients?" asks Phil Lawson, vice president of sales for Allstate Insurance. "It's an obvious competitive advantage when you can mirror the clients that you serve."

Allstate actively recruits, develops, and promotes diverse employees. Its percentages of minority employees, female executives, and minority executives are all well above the national average. However, the company's concept of diversity is a broad one that goes beyond race and gender to include diversity in terms of age, religion, sexual orientation, disability, and other dimensions as well.

Allstate's diversity initiatives have earned the company a string of awards, such as the "1999 Best Companies for Hispanics to Work," the "1998 Top 10 Companies for Minority Managers," and the 2002 "50 Best Companies for Minorities." They've also led to some solid business results. A study by Simmons Research Group found that Allstate is the number-one life and auto insurer among African Americans and the number-one homeowner's and life insurance firm among Hispanic Americans. Allstate's internal measurement systems show a steady increase in the customer base and growing levels of customer satisfaction.

The company's diverse workforce has helped Allstate establish solid relationships with culturally and ethnically diverse communities. At the Sunnyside neighborhood office in Queens, New York, one of the most ethnically diverse communities in the country, customers often relate to sales reps like members of their family, consulting them on problems that might have no relation to insurance. Mike Kalkin, the agent who heads up the office (and who is himself from an immigrant family), often recruits employees from within the community because they understand the local people's unique needs. A different situation exists at a northwestern Arkansas office, where a growing retired population means placing more emphasis on serving the needs of older customers.

"We want to outperform the competition," says Joan Crockett, senior vice president for human resources. "[For us] the best talents are diverse because the customers are."[19]

Action Memo

As a leader: Hire and promote people from diverse cultures and with diverse human characteristics. Use organizational diversity to improve creativity and decision-making, better serve customers, attract and retain the best people, and enhance organizational flexibility.

Another need for diversity is to develop employee and organizational potential. When organizations support diversity, people feel valued for what they can bring to the organization, which leads to higher morale. A story from furniture manufacturer Herman Miller, told in the Living Leadership box, illustrates that each of us has unique talents and gifts. Incorporating diversity can help people feel good about themselves and the special contributions they can make to the organization. People can also build better relationships at work when they develop the skills to understand and accept cultural differences. Allstate's diversity training emphasizes that employees can expect to be treated with respect and dignity, but they are also expected to treat others the same way and to cultivate their business as well as relationship skills to help Allstate succeed.

By seriously recruiting and valuing individuals without regard to race, nationality, gender, age, sexual preference, or physical ability, organizations can attract and retain the best human talent. Myrtle Potter, described in the chapter opening case, believes that when leaders "keep [their] eyes focused on identifying the best people possible, remain open-minded about what constitutes being the best, and have no preconceived notion about what talent looks like, then [organizations] find the best people."[20]

Finally, diversity develops greater organizational flexibility. For one thing, diversity within an organization provides a broader and deeper base of experience for problem solving, creativity, and innovation. Bell Atlantic CEO Ivan Seidenberg promotes diversity at his company primarily because he believes diverse groups make better decisions and bring the creativity and innovation needed to keep pace with massive changes in technology and competition. "If everybody in the room is the same," Seidenberg says, "you'll get a lot fewer arguments and a lot worse answers."[21]

LIVING LEADERSHIP

Honoring Our Diversity of Gifts

One day the millwright died.

My father, being a young manager at the time, did not particularly know what he should do when a key person died, but thought he ought to go visit the family. He went to the house and was invited to join the family in the living room. There was some awkward conversation—the kind with which many of us are familiar.

The widow asked my father if it would be all right if she read aloud some poetry. Naturally, he agreed. She went into another room, came back with a bound book, and for many minutes, read selected pieces of beautiful poetry. When she finished, my father commented on how beautiful the poetry was and asked who wrote it. She replied that her husband, the millwright, was the poet.

It is now nearly sixty years since the millwright died, and my father and many of us at Herman Miller continue to wonder: Was he a poet who did millwright's work, or was he a millwright who wrote poetry?

* * *

Understanding diversity enables us to see that each of us is needed. . . .

The simple act of recognizing diversity in corporate life helps us to connect the great variety of gifts that people bring to the work and service of the organization. Diversity allows each of us to contribute in a special way, to make our special gift a part of the corporate effort.

SOURCE: From *Leadership Is an Art,* by Max DePree, copyright © 1987 by Max DePree. Used with permission of Doubleday, a division of Random House, Inc.

Diversity of thought is essential to today's learning organization, which will be described in Chapter 15. Competitive pressures are challenging leaders to create organizational environments that foster and support creative thinking and sharing of diverse viewpoints. Diverse groups tend to be more creative than homogeneous groups in part because of the different perspectives people can bring to the problem or issue. One study reported that companies that are high on creativity and innovation have a higher percentage of women and nonwhite male employees than less innovative companies.[22]

One aspect of diversity that is of particular interest in organizations is the way in which women's style of leadership may differ from men's. As women move into higher positions in organizations, it has been observed that they often use a style of leadership that is highly effective in today's turbulent, culturally diverse environment.[23]

Ways Women Lead

Action Memo

As a leader: Use an interactive, collaborative leadership process. Develop personal, caring relationships with your followers. Make everyone feel like an important part of your group or organization.

Leadership traits traditionally associated with white, American-born males include aggressiveness or assertiveness, rational analysis, and a "take charge" attitude. Male leaders tend to be competitive and individualistic and prefer working in vertical hierarchies. They rely on formal authority and position in their dealings with subordinates.

Although women may also demonstrate these traits, research has found that in general, women tend to be more concerned with relationship building, inclusiveness, participation, and caring.[24] Female leaders such as Deborah Kent, the first woman to head a vehicle assembly plant for Ford Motor Co., are often more willing to share power and information, to encourage employee development, and to strive to enhance others' feelings of self-worth. "It does no good to have a diverse workforce if you don't listen to their opinions and thoughts," says Kent. "I treat people the way I want to be treated."[25]

There is some evidence that men may become less influential in the workforce with women becoming dominant players because women's approach is more attuned to the needs and values of a multicultural environment. There is a stunning gender reversal in U.S. education, with girls taking over almost every leadership role from kindergarten to graduate school. In addition, women of all races and ethnic groups are outpacing men in earning bachelor's and master's degrees. They're rapidly closing the M.D. and Ph.D. gap and make up almost half of law students. Overall, women's participation in the labor force has steadily increased since the mid-1950s, while men's participation has slowly but steadily declined. According to James Gabarino, an author and professor of human development at Cornell University, women "are better able to deliver in terms of what modern society requires of people—paying attention, abiding by rules, being verbally competent, and dealing with interpersonal relationships in offices."[26]

Interactive leadership
a leadership style in which people develop personal relationships with followers, share power and information, empower employees, and strive to enhance others' feelings of self-worth

Professor and author Judy B. Rosener has called women's approach to leadership **interactive leadership**.[27] The leader favors a consensual and collaborative process, and influence derives from relationships rather than position power and authority. Some psychologists have suggested that women may be more relationship-oriented than men because of different psychological needs stemming from early experiences. This difference between the relationship orientations of men and women has sometimes been used to suggest that women cannot lead effectively because they fail to exercise power. However, whereas male leaders may associate effective leadership with a top-down command-and-control process, women's interactive leadership seems appropriate for the future of diversity and learning organizations.

Although the values associated with interactive leadership, such as inclusion, relationship building, and caring, are generally considered "feminine" values, interactive leadership is not gender-specific. These values are becoming increasingly

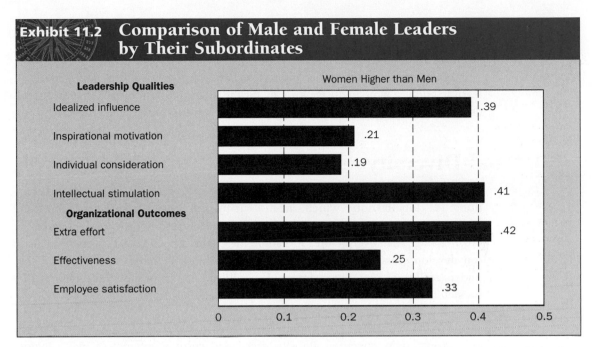

Exhibit 11.2 **Comparison of Male and Female Leaders by Their Subordinates**

NOTE: *Ratings of leaders were on a scale of 1–5. Women leaders were rated higher, on average, by the amount indicated for each item.*
SOURCE: *Based on Bernard M. Bass and Bruce J. Avolio, "Shatter the Glass Ceiling: Women May Make Better Managers," Human Resource Management 33, no. 4 (Winter 1994); 549–560.*

valuable for both male and female leaders. Today's flatter, team-based organizations are no longer looking for top-down authority figures but for more collaborative and inclusive approaches to leadership.[28]

As illustrated in Exhibit 11.2, one survey of followers rated women leaders significantly higher than men on several characteristics that are crucial for developing fast, flexible, learning organizations. Female leaders were rated as having more idealized influence, providing more inspirational motivation, being more individually considerate, and offering more intellectual stimulation.[29] *Idealized influence* means that followers identify with and want to emulate the leader; the leader is trusted and respected, maintains high standards, and is considered to have power because of who she is rather than what position she holds. *Inspirational motivation* is derived from the leader who appeals emotionally and symbolically to employees' desire to do a good job and help achieve organizational goals. *Individual consideration* means each follower is treated as an individual but all are treated equitably; individual needs are recognized and assignments are delegated to followers to provide learning opportunities. *Intellectual stimulation* means questioning current methods and challenging employees to think in new ways. In addition, women leaders were judged by subordinates as more effective and satisfying to work for and were considered able to generate extra levels of effort from employees.

Again, the interactive leadership style is not exclusive to women. Any leader can learn to adopt a more inclusive style by paying attention to nonverbal behavior and developing skills such as listening, empathy, cooperation, and collaboration.[30]

Global Diversity

One of the most rapidly increasing sources of diversity in North American organizations is globalization, which means hiring employees in many countries. Globalization means that organizations are confronting diversity issues across a broader stage than ever before. To handle the challenges of global diversity, leaders can develop cross-cultural understanding, the ability to build networks, and the understanding of geopolitical forces. A significant aspect of global diversity is the sociocultural environment and its effect on leadership actions.

The Sociocultural Environment

For organizations operating globally, social and cultural differences may provide more potential for difficulties and conflicts than any other source. Managers in some U.S. corporations operating internationally have run into problems trying to transfer their diversity policies and practices to European divisions. Policies designed to address diversity issues in the United States don't take into consideration the complex social and cultural systems in Europe. Even the meaning of the term diversity presents problems. In many European languages, the closest word implies separation rather than the inclusion sought by U.S. diversity programs.[31]

National cultures are intangible, pervasive, and difficult to comprehend. However, it is imperative that leaders in international organizations learn to understand local cultures and deal with them effectively. As C. R. "Dick" Shoemate, chairman and CEO of Bestfoods, says, "It takes a special kind of leadership to deal with the differences in a multicountry, multicultural organization. . . . " Bestfoods uses cross-border assignments and extensive individual coaching to train people to lead in different cultures.[32] One approach to understanding other cultures is to look at how social value systems differ.

Social Value Systems Research done by Geert Hofstede on IBM employees in 40 countries discovered that mind-set and cultural values on issues such as individualism versus collectivism strongly influence organizational and employee relationships and vary widely among cultures.[33] Exhibit 11.3 shows examples of how countries rate on four significant dimensions.

Exhibit 11.3   Rank Orderings of 10 Countries Along Four Dimensions of National Value System

Country	Power[a]	Uncertainty[b]	Individualism[c]	Masculinity[d]
Australia	7	7	2	5
Costa Rica	8	2 (tie)	10	9
France	3	2 (tie)	4	7
India	2	9	6	6
Japan	5	1	7	1
Mexico	1	4	8	2
Sweden	10	10	3	10
Thailand	4	6	9	8
United States	6	8	1	4

[a]1 = highest power distance
10 = lowest power distance
[b]1 = highest uncertainty avoidance
10 = lowest uncertainty avoidance

[c]1 = highest individualism
10 = highest collectivism
[d]1 = highest masculinity
10 = highest femininity

SOURCE: From Dorothy Marcic, *Organizational Behavior and Cases*, 4th ed. (St. Paul, MN: West, 1995). Based on Geert Hofstede, *Culture's Consequences* (London: Sage Publications, 1984); and *Cultures and Organizations: Software of the Mind* (New York:McGraw-Hill, 1991).

❋ *Power distance.* High power distance means people accept inequality in power among institutions, organizations, and individuals. Low power distance means people expect equality in power. Countries that value high power distance are Malaysia, the Philippines, and Panama. Countries that value low power distance include Denmark, Austria, and Israel.

❋ *Uncertainty avoidance.* High uncertainty avoidance means that members of a society feel uncomfortable with uncertainty and ambiguity and thus support beliefs and behaviors that promise certainty and conformity. Low uncertainty avoidance means that people have a high tolerance for the unstructured, the unclear, and the unpredictable. High uncertainty avoidance cultures include Greece, Portugal, and Uruguay. Singapore and Jamaica are two countries with low uncertainty avoidance values.

❋ *Individualism and collectivism.* Individualism reflects a value for a loosely knit social framework in which individuals are expected to take care of themselves. Collectivism is a preference for a tightly knit social framework in which people look out for one another and organizations protect their members' interests. Countries with individualist values include the United States, Great Britain, and Canada. Countries with collectivist values are Guatemala, Ecuador, and Panama.

Power distance
how much people accept equality in power; high power distance reflects an acceptance of power inequality among institutions, organizations, and individuals. Low power distance means people expect equality in power

Uncertainty avoidance
the degree to which members of a society feel uncomfortable with uncertainty and ambiguity and thus support beliefs and behaviors that promise certainty and conformity

Individualism
a value for a loosely knit social framework in which individuals are expected to take care of themselves

Collectivism
a preference for a tightly knit social framework in which people look out for one another and organizations protect their members' interests

Masculinity
a preference for achievement, heroism, assertiveness, work centrality, and material success

Femininity
a preference for relationships, cooperation, group decision making, and quality of life

※ *Masculinity and femininity.* **Masculinity** reflects a preference for achievement, heroism, assertiveness, work centrality, and material success. **Femininity** reflects the values of relationships, cooperation, group decision making, and quality of life. Japan, Austria, and Mexico are countries with strong masculine values. Countries with strong feminine values include Sweden, Norway, Denmark, and the former Yugoslavia. Both men and women subscribe to the dominant value in masculine or feminine cultures.

Social value differences can significantly affect leadership, working relationships, and organizational functioning. Answering the questions in Leader's Self-Insight 11.1 can help you better understand the social values of your classmates or co-workers. Terry Neill, a managing partner at a London-based change management practice, uses Hofstede's findings in his work with companies. Based on his experiences with global companies such as Unilever PLC, Shell Oil, and British Petroleum, Neill points out that the Dutch, Irish, Americans, and British are generally quite comfortable with open argument. However, Japanese and other Asian employees often feel uneasy or even threatened by such directness.[34] In many Asian countries, leaders perceive the organization as a large family and emphasize cooperation through networks of personal relationships. In contrast, leaders in Germany and other central European countries typically strive to run their organizations as impersonal well-oiled machines.[35] How leaders handle these and other cultural differences has tremendous impact on the satisfaction and effectiveness of diverse employees.

Other Cultural Characteristics Other cultural characteristics that can affect international leadership are language, religion, attitudes, social organization, and education. Some countries, such as India, are characterized by *linguistic pluralism,* meaning several languages are spoken there. Other countries may rely heavily on spoken rather than written language. Religion includes sacred objects, philosophical attitudes toward life, taboos, and rituals. Attitudes toward time, space, authority, and achievement can all affect organizations. People from urban cultures tend to follow rigid time schedules, for example, while those from rural cultures are less concerned with clock time, which can lead to disputes regarding tardiness. In some cultures, the amount of space an employee is given to work in is a status symbol, while other cultures treat space as inconsequential. Elements of social organization include kinship and families, status systems, and opportunities for social mobility. For example, leadership in Japan is a way to move up in the social "pecking order." Age commands more status and respect in Europe and the Middle East than in the United States.[36]

Leaders working in a global context have found that social and cultural differences cannot be ignored. Consider how addressing cultural differences has helped McDonald's thrive in France even as the corporation's U.S. business stalled.

Social Values

Instructions: Different social groups (work colleagues, family, professional groups, and national, religious, and cultural groups) are all around us. Focus on the group of individuals whom you consider to be your colleagues (e.g., team members, co-workers, classmates). Respond to each of the following statements and indicate its level of importance to your colleague group on the scale of (1) Not at all important to (5) Very important.

How Important Is It:	Not at all important				Very important
1. To compromise one's wishes to act together with your colleagues?	1	2	3	4	5
2. To be loyal to your colleagues?	1	2	3	4	5
3. To follow norms established by your colleagues?	1	2	3	4	5
4. To maintain a stable environment rather than "rock the boat"?	1	2	3	4	5
5. To not break the rules?	1	2	3	4	5
6. To be a specialist or professional rather than a manager?	1	2	3	4	5
7. To have an opportunity for high earnings?	1	2	3	4	5
8. To have an opportunity for advancement to higher level jobs?	1	2	3	4	5
9. To work with people who cooperate well with one another?	1	2	3	4	5
10. To have a good working relationship with your manager?	1	2	3	4	5
11. To have a manager that gives detailed instructions?	1	2	3	4	5
12. To avoid disagreement with a manager?	1	2	3	4	5

Scoring and Interpretation

There are four subscale scores that measure the four social values described by Hofstede. For the dimension of *individualism–collectivism*, compute your **average** score based on responses to questions 1, 2, and 3. For the dimension of *uncertainty avoidance*, compute your **average** score based on responses to questions 4, 5, and 6. For the dimension of *masculinity–femininity*, reverse score your responses to questions 9 and 10 (5 = 1, 4 = 2, 2 = 4, and 1 = 5) and then compute your **average** score for questions 7, 8, 9, and 10. For the dimension of *power distance*, compute the **average** score for questions 11 and 12.

My average social value scores are:

Individualism–collectivism (I–C) _____.   Masculinity–femininity (M–F) _____.
Uncertainty avoidance (UA) _____.   Power distance (PD) _____.

An average score of 4 or above on the I–C scale means that *collectivism* is a social value in your colleague group, and a score of 2 or below means that the value of *individualism* dominates. A score of 4 or above on the UA scale means that your group values the absence of ambiguity and uncertainty (*high uncertainty avoidance*), and a score below 2 means that uncertainty and unpredictability are preferred. A score of 4 or above on the M–F scale means that *masculinity* is a social value in your colleague group, and a score of 2 or below means that the value of *femininity* dominates. A score of 4 or above on the PD scale means that *high power distance*, or hierarchical differences, is a social value in your colleague group, and a score of 2 or below means that the value of *low power distance*, or equality, dominates.

Compare your four scores to one another to understand your perception of the different values in your colleague group. On which of the four values would you like to score higher? Lower? Analyze the specific questions on which you scored higher or lower to analyze the pattern of your group's social values. Show your scores to a student from another country and explain what they mean. How do the social values of your colleague group differ from the social values of the international student's colleague group? How do these social values differ across the different nationalities represented in your class?

SOURCE: Adapted from Geert Hofstede, *Culture's Consequences* (London: Sage Publications, 1984); and D. Matsumoto, M. D. Weissman, K. Preston, B. R. Brown, and C. Kupperbausch, "Context-specific Measurement of Individualism–Collectivism on the Individual Level: The Individualism-Collectivism Interpersonal Assessment Inventory," *Journal of Cross-Cultural Psychology* 28, no. 6 (1997): 743–767.

In the Lead   Denis Hennequin, McDonald's France

In December 2002, McDonald's, the long-time king of fast food, posted its first ever quarterly loss and announced the closing of 175 outlets worldwide. Yet, during that same time period, a new McDonald's restaurant was opening in France every six days.

McDonald's French subsidiary is booming, thanks to leaders who responded to local and national differences rather than trying to transfer the American fast-food concept wholesale. Consumers in France were initially resentful of the U.S.-based chain's incursion. It wasn't so long ago that an anti-globalization activist was hailed as a national hero for razing a partially built McDonald's in the south of France. Denis Hennequin, the French subsidiary's CEO, responded by running a series of edgy advertisements depicting fat, ignorant Americans who couldn't understand why McDonald's France used locally produced food that wasn't genetically modified. Hennequin knows the French are distrustful of all things American, and he believes leaders should keep a sense of humor to help them address cultural issues.

Hennequin has followed a clever strategy for giving McDonald's France its own identity and boosting the chain's attractiveness to customers. Rather than building red and yellow boxes, leaders are adapting restaurant designs to fit with the local architecture and remodeling existing outlets to include features such as hardwood floors, wood-beam ceilings, comfortable armchairs, and music videos. Rather than streamlining the menu, they've added items such as espresso, brioche, and more upscale sandwiches, including a hot ham and cheese sandwich dubbed the Croque McDo. The upscale styling doesn't come cheap, but the Gallic twists have helped sales soar. Unlike in the United States, where customers want quick service and cheap, tasty eats, the French want higher-quality food and a friendly atmosphere that encourages them to linger. The average McDonald's customer in France spends $9 per visit, compared to an average of $4 per visit in the United States.[37]

Responding to local needs and cultural values can help organizations like McDonald's be more competitive and successful. However, blending cultures isn't always easy. Cultural differences can create significant barriers to successful communication and collaboration. The merger of U.S.-based Upjohn and Sweden's Pharmacia floundered, partly because of cross-cultural misunderstandings. Similarly, leaders at Chrysler Corp. and Germany's Daimler Benz have had a difficult time integrating the two companies because of cultural differences.[38]

Leadership Implications

A study of executives in five countries found that although the globalization of business seems to be leading to a convergence of managerial values and attitudes, executives in different countries differ significantly in some areas, which can create problems for leadership.[39] To lead effectively in a diverse global environment, leaders should be aware of cultural and subcultural differences. Chapter 3 examined contingency theories of leadership that explain the relationship between leader style and a given situation. It is important for leaders to recognize that culture affects both style and the leadership situation. For example, in cultures with high uncertainty avoidance, a leadership situation with high task structure as described in Chapter 3 is favorable, but those in low uncertainty avoidance cultures prefer less structured work situations.

In addition, how behavior is perceived differs from culture to culture. To criticize a subordinate in private directly is considered appropriate behavior in individualistic societies such as the United States. However, in Japan, which values collectivism over individualism, the same leader behavior would be seen as inconsiderate. Japanese employees lose face if they are criticized directly by a supervisor. The expectation is that people will receive criticism information from peers rather than directly from the leader.[40] Research into how the contingency models apply to cross-cultural situations is sparse. However, all leaders need to be aware of the impact that culture may have and consider cultural values in their dealings with employees.

Action Memo

As a leader: Develop a global mindset. Study other languages and cultures. Form relationships with people from different countries. Be sensitive to differences in social value systems, and find creative ways to address delicate diversity issues.

Challenges Minorities Face

Valuing diversity and enabling all individuals to develop their unique talents is difficult to achieve. Ethnocentrism, the belief that one's own culture and subculture are inherently superior to other cultures, is a natural tendency of most people.[41] Many leaders relate to people in the organization as if everyone shares similar values, beliefs, motivations, and attitudes about work and life. This assumption is typically false even when dealing with people who share the same cultural background. Ethnocentric viewpoints combined with a standard set of cultural assumptions and practices create a number of challenges for minority employees and leaders.

Ethnocentrism
the belief that one's own culture and subculture are inherently superior to other cultures

Unequal Expectations/Difference as Deficiency The one-best-way approach leads to a mind-set that views difference as deficiency or dysfunction.[42] The perception by many career women and minorities is that no matter how many college degrees they earn, how many hours they work, how they dress, or how much effort and enthusiasm they invest, they are never considered to "have the right stuff." For example, a Hispanic executive, in discussing the animosity he felt at one job, said, "The fact that I graduated first in my class didn't make as much difference as the fact that I looked different."[43] If the standard of quality were based, for instance, on being white and male, anything else would be seen as deficient. This dilemma is often difficult for white men to understand because most of them are not intentionally racist and sexist. Many men feel extremely uncomfortable with the prevailing attitudes and stereotypes, but don't know how to change them. These attitudes are deeply rooted in our society as well as in our organizations. Only through conscious leadership can the status quo be changed.

Racism and sexism in the workplace often show up in subtle ways—the disregard by a subordinate for an assigned chore; a lack of urgency in completing an important assignment; the ignoring of comments or suggestions made at a meeting. Many minority leaders struggle daily with the problem of delegating authority and responsibility to employees who show them little respect. Passive bias is perhaps a bigger problem than blatant discrimination in today's organizations. Take the quiz in Leader's Self-Insight 11.2 to evaluate your personal degree of passive bias and think about ways you can become more diversity-aware.

Many women and minorities also feel that they are not evaluated by the same standards as their male counterparts. For example, where having a family is often considered a plus for a male executive, it can be perceived as a hindrance for a woman who wants to reach the top. One term heard frequently is the *mommy track*, which implies that a woman's commitment to her children limits her commitment to the company or her ability to handle the rigors of corporate leadership.[44] Indeed, women leaders frequently do give up personal time, outside friendships, or hobbies because they still do most of the child care and housework in addition to their business responsibilities. Exhibit 11.4 shows the discrepancy between high-achieving men and women in terms of the time they devote to domestic duties, based on one survey.

Biculturalism

the sociocultural skills and attitudes used by racial minorities as they move back and forth between the dominant culture and their own ethnic or racial culture

Living Biculturally Research on differences between whites and blacks has focused on issues of biculturalism and how it affects employees' access to information, level of respect and appreciation, and relation to superiors and subordinates. Biculturalism can be defined as the sociocultural skills and attitudes used by racial minorities as they move back and forth between the dominant culture and their own ethnic or racial culture.[45] More than 90 years ago, W. E. B. DuBois referred to this as a "double-consciousness.... One always feels his twoness—an American, a Negro; two souls, two thoughts, two unreconciled strivings...."[46] In general, African Americans feel less accepted in their organizations, perceive themselves to have less discretion on their jobs, receive lower ratings on job performance, experience lower levels of job satisfaction, and reach career plateaus earlier than whites.

Eula Adams, head of card operations for First Data, recalls the feeling of loneliness that can come from living biculturally. Adams began his career in 1972 at Touche Ross, the accounting firm that is today known as Deloitte & Touche, and

LEADER'S SELF-INSIGHT 11.2

A Passive Bias Quiz

	Yes	No
1. What you notice first about people around you are the characteristics that make them different from you.	___	___
2. You make it a general rule never to discuss the subjects of race, ethnicity, politics, age, religion, gender, and sexuality when you are at work.	___	___
3. When others make bigoted remarks or jokes, you either laugh or say nothing because you don't want to seem sensitive or self-righteous.	___	___
4. When you see media that are targeted at an ethnic, gender, or religious group that you do not represent, you usually ignore them.	___	___
5. When you look for a mentor or protégé, you pick someone like yourself.	___	___
6. If someone tells you about a cultural difference that you have never heard of, you rarely ask questions.	___	___
7. You are affiliated with organizations that practice subtle discrimination, but you say nothing because you didn't create the rules.	___	___
8. Before you hire someone for a position, you have a vague picture in mind of what the ideal candidate would look like.	___	___
9. Your conversations make use of phrases like "you people" or "our kind."	___	___
10. You avoid talking about cultural differences when dealing with people different from you because you're afraid of saying the wrong thing.	___	___
11. When complimenting someone from a different background, you might tell them, "You are nothing like the others" or "I really don't think of you as a ____."	___	___
12. There are people in your organization whom you like and respect but whom you would feel uncomfortable introducing to your family or close friends.	___	___

Scoring and Interpretation
Give yourself five points for each "yes" answer.

The appropriate score for today's world is "0." However, if you scored less than 20, you're probably making a good attempt to eliminate personal passive bias. A score of 20 to 40 means you need to watch it—you reveal passive bias that is inappropriate in organizations and society. If you scored more than 40, your level of bias could get you into trouble. You should definitely consider ways to become more diversity-aware and culturally sensitive.

SOURCE: Adapted from Lawrence Otis Graham, *Proversity: Getting Past Face Values and Finding the Soul of People* (New York: John Wiley & Sons, 1997). Used with permission of Lawrence Otis Graham.

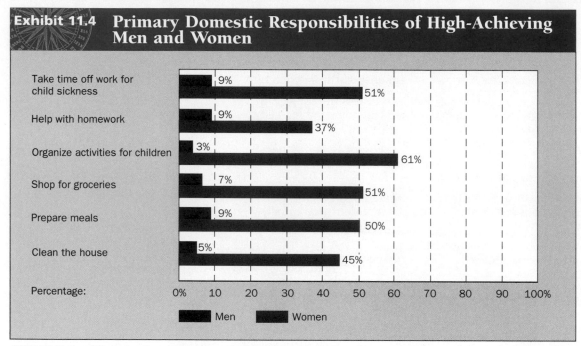

Exhibit 11.4   **Primary Domestic Responsibilities of High-Achieving Men and Women**

SOURCE: National Parenting Association, as reported in Sylvia Ann Hewlett, "Executive Women and the Myth of Having It All," *Harvard Business Review* (April 2002): 66–73.

became the firm's first African-American partner in 1983. "The loneliness, especially in the early days, was the hardest," Adams now says. "I lived in two worlds. I'd leave work and go home to one world and then wake up and go back to work in that other world."[49] Other minority groups struggle with biculturalism as well. They find themselves striving to adopt behaviors and attitudes that will help them be successful in the white-dominated corporate world while at the same time maintaining their ties to their racial or ethnic community and culture. J. D. Hokoyama started a nonprofit organization to teach Asian Americans how to be bicultural.

In the Lead   J. D. Hokoyama, Leadership Education for Asian Pacifics, Inc.

Asian Americans who aspire to leadership positions are often frustrated by the stereotype that they are hard workers but not executive material. Many times Asian Americans are perceived as too quiet or not assertive enough. One Chinese American woman says her boss claimed she wasn't strong enough for an executive-level job because she didn't raise her voice in discussions as he did.

J. D. Hokoyama, a 47-year-old Japanese American, started a nonprofit organization to try to change these perceptions. Hokoyama runs workshops to alert Asian Americans to the ways in which their communication style may hold them back in the American workplace. Participants are taught to use more eye contact, start more sentences with "I," and use more assertive body language. Many Asian Americans are offended by the implication that they should abandon their cultural values to succeed. Hokoyama, however, looks at this as a way to help more Asian Americans adjust their style so they can move into leadership positions. Pauline Ho, a senior technical staff member at Sandia National Laboratories, agrees. She has seen the obstacles her parents and other immigrants faced and knows how difficult it is to succeed in the mainstream culture: "They want to get ahead, but they don't understand what they should be doing."

Hokoyama says Asian Americans and other minorities should not have to give up their own culture; however, he believes that only by understanding the differences between Asian values and mainstream American values can more Asians and Asian Americans move into leadership positions.[48]

The workshops offered by Leadership Education for Asian Pacifics, Inc. are a sad commentary on the opportunities for minorities in America's organizations. Many minorities feel they have a chance for career advancement only by becoming bicultural or abandoning their native cultures altogether. Culturally sensitive leadership can work to remove these barriers.

The Glass Ceiling Another issue is the glass ceiling, an invisible barrier that separates women and minorities from top leadership positions. They can look up through the ceiling, but prevailing attitudes are invisible obstacles to their own advancement. Although a few women and minorities have recently moved into highly visible top leadership positions, evidence that the glass ceiling still exists is that most women and minorities are clustered at the bottom of the organizational hierarchy. Overall, women make up 12.5 percent of corporate officers in *Fortune* 500 companies, and 7.3 percent of managers in line positions. Statistics for women of color are even more dismal. Although women of color make up 23 percent of the U.S. women's workforce, they account for only 14 percent of the women in all management positions.[49] Moreover, about 65 percent of women of color surveyed said they plan to leave their management positions because of their organizations' failure to address subtle bias in the workplace.[50]

Women and minorities also earn considerably less than their male peers, with women of color earning the least. As women move up the career ladder, the wage gap widens. Moreover, the gap between male and female managers actually grew during the prosperous years between 1995 and 2000.[51]

Glass ceiling
an invisible barrier that separates women and minorities from top leadership positions

Action Memo

As a leader: Fight ethnocentric attitudes. Create an environment in which people value other ways of thinking, dressing, or behaving. Break down the barriers of unequal expectations, stereotypes, unequal pay, and the glass ceiling. Close the opportunity gap so minorities have an equal chance to succeed.

The glass ceiling persists because top-level corporate culture in most organizations still revolves around traditional management thinking, a vertical hierarchy populated by white, American-born males, who often hire and promote people who look, act, and think like them. Many organizations were originally created by and for men, and the prevailing work practices and patterns of social interaction tend to privilege men and disadvantage women, often in subtle ways.[52] One recent study supports the idea that in organizations with strong male hierarchies, women are less likely than men to advance to higher-level positions and more likely to decline in hierarchical level. Networks and other social factors often play a significant role in advancement to higher organizational levels, which tends to handicap women and minorities. In addition, women are more likely to advance if they demonstrate traits associated with masculinity, such as assertiveness, achievement-orientation, and focus on material success.[53]

Although hiring and promotion patterns may be well intended, women and minority employees are often relegated to less visible positions and projects; hence, their work fails to come to the attention of top executives. Research has suggested the existence of "glass walls" that serve as invisible barriers to important lateral movement within the organization. Glass walls bar experience in areas such as line supervision or general management that would enable women and minorities to advance to senior-level positions.[54] In general, women and minorities feel that they must work harder and perform at higher levels than their white male counterparts in order to be noticed, recognized, fully accepted, and promoted.

The Opportunity Gap In some cases, people fail to advance to higher levels in organizations because they don't have the necessary education and skills. A final challenge is the lack of opportunities for many minorities to obtain the same level of education as white, American-born individuals. Only 62 percent of Hispanics, the fastest growing segment of the U.S. population, complete high school. Both African Americans and Hispanics lag behind whites in college attendance, and only 10 percent of adults with disabilities have graduated from college.[55] Eric Adolphe, president and CEO of Optimus Corporation, who managed to stay in college because of a scholarship from the National Association Council for Minorities in Engineering, recalls many of the kids he grew up with in New York City: "There are a lot of people more gifted than myself who never made it—not because of their lack of ability, but because of their lack of opportunity."[56] Many African Americans and other minorities also have fewer skills because of inadequate inner city schools and lack of exposure to the ideas, technologies, and disciplines that are needed to succeed in today's knowledge-based organizations. There is not yet a level playing field in our schools and in society, which is, in turn, reflected in unequal opportunities in organizations. Some companies and leaders are taking the lead to ensure that minorities get the education, skills, and opportunities they need to participate fully in today's economy. Consider the example of Ernst & Young.

In the Lead   Ernst & Young LLP

Ernst & Young has long had a sterling reputation in the field of accounting services, but the firm is striving to become a leader in diversity as
well. Leaders launched two diversity initiatives aimed at increasing the
recruitment and retention of women and minorities and have invested
significant resources in training and mentoring programs. These programs
have had a positive impact, with the number of minorities recruited each
year rising from around 10 percent to around 24 percent. The number of
women and minorities in senior management positions is also edging up.

What's more important is that E & Y is aiming toward the future by giving
minority high school and college students greater opportunities. Through
the Office of Minority Recruitment and Retention, headed by Allen Boston,
an African-American partner at E & Y, the company is providing for minority
scholarships at both undergraduate and graduate institutions. E & Y also
sponsors two organizations that give minority high school students an inside
look at the accounting and engineering professions. An innovative program
called Your Master Plan (YMP) gives recent college graduates a chance to
work at E & Y while they pursue a Master's degree in accounting, paid for
by the firm. These initiatives give young minority individuals opportunities
for career advancement that they might not otherwise have—and they give
E & Y access to high-quality minority employees. According to Miriam
Nalumansi, who began the YMP program recently, "One of the things that
attracted me to Ernst & Young was the firm's commitment to diversity. I'm
black, I'm female—those are things I have to consider."[57]

Leadership Initiatives Toward
Organizational Diversity

One goal for today's global organizations is to ensure that *all* employees—women,
ethnic and racial minorities, gay people, the disabled, the elderly, as well as white
males—are given equal opportunities in the workplace.[58] Strong, culturally sensitive
leadership can move organizations toward diversity, where all people are valued and
respected for the unique abilities they can bring to the workplace.

Organizational Stages of Diversity Awareness

Organizations as well as individuals vary in their sensitivity and openness to other
cultures, attitudes, values, and ways of doing things. Exhibit 11.5 shows a model
of five organizational stages of diversity awareness and action.[59] The continuum

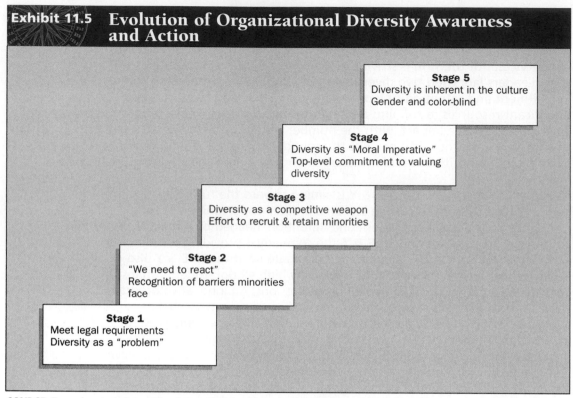

Exhibit 11.5   Evolution of Organizational Diversity Awareness and Action

Stage 5
Diversity is inherent in the culture
Gender and color-blind

Stage 4
Diversity as "Moral Imperative"
Top-level commitment to valuing
diversity

Stage 3
Diversity as a competitive weapon
Effort to recruit & retain minorities

Stage 2
"We need to react"
Recognition of barriers minorities
face

Stage 1
Meet legal requirements
Diversity as a "problem"

SOURCE: From *America's Competitive Secret: Utilizing Women as a Management Strategy*, by Judy Rosener. Copyright 1995 by Oxford University Press, Inc. Used by permission of Oxford University Press, Inc.

ranges from meeting the minimum legal requirements regarding affirmative action and sexual harassment to valuing diversity as an inherent part of the organizational culture.

Stage 1 organizations and leaders consider themselves successful if their legal record is good. Women and minorities are viewed primarily as a "problem" that must be dealt with, and typically there are only a few minorities in executive-level jobs to meet legal requirements. At Stage 2, leaders become aware that women and minorities face challenges not faced by white males, and that higher absenteeism and turnover rates among minorities are detrimental to the organization. However, awareness is seldom translated into action until the organization moves into Stage 3. Leaders become proactive and acknowledge that addressing issues of gender, race, disability, and so forth, is important not just for the minority employees but for the health of the organization. They recognize that women and minorities can bring needed insight into developing and marketing products for new customers, so they look for ways to attract and retain high-quality minority employees. In

Stage 3 organizations, more women and minorities make it to high-level positions, and the organization begins providing some diversity awareness training to all employees. The motivation for diversity at Stage 3 is to remain competitive.

When the organization reaches Stage 4, there is a top-level leadership commitment to broad equality and community. Leaders rectify the undervaluation and underutilization of women and minorities. Top leaders allocate significant resources for diversity training and other programs to bring about organizational change. A genuine attempt is made to develop policies and practices that are inclusive rather than exclusive, and executives at all levels are generally required to provide evidence that they are recruiting, retaining, and promoting quality female and minority employees. For example, at Allstate Insurance, described earlier, leaders are held responsible for proactive hiring and promotion.

Stage 5 organizations are gender- and color-blind. All employees are judged on their competence, and stereotypes and prejudices are completely erased. No group of employees feels different or disadvantaged. This stage represents the ideal organization. Although it may seem unreachable, many of today's best organizations, such as Marriott International, Pep Boys, Union Bank of California, and McDonald's, which won the top spot on *Fortune* magazine's 2003 list of the "50 Best Companies for Minorities," are striving to reach this stage of diversity awareness and acceptance.

Barriers to Evolution

Leaders face a number of personal and organizational barriers to achieving a high level of diversity awareness, acceptance, and appreciation. Five of these barriers are discussed below.[60]

Ethnocentrism Recall that ethnocentrism is the belief that one's own group and subculture are inherently superior to other groups and cultures. Viewing one's own culture as the best culture is a natural tendency among most people and contributes to cultural cohesiveness. However, ethnocentrism makes it difficult to value diversity because it tends to produce a monoculture, a culture that accepts only one way of doing things and one set of values and beliefs. The goal for organizations seeking cultural diversity is to develop *ethnorelativism*, or the belief that all groups, cultures, and subcultures are inherently equal.

Stereotypes and Prejudice Carried to an extreme, ethnocentrism becomes outright prejudice, which is perhaps the single biggest obstacle to providing equal opportunities for women and minorities. *Prejudice* can be defined as the tendency to view people who are different from the mainstream in terms of sex, race, ethnic background, or physical ability as being deficient. Prejudice is the assumption, without evidence, that minorities are inherently inferior, less competent at their jobs, and less suitable for leadership positions. Recent surveys have found that stereotypes are

Action Memo

As a leader: Advance your organization to higher stages of diversity awareness and action. Commit to valuing diversity and providing equal opportunities for everyone. Allocate resources for diversity training and other programs that will shift attitudes toward greater understanding and acceptance of differences.

still prevalent in our society, and prejudice is a contributing factor in most other barriers to accepting and valuing diversity in the workplace.[61]

The "White Male" Club The work environment for many minorities is lonely, unfriendly, and stressful, which is partly attributed to the so-called *white male club*. Particularly in executive-level positions, women and minorities are heavily outnumbered by white men, many of whom treat them differently from the way they treat their white male colleagues. Women and minorities may be excluded, often unintentionally, from social functions, lunches, and even regular office banter. In addition, there are few role models or mentors for women and minorities trying to reach senior-level positions. Minorities feel they have no one to talk to about their fears, their mistakes, and even their ideas for the organization. They have difficulty fitting into the white male club, yet if they remain isolated, they are perceived as aloof and arrogant.

The Paradox of Diversity Leaders also face a significant challenge in simultaneously promoting diversity and maintaining a strong, unified corporate culture.[62] Homogeneous organizations provide a firmer basis for building a strong culture, which is considered critical to organizational success. One reason is that, in general, people feel more comfortable and satisfied dealing with others who are like themselves. Also, in many communities, ethnic groups still do not interact socially, and this carries over into unfamiliarity and discomfort in the workplace. Diverse racial and ethnic groups within a work environment can be competitive with and even antagonistic toward one another, and the time and energy leaders spend dealing with interpersonal issues dramatically increases in a diverse environment. Leaders have to work harder than ever to unite employees around a common purpose while also allowing individual differences to flourish.

Actual Cultural Differences Finally, real cultural differences can cause problems in the workplace. As we discussed earlier in the chapter, culture influences attitudes toward such things as time, physical space, and authority. Leaders may face enormous challenges in relating to employees from different cultures. For example, most organizations will not accept routine tardiness or absenteeism from employees simply because their time orientation is culturally different from the mainstream values.

As another example of how cultural differences complicate leadership, one supervisor declined a gift from a new employee, an immigrant who wanted to show gratitude for her job. He was concerned about ethics and explained the company's policy about not accepting gifts. The employee was so insulted that she quit, even though she desperately needed the work.[63] The potential for communication difficulties is much greater in heterogeneous groups, leading to misunderstandings, conflict, and anxiety for leaders as well as employees.

Leadership Solutions

In the past, the pressure to change has been on the new employee coming into the workplace. Today, however, the idea that diverse individuals have to assimilate into the mainstream culture is dead. The pressure is now on organizations to change, and strong leadership is needed. Many of today's leaders have had little experience with people different from themselves and are unprepared to deal with emerging diversity in the workplace. The benefits of diversity are not automatic, and working with people different from oneself can be difficult and frustrating. Without strong leadership, increased cultural diversity can lead to decreased work effort and lower organizational performance.

Personal Qualities for Leading Diverse Organizations

To successfully lead in diverse organizations, leaders must develop personal characteristics that support diversity. Four characteristics have been identified as important for leadership of diverse organizations.[64]

* *A personal, long-range vision that recognizes and supports a diverse organizational community.* Leaders should have long-term plans to include employees of various ethnic and cultural groups, races, ages, and so on at all levels of the organization. In addition, they express the vision through symbols and rituals that reinforce the value of a diverse workforce.
* *A broad knowledge of the dimensions of diversity and awareness of multicultural issues.* Leaders need a basic knowledge of the primary dimensions of diversity as discussed earlier in this chapter: age, race, ethnicity, gender, mental or physical abilities, and sexual orientation, as well as some understanding of secondary dimensions. Knowledge is also put into action through the use of inclusive language and showing respect for differences.
* *An openness to change themselves.* Leaders in diverse organizations encourage feedback from their employees, can accept criticism, and are willing to change their behavior. It is leaders' behavior that has the most impact on whether diversity is truly valued within the organization. At Baxter Healthcare Corp., for example, Chairman and CEO Harry Jansen Kraemer, Jr. writes a newsletter called *CEO Update* for the company intranet. Rather than just talking about business issues, he includes a section updating people on his family life. For women who are juggling career and family, it is a clear signal that the company values family and considers work/life balance important.[65]
* *Mentoring and empowerment of diverse employees.* Leaders take an active role in creating opportunities for all employees to use their unique abilities. They also

offer honest feedback and coaching as needed, and they reward those in the organization who show respect to culturally different employees.

Once leaders examine and change themselves, they can lead change in the organization.

Changing Corporate Culture

A leader's ability to create and communicate a shared vision and values for the organization becomes even more critical in an organization made up of diverse individuals. Leaders are also challenged to ensure that the organizational culture is continually open to new and different ideas and ways of doing things, while maintaining a focus on the common purpose and vision.[66] Shaping culture and values will be discussed in detail in Chapter 14.

Today's organizational cultures for the most part reflect the white male model of doing business. R. Roosevelt Thomas Jr., founder of the American Institute for Managing Diversity and co-author of *Building a House for Diversity*, illustrates this situation with a fable about a giraffe who built a wonderful home with raised ceilings, narrow hallways, and high windows. The home was great for his family, but it wasn't so comfortable for his elephant friend. When companies say they've built a wonderful environment for diversity but all their managers have to work 70-hour weeks and they recruit from the same sources every time, Thomas observes, they've built a home for giraffes. No matter how hard they try to get elephants or lions or kangaroos to live in it, it's still a home for giraffes.[67] When the organizational environment reflects one limited perspective, diverse employees are not going to feel comfortable, no matter how much leaders tout diversity initiatives.

As a result of the mismatch between the dominant culture and the growing employee population of minorities and women, many employees' talents and abilities are not being fully used. To help an organization thrive in today's diverse environment, leaders should develop a culture that supports the inclusion and full participation of all individuals, regardless of race, gender, age, cultural or ethnic group, physical ability, or other characteristics. Leaders have to examine everything from formal policies and practices, to informal patterns of social interaction, to the basic mind-sets of managers throughout the organization. One way leaders begin to shift cultural values is by using symbols, such as encouraging and celebrating the promotion of minorities or by symbolizing the importance of work/life balance, as the CEO of Baxter Healthcare does with his newsletter columns. Leaders also examine the unwritten rules and assumptions in the organization. What are the values that exemplify the existing culture? What are the myths and stereotypes about minorities? Are unwritten rules communicated from one person to another in ways that exclude women and minority workers?

The most important element in changing the corporate culture to one that values diversity is leadership. After blatant acts of racism were exposed at Texaco some

Action Memo

As a leader: Create a personal vision for a diverse community. Develop a mentoring relationship with people who are different from you. Use words, actions, and symbols to create an organizational culture that includes the participation of all people regardless of race, age, gender, cultural or ethnic group, or physical ability.

years ago, CEO Peter Bijur and other top leaders consciously established a detailed plan for a total cultural overhaul. "I drew a line in the sand and said that we will not tolerate disrespect," Bijur said. The CEO set specific goals with timetables and made it clear to executives that their future career advancement would depend on how well they implemented the new diversity initiatives. Bijur also recruited several high-profile African Americans, who agreed to join Texaco's top ranks because of top leaders' ardent personal commitment to culture change.[68]

Diversity Awareness Training

Many organizations provide diversity awareness training to help employees become aware of their own cultural boundaries, their prejudices and stereotypes, so they can learn to work together successfully. Leaders in these companies understand that their future competitiveness may depend on how well they handle diversity issues.[69]

Diversity awareness training
training that helps employees become aware of their own cultural boundaries, their prejudices and stereotypes, so they can learn to work together successfully

People vary in their sensitivity and openness to other cultures and ways of doing things. Exhibit 11.6 shows a model of five stages of individual diversity awareness, which are roughly comparable to the organizational stages shown in Exhibit 11.5. The continuum ranges from a defensive, ethnocentric attitude to a complete understanding and acceptance of people's differences. The model can help leaders assess their own and employees' openness to change. People at different levels may require different kinds of training. A primary aim of diversity awareness training is to help people recognize that their own hidden and overt biases direct their thinking about specific individuals and groups. Diversity awareness programs also focus on helping people of varying backgrounds communicate effectively with one another and understand the language and context used in dealing with people from other cultural groups. One of the most important aspects of diversity training is to bring together people of differing perspectives so that they can engage in learning new interpersonal communication skills.

Diversity presents many challenges, yet it also provides leaders with an exciting opportunity to build organizations as integrated communities in which all people feel encouraged, respected, and committed to common purposes and goals. Consider how leaders at Denny's Restaurants have used diversity training and culture change initiatives to transform the company from an icon of racism to a paragon of diversity.

In the Lead   Denny's Restaurants (Advantica)

Advantica, the parent of Denny's Restaurants, recently closed down its minority mentoring program. Diversity has become such an integral, everyday part of the way the company does business that the special program is no longer needed. However, leaders remain firmly committed to fostering an inclusive environment where everyone feels respected and valued.

Exhibit 11.6   Stages of Personal Diversity Awareness

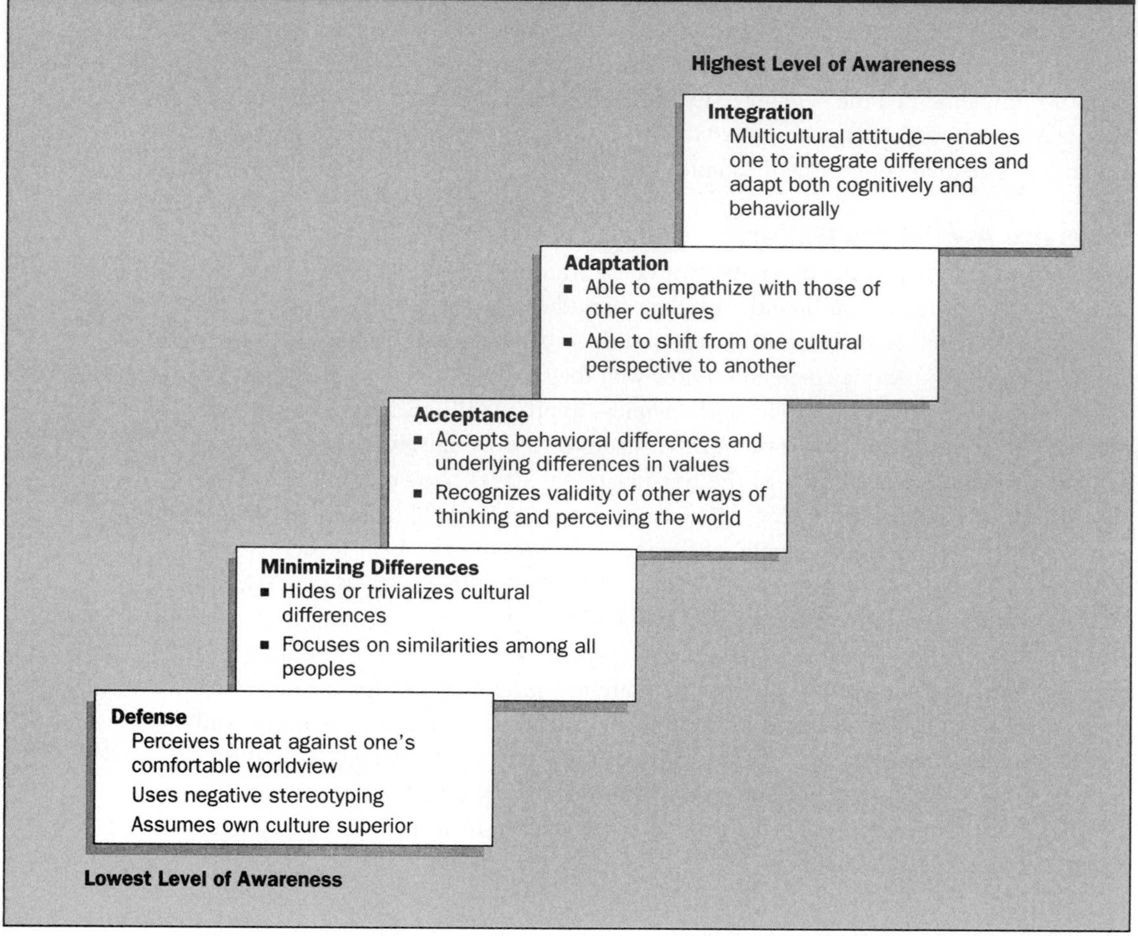

Highest Level of Awareness

Integration
Multicultural attitude—enables
one to integrate differences and
adapt both cognitively and
behaviorally

Adaptation
- Able to empathize with those of
  other cultures
- Able to shift from one cultural
  perspective to another

Acceptance
- Accepts behavioral differences and
  underlying differences in values
- Recognizes validity of other ways of
  thinking and perceiving the world

Minimizing Differences
- Hides or trivializes cultural
  differences
- Focuses on similarities among all
  peoples

Defense
Perceives threat against one's
comfortable worldview
Uses negative stereotyping
Assumes own culture superior

Lowest Level of Awareness

SOURCE: Based on M. Bennett, "A Developmental Approach to Training for Intercultural Sensitivity, "*International Journal of Intercultural Relations* 10 (1986), 179–196.

Things have certainly changed. In the early 1990s, Denny's Restaurants became an icon for racism in the United States when six black Secret Service officers accused servers and managers at an Annapolis, Maryland, restaurant of humiliating and discriminating against them while their white colleagues were welcomed to a hearty breakfast. Other incidents of racism and discrimination soon surfaced, including managers barring black customers or asking them to prepay their dinner bills. At that time, only one of the chain's franchises was minority-owned, the company had virtually no minority suppliers, and the board was made up primarily of white males. Today, however, a sweeping cultural overhaul has transformed Denny's into a model for diversity. Consider these statistics:

❊ Forty-six percent of Denny's franchises are owned by minorities.

❊ The company does more than $125 million in business with minority suppliers each year. That represents at least 19 percent of the company's contracts, as compared to a national average of 3 to 4 percent.

❊ Thirty-three percent of the board of directors is composed of people of color.

❊ At the senior management level, nearly 29 percent are women and people of color.

❊ For the past three years, Advantica has ranked in the top three on *Fortune* magazine's list of the best companies for minorities.

The biggest factor in the culture change has been top leaders' "absolute commitment to doing what was right, no matter what," as Advantica chairman and CEO Jim Adamson puts it. Extensive training has also played an important role. Every single person employed by Denny's Restaurants—not just managers and servers, but also media planners and leased security guards—receives training in diversity awareness with specific guidelines on how to apply diversity understanding and sensitivity to working in the restaurant business. In the "We Can" training program, for example, employees learn a three-step model: (1) *prevention*, such as how to behave in order to reduce the possibility of a guest or fellow employee feeling that he or she has been discriminated against; (2) *intervention*, which teaches people to "acknowledge, apologize, and act" when something goes wrong; and (3) *managing escalation*, in which employees learn how to genuinely listen, show empathy, and reduce the anger and frustration level.

Advantica spends several million dollars a year on compliance and training, and its diversity training system is one of the most comprehensive in the industry. Results of the training have been so strong that the company was released from the oversight of the Office of the Civil Rights Monitor (OCRM) more than a year ahead of schedule. However, leaders are quick to point out that just because they no longer face daily oversight doesn't mean they will stop their efforts to be a diverse, inclusive, and nondiscriminatory company. "Inclusion and diversity are something we focus on each day," says Adamson. "And what we've done here can be done by any company that's committed."[70]

Summary and Interpretation

The main point of this chapter is that diversity is a fact of life in today's world, and leaders can create change in organizations to keep up. The U.S. population, the workforce, and the customer base are changing. In addition, people of different national origins, races, and religions are no longer willing to be assimilated into the mainstream culture. Organizations are also operating in an increasingly global world, which means dealing with diversity on a broader stage than ever before.

Dimensions of diversity are both primary, such as age, gender, and race, and secondary, such as education, marital status, and religion. There are several reasons why organizations are recognizing the need to value and support diversity. Diversity helps organizations build better relationships with diverse customers and helps develop employee potential. Diversity provides a broader and deeper base of experience for creativity and problem solving, which is essential to building learning organizations. One aspect of diversity of particular interest is women's style of leadership, referred to as interactive leadership. The values associated with interactive leadership, such as inclusion, relationship building, and caring, are emerging as valuable qualities for both male and female leaders in the twenty-first century.

Another important idea in this chapter is global diversity. Leaders can be aware of the impact culture may have and consider cultural differences in their dealings with followers. Within organizations, people who do not fit the mainstream white, U.S.-born, male culture face a number of challenges, including unequal expectations, the need to live biculturally, the glass ceiling, and the opportunity gap.

Organizations generally evolve through stages of diversity awareness and action, ranging from minimum efforts to meet affirmative action guidelines to valuing diversity as an integral part of organizational culture. The barriers to successful evolution include ethnocentrism, prejudice, the so-called white male club, the paradox of diversity, and actual cultural differences. Strong, culturally sensitive leadership is the only way organizations can move through the stages of diversity awareness. Leaders first change themselves by developing personal characteristics that support diversity. They use these personal characteristics to change the organization. The ultimate goal for leaders in the twenty-first century is to build organizations as integrated communities in which all people feel encouraged, respected, and committed to common purposes and goals.

Discussion Questions

1. How might a leader's role and responsibility change as a company becomes more diverse? Explain.
2. How might diversity within the organization ultimately lead to better problem solving and greater creativity?

3. What is interactive leadership, and why might this approach be increasingly important in the twenty-first century?

4. Discuss ways in which low power distance as a social value among followers could affect their interaction with a leader who displays high power distance.

5. Why do you think the glass ceiling persists in organizations?

6. What is the paradox of diversity and how could it be a barrier to valuing and supporting diversity within organizations?

7. In preparing organizations to accept and value diversity, do you think leaders should focus primarily on changing the underlying culture or on diversity awareness training? Discuss.

8. Recall a company you worked for. At what stage of diversity awareness (refer to Exhibit 11.5) was it? Explain.

9. Do you think people and organizations can ever become gender and color-blind? Discuss.

Leadership at Work

Personal Diversity

Each of us feels different in many ways from the average behavior or expectations that other people seem to value. This reflects our own feelings of diversity. The differences you feel compared to others could be about your physical characteristics (height, age, skin color), but also could reflect a difference in your thinking style, feelings, personality or behavior, especially when you feel different from what other people expect or what you perceive are the social norms. Write in the list below six ways you feel different from others:

1. _____   4. _____

2. _____   5. _____

3. _____   6. _____

Now answer the following questions with respect to your perceived diversity.

What are your feelings about being different?

_____

_____

_____

Which elements of diversity are you proud of? Why?

_____

_____

_____

What element would you like to change to be less diverse? Why?

_____

_____

_____

How do your differences contribute to a student team or work organization?

_____

_____

_____

In Class: This exercise can be adapted for group discussion in class about underlying diversity. The instructor can ask students to sit in teams of 3 to 5 members in a circle facing each other. A student (focal person) then volunteers to describe the way he or she feels different from others based on the list above. Other students take turns providing feedback to the focal person on what the perceived differences mean to them with respect to team or class contributions. Each student takes a turn as the focal person, describing their feelings of being different and hearing feedback from others on the perception and impact of those differences.

Here are the key questions for this exercise: What did you learn about perceived diversity and interpersonal relations? What does it mean when our differences appear larger to ourselves than they appear to others? How does personal diversity affect team or organizational performance? (A list can be written on the board.)

 ## Leadership Development: Cases for Analysis

Northern Industries

Northern Industries asked you, a consultant in organizational change and diversity management, to help them resolve some racial issues that, according to president Jim Fisher, are "festering" in their manufacturing plant in Springfield, Massachusetts. Northern Industries is a family-owned enterprise that manufactures greeting cards and paper and plastic holiday decorations. It employs 125 people full time, including African Americans and Asians. About 80 percent of the full-time workforce is female. During the peak production months of September and January (to produce orders primarily for Christmas/Hanukah and Mother's Day), the company runs a second shift and adds about 50 part-time workers, most of whom are women and minorities.

All orders are batch runs made to customer specifications. In a period of a week, it is not unusual for 70 different orders to be filled requiring different paper stocks, inks, plastics, and setups. Since these orders vary greatly in size, the company has a long-term policy of giving priority to high-volume customers and processing other orders on a first-come first-served basis. Half a dozen of the company's major customers have been doing business with Northern for more than 20 years, having been signed on by Jim Fisher's father (now retired).

To begin your orientation to the company, Fisher asks his production manager, Walter Beacon, to take you around the plant. Beacon points out the production areas responsible for each of the various steps in the manufacture of a greeting card, from purchasing to printing to quality control and shipping. The plant is clean, but the two large printing rooms, each the workplace for about 25 workers, are quite noisy. You catch snatches of the employees' conversations there, but you cannot figure out what language they are speaking. In the shipping and receiving department you notice that most workers are black, perhaps African American. Beacon confirms that 8 out of 10 of the workers in that department are black males, and that their boss, Adam Wright, is also African American.

It has been previously arranged that you would attend a meeting of top management in order to get a flavor of the organizational culture. The president introduces you as a diversity consultant and notes that several of his managers have expressed concerns about potential racial problems in the company. He says, "Each of the minority groups sticks together. The African Americans and Orientals rarely mix. Recently there has been a problem with theft of finished product, especially on the second shift, and we had to fire a Thai worker." Fisher has read a lot lately about "managing diversity" and hopes you will be able to help the company. Several managers nod their heads in agreement.

Fisher then turns his executive team to its daily business. The others present are the general manager, personnel manager (the only woman), sales manager, quality control manager, production manager (Beacon), and the shipping and receiving manager (the only nonwhite manager). Soon an angry debate ensues between the sales and shipping/receiving managers. It seems that orders are not being shipped quickly enough, according to the sales manager, and several complaints have been received from smaller customers about the quality of the product. The shipping/receiving manager argues that he needs more hands to do the job, and that the quality of incoming supplies is lousy. While this debate continues, the other managers are silent and seemingly uncomfortable. Finally one of them attempts to break up the argument with a joke about his wife. Fisher and the other men laugh loudly, and the conversation shifts to other topics.

SOURCE: Copyright 1991 by Rae Andre of Northeastern University. Used with permission.

Questions
1. What recommendations would you make to Northern's leaders to help them move toward successfully managing diversity issues?
2. If you were the shipping and receiving or personnel manager, how do you think you would feel about your job? Discuss some of the challenges you might face at Northern.
3. Refer to Exhibit 11.6. Based on the information in the case, at what stage of personal diversity awareness do leaders at Northern seem to be? Discuss.

The Trouble with Bangles

Leela Patel was standing by her machine, as she had for eight hours of each working day for the past six years. Leela was happy; she had many friends among the 400 or so women at the food processing plant. Most of them were of Indian origin like herself, although Asian women formed less than a fifth of the female workforce. Leela was a member of a five-woman team that reported to supervisor Bill Evans.

Leela saw Evans approaching now, accompanied by Jamie Watkins, the shop steward. "Hello, Leela; we've come to explain something to you," Evans began. "You must have heard about the accident last month when one of the girls caught a bangle in the machine and cut her wrist. Well, the Safety Committee has decided that no one will be allowed to wear any bangles, engagement rings, earrings, or necklaces at work—only wedding rings, sleepers for pierced ears, and wristwatches will be allowed. So I'm afraid you'll have to remove your bangles." Leela, as was her custom, was wearing three bangles, one steel, one plastic, and one gold. All the married Asian women wore bangles, and many of the

English girls had also begun wearing them. Leela explained that she was a Hindu wife and the bangles were important to her religion.

"Don't make a fuss, Leela," Evans said between clenched teeth. "I've already had to shout at Hansa Patel and Mira Desai. Why can't you all be like Meena Shah? She didn't mind taking her bangles off; neither did the English girls." Leela could see that Evans was very angry so, almost in tears, she removed the bangles. When the two had moved off, however, she replaced the gold bangle and carried on with her work.

Within two or three days, the plant manager, Sam Jones, noticed that all the Asian women were wearing their bangles again—some, in fact, were wearing more than ever before. "I'm staggered by the response which this simple, common-sense restriction on the wearing of jewelry has brought," Jones remarked to the regional race relations employment advisor. "I have had several deputations from the Asian women protesting the ban, not to mention visits by individuals on the instruction of their husbands. In addition, I've just had a letter from something called the Asian Advisory Committee, asking that the ban be lifted until we meet with their representatives. The strength of this discontent has prompted me to talk to you. Jewelry constitutes both a safety and a hygiene hazard on this site, so it must be removed. And I'm afraid if I talk to this Asian Committee, they'll turn out to be a bunch of militants who'll cause all sorts of trouble. At the same time, we can't afford any work stoppages. What do you suggest?"

Several days later, the advisor had arranged for Mr. Singh from the local Council for Community Relations to talk to Jones and other managers. Singh explained that in his opinion there were no obstacles arising from *religious* observance that prevented implementation of the ban on bangles. However, he pointed out, the bangles do have a custom base which is stronger than the English tradition base for wedding rings. "The bangles are a mark not only of marriage but of the esteem in which a wife is held by her husband. The more bangles and the greater their value, the higher her esteem and the greater her social standing. The tradition also has religious overtones, since the wearing of bangles by the wife demonstrates that each recognizes the other as "worthy" in terms of the fulfillment of their religious obligations. This position is further complicated in that women remove their bangles if they are widowed, and some fear that the removal of the bangles may lead to their husbands' deaths."

SOURCE: Adapted from "Bangles," in Allan R. Cohen, Stephen L. Fink, Herman Gadon, and Robin D. Willits, *Effective Behavior in Organizations: Cases, Concepts, and Student Experiences*, 7th ed. (Burr Ridge, IL: McGraw-Hill Irwin, 2001), 413–414.

Questions

1. What is your initial reaction to this story? Why do you think you had this reaction?
2. Based on this limited information, how would you rate this organization in terms of developing leadership diversity? Discuss.
3. If you were a top manager at this company, how would you handle this problem?

References

1. Robin Madell, "Uniting People and Products: Myrtle Potter–2000 HBA Woman of the Year," *Pharmaceutical Executive* 20, no. 4 (April 2000): 48–60; and Cora Daniels, "The Most Powerful Black Executives in America," *Fortune* (July 22, 2002): 60–80.
2. "Diversity in the New Millennium," *Working Woman* (September 2000): Special Advertising Section.
3. Louisa Wah, "Diversity at Allstate: A Competitive Weapon," *Management Review* (July–August 1999): 24–30.
4. G. Pascal Zachary, "The Rage for Global Teams," *Technology Review* (July–August 1998): 33; G. Pascal Zachary, "Mighty is the Mongrel," *Fast Company* (July 2000): 270–284.
5. Frances J. Milliken and Luis I. Martins, "Searching for Common Threads: Understanding the Multiple Effects of Diversity in Organizational Groups," *Academy of Management Review* 21, no. 2 (1996), 402–433.
6. Timothy Aeppel, "A 3Com Factory Hires a Lot of Immigrants, Gets Mix of Languages," *The Wall Street Journal* (March 30, 1998): A1; Mike Hofman, "Lost in the Translation," *Inc.* (May 2000): 161–162.
7. Roger O. Crockett, with Andy Reinhardt, Peter Burrows, and Leah Nathans Spiro, "Jesse's New Target: Silicon Valley," *BusinessWeek* (July 12, 1999): 111–112.
8. Marilyn Loden and Judy B. Rosener, *Workforce America!* (Homewood, IL: Business One Irwin, 1991); and Marilyn Loden, *Implementing Diversity* (Homewood, IL: Irwin, 1996).
9. Milliken and Martins, "Searching for Common Threads."
10. C. Keen, "Human Resource Management Issues in the '90s," *Vital Speeches* 56, no. 24 (1990): 752–754.
11. Richard W. Judy and Carol D'Amico, *Workforce 2020: Work and Workers in the 21st Century* (Indianapolis, IN: Hudson Institute, 1997).
12. Steven Greenhouse, N.Y. Times News Service, "Influx of Immigrants Having Profound Impact on Economy," *Johnson City Press* (September 4, 2000): 9.

13. Sharon Cohany, Bureau of Labor Statistics, as reported in Michelle Conlin, "The New Gender Gap," *BusinessWeek* (May 26, 2003): 75–82.

14. Judy and D'Amico, *Workforce 2020*.

15. Zachary, "Mighty is the Mongrel."

16. Orlando C. Richard, "Racial Diversity, Business Strategy, and Firm Performance: A Resource-Based View," *Academy of Management Journal* 43, no. 2 (2000): 164–177.

17. Sharon Nelton, "Nurturing Diversity," *Nation's Business* (June 1995): 25–27.

18. Bernice Kanner, "Are You Selling to Me?" *Working Woman* (March 1999): 62–65.

19. Wah, "Diversity at Allstate: A Competitive Weapon."

20. Madell, "Uniting People and Products."

21. Geoffrey Colvin, "The 50 Best Companies for Asians, Blacks, and Hispanics," *Fortune* (July 19, 1999): 53–58.

22. Taylor H. Cox, *Cultural Diversity in Organizations* (San Francisco: Berrett-Koehler, 1994).

23. Judy B. Rosener, *America's Competitive Secret: Women Managers* (New York: Oxford University Press, 1995), and "Ways Women Lead," *Harvard Business Review* (November–December 1990): 119–125; Sally Helgesen, *The Female Advantage: Women's Ways of Leadership* (New York: Currency/Doubleday, 1990); Joline Godfrey, "Been There, Doing That," *Inc.* (March 1996) 21–22; Chris Lee, "The Feminization of Management," *Training* (November 1994): 25–31; and Bernard M. Bass and Bruce J. Avolio, "Shatter the Glass Ceiling: Women May Make Better Managers," *Human Resource Management* 33, no. 4 (Winter 1994): 549–560.

24. One recent review of the research on gender differences in leadership is Nicole Z. Stelter, "Gender Differences in Leadership: Current Social Issues and Future Organizational Implications," *The Journal of Leadership Studies* 8, no. 4 (2002): 88–99.

25. Lena Williams, "A Silk Blouse on the Assembly Line? (Yes, the Boss's)," *The New York Times* (February 5, 1995) Business Section, 7.

26. Michelle Conlin, "The New Gender Gap," *BusinessWeek* (May 26, 2003): 74–82.

27. Based on Judy B. Rosener, *America's Competitive Secret: Women Managers* (New York: Oxford University Press, 1997), 129–135.

28. Susan J. Wells, "A Female Executive Is Hard to Find," *HR Magazine* (June 2001): 40–49; and Helgesen, *The Female Advantage*.

29. Bass and Avolio, "Shatter the Glass Ceiling."

30. M. Fine, F. Johnson, and M. S. Ryan, "Cultural Diversity in the Workforce," *Public Personnel Management* 19 (1990): 305–319; and Dawn Hill, "Women Leaders Doing It Their Way," *New Woman* (January 1994): 78.

31. Helen Bloom, "Can the United States Export Diversity?" *Across the Board* (March/April 2002): 47–51.

32. "Molding Global Leaders," *Fortune* (October 11, 1999): 270.

33. Geert Hofstede, "The Interaction between National and Organizational Value Systems," *Journal of Management Studies* 22 (1985): 347–357; and "The Cultural Relativity of the Quality of Life Concept," *Academy of Management Review* 9 (1984): 389–398.

34. Debby Young, "Team Heat," *CIO*, Section 1 (September 1, 1998): 43–51.

35. Geert Hofstede, "Cultural Constraints in Management Theories," excerpted in Dorothy Marcic and Sheila M. Puffer, *Management International: Cases, Exercises, and Readings* (St. Paul, MN: West Publishing, 1994), 24.

36. Gilbert W. Fairholm, *Leadership and the Culture of Trust* (Westport, CT: Praeger, 1994), 187–188.

37. Carol Matlack with Pallavi Gogoi, "What's This? The French Love McDonald's?" *BusinessWeek* (January 13, 2003): 50; and Shirley Leung, "'McHaute Cuisine,' Armchairs, TVs, and Espresso–Is It McDonald's?" *The Wall Street Journal* (August 30, 2002): A1, A6.

38. R. Frank and T. Burton, "Culture Clash Causes Anxiety for Pharmacia and Upjohn Inc.," *The Wall Street Journal* (February 4, 1997): A1, A12; J. Ball, "DaimlerChrysler's Transfer Woes," *The Wall Street Journal* (August 24, 1999): B1, B2; "DaimlerChrysler Moves Shift Power to Germans," *Columbus Dispatch* (September 25, 1999): E1, E2; Douglas A. Blackmon, "A Factory in Alabama is the Merger in Microcosm," *The Wall Street Journal* (May 8, 1998): B1.

39. Alison M. Konrad, Roger Kashlak, Izumi Yoshioka, Robert Waryszak, and Nina Toren, "What Do Managers *Like* to Do?" *Group and Organization Management* 26, no. 4 (December 2001): 401–433.

40. Harry C. Triandis, "The Contingency Model in Cross-Cultural Perspective," in Martin M. Chemers and Roya Ayman, eds., *Leadership Theory and Research: Perspectives and Directions* (San Diego, CA: Academic Press, Inc., 1993): 167–188; and Peter B. Smith and Mark F. Peterson, *Leadership, Organizations, and Culture: An Event Management Model* (London: Sage, 1988).

41. G. Haight, "Managing Diversity," *Across the Board* 27, No. 3 (1990): 22–29.

42. This section is based on Rosener, *America's Competitive Secret*, 33–34.

43. Ann Morrison, *The New Leaders: Guidelines on Leadership Diversity in America* (San Francisco: Jossey-Bass, 1992): 37.

44. Deborah L. Jacobs, "Back from the Mommy Track," *The New York Times* (October 9, 1994): F1, F6; Lisa Cullen, "Apple Pie, My Eye," *Working Woman* (May–June 2001): 19-20; Ann Crittenden, *The Price of Motherhood* (New York: Metropolitan Books 2001); and Michelle Conlin, "The New Debate over Working Moms," *BusinessWeek* (September 18, 2000): 102–104.

45. Robert Hooijberg and Nancy DiTomaso, "Leadership in and of Demographically Diverse Organizations," *Leadership Quarterly* 7, no. 1 (1996): 1–19.

46. W. E. B. DuBois, *The Souls of Black Folks* (Chicago: Chicago University Press, 1903), quoted in Hooijberg and DiTomaso, "Leadership in and of Demographically Diverse Organizations."

47. Cora Daniels, "The Most Powerful Black Executives in America," *Fortune* (July 22, 2002): 60–80.

48. Vivian Louie, "For Asian-Americans, A Way to Fight a Maddening Stereotype," *The New York Times*, August 8, 1993, 9.

49. Debra E. Meyerson and Joyce K. Fletcher, "A Modest Manifesto for Shattering the Glass Ceiling," *Harvard Business Review* (January–February 2000): 127–136; and Eileen Alt Powell, "Survey: Women Make Up 12.5 Percent of Fortune 500 Executives," AP report, *Johnson City Press*, November 14, 2000.

50. "Diversity in the New Millennium," *Working Woman* (September 2000): Special Advertising Section.

51. C. Solomon, "Careers under Glass," *Personnel Journal* 69, no. 4 (1990): 96–105; and *Population Profile of the United States* 1995, U.S. Department of Commerce, Bureau of the Census, July 1995; Margaret Heffernan, "The Female CEO ca. 2002," *Fast Company* (August 2002): 58–66.

52. Robin J. Ely and Debra E. Meyerson, "Theories of Gender in Organizations: A New Approach to Organizational Analysis and Change," *Research in Organizational Behaviour* 22 (2000): 103–151.

53. Phyllis Tharenou, "Going Up? Do Traits and Informal Social Processes Predict Advancing in Management?" *Academy of Management Journal* 44, no. 5 (2001): 1005–1017.

54. Meyerson and Fletcher, "A Modest Manifesto for Shattering the Glass Ceiling"; Julie Amparano Lopez, "Study Says Women Face Glass Walls as Well as Glass Ceiling," *The Wall Street Journal*, March 3, 1992, B1, B2; and Joann S. Lublin, "Women at Top Still Are Distant from CEO Jobs," *The Wall Street Journal*, February 28, 1996, B1, B8.

55. U.S. Department of Labor, *Futurework: Trends and Challenges for Work in the 21st Century.*

56. "Diversity: Developing Tomorrow's Leadership Today," *BusinessWeek* (December 20, 1999): Special Advertising Section.

57. "Ernst & Young LLP: An Aggressive Approach," in "Diversity Today: Developing and Retaining the Best Corporate Talent," special advertising section, *Fortune* (June 21, 1999); and "Leveraging Diversity: Opportunities in the New Market," Part III of "Diversity: The Bottom Line," special advertising section, *Forbes* (November 13, 2000).

58. Renee Blank and Sandra Slipp, "The White Male: An Endangered Species?" *Management Review* (September 1994): 27–32; and Nelton, "Nurturing Diversity."

59. Based on Rosener, *America's Competitive Secret*, 142–148.

60. Based on Fairholm, *Leadership and the Culture of Trust*, 189–192; Cox, *Cultural Diversity in Organizations*; and Morrison, *The New Leaders*, 29–56.

61. Morrison, *The New Leaders*, 35.

62. Based on Nicholas Imparato and Oren Harari, *Jumping the Curve: Innovation and Strategic Choice in an Age of Transition* (San Francisco: Jossey-Bass, 1994), 186–203.

63. Lennie Copeland, "Learning to Manage a Multicultural Workforce," *Training* (May 25, 1988): 48–56.

64. Martin M. Chemers and Roya Ayman, *Leadership Theory and Research: Perspectives and Directions* (San Diego, CA: Academic Press, 1993), 209.

65. Susan J. Wells, "Smoothing the Way," *HR Magazine* (June 2001): 52–58.

66. Fairholm, *Leadership and the Culture of Trust*, 194.

67. Reported by Dave Murphy of the *San Francisco Chronicle* in "Diversity at Work Hard to Uphold," *Johnson City Press*, February 11, 2001, 29.

68. Kenneth Labich, "No More Crude at Texaco," *Fortune* (September 6, 1999): 205–212.

69. Jenny C. McCune, "Diversity Training: A Competitive Weapon," *Management Review* (June 1996): 25–28.

70. Jim Adamson, "How Denny's Went from Icon of Racism to Diversity Award Winner," *Journal of Organizational Excellence* (Winter 2000): 55–68; Jonathan Hickman, "America's 50 Best Companies for Minorities," *Fortune* (July 8, 2002): 110–120; Jonathan Hickman, "50 Best Companies for Minorities," *Fortune* (July 7, 2003): 103–120.

Chapter

Your Leadership Challenge

After reading this chapter, you should be able to:

- Recognize your natural leadership frame of reference and how you can expand your perspective.

- Use power and politics to help accomplish important organizational goals.

- Identify types and sources of power in organizations and know how to increase power through political activity.

- Use the influence tactics of rational persuasion, friendliness, reciprocity, developing allies, direct appeal, and scarcity.

After 10 hours of meetings focused on his company's Six Sigma initiative, all Jim Goetz wanted to do was head to his hotel room. Goetz is CIO of ServiceMaster, an organization based in Downers Grove, Illinois, that owns and operates a variety of home service companies, including Terminix pest control and Merry Maids cleaning service. CEO Jon Ward had recently announced a Six Sigma project to improve customer service, which required gathering information on what customers wanted and compiling statistics on service representatives' performance in the field. Goetz created a database along with Web-enabled reporting tools so that reporting and accessing the data would be convenient for branch employees as well as managers and the Six Sigma team. The problem was, some of the branches and divisions were resistant to using the new system. Divisional executives who were used to initiating and implementing their own projects weren't happy about a centralized database that all the divisions were required to use.

So, as tired as he was after the long day of meetings at the Peabody Hotel in Memphis, Tennessee, Jim Goetz headed toward the lobby to do some politicking. He saw an opportunity to build a coalition of people to support the use of the Internet as a way to deliver Six Sigma improvements, and he wasn't about to let it pass. Goetz approached people from all divisions and involved them in informal conversations about the Six Sigma project, their goals and interests, and their expectations for how IT could help them meet their own division's or department's objectives. He knew that for the IT project to be successful, he needed to understand his colleagues' needs and goals as well as his own.

When he finally got to his room several hours later, Goetz still had two challenges: to sell branch employees on the ease of the Internet as a way to report data, and to convince the various divisions of the value of centralized implementation. But thanks to his informal talks, he now had a pretty good idea who his allies were, and he was already formulating strategies to influence others to support the project by aligning it with their own interests.[1]

Leaders like Jim Goetz understand the importance of using power, politics, and influence to get things done. Successful leaders take the time to build relationships all across the organization and talk with others informally about important projects and priorities. Much of a leader's influence occurs outside of formal meetings and work situations, in informal conversations such as those following the ServiceMaster meetings at the Peabody Hotel.

Recall that one of the key elements in the definition of leadership is *influence*. A central concern for leaders is getting other people to do what is necessary to reach specific goals. Some do so by exercising their formal position of authority in the organization. Others, such as Admiral Albert Konetzni, described in Chapter 5, and Myrtle Potter, described in Chapter 11, do so by building personal relationships with followers based on trust, respect, and genuine caring for one another. Another way leaders gain power and influence is through political activity, such as building a coalition, as Jim Goetz is doing at ServiceMaster.

This chapter explores the topic of leadership power and influence in detail. The chapter opens with a consideration of leadership frames of reference and how a political approach to leadership combines with other leadership philosophies. We will also examine the concepts of power and influence, look at some sources and types of power, and outline ways leaders exercise power and influence through political activity. Finally, we will briefly consider some ethical aspects of using power and influence.

Leadership Frames of Reference

Frame

a perspective from which a leader views the world

A **frame** is a perspective from which a leader views the world. The concept of frames of reference calls attention to the way people gather information, make decisions, and exercise power. The four frames of reference, illustrated in Exhibit 12.1 as a set of stairsteps, are structural, human resource, political, and symbolic. These frames of reference determine how situations are defined and what actions are taken.[2] Leaders often begin with a limited structural perspective of the organization and develop the other frames based on their own personal development and experience with the organization. One study found the structural frame of reference was used about 60 percent of the time, while the symbolic frame was used only about 20 percent of the time.[3]

Each frame of reference has strengths and weaknesses, and effective leaders strive for a balanced perspective so that all the needs of the organization are met. Previous chapters of this book have dealt primarily with leadership approaches relating to the first two frames (structural and human resource). This chapter examines leadership as a *political process*. The final chapters of the book will focus on the symbolic frame, considering how leaders influence others through vision, culture, and values. Effective leaders balance their view of the organization by

Exhibit 12.1   Four Leader Frames of Reference

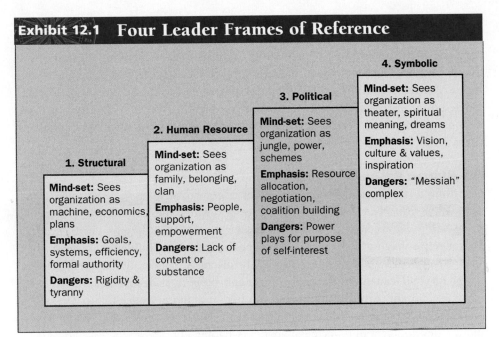

4. Symbolic

Mind-set: Sees organization as theater, spiritual meaning, dreams

Emphasis: Vision, culture & values, inspiration

Dangers: "Messiah" complex

3. Political

Mind-set: Sees organization as jungle, power, schemes

Emphasis: Resource allocation, negotiation, coalition building

Dangers: Power plays for purpose of self-interest

2. Human Resource

Mind-set: Sees organization as family, belonging, clan

Emphasis: People, support, empowerment

Dangers: Lack of content or substance

1. Structural

Mind-set: Sees organization as machine, economics, plans

Emphasis: Goals, systems, efficiency, formal authority

Dangers: Rigidity & tyranny

SOURCE: Based on Lee G. Bolman and Terrence E. Deal, *Reframing Organizations* (San Francisco: Jossey-Bass, 1991); and Bolman and Deal, "Leadership and Management Effectiveness: A Multi-Frame, Multi-Sector Analysis," *Human Resource Management* 30, no. 4 (Winter 1991), 509–534. Thanks to Roy Williams for suggesting the stair sequence.

becoming aware of all four frames of reference, the importance of each, and how using multiple frames can help leaders better understand organizational needs and problems.

The Structural Frame

The organization as machine is the dominant image in the structural frame of reference. Leaders strive for machine-like efficiency and make decisions based on economic efficiency. Plans and goals are the primary tools of management, and leaders rely heavily on the power and authority granted through their organizational position to influence others.

The structural frame of reference places emphasis on goal setting and clarifying job expectations as a way to provide order, efficiency, and continuity. Leaders emphasize clear job descriptions, specific policies and procedures, and the view of the organization as a rational system. Leaders value hard data and analysis, keep an eye on the bottom line, and stress adherence to accepted standards, conformity to rules, and the creation of administrative systems as a way to bring order and logic to the organization. Clarity of direction and control of results are important

Structural frame

frame of reference that places emphasis on goal setting and clarifying job expectations as a way to provide order, efficiency, and continuity characteristics in this frame. The task-oriented leadership styles described in Chapter 2 and some of the contingency approaches discussed in Chapter 3 illustrate the structural frame of reference. Transactional leadership, described in Chapter 4, also relies heavily on the structural frame. Structure, plans, and rationality are needed in all organizations, but not to the exclusion of other frames. Carried to an extreme, the structural frame of reference leads to rigidity and even tyranny among leaders, who will quote the rules and insist that they be followed to the letter.[4]

The Human Resource Frame

Human resource frame

frame of reference in which people are treated as the organization's most valuable resource

According to the **human resource frame** of reference, people are the organization's most valuable resource. This frame defines problems and issues in interpersonal terms and looks for ways to adjust the organization to meet human needs. Leaders do not rely solely on the power of their position to exert influence. Instead, they focus on relationships and feelings (recall the discussion of emotional intelligence in Chapter 5) and lead through empowerment and support, as described in the empowerment section of Chapter 8 and in our discussion of moral leadership in Chapter 6. Leaders also encourage open communication (Chapter 9), teamwork (Chapter 10), and the development of diverse employees (Chapter 11).

Effective leaders use the human resource perspective to involve others and give them opportunities for personal and professional development. They value people, are visible and accessible, and serve others. The images in this view are a sense of family, belonging, and the organization as a clan. This frame of reference, however, can also lead to ineffectiveness if leaders are wishy-washy and always bending to the whims of others, in essence using caring and participation as an excuse to avoid leadership responsibility.[5]

The Political Frame

Political frame

frame of reference that views organizations as arenas of ongoing conflict over the allocation of scarce resources

The **political frame** of reference views organizations as arenas of ongoing conflict or tension over the allocation of scarce resources. Leaders spend their time networking and building alliances and coalitions to influence decisions. These leaders consciously strive to build a power base, and they frequently exercise both personal and organizational power to achieve their desired results. Carried to an extreme, the political frame of reference can lead to deception, dishonesty, and power plays for purposes of individual self-interest. However, effective political leaders typically use their negotiating, bargaining, and coalition-building skills to serve organizational needs.[6]

Power and politics are an important, although often hidden, part of all organizations. The mind-set in the political frame is to be aware of the organization as a jungle. Power is a reality, and political schemes are a natural part of organizational life. Embracing this frame, although not to the exclusion of the other frames, is an important part of effective leadership in most organizations. The remaining sections of this chapter will examine the political approach to leadership in more detail.

The Symbolic Frame

To use full leadership potential requires that leaders also develop a fourth frame of reference—the **symbolic frame**, in which leaders perceive the organization as a system of shared meaning and values.[7] Rather than relying only on formal power and the use of politics, the symbolic leader focuses on shared vision, culture, and values to influence others and lead the organization. We have touched on topics related to the symbolic frame of reference throughout this book. For example, charismatic and transformational leadership, described in Chapter 4, rely heavily on this frame. The communication chapter (Chapter 9) discussed how leaders use stories and symbols to build shared values, and Chapter 11 touched on changing cultural values to support diversity. The symbolic frame of reference will be explored in more depth in the remaining chapters of this book. Chapter 13 will focus on how leaders create and communicate a vision for the organization, and Chapter 14 will look closely at building and changing organizational culture. In Chapter 15, we will examine how leaders design learning organizations, including shaping the values required to promote continuous learning and change. The final chapter of the book looks specifically at the topic of leading change.

Symbolic frame
frame of reference in which the organization is perceived as a system of shared meaning and values

Symbolic leaders frequently inspire people to higher levels of performance and commitment; however, this frame of reference can also lead to problems when used exclusively. One danger of relying too heavily on the symbolic frame is that leaders develop a "messiah" complex. The focus shifts to the leader rather than the organization and all its members (recall our discussion of the "black hat of charisma" in Chapter 4). Symbols can also be used for dishonest, unethical, and self-serving purposes. Symbolic leaders are effective when they articulate a vision that is widely shared and understood, and when they support the deepest values and concerns of followers. The leader thinks in terms of the organization as theater, is concerned with spirit and meaning, and focuses on harnessing people's dreams and desires for the benefit of everyone and the organization.

Each of the four frames illustrated in Exhibit 12.1 provides significant possibilities for enhancing leadership effectiveness, but each is incomplete. Leaders can understand their own natural frame of reference and recognize its limitations. In addition, they can learn to integrate multiple frames to fully use their leadership potential. Complete the questionnaire in Leader's Self-Insight 12.1 to understand your own dominant frame of reference. Not every leader can develop abilities in all areas. However, effective leaders "understand their own strengths, work to expand them, and build teams that together can provide leadership in all four modes—structural, human resource, political, and symbolic."[8]

Action Memo

As a leader: Use each of the structural, human resource, political, and symbolic frames of reference to maximize your leadership effectiveness. Recognize the limits of your dominant frame. Surround yourself with followers who can help you view the organization from multiple perspectives.

LEADER'S SELF-INSIGHT 12.1

Your Leadership Orientation

This questionnaire asks you to describe yourself as a leader. Rank each item as follows: 4 = Best describes you, 3 = Next best describes you, 2 = Does not describe you well, 1 = Does not describe you at all.

1. My strongest skills are
   _____a. analytical skills.
   _____b. interpersonal skills.
   _____c. political skills.
   _____d. flair for drama.

2. The best way to describe me is
   _____a. technical expert.
   _____b. good listener.
   _____c. skilled negotiator.
   _____d. inspirational leader.

3. What has helped me the most to be successful is my ability to
   _____a. make good decisions.
   _____b. coach and develop people.
   _____c. build strong alliances and a power base.
   _____d. inspire and excite others.

4. What people are most likely to notice about me is my
   _____a. attention to detail.
   _____b. concern for people.
   _____c. ability to succeed in the face of conflict and opposition.
   _____d. charisma.

5. My most important leadership trait is
   _____a. clear, logical thinking.
   _____b. caring and support of others.
   _____c. toughness and aggressiveness.
   _____d. imagination and creativity.

6. I am best described as a(n)
   _____a. analyst.
   _____b. humanist.
   _____c. politician.
   _____d. visionary.

Scoring and Interpretation

Compute your scores as follows:
Structural = 1a + 2a + 3a + 4a + 5a + 6a = _____
Human resource = 1b + 2b + 3b + 4b + 5b + 6b = _____
Political = 1c + 2c + 3c + 4c + 5c + 6c = _____
Symbolic = 1d + 2d + 3d + 4d + 5d + 6d = _____

The Leadership Orientation instrument reveals your leadership preferences for the four frames of reference discussed in the text. The higher the score, the greater your preference. Compare your scores to other people. What have you learned about your leader frames? How will you expand your leadership thinking to incorporate other frames of reference?
_____

SOURCE: Leadership Framework, 440 Boylston Street, Brookline, MA 02146, (1988). All rights reserved.

Power, Influence, and Leadership

One distinction in the four frames of reference is how leaders gain and use power and influence. Power may be one of the most important concepts in the study of leadership. However, getting a grasp on the meaning of the terms power and influence can be difficult.[9]

Power is an intangible force in organizations. It cannot be seen, but its effect can be felt. Power is often defined as the potential ability of one person (or department) to influence other persons (or departments) to carry out orders[10] or to do something they otherwise would not have done.[11] Other definitions stress that power is the ability to achieve goals or outcomes that power holders desire.[12] The achievement of desired outcomes is the basis of the definition used here. Power is the ability of one person or department in an organization to influence other people to bring about desired outcomes. It is the potential to influence others within the organization with the goal of attaining desired outcomes for power holders. Potential power is realized through the processes of politics and influence.[13] Sometimes, the terms power and influence are used synonymously, but there are distinctions between the two. Basically, **influence** is the effect a person's actions have on the attitudes, values, beliefs, or actions of others. Whereas power is the capacity to cause a change in a person, influence may be thought of as the degree of actual change. For example, as a child you may have had the experience of playing a game you didn't really want to play because one person in the group influenced others to do what he or she wanted. Or you may have changed your college major because of the influence of someone important in your life, or shifted your beliefs about some social issue based on the influence of political or religious leaders. Although we usually think of power and influence as belonging to the leader, in reality they result from the interaction of leaders and followers in specific situations. As we learned in Chapter 7 on followership, followers may also influence a leader's behavior in any number of ways, for better or worse. Later in this chapter, we will examine some specific *influence tactics* that may be used to change another's attitudes or behavior. Leaders can improve their effectiveness by understanding the various types and sources of power as well as the influence tactics they or their followers may use.

Five Types of Leader Power

Power is often described as a personal characteristic, but as described above, organizational position also influences a leader's power. Most discussions of power include five types that are available to leaders.[14]

The five types of leader power are illustrated in Exhibit 12.2. The first three—legitimate, reward, and coercive power—may all be considered types of *position power* that are defined largely by the organization's policies and procedures. A person's

Power
the ability of one person or department in an organization to influence other people to bring about desired outcomes

Influence
the effect a person's actions have on the attitudes, values, beliefs, or actions of others

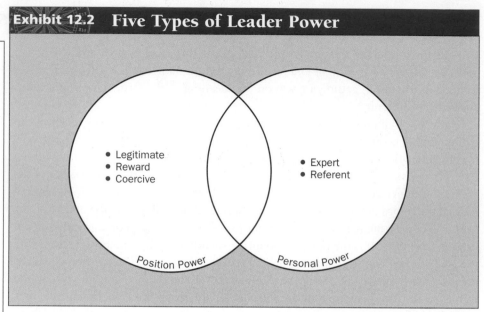

Exhibit 12.2   Five Types of Leader Power

- Legitimate
- Reward
- Coercive

- Expert
- Referent

Position Power

Personal Power

position in the organization determines what amount of power he or she has, particularly in regard to the ability to reward or punish subordinates to influence their behavior. However, it is important to remember that position power and leadership are not the same thing. As we discussed in Chapter 1, a person might hold a formal position of authority and yet not be a leader. Effective leaders don't rely solely on formal position to influence others to accomplish goals. Two sources of *personal power*, called expert power and referent power, are based on the leader's special knowledge or personal characteristics.

Legitimate
power
───────
authority
granted from a
formal position

Legitimate Power Legitimate power is the authority granted from a formal position in an organization. For example, once a person has been selected as a supervisor, most workers understand that they are obligated to follow his or her direction with respect to work activities. Subordinates accept this source of power as legitimate, which is why they comply. Certain rights, responsibilities, and prerogatives accrue to anyone holding a formal leadership position. Followers accept the legitimate rights of formal leaders to set goals, make decisions, and direct activities. Most North Americans accept the legitimate right of appointed leaders to direct an organization.

Reward Power This kind of power stems from the authority to bestow rewards on other people. For example, appointed leaders may have access to formal rewards, such as pay increases or promotions. Moreover, organizations allocate huge amounts of resources downward from top leaders. Leaders control resources and their distribution. Lower-level followers depend on leaders for the financial and physical resources to perform their tasks. Leaders with **reward power** can use rewards to influence subordinates' behavior.

Reward power
authority to bestow rewards on other people

Coercive Power The opposite of reward power is **coercive power**. It refers to the power to punish or recommend punishment. Supervisors have coercive power when they have the right to fire or demote subordinates, criticize, or withdraw pay increases. For example, if Paul, a salesman, does not perform as well as expected, his supervisor has the coercive power to criticize him, reprimand him, put a negative letter in his file, and hurt his chance for a raise. Coercive power is the negative side of legitimate and reward power.

Coercive power
authority to punish or recommend punishment

Expert Power Power resulting from a leader's special knowledge or skill regarding tasks performed by followers is referred to as **expert power**. When a leader is a true expert, subordinates go along with recommendations because of his or her superior knowledge. Leaders at supervisory levels often have experience in the production process that gains them promotion. At top management levels, however, leaders may lack expert power because subordinates know more about technical details than they do. For example, a lower-level communications manager gained power at Empire Blue Cross and Blue Shield after the September 11, 2001, attack on the World Trade Center, where the company had offices. The manager worked around the clock to get phone lines and voice mail working again. "He acted on his own and knew what to do, even though we'd never anticipated losing all our exchanges," said Empire's CEO.[15] People with expertise and knowledge can use it to influence or place limits on decisions made by people above them in the organization.[16] Furthermore, specialized information may be withheld or divulged in ways designed to achieve particular outcomes desired by the leaders.[17]

Expert power
authority resulting from a leader's special knowledge or skill

Referent Power This kind of power comes from leader personality characteristics that command followers' identification, respect, and admiration so they want to emulate the leader. When workers admire a supervisor because of the way he or she deals with them, the influence is based on referent power. **Referent power** depends on the leader's personal characteristics rather than on a formal title or position and is visible in the area of charismatic leadership as described in Chapter 4. The Living Leadership box talks about the far-reaching impact of referent power.

One leader who illustrates referent power is Lorraine Monroe, former principal of Harlem's Frederick Douglass Academy. After leaving Frederick Douglass, Monroe founded the School Leadership Academy at the Center for Educational Innovation, a business-sponsored group designed to foster creative educational leadership.

Referent power
authority based on personality characteristics that command followers' attention, respect, and admiration so that they want to emulate the leader

LIVING LEADERSHIP

The Ripple Effect

Do you want to be a positive influence in the world? First, get your own life in order. Ground yourself in the single principle so that your behavior is wholesome and effective. If you do that, you will earn respect and be a powerful influence.

Your behavior influences others through a ripple effect. A ripple effect works because everyone influences everyone else. Powerful people are powerful influences.

If your life works, you influence your family.

If your family works, your family influences the community.

If your community works, your community influences the nation.

If your nation works, your nation influences the world.

If your world works, the ripple effect spreads throughout the cosmos.

SOURCE: John Heider, *The Tao of Leadership: Leadership Strategies for a New Age* (New York: Bantam Books, 1985), 107. Copyright 1985 Humanic Ltd., Atlanta, GA. Used with permission.

In the Lead   Lorraine Monroe, Frederick Douglass Academy

When Lorraine Monroe became principal of Harlem's Frederick Douglass School (which she renamed Frederick Douglass Academy), the school was known for excessive violence, poor attendance, and low achievement. Only five years later, test scores of Frederick Douglass students ranked among the best in New York City, and 96 percent of graduates went on to college.

To turn around the troubled school, Monroe relied more on referent power than position power for influencing followers. Her personal energy, genuine caring, and ability to understand and respond to the unspoken fears and longings of others inspired both teachers and students to imagine greater possibilities for themselves and believe they could achieve them. She lived her own life by her "Twelve Non-Negotiable Rules and Regulations," rules based in respect for oneself, for one's associates, and for the school, and others soon followed her example.

Monroe believes a leader has a responsibility to turn a workplace into a community by making sure people are nurtured, respected, and given an opportunity to make genuine, lasting contributions. She demands the best from people and helps them achieve it. "People want to be about good things," Monroe says. "They want to believe that the work they do has meaning, some purpose beyond making a salary."[18]

Responses to the Use of Power

Leaders use the various types of power to influence others to do what is necessary to accomplish organizational goals. The success of any attempt to influence is a matter of degree, but there are three distinct outcomes that may result from the use of power: compliance, resistance, and commitment, as illustrated in Exhibit 12.3.[19]

When people successfully use position power (legitimate, reward, coercive), the response is compliance. **Compliance** means that people follow the directions of the person with power, whether or not they agree with those directions. They will obey orders and carry out instructions even though they may not like it. The problem is that in many cases, followers do just enough work as is necessary to satisfy the leader and may not contribute their full potential. In addition, if the use of position power, especially the use of coercion, exceeds a level people consider legitimate, people may resist the attempt to influence. **Resistance** means that employees will deliberately try to avoid carrying out instructions or they will attempt to disobey orders. Thus, the effectiveness of leaders who rely solely on position power is limited.

The follower response most often generated by personal power (expert, referent) is commitment. **Commitment** means that followers adopt the leader's viewpoint and enthusiastically carry out instructions, as they did at Frederick Douglass Academy. Needless to say, commitment is preferred to compliance or resistance. Although compliance alone may be enough for routine matters, commitment is particularly important when the leader is promoting change. Change carries risk or uncertainty, and follower commitment helps to overcome fear and resistance associated with change efforts. Successful leaders exercise both personal and position power to influence others. What types of power do you prefer using to influence others? Complete Leader's Self-Insight 12.2 to find out.

Compliance
following the directions of the person with power, regardless of how much agreement there is with that person's directions

Resistance
the act of disobeying orders or deliberately avoiding carrying out instructions

Commitment
adopting the leader's viewpoint and enthusiastically carrying out instructions

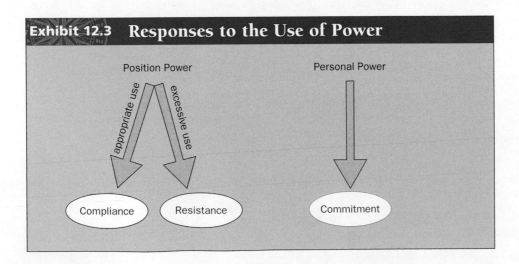

Exhibit 12.3   Responses to the Use of Power

LEADER'S SELF-INSIGHT 12.2

Personal Power Profile

Below is a list of statements that describe behaviors that leaders in work organizations can direct toward their followers. Read each descriptive statement, thinking in terms of how you prefer to influence others. Mark the number that most closely represents how you feel. Use the following numbers for your answers: 1 = Strongly disagree; 2 = Disagree, 3 = Neither agree nor disagree; 4 = Agree; 5 = Strongly agree

To influence others, I would prefer to:	Strongly disagree				Strongly agree
1. Increase their pay level	1	2	3	4	5
2. Make them feel valued	1	2	3	4	5
3. Give undesirable job assignments	1	2	3	4	5
4. Make them feel that I approve of them	1	2	3	4	5
5. Make them feel that they have commitments to meet	1	2	3	4	5
6. Make them feel personally accepted	1	2	3	4	5
7. Make them feel important	1	2	3	4	5
8. Give them good technical suggestions	1	2	3	4	5
9. Make the work difficult for them	1	2	3	4	5
10. Share my experience and/or training	1	2	3	4	5
11. Influence a pay increase	1	2	3	4	5
12. Make working here unpleasant	1	2	3	4	5
13. Make being at work distasteful	1	2	3	4	5
14. Make them feel that they should satisfy their job requirements	1	2	3	4	5
15. Provide them with sound job-related advice	1	2	3	4	5
16. Provide them with special benefits	1	2	3	4	5
17. Influence promotions	1	2	3	4	5
18. Give them the feeling that they have responsibilities to fulfill	1	2	3	4	5
19. Provide them with needed technical knowledge	1	2	3	4	5
20. Make them recognize that they have tasks to accomplish	1	2	3	4	5

Scoring and Interpretation

Compute your scores from the 20 questions according to the following procedure: Reward power—sum your responses to items 1, 11, 16, and 17. Coercive power—sum your responses to items 3, 9, 12, and 13. Legitimate power—sum your responses to questions 5, 14, 18, and 20. Referent power—sum your responses to questions 2, 4, 6, and 7. Expert power—sum your responses to questions 8, 10, 15, and 19.

Scores: Reward = _____   Coercive = _____   Legitimate = _____

Referent = _____   Expert = _____

A high score (16 and greater) on any of the five dimensions of power implies that you prefer to influence others by employing that particular form of power. A low score (8 and less) implies that you prefer not to employ this particular form of power to influence others. These scores represent your power profile.

SOURCE: Modified version of T. R. Hinkin and C. A. Schriesheim, "Development and Application of New Scales to Measure the French and Raven Bases of Social Power," *Journal of Applied Psychology* 74 (1989), 561–567, copyright (c) 1989 by the American Psychological Association, as appeared in Jon L. Pierce and John W. Newstrom, *Leaders and the Leadership Process: Readings, Self-Assessments, and Applications* (Chicago: Richard D. Irwin, 1995), 25–26.

The Role of Dependency

You probably know from personal experience that when a person has control over something that others want and need, he or she gains power. A simple example is a star high school quarterback graduating at a time when there are few excellent quarterbacks coming out of high schools. The star will be courted by numerous colleges who will vie for his interest and make increasingly attractive offers to entice him to sign on with their team.

One of the key aspects of power is that it is a function of dependence—that is, the greater Individual B's dependence on Individual A, the greater power A will have over B. People in organizations, as elsewhere, have power because other people depend on them—for information, resources, cooperation, and so forth. The more people depend on someone, the greater that person's power.[20] The nature of dependency relationships between leaders and subordinates in organizations changed during the prosperous years of the 1990s because of low unemployment and a tight labor market. When good jobs are plentiful, people feel less dependent on their supervisors, while managers are more dependent on employees because they are difficult to replace. Only a few years ago, for example, the shortage of engineers and other high-tech talent was so severe that many employees could shop around, gather several offers, and then demand more money and benefits from their employers. In the early 2000s, with a struggling economy and massive downsizing, the situation reversed, with employers again gaining more clout over workers.[21] When jobs are hard to come by and unemployment is high, organizational leaders have greater power over employees because most people are dependent on the organization for their livelihood. They know that if they lose their job it might be very difficult to find another one.

This type of dependency primarily affects a leader's position power, which is based on formal authority and the ability to bestow rewards and punishments. When supervisors are dependent on employees, such as in a tight labor market, leaders must gain and exercise personal power to a greater extent, because people will often stay in a job where they admire and respect the leader, even if other opportunities are plentiful. When jobs are scarce, it is easier for leaders to get by relying on position power, but they won't get the full benefit of employees' enthusiasm and commitment.

Dependency in organizations is related to a person's control over resources. Resources include such things as jobs, rewards, financial support, expertise, knowledge, materials, information, and time. As illustrated in Exhibit 12.4, people are more dependent—therefore leaders and organizations have more control and power—when resources are high on three characteristics—importance, scarcity, and nonsubstitutability.[22] People in the organization must perceive the resource to be *important*—that is, if nobody wants what you've got, it's not going to create dependency. Resources can be important for a variety of reasons. For example, they may be

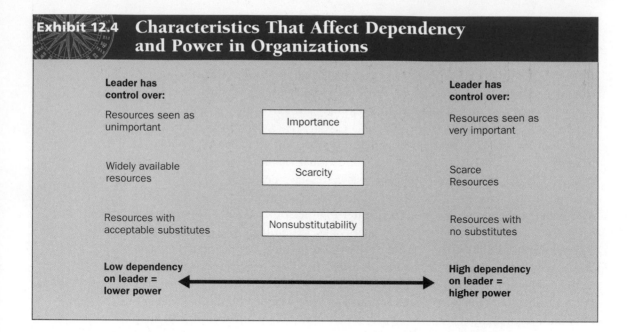

Exhibit 12.4   Characteristics That Affect Dependency and Power in Organizations

Leader has control over:		Leader has control over:
Resources seen as unimportant	Importance	Resources seen as very important
Widely available resources	Scarcity	Scarce Resources
Resources with acceptable substitutes	Nonsubstitutability	Resources with no substitutes

Low dependency on leader = lower power ⬌ High dependency on leader = higher power

essential elements of a key product, they may directly generate sales, or they may be critical to reducing or avoiding uncertainty for the organization's top decision makers. Chief information officers have gained a tremendous amount of power in many organizations because of the critical role of information technology in today's business world.

Scarcity refers to whether the resource is easy or difficult to obtain. A resource that is difficult or expensive to acquire is more valuable and creates more dependency than one that is widely available. For example, Wal-Mart has decided that it will stop selling point-of-sales data from its cash registers to market research firms like AC Nielsen and IRI. Without data from the world's largest retailer, it will be much more difficult, expensive, and time-consuming for these firms to find out who's buying what. Wal-Mart could use its powerful position to squeeze more money out of the research firms that want the data.[23] Leaders and employees with specialized knowledge also illustrate this aspect of dependency. In companies moving toward e-business, some young Internet-literate managers have gained power over senior leaders with no computer expertise.

The third characteristic, *nonsubstitutability*, means that leaders or employees with control over resources with no viable substitute will have more power. These resources may include knowledge and expertise as well as access to people with high power. For example, an executive secretary who has daily access to the CEO might have more power than middle managers, who must compete for a few minutes of the top leader's time.

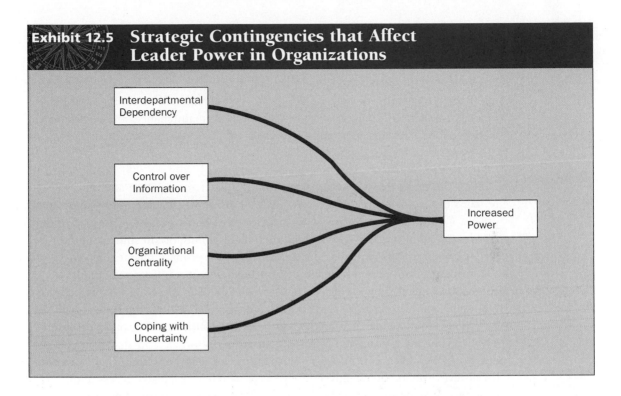

Exhibit 12.5 Strategic Contingencies that Affect Leader Power in Organizations

Sources of Leader Power in Organizations

An understanding of dependency provides the foundation for examining several sources of leader power in organizations. The five types of power we discussed earlier are derived from either formal position or the leader's personal qualities. These sources provide a basis for much of a leader's influence. In organizations, however, additional sources of power and influence have been identified. The strategic contingencies theory identifies power sources not linked to the specific person or position, but to the role the leader plays in the overall functioning of the organization.[24] Sources of power in this regard are interdepartmental dependency, control over information, centrality, and coping with uncertainty, as illustrated in Exhibit 12.5.

Interdepartmental Dependency

One key source of leader power in many organizations is interdepartmental dependency. Materials, resources, and information may flow between departments in one direction. In such cases, leaders in the department receiving resources will have less power than those in the department that provides them. For example, consider the case of leaders at a cigarette factory.[25] One might expect that the production department would be more powerful than the maintenance department, but this was not the case in a cigarette plant near Paris. The production of cigarettes was a routine process. The machinery was automated. On the other hand, maintenance department workers and their leaders were responsible for repair of the automated machinery, which was a complex task, and they had many years of experience. Because the maintenance department had the ability to fix unpredictable assembly-line breakdowns, production managers became dependent on maintenance, and maintenance leaders called the shots about machine repair and assembly line maintenance.

Control Over Information

Despite the trend toward empowerment and broader information-sharing, the fact remains that some people will almost always have access to more information than others. Control over information—which involves both access to information and control over how and to whom it is distributed—is an important source of power for leaders. Most leaders recognize that information is a primary business resource and that by controlling what information is collected, how it is interpreted, and how it is shared, they can influence how decisions are made.[26] To some extent, access to information is determined by a person's position in the organization. Top leaders typically have access to more information than do lower-level supervisors or other employees. They can release information selectively to influence others and shape actions and decisions. However, control over information can also be a source of power for lower-level leaders and employees. Employees who have exclusive access to information needed by leaders to make decisions gain power as a result. For example, top executives may be dependent on the operating manager for analyzing and interpreting complex operations data.

Some leaders actively seek to increase their power by gaining control over information. At a not-for-profit organization that sponsors a regional book fair, the fair's coordinator developed contacts with publishing houses that gave her early access to information about new books and authors who would be touring the country. She could selectively provide information to the executive director and steering committee to shape the content of the program. Sometimes, the committee approved authors that the coordinator wanted on the program, even though these authors might not have been chosen had the committee known the full slate of potential participants.

Organizational Centrality

Centrality
a leader's or a deparment's role in the primary activity of an organization

Centrality reflects a leader's or a department's role in the primary activity of an organization.[27] One measure of centrality is the extent to which the work of the leader's department affects the final output of the organization. At a company such as Intel, which is heavily technology-oriented, engineers have a high degree of power because the organization depends on them to maintain the technical superiority of its products. In contrast, engineers at a company such as Procter & Gamble or Kimberly-Clark, where marketing is the name of the game, have a lower degree of power. In these organizations, marketers are typically the most powerful group of employees.[28] Centrality is associated with more power because it reflects the contribution made to the organization. At the University of Illinois, for example, important resources come from research grants and the quality of students and faculty. Departments that provide the most resources to the university are rated as having the most power. Also, departments that generate large research grants are more powerful because the grants contain a sizable overhead payment to university administration.[29]

Coping with Uncertainty

The environment can change swiftly and create uncertainty and complexity for leaders. In the face of uncertainty, little information is available to leaders on appropriate courses of action. Leaders in departments that cope well with this uncertainty will increase their power.[30] When market research personnel accurately predict changes in demand for new products, for example, they gain power and prestige because they have reduced a critical uncertainty. Leaders in industrial relations departments may gain power by helping the organization deal with uncertainties created by labor unions. Consider how public relations leaders at PepsiCo helped cope with uncertainty during the "syringe in the Pepsi can" scare of the early 1990s.

In the Lead   PepsiCo

It has been more than a decade, but PepsiCo's handling of a crisis that occurred when a couple claimed to have found a hypodermic syringe in an unopened can of Pepsi still ranks as one of the classic stories of how to cope with crisis and uncertainty. The couple's lawyer contacted the county health department, the bottler and distributor, and the media. Within days, the story was splashed across every front page in the country, and copycats emerged by the dozens, claiming that they, too, had found needles in their Pepsis.

Jerry Gregoire was chief information officer at PepsiCo at the time and recalls the response of top executives: "Those of us who were familiar with the bottling process, the lightning speed of the production line, and the particulars of how the cans are handled during filling and capping knew these claims were a pack of lies." Some leaders wanted to run to the nearest television camera and say just that. However, leaders in the public relations department cautioned that doing so would be a huge mistake considering the media feeding frenzy that was going on at the time. PR leaders worked with top executives to respond quickly to consumer fears—whether they were true of not—with a massive public relations and education campaign. Company leaders took to the airwaves to express deep concern, recalled their product, and aggressively inspected their bottling plants, despite their certainty that there was nothing to find. At one point, PepsiCo's then-CEO Craig Weatherup appeared on ABC's *Nightline* with FDA Commissioner David Kessler to explain the situation as it was emerging.

Before long, most of the supposed victims had confessed that it was all a hoax. Pepsi's market standing was temporarily damaged by the syringe scare, but its reputation as an ethical and trustworthy company was still intact. If leaders had failed to successfully manage the company's public image, the crisis could have seriously threatened Pepsi's future competitiveness.[31]

Leaders in the public relations department at PepsiCo took action to help the company cope with a critical uncertainty after it appeared, giving them and their department increased power. PR departments in many companies have gained greater power today, when even minor problems can suddenly balloon into major crises in the media. Strategic issues and uncertainties are continually changing for organizations, which leads to shifting power relationships. Departments that help organizations cope with new uncertainties will increase their power.

Increasing Power Through Political Activity

Politics

activities to acquire, develop, and use power and other resources to obtain desired future outcomes when there is uncertainty or disagreement about choices

Another aspect of power is that it isn't enough to be performing central activities or coping with organizational uncertainties—one's efforts must also be recognized as important by others.[32] People who want to increase their power make sure their activities are visible and appreciated by others. Acquiring and using power is largely a political process. **Politics** involves activities to acquire, develop, and use power and other resources to obtain desired future outcomes when there is uncertainty or disagreement about choices.[33] For example, many organizations engage in political activity to influence government policies because government choices represent a critical source of uncertainty for businesses as well as nonprofit organizations.[34] Consider such recent U.S. government decisions as the activation of a national "do not call" registry, which dramatically changes the rules of the game for telemarketers, a Supreme Court ruling that endorsed the continuation of affirmation action guidelines for hiring and college admissions, or changes in Medicare and Medicaid that enable states to wring discounts from health care providers. Organizations use political activity to try to influence decisions that will be to their benefit.

Individuals and departments within organizations also engage in political activity. Political behavior can be either a positive or negative force. Uncertainty and conflict are natural in organizations, and politics is the mechanism for accomplishing things that can't be handled purely through formal policies or position power. The appropriate use of power and politics to get things done is an important aspect of leadership, as further discussed in this chapter's Leader's Bookshelf.

Leaders use politics to increase their personal power in a number of ways. One way leaders increase their power is by seeking greater responsibility, such as serving on committees or volunteering for difficult projects. This often enables them to make connections with powerful people in the organization and build their reputation among those people. When lower-level leaders are perceived as having "friends in higher places," their own power is increased.

Another political approach is called *impression management*, which means leaders seek to control how others perceive them. In other words, they strive to create an impression of greater power. A whole industry, known as *executive coaching*, is aimed at helping leaders develop this ability. For example, coach Debra Benton helps executives at companies such as Mattel, Hewlett-Packard, and PepsiCo develop what she calls executive presence—"the impact you have when you walk into a room, a collection of subtle . . . visual cues, including everything from how your clothes fit to how you walk."[35] Impression management may include a wide variety of tactics. Subtle name-dropping can give the impression that a leader associates with high-status people. Likewise, flattery is a form of impression management that can help a person appear to be perceptive and pleasant. These political tactics can be helpful when they enable others to perceive a leader's value to the organization. However, they can also backfire if leaders are perceived as being insincere, dishonest, or arrogant. One example of the effective use of impression management is Steve Harrison, who at the age of 50 was afraid younger superiors as well as subordinates might perceive him as behind the times. Not only does Harrison make sure others know that he keeps up with current business issues, but he also peppers his informal conversations with references to his "youthful" hobbies of running and collecting electric guitars.[36]

Tactics for Asserting Leader Influence

The next issue is how leaders use their power to implement decisions, facilitate change, and pursue organizational goals. That is, leaders use power to influence others, which requires both skill and willingness. Much influence is interpersonal and one-on-one. This is social influence, which involves coalitions, rewards, and inspiration. Other influence has broader appeal, such as to influence the organization as a whole, or to influence those outside the organization. However, not all attempts to use power result in actual influence. Some power moves are rejected by followers, particularly if they are seen to be self-serving. Leaders have to determine the best approach for using their power—that is, the approach that is most likely to influence

LEADER'S BOOKSHELF

Leadership on the Line: Staying Alive Through the Dangers of Leading
By Ronald A. Heifetz and Marty Linsky

In *Leadership on the Line*, Ronald Heifetz and Marty Linsky start with the premise that leadership is hard and lonely work. Each of us has opportunities to lead every day, but many avoid the challenge. And with good reason, say the authors: "To lead is to live dangerously because when leadership counts, when you lead people through difficult change, you challenge what people hold dear—their daily habits, tools, loyalties, and ways of thinking—with nothing more to offer perhaps than a possibility." Heifetz and Linsky, who teach at Harvard University's Kennedy School of Government, wrote *Leadership on the Line* as a guide for "surviving and thriving amidst the dangers of leadership."

Strategies for Thriving as a Leader
Here are a few of the strategies Heifetz and Linsky offer for how leaders can accomplish change and avoid being put down or pushed aside.

* *Think politically.* A key step is acknowledging the political nature of leadership. Leaders cannot get anything done unless they create and nurture networks of people they can call on and work with to accomplish goals. At the start of any change campaign, good leaders line up their supporters, start working closely with their opponents, and develop tactics for influencing the uncommitted.

* *Manage conflict.* Any tough issue is bound to be accompanied by conflict. While the natural tendency for most of us is to limit conflict, Heifetz and Linsky point out that people learn and grow only when they encounter ideas that challenge their own experience and assumptions. The job for leaders is to work with differing ideas, opinions, emotions, and attitudes in a way that harnesses the energy of conflict but minimizes its destructive potential.

* *Keep your hungers in check.* Everyone has *hungers,* expressions of our normal human needs, but leaders are careful not to let their hungers disrupt their capacity for acting with wisdom and purpose. For example, a lust for power becomes an end in itself, distracting a leader's attention from organizational needs and goals. Inappropriate personal behavior damages trust, creates confusion, and destroys relationships. An inflated sense of self-importance limits the capacity for self-understanding and meaningful, caring relationships with others. Good leaders understand where their vulnerabilities are and work to keep them from taking charge of their lives.

Emotional and Practical Support
Leadership on the Line can help people from all walks of life accept the challenge of leadership and "survive to delight in the fruits of your labor." Taking the opportunity to lead—to make a difference in the lives of people around you—is not always easy, but it is worth the costs. With the tips, strategies, and guidelines in *Leadership on the Line*, Heifetz and Linsky lend emotional and practical support for those who rise to the challenge.

Leadership on the Line: Staying Alive Through the Dangers of Leading, by Ronald A. Heifetz and Marty Linsky, is published by Harvard Business School Press.

others—by considering the individuals, groups, and situations involved.[37] In addition, they understand the basic principles that can cause people to change their behavior or attitudes. Leaders frequently use a combination of influence strategies, and people who are perceived as having greater power and influence typically are those who use a wider variety of tactics. One survey of a few hundred leaders identified more than 4,000 different techniques by which these people were able to influence others to do what the leader wanted.[38]

However, the myriad successful influence tactics used by leaders fall into basic categories of influence actions. Exhibit 12.6 lists seven principles for asserting leader influence. Notice that most of these involve the use of personal power, rather than relying solely on position power or the use of rewards and punishments.

1. *Use rational persuasion.* Perhaps the most frequently used influence tactic is rational persuasion, which means using facts, data, and logical arguments to persuade others that a proposed idea or request is the best way to complete a task or accomplish a desired goal. It can be effective whether the influence attempt is directed upward toward superiors, downward toward subordinates, or horizontally, because most people have faith in facts and analysis.[39] Rational persuasion is most effective when a leader has technical knowledge and expertise related to the issue (expert power), although referent power is also used. Frequently, some parts of a rational argument cannot be backed up with facts and figures, so people have to believe in the leader's credibility to accept his or her argument.

2. *Make people like you.* People would rather say yes to someone they like than someone they don't like.[40] One author of a book on influence tells a story about an American working in Saudi Arabia, who learned that getting information or action from government offices was easy when he'd drop by, drink tea, and chat for a while.[41] Cultural values in Saudi Arabia put great

Action Memo

As a leader: Use political activity to achieve important organizational goals when there is uncertainty or disagreement about choices. Develop connections with powerful people by volunteering for difficult projects and serving on committees. Use impression management to shape how others perceive you.

Exhibit 12.6   Seven Principles for Asserting Leader Influence

1. Use rational persuasion.
2. Make people like you.
3. Rely on the rule of reciprocity.
4. Develop allies.
5. Ask for what you want.
6. Remember the principle of scarcity.
7. Extend formal authority with expertise and credibility.

emphasis on personal relationships, but people in all cultures respond to friendliness and consideration. When a leader shows concern for others, demonstrates trust and respect, and treats people fairly, people are more likely to want to help and support the leader by doing what he or she asks. In addition, most people will like a leader who makes them feel good about themselves. Leaders never underestimate the importance of praise.

3. *Rely on the rule of reciprocity.* Recall the discussion of dependency, and how leaders gain power by having something that others value. A primary way to turn that power into influence is to share what you have—whether it be time, resources, services, or emotional support. There's a near universal feeling among people that others should be paid back for what they do in one form or another. This "unwritten law of reciprocity" means that leaders who do favors for others can expect others to do favors for them in return. Leaders also elicit the kind of cooperative and sharing behavior they want from others by first demonstrating it with their own actions.[42]

4. *Develop allies.* Reciprocity also plays an important role in developing networks of allies, people who can help the leader accomplish his or her goals. Leaders can influence others by taking the time to talk with followers and other leaders outside of formal meetings to understand their needs and concerns, as well as to explain problems and describe the leader's point of view.[43] Leaders consult with one another and reach a meeting of minds about a proposed decision, change, or strategy.[44]

A leader can expand his or her network of allies by reaching out to establish contact with additional people. Some leaders expand their networks through the hiring, transfer, and promotion process. Identifying and placing in key positions people who are sympathetic to the desired outcomes of the leader can help achieve the leader's goals. The following example illustrates a successful use of power and influence that followed the merger of Morgan Stanley and Dean Witter, where the Dean Witter boss gained complete control over the newly merged firm by surrounding himself with loyal allies and edging out his Morgan Stanley counterpart.

In the Lead   Philip Purcell, Morgan Stanley Dean Witter

During negotiations for the merger of Morgan Stanley and Dean Witter, Dean Witter's long-time head, Philip Purcell, argued that since his firm was technically the acquirer in the deal, it was only right that the first CEO come from Dean Witter. Morgan's heir apparent, John Mack, agreed to the terms, saying the merger was too important to make an issue over the top job.

Morgan's then-CEO and chairman, Richard Fisher, cautioned Mack to guard against losing too much power to Purcell, and the three hammered out an informal arrangement whereby Purcell would run the company for approximately five years and then Mack would succeed him. But the Morgan managers soon began to suspect that Purcell was out to gain total control for himself. He quickly installed trusted Dean Witter veterans in key positions and often supported them over higher-level Morgan managers. Executives loyal to Purcell successfully resisted any efforts Mack made for change in the business. Purcell gradually shifted more and more aspects of the business away from Mack and to his trusted aides. Frustrated, Mack launched a campaign to have himself named co-CEO, but the balance of power had already swung too far toward Purcell. A series of departures from the board, including Mack's biggest supporter, Richard Fisher, allowed Purcell to appoint new directors who were loyal to him and would support his proposals for management changes over those of Mack.[45]

When the dust settled at Morgan Stanley Dean Witter, Phillip Purcell had gained complete control of the firm, with all core operations reporting directly to him. Mack gave a short departure speech to the staff and, after a standing ovation, he was gone. By surrounding himself with trusted allies within the firm and on the board, Purcell gained the influence needed to push his rival for the top job out of the firm.

> **Action Memo**
>
> As a leader: Find your best approach for influencing others. Use rational persuasion, develop allies, and expand your expertise and credibility. Remember that people respond to friendliness and consideration. Do favors for others that will encourage them to reciprocate. Ask for what you want. Frame your requests in a way that captures people's interest and makes them feel important.

5. *Ask for what you want.* Another way to have influence is to make a direct appeal by being clear about what you want and asking for it. If leaders do not ask, they seldom receive. Political activity is effective only when the leader's vision, goals, and desired changes are made explicit so the organization can respond. Leaders can use their courage to be assertive, saying what they believe to persuade others. An explicit proposal may be accepted simply because other people have no better alternatives. Also, an explicit proposal for change or for a specific decision alternative will often receive favorable treatment when other options are less well defined. Effective political behavior requires sufficient forcefulness and risk-taking to at least try to achieve desired outcomes.[46]

6. *Remember the principle of scarcity.* This principle means that people usually want more of what they can't have. When things are less available, they become more desirable. An interesting dissertation study on the purchase decisions of wholesale beef buyers found that buyers more than doubled their orders when they were told that because of weather conditions there was likely to be a scarcity of foreign beef in the near future. Interestingly, though, their orders increased 600 percent when they were informed that

no one else had that information yet.[47] Leaders can learn to frame their requests or offers in such a way as to highlight the unique benefits and exclusive information being provided. One approach is to selectively release information that is not broadly available and that supports the leaders' ideas or proposals. Letting people know they're getting a sneak peak at information captures their interest and makes them more likely to support the leader's position.

7. *Extend formal authority with expertise and credibility.* The final principle for asserting influence is the leader's legitimate authority in the organization. Legitimate authorities are in a position to be particularly influential. However, research has found that the key to successful use of formal authority is to be knowledgeable, credible, and trustworthy. Managers who become known for their expertise, who are honest and straightforward with others, and who inspire trust can exert greater influence than those who simply try to issue orders.[48] In addition, effective leaders keep the six previous influence principles in mind, realizing that influence depends primarily on personal rather than position power. By understanding the importance of rational persuasion, liking and friendship, reciprocity, networks of alliances, direct appeal, and scarcity, leaders can extend the power of their formal position and strengthen their influence over others.

Ethical Considerations in Using Power and Politics

Harry Truman once said that leadership is the ability to get people to do what they don't want to do and like it.[49] His statement raises an important issue: Leadership can be an opportunity to use power and influence to accomplish important organizational goals, but power can also be abused. We all know that some people use power primarily to serve their own interests, at the expense of others and the organization. Recall from Chapter 4 our discussion of *personalized* versus *socialized* charismatic leaders. This distinction refers primarily to their approach to the use of power.[50] Personalized leaders are typically selfish, impulsive, and exercise power for their own self-centered needs and interests rather than for the good of the organization. Socialized leaders exercise power in the service of higher goals that will benefit others and the organization as a whole.

One specific area in which the unethical use of power has become of increasing concern for organizations is sexual harassment. People in organizations depend on one another—and especially on leaders—for many resources, including information, cooperation, and even their jobs. When access to resources seems to depend on granting sexual favors or putting up with sexually intimidating or threatening comments, the person in a dependent position is being personally violated, whether or not the leader actually withholds the resources. Partly in response to pressures from the courts, many organizations are developing policies and procedures that protect individuals from sexual harassment on the job and offer mechanisms for reporting complaints. Sexual harassment is not just unethical, it is illegal, and it is a clear abuse of power.

Action Memo

As a leader: Be ethical in your use of power and politics. Build long-term productive relationships that can achieve important goals and benefit the entire team or organization.

However, there are many other situations in organizations that are not so clear-cut, and leaders may sometimes have difficulty differentiating ethical from unethical uses of power and influence. Exhibit 12.7 summarizes some criteria that can guide ethical actions. First and foremost is the question of whether the action is motivated by self-interest or whether it is consistent with the organization's goals. At Phone.com, any employee can be terminated for a political act that is in the individual's own self-interest rather than in the interest of the company, or that harms another person in the company.[51] Once a leader answers this primary question, there are several other questions that can help determine whether a potential influence action is ethical, including whether it respects the rights of individuals and groups affected by it, whether it meets the standards of fairness, and whether the leader would want others to behave in the same way. If a leader answers these questions honestly, they can serve as a guide to whether an intended act is ethical. However, in the complex world of organizations, there will always be situations that are difficult to interpret. The most important point is for leaders to be aware of the ethical responsibilities of possessing power and take care to use their power to help rather than harm others. Leaders should think not in terms of getting their own way, but rather, in terms of building long-term productive relationships that can achieve goals and benefit the entire organization.

Exhibit 12.7   Guidelines for Ethical Action

| Is the action consistent with the organization's goals, rather than being motivated purely by self-interest? | Does the action respect the rights of individuals and groups affected by it? | Does the action meet the standards of fairness and equity? | Would you wish others to behave in the same way if the action affected you? | Ethical Choice |

SOURCES: Based on G. F. Cavanaugh, D. J. Mobert, and M. Valasques, "The Ethics of Organizational Politics, "*Academy of Management Journal*, (June 1981, 363–374); and Stephen P. Robbins, *Organizational Behavior*, 8th ed. (Upper Saddle River, NJ: Prentice Hall, 1998), 422.

Summary and Interpretation

Leaders use various frames of reference to view the organization and its needs. Frames of reference determine how people gather information, make decisions, and exercise power. There are four frames of reference leaders may use: structural, human resource, political, and symbolic. Most leaders rely heavily on one or the other, but they can learn to use multiple frames of reference to expand their influence and better meet the needs of the organization.

This chapter focused largely on the political frame of reference. Power and politics are an important, though often hidden, part of all organizations. Power is the ability to influence others to reach desired outcomes. The best known types of power are legitimate, reward, expert, referent, and coercive, which are associated with a leader's position and personal qualities. Three distinct outcomes may result from the use of power to influence others: compliance, resistance, and commitment. The effective use of position power generally leads to follower compliance, whereas the excessive use of position power—particularly coercive power—may result in resistance. The follower response most often generated by personal power is commitment.

A key aspect of power is that it is a function of dependency, which is related to a person's control over resources. Dependency is greatest for resources that are highly important, scarce, and have no readily available substitutes. Leaders may gain power by contributing to the organization's purpose via interdepartmental dependencies, centrality, control over information, and coping with uncertainty.

Power is acquired, developed, and exercised through political activities. Leaders use a wide variety of influence tactics, but they fall within some broad categories based on general principles for asserting influence. Seven principles for asserting leader influence are rational persuasion, liking and friendliness, reciprocity, developing allies, direct appeal, scarcity, and formal authority. Leadership action depends on forming effective social relationships and achieving the desired future through agreements and cooperation in today's complex world. One important consideration for leaders is how to use power and politics ethically and responsibly. Ethical leaders use power to serve the organization's goals, respect the rights of individuals and groups, and strive to be fair in their dealings with others.

Discussion Questions

1. Which organizational frame of reference do you most identify with? How do you think this frame of reference could be beneficial or detrimental to your leadership capability?
2. Discuss why symbolic leadership needs to be balanced by other leadership perspectives in order to meet organizational needs.

3. Do you agree that politics is a natural and healthy part of organizational life? Discuss.
4. What types and sources of power would be available to a leader of a student government organization? To a head nurse in a small hospital?
5. Do you think impression management is an appropriate political approach for a business leader? Discuss. Can you name some ways in which you have personally used this tactic?
6. How does control over information give power to a person? Have you ever used control over information to influence a decision with friends or coworkers? Explain.
7. Describe ways in which you might increase your personal power.
8. Which of the seven influence tactics would you be most comfortable with as leader of a study group? Of a work team? Discuss.

Leadership at Work

Circle of Influence

How do you personally try to influence others? Think carefully about how you get others to agree with you or do something you want. Watch the way you influence others in a team, at home, or during your work. Make a list below of your influence tactics:

1. _____   4. _____

2. _____   5. _____

3. _____   6. _____

Of the influence and political tactics discussed in the chapter, which ones do you typically not use?

_____

_____

_____

During the next two days, your assignment is to (1) monitor the influence tactics you typically use, and (2) try one new tactic that you don't normally use. The new influence tactic you will try is: _____

_____

Another important concept is called the *circle of influence*. Think carefully about the people who have influence *over you*. These people are your circle of influence. You may have one circle of influence at work, another at home, and others for your social life or career. Write down the people who would have some influence over you at work or school:

_____

_____

This is your circle of influence.

A person's circle of influence can be important when you really want to influence that person. If the person doesn't respond to your normal influence attempts, think about identifying their circle of influence—the people who have influence over them. You can then influence people in the "circle" as an indirect way to influence the person you want to change.

Pick a person at work or school, or even your instructor, and plot out their circle of influence. List the key people you believe are in their circle of influence:

_____

_____

_____

How would you get more information on the person's true circle of influence?

_____

_____

_____

How can you use your knowledge of the person's circle to have influence over him/her? What are possible disadvantages of using this approach to influence someone?

_____

_____

_____

In Class: The instructor can ask students to sit in small groups of three to five people and share the circles of influence they identified for themselves. After listing the circle of influence at work or school, students can also talk about the circles of people who might influence them in their professional, social or family activities. Key questions for this discussion are: What are the common themes in the students' circles of influence? When and how could the circle idea be applied to influence someone? How might it be misapplied and backfire on your effort to influence another?

Leadership Development: Cases for Analysis

The Unhealthy Hospital

When Bruce Reid was hired as Blake Memorial Hospital's new CEO, the mandate had been clear: Improve the quality of care, and set the financial house in order.

As Reid struggled to finalize his budget for approval at next week's board meeting, his attention kept returning to one issue—the future of six off-site clinics. The clinics had been set up six years earlier to provide primary health care to the community's poorer neighborhoods. Although they provided a valuable service, they also diverted funds away from Blake's in-house services, many of which were underfunded. Cutting hospital personnel and freezing salaries could affect Blake's quality of care, which was already slipping. Eliminating the clinics, on the other hand, would save $256,000 without compromising Blake's internal operations.

However, there would be political consequences. Clara Bryant, the recently appointed commissioner of health services, repeatedly insisted that the clinics were an essential service for the poor. Closing the clinics could also jeopardize Blake's access to city funds. Dr. Winston Lee, chief of surgery, argued forcefully for closing the off-site clinics and having shuttle buses bring patients to the hospital weekly. Dr. Susan Russell, the hospital's director of clinics, was equally vocal about Blake's responsibility to the community, and suggested an entirely new way of delivering health care: "A hospital is not a building," she said, "it's a service. And wherever the service is needed, that is where the hospital should be." In Blake's case, that meant funding *more* clinics. Russell wanted to create a network of neighborhood-based centers for all the surrounding neighborhoods, poor and middle income. Besides improving health care, the network would act as an inpatient referral system for hospital services. Reid considered the proposal: If a clinic network could tap the paying public and generate more inpatient business, it might be worth looking into. Blake's rival hospital, located on the affluent side of town, certainly wasn't doing anything that creative. Reid was concerned, however, that whichever way he decided, he was going to make enemies.

SOURCE: Based on Anthony R. Kovner, "The Case of the Unhealthy Hospital," *Harvard Business Review* (September–October 1991): 12–25.

Questions

1. What sources of power does Reid have in this situation? Do you believe using legitimate power to implement a decision would have a positive effect at Blake Memorial? Discuss.

2. What influence tactics might you use to resolve this dilemma?
3. How might Reid's predominant frame of reference influence his actions? Consider how he might act based on each of the four frames.

Waite Pharmaceuticals

Amelia Lassiter is chief information officer at Waite Pharmaceuticals, a large California-based company. In an industry where it generally takes $500 million and 10 to 12 years to bring a new drug to market, companies such as Waite are always looking for ways to increase productivity and speed things up. After about eight months on the job, Lassiter suggested to company president James Hsu that Waite implement a new global knowledge-sharing application that promises to cut development time and costs in half. She has done extensive research on knowledge-sharing systems, and has talked closely with an IT director at global powerhouse Novartis, a company on the cutting edge in pharmaceuticals and animal health care, as well as other diverse products. The Novartis director believes the knowledge-sharing system plays an important role in that company's competitiveness.

Hsu presented the idea to the board of directors, and everyone agreed to pursue the project. He has asked Lassiter to investigate firms that could assist Waite's IT department in developing and implementing a global knowledge-sharing application that would be compatible with Waite's existing systems. Hsu explained that he wants to present the information to the board of directors for a decision next month.

Lassiter identified three major firms that she believed could handle the work and took a summary of her findings to Hsu's office, where she was greeted by Lucy Lee, a young, petite, attractive woman who served as a sort of executive assistant to Hsu. Word was that the relationship between Lee and Hsu was totally proper, but besides the value of her good looks, no one in the company could understand why she was working there. Her lack of talent and experience made her a liability more than a help. She was very deferential to Hsu, but condescending to everyone else. Lee was a constant source of irritation and ill will among managers throughout the company, but there was no doubt that the only way to get to Hsu was through Lucy Lee. Lee took the information from Lassiter and promised the president would review it within two days.

The next afternoon, Hsu called Lassiter to his office and asked why Standard Systems, a small local consulting firm, was not being considered as a potential provider. Lassiter was surprised—Standard was known primarily for helping small companies computerize their accounting systems. She was not aware that they had done any work related to knowledge-sharing applications, particularly on a global basis. Upon further investigation into the company, she learned that Standard was owned by an uncle of Lucy Lee's, and things began to fall into place. Fortunately, she also learned that the firm did have some limited experience in more complex applications. She tried to talk privately with Hsu about his reasons for wanting to consider Standard, but Hsu insisted that Lee participate in all his internal meetings. At their most recent meeting, Hsu insisted that Standard be included for possible consideration by the board.

During the next two weeks, representatives from each company met with Hsu, his two top executives, and the IT staff to explain their services and give demonstrations. Lassiter had suggested that the board of directors attend these presentations, but Hsu said they wouldn't have the time and he would need to evaluate everything and make a recommendation to the board. At the end of these meetings, Lassiter prepared a final report evaluating the pros and cons of going with each firm and making her first and second-choice recommendations. Standard was dead last on her list. Although the firm had some excellent people and a good reputation, it was simply not capable of handling such a large and complex project.

Lassiter offered to present her findings to the board, but again, Hsu declined her offer in the interest of time. "It's best if I present them with a final recommendation; that way, we can move on to other matters without getting bogged down with a lot of questions and discussion. These are busy people." The board meeting was held the following week. Lassiter was shocked when the president returned from the meeting and informed her that the board had decided to go with Standard Systems as the consulting firm for the knowledge-sharing application.

SOURCES: Based on "Restview Hospital," in Gary Yukl, *Leadership*, 4th ed. (Upper Saddle River, NJ: Prentice Hall, 1998), 203–204; "Did Somebody Say Infrastructure?" in Polly Schneider, "Another Trip to Hell," *CIO*, (February 15, 2000): 71–78; and Joe Kay, "Digital Diary," Part I, http://*www.forbes.com/asap/ 2000/*, accessed on November 19, 2000.

Questions
1. How would you explain the board's selection of Standard Systems?
2. Discuss the types, sources, and relative amount of power for the three main characters in this story.
3. How might Lassiter have increased her power and influence over this decision? If you were in her position, what would you do now?

References

1. Meridith Levinson, "The Art of the Shmooze," *CIO* (April 15, 2002): 99–104.
2. Based on Lee G. Bolman and Terrence E. Deal, *Reframing Organizations: Artistry, Choice, and Leadership* (San Francisco: Jossey-Bass, 1991), and "Leadership and Management Effectiveness: A Multi-Frame, Multi-Sector Analysis," *Human Resource Management* 30, no. 4 (Winter 1991): 509–534.
3. Bolman and Deal, "Leadership and Management Effectiveness."
4. Richard D. Heimovics, Robert D. Herman, and Carole L. Jurkiewicz Coughlin, "Executive Leadership and Resource Dependence in Nonprofit Organizations: A Frame Analysis," *Public Administration Review* 53, no. 5 (September–October 1993): 419–427.
5. Bolman and Deal, *Reframing Organizations*, 431.
6. Jeffrey Pfeffer, *Managing with Power: Politics and Influence in Organizations* (Boston, Harvard Business School Press, 1992); and Peter Moroz and Brian H. Kleiner, "Playing Hardball in Business Organizations," *IM* (January–February 1994), 9–11.
7. Bolman and Deal, "Leadership and Management Effectiveness."
8. Bolman and Deal, *Reframing Organizations*, 445.
9. James MacGregor Burns, *Leadership* (New York: Harper & Row, 1978); and Earle Hitchner, "The Power to Get Things Done," *National Productivity Review* 12 (Winter 1992/93): 117–122.
10. Robert A. Dahl, "The Concept of Power," *Behavioral Science* 2 (1957): 201–215.
11. W. Graham Astley and Paramijit S. Pachdeva, "Structural Sources of Intraorganizational Power: A Theoretical Synthesis," *Academy of Management Review* 9 (1984): 104–113; and Abraham Kaplan, "Power in Perspective," in Robert L. Kahn and Elise Boulding, eds., *Power and Conflict in Organizations* (London: Tavistock, 1964), 11–32.
12. Gerald R. Salancik and Jeffrey Pfeffer, "The Bases and Use of Power in Organizational Decision Making: The Case of the University," *Administrative Science Quarterly* 19 (1974): 453–473.
13. Earle Hitchner, "The Power to Get Things Done."
14. John R. P. French, Jr. and Bertram Raven, "The Bases of Social Power," in *Group Dynamics*, D. Cartwright and A. F. Zander, eds. (Evanston, IL: Row Peterson, 1960), 607–623.
15. Carol Hymowitz, "Companies Experience Major Power Shifts as Crises Continue," (In the Lead column), *The Wall Street Journal*, October 9, 2001, B1.
16. Jeffrey Pfeffer, *Power in Organizations* (Marshfield, MA: Pitman Publishing, 1981).
17. Erik W. Larson and Jonathan B. King, "The Systemic Distortion of Information: An Ongoing Challenge to Management," *Organizational Dynamics*, 24, no. 3 (Winter 1996), 49–61; Thomas H. Davenport, Robert G.

Eccles, and Lawrence Prusak, "Information Politics," *Sloan Management Review* (Fall 1992): 53–65.

18. Keith H. Hammonds, "The Monroe Doctrine," *Fast Company* (October 1999): 230–236; and Lorraine Monroe, *Nothing's Impossible: Leadership Lessons from Inside and Outside the Classroom* (New York: Times Books, 1997).

19. Gary A. Yukl and T. Taber, "The Effective Use of Managerial Power," *Personnel* (March–April 1983): 37–44.

20. R. E. Emerson, "Power-Dependence Relations," *American Sociological Review* 27 (1962): 31–41.

21. Carol Hymowitz, "Managers Are Starting to Gain More Clout Over Their Employees," (In the Lead column), *The Wall Street Journal* (January 30, 2001), B1.

22. Henry Mintzberg, *Power In and Around Organizations* (Englewood Cliffs, NJ: Prentice-Hall, 1963).

23. Megan Barnett, Greg Dalton, and Maryann Jones Thompson, "Wal-Mart's Power Play," *The Industry Standard* (May 28, 2001): 26.

24. Jeffrey Pfeffer, *Managing with Power: Politics and Influence in Organizations* (Boston: Harvard University Press, 1992); Gerald R. Salancik and Jeffrey Pfeffer, "Who Gets Power—and How They Hold onto It: A Strategic Contingency Model of Power," *Organizational Dynamics* (Winter 1977): 3–21; Pfeffer, *Power in Organizations*; Carol Stoak Saunders, "The Strategic Contingencies Theory of Power: Multiple Perspectives," *Journal of Management Studies* 27 (1990): 1–18.

25. Michel Crozier, *The Bureaucratic Phenomenon* (Chicago: University of Chicago Press, 1964).

26. Larson and King, "The Systemic Distortion of Information;" and Davenport, Eccles, and Prusak, "Information Politics."

27. D. J. Hickson, C. R. Hinings, C. A. Lee, R. C. Schneck, and J. M. Pennings, "A Strategic Contingencies Theory of Intraorganizational Power," *Administrative Science Quarterly* 16 (1971): 216–229.

28. Stephen P. Robbins, *Organizational Behavior*, 8th ed. (Upper Saddle River, NJ: Prentice Hall, 1998), 401.

29. Jeffrey Pfeffer and Gerald Salancik, "Organizational Decision Making as a Political Process: The Case of a University Budget," *Administrative Science Quarterly* (1974), 135–151.

30. Hickson, et al., "Strategic Contingencies Theory."

31. Jerry Gregoire, "On Assignment," *CIO* (July 1, 2002): 48–51; Michael J. McCarthy, "Pepsi Faces Problem in Trying to Contain Syringe Scare," *The Wall Street Journal*, June 17, 1993, B1; Elizabeth Lesly and Laura Zinn, "The Right Moves Baby," *BusinessWeek* (July 5, 1993): 30–31; and "The Pepsi Hoax: What Went Right?" The Pepsi-Cola Company Public Affairs Office, 1993.

32. Allan R. Cohen, Stephen L. Fink, Herman Gadon, and Robin D. Willits, *Effective Behavior in Organizations*, 7th ed. (New York: McGraw-Hill Irwin,

2001), 264; Rosabeth Moss Kanter, *Men and Women of the Corporation* (New York: Basic Books, 1977).

33. Pfeffer, *Power in Organizations*, 70.

34. See Amy J. Hillman and Michael A. Hitt, "Corporate Political Strategy Formulation: A Model of Approach, Participation, and Strategy Decisions," *Academy of Management Review* 24, no. 4 (1999): 825–842, for a recent examination of organizational approaches to political action.

35. Anne Fisher, "Ask Annie: Studying in Charm School, and Meeting Laggards," *Fortune* (June 7, 1999): 226.

36. Hal Lancaster, "For Some Managers, Hitting Middle Age Brings Uncertainties," *The Wall Street Journal*, April 20, 1999, B1.

37. John R. Carlson, Dawn S. Carlson, and Lori L. Wadsworth, "The Relationship Between Individual Power Moves and Group Agreement Type: An Examination and Model, *SAM Advanced Management Journal* (Autumn 2000): 44–51.

38. D. Kipnis, S. M. Schmidt, C. Swaffin-Smith, and I. Wilkinson, "Patterns of Managerial Influence: Shotgun Managers, Tacticians, and Bystanders," *Organizational Dynamics* (Winter 1984): 58–67.

39. Ibid., and Pfeffer, *Managing with Power*, Chapter 13.

40. This discussion is based partly on Robert B. Cialdini, "Harnessing the Science of Persuasion," *Harvard Business Review* (October 2001): 72–79.

41. Judith Tingley, *The Power of Indirect Influence* (New York: AMACOM, 2001), as reported by Martha Craumer, "When the Direct Approach Backfires, Try Indirect Influence," *Harvard Management Communication Letter* (June 2001): 3–4.

42. Cialdini, "Harnessing the Science of Persuasion."

43. Pfeffer, *Power in Organizations*, 70.

44. V. Dallas Merrell, *Huddling: The Informal Way to Management Success* (New York: AMACON, 1979).

45. Charles Gasparino and Anita Raghavan, "Survivor: How Dean Witter Boss Got the Upper Hand in Merger with Morgan," *The Wall Street Journal*, March 22, 2001, A1, A6.

46. Richard L. Daft, *Organization Theory and Design*, 6th ed. (Cincinnati, OH: South-Western, 1998), Chapter 12.

47. Cialdini, "Harnessing the Science of Persuasion."

48. Robert B. Cialdini, *Influence: Science and Practice*, 4th ed. (Boston: Pearson Allyn & Bacon, 2000).

49. Quoted in Cohen, Fink, Gadon, and Willits, *Effective Behavior in Organizations*, 254.

50. For a discussion of personalized and socialized power, see David C. McClelland, *Power: The Inner Experience* (New York: Irvington, 1975).

51. "Stop the Politics," *Forbes ASAP* (April 3, 2000): 126.

The Leader as Social Architect

Chapter

Your Leadership Challenge

After reading this chapter, you should be able to:

- Explain the relationship among vision, mission, strategy, and implementation mechanisms.

- Create your personal leadership vision.

- Use the common themes of powerful visions in your life and work.

- Understand how leaders formulate and implement strategy.

- Apply the elements of effective strategy.

As you enter The Children's Hospital at Montefiore, the first thing you see is a glowing glass mural of the Milky Way, the center of a model of the solar system that serves as a gateway to a journey of healing, discovery, and opportunity. When Dr. Irwin Redlener was recruited to take a leadership role in creating a children's addition to the Montefiore Medical Center in the northwest corner of the Bronx, New York, he jumped at the chance to shape a new kind of children's hospital. Redlener had long had a personal vision that health care could be used as a lever to address the myriad problems of the world's most disenfranchised children and families.

His vision for the Children's Hospital at Montefiore (CHAM) was that people broaden their mind-set about the role of doctors, the nature of medical institutions, and the standard approach to health care. He inspired others with his dream that CHAM could go beyond healing to focus instead on changing lives by unlocking the future for millions of kids with no sense of hope. He urged that the facility be the center of a comprehensive children's health system throughout the Bronx, involving a dynamic relationship between the hospital and the community. Today, CHAM is linked to a network of more than 30 community-based health facilities, the largest school-based health program in the country, a cutting-edge neonatal intensive care unit, New York City's leading child-protection program, and a fleet of mobile medical units.

The ideas and imagination of the late astronomer and author Carl Sagan served as a road map for Redlener. "He believed that the process of finding where you fit into the universe and the inspiration that comes from learning something about your world can be a gateway to a whole set of possibilities for children who have otherwise been contained in a very limited worldview," Redlener says. Practically every inch of CHAM's gleaming new facility is loaded with information and thoughts about the universe, from the microscopic functions of life to the wonders of outer space. Design elements such as exhibit-quality artistry and layers of detail combine with technological features such smart cards and bedside gigabit ethernet to create an environment that seems like a high-tech classroom, an innovative science museum, and a futuristic playground all in one. Redlener sees health care as a foot in the door to the future for disadvantaged children. But he also knows they have to envision a better future and find the hope and inspiration to believe they can get there.[1]

One of the most important functions of a leader is to articulate and communicate a compelling vision that will motivate and energize people toward the future, as Dr. Irwin Redlener did at The Children's Hospital at Montefiore. Working together, doctors, nurses, administrators, and others have created a totally new and powerful statement of what a children's hospital can be and do. Leaders provide a vision for the future and develop strategies to achieve it. Good leaders are always looking forward, setting a course for the future and getting everyone moving in the same direction. Lorraine Monroe, the leader profiled at the beginning of Chapter 12, refers to a leader as "the drum major, the person who keeps a vision in front of people and reminds them of what they're about." People naturally "gravitate toward leaders who have a vision." Monroe says. When people see that you love your work, they want to catch your energy."[2]

Follower motivation and energy are crucial to the success of any endeavor; the role of leadership is to focus everyone's energy on the same path. For Irwin Redlener, this means focusing people on providing not only excellent health care but a total environment that ignites children's imaginations. At City Bank, the predecessor of Citigroup, leaders energized employees with a vision of becoming "the most powerful, the most serviceable, the most far-reaching world financial institution that has ever been." That vision, first articulated in 1915 by a small regional bank, motivated and inspired generations of employees until it was eventually achieved.[3]

In this chapter, we will first provide an overview of the leader's role in creating the organization's future. Then, we examine what vision is, the underlying themes that are common to effective visions, and how vision works on multiple levels. The distinction between vision and the organization's mission will also be explained. We will discuss how leaders formulate vision and strategy and the leader's contribution to actually achieving the vision. The last section discusses the impact this leadership has on organizations.

Strategic Leadership

Superior organizational performance is not a matter of luck. It is determined largely by the choices leaders make. Top leaders are responsible for knowing the organization's environment, considering what it might be like in 5 or 10 years, and setting a direction for the future that everyone can believe in. Strategic leadership is one of the most critical issues facing organizations.[4] **Strategic leadership** means the ability to anticipate and envision the future, maintain flexibility, think strategically, and work with others to initiate changes that will create a competitive advantage for the organization in the future.[5] In a fast-changing environment, leaders are faced with a bewildering array of complex and ambiguous information, and no two leaders will see things the same way or make the same choices.

The complexity of the environment and the uncertainty of the future can overwhelm an executive. Thus, many are inclined to focus on internal organizational issues rather than strategic activities. It is easier and more comforting for leaders to deal with routine, operational issues where they can see instant results and feel a sense of control. In addition, many leaders today are inundated with information and overwhelmed by minutia. Years of downsizing and reengineering have reduced support staff in many organizations, and as data and information become easier to access and share, it grows harder and harder for leaders to keep pace. Most leaders today have difficulty finding the quiet time needed for "big-picture thinking." One study looked at the time executives in various departments spend on long-term, strategic activities and found discouraging results. In the companies studied, 84 percent of finance executives' time, 70 percent of information technology executives' time, and 76 percent of operational managers' time is focused on routine, day-to-day activities.[6] Another study found that, on average, senior executives in today's organizations spend less than 3 percent of their energy on building a corporate perspective for the future, and in some companies, the average is less than 1 percent.[7]

The first essential step in keeping an organization competitive is to develop an understanding of the trends and discontinuities that can be used to gain an edge. Rather than reacting to environmental changes, strategic leaders study the events that have already taken place and act to anticipate what these might mean for the future.[8] Leaders need massive amounts of information, but they also need quiet time and mental space to think creatively about all the information they're absorbing and how to put it to use. Microsoft chairman Bill Gates has a habit of hiding himself away for a week at a time to give himself time for thinking strategically.[9]

Sander Flaum, chairman and CEO of Robert A Becker, a health care strategic marketing firm, says great leaders are constantly looking toward the future. "They aren't afraid to go outside the box. . . . ," Flaum says. "The great ones are always focused on discontinuity, not building the future based upon the past, but building a future on what [they] think it can be."[10] For example, leaders at Charles Schwab recognized the potential of the Internet for online securities trading as early as 1995, the first year more personal computers were sold in the United States than televisions. Leaders at other firms had the same information, but they didn't have the same vision or didn't want to take a chance on the new technology, enabling Schwab to capture a huge share of the online securities market.[11] Another example comes from Sony Corporation, which has remained one of the world's most successful companies partly because it venerates mavericks and dreamers. Ken Kutaragi, for example, pushed Sony into the risky videogames business in the early 1990s with the original PlayStation game machine. Sony's profits suffered for a while, but today Kutaragi's division produces a huge portion of the company's profits.[12]

Strategic leadership
the ability to anticipate and envision the future, maintain flexibility, think strategically, and initiate changes that will create a competitive advantage for the organization in the future

Action Memo

As a leader: Think strategically. Anticipate and envision the future. Initiate changes that can help the organization be competitive over the long term.

Thinking about how to meet future customer needs is more important now than ever. Globalization, deregulation, advancing technology, and changing demographics and lifestyles are profoundly altering the way businesses are perceived and operate. The world in 2015 will be different from the world of today, and leaders are responsible for determining how their organizations can fit into that world. No organization can thrive for long without a clear viewpoint and framework for the future.

Exhibit 13.1 illustrates the levels that make up the domain of strategic leadership. Strategic leadership is responsible for the relationship of the external environment to choices about vision, mission, strategy, and their implementation.[13] At the top of Exhibit 13.1 is a clear, compelling vision of where the organization wants to be in 5 to 10 years. The vision reflects the environment and works in concert with the company's mission—its core values, purpose, and reason for existence. Strategy provides direction for translating the vision into action and is the basis for the development of specific mechanisms to help the organization achieve goals. Strategies are intentions, whereas implementation is through the basic organization architecture (structure, incentives) that makes things happen. Each level of the hierarchy in Exhibit 13.1 supports the level above it. Each part of this framework will be discussed in the remainder of this chapter.

Leadership Vision

A vision can be thought of as a dream for the future. Rebekka Weinstein, the daughter of an entrepreneur, has grown up with the dream of going into business for herself, of not being "harnessed and restricted by the corporate world." Her dream motivated her to study hard and achieve high academic honors at Richardson High School in Texas, which in turn enabled her to win a scholarship that will help finance her studies at Brown University. Moreover, Rebekka has already started her

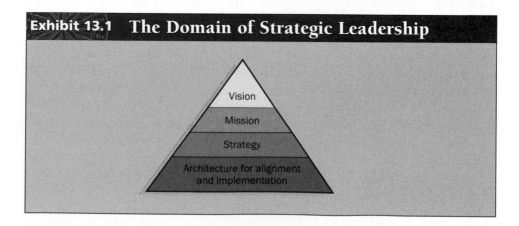

Exhibit 13.1   The Domain of Strategic Leadership

Vision

Mission

Strategy

Architecture for alignment and implementation

own jewelry-making business, creating custom pieces for individuals and selling original designs through the museum store at the Dallas Museum of Art and through a few independent retailers.[14] Rebekka's dream has played a powerful role in motivating her behavior and guiding her decisions and actions. Rebekka's dream is a personal one, but if her vision becomes a reality, she will someday have to create a vision that will inspire and motivate her employees as well as herself.

For organizations, a **vision** is an attractive, ideal future that is credible yet not readily attainable. A vision is not *just* a dream—it is an ambitious view of the future that everyone in the organization can believe in, one that can realistically be achieved, yet offers a future that is better in important ways than what now exists. In the 1950s, Sony Corporation wanted to "[b]ecome the company most known for changing the worldwide poor-quality image of Japanese products."[15] It may be hard to believe today, but in the 1950s this was a highly ambitious goal. Similarly, when Korea's Samsung Group announced it would enter the automobile manufacturing industry in the late 1990s, leaders inspired employees with a vision that Samsung would rank among the world's top 10 automakers by 2010—even though the company at that time had never built a single automobile.[16] Sometimes, visions are brief, compelling, and slogan-like, easily communicated to and understood by everyone in the organization. For example, Coca-Cola's "A Coke within arm's reach of everyone on the planet" and Komatsu's "Encircle Caterpillar" serve to motivate all employees. BP's new slogan, "Beyond Petroleum," captures the organization's vision to be leader in moving civilization out of the fossil-fuel era.[17] Exhibit 13.2 lists a few more brief vision statements that let people know where the organization wants to go in the future.

Vision
an attractive, ideal future that is credible yet not readily attainable

As these visions illustrate, a vision presents a challenge—it is an ambitious view of the future that requires employees to give their best. Many successful organizations don't have short, easily communicated slogans, but their visions are powerful because leaders paint a compelling picture of where the organization wants to go. Strong, inspiring visions have been associated with higher organizational performance.[18] When people are encouraged by a picture of what the organization can be in the future, they can help take it there.

Recall from Chapter 4 that vision is an important aspect of transformational leadership. Transformational leaders typically articulate visions that present a highly optimistic view of the future and express high confidence that the better future can be realized.[19] The vision expressed by civil rights leader Martin Luther King Jr. in his "I Have a Dream" speech is a good example. King articulated a vision of racial harmony, where discrimination was nonexistent, and he conveyed the confidence and conviction that his vision would someday be achieved. The new leader of United Way of America has a vision of transforming the charitable agency with a new approach to solving social problems.

Exhibit 13.2   Examples of Brief Vision Statements

Motorola: Become the premier company in the world.

Ritz-Carlton (Amelia Island) engineering department: To boldly go where no hotel has gone before—free of all defects.

Johnson Controls Inc.: Continually exceed our customers' increasing expectations.

New York City Transit: No graffiti.

Texas Commerce Bank: Eliminate what annoys our bankers and our customers.

AT&T Business and Commercial Services: Be our customers' best sales relationship.

Egon Zehnder: Be the worldwide leader in executive search.

SOURCES: These examples are from Jon R. Katzenbach and the RCL Team, *Real Change Leaders: How You Can Create Growth and High Performance in Your Company* (New York: Times Business, 1995), 68–70; Andrew Campbell and Sally Yeung, "Creating a Sense of Mission," *Long Range Planning,* (August, 1991): 10–20; Alan Farnham, "State Your Values, Hold the Hot Air," *Fortune* (April 19, 1993): 117–124; and Christopher K. Bart, "Sex, Lies, and Mission Statements," *Business Horizons* (November–December): 1997, 23–28.

In the Lead   Brian Gallagher, United Way of America

The nation's largest charity, United Way of America, may be on the verge of a transformation if CEO Brian Gallagher can inspire people with his vision of a new approach to fighting hunger, homelessness, or crime. Gallagher hopes to transform the nation's largest charitable group from an organization that just raises money and gives it away to other charities into a community partner that works actively to solve specific social problems.

Gallagher began testing his vision when he was head of the United Way of Central Ohio, based in Columbus. Instead of simply funding various charities that provided beds for the homeless, he formed a community coalition that devised specific strategies for fighting homelessness. The group created the Family Housing Collaborative, which helps homeless families get low-cost apartments and provides them with job training and day care services. The collaborative approach helped push down the number of families in Columbus, Ohio, shelters by 39 percent from 1998 to 2000. However, it also created hard feelings with some agencies that weren't getting the same level of funding from United Way because of funds targeted to the Housing Collaborative.

Selling the vision on a national scale will be even more of a challenge for Gallagher, but some people believe a new approach is needed to keep the United Way relevant in today's changing environment. "These days, stakeholders are looking at the outcome of their donations," says Evern D. Cooper, head of the UPS Foundation. It remains to be seen if Gallagher can articulate his vision in a way that will inspire and motivate followers to make the difficult changes needed to transform the United Way into a dynamic community problem solver.[20]

Vision is just as important for nonprofit agencies like the United Way and the Salvation Army as it is for businesses such as Coca-Cola or Microsoft. In Exhibit 13.3, vision is shown as a guiding star, drawing everyone along the same path toward the future. Vision is based in the current reality but is concerned with a future that is substantially different from the status quo.[21] Taking the group or organization along this path requires leadership. Compare this to rational management (as described in Chapter 1), which leads to the status quo. When employees have a guiding vision, everyday decisions and actions throughout the organization respond

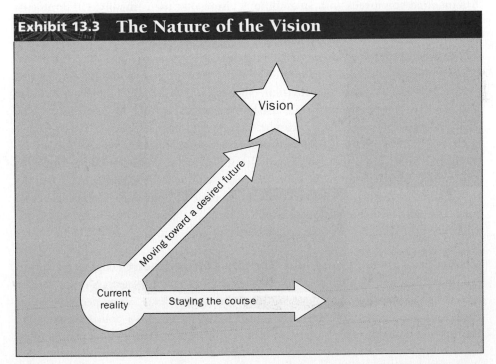

Exhibit 13.3   The Nature of the Vision

SOURCE: Based on William D. Hitt, *The Leader-Manager: Guidelines for Action* (Columbus, OH: Battelle Press, 1988).

to current problems and challenges in ways that move the organization toward the future rather than maintain the status quo. You can evaluate your potential for visionary leadership by completing Leader's Self-Insight 13.1.

What Vision Does

Vision works in a number of important ways. An effective vision provides a link between today and tomorrow, serves to energize and motivate employees toward the future, provides meaning for people's work, and sets a standard of excellence and integrity in the organization.[22]

Vision Links the Present to the Future Vision connects what is going on right now with what the organization aspires to. A vision is always about the future, but it begins with the here and now. Consider Microsoft, which uses the advertising slogan, "Your potential inspires us to create products that help you reach it." Microsoft employees create software products that help meet current needs, but they also strive to envision and create products that might encourage other, broader applications for the future. Another example is Dell Computer. Today, Dell is the hottest manufacturer of PCs but chairman and CEO Michael Dell has inspired employees with an ambitious vision that the company will double its sales by 2007, with half of that coming from non-PC businesses such as corporate computing and services.[23]

In organizations, the pressures to meet deadlines, make the big sale, solve immediate problems, and complete specific projects are very real. Some have suggested that today's leaders need "bifocal vision," the ability to take care of the needs of today and meet current obligations while also aiming toward dreams for the future.[24] The ability to operate on both levels can be seen in a number of successful companies, such as DuPont. Top executives routinely review short-term operational goals with managers throughout the company, reflecting a focus on the present. However, DuPont has succeeded over the long haul because of its leaders' ability to look to the future and shift gears quickly to take advantage of new opportunities. Since its beginning, DuPont's business portfolio has shifted from gunpowder to specialty chemicals, and today, the company is moving into biotechnology and life sciences.[25]

Vision Energizes People and Garners Commitment People want to feel enthusiastic about their work. A powerful vision frees people from the mundane by providing them with a challenge worthy of their best efforts. Many people commit their time and energy voluntarily to causes they believe in—a political campaign, feeding the homeless and hungry, environmental causes. These same people often leave their energy and enthusiasm at home when they go to work, because they don't have anything to inspire them. Employees are not generally willing to make

Visionary Leadership

Think about a situation in which you either assumed or were given a leadership role in a group. Imagine your own behavior as leader. To what extent does each of the following statements characterize your leadership?

1 = Very little; 2 = A little; 3 = A moderate amount; 4 = Quite a bit; 5 = Very much

	Very little				Very much
1. I have a clear understanding of where we are going.	1	2	3	4	5
2. I work to get others to be committed to our desired future.	1	2	3	4	5
3. I paint an interesting picture for my group.	1	2	3	4	5
4. I get the group to work together for the same outcome.	1	2	3	4	5
5. I initiate discussion with others about the kind of future I would like us to create together.	1	2	3	4	5
6. I clearly and repeatedly communicate a positive outlook for the group's future.	1	2	3	4	5
7. I look ahead and forecast what I expect in the future.	1	2	3	4	5
8. I show others how their interests can be realized by working toward a common vision.	1	2	3	4	5
9. I am excited and enthusiastic about future possibilities.	1	2	3	4	5
10. I make certain that the activities I manage are broken down into manageable chunks.	1	2	3	4	5
11. I seek future challenges for the group.	1	2	3	4	5
12. I spend time and effort making certain that people adhere to the values and outcomes that have been agreed on.	1	2	3	4	5
13. I inspire others with my ideas for the future.	1	2	3	4	5
14. I give special recognition when others' work is consistent with the vision.	1	2	3	4	5

Scoring and Interpretation

The odd-numbered questions pertain to creating a vision for the group. The even-numbered questions pertain to implementing the vision. Calculate your score for each set of questions. Which score is higher? Compare your scores with other students.

This questionnaire pertains to two dimensions of visionary leadership. Creating the vision has to do with whether you think about the future, whether you are excited about the future, and whether you engage others in the future. Implementing the vision is about the extent to which you communicate, allocate the work, and provide rewards for activities that achieve the vision. Which of the two dimensions is easiest for you? Are your scores consistent with your understanding of your own strengths and weaknesses? What might you do to improve your scores?

emotional commitments just for the sake of increasing profits and enhancing shareholder wealth. Vision needs to transcend the bottom line because people are willing, and even eager, to commit to something truly worthwhile, something that makes life better for others or improves their communities.[26] Consider Henry Ford's original vision for Ford Motor Company:

> I will build a motor car for the great multitude. . . . It will be so low in price that no man making a good salary will be unable to own one and enjoy with his family the blessings of hours of pleasure in God's open spaces. . . . When I'm through, everybody will be able to afford one, and everyone will have one. The horse will have disappeared from our highways, the automobile will be taken for granted [and we will give many people] employment at good wages.[27]

Employees were motivated by Ford's vision because they saw an opportunity to make life better for themselves and others.

Action Memo

As a leader: Frame a vision that sets a standard of excellence and integrity, connects to core values, and helps people find meaning and dignity in their work.

Vision Gives Meaning to Work People need to find dignity and meaning in their work. Even people performing routine tasks can find pride in their work when they have a larger purpose for what they do. For example, a clerk who thinks of his job as "processing insurance claims" will feel very differently than one who thinks of her job as helping victims of fire or burglary put their lives back in order.[28] As another example, one housekeeper at ServiceMaster Co. explained that she is enthusiastic about her work at a community hospital because leaders help her see her job as more than just cleaning floors. The housekeeper considers herself an important member of a team that is dedicated to helping sick people get well. Without quality cleaning, she points out, the hospital could not serve its patients well and would soon be out of business.[29]

People are drawn to companies that offer them a chance to do something meaningful. Today, prospective employees often ask about a company's vision when interviewing for a job because they want to know what the organization stands for and how, or whether, they will fit in.

Vision Establishes a Standard of Excellence and Integrity Vision provides a measure by which employees can gauge their contributions to the organization. Most workers welcome the chance to see how their work fits into the whole. Think of how frustrating it is to watch a movie when the projector is out of focus. Today's complex, fast-changing business environment often seems just like that—out of focus.[30] A vision is the focus button. It clarifies an image of the future and lets people see how they can contribute. A vision presents a challenge, asks people to go where they haven't gone before. Thus, it encourages workers to take risks and find new ways of doing things. The Living Leadership box discusses three qualities a powerful vision can inspire.

In addition, vision clarifies and connects to the core values and ideals of the organization and thus sets a standard of integrity for employees. A good vision brings out the best in people by illuminating important values, speaking to people's hearts, and letting them be part of something bigger than themselves. Consider how Walt Disney painted a picture of Disneyland that unified and energized employees.

In the Lead   Walt Disney

Walt Disney created a clear picture of what he wanted Disneyland to be. His vision translated hopes and dreams into words and allowed employees to help create the future. Notice how the vision says nothing about making money—the emphasis is on a greater purpose that all employees could believe in.

"The idea of Disneyland is a simple one. It will be a place for people to find happiness and knowledge. It will be a place for parents and children to spend pleasant times in one another's company, a place for teachers and pupils to discover greater ways of understanding and education. Here the older generation can recapture the nostalgia of days gone by, and the younger generation can savor the challenge of the future. Here will be the wonders of Nature and Man for all to see and understand. Disneyland will be based on and dedicated to the ideals, the dreams, and hard facts that have created America. And it will be uniquely equipped to dramatize these dreams and facts and send them forth as a source of courage and inspiration for all the world. Disneyland will be something of a fair, an exhibition, a playground, a community center, a museum of living facts, and a showplace of beauty and magic. It will be filled with the accomplishments, the joys and hopes of the world we live in. And it will remind us and show us how to make these wonders part of our lives."[31]

A clear, inspiring picture such as that painted by Walt Disney can have a powerful impact on people. His vision gave meaning and value to workers' activities. Painting a clear picture of the future is a significant responsibility of leaders, yet it cannot always be the leader's alone. To make a difference, a vision can be widely shared and is often created with the participation of others. Every good organizational vision is a shared vision.

Common Themes of Vision

Five themes are common to powerful, effective visions: they have broad, widely shared appeal; they help organizations deal with change; they encourage faith and hope for the future; they reflect high ideals; and they define both the organization's destination and the basic rules to get there.

LIVING LEADERSHIP

Vision's Offspring

A compelling vision inspires and nurtures three qualities, here personified as individuals. Do you think followers would benefit from contact with the following "people" in an organization?

Clarity

My visits to Clarity are soothing now. He never tells me what to think or feel or do but shows me how to find out what I need to know . . . he presented me with a sketchbook and told me to draw the same thing every day until the drawing started to speak to me.

Commitment

Commitment has kind eyes. He wears sturdy shoes. . . . You can taste in [his] vegetables that the soil has been cared for. . . . He is a simple man, and yet he is mysterious. He is more generous than most people. His heart is open. He is not afraid of life.

Imagination

Some people accuse Imagination of being a liar. They don't understand that she has her own ways of uncovering the truth. . . . Imagination has been working as a fortuneteller in the circus. She has a way of telling your fortune so clearly that you believe her, and then your wishes start to come true. . . . Her vision is more complex, and very simple. Even with the old stories, she wants us to see what has never been seen before.

SOURCE: J. Ruth Gendler, *The Book of Qualities* (New York: Harper & Row, 1988). Used with permission.

Vision Has Broad Appeal   Although it may be obvious that a vision can be achieved only through people, many visions fail to adequately involve employees. The vision cannot be the property of the leader alone.[32] If Brian Gallagher cannot effectively involve local chapters in his vision for a more active United Way, for example, the vision will fail. The ideal vision is identified with the organization as a whole, not with a single leader or even a top leadership team. It "grabs people in the gut" and motivates them to work toward a common end.[33] It allows each individual to act independently but in the same direction.

Vision Deals with Change   Visions that work help the organization achieve bold change. Vision is about action and challenges people to make important changes toward a better future. Change can be frightening, but a clear sense of direction helps people face the difficulties and uncertainties involved in the change process.

Vision Encourages Faith and Hope   Vision exists only in the imagination— it is a picture of a world that cannot be observed or verified in advance. The future is shaped by people who believe in it, and a powerful vision helps people believe that they can be effective, that there is a better future they can move to through their own commitment and actions. Vision is an emotional appeal to our fundamental human needs and desires—to feel important and useful, to believe we can make a real difference in the world.[34] John F. Kennedy's vision for NASA to send a man to the moon by the end of the 1960s was so powerful that hundreds of thousands of people throughout the world believed in a future they couldn't see.[35]

Vision Reflects High Ideals Good visions are idealistic. Vision has power to inspire and energize people only when it paints an uplifting future. When Kennedy announced the "man on the moon" vision, NASA had only a small amount of the knowledge it would need to accomplish the feat. William F. Powers, who worked at NASA during the 1960s, later helped Ford Motor Company develop an idealistic vision for the world's first high-volume, aerodynamically styled car that featured fuel economy (the 1980s Taurus). It was a big risk for Ford at a time when the company was down and out. But leaders painted this as a chance not only to save the company but to establish a whole new path in automotive engineering, which tapped into employees' imaginations and idealism.[36]

Vision Defines the Destination and the Journey A good vision for the future includes specific outcomes that the organization wants to achieve. It also incorporates the underlying values that will help the organization get there. For example, a private business school might specify certain outcomes such as a top 20 ranking, placing 90 percent of students in summer internships, and getting 80 percent of students into jobs by June of their graduating year. Yet in the process of reaching those specific outcomes, the school wants to increase students' knowledge of business, values, and teamwork, as well as prepare them for lifelong learning. Additionally, the vision may espouse underlying values such as no separation between fields of study or between professors and students, a genuine concern for students' welfare, and adding to the body of business knowledge. A good vision includes both the desired future outcomes and the underlying values that set the rules for achieving them.[37]

A powerful vision can have a significant impact on an organization and its employees, but only if it is communicated clearly to everyone throughout the organization. Some companies, such as Merix Corp., a $140 million electronic interconnect supplier that was spun out of Tektronix in 1994, are experimenting with graphical vision statements that help people think in new, metaphorical ways about their work.

> **Action Memo**
>
> As a leader: Encourage people to share their hopes and dreams for the future. Create a shared vision so that every individual, team, and department is moving in the same direction. Help people see the values, activities, and objectives that can attain the vision.

In the Lead   Merix Corp.

Most of us have heard the saying that a picture is worth a thousand words. Leaders at Merix Corp., based in Forest Grove, Oregon, took the saying to heart and used graphics as a tool to articulate the company's strategic vision.

Former chair and CEO Debi Coleman held a company retreat where employees talked about their feelings about Merix and where it should be headed. A consultant then mapped out the themes that emerged. The resulting graphical vision statement, shown in Exhibit 13.4, conveys the image of a futuristic company on the leading edge of technology. Under current Chairman and CEO Mark Hollinger, the company's continuing goal is to be the best global provider of printed circuit boards and interconnect solutions. The image conveys the vision and its challenges in a powerful way. It also incorporates the core values of the company and tells a story about Merix and its relationships with Tektronix and a variety of suppliers and partners. The statement portrays Merix as a mother ship, moving fast in a fast-changing and complex industry, constantly sharing goods, information, and technology with partner organizations.

Each of the images has meaning for Merix employees. As Coleman explained it, "If you could put this drawing on a computer and double-click on each image, underneath each one you'd find serious plans, strategies with time lines, and performance measures. If you look around Merix, this picture is on people's walls, on workbenches, even on T-shirts."[38]

Merix leaders believe the image in Exhibit 13.4 conveys the company's vision and worldview more powerfully than words ever could. A visual statement can be more broadly shared—a written statement on posters and T-shirts wouldn't have the same aesthetic and emotional impact that the image has. Other companies are also using graphics as a tool to more vividly convey their visions.

A Vision Works at Multiple Levels

Most of the visions we have talked about so far are for the company as a whole. However, divisions, departments, and individuals also have visions, which are just as important and powerful. For example, Benjamin Zander, world-renowned conductor of the Boston Philharmonic Orchestra, has a personal vision to "share the most powerful language ever devised by human beings" by putting a recording of Beethoven's Fifth Symphony in the hands of every person on earth.[39] Successful individuals usually have a clear mental picture of their vision and how to achieve it. People who do not have this clear vision of the future have less chance of success.

Top leaders of an effective organization develop a vision for the organization as a whole, and at the same time a project team leader five levels beneath the CEO can develop a vision with team members for a new product they are working on. Leaders of functional departments, divisions, and teams can use vision with the same positive results as do top leaders.

Consider the facility manager for a large corporation. His department received requests to fix toilets and air conditioners. The manager took this to mean that people

Exhibit 13.4   Merix Vision Statement

cared about their physical space, which became the basis for his vision to "use physical space to make people feel good." People in his department started planting flowers outside office windows and created an environment that lifted people's spirits.[40] In innovative companies, every group or department creates its own vision, as long as the vision is in line with the overall company's direction.

When a vision for the organization as a whole is shared among individuals and departments, it has real impact. Therefore top leaders' real work is to share the vision with others, and to help them develop their part of the vision so that everyone has the picture. The vision becomes the common thread connecting people, involving them personally and emotionally in the organization.[41]

When every person understands and embraces a vision, the organization becomes self-adapting. Although each individual acts independently, everyone is working in the same direction. In the new sciences, this is called the principle of self-reference. **Self-reference** means that each element in a system will serve the goals of the whole system when the elements are imprinted with an understanding of the whole. Thus the vision serves to direct and control people for the good of themselves and the organization. Leaders at Dell Computer have imprinted the vision so clearly in employees' minds that one CEO who has studied the company says Dell is "like a living organism. It is constantly adapting and changing and finding ways to master its environment, as opposed to just respond to it. . . . Somehow Dell has been able to take speed and flexibility and build it into their DNA."[42]

To develop a shared vision, leaders share their personal visions with others and encourage others to express their dreams for the future. This requires openness, good listening skills, and the courage to connect with others on an emotional level. Good leaders give up the idea that vision emanates from only the top. A leader's ultimate responsibility is to be in touch with the hopes and dreams that drive employees and find the common ground that binds personal dreams into a shared vision for the organization. As one successful top leader put it, "My job, fundamentally, is listening to what the organization is trying to say, and then making sure it is forcefully articulated."[43] Another successful leader refers to leadership as "discovering the company's destiny and having the courage to follow it."[44]

Self-reference
a principle stating that each element in a system will serve the goals of the whole system when the elements are imprinted with an understanding of the whole

▚ Mission

Mission
the organization's core broad purpose and reason for existence

Mission is not the same thing as a company's vision, although the two work together. The **mission** is the organization's core broad purpose and reason for existence. It defines the company's core values and reason for being, and it provides a basis for creating the vision. Whereas vision is an ambitious desire for the future, mission is what the organization "stands for" in a larger sense. James Collins compares Zenith and Motorola to illustrate the importance of a solid organizational mission. Both

Zenith and Motorola were once successful makers of televisions. Yet while Zenith stayed there, Motorola continued to move forward—to making microprocessors, integrated circuits, cellular phones, and other products—and became one of the most highly regarded companies in the country. The difference is that Motorola defined its mission as "applying technology to benefit the public," not as "making television sets."[45] Whereas visions continue to grow and change, the mission persists in the face of changing technologies, economic conditions, or other environmental shifts. The mission defines the enduring character—the spiritual DNA—of the organization and can be used as a leadership tool to help employees find genuine meaning in their work.[46] Recall the discussion of intrinsic rewards from Chapter 8. When people connect their jobs to a higher purpose, the work itself becomes a great motivator. The Gallup organization's Q12 study, also discussed in Chapter 8, has found that when employees believe the company mission makes their job important, they are typically more engaged with their work, feel a greater sense of pride and loyalty, and are more productive. Exhibit 13.5 compares the Gallup results for those who agree that the mission makes their job important to those who do not feel that the mission of the company makes their job important. The differences are quite striking. For example, 60 percent of respondents who agreed that the mission made their job important reported feeling engaged with

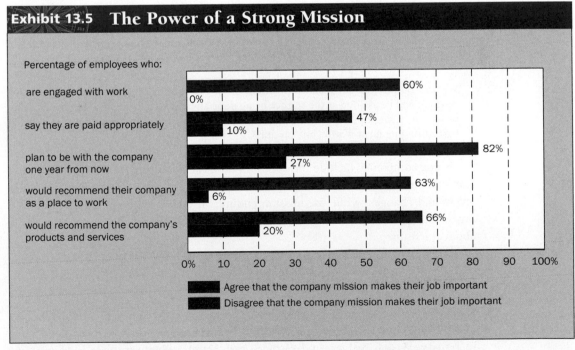

Exhibit 13.5   The Power of a Strong Mission

Percentage of employees who:

- are engaged with work — 60% / 0%
- say they are paid appropriately — 47% / 10%
- plan to be with the company one year from now — 82% / 27%
- would recommend their company as a place to work — 63% / 6%
- would recommend the company's products and services — 66% / 20%

■ Agree that the company mission makes their job important
■ Disagree that the company mission makes their job important

SOURCE: Susan Ellingwood, "On a Mission," *Gallup Management Journal* (Winter 2001): 6–7.

Action Memo

As a leader: Remember what the organization stands for in a broader sense—its core purpose and values. Create the vision around that central mission.

their work, whereas none of the respondents who disagreed felt engaged with their work. Sixty-six percent would recommend their company's products or services, compared to only 20 percent of those who did not believe the mission made their job important.[47]

Typically, the mission is made up of two critical parts: the core values and the core purpose. The *core values* guide the organization "no matter what." As Ralph Larsen, former CEO of Johnson & Johnson, explained it, "The core values embodied in our credo might be a competitive advantage, but that is not *why* we have them. We have them because they define for us what we stand for, and we would hold them even if they became a competitive *dis*advantage in certain situations."[48] Johnson & Johnson's core values led the company, for example, to voluntarily remove Tylenol from the market after the cyanide poisoning of some Tylenol capsule users, even though this act cost the company more than $100 million.

The mission also includes the company's *core purpose*. An effective purpose statement doesn't just describe products or services; it captures people's idealistic motivations for why the organization exists. Most successful companies have missions that proclaim a noble purpose of some type, such as Motorola's "applying technology to benefit the public," Mary Kay's "to enrich the lives of women," or Wal-Mart Stores' "to give ordinary folk the chance to buy the same things as rich people."[49]

The core values and core purpose are frequently expressed in a *mission statement*. Exhibit 13.6 shows the mission statement for Merck & Co., Inc. Read the mission statement and then consider how Merck's specific vision grows out of the company's mission and works with it:

> We will be the first drug maker with advanced research in every disease category. Our research will be as good as the science being done anywhere in the world. Our drugs won't be used by a single person who doesn't need them. Merck will continue to grow on a steady basis, bringing forth worthwhile products. . . . [50]

Some companies include the specific vision for the future as a part of their mission statements. However, it is important to remember that the vision continually grows and changes, while the mission endures. It serves as the glue that holds the organization together in times of change and guides strategic choices and decisions about the future.

Strategy Formulation

Strong missions and guiding visions are important, but they are not enough alone to make strong, powerful organizations. For organizations to succeed, they need ways to translate vision, values, and purpose into action, which is the role of strategy.

Exhibit 13.6   Merck's Mission Statement

Merck & Co., Inc. is a leading research-driven pharmaceutical products and services company. Merck discovers, develops, manufactures, and markets a broad range of innovative products to improve human and animal health. The Merck-Medco Managed Care Division manages pharmacy benefits for more than 40 million Americans, encouraging the appropriate use of medicines and providing disease management programs.

OUR MISSION

The mission of **Merck** is to provide society with superior products and services—innovations and solutions that improve the quality of life and satisfy customer needs—to provide employees with meaningful work and advancement opportunities and investors with a superior rate of return.

OUR VALUES

1. **Our business is preserving and improving human life.** All of our actions must be measured by our success in achieving this goal. We value above all our ability to serve everyone who can benefit from the appropriate use of our products and services, thereby providing lasting consumer satisfaction.

2. **We are committed to the highest standards of ethics and integrity.** We are responsible to our customers, to Merck employees and their families, to the environments we inhabit, and to the societies we serve worldwide. In discharging our responsibilities, we do not take professional or ethical shortcuts. Our interactions with all segments of society must reflect the high standards we profess.

3. **We are dedicated to the highest level of scientific excellence and commit our research to improving human and animal health and the quality of life.** We strive to identify the most critical needs of consumers and customers, we devote our resources to meeting those needs.

4. **We expect profits, but only from work that satisfies customer needs and benefits humanity.** Our ability to meet our responsibilities depends on maintaining a financial position that invites investment in leading-edge research and that makes possible effective delivery of research results.

5. **We recognize that the ability to excel—to most competitively meet society's and customers' needs—depends on the integrity, knowledge, imagination, skill, diversity, and teamwork of employees, and we value these qualities most highly.** To this end, we strive to create an environment of mutual respect, encouragement and teamwork—a working environment that rewards commitment and performance and is responsive to the needs of employees and their families.

SOURCE: *http://www.merck.com/overview/philosophy.html*

Strategic management

the set of decisions and actions used to formulate and implement specific strategies that will achieve a competitively superior fit between the organization and its environment so as to achieve organizational goals

Formulating strategy is the hard, serious work of taking a specific step toward the future. **Strategic management** is the set of decisions and actions used to formulate and implement specific strategies that will achieve a competitively superior fit between the organization and its environment so as to achieve organizational goals.[51] It is the leader's job to find this fit and translate it into action.

Strategy can be defined as the general plan of action that describes resource allocation and other activities for dealing with the environment and helping the organization attain its goals. In formulating strategy, leaders ask questions such as "Where is the organization now? Where does the organization want to be? What changes and trends are occurring in the competitive environment? What courses of action can help us achieve our vision?" Developing effective strategy requires actively listening to people both inside and outside the organization, as well as examining trends and discontinuities in the environment. Good leaders anticipate, look ahead, and prepare for the future based on trends they see in the environment today, which often requires radical thinking. Lindsay Owens-Jones, chairman and CEO of L'Oreal, turned his company into a global powerhouse by thinking radically. When Owens-Jones was running L'Oreal's U.S. division in the early 1980s, his Parisian colleagues told him European brands like L'Oreal's Lancôme could never compete with established U.S. cosmetics such as Estee Lauder and Revlon. Owens-Jones refused to accept that, and before long Lancôme was competing head-to-head with Estee Lauder in American department stores. After becoming CEO, Owens-Jones set out on an aggressive strategy of acquiring local brands, repackaging them, and sending them around the world. Maybelline, for example, once considered the dowdy choice of Middle America, has become one of the hottest brands among Japanese teenagers under the ownership of L'Oreal. Other L'Oreal brands are also capturing huge market share in Asia, Africa, and other parts of the world.[52] The Leader's Bookshelf describes another successful application of radical thinking in the Oakland A's baseball team.

Innovative thinking carries a lot of risk. Sometimes leaders have to shift their strategy several times before they get it right.[53] In addition, strategy necessarily changes over time to fit shifting environmental conditions. To improve the chances for success, leaders develop strategies that focus on three qualities: core competence, developing synergy, and creating value for customers.

Strategy

the general plan of action that describes resource allocation and other activities for dealing with the environment and helping the organization attain its goals

Core Competence

Core competence

something the organization does extremely well in comparison to competitors

An organization's **core competence** is something the organization does extremely well in comparison to competitors. Leaders try to identify the organization's unique strengths—what makes their organization different from others in the industry. L'Oreal has a core competence in global brand management. At Amgen, a pharmaceutical company, strategy focuses on the company's core competence of high-quality scientific research. Rather than starting with a specific disease and

LEADER'S BOOKSHELF

Moneyball: The Art of Winning an Unfair Game
by Michael Lewis

How do you turn a bunch of undervalued baseball players, many of them deemed unfit for the big leagues, into one of the Major League's most successful franchises? The Oakland A's general manager Billy Beane did it by having a different vision than the rest of the pack. Beane's unique vision and strategy built one of Major League Baseball's winningest teams with one of its smallest budgets. Unlike successful teams such as the New York Yankees, which can afford to lavish millions on high-profile free-agents, Beane looks for the hidden talents among unwanted or undiscovered players.

Finding a Diamond in the Rough
Beane's skill at finding baseball's hidden gems comes partly from his own rocky experiences as a big-league outfielder, where he learned that there's more to being a good ball player than raw talent. The other part is his unique vision and strategy for fielding a ball team. Here are some of Beane's guiding principles:

❋ *Buy low and sell high.* Beane and his managers look for players at all levels—from high school and college to the minor and major leagues—who are undervalued by others, whether because of a quirk in their playing style or other managers' narrow mindsets. When other managers don't see a player's potential, Beane can swoop in and get him for a bargain. Then, he has the discipline and sense of timing to trade a player once he's turned him into a star who is highly desired by other teams. Beane picks up several new, low-cost players with combined talents that roughly equal that of the player traded.

❋ *Forget the traditional measures.* In choosing players, Beane makes much greater use of sophisticated statistical analysis than other general managers, and he looks at different measures. For example, he favors stats such as on-base percentage over batting average. Beane believes the ability to get on base—even with a walk—is a valuable long-term asset whereas traditional measures such as batting average or base steals may mean nothing over the long haul.

❋ *The stats always rule.* Scouting is de-emphasized in Oakland. Other managers sometimes reject a player because he doesn't "look" like a major-leaguer, but not Beane. If the statistics say an overweight college catcher that nobody else wants should be a number-one draft pick, Beane goes for it. One player was signed on without anyone from the A's ever seeing him.

Thinking Radically
The new statistical models and sophisticated tools Beane is using to spot high-potential players have been around for years, but they were used mostly by amateur baseball enthusiasts: software engineers, statisticians, Wall Street analysts, lawyers, physics professors, and just run-of-the-mill geeks. Billy Beane looked at the cache of numbers compiled over the years and saw a new vision: the traditional yardsticks of success for baseball players are fatally flawed. By thinking differently and paying attention to obscure numbers, Beane has built a highly successful organization—and perhaps revolutionized baseball management.

Moneyball: The Art of Winning an Unfair Game, by Michael Lewis, is published by W. W. Norton & Company.

working backward, Amgen takes brilliant science and finds unique uses for it.[54] Chase Brass Industries, a manufacturer of brass rods and steel tubing, has a core competence in the mastery of specific technologies and production processes.[55] Dell Computer Corp. has thrived even during the industry's hard times by focusing on core competencies of speed and cost efficiency. In each case, leaders identified what their company does particularly well and built strategy around it. Another organization that has found renewed competitiveness with core competencies of speed and efficiency is England, Inc., a furniture maker.

In the Lead   Rodney England, England Inc.

Go into any Wal-Mart or Big Lots and you'll likely see low-priced, imported furniture ready to take home. U. S. furniture makers have taken a beating in recent years from manufacturers in China and other countries who offer low prices, rising quality, and instant gratification.

One of the few advantages U.S. manufacturers have is offering an array of fabric choices and building a sofa to match the customer's decor. The only problem is that delivery time sometimes stretches to months. England, Inc., now owned by La-Z-Boy and based in New Tazewell, Tennessee, has managed to cut that delivery time to three weeks. "In the furniture business, that's like greased lightening," says Tom Rose, owner of Thomas Everett's Fine Furniture in Abilene, Texas. The company, under the leadership of Rodney England, builds about 11,000 sofas and chairs a week, all made to order. England pushes its suppliers for smaller, more frequent deliveries and drops the ones who can't keep pace. The number of fabric vendors, for example, is down from 40 about 7 years ago to 4 key vendors who can meet England's need for speedy deliveries and lower prices. Another key to speed is that England runs its own trucks, which is highly unusual among sofa makers.

The other advantage England has over competitors is the discipline to keep costs—and therefore prices—comparatively low. To recoup transportation costs, four employees continuously work the phones and the Internet searching for paying loads that England's trucks can haul back to Tennessee. The company refuses to take an order that arrives even five minutes after the weekly production deadline because it will create chaos with the production and delivery schedules. Unlike computer maker Dell, England can't start a sofa the minute—or even the day—an order is placed because it has to build up its production and delivery schedule to maximize efficiency. Every Monday night, England's computers take all the orders for the week, plot out delivery schedules, and schedule production tasks down to the minute, printing out bar-code tickets that are attached to various pieces. Production is grouped by various furniture styles. The goal is to never program the wood routers to cut a single frame when they can cut 25, and never cut a single fabric pattern when they can cut a stack of 50.

Some retailers think England has the best speed and discipline in the industry. The bottom line for leaders is that the strategy is working. Although sales for the entire domestic upholstery-manufacturing industry have been falling, England's sales jumped 8.3 percent in one recent year. La-Z-Boy executives are pushing the rest of the company to move as fast. "I wish we could," says La-Z-Boy Chairman Pat Norton. "We would own the market."[56]

Synergy

Synergy occurs when organizational parts interact to produce a joint effect that is greater than the sum of the parts acting alone. As a result the organization may attain a special advantage with respect to cost, market power, technology, or employee skills. PepsiCo's "Power of One" strategy is aimed at leveraging the synergies of its soft drink and snack divisions to achieve greater market power. The business that drives PepsiCo these days is snack foods, with the Frito-Lay division enjoying near total dominance of the snack food market. PepsiCo CEO Roger Enrico used the company's clout with supermarkets to move Pepsi drinks next to Frito-Lay snacks on store shelves, increasing the chance that when shoppers pick up chips and soda, the soda of choice will be a Pepsi product. Enrico personally visited the heads of the twenty-five largest supermarket chains to sell the strategy. Leaders are betting that the strength of Frito-Lay can not only gain greater shelf space for Pepsi, but increased market share as well.[57]

Alliances between companies can also be a source of synergy. For example, Erie Bolt, a small Erie, Pennsylvania, company, teamed up with 14 other area companies to give itself more muscle in tackling competitive global markets. Team members share equipment, customer lists, and other information that enables each small company to go after more business than it ever could without the team approach.[58]

Synergy
the interaction of organizational parts to produce a joint effect that is greater than the sum of the parts

Value Creation

Focusing on core competencies and attaining synergy helps companies create value for their customers. Value can be defined as the combination of benefits received and costs paid by the customer.[59] Delivering value to the customer is at the heart of strategy. At Pottery Barn, for example, president Laura Alber points to a thick, $24 bath towel as an icon of what Pottery Barn aspires to: "For us this represents a combination of design, quality, and price," Alber says. "If this were $60, you'd still like it. But at $24, you go, 'This is incredible.'"[60] Value is also key to strategy for leaders at General Mills.

Value
the combination of benefits received and costs paid by the customer

In the Lead   Steve Sanger, General Mills Inc.

Steve Sanger's first question when a new product is being developed or an old product needs a boost is, "Can we make it 'one-handed'?" Growth has stalled for most food companies, but General Mills has fared better than most, largely because of chairman and CEO Sanger's strategy of designing everyday, reasonably priced foods for people who like to keep one hand free for typing or driving while they eat.

With the way people are eating today, convenience is the byword. Few companies have adapted to the American pursuit of mobility as well as General Mills. Its Hamburger Helper line of meals has been stressing convenience for years, but new products are making even that look complicated. The company has zoomed to the top of the yogurt business since introduction of Go-Gurt, a kid-friendly yogurt in a squeezable tube, and a squeezable version for adults isn't far behind. Cereals pressed into the shape of a candy bar, containing real milk solids and the same nutrition as a bowl of milk and cereal, have also been a hit. Though not quite one-handed, the Bowl Appetit line of single-serving rice- and pasta-based meals is making lunch at the office easier than ever.

A couple of years ago, General Mills acquired Pillsbury Co. from Diageo PLC of Britain to gain synergy with Pillsbury's food lines. "If you think about hand-held foods," Sanger says, "most of them are dough wrapped around something,"[61]

Strategy in Action

Strategy formulation

integrating knowledge of the environment, vision, and mission with the core competence in such a way as to achieve synergy and create customer value

Strategy formulation integrates knowledge of the environment, vision, and mission with the company's core competence in such a way as to achieve synergy and create value for customers. When these elements are brought together, the company has an excellent chance to succeed in a competitive environment. But to do so, leaders have to ensure that strategies are implemented—that actual behavior within the organization reflects the desired direction.

Strategy is implemented through specific mechanisms, techniques, or tools for directing organizational resources to accomplish strategic goals. This is the basic architecture for how things get done in the organization. Strategy implementation is the most important as well as the most difficult part of strategic management.[62] Recent research has estimated that as much as 70 percent of business strategies never get implemented, reflecting the complexity of implementation.[63] Strategy implementation involves using several tools or parts of the organization that can be adjusted to put strategy into action. Strong leadership is one of the most important tools for strategy implementation. Employee support for the strategic plan is essential for successful implementation, and leaders create the environment that determines whether people understand and feel committed to the company's strategic direction. People who feel trust in their leaders and commitment to the organization are typically more supportive of strategy and put forth more effort to implement strategic decisions.[64]

As an example of using leadership in strategy implementation, the manager of a department store might implement a strategy of increased sales by pumping up morale, encouraging aggressive selling, being physically present on the sales floor, and speaking enthusiastically with employees about meeting the high sales goals. Strategy is also implemented through organizational elements such as structural design, pay or reward systems, budget allocations, and organizational rules, policies, or procedures. An example comes from Intuit, where a new CEO has transformed the complacent firm into a hot growth company and the eighth largest software company in the world. To support his strategy for growth, CEO Steve Bennett sold off underperforming units, demolished the old budget system in favor of a model that requires managers to justify expenditures, and replaced guaranteed raises with a pay-for-performance system.[65]

Leaders are responsible for making decisions about changes in structure, systems, policies, and so forth, to support the company's strategic direction. Leaders make decisions every day—some large and some small—that support company strategy. Exhibit 13.7 provides a simplified model for how leaders make strategic decisions. The two dimensions considered are whether a particular choice will have a high or low strategic impact on the business and whether implementation of the decision will be easy or difficult. A change that both produces a high strategic

Strategy implementation putting strategy into action by adjusting various parts of the organization and directing resources to accomplish strategic goals

Action Memo

As a leader: Formulate strategies that focus on the organization's core competencies, attain synergy, and create value for customers. Prepare for the future based on trends in the environment today. Don't be afraid to think radically. Shift your strategies to fit changing environmental conditions.

Exhibit 13.7	**Making Strategic Decisions**

	Ease of Implementation	
	Hard	Easy
High	**High Impact, Hard to Implement.** Major changes, but with potential for high payoff	**High Impact, Easy to Implement.** Simple changes that have high strategic impact—take action here first
Strategic Impact		
Low	**Low Impact, Hard to Implement.** Difficult changes with little or no potential for payoff—avoid this category	**Low Impact, Easy to Implement.** Incremental improvements, "small wins;" pursue for symbolic value of success

SOURCE: Adapted from Amir Hartman and John Sifonis, wtih John Kador, *Net Ready: Strategies for the New E-conomy* (McGraw-Hill, 2000), 95.

impact and is easy to implement would be a leader's first choice for putting strategy into action. For example, when Emerson Electric Company wanted to pursue a high-growth strategy, one of the first things leaders did was change hiring practices and begin recruiting experienced marketers from companies such as Procter & Gamble, Johnson & Johnson, and Black & Decker to put more muscle into Emerson's industrial brands.[66] The decision had a tremendous impact because it gave Emerson the marketing talent it needed to pursue growth, but the change was relatively easy to implement. Pursuing growth through acquisitions, on the other hand, is much more difficult to implement. Mergers and acquisitions can present difficulties of blending production processes, accounting procedures, corporate cultures, and other aspects of the organizations into an effectively functioning whole. Leaders frequently initiate major changes despite the risks and difficulties because the potential strategic payoff is very high. Other high-risk strategic decisions include structural reorganizations, such as a shift to horizontal teams or breaking a corporation into separate divisions.

Leaders also sometimes pursue activities that have a low strategic impact but which are relatively easy to implement. Incremental improvements in products, work processes, or techniques are examples. Over time, incremental improvements can have an important effect on the organization. In addition, small changes can sometimes be needed to symbolize improvement and success to people within the organization. It may be important for leaders to produce quick, highly visible improvements to boost morale, keep people committed to larger changes, or keep followers focused on the vision. For example, the manager of a purchasing department wanted to reengineer the purchasing process to increase efficiency and improve relationships with suppliers. He wanted requisitions and invoices to be processed within days rather than the several weeks it had been taking. Employees were skeptical that the department could ever meet the new standards and pointed out that some invoices currently awaiting processing were almost two months old. The manager decided to make some simple revisions in the flow of paperwork and employee duties which enabled the department to process all the old invoices so that no remaining invoice was more than a week old. This "small win" energized employees and helped keep them focused on the larger goal.[67] The positive attitude made implementation of the larger change much smoother.

The final category shown in Exhibit 13.7 relates to changes that are both difficult to implement and have low strategic impact. An illustration of a decision in this category was the attempt by new management at a highly successful mail-order clothing company to implement teams. In this case, the decision was not made to support a new strategic direction but simply to try out a new management trend—and it was a miserable failure that cost the organization much time, money, and employee goodwill before the teams were finally disbanded.[68] Effective leaders strive to avoid making decisions that fall within this category.

The Leader's Contribution

Although good leadership for today's organizations calls for actively involving everyone in the organization, leaders are still ultimately responsible for establishing direction through vision and strategy. When leadership fails to provide direction, organizations flounder. For example, McDonald's is a well-managed company, but when franchisees saw per-store profits sink as much as 30 percent in the 1990s, they criticized leaders for their failure to provide vision and strategy. Since Jack M. Greenberg took over as chairman and CEO, he has been striving to provide the clear, focused direction McDonald's needs to stay strong in the future.[69] Strategic management is one of the most critical jobs of a leader, but leaders may exhibit different strategy styles that can be effective. Leader's Self-Insight 13.2 lets you determine your strengths based on two important ways leaders can bring creativity to strategic management.

Stimulating Vision and Action

In the waiting lounge of a fine lakeside restaurant a sign reads, "Where there is no hope in the future, there is no power in the present." The owner explains its presence there by telling the story of how his small, picturesque village with its homes and businesses was sacrificed to make way for a flood-control project. After losing their fight to reverse the decision, most business leaders simply let their businesses decline and die. Soon, the only people who came to the village did so to eat at the cheery little diner, whose owner became the butt of jokes because he continued to work so hard. Everyone laughed when he chose to open a larger and fancier restaurant on the hill behind the village. Yet, when the flood-control project was finally completed, he had the only attractive restaurant on the edge of a beautiful, newly constructed lake that drew many tourists. Anyone could have found out, as he did, where the edge of the lake would be, yet most of the business owners had no vision for the future. The restaurant owner had a vision and he took action on it. Hopes and dreams for the future are what keep people moving forward. However, for leaders to make a real difference, they have to link those dreams with strategic actions. Vision has to be translated into specific goals, objectives, and plans so that employees know how to move toward the desired future. An old English churchyard saying applies to organizations as it does to life:

> Life without vision is drudgery.
> Vision without action is but an empty dream.
> Action guided by vision is joy and the hope of the earth.[70]

Exhibit 13.8 illustrates four possibilities of leadership in providing direction. Four types of leader are described based on their attention to vision and attention to action. The person who is low both on providing vision and stimulating action is *uninvolved*, not really a leader at all. The leader who is all action and little vision is

Everything

Action Memo

As a leader: Build the trust and commitment of employees to support the strategy. Direct resources toward the achievement of strategic goals. Revise policies, procedures, reward systems, budget allocations, organizational design, or other elements as needed to effectively implement the strategy.

Your Strategy Style

Think about *how you handle challenges and issues* in your current or a recent job. Then circle a or b for each item below depending on which is generally more descriptive of your behavior. There are no right or wrong answers. Respond to each item as it best describes how you respond to work situations.

1. When keeping records, I tend to
   a. be very careful about documentation.
   b. be more haphazard about documentation.

2. If I run a group or a project, I
   a. have the general idea and let others figure out how to do the tasks.
   b. try to figure out specific goals, time lines, and expected outcomes.

3. My thinking style could be more accurately described as
   a. linear thinker, going from A to B to C.
   b. thinking like a grasshopper, hopping from one idea to another.

4. In my office or home, things are
   a. here and there in various piles.
   b. laid out neatly or at least in reasonable order.

5. I take pride in developing
   a. ways to overcome a barrier to a solution.
   b. new hypotheses about the underlying cause of a problem.

6. I can best help strategy by making sure there is
   a. openness to a wide range of assumptions and ideas.
   b. thoroughness when implementing new ideas.

7. One of my strengths is
   a. commitment to making things work.
   b. commitment to a dream for the future.

8. For me to work at my best, it is more important to have
   a. autonomy.
   b. certainty.

9. I work best when
   a. I plan my work ahead of time.
   b. I am free to respond to unplanned situations.

10. I am most effective when I emphasize
    a. inventing original solutions.
    b. making practical improvements.

Scoring and Interpretation

For *Strategic Innovator* style, score one point for each "a" answer circled for questions 2, 4, 6, 8, 10 and for each "b" answer circled for questions 1, 3, 5, 7, and 9. For *Strategic Adaptor* style, score one point for each "b" answer circled for questions 2, 4, 6, 8, 10, and for each "a" answer circled for questions 1, 3, 5, 7, and 9. Which of your two scores is higher and by how much? The higher score indicates your Strategy Style.

Strategic Innovator and Strategic Adaptor are two important ways leaders bring creativity to strategic management. Leaders with an adaptor style tend to work within the situation as it is given and improve it by making it more efficient and reliable. They succeed by building on what they know is true and proven. Leaders with the innovator style push toward a new paradigm and want to find a new way to do something. Innovators like to explore uncharted territory, seek dramatic break-throughs, and may have difficulty accepting an ongoing strategy. Both innovator and adaptor styles are essential to strategic management, but with different approaches. The strategic adaptor asks, "How can I make this better?" The strategic innovator asks, "How can I make this different?" Strategic innovators often use their skills in the formulation of whole new strategies, and strategic adaptors are often associated with strategic improvements and strategy implementation.

If the difference between the two scores is two or less, you have a mid-adaptor/innovator style, and work well in both arenas. If the difference is 4 to 6, you have a moderately strong style and probably work best in the area of your strength. And if the difference is 8 to 10, you have a strong style and almost certainly would want to work in the area of your strength rather than in the opposite domain.

SOURCES: Adapted from Dorothy Marcic and Joe Seltzer, *Organizational Behavior: Experiences and Cases* (Cincinnati: South-Western, 1998), 284–287; and William Miller, *Innovation Styles* (Global Creativity Corporation, 1997). The adaptor-innovator concepts are from Michael J. Kirton, "Adaptors and Innovators: A Description and Measure," *Journal of Applied Psychology* 61, no. 5 (1976): 623.

a *doer*. He or she may be a hard worker and dedicated to the job and the organization, but the doer is working blind. Without a sense of purpose and direction, activities have no real meaning and do not truly serve the organization, the employees, or the community. The *dreamer*, on the other hand, is good at providing a big idea with meaning for self and others. This leader may effectively inspire others with a

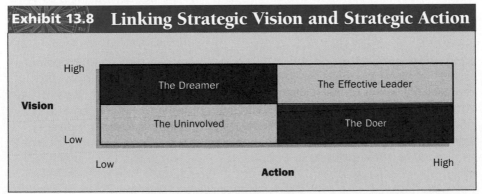

Exhibit 13.8 Linking Strategic Vision and Strategic Action

SOURCE: Based on William D. Hitt, *The Leader–Manager: Guidelines for Action* (Columbus, OH: Battelle Press, 1988), 7.

vision, yet he or she is weak on implementing strategic action. The vision in this case is only a dream, a fantasy, because it has little chance of ever becoming reality. To be an *effective leader*, one both dreams big *and* transforms those dreams into significant strategic action, either through his or her own activities or by hiring other leaders who can effectively implement the vision and strategy. For example, Jeff Bezos, founder and CEO of Amazon.com, has been hailed as a visionary for taking something right in front of everyone—selling books—and putting it together with new technology to create a whole new business model. However, Bezos has also shown himself to be a shrewd strategic leader who can take action and implement decisions to keep the company moving forward through bad times as well as good. Not so long ago, conventional wisdom said Amazon would soon join the trash heap of dot-com failures, but Bezos's strategic leadership has proved the critics wrong. Revenues, around $4 billion in 2003, are growing by more than 20 percent a year. Operating costs, once outrageously high, are now so low that few companies can claim to be better. Moreover, Amazon's profit margin, at 5 percent, is better than most retailers and edging close to leader Wal-Mart's.[71]

Action Memo

As a leader: Combine vision with action. Don't be a dreamer who never gets anything done. Make a difference for your team or organization by both having big dreams and transforming them into significant strategic action.

How Leaders Decide

To determine strategic direction for the future, leaders look inward, outward, and forward. Leaders scan both the internal and external organizational environment to identify trends, threats, and opportunities for the organization. Consider how Andrea Jung looked at changes and trends in the environment to develop a new strategic plan for Avon.

In the Lead   Andrea Jung, Avon Products Inc.

Andrea Jung recently stood before thousands of Avon representatives and vowed that Avon Products Inc. can be as big in the beauty business as Walt Disney Co. is in entertainment. The audience rose to a standing ovation as Jung continued: "We will change the future of women around the world!"

Jung, who landed the top job at Avon in November 1999, began formulating a new vision and strategy by looking at where Avon is now and where it needs to go in the future. One environmental trend of particular concern for Avon is that most women, particularly in the United States, now work outside the home, making the company's traditional direct-sales approach impractical. Another trend is the explosion of the Internet as a place for doing business. People no longer have the time or the desire to have a cup of coffee with the "Avon lady." Jung's vision for a new Avon is what she calls the "ultimate relationship marketer of products and services for women." She is rebuilding the organization from the ground up, making it a source for anything and everything today's busy woman wants to buy. In addition, Avon now gives women a choice of buying through a traditional representative, from a store, or over the Web.

Putting strategy into action involves setting up Avon kiosks in shopping malls, which are effectively luring younger customers who have never tried Avon products. Jung has updated and revitalized the Avon image with new products, new packaging, and a contemporary advertising campaign. In addition to the traditional beauty catalog, items such as vitamins, nutritional supplements, exercise gear, and other health products have been added to the list of Avon offerings. The sales force has been reinvigorated with a revised compensation and training program that makes the job more attractive to ambitious women. Since the program went into effect, the number of sales reps has been steadily climbing, as have revenues and profits. Far from becoming obsolete, independent sales contractors have been a driving force behind Avon's turnaround.

The riskiest part of the strategy is the push toward e-commerce, but Jung has handled this smoothly as well. She set up focus groups with both Net-savvy and technologically illiterate sales reps to help plan the best way to merge an Internet strategy with the company's direct sales model. She has invested millions of dollars to build a Web site that includes the full range of products, but also focuses on sales reps and helps them increase their earnings.

Jung believes Avon has an opportunity to provide a new kind of Web experience. "If we don't include [our sales reps] in everything we do, then we're just another retail brand, just another Internet site, and I don't see the world needing more of those," she says. Former CEO James E. Preston, who was Jung's mentor, praises her for having a "fresh take on what Avon could be." However, analysts warn that the key to moving Avon forward is careful, step-by-step execution. So far, Jung has done a superb job of executing her strategy and reinventing Avon for a new generation. As one investor put it, "at this point, it would be hard to give her anything less than A's."[72]

Leaders like Andrea Jung recognize that organizations need both a broad and inspiring vision and an underlying plan for how to achieve it. To decide and map a strategic direction, leaders strive to develop industry foresight based on trends in technology, demographics, government regulation, values and lifestyles that will help them identify new competitive advantages.

One approach leaders take in setting a course for the future is through hard analysis. Situation analysis, for example, includes a search for SWOT—strengths, weaknesses, opportunities, and threats that affect organizational performance. Leaders using situation analysis obtain external information from a variety of sources, such as customers, government reports, suppliers, consultants, or association meetings. They gather information about internal strengths and weaknesses from sources such as budgets, financial ratios, profit and loss statements, and employee surveys. Another formula often used by companies is a five-force analysis developed by Michael Porter, who studied a number of businesses and proposed that strategy is often the result of five competitive forces: potential new entrants into an industry; the bargaining power of buyers; the bargaining power of suppliers; the threat of substitute products; and rivalry among competitors. By carefully examining these five forces, leaders can develop effective strategies to remain competitive.

Vision and strategy have to be based on a solid factual foundation, but too much rationality can get in the way of creating a compelling vision. When leaders rely solely on formal strategic planning, competitor analysis, or market research, they miss new opportunities. For example, when Ted Turner first talked about launching a 24-hour news and information channel in the 1970s, many dismissed him as delusional. Every source of conventional wisdom, from market research to broadcast professionals, said the vision was crazy and bound to fail. Yet Turner looked at emerging social and demographic trends, listened to his intuition, and launched a global network that generates 35 percent gross margins.[73]

To formulate a vision, leaders also look inward to their hopes and dreams. Foresight and the ability to see future possibilities emerge not just from traditional strategic planning tools and formulas, but from curiosity, instinct and intuition, emotions, deep thinking, personal experience, and hope.

Another good reason for not relying too heavily on rational analysis is that rationality can kill a vision. Overly rational people have a hard time letting go and dreaming big. At Sewell Village Cadillac in Dallas, antique lamps are used instead of fluorescent lights. The expensive fixtures don't make sense in a rational, economic sense, but the setting captures people's imaginations, making the dealership seem special. To connect with people's deeper yearning for something great, vision can transcend the rational. Although it is based on reality, it comes from the heart rather than the head. One writer has suggested that leaders take a tip from Helen Keller, who was blind and deaf since early childhood and in order to see had to go out and touch the world, relying on instinct, emotion, and cues from others.[74]

The Leader's Impact

When leaders link vision and strategy, they can make a real difference for their organization's future. A leader's greatest discretion is often over strategic vision and strategic action. Research has shown that strategic thinking and planning for the future can positively affect a company's performance and financial success.[75] Another study has shown that as much as 44 percent of the variance in profitability of major firms may be attributed to strategic leadership.[76]

One way leader impact has been evaluated is to examine whether top executive turnover makes a difference. Several studies of chief executive turnover have been conducted, including a sample of 167 corporations studied over a twenty-year period, 193 manufacturing companies, a large sample of Methodist churches, and retail firms in the United Kingdom.[77] These studies found that leader succession was associated with improved profits and stock prices and, in the case of churches, with improved attendance, membership, and donations. Although good economic conditions and industry circumstances play a part in improved performance for any organization, the top leader had impact beyond these factors. Overall, when research has been carefully done, top leader succession typically explains from 20 percent to 45 percent of the variance in organizational outcomes.[78]

More recent research has explored the notion of top leadership teams, as opposed to an individual executive. The makeup of the top leadership group is believed to affect whether an organization develops organizational capability and the ability to exploit strategic opportunities. A team provides diverse aptitudes and skills to deal with complex organizational situations. Many researchers believe the configuration of the top leadership team to be more important for organizational success than the characteristics of a single CEO. For example, the size, diversity, attitudes, and skills of the team affect patterns of communication and collaboration, which, in turn, affect company performance.[79]

The emerging focus on teams is more realistic in some ways than focusing on individual leadership. In a complex environment, a single leader cannot do all things. An effective team may have a better chance of identifying and implementing a successful strategy, of discerning an accurate interpretation of the environment, and of developing internal capability based on empowered employees and a shared vision. Without a capable and effectively interacting top leadership team, a company may not adapt readily in a shifting environment. Although research in the area of leader impact is still relatively limited, it does seem to affirm the belief that the choices leaders make have significant impact on an organization's performance.

Summary and Interpretation

Leaders establish organizational direction through vision and strategy. They are responsible for studying the organization's environment, considering how it may be different in the future, and setting a direction everyone can believe in. The shared vision is an attractive, ideal future for the organization that is credible yet not readily attainable. A clear, powerful vision links the present and the future by showing how present actions and decisions can move the organization toward its long-range goals. Vision energizes employees and gives them an inspiring picture of the future to which they are eager to commit themselves. The vision can also give meaning to work and establish a standard of excellence by presenting a challenge that asks all workers to give their best.

The mission includes the company's core values and its core purpose or reason for existence. Visions for the future change, whereas the mission should persist, as a reflection of the enduring character of the organization.

Strategy is the serious work of figuring out how to translate vision and mission into action. Strategy is a general plan of action that describes resource allocation and other activities for dealing with the environment and helping the organization reach its goals. Like vision, strategy changes, but successful companies develop strategies that focus on core competence, develop synergy, and create value for customers. Strategy is implemented through the systems and structures that are the basic architecture for how things get done in the organization.

Leaders decide on direction through rational analysis as well as intuition, personal experience, and hopes and dreams. Leaders make a real difference for their organization only when they link vision to strategic action, so that vision is more than just a dream. Superior organizational performance is not a matter of luck. It is determined by the decisions leaders make.

Discussion Questions

1. A management consultant said that strategic leaders are concerned with vision and mission, while strategic managers are concerned with strategy. Do you agree? Discuss.

2. A vision can apply to an individual, a family, a college course, a career, or decorating an apartment. Think of something you care about for which you want the future to be different from the present and write a vision statement for it.

3. If you worked for a company like Microsoft or Dell that has a strong vision for the future, how would that affect you compared to working for a company that did not have a vision?

4. Do you agree with the principle of self-reference? In other words, do you believe if people know where the organization is trying to go, they will make decisions that support the desired organizational outcome?

5. What does it mean to say that the vision can include a description of both the journey and the destination?

6. Many visions are written and hung on a wall. Do you think this type of vision has value? What would be required to imprint the vision within each person?

7. What is the difference between mission and vision? Can you give an example of each?

8. What is the difference between synergy and value creation with respect to strategy?

9. Strategic vision and strategic action are both needed for a leader to be effective. Which do you think you are better at doing? Why?

10. If a new top leader is hired for a corporation, and performance improves, to what extent do you think the new top leader was responsible compared to other factors? To what extent do you think a new coach is responsible if her basketball team did better after she took over?

Leadership at Work

Future Thinking

Think of some problem you have in your life right now. It could be any problem you are having at school, home, or work that you would like to solve. Write a few words that summarize the problem:

_____

_____

_____

Now write brief answers to the following questions for that specific problem. (Do not look ahead to the next set of four questions below. This exercise is more effective if the questions are seen in sequence.)

1. Why do I have this problem?

_____

_____

_____

2. Who/what caused this problem?

_____

_____

_____

3. What stands in the way of a solution?

_____

_____

_____

4. How likely is it that I'll solve this problem?

_____

_____

_____

After you have answered these four questions, write down what are you feeling about the problem.

_____

_____

_____

Now, for the same problem, write brief answers to the four questions below.

1. What do I really want instead of this problem? (Your answer equals your desired future outcome.)

_____

_____

_____

2. How will I know I've achieved this future outcome? (What will I see, hear, and feel?)

_____

_____

_____

3. What resources do I need to pursue this future outcome?

_____

_____

_____

4. What is the first step I can take to achieve this outcome?

_____

_____

_____

After you have answered these four questions, what are you feeling about the problem?

_____

_____

_____

The human mind is effective at focusing on problems to diagnose what is wrong and who to blame. The first four questions reflect that approach, which is called problem-focused thinking.

The second set of four questions reflects a different approach, called outcome-directed thinking. It focuses the mind on future outcomes and possibilities rather than on the causes of the problem. Most people feel more positive emotion, more creative ideas, and more optimism about solving the problem after answering the second four questions compared to the first four questions. Shifting the mind to the future harnesses the same power that a vision has to awaken creativity and inspire people to move forward. Future thinking is using the idea of future vision on a small, day-to-day scale.

In Class: This exercise is very effective when each student selects a problem, and then students interview each other about their problems. Students should work in pairs—one acting the role of leader and the other acting as a subordinate. The subordinate describes his or her problem (one minute), and then the leader simply asks the first four questions above (*changing each "I" to "you"*) and listens to the answers (four minutes). Then the two students can switch leader/subordinate roles and repeat the process for the same four questions. The instructor can then gather students' observations about what they felt when answering the four questions.

Then, students can be instructed to find a new partner, and the pairs can again adopt the role of leader and subordinate. The subordinate will relate the same problem as before to the leader, but this time the leader will ask the second four questions (outcome-directed thinking, *again changing each "I" to "you"*). After the subordinate answers the four questions, the pair switches leader/subordinate roles and repeats the process. Then the instructor can ask for student observations about how they felt answering these four questions compared to the first four questions. Generally the reaction is quite positive. The key questions for students to consider are: How did the questions about future outcomes affect your creative thoughts for solving the problem compared to the first four questions that were problem-oriented? As a leader, can you use future oriented questions in your daily life to shape your thinking and the thinking of others toward more creative problem solving? Future-oriented thinking is a powerful leadership tool.

SOURCES: This approach to problem solving was developed by Robert P. Bostrom and Victoria K. Clawson of Bostrom and Associates, Columbia Missouri, and is based on a write-up appearing in "Inside USAA," September 11, 1996, 8–10; and Victoria K. Clawson and Robert P. Bostrom, "Research-Driven Facilitation Training for Computer-Supported Environments," *Group Decision and Negotiation* 5 (1996), 7–29.

Leadership Development: Cases for Analysis

Metropolis Police Department

You are in a hotel room watching the evening news as a local reporter interviews people who complain about abuse and mistreatment by police officers. These reports have been occurring in the news media with increasing frequency over the last three years. Some observers believe the problem is the police department's authoritarian style. Police managers encourage paramilitary values and a "them-against-us" attitude. The police orientation has been toward a spit-and-polish force that is efficient and tolerates no foolishness. The city believes that a highly professional, aloof police force is the best way to keep the city under control. Training emphasizes police techniques, the appropriate use of guns, and new technology, but there is no training on dealing with people. Several citizens have won large lawsuits against the police force, and many suits originated with minority groups. Critics believe the police chief is a major part of the problem. He has defended the rough actions of police officers, giving little public credence to complaints of abuse. He resists the community-oriented, people-friendly attitudes of other city departments. The chief has been considered insensitive toward minorities and has been heard to make disparaging public comments about African Americans, women, and Hispanics.

One vocal critic alleges that police brutality depends on the vision and moral leadership set by the chief of police and lays responsibility for incidents of abuse on the current chief. Another critic believes there is a relationship between his intemperate remarks and the actions of police officers.

The reason you are in Metropolis, watching the news in a hotel room, is that you have been invited to interview for the job of police chief. The mayor and selected council members are preparing to fire the chief and name a replacement. You are thinking about what you would do if you took the job.

Questions

1. Identify themes that you would like to make a part of your vision for the police department.
2. If you get the job, how will you gain acceptance for your vision? How will you implement changes that will support the new vision and values?
3. Would you relish the challenge of becoming police chief of Metropolis? Why or why not?

The Visionary Leader

When Frank Coleman first began his job as president of Hi-Tech Aerostructures, most managers and employees felt a surge of hope and excitement. Hi-Tech Aerostructures is a 50-year-old family-owned manufacturing company that produces parts for the aircraft industry. The founder and owner had served as president until his health began to decline, and he felt the need to bring in someone from outside the company to get a fresh perspective. It was certainly needed. Over the past several years, Hi-Tech had just been stumbling along.

Coleman came to the company from a smaller business, but one with excellent credentials as a leader in advanced aircraft technology. He had a vision for transforming Hi-Tech into a world-class manufacturing facility. In addition to implementing cutting-edge technology, the vision included transforming the sleepy, paternalistic culture to a more dynamic, adaptive one and empowering employees to take a more active, responsible role in the organization. After years of just doing the same old thing day after day, vice president David Deacon was delighted with the new president and thrilled when Coleman asked him to head up the transformation project.

Deacon and his colleagues spent hours talking with Coleman, listening to him weave his ideas about the kind of company Hi-Tech could become. He assured the team that the transformation was his highest priority, and inspired them with stories about the significant impact they were going to have on the company as well as the entire aircraft industry. Together, the group crafted a vision statement that was distributed to all employees and posted all over the building. At lunchtime, the company cafeteria was abuzz with talk about the new vision. And when the young, nattily dressed president himself appeared in the cafeteria, as he did once every few weeks, it was almost as if a rock star had walked in.

At the team's first meeting with Coleman, Deacon presented several different ideas and concepts they had come up with, explaining the advantages of each for ripping Hi-Tech out of the past and slamming it jubilantly into the twenty-first century. Nothing, however, seemed to live up to Coleman's ambitions for the project—he thought all the suggestions were either too conventional or too confusing. After three hours the team left Coleman's office and went back to the drawing board. Everyone was even more fired up after Coleman's closing remarks about the potential to remake the industry and maybe even change the world.

Early the next day, Coleman called Deacon to his office and laid out his own broad ideas for how the project should proceed. "Not bad," thought Deacon, as he took the notes and drawings back to the team. "We can take this broad concept and really put some plans for action into place." The team's work over the next few months was for the most part lively and encouraging. Whenever Coleman would attend the meetings, he would suggest changes in many of their specific plans and goals, but miraculously, the transformation plan began to take shape. The team sent out a final draft to colleagues and outside consultants and the feedback was almost entirely positive.

The plan was delivered to Coleman on a Wednesday morning. When Deacon had still not heard anything by Friday afternoon, he began to worry. He knew Coleman had been busy with a major customer, but the president had indicated his intention to review the plan immediately. Finally, at 6 P.M., Coleman called Deacon to his office. "I'm afraid we just can't run with this," he said, tossing the team's months of hard work on the desk. "It's just . . . well, just not right for this company."

Deacon was stunned. And so was the rest of the team when he reported Coleman's reaction. In addition, word was beginning to get out around the company that all was not smooth with the transformation project. The cafeteria conversations were now more likely to be gripes that nothing was being done to help the company improve. Coleman assured the team, however, that his commitment was still strong; they just needed to take a different approach. Deacon asked that Coleman attend as many meetings as he could to help keep the team on the right track. Nearly a year later, the team waited in anticipation for Coleman's response to the revised proposal.

Coleman called Deacon at home on Friday night. "Let's meet on this project first thing Monday morning," he began. "I think we need to make a few adjustments. Looks like we're more or less headed in the right direction, though." Deacon felt like crying as he hung up the phone. All that time and work. He knew what he could expect on Monday morning. Coleman would lay out his vision and ask the team to start over.

SOURCES: Based on "The Vision Failed," Case 8.1 in Peter G. Northouse, *Leadership—Theory and Practice*, 2nd ed. (Thousand Oaks, CA: Sage, 2001), 150–151; and Joe Kay, "My Year at a Big High Tech Company," *Forbes ASAP* (May 29, 2000): 195–198; "Digital Diary (My Year at a Big High Tech Company)," *http://www.forbes.com/asap/2000/* accessed on November 19, 2000; and "Digital Diary, Part Two: The Miracle," *Forbes ASAP* (August 21, 2000): 187–190.

Questions

1. How effective would you rate Coleman as a visionary leader? Discuss.
2. Where would you place Coleman on the chart of types of leaders in Exhibit 13.8? Where would you place Deacon?
3. If you were Deacon, what would you do?

References

1. Polly LaBarre, "Hospitals Are About Healing. This One Is Also About Changing Lives,'" *Fast Company* (May 2002): 64–78.
2. Keith H. Hammonds, "The Monroe Doctrine," *Fast Company* (October 1999): 230–236.
3. James C. Collins and Jerry I. Porras, "Building Your Company's Vision," *Harvard Business Review* (September–October 1996): 65–77.
4. R. Duane Ireland and Michael A. Hitt, "Achieving and Maintaining Strategic Competitiveness in the 21st Century: the Role of Strategic Leadership," *Academy of Management Executive* 13, no. 1 (1999): 43–57; M. Davids, "Where Style Meets Substance", *Journal of Business Strategy* 16, no. 1 (1995): 48–60; and R. P. White, P. Hodgson, and S. Crainer, *The Future of Leadership* (London: Pitman Publishing, 1997).
5. Ireland and Hitt, "Achieving and Maintaining Strategic Competitiveness."
6. Louisa Wah, "The Dear Cost of 'Scut Work,'" *Management Review* (June 1999): 27–31.
7. Gary Hamel and C. K. Prahalad, "Seeing the Future First," *Fortune* (September 5, 1994): 64–70.
8. Ireland and Hitt, "Achieving and Maintaining Strategic Competitiveness."
9. Carol Hymowitz, "Taking Time to Focus on the Big Picture Despite Flood of Data" (In the Lead column), *The Wall Street Journal* (February 27, 2001), B1.
10. Quoted in Wah, "The Dear Cost of 'Scut Work.'"
11. Nanette Byrnes and Paul C. Judge, "Internet Anxiety," *BusinessWeek* (June 28, 1999): 79–88.
12. Robert A. Guth, "Sharp Shooter: Sony Is Grooming Games Maverick for the Next Level," *The Wall Street Journal*, November 18, 2002, A1, A19.
13. Ray Maghroori and Eric Rolland, "Strategic Leadership: The Art of Balancing Organizational Mission with Policy, Procedures, and External Environment," *The Journal of Leadership Studies* no. 2 (1997): 62–81.

14. Suzanne Martin, "Family Inspires a Bright Future for Young Entrepreneur," *Self-Employed America* (September–October 1997): 12–13.

15. Collins and Porras, "Building Your Company's Vision."

16. Ireland and Hitt, "Achieving and Maintaining Strategic Competitiveness."

17. Art Kleiner, George Roth, and Nina Kruschwitz, "Should a Company have a Noble Purpose?" *Across the Board* (January 2001): 18–24.

18. R. J. Baum, E. A. Locke, and S. Kirkpatrick, "A Longitudinal Study of the Relations of Vision and Vision Communication to Venture Growth in Entrepreneurial Firms," *Journal of Applied Psychology* 83 (1998): 43–54.

19. Yair Berson, Boas Shamir, Bruce J. Avolio, and Micha Popper, "The Relationship Between Vision Strength, Leadership Style, and Context," *The Leadership Quarterly* 12 (2001): 53–73.

20. Darnell Little, "A Better Way to Make a Difference?" *BusinessWeek* (March 18, 2002): 66, 68.

21. Andrew Douglas, John O. Burtis, and L. Kristine Pond-Burtis, "Myth and Leadership Vision: Rhetorical Manifestation of Cultural Force," *The Journal of Leadership Studies* 7, no. 4 (2001): 55–69.

22. This section is based on Burt Nanus, *Visionary Leadership* (San Francisco: Jossey-Bass, 1992), 16–18; and Richard L. Daft and Robert H. Lengel, *Fusion Leadership: Unlocking the Subtle Forces that Change People and Organizations* (San Francisco: Berrett-Koehler, 1998).

23. Steve Lohr, "On a Roll, Dell Enters Uncharted Territory," *The New York Times* (August 25, 2002), Section 3,1,10; and Andrew Park with Faith Keenan and Cliff Edwards, "Whose Lunch Will Dell Eat Next?" *BusinessWeek* (August 12, 2002):66–67.

24. Oren Harari, "Looking Beyond the Vision Thing," *Management Review* (June 1997): 26–29; and William D. Hitt, *The Leader-Manager: Guidelines for Action* (Columbus, OH: Battelle Press, 1988), 54.

25. Nancy Chambers, "The Really Long View," *Management Review* (January 1998): 11–15, and Arie de Geus, "The Living Company," *Harvard Business Review* (March–April 1997): 51–59.

26. Nanus, *Visionary Leadership*, 16.

27. Collins and Porras, "Building Your Company's Vision," 74.

28. Roger E. Herman and Joyce L. Gioia, "Making Work Meaningful: Secrets of the Future-Focused Corporation," *The Futurist* (December 1998): 24–26.

29. Stephen J. Garone, "Motivation: What Makes People Work?" *Across the Board* (May–June 2001): 79–80.

30. James M. Kouzes and Barry Z. Posner, *The Leadership Challenge: How to Get Extraordinary Things Done in Organizations* (San Francisco: Jossey-Bass, 1988), 98.

31. B. Thomas, *Walt Disney: An American Tradition* (New York: Simon & Schuster, 1976), 246–247.

32. Marshall Sashkin, "The Visionary Leader," in Jay Conger and Rabindra N. Kanungo, eds., *Charismatic Leadership: The Elusive Factor in Organizational Effectiveness* (San Francisco: Jossey-Bass, 1988): 122–160.

33. James C. Collins and Jerry I. Porras, "Organizational Vision and Visionary Organizations," *California Management Review* (Fall 1991): 30–52.

34. Nanus, *Visionary Leadership*, 26; John W. Gardner, "Leadership and the Future," *The Futurist* (May–June 1990): 9–12; and Warren Bennis and Burt Nanus, *Leaders: The Strategies for Taking Charge* (New York: Harper & Row, 1985), 93.

35. Gardner, "Leadership and the Future."

36. William F. Powers, segment in Polly LaBarre, ed., "What's New, What's Not," (Unit of One), *Fast Company* (January 1999), 73.

37. Daft and Lengel, *Fusion Leadership*.

38. Kate A. Kane, "Vision for All to See," *Fast Company* (April–May 1996): 44–45.

39. Polly LaBarre, "Leadership—Ben Zander," segment in "Who's Fast 99: Unsung Heroes, Rising Stars," *Fast Company* (December 1998): 111–116.

40. Kouzes and Posner, *The Leadership Challenge*, 82.

41. This section is based on Peter M. Senge, *The Fifth Discipline: The Art and Practice of the Learning Organization* (New York: Doubleday/Currency, 1990): 205–225.

42. Betsy Morris, "Can Michael Dell Escape The Box?" *Fortune* (October 16, 2000): 92–110.

43. Quoted in Senge, *The Fifth Discipline*, 218.

44. Joe Jaworski, quoted in Alan M. Webber, "Destiny and the Job of the Leader," *Fast Company* (June–July 1996), 40, 42.

45. James Collins, "It's Not What You Make, It's What You Stand For," *Inc.* (October 1997): 42–45.

46. Susan Ellingwood, "On a Mission," *Gallup Management Journal* (Winter 2001): 6–7.

47. Ibid.

48. Collins and Porras, "Building Your Company's Vision."

49. Kleiner, et al., "Should a Company Have a Noble Purpose?"

50. Collins and Porras, "Building Your Company's Vision."

51. John E. Prescott, "Environments as Moderators of the Relationship between Strategy and Performance," *Academy of Management Journal* 29 (1986): 329–346.

52. Richard Tomlinson, "L'Oreal's Global Makeover," *Fortune* (September 30, 2002): 141–146.

53. Christopher Hoenig, "True Grit," *CIO* (May 1, 2002): 50–52.

54. Ronald B. Lieber, "Smart Science," *Fortune* (June 23, 1997), 73.

55. Gail Dutton, "What Business Are We In?" *Management Review* (September 1997): 54–57.

56. Dan Morse, "Fast Furniture—Tennessee Producer Tries New Tactic in Sofas: Speed," *The Wall Street Journal* (November 19, 2002), A1, A20.

57. John A. Byrne, "PepsiCo's New Formula," *BusinessWeek* (April 10, 2000): 172–184.

58. John S. DeMott, "Company Alliances for Market Muscle," *Nation's Business* (February 1994): 52–53.

59. Gregory M. Bounds, Gregory H. Dobbins, and Oscar S. Fowler, *Management: A Total Quality Perspective* (Cincinnati, OH: South-Western, 1995), 244 and Michael Treacy, "You Need a Value Discipline—But Which One?" *Fortune* (April 17, 1995): 195.

60. Linda Tischler, "How Pottery Barn Wins With Style," *Fast Company* (June 2003): 106.

61. Jonathan Eng, "Forsaking the Fork: General Mills Intends to Reshape Doughboy In Its Own Image," *The Wall Street Journal*, July 18, 2000, A1, A8.

62. L. J. Bourgeois III and David R. Brodwin, "Strategic Implementation: Five Approaches to an Elusive Phenomenon," *Strategic Management Journal* 5 (1984), 241–264; and Anil K. Gupta and V. Govindarajan, "Business Unit Strategy, Managerial Characteristics, and Business Unit Effectiveness at Strategy Implementation," *Academy of Management Journal* (1984), 25–41.

63. M. Corboy and D. O'Corrbui, "The Seven Deadly Sins of Strategy," *Management Accounting* 77, no. 10 (1999), 29–33.

64. W. Robert Guffey and Brian J. Nienhaus, "Determinants of Employee Support for the Strategic Plan," *SAM Advanced Management Journal* (Spring 2002): 23–30.

65. Eric Nee, "The Hottest CEO in Tech," *Business 2.0* (June 2003): 86–92.

66. Rajan Anandan, Mehrdad Baghai, Stephen Coley, and David White, "Seven Paths to Growth," *Management Review* (November 1999): 39–45.

67. Thanks to Russell Guinn for the story on which this example is based.

68. Based on Gregory A. Patterson, "Land's End Kicks Out Modern New Managers, Rejecting a Makeover," *The Wall Street Journal* (April 3, 1995), A1, A6.

69. Shelly Branch, "What's Eating McDonald's?" *Fortune* (October 13, 1997): 122–125; and Michael Arndt, "Did Somebody Say McBurrito?" *BusinessWeek* (April 10, 2000): 166, 170.

70. Quoted in Pat McHenry Sullivan, "Finding Visions for Work and Life," *Spirit at Work* (April 1997), 3.

71. Fred Vogelstein, "Mighty Amazon," *Fortune* (May 26, 2003): 60–74.

72. Nanette Byrnes, "Avon: The New Calling," *BusinessWeek* (September 18, 2000): 136–148; Nanette Byrnes, "Avon Calling—Lots of New Reps," *BusinessWeek* (June 2, 2003): 53–54.

73. Oren Harari, "Catapult Your Strategy Over Conventional Wisdom," *Management Review* (October 1997): 21–24.

74. Pat McHenry Sullivan, "Finding Visions for Work and Life," 3.

75. C. Chet Miller and Laura B. Cardinal, "Strategic Planning and Firm Performance: A Synthesis of More than Two Decades of Research," *Academy of Management Journal* 37, no. 6 (1994), 1649–1665.

76. Sydney Finkelstein and Donald C. Hambrick, *Strategic Leadership: Top Executives and Their Effect on Organizations* (St. Paul, MN: West Publishing, 1996), 23.

77. Stanley Lieberson and James F. O'Connor, "Leadership and Organizational Performance: A Study of Large Corporations," *American Sociological Review* 37 (1972): 119; Nan Weiner and Thomas A. Mahoney, "A Model of Corporate Performance as a Function of Environmental, Organizational, and Leadership Influences," *Academy of Management Journal* 24 (1981): 453–470; Ralph A. Alexander, "Leadership: It Can Make a Difference," *Academy of Management Journal* 27 (1984): 765–776; and Alan Berkeley Thomas, "Does Leadership Make a Difference to Organizational Performance?" *Administrative Science Quarterly* 33 (1988): 388–400.

78. David G. Day and Robert G. Lord, "Executive Leadership and Organizational Performance: Suggestions for a New Theory and Methodology," *Journal of Management* 14 (1988): 453–464.

79. Ken G. Smith, Ken A. Smith, Judy D. Olian, Henry P. Sims, Jr., Douglas P. O'Bannon, and Judith A. Scully, "Top Management Team Demography and Process: The Role of Social Integration and Communication," *Administrative Science Quarterly* 39 (1994): 412–438

Chapter

Your Leadership Challenge

After reading this chapter, you should be able to:

- Understand why shaping culture is a critical function of leadership.

- Recognize the characteristics of an adaptive, as opposed to an unadaptive, culture.

- Understand and apply how leaders shape culture and values through ceremonies, stories, symbols, language, selection and socialization, and daily actions.

- Identify the cultural values associated with adaptability, achievement, clan, and bureaucratic cultures and the environmental conditions associated with each.

- Use the concept of values-based leadership.

Commerce Bank is one of the fastest growing banks in the United States—but it's also one of the goofiest places of business you're likely to find. Commerce's two costumed mascots regularly visit branches and mingle with customers at special events. Mr. C, a jolly, oversized, red letter, serves as the bank's walking logo. On "Red Fridays," Mr. C joins the "Wow Patrol" visiting branches and taking photos of staffers and customers. The second mascot, Buzz, an exuberant giant bee, also gets in on the act, making sure employees are creating buzz within the branches. "It sounds juvenile, but people love getting their picture taken with Mr. C," says John Manning, vice president of the Wow Department.

The *What* Department? "*Wow* is more than a word around here," Manning emphasizes. "It's a feeling that you give and get." That's right—all this silliness has a very serious purpose. Leaders rely on this playful culture to create and maintain Commerce Bank's obsession with customer service. In Commerce lingo, that means its focus on "wowing" customers. Through the company's *Kill a Stupid Rule* program, any employee who identifies a rule that prevents Commerce from wowing customers wins $50. Each week, Dr. Wow (no one knows his or her real identity) reviews hundreds of letters and e-mails from employees and customers. Branches compete to out-wow one another and take home the coveted Hill Cup (named for president and CEO Vernon Hill).

Whereas most banks try to steer customers from branches to ATMs and online banking, Commerce looks for ways to lure more customers in. Buildings are designed to attract visitors, with floor-to-ceiling windows and historic murals on the walls. Most are open from 7:30 A.M. to 8:00 P.M. seven days a week—and the company's 10-minute rule means that if you arrive at 7:20 A.M. or 8:10 P.M. you can still get service.

Commerce Bank's approach is working. Customers who are tired of being treated shabbily by other banks are enamored of Commerce's service and convenience orientation. "There's a different attitude around here, like we're all in this together," said one customer. As the organization grows, what tools does Commerce plan to use to keep its focus on superior service? President and CEO Vernon Hill gives one answer: "Culture, culture, culture." Without the wow, he says, Commerce would be just another bank.[1]

Commerce Bank has definite cultural values that make it unique in the banking industry. New managers and employees who attend sessions at Commerce University, the bank's training department inspired by McDonald's Hamburger University, learn that they've joined a service cult. A one-day course called Traditions—part game show, part training session, and part culture festival—begins socializing people into Commerce's unique way of doing things. Weekly activities such as Red Fridays and the care and attention of Dr. Wow help to keep the culture strong.

In the previous chapter, we talked about creating a vision that inspires and motivates people to strive for a better future. This chapter will focus on how leaders align people with the vision by influencing organizational culture and shaping the environment that determines employee morale and performance. The nature of the culture is highly important because it impacts a company for better or worse. Southwest Airlines and Starbucks Coffee Company have often attributed their success to the cultures their leaders helped create. Louis V. Gerstner's cultural overhaul of IBM revived the company's reputation and profitability. Leaders at other companies, including Kodak and Xerox, are trying to shift their cultural values to remain competitive in today's environment. In a *Fortune* magazine survey, CEOs cited organizational culture as their most important mechanism for attracting, motivating, and retaining talented employees, a capability that may be the single best predictor of overall organizational excellence.[2] One long-term study discovered that organizations with strong cultures outperform organizations that have weak cultures two-to-one on several primary measures of financial performance.[3]

This chapter explores ideas about organizational culture and values, and the role of leaders in shaping them. The first section will describe the nature of corporate culture and its importance to organizations. Then we turn to a consideration of how shared organizational values can help the organization stay competitive and how leaders influence culture. Leaders emphasize specific cultural values depending on the organization's situation. The final section of the chapter will briefly discuss ethical values in organizations and examine how values-based leadership shapes an ethical atmosphere.

Organizational Culture

The concept of organizational culture is fairly recent. It became a topic of significant concern in the United States during the early 1980s, primarily due to an interest in learning why U.S. corporations were not performing as well as their counterparts in Japan. Observers and researchers thought that the national culture and corporate culture could explain differences in performance.[4] Leaders now understand that when a company's culture fits the needs of its external environment and company strategy, employees can create an organization that is tough to beat.[5]

What Is Culture?

Some people think of culture as the character or personality of an organization. How an organization looks and "feels" when you enter it is a manifestation of the organizational culture. For example, you might visit one company where you get a sense of formality the minute you walk in the door. Desks are neat and orderly, employees wear professional business attire, and there are few personal items such as family photos or other decorations on walls and desks. At another company, employees may be wearing jeans and sweaters, have empty pizza boxes and cola cans on their desks, and bring their dogs to work with them. Both companies may be highly successful, but the underlying cultures are very different.

Culture can be defined as the set of key values, assumptions, understandings, and norms that is shared by members of an organization and taught to new members as correct.[6] Norms are shared standards that define what behaviors are acceptable and desirable within a group of people. At its most basic, culture is a pattern of shared assumptions about how things are done in an organization. As organizational members cope with internal and external problems, they develop shared assumptions and norms of behavior that are taught to new members as the correct way to think, feel, and act in relation to those problems.[7]

Culture can be thought of as consisting of three levels, as illustrated in Exhibit 14.1, with each level becoming less obvious.[8] At the surface level are visible artifacts such as manner of dress, patterns of behavior, physical symbols, organizational

Culture

the set of key values, assumptions, understandings, and norms that is shared by members of an organization and taught to new members as correct

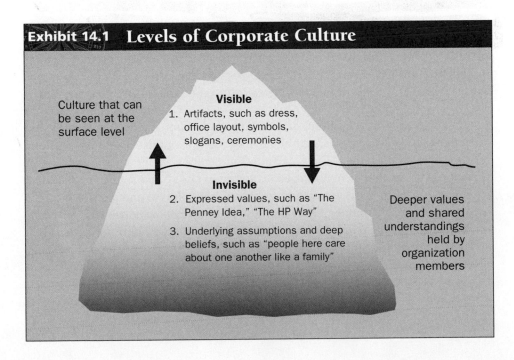

Exhibit 14.1   Levels of Corporate Culture

Culture that can be seen at the surface level

Visible
1. Artifacts, such as dress, office layout, symbols, slogans, ceremonies

Invisible
2. Expressed values, such as "The Penney Idea," "The HP Way"

3. Underlying assumptions and deep beliefs, such as "people here care about one another like a family"

Deeper values and shared understandings held by organization members ceremonies, and office layout—all the things one can see, hear, and observe by watching members of the organization. For example, Commerce Bank's mascots and employees dressing in red for Red Fridays are visible manifestations of the corporate culture. At a deeper level are the expressed values and beliefs, which are not observable but can be discerned from how people explain and justify what they do. These are values that members of the organization hold at a conscious level. Commerce Bank's employees consciously know that service is highly valued and rewarded in the company culture.

Some values become so deeply embedded in a culture that organizational members may not be consciously aware of them. These basic, underlying assumptions are the deepest essence of the culture. At Commerce Bank, these assumptions might include (1) that the bank cares about its employees as much as it expects them to care about customers, (2) that individual employees should think for themselves and do what they believe is right to provide exceptional customer service, and (3) that work should be as natural and joyful a part of life as play. Assumptions generally start out as expressed values, but over time they become more deeply embedded and less open to question—organization members take them for granted and often are not even aware of the assumptions that guide their behavior, language, and patterns of social interaction.

Importance of Culture

When people are successful at what they undertake, the ideas and values that led to that success become institutionalized as part of the organization's culture.[9] Culture gives employees a sense of organizational identity and generates a commitment to particular values and ways of doing things. Culture serves two important functions in organizations: (1) it integrates members so that they know how to relate to one another, and (2) it helps the organization adapt to the external environment.

Internal Integration Culture helps members develop a collective identity and know how to work together effectively. It is culture that guides day-to-day working relationships and determines how people communicate in the organization, what behavior is acceptable or not acceptable, and how power and status are allocated. Culture can imprint a set of unwritten rules inside employees' minds, which can be very powerful in determining behavior, thus affecting organizational performance.[10]

Organizations are putting increased emphasis on developing strong cultures that encourage teamwork, collaboration, and mutual trust.[11] In an environment of trust, people are more likely to share ideas, be creative, and be generous with their knowledge and talents. At the Container Store, a chain of retail stores that sells boxes, garbage cans, shelving, and just about anything else you might need to organize your home, office, or car, the culture encourages employees to do whatever needs to be done. Simple maxims like "treat people the way you want to be treated" and "be helpful to others" are granted policy status at the Container Store. Cultural values that promote open communication, cooperation, and equality helped the company win the No. 1 spot two years in a row on *Fortune* magazine's list of the best companies to work for in America. It was edged out of the top spot in 2003 by Edward Jones, another company with a strong, collaborative culture.[12]

External Adaptation Culture also determines how the organization meets goals and deals with outsiders. The right cultural values can help the organization respond rapidly to customer needs or the moves of a competitor. Culture can encourage employee commitment to the core purpose of the organization, its specific goals, and the basic means used to accomplish goals.

The culture should embody the values and assumptions needed by the organization to succeed in its environment. If the competitive environment requires speed and flexibility, for example, the organizational culture should embody values that support adaptability, collaboration across departments, and a fast response to customer needs or environmental changes. Consider how PSS World Medical's values meet the needs of its competitive environment.

In the Lead   Pat Kelly, PSS World Medical

PSS World Medical, a specialty marketer and distributor of medical products and supplies, has thrived in a fiercely competitive industry by offering superior service and responsiveness to customers. Company practices such as same-day delivery, no minimum order sizes, and a no-hassles return policy have earned PSS a loyal following among physicians, long-term care facilities, and hospitals. But what really distinguishes the company is its employees, who approach their jobs with energy, enthusiasm, and commitment. Delivery drivers have business cards with their name and "CEO" on them, because founder and top executive Pat Kelly believes "when you're standing in front of the customer, you *are* the CEO." Decision making is decentralized so that each person can do whatever is needed to make the jobs of their harried customers easier.

Kelly attributes his organization's success primarily to its corporate culture, which is based on the idea of personal responsibility and values of honesty, trust, and mutual respect. The company not only practices open book management, sharing all financial and operating information with employees, but managers also encourage employees to ask any question of anyone in the company without fear of punishment. When top executives visit a branch, they pass out $2 bills to anyone with a question as a fun way to get people to participate. Leaders see themselves as working for their employees, rather than vice versa. The responsibility of leaders is to teach, guide, and develop employees, helping them achieve their highest potential. The unique cultural ritual of "Firing the Boss" shows that PSS is sincere about employee empowerment. In most cases, supervisors don't really get fired (although sometimes they do); the ritual simply provides a way to get problems out into the open, prompt better communication, and make sure leaders understand the importance of listening to and serving employees. Personal accountability is another core value, and people at all levels are given the authority to make decisions and solve problems. No one is ever fired for making an honest mistake, because taking risks and making mistakes is seen as a key to learning and growth. Rather than pushing and prodding people to perform, PSS creates an environment in which people want to excel and have the opportunity to do so. By creating a culture that unleashes all employees' energy and enthusiasm, PSS has grown and flourished.[13]

Strong cultures bind people together, making the organization a community rather than just a collection of individuals. However, as at PSS, the culture also needs to encourage adaptation to the environment in order to keep the organization healthy and profitable. This chapter's Living Leadership highlights the importance of adaptability.

Culture Strength and Adaptation

Culture strength

the degree of agreement among employees about the importance of specific values and ways of doing things

Culture strength refers to the degree of agreement among employees about the importance of specific values and ways of doing things. If widespread consensus exists, the culture is strong and cohesive; if little agreement exists, the culture is weak.[14] The effect of a strong culture is not always a positive one. Sometimes a strong culture can encourage the wrong values and cause harm to the organization and its members. Think of Enron Corp., which failed largely because of a strong culture that supported pushing everything to the limits: business practices, rules, personal behavior, and laws. Executives drove expensive cars, challenged employees to participate in dangerous competitive behavior, and often celebrated big deals by heading off to a bar or club for a night of carousing.[15]

Thus, a strong culture increases employee cohesion and commitment to the values, goals, and strategies of the organization, but companies can sometimes have unethical values or values that are unhealthy for the organization because they don't fit the needs of the environment. Research at Harvard into some 200 corporate cultures found that a strong culture does not ensure success unless it also encourages a healthy adaptation to the external environment.[16] A strong culture that does not encourage adaptation can be more damaging to an organization than a weak culture.

LIVING LEADERSHIP

Flexible or Rigid

The ability to embrace change is characteristic of growth and vibrancy. This metaphor illustrates that organizations should remain adaptable:

At birth, a person is flexible and flowing. At death, a person becomes rigid and blocked. Consider the lives of plants and trees: during their time of greatest growth, they are relatively tender and pliant. But when they are full grown or begin to die, they become tough and brittle.

The tree which has grown up and become rigid is cut into lumber. . . .

Whatever is flexible and flowing will tend to grow. Whatever is rigid and blocked will atrophy and die.

SOURCE: John Heider, *The Tao of Leadership: Leadership Strategies for a New Age* (New York: Bantam Books, 1985), 151. Copyright © 1985 Humanic Ltd., Atlanta, GA. Used with permission.

For example, Motorola's strong culture based on encouraging internal competition among divisions almost destroyed the company. After many years of success, Motorola's culture had become "set," as if in concrete, and the company failed to adapt as the environment changed. The company that had invented the cellular telephone industry was being pounded by more innovative rivals such as Nokia and was infuriating customers with its arrogant approach. Moreover, leaders viewed the Internet as an oddball curiosity, rather than a trend the company needed to embrace. Fortunately, Motorola CEO Christopher B. Galvin recognized the need for a corporate makeover and began working with other leaders to change the insular and competitive culture. Today employees and executives are focused on collaboration rather than competition to spur development of Internet-based products and improve customer service. The makeover isn't complete, but most observers agree that Motorola is on the right path, toward providing the best lineup of Web phones in the world. Shifting to a more adaptive culture has made Motorola once again a name to fear in the wireless industry.[17]

As illustrated in Exhibit 14.2, adaptive corporate cultures have different values and behavior from unadaptive cultures. In adaptive cultures, leaders are concerned with customers and those internal people, processes, and procedures that bring about useful change. In unadaptive cultures, leaders are concerned with themselves or their own special projects, and their values tend to discourage risk-taking and change. Thus, a strong culture is not enough, because an unhealthy culture may encourage the organization to march resolutely in the wrong direction. Healthy cultures help companies adapt to the external environment. Leader's Self-Insight 14.1 gives you an opportunity to assess the cultural values of a place you have worked.

Exhibit 14.2 **Adaptive Versus Unadaptive Cultures**		
	Adaptive Organizational Culture	**Unadaptive Organizational Culture**
Visible Behavior	Leaders pay close attention to all their constituencies, especially customers, and initiate change when needed to serve their legitimate interests, even if it entails taking some risks.	Managers tend to behave somewhat insularly, politically, and bureaucratically. As a result, they do not change their strategies quickly to adjust to or take advantage of changes in their business environments.
Expressed Values	Leaders care deeply about customers, stockholders, and employees. They also strongly value people and processes that can create useful change (e.g., leadership initiatives up and down the management hierarchy).	Managers care mainly about themselves, their immediate work group, or some product (or technology) associated with that work group. They value the orderly and risk-reducing management process much more highly than leadership initiatives.
Underlying Assumption	Serve whole organization, trust others.	Meet own needs, distrust others.

SOURCE: Reprinted with the permission of The Free Press, a Division of Simon & Schuster Adult Publishing Group, from *Corporate Culture and Performance* by John P. Kotter and James L. Heskett. Copyright © 1992 by Kotter Associates, Inc. and James L. Heskett. All rights reserved.

An organization's culture may not always be in alignment with the needs of the external environment. The values and ways of doing things may reflect what worked in the past, as they did at Motorola. The difference between desired and actual values and behaviors is called the culture gap.[18] Organizations can be much more effective when the culture fits the external environment. Many organizations have some degree of culture gap, though leaders often fail to realize it. An important step toward shifting the culture toward more adaptive values is to recognize when people are adhering to the wrong values or when important values are not held strongly enough.[19]

Culture gap
the difference between desired and actual values and behaviors

Culture gaps can be immense, particularly in the case of mergers. Despite the popularity of mergers and acquisitions as a corporate strategy, many fail. Almost one-half of all acquired companies are sold within five years, and some experts claim that 90 percent of mergers never live up to expectations.[20] One reason for this is the difficulty of integrating cultures.

LEADER'S SELF-INSIGHT 14.1

Working in an Adaptive Culture

Think of a specific full-time job you have held. Please answer the questions below according to your perception of the *managers above you* in that job. Circle a number on the 1–5 scale based on the extent to which you agree with each statement about the managers above you: 5 = Strongly agree; 4 = Agree; 3 = Neither agree nor disagree; 2 = Disagree; 1 = Strongly disagree

	Strongly disagree				Strongly agree
1. Good ideas got serious consideration from management above me.	1	2	3	4	5
2. Management above me was interested in ideas and suggestions from people at my level in the organization.	1	2	3	4	5
3. When suggestions were made to management above me, they received fair evaluation.	1	2	3	4	5
4. Management did not expect me to challenge or change the status quo.	1	2	3	4	5
5. Management specifically encouraged me to bring about improvements in my workplace.	1	2	3	4	5
6. Management above me took action on recommendations made from people at my level.	1	2	3	4	5
7. Management rewarded me for correcting problems.	1	2	3	4	5
8. Management clearly expected me to improve work unit procedures and practices.	1	2	3	4	5
9. I felt free to make recommendations to management above me to change existing practices.	1	2	3	4	5
10. Good ideas did not get communicated upward because management above me was not very approachable.	1	2	3	4	5

Scoring and Interpretation

To compute your score: Subtract each of your scores for questions 4 and 10 from 6. Using your adjusted scores, add the numbers for all 10 questions to give you the total score: _____. Divide by 10 to get your average score: _____.

An adaptive culture is shaped by the values and actions of top and middle managers. When managers actively encourage and welcome change initiatives from below, the organization will be infused with values for change. The 10 questions above measure your management's openness to change. A typical average score for management openness to change is about 3. If your average score was 4 or higher, you worked in an organization that expressed strong cultural values of adaptation. If your average score was 2 or below, the culture was probably unadaptive.

Thinking about your job, is the level of management openness to change correct for the organization? Why? Compare your scores to those of another student, and take turns describing what it was like working for the managers above your jobs. Do you sense that there is a relationship between job satisfaction and your management's openness to change? What specific management characteristics and corporate values explain the openness scores in the two jobs?

SOURCES: S. J. Ashford, N. P. Rothbard, S. K. Piderit, and J. E. Dutton, "Out on a Limb: The Role of Context and Impression Management in Issue Selling," *Administrative Science Quarterly* 43 (1998): 23–57; and E. W. Morrison and C. C. Phelps, "Taking Charge at Work: Extrarole Efforts to Initiate Workplace Change," *Academy of Management Journal* 42, (1999): 403–419.

For example, when Harty Press acquired Pre-Press Graphics to move their company into the digital age, the two cultures clashed from the beginning. Executives initially focused on integrating the acquired firm's financial systems and production technologies, but their failure to pay attention to culture seriously damaged the company. According to general manager Michael Platt, "I thought all that stuff people said about culture when it came to mergers was a bunch of fluff—until it happened."[21] Organizational leaders should remember that the human systems—in particular, the norms and values of corporate culture—are what make or break any change initiative. The problem of integrating cultures increases in scope and complexity with global companies and cross-cultural mergers or acquisitions.

Shaping Culture

An organization exists only because of the people who are a part of it, and those people both shape and interpret the character and culture of the organization. That is, an organization is not a slice of objective reality; different people may perceive the organization in different ways and relate to it in different ways. Leaders in particular formulate a viewpoint about the organization and the values that can help people achieve the organization's mission, vision, and goals. Therefore, leaders enact a viewpoint and a set of values that they think are best for helping the organization succeed. An organization's culture is often a reflection of the values advocated by a founder or top leader. For example, Kingston Technology Co. reflects the values of founders David Sun and John Tu.

In the Lead   David Sun and John Tu, Kingston Technology Co.

"Business is not about money," says David Sun, vice president and chief operating officer of Kingston Technology Co., which manufactures memory products for personal computers, laser printers, digital cameras, and other products. "It's about relationships." Sun and his co-founder, president John Tu, have instilled values of caring, trust, collaboration, and sharing in their company. "They are part of the team," says one employee of the partnership workers feel with leaders at Kingston. "They are not owners, they are employees. And that culture, that value system is passed on."

When Sun and Tu sold 80 percent of Kingston to Softbank Corp. of Japan for $1.5 billion, they set aside $100 million of the proceeds for employee bonuses. The initial distribution of $38 million went to around 550 employees who were with the company at the time of its sale. Another $40 million has since been divvied out among the company's current 1,500 workers. Sun and Tu seem genuinely puzzled by the astonishment that they would give $100 million to employees. Yet, despite this generosity, when people talk about why they like working for Kingston, they rarely mention money and benefits. Instead, they talk about personal acts of gentleness or kindness performed by the two top leaders. There are many stories of these leaders quietly offering money, time, other resources—or just genuine concern—to employees who were dealing with family or personal troubles. This approach to leadership creates an emotional bond with employees that builds trust and respect. Because employees are treated with kindness, care, and respect, they pass that on in their relationships with each other and with customers, suppliers, and other outsiders. Employees are highly motivated to meet organizational goals and keep the company's reputation for doing the right thing. Says one, "We try to keep the family name a good name."[22]

Action Memo

As a leader: Build a culture that is strong and adaptive. Show concern for customers and other stakeholders in the external environment. Support people and projects that bring about useful change. Be alert to culture gaps and shift values to close them.

Once a healthy culture is established, leaders use a variety of techniques to maintain a strong culture that provides both smooth internal integration and external adaptation. Leaders can use organizational rites and ceremonies, stories, symbols, and specialized language to enact cultural values. In addition, they can emphasize careful selection and socialization of new employees to keep cultures strong. Perhaps most importantly, leaders signal the cultural values they want to instill in the organization through their day-to-day actions.

Ceremonies

A **ceremony** is a planned activity that makes up a special event and is generally conducted for the benefit of an audience. Leaders can schedule ceremonies to provide dramatic examples of what the company values. Ceremonies reinforce specific values, create a bond among employees by allowing them to share an important event, and anoint and celebrate employees who symbolize important achievements.[23]

Ceremony
a planned activity that makes up a special event and is generally conducted for the benefit of an audience

A ceremony often includes the presentation of an award. At Mary Kay Cosmetics, one of the most effective companies in the world at using ceremonies, leaders hold elaborate award ceremonies at an annual event called "Seminar," presenting jewelry, furs, and luxury cars to high-achieving sales consultants. The most successful consultants are introduced by film clips like the ones used to present award nominees in the entertainment industry.[24] These ceremonies recognize and celebrate high-performing employees and help bind sales consultants together. Even when they know they will not personally be receiving awards, consultants look forward to Seminar all year because of the emotional bond it creates with others.

Stories

Story

a narrative based on true events that is repeated frequently and shared among employees

A **story** is a narrative based on true events that is repeated frequently and shared among employees. Stories are told to new employees to illustrate the company's primary values. Leaders can use stories to reinforce important cultural values and provide a shared meaning for employees. One frequently told story at UPS concerns an employee who, without authority, ordered an extra Boeing 737 to ensure timely delivery of a load of Christmas packages. As the story goes, rather than punishing the worker, UPS rewarded his initiative. By telling this story, UPS workers communicate that the company stands behind its commitment to worker autonomy and customer service.[25] In some cases, stories may not be supported by facts, but they are consistent with the values and beliefs of the organization. At Nordstrom, for example, leaders do not deny the story about a customer who got his money back on a defective tire, even though Nordstrom does not sell tires. The story reinforces the company's no-questions-asked return policy.[26]

As we discussed in Chapter 9, storytelling is a powerful way to connect with others on an emotional level, helping to convey and transmit important cultural values. Richard Stone runs a company called StoryWork Institute that helps organizations find and circulate stories as a way to strengthen or change cultural values. One client, Nighttime Pediatrics Clinics, which runs after-hours clinics in the Salt Lake City area, hired Stone when CEO Teresa Lever-Pollary became concerned that the organization was losing its values in the face of rapid growth and the strictures of managed care. To solidify values such as individual-centered care, teamwork, and informality, Stone collected stories from patients, doctors, nurses, clerks, and others and put them together in a collection called *Nighttime Stories*, which was given out at the company's fifteenth birthday celebration. "It has helped people remember what is special about us," says Lever-Pollary. One story tells of a doctor who bent the clinic's rules to treat a disoriented elderly woman. Another focuses on a payroll employee who convinced management to scrap an expensive investment in flawed new software.[27]

Symbols

Symbol

an object, act, or event that conveys meaning to others

Another tool for conveying cultural values is the symbol. A **symbol** is an object, act, or event that conveys meaning to others. In a sense, stories and ceremonies are symbols, but physical artifacts can also be used by leaders to symbolize particular values. For example, Stephen Quesnelle, head of quality programs at Mitel Corp., placed a nearly life-size wooden heifer outside his office to symbolize the importance of tracking down and destroying sacred cows, "the barriers that everyone knows about but nobody talks about."[28]

At Siebel Systems in San Mateo, California, employees are surrounded by symbolic reminders that the customer always comes first. Every conference room is named after a major Siebel customer. All the artwork on office walls comes from customer ads or annual reports. "The cornerstone of our corporate culture," says Siebel, "is that we are committed to do whatever it takes to make sure that each and every one of our customers succeeds."[29]

Specialized Language

Language can shape and influence organizational values and beliefs. Leaders sometimes use slogans or sayings to express key corporate values. Slogans can easily be picked up and repeated by employees. For example, at Averitt Express, the slogan "Our driving force is people," applies to customers and employees alike. The culture emphasizes that drivers and customers, not top executives, are the power that fuels the company's success.

Leaders also express and reinforce cultural values through written public statements, such as corporate mission statements or other formal statements that express the core values of the organization. Leaders at Eli Lilly and Company developed a formal statement of corporate values, including respect for all people, honesty and integrity, and striving for continuous improvement.[30] Eaton Corporation's philosophy statement, called "Excellence Through People," includes values such as encouraging employee involvement in all decisions, regular face-to-face communication between executives and employees, emphasizing promotion from within, and always focusing on the positive behavior of workers.[31]

Selection and Socialization

Selection and socialization of new employees helps maintain cultural values. Companies with strong, healthy cultures, such as Southwest Airlines, Nordstrom, Commerce Bank, and PSS World Medical, often have careful and rigorous hiring practices. PSS doesn't call candidates back for follow-up interviews. Requiring the candidate to take the initiative through every step of the recruiting and hiring process, which takes six to eight weeks, ensures that PSS hires the kind of people with the right values and attitudes to fit its culture. Commerce Bank looks for a sense of humor, outgoing personality, and enthusiasm. "This is not a job for someone who's interested in being cool or indifferent," says John Manning of Commerce.[32]

Once the right people are hired, the next key to a strong, healthy culture is socializing them into the culture. Starbucks Coffee emphasizes socialization to maintain its strong culture. CEO Howard Schultz compares an employee's first days with the company to the early years of childhood, when you want to instill good values, high self-esteem, and the confidence to begin taking risks and making decisions. Schultz himself welcomes each new employee by video, tells about the company's history and culture, and shares some of his own personal experiences at Starbucks. All employees receive 24 hours of training, during which they talk about the Starbucks mission and values and the qualities that make Starbucks a unique

Action Memo

As a leader: Shape cultural values through rites and ceremonies, stories, symbols, and language. Select and socialize people to keep the culture strong. Match your actions to espoused values.

company.[33] Even though Schultz believes an employee's first two weeks may be the most important, socialization also continues throughout an employee's tenure with the organization.

Daily Actions

Ceremonies, stories, slogans, and symbols are useless if leaders don't signal and support important cultural values through their daily actions. Employees learn what is valued most in a company by watching what attitudes and behaviors leaders pay attention to and reward, how leaders react to organizational crises, and whether the leader's own behavior matches the espoused values.[34] At Levi Strauss, for example, managers' bonus pay, which can be two-thirds of their total compensation, is tied explicitly to how well they follow the organization's list of "corporate aspirations"—a list of stated core values that includes an emphasis on teamwork, trust, diversity, recognition, ethics, and empowerment.[35] Because leaders at Levi Strauss create linkages between stated values, training, everyday action, and appraisal and reward systems, employees rely on the aspirations as a standard of behavior.

Good leaders understand how carefully they are watched by employees. The story of Bob Kierlin, chairman, president, and CEO of Fastenal, illustrates clearly that the leader's greatest impact on culture comes from what he or she does on a day-by-day basis.

In the Lead   Bob Kierlin, Fastenal Co.

Inc. magazine once referred to Bob Kierlin, the top leader of Fastenal Co. of Winona, Minnesota, as "the cheapest CEO in America." It may sound like a dubious honor, but Kierlin runs a national powerhouse that operates almost 800 branch sites in 48 states, Canada, and Puerto Rico. The company sells and custom manufactures nuts and bolts, fasteners, safety supplies, tools, and other industrial and construction products. Despite Kierlin's "cheapness," Fastenal is a growing company because it invests wisely in new equipment and technology. In addition, Fastenal's employees are happy and feel a strong commitment to the company.

Bob Kierlin is the kind of guy who just loves a bargain. He clips coupons from the Sunday paper, eats McDonald's Extra Value Meals, and has taken home the same $120,000 yearly paycheck for the last decade. He buys his suits used from the manager of a men's clothing store. Fastenal's culture very much reflects Kierlin's values—scratch pads are made from used paper, annual reports are produced in-house for 40 cents a copy, and the warehouse shelving was bought used for 25 cents on the dollar.

Kierlin sets the example daily. Rather than flying to a conference in Chicago, he and the chief financial officer drove five and a half hours in a van, saving Fastenal hundreds of dollars. They lunched at A&W on burgers and root beer for $5 each and spent the night in a suburb to avoid high city prices—they even shared a room. Top executives have no special privileges. Kierlin fights for a good parking space just like anyone else in the company. Until recently, he shoveled snow at corporate headquarters and sorted the mail himself. That kind of social leveling has created a bond between workers and executives that most companies can only dream of. Workers respect Kierlin—he treats everyone the same, whether you're a janitor or a vice president, and he comes in at 6 A.M. and works as hard as anyone in the company. They also share the cultural values Kierlin models every day—not just the value of a buck, but the importance of being fair and treating everyone as an equal. Because of a profit-sharing plan, they know that cutting costs fattens everyone's paycheck, but the quality of their relationships is just as important.

Kierlin doesn't see anything unusual about his leadership or his company's culture—he thinks it's just good, old-fashioned common sense.[36]

A culture of frugality and fairness is powerful at Fastenal, but not just because it saves money. The company's constant obsession with costs promotes a kind of attentiveness to the mundane that inevitably improves quality. In addition, the culture spreads accountability and responsibility everywhere—at Fastenal, you never call somebody else to fix a problem, you fix it yourself. The culture is strong primarily because the company's top leaders live the cultural values every day.

Leaders can also change unadaptive cultures by their actions. For example, at Mariott, as at many hotels, the pursuit of superior round-the-clock performance had led to a deeply ingrained culture of *face time*—the more hours a manager put in, the better. By the late 1990s, though, this philosophy was making it tough for Marriott to find and keep talented people. When leaders wanted to instill values that encouraged work–life balance and an emphasis on results rather than hours worked, one of their most important steps was to make a point of leaving work early whenever possible. Encouraging lower-level managers to take more time off did no good until top leaders demonstrated the new value with their own behavior.[37]

Through ceremonies, stories, symbols, language, hiring and training practices, and their own behavior, leaders influence culture. When culture change is needed to adapt to the environment or bring about smoother internal integration, leaders are responsible for instilling new cultural values. Changing cultures is not easy, but through their words, and particularly their actions, leaders let other members know what really counts in the company.

The Competing Values Approach to Shaping Culture

Organizational values

the enduring beliefs that have worth, merit, and importance for the organization

Today's leaders recognize the importance of shared values and invest time in thinking about and discussing them. **Organizational values** are the enduring beliefs that have worth, merit, and importance for the organization. The crisis in corporate ethics and the crash of once-promising companies such as WorldCom, Qwest, Enron, and Arthur Andersen have brought values to the forefront. One review of recent company failures revealed that unhealthy cultural values played a crucial role in many of the mistakes these companies made.[38] Ethical values will be discussed later in the chapter. Changes in the nature of work, increasing diversity in the workforce, and other shifts in the larger society have also made the topic of values one of considerable concern to leaders. They are faced with such questions as, "How can I determine what cultural values are important? Are some values 'better' than others? How can the organization's culture help us be more competitive?"

In considering what values are important for the organization, leaders consider the external environment and the company's vision and strategy. Cultures can vary widely across organizations; however, organizations within the same industry often reveal similar values because they are operating in similar environments.[39] Key values should embody what the organization needs to be effective. Rather than looking at values as either "good" or "bad," leaders look for the right combination. The correct relationship among cultural values, organizational strategy, and the external environment can enhance organizational performance.

Organizational cultures can be assessed along many dimensions, such as the extent of collaboration versus isolation among people and departments, the importance of control and where control is concentrated, or whether the organization's time orientation is short-range or long-range.[40] Here, we will focus on two specific dimensions: (1) the extent to which the competitive environment requires flexibility or stability; and (2) the extent to which the organization's strategic focus and strength is internal or external. Four categories of culture associated with these differences, as illustrated in Exhibit 14.3, are adaptability, achievement, clan, and bureaucratic.[41] These four categories relate to the fit among cultural values, strategy, structure, and the environment, with each emphasizing specific values, as shown in the exhibit.

An organization may have cultural values that fall into more than one category, or even into all categories. However, successful organizations with strong cultures will lean more toward one particular cultural category. For example, Fastenal, described in the previous section, clearly values economy, listed in the bureaucratic culture category. However, its overall set of values places it more clearly in the clan culture category because of its strong emphasis on fairness, social equality, and caring for people.

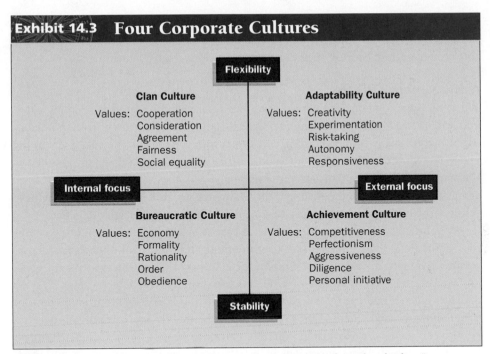

Exhibit 14.3   Four Corporate Cultures

Flexibility

Clan Culture

Values: Cooperation
Consideration
Agreement
Fairness
Social equality

Adaptability Culture

Values: Creativity
Experimentation
Risk-taking
Autonomy
Responsiveness

Internal focus — External focus

Bureaucratic Culture

Values: Economy
Formality
Rationality
Order
Obedience

Achievement Culture

Values: Competitiveness
Perfectionism
Aggressiveness
Diligence
Personal initiative

Stability

SOURCES: Based on Paul McDonald and Jeffrey Gandz, "Getting Value from Shared Values," *Organizational Dynamics* 21, no. 3 (Winter 1992): 64–76; Deanne N. Den Hartog, Jaap J. VanMuijen, and Paul L. Koopman, "Linking Transformational Leadership and Organizational Culture," *The Journal of Leadership Studies* 3, no. 4 (1996): 68–83; Daniel R. Denison and Aneil K. Mishra, "Toward a Theory of Organizational Culture and Effectiveness," *Organizational Studies* 6, no. 2 (March–April 1995): 204–223; Robert Hooijberg and Frank Petrock, "On Cultural Change: Using the Competing Values Framework to Help Leaders Execute a Transformational Strategy," *Human Resource Management* 32, no. 1 (1993): 29–50; R.E. Quinn, *Beyond Rational Management: Mastering the Paradoxes and Competing Demands of High Performance* (San Francisco: Jossey-Bass, 1998).

Adaptability Culture

The adaptability culture is characterized by strategic leaders encouraging values that support the organization's ability to interpret and translate signals from the environment into new behavior responses. Employees have autonomy to make decisions and act freely to meet new needs, and responsiveness to customers is highly valued. Leaders also actively create change by encouraging and rewarding creativity, experimentation, and risk-taking. A good example of an adaptability culture is 3M Corp., where leaders encourage experimentation and taking risks as an everyday way of life. All employees attend a class on risk-taking where they are encouraged to defy their supervisors if necessary to pursue a promising idea. Researchers are allowed to use 15 percent of their time to explore ideas outside their assigned projects. This encouragement of *experimental doodling*, as an early 3M manager called it, has led to the creation

Adaptability culture

culture characterized by values that support the organization's ability to interpret and translate signals from the environment into new behavior responses of hundreds of innovative projects and entrenched 3M as a leader in some of today's most dynamic global markets.[42] Many technology and Internet companies also use this type of culture because they must move quickly to satisfy customers.

Achievement Culture

Achievement culture

culture characterized by a clear vision of the organization's goals and leaders' focus on the achievement of specific targets

The **achievement culture** is characterized by a clear vision of the organization's goals, and leaders focus on the achievement of specific targets such as sales growth, profitability, or market share. An organization concerned with serving specific customers in the external environment but without the need for flexibility and rapid change is suited to the achievement culture. This is a results-oriented culture that values competitiveness, aggressiveness, personal initiative, and the willingness to work long and hard to achieve results. An emphasis on winning is the glue that holds the organization together.[43]

A good example of an achievement culture is Siebel Systems, which sells complex software systems. Siebel, like its cofounder and CEO Tom Siebel, is intense, competitive, and driven to win. Employees who perform and meet stringent goals are handsomely rewarded; those who don't are fired. Nearly every employee at Siebel is given a ranking within each department, and every six months the bottom 5 percent are axed. Siebel has procedures and systems for carefully measuring employees on key performance variables such as responsiveness to customers. Succeeding at Siebel Systems means being smart, competitive, aggressive, and thorough. Employees who thrive on the competitive culture have helped Siebel's revenues grow rapidly.[44]

Clan Culture

Clan culture

culture with an internal focus on the involvement and participation of employees to meet changing expectations from the external environment

The **clan culture** has an internal focus on the involvement and participation of employees to meet changing expectations from the external environment. More than any other, this culture places value on meeting the needs of organization members. These organizations are generally friendly places to work and employees may seem almost like a family. Leaders emphasize cooperation, consideration of both employees and customers, and avoiding status differences. Leaders put a premium on fairness and reaching agreement with others.

One company that achieves success with a clan culture is Motek, a software company whose motivational practices were described in Chapter 8. The most important value is taking care of employees and making sure they have whatever they need to be satisfied and productive. Employees get housing subsidies, earn travel bonuses, and are forbidden to work after 5:00 P.M. or on weekends. Everyone gets five weeks of vacation, plus 10 paid holidays. Leaders encourage people to live a balanced life rather than work long hours and express a hard-charging, competitive spirit. Other key values include equality, fairness, and cooperation. At Motek, employees care about each other and the company, a focus that has helped the organization adapt to stiff competition and changing markets.[45]

Bureaucratic Culture

The **bureaucratic culture** has an internal focus and consistency orientation for a stable environment. The culture supports a methodical, rational, orderly way of doing business. Following the rules and being thrifty are valued. The organization succeeds by being highly integrated and efficient.

Safeco Insurance has functioned well with a bureaucratic culture. Employees take their coffee breaks at an assigned time, and a dress code specifies white shirts and suits for men and no beards. However, employees like this culture—reliability is highly valued and extra work isn't required. The bureaucratic culture works for the insurance company, and Safeco succeeds because it can be trusted to deliver on insurance policies as agreed.[46] In today's fast-changing world, very few organizations operate in a stable environment, and most leaders are shifting away from bureaucratic cultures because of a need for greater flexibility.

Each of the four cultures can be successful. The relative emphasis on various cultural values depends on the organization's strategic focus and on the needs of the external environment. Leaders might have preferences for the values associated with one type of culture, but they learn to adjust the values they emulate and encourage, depending on the needs of the organization. You can determine your own cultural preferences by completing the exercise in Leader's Self-Insight 14.2. It is the responsibility of leaders to ensure that organizations don't get "stuck" in cultural values that worked in the past but are no longer successful. As environmental conditions and strategy change, leaders work to instill new cultural values to help the organization meet new needs. For example, when Dick Brown took over at EDS, he realized that the company was out of phase with the current environment for the technology industry. To revitalize the company and take advantage of new opportunities, Brown started by redefining the culture.

In the Lead   Dick Brown, Electronic Data Systems

Electronic Data Systems (EDS) was a pioneer in the information technology services industry, but as the environment changed and became more competitive, EDS failed to shift its cultural values. Faster, nimbler start-ups were beating EDS at its own game—and when IBM launched its own innovative IT-services unit, the game seemed all but over for EDS. When Dick Brown took over as chairman and CEO, he quickly discovered part of the problem. On his first day of work, when Brown asked a phone technician why his phone wasn't working, the technician explained that the previous CEO had the lines cut to avoid disruptive incoming calls. When he tried to send an e-mail to EDS's 140,000 employees, he learned that the company's systems didn't allow it. Brown knew he had to "reconnect" the company in a hurry.

Bureaucratic culture

culture with an internal focus and consistency orientation for a stable environment

Action Memo

As a leader: Align the organizational culture to strategy and the needs of the external environment. Implement an adaptability, achievement, clan, or bureaucratic culture depending on environmental requirements for either flexibility or stability and the organization's internal or external strategic focus.

The old culture of isolationism, information hoarding, rampant individualism, slow response time, and separation between managers and employees on the front lines had worked fine for EDS in the 1980s, but the fast-paced, high-stakes world of the 21st century demanded new values. Brown implemented initiatives designed to foster a companywide culture based on individual autonomy and responsibility, quick feedback, open communication, and rapid response. One technique is the "monthly performance call," during which 125 of EDS's top worldwide executives join in a conference call to review the past month's operational details. Executives know if they don't meet their targets, they'll have to explain to everyone why, but the real value of the calls is that they emphasize sharing information and helping one another better meet clients' needs. Brown also began personally visiting customers to model a new commitment to customer service and responsiveness. Information and reward systems were altered to support the new values of client focus and innovation.

"At the old EDS, the culture was 'Fix the problem yourself,'" says one manager. Now, employees at EDS are focused on collaborating to better serve clients. Shifting to a more open, adaptability culture has helped EDS reap increases in sales, profits, and market share. The company's famous "Cat Herders" Super Bowl commercial was a symbol of the cultural changes at EDS. In the commercial, rugged cowboys are herding 10,000 house cats under big open skies, accompanied by a stirring musical score. By allowing EDS to poke a little bit of fun at itself at the same time it symbolized the company's commitment to riding herd over clients' technological problems, the commercial was an outward representation of the substantial changes in corporate culture.[47]

Ethical Values in Organizations

Of the values that make up an organization's culture, ethical values are considered highly important for leaders and have gained renewed emphasis in today's era of financial scandals and moral lapses. Most organizations that remain successful over the long term have leaders who include ethics as part of the formal policies and informal cultures of their companies. Some companies place significant emphasis on ethics in their business conduct. For example, leaders at Baxter International Inc. quickly yanked a product from the market when a number of people died after undergoing dialysis using a Baxter blood filter. It's a CEO's nightmare, but top leaders at Baxter did the right thing by investigating the problem, admitting their role in the deadly mistake, and providing financial compensation to families of the victims. Moreover, in atonement for the error, CEO Harry M. Jansen Kraemer, Jr. slashed his annual bonus by 40 percent and the bonuses of other top executives by 20 percent.

LEADER'S SELF-INSIGHT 14.2

Culture Preference Inventory

The inventory below consists of 14 sets of four responses that relate to typical values or situations facing leaders in organizations. Although each response to a question may appear equally desirable or undesirable, your assignment is to rank the four responses in each row according to your preference. Think of yourself as being in charge of a major department or division in an organization. Rank the responses in each row according to how much you would like each one to be a part of your department. There are no correct or incorrect answers; the scores simply reflect your preferences for different responses.

Rank each of the four in each row using the following scale. You must use all four numbers for each set of four responses.

1. Would not prefer at all
2. Would prefer on occasion
4. Would prefer often
8. Would prefer most of all

	I	II	III	IV
1.	Aggressiveness	Cost-efficiency	Experimentation	Fairness
2.	Perfection	Obedience	Risk-taking	Agreement
3.	Pursue future goals	Solve current problems	Be flexible	Develop people's careers
4.	Apply careful analysis	Rely on proven approaches	Look for creative approaches	Build consensus
5.	Initiative	Rationality	Responsiveness	Collaboration
6.	Highly capable	Productive and accurate	Receptive to brainstorming	Committed to the team
7.	Be the best in our field	Have secure jobs	Recognition for innovations	Equal status
8.	Decide and act quickly	Follow plans and priorities	Refuse to be pressured	Provide guidance and support
9.	Realistic	Systematic	Broad and flexible	Sensitive to the needs of others
10.	Energetic and ambitious	Polite and formal	Open-minded	Agreeable and self-confident
11.	Use key facts	Use accurate and complete data	Use broad coverage of many options	Use limited data and personal opinion
12.	Competitive	Disciplined	Imaginative	Supportive
13.	Challenging assignments	Influence over others	Achieving creativity	Acceptance by the group
14.	Best solution	Good working environment	New approaches or ideas	Personal fulfillment

Scoring and Interpretation

Add the points in each of the four columns—I, II, III, IV. The sum of the point columns should be 210 points. If your sum does not equal 210 points, check your answers and your addition.

The scores represent your preference for I, achievement culture; II, bureaucratic culture; III, adaptability culture; and IV, clan culture. Your personal values are consistent with the culture for which you achieved the highest score, although all four sets of values exist within you just as they exist within an organization. The specific values you exert as a leader may depend on the group situation, particularly the needs of the external environment. Compare your scores with other students and discuss their meaning. Are you pleased with your preferences? Do you think your scores accurately describe your values?

SOURCE: Adapted from Alan J. Rowe and Richard O. Mason, *Managing with Style: A Guide to Understanding, Assessing, and Improving Decision Making* (San Francisco: Jossey-Bass, 1987).

Semiconductor maker Xilinx has adhered to its strict no-layoffs policy throughout the technology downturn by negotiating with workers to take pay cuts. Significantly, top leaders took the hardest hit, with the CEO cutting his salary by 20 percent.[48]

Ethics

the code of moral principles and values that governs the behavior of a person or group with respect to what is right and wrong

Ethics is difficult to define in a precise way. In general, **ethics** is the code of moral principles and values that governs the behavior of a person or group with respect to what is right or wrong. Ethics sets standards as to what is good or bad in conduct and decision making.[49] Many people believe that if you are not breaking the law, then you are behaving in an ethical manner, but ethics often goes far beyond the law.[50] The law arises from a set of codified principles and regulations that are generally accepted in society and are enforceable in the courts. Ethical standards for the most part apply to behavior not covered by law. Although current laws often reflect minimum moral standards, not all moral standards are codified into law. The morality of aiding a drowning person, for example, is not specified by law.

The standards for ethical conduct are embodied within each employee as well as within the organization itself. In a survey about unethical conduct in the workplace, more than half of the respondents cited poor leadership as a factor.[51] Leaders can create and sustain a climate that emphasizes ethical behavior for all employees.

 # Values-Based Leadership

Values-based leadership

a relationship between leaders and followers that is based on shared, strongly internalized values that are advocated and acted upon by the leader

Ethical values in organizations are developed and strengthened primarily through **values-based leadership**, a relationship between leaders and followers that is based on shared, strongly internalized values that are advocated and acted upon by the leader.[52] Leaders influence ethical values through their personal behavior as well as through the organization's systems and policies.

Personal Ethics

Employees learn about values from watching leaders. Values-based leaders generate a high level of trust and respect from employees, based not just on stated values but on the courage, determination, and self-sacrifice they demonstrate in upholding those values. When leaders are willing to make personal sacrifices for the sake of values, employees become more willing to do so.

For organizations to be ethical, leaders need to be openly and strongly committed to ethical conduct. Leader's Self-Insight 14.3 lets you see how you feel about some ethical issues that students typically face. Several factors contribute to an individual leader's ethical stance. Every individual brings a set of personal beliefs, values, personality characteristics, and behavior traits to the job. The family backgrounds and spiritual beliefs of leaders often provide principles by which they conduct business. Personality characteristics such as ego strength, self-confidence, and a strong sense of independence may enable leaders to make ethical decisions even if those decisions might be unpopular.

Personal Ethical Beliefs

Cheating is a common problem on college campuses today; 67 percent of students confess that they have cheated at least once. Many pressures cause students to engage in unethical behavior, and these are similar to pressures they will later face in the workplace. Answer the following questions to see how you think and feel about certain student behaviors that could be considered unethical. Circle a number on the 1–5 scale based on the extent to which you approve of the behavior described, with 5 = Strongly approve and 1 = Strongly disapprove. *Please answer based on whether you approve or disapprove of the behavior, not whether you have ever acted in such a way.*

	Strongly disapprove				Strongly approve
1. Receiving a higher grade through the influence of a family or personal connection	1	2	3	4	5
2. Communicating answers to a friend during a test	1	2	3	4	5
3. Using a faked illness as an excuse for missing a test	1	2	3	4	5
4. Visiting a professor's office frequently to seek help in a course	1	2	3	4	5
5. "Hacking" into the university's computer system to change your grade	1	2	3	4	5
6. Getting extra credit because the professor likes you	1	2	3	4	5
7. Using formulas programmed into your pocket calculator during an exam	1	2	3	4	5
8. Attending commercial test preparatory courses such as those offered by Kaplan	1	2	3	4	5
9. Asking a friend to sign you in as attending when you are absent from a large class	1	2	3	4	5
10. Peeking at your neighbor's exam during a test	1	2	3	4	5
11. Brown-nosing your professor	1	2	3	4	5
12. Overhearing the answers to exam questions when your neighbor whispers to another student	1	2	3	4	5
13. Using a term paper that you purchased or borrowed from someone else	1	2	3	4	5
14. Contributing little to group work and projects but receiving the same credit and grade as other members	1	2	3	4	5
15. Hiring someone or having a friend take a test for you in a very large class	1	2	3	4	5
16. Comparing work on assignments with classmates before turning the work in to the instructor	1	2	3	4	5
17. Receiving favoritism because you are a student athlete or member of a campus organization	1	2	3	4	5
18. Using unauthorized "crib notes" during an exam	1	2	3	4	5
19. Taking advantage of answers you inadvertently saw on another student's exam	1	2	3	4	5
20. Having access to old exams in a particular course that other students do not have access to	1	2	3	4	5
21. Receiving information about an exam from someone in an earlier section of the course who has already taken the test	1	2	3	4	5
22. Being allowed to do extra work, which is not assigned to all class members, to improve your grade	1	2	3	4	5

Scoring and Interpretation

There are five subscale scores that reflect your attitudes and beliefs about different categories of behavior.

For the category of *actively benefiting from unethical action*, sum your scores for questions 2, 5, 10, 13, 15, and 18 and divide by 6 _____.

For the category of *passively benefiting from questionable action*, sum your scores for questions 1, 6, 11, 14, 17, 20, and 22 and divide by 7_____.

For the category of *actively benefiting from questionable action*, sum your scores for questions 3, 7, 9, and 21 and divide by 4 _____.

For the category of *acting on an opportunistic situation*, sum your scores for questions 12 and 19 and divide by 2 _____.

For the category of *no harm/no foul* (actions perceived to cause no harm to anyone are considered okay) sum your scores for questions 4, 8, and 16 and divide by 3 _____.

The higher the score, the more you find that category of behaviors acceptable. When the scale was administered to 291 students in marketing and finance classes at a medium-sized university, the mean scores were as follows: *actively benefiting from unethical behavior*: 1.50; *passively benefiting from questionable action*: 2.31; *actively benefiting from questionable action*: 2.46; *acting on an opportunistic situation*: 2.55; and *no harm/no foul*: 4.42. How do your scores compare to these averages? The students in this sample had high approval for the *no harm/no foul* category. Do you agree that these behaviors are acceptable? Why might some people consider them unethical? If you feel comfortable doing so, compare your scores to another student's and discuss your beliefs about categories that you strongly disapprove or strongly approve of.

SOURCE: Mohammed Y. A. Rawwas and Hans R. Isakson, "Ethics of Tomorrow's Business Managers: The Influence of Personal Beliefs and Values, Individual Characteristics, and Situational Factors," *Journal of Education for Business* (July 2000): 321. Reprinted with permission of the Helen Dwight Reid Educational Foundation. Published by Heldref Publications, 1319 Eighteenth St., NW, Washington, DC 20036-1802. Copyright © 2000.

One important personal factor is the leader's stage of moral development, as described in Chapter 6, which affects an individual's ability to translate values into behavior.[53] For example, some people make decisions and act only to obtain rewards and avoid punishment for themselves. Others learn to conform to expectations of good behavior as defined by society. This means willingly upholding the law and responding to the expectations of others. At the highest level of moral development are people guided by high internal standards. These are self-chosen ethical principles that don't change with reward or punishment. Leaders can strive to develop higher moral principles so that their daily actions reflect important ethical values. When faced with difficult decisions, values-based leaders know what they stand for, and they have the courage to act on their principles. This chapter's Leader's Bookshelf describes a unique, 450-year old organization that has succeeded by emphasizing personal values as the basis of leadership.

LEADER'S BOOKSHELF

Heroic Leadership: Best Practices From a 450-Year Old Company That Changed the World
by Chris Lowney

Many of today's organizations struggle to find leadership. Top executives hire talented, ambitious young people only to find that they crumble under pressure, can't inspire and motivate their teams, or lack the courage to innovate and take risks. Chris Lowney, author of *Heroic Leadership*, believes these companies can look to a 16th century priest for guidance. In 1540, St. Ignatius Loyola founded the 10-man Jesuits with no capital and molded it into the most successful "company" of its time. Now the world's largest religious order, the Jesuits have operated a highly-efficient international network of trade, education, military work, and scholarship for almost five centuries.

Pillars of Leadership Success
With fascinating historical examples and anecdotes, Lowney explores how the Jesuits have grappled with many of the same problems that face today's organizations—"forging seamless multinational teams, motivating inspired performance, remaining change ready and strategically adaptable." He believes the Jesuits' enduring success comes from molding leaders at all levels based on four core leadership pillars:

* *Self-Awareness*. To be a leader, one must understand his or her strengths, weaknesses, values, and beliefs. The Jesuits are trained to reflect on their goals, values, and performance throughout each day. Once a year, each sits down with a superior for an "account of conscience" to reinforce an understanding of common goals and success.

* *Ingenuity*. Innovating and adapting to a changing world is one of the things the Jesuits have done best. St. Ignatius Loyola described the ideal Jesuit as "living with one foot raised," always ready to respond to opportunities. Although education was not one of the Jesuit's initial goals, for example, they spotted a need and began plowing money into building a college. Within a decade, they had opened more than 30 colleges all over the world.

* *Love*. Loyola believed people perform best in environments that are supportive, caring, and charged with positive emotion. He counseled leaders to create a climate filled with "greater love than fear," and be passionately committed to unlocking the potential in themselves and others.

* *Heroism*. "Heroes extract gold from the opportunities around them rather than waiting for golden opportunities to be handed to them." Leaders aim high and energize others with their ambitions for something *more*, something greater than what is. This Jesuit idea contributed to the first European forays into Tibet, for example, and created the world's highest-quality secondary education available.

Living Leadership
The Jesuit approach focuses not on what leaders do, but on who they are. The principles aim to make each individual a better person, which in turn makes a stronger organization. Leadership cannot be separated from everyday life. The four pillars of leadership form a foundation for a way of living that is based on strong values and allows any individual to respond positively to the leadership opportunities all around us every day.

Heroic Leadership, by Chris Lowney, is published by Loyola Press.

In a study of ethics policy and practice in successful, ethical companies such as Boeing, Chemical Bank, General Mills, GTE, Johnson & Johnson, and Hewlett-Packard, no point emerged more clearly than the crucial role of top leaders.[54] Leaders set the tone for an organization's ethics through their own actions.

Organizational Structure and Systems

Leaders also influence ethical values through formal systems, programs, and policies. Formal systems that effectively influence organizational ethics are codes of ethics, ethical structures, training programs, and disclosure mechanisms.

Code of Ethics

Code of Ethics   A code of ethics is a formal statement of the company's ethical values. It communicates to employees what the company stands for. Codes of ethics state the values and behavior that are expected and those that will not be tolerated. A recent survey of *Fortune* 1,000 companies found that 98 percent address issues of ethics and business conduct in formal corporate policies, and 78 percent have separate codes of ethics that are widely distributed to employees.[55] When leaders support and enforce these codes, they can uplift a company's ethical climate.

Some companies include ethics as a part of broader statements that also define their mission. These statements generally define ethical values as well as corporate culture and contain language about company responsibility, quality of product, and treatment of employees. For example, Northern Telecom's *Code of Business Conduct*, which is provided to all employees and is also available on the Internet, is a set of guidelines and standards that illustrates how the company's mission and core values translate into ethical business practices.

Structure   Ethical structure represents the various positions or programs an organization uses to encourage ethical behavior. One example is an ethics committee—a group of employees appointed to oversee the company's ethics and provide rulings on questionable ethics issues. The committee typically includes high-level executives to signal the importance of ethical issues. Vic Sarni, former CEO of PPG Industries, for example, personally headed his firm's ethics committee.[56]

Many organizations are setting up ethics departments that manage and coordinate all corporate ethics activities. These departments are headed by a **chief ethics officer**, a high-level company executive who oversees all aspects of ethics, including establishing and broadly communicating ethical standards, setting up ethics training programs, supervising the investigation of ethical problems, and advising managers in the ethical aspects of corporate decisions.[57] Most ethics offices also work as counseling centers to help employees resolve difficult ethical dilemmas. The focus is as much on helping employees make the right decisions as on disciplining wrongdoers.

Action Memo

As a leader: Be ethical. Act on high moral principles in your daily behavior. Use a code of ethics, an ethics office, and training programs to instill ethical values in the organization. Value and support whistleblowers. Investigate reported ethical concerns.

Code of ethics

a formal statement of the company's ethical values

Chief ethics officer

a high-level company executive who oversees all aspects of ethics

Training To make sure ethical issues are considered in daily actions, leaders often implement training programs to supplement a written code of ethics. Texas Instruments developed an eight-hour ethics-training course for all employees. In addition, leaders incorporate ethics into every course the company offers.[58]

Companies with a strong commitment to ethical values make ethical issues a part of all training. Starbucks Coffee uses new employee training to begin instilling values such as taking personal responsibility, treating everyone with respect, and doing the right thing even if others disagree with you.[59] At the Holt Companies, all employees attend a two-day training program where they learn about the company's values and talk about values-related cases and dilemmas. In addition, all managers and supervisors attend another two-day session focused specifically on ethics awareness.[60]

Disclosure Mechanisms Finally, leaders can support employees who do the right thing and voice their concerns about unethical practices. One important step is to develop policies about **whistle-blowing**, employee disclosure of illegal or immoral practices on the part of the organization. As discussed in Chapter 6, it can be risky for employees to blow the whistle—they can lose their jobs, be transferred to lower-level positions, or be ostracized by co-workers.

Leaders set the standard for how whistleblowers are treated. If the organization genuinely wants to maintain ethical standards, whistleblowers are valued and leaders make dedicated efforts to protect them.[61] Leaders can create a climate where people feel free to point out problems without fear of punishment. In addition, they can set up hot lines to give employees a confidential way to report problems, and then make sure action is taken to investigate reported concerns.

In summary, leaders create an ethical climate for the organization through systems and programs such as codes of ethics, ethics committees or offices, training programs, and mechanisms to protect whistleblowers. Leaders instill and encourage ethical values most clearly through their own personal actions. Organizations can be ethical only when leaders are ethical.

Whistle-blowing
employee disclosure of illegal or immoral practices on the part of the organization

Summary and Interpretation

Leaders influence organizational culture and ethical values. Culture is the set of key values, norms, and assumptions that is shared by members of an organization and taught to new members as correct. Culture serves two critically important functions—to integrate organizational members so they know how to relate to one another and to help the organization adapt to the environment. Strong, adaptive cultures have a positive impact on organizational outcomes. A culture gap exists when an organization's culture is not in alignment with the needs of the external environment or company strategy. Leaders use ceremonies, stories, symbols, specialized language, selection, and socialization to influence cultural values. In addition, leaders shape cultural values most strongly through their daily actions.

Leaders consider the external environment and the company's vision and strategy in determining which values are important for the organization. Four types of culture may exist in organizations: Adaptability, Achievement, Clan, and Bureaucratic. Each type emphasizes different values, although organizations may have values that fall into more than one category.

Of the values that make up an organization's culture, ethical values are among the most important. Ethics is the code of moral principles and values that governs the behavior of a person or group with respect to what is right or wrong. Leaders shape ethical values through values-based leadership, including their own personal behavior as well as the organization's systems and policies. Leaders' personal beliefs and level of moral development influence their personal ethics. For organizations to be ethical, leaders have to be openly and strongly committed to ethical conduct in their daily actions. Leaders can also influence ethical values in the organization through codes of ethics, ethics committees and ethics offices, training programs, and disclosure mechanisms to support employees who voice concerns about ethical practices.

 ## Discussion Questions

1. Describe the culture for an organization you are familiar with. Identify the physical artifacts and underlying values and assumptions. What did you learn?
2. Discuss how a strong culture could have either positive or negative consequences for an organization.
3. What is a culture gap? What are some techniques leaders might use to influence and change cultural values when necessary?
4. Compare and contrast the achievement culture with the clan culture. What are some possible *disadvantages* of having a strong clan culture? A strong achievement culture?
5. Which do you think is more important for improving ethical values in an organization: a code of ethics, leader behavior, or employee training? Discuss.
6. In which of the four types of culture (adaptability, achievement, clan, bureaucratic) might you expect to find the greatest emphasis on ethical issues? Why?
7. If a leader directs her health care company to reward hospital managers strictly on hospital profits, is the leader being ethically responsible? Discuss.
8. What is meant by the idea that culture helps a group or organization solve the problem of internal integration?

Leadership at Work

Walk the Talk

Often in an organization the culture is characterized both by what people say (talk) and by what people actually do (walk). When this happens there is a gap between organizational leaders' espoused values and the values in action within the company. One example would be an espoused value of "a balanced life for employees," while managers and employees are actually expected to work nights and weekends to meet demanding performance goals. This is the difference between the "walk" and the "talk" in an organization.

Your assignment for this exercise is to think of one example in your own student or work experience where the walk and talk in a corporate culture did not align. Why do you think the gap occurred? Then interview four other people for examples of when an organization's espoused values did not align with the values in action. Also ask them why they think the walk and talk differed. Summarize the findings from your interviews below:

My example (and why):

_____

_____

_____

Second person's examples (and why):

_____

_____

_____

Third person's examples (and why):

_____

_____

_____

Fourth person's examples (and why):

_____

_____

_____

Fifth person's examples (and why):

_____

_____

_____

What patterns and themes do you see in the responses? Is there a common type of walk/talk gap? What is the most common reason why these gaps occur? Which is the real culture—the leader's espoused values or the values in action?

In Class: Students can be organized into small groups in class and do the above exercise all at once. Each person in the circle can give examples of an organization's walk not fitting its talk from their work and student experiences, and explain why they think the gaps occurred. Then students can identify the common themes from their discussion. The instructor can help students probe into this issue by writing good examples from students on the board and asking students to help identify key themes. Students can be engaged to discuss the walk versus talk phenomenon via key questions, such as: What does it mean to you when you discover a walk/talk gap in your organization? Are espoused values or values-in-action more indicative of a company's culture (or are both the culture)? Are walk/talk gaps likely to be associated with an adaptive culture? A strong culture? Do symbols, stories, ceremonies, and other signals of corporate culture mean what they imply?

Leadership Development: Cases for Analysis

Lisa Benavides, Forest International

Lisa Benavides has just been hired as the vice president of human resources for Forest International. Previously, the company had only a personnel officer and a benefits specialist, who spent most of their time processing applications and benefit forms and tracking vacation and sick days. However, a new CEO came to Forest believing that HR can play a key strategic role in the organization, and he recruited Benavides from a well-known HR consulting firm soon after he took over the top job. The new CEO has lots of ideas about empowerment, shared leadership, and teamwork that he hopes to eventually implement at the company.

Forest International operates in one of the most dangerous industries around. Paper mills, sawmills, and plywood factories are filled with constant noise, giant razor-toothed saw blades, caustic chemicals, and chutes loaded with tons of lumber. Even in this notoriously hazardous industry, Forest's safety record stinks. Within a four-year period, 29 workers were killed on the job. There are an average of 9 serious injuries per 100 employees each year. In addition, productivity has been declining in recent years, and Forest's competitors are gaining market share. As one of her first major projects, the CEO has asked Benavides for her advice on how to improve the company's safety record and increase productivity.

The company, based outside Atlanta, Georgia, has around $11 billion in annual revenues and employs 45,000 people. Many employees' parents and grandparents also worked in Forest's mills and factories. Among many of the workers, missing a finger or two is considered a badge of honor. Taking chances is a way of proving that you're a true *Forest-man* (the term persists even though the company now has a good percentage of female workers). During lunch or break, groups of workers routinely brag about their "close calls" and share stories about parents or grandparents' dangerous encounters with saw blades or lumber chutes.

It is clear to Benavides that worker attitudes are part of the problem, but she suspects that management attitudes may play a role as well. Production managers emphasize the importance of keeping the line moving, getting the product out no matter what. Rather than finding a supervisor and asking that the production line be shut down, most line employees take chances on sticking their hands into moving equipment whenever there is a minor problem. As Benavides talks with workers, she learns that most of them believe managers care more about productivity and profits than they do about the well-being of people in the plant. In fact, most Forest employees don't feel that they're valued at all by the company. One saw operator told Benavides that he has made several suggestions for improving productivity and safety on his line but has been routinely ignored by management. "They never listen to us; they just expect us to do what we're told," he said. This same employee was one of the most vocal in opposing some recent safety-oriented changes requiring that all workers wear safety gear anytime they're on the production floor, not just when they are on the line. "They don't really care about our safety," he boomed. "They just want another way to push us around." Many of the other workers also oppose the new rules, saying that "managers walk around the production floor all the time without goggles and ear plugs, so why shouldn't we?"

SOURCES: Based in part on information in Anne Fisher, "Danger Zone," *Fortune* (September 8, 1997): 165–167; and Robert Galford, "Why Doesn't This HR Department Get Any Respect?" *Harvard Business Review* (March–April 1998): 24–26.

Questions

1. How would you describe the culture of Forest International as it relates to internal integration and external adaptation?
2. Would you expect that changing the culture at Forest would be easily accomplished now that a new CEO is committed to change? Why or why not?
3. If you were Lisa Benavides, what suggestions would you make to Forest's new CEO?

Acme and Omega

Acme Electronics and Omega Electronics both manufacture integrated circuits and other electronic parts as subcontractors for large manufacturers. Both Acme and Omega are located in Ohio and often bid on contracts as competitors. As subcontractors, both firms benefited from the electronics boom of the 1980s, and both looked forward to growth and expansion. Acme has annual sales of about $100 million and employs 950 people. Omega has annual sales of $80 million and employs about 800 people. Acme typically reports greater net profits than Omega.

The president of Acme, John Tyler, believed that Acme was the far superior company. Tyler credited his firm's greater effectiveness to his managers' ability to run a "tight ship." Acme had detailed organization charts and job descriptions. Tyler believed that everyone should have clear responsibilities and narrowly defined jobs, which generates efficient performance and high company profits. Employees were generally satisfied with their jobs at Acme, although some managers wished for more empowerment opportunities.

Omega's president, Jim Rawls, did not believe in organization charts. He believed organization charts just put artificial barriers between specialists who should be working together. He encouraged people to communicate face-to-face rather than with written memos. The head of mechanical engineering said, "Jim spends too much time making sure everyone understands what we're doing and listening to suggestions." Rawls was concerned with employee satisfaction and wanted everyone to feel part of the organization. Employees were often rotated among departments so they would be familiar with activities throughout the organization. Although Omega wasn't as profitable as Acme, they were able to bring new products on line more quickly, work bugs out of new designs more accurately, and achieve higher quality because of superb employee commitment and collaboration.

It is the end of May, and John Tyler, president of Acme, has just announced the acquisition of Omega Electronics. Both management teams are proud of their cultures and have unflattering opinions of the other's. Each company's customers are rather loyal, and their technologies are compatible, so Tyler believes a combined company will be even more effective, particularly in a time of rapid change in both technology and products.

The Omega managers resisted the idea of an acquisition, but the Acme president is determined to unify the two companies quickly, increase the new firm's marketing position, and revitalize product lines—all by year end.

SOURCES: Adapted from John F. Veiga, "The Paradoxical Twins: Acme and Omega Electronics," in John F. Veiga and John N. Yanouzas, *The Dynamics of Organization Theory* (St. Paul: West Publishing, 1984), 132–138; and "Alpha and Omega," Harvard Business School Case 9-488-003, published by the President and Fellows of Harvard College, 1988.

Questions

1. Using the competing values model in Exhibit 14.3, what type of culture (adaptability, achievement, clan, bureaucratic) would you say is dominant at Acme? At Omega? What is your evidence?
2. Is there a culture gap? Which type of culture do you think is most appropriate for the newly merged company? Why?
3. If you were John Tyler, what techniques would you use to integrate and shape the culture to overcome the culture gap?

References

1. Chuck Salter, "The Problem with Most Banks Is That They Abuse Their Customers Every Day. We Want to Wow Ours," *Fast Company* (May 2002): 80–91.
2. Jeremy Kahn, "What Makes a Company Great?" *Fortune* (October 26, 1998): 218; James C. Collins and Jerry I. Porras, *Built to Last: Successful Habits of Visionary Companies* (New York: HarperBusiness, 1994); and James C. Collins, "Change is Good—But First Know What Should Never Change," *Fortune* (May 29, 1995): 141.
3. T. E. Deal and A. A. Kennedy, *The New Corporate Cultures: Revitalizing the Workforce after Downsizing, Mergers, and Reengineering* (Perseus Books, 1999).
4. Edgar H. Schein, "Organizational Culture," *American Psychologist* 45, no. 2 (February 1990): 109–119.

5. Yoash Wiener, "Forms of Value Systems: A Focus on Organizational Effectiveness and Culture Change and Maintenance," *Academy of Management Review* 13 (1988): 534–545; V. Lynne Meek, "Organizational Culture: Origins and Weaknesses," Organization Studies 9 (1988): 453–473; and John J. Sherwood, "Creating Work Cultures with Competitive Advantage," *Organizational Dynamics* (Winter 1988): 5–27.

6. W. Jack Duncan, "Organizational Culture: Getting a 'Fix' on an Elusive Concept," *Academy of Management Executive* 3 (1989): 229–236; Linda Smircich, "Concepts of Culture and Organizational Analysis," *Administrative Science Quarterly* 28 (1983): 339–358; and Andrew D. Brown and Ken Starkey, "The Effect of Organizational Culture on Communication and Information," *Journal of Management Studies* 31, no. 6 (November 1994): 807–828.

7. Schein, "Organizational Culture."

8. This discussion of the levels of culture is based on Edgar H. Schein, *Organizational Culture and Leadership*, 2nd ed. (San Francisco: Jossey-Bass, 1992), 3–27.

9. John P. Kotter and James L. Heskett, *Corporate Culture and Performance* (New York: The Free Press, 1992), 6.

10. Peter B. Scott-Morgan, "Barriers to a High-Performance Business," *Management Review* (July 1993): 37–41.

11. Arthur Ciancutti and Thomas Steding, "Trust Fund," *Business 2.0* (June 13, 2000): 105–117.

12. Daniel Roth, "My Job at the Container Store," *Fortune* (January 10, 2000): 74–78; and Robert Levering and Milton Moskowitz, "The 100 Best Companies to Work For," *Fortune* (January 20, 2003): 127–152.

13. Charles A. O'Reilly III and Jeffrey Pfeffer, "PSS World Medical: Opening the Books Boosts Commitment and Performance," *Journal of Organizational Excellence* (Spring, 2001): 65–80.

14. Bernard Arogyaswamy and Charles M. Byles, "Organizational Culture: Internal and External Fits," *Journal of Management* 13 (1987): 647–659.

15. Anita Raghavan, Kathryn Kranhold, and Alexei Barrionuevo, "Full Speed Ahead: How Enron Bosses Created a Culture of Pushing Limits," *The Wall Street Journal,* August 26, 2002, A1, A7.

16. Kotter and Heskett, *Corporate Culture and Performance.*

17. Roger O. Crockett, "A New Company Called Motorola," *BusinessWeek* (April 17, 2000): 86ff.

18. Ralph H. Kilmann, Mary J. Saxton, Roy Serpa, and Associates, *Gaining Control of the Corporate Culture* (San Francisco: Jossey-Bass, 1985).

19. Larry Mallak, "Understanding and Changing Your Organization's Culture, *Industrial Management* (March–April 2001): 18–24.

20. Oren Harari, "Curing the M&A Madness," *Management Review* (July/August 1997): 53–56; Morty Lefkoe, "Why So Many Mergers Fail," *Fortune* (June 20, 1987): 113–114.

21. Edward O. Welles, "Mis-Match," *Inc.* (June 1994): 70–79; Thomas A. Stewart, "Rate Your Readiness to Change," *Fortune* (February 7, 1994): 106–110.

22. Richard Osborne, "Kingston's Family Values," *Industry Week*, August 13, 2001, 51–54.

23. Harrison M. Trice and Janice M. Beyer, "Studying Organizational Culture Through Rites and Ceremonials," *Academy of Management Review* 9 (1984): 653–669.

24. Alan Farnham, "Mary Kay's Lessons in Leadership," *Fortune* (September 20, 1993): 68–77.

25. Robert E. Quinn and Gretchen M. Spreitzer, "The Road to Empowerment: Seven Questions Every Leader Should Consider," *Organizational Dynamics* (Autumn 1997): 37–49.

26. Joan O'C. Hamilton, "Why Rivals Are Quaking As Nordstrom Heads East," *BusinessWeek* (June 15, 1987): 99–100.

27. Thomas A. Stewart, "The Cunning Plots of Leadership," *Fortune* (September 7, 1998): 165–166.

28. David Beardsley, "This Company Doesn't Brake for (Sacred) Cows," *Fast Company* (August 1998): 66–68.

29. Melanie Warner, "Confessions of a Control Freak," *Fortune* (September 4, 2000): 130–140.

30. "About Lilly: Overview: Our Values," *http://www.lilly.com/about/overview/ values.html* accessed on August 9, 2000.

31. Gerald E. Ledford, Jr., Jon R. Wendenhof, and James T. Strahley, "Realizing a Corporate Philosophy," *Organizational Dynamics* 23, no. 3, (Winter 1995): 5–19.

32. Salter, "The Problem with Most Banks."

33. Stephanie Gruner, "Lasting Impressions," *Inc.* (July 1998): 126.

34. Deanne N. Den Hartog, Jaap J. Van Muijen, and Paul L. Koopman, "Linking Transformational Leadership and Organizational Culture," *The Journal of Leadership Studies* 3, no. 4 (1996): 68–83; and Schein, "Organizational Culture."

35. Stratford Sherman, "Levi's: As Ye Sew, So Shall Ye Reap," *Fortune* (May 12, 1997): 104–116.

36. Marc Ballon, "The Cheapest CEO in America," *Inc.* (October 1997): 53–61; and *http://www.fastenal.com*, accessed on November 21, 2000.

37. Bill Munck, "Changing a Culture of Face Time," *Harvard Business Review* (November 2001): 125–131.

38. Ram Charan and Jerry Useem, "Why Companies Fail," *Fortune* (May 27, 2002): 50–62.

39. Jennifer A. Chatman and Karen A. Jehn, "Assessing the Relationship Between Industry Characteristics and Organizational Culture: How Different Can You Be?" *Academy of Management Journal* 37, no. 3 (1994): 522–553.

40. James R. Detert, Roger G. Schroeder, and John J. Mauriel, "A Framework for Linking Culture and Improvement Initiatives in Organizations," *Academy of Management Review* 25, no. 4 (2000): 850–863.

41. Paul McDonald and Jeffrey Gandz, "Getting Value from Shared Values," *Organizational Dynamics* 21, no. 3 (Winter 1992): 64–76; Daniel R. Denison and Aneil K. Mishra, "Toward a Theory of Organizational Culture and Effectiveness," *Organization Science* 6, no. 2 (March–April 1995): 204–223.

42. Joel Hoekstra, "3M's Global Grip," *WorldTraveler* (May 2000): 31–34; and Thomas A. Stewart, "3M Fights Back," *Fortune* (February 5, 1996): 94–99.

43. Robert Hooijberg and Frank Petrock, "On Cultural Change: Using the Competing Values Framework to Help Leaders Execute a Transformational Strategy," *Human Resource Management* 32, no. 1 (1993): 29–50.

44. Warner, "Confessions of a Control Freak."

45. Ellyn Spragins, Is This the Best Company to Work for Anywhere?" *FSB* (November 2002): 66–70.

46. Carey Quan Jelernter, "Safeco: Success Depends Partly on Fitting the Mold," *Seattle Times* (June 5, 1986), D8.

47. Bill Breen, "How EDS Got Its Groove Back," *Fast Company* (October 2001): 106–116.

48. Michael Arndt, "How Does Harry Do It?" *BusinessWeek* (July 22, 2002): 66–67.

49. Gordon F. Shea, *Practical Ethics* (New York: American Management Association, 1988); and Linda Klebe Treviño, "Ethical Decision Making in Organizations: A Person-Situation Interactionist Model," *Academy of Management Review* 11 (1986): 601–617.

50. Dawn-Marie Driscoll, "Don't Confuse Legal and Ethical Standards," *Business Ethics* (July/August 1996): 44.

51. Alison Boyd, "Employee Traps—Corruption in the Workplace," *Management Review* (September 1997): 9.

52. Robert J. House, Andre Delbecq, and Toon W. Taris, "Values-Based Leadership: An Integrated Theory and an Empirical Test" (Working Paper).

53. Lawrence Kohlberg, "Moral Stages and Moralization: The Cognitive-Developmental Approach," in *Moral Development and Behavior: Theory, Research, and Social Issues*, T. Likona, ed. (New York: Holt, Rinehart & Winston, 1976): 31–53; and Jill W. Graham, "Leadership, Moral Development, and Citizenship Behavior," *Business Ethics Quarterly* 5, no. 1, (January 1995): 43–54.

54. "Corporate Ethics: A Prime Business Asset," The Business Roundtable, 200 Park Avenue, Suite 2222, New York, NY 10166, February 1988.

55. Linda Klebe Treviño, Gary R. Weaver, David G. Gibson, and Barbara Ley Toffler, "Managing Ethics and Legal Compliance: What Works and What Hurts?" *California Management Review* 41, no. 2 (Winter 1999): 131–151.

56. Linda K. Treviño and Katherine A. Nelson, *Managing Business Ethics: Straight Talk about How to Do It Right*, (New York: Wiley , 1995), 201.

57. Alan Yuspeh, "Do the Right Thing," *CIO* (August 1, 2000): 56–58; and Beverly Geber, "The Right and Wrong of Ethics Offices," *Training* (October 1995): 102–118.

58. Mark Henricks, "Ethics in Action," *Management Review* (January 1995): 53–55.

59. Jennifer Reese, "Starbucks: Inside the Coffee Cult," *Fortune* (December 9, 1996): 190–200.

60. Linda Klebe Treviño and Katherine A. Nelson, *Managing Business Ethics: Straight Talk about How to Do It Right*, 2nd ed. (New York: John Wiley & Sons, Inc., 1999): 274–283.

61. Eugene Garaventa, "*An Enemy of the People* by Henrik Ibsen: The Politics of Whistle-Blowing," *Journal of Management Inquiry* 3, no. 4 (December 1994): 369–374; and Marcia P. Miceli and Janet P. Near, "Whistleblowing: Reaping the Benefits," *Academy of Management Executive* 8, no. 3 (1994), 65–74.

Chapter

Your Leadership Challenge

After reading this chapter, you should be able to:

- Trace the evolution of leadership through four eras to the learning leadership required in many organizations today.

- Recognize how leaders build learning organizations through changes in structure, tasks, systems, strategy, and culture.

- Know when and how horizontally organized structures provide advantages over vertical, functionally organized ones.

- Distinguish between tasks and roles and how each impacts employee satisfaction and organizational performance.

- Meet the dual challenge of supporting both efficiency and learning by using ambidextrous organization design elements, embracing technology, and using after-action reviews.

15 Designing and Leading a Learning Organization

Cementos Mexicanos (Cemex) specializes in developing areas of the world—places where anything can, and usually does, go wrong. To cope with the extreme complexity of their business, CEO Lorenzo Zambrano and other leaders developed a new approach to delivering cement, which they call "living with chaos." Rather than trying to change the customers, the weather, the traffic, or the labor conditions, Cemex designed a company in which last-minute changes and unexpected problems are routine.

A core element of the new approach is the company's complex information technology infrastructure, which includes a global positioning satellite system and on-board computers in all delivery trucks that are continuously fed with streams of day-to-day data on customer orders, production schedules, traffic problems, weather conditions, and so forth. Even more important are changes in how employees think about and do their work. All drivers and dispatchers (many of whom had only a sixth-grade education) attended weekly secondary education classes for two years. Regular training in quality, customer service, and computer skills continues, with Cemex devoting at least 8 percent of total work time to employee training and development. Strict and demanding work rules have been abolished so that workers have more discretion and responsibility for identifying and solving problems. As a result, Cemex trucks now operate as self-organizing business units, run by well-trained employees who think like businesspeople. According to Francisco Perez, operations manager at Cemex in Guadalajara, "They used to think of themselves as drivers. But anyone can deliver concrete. Now our people know that they're delivering a service that the competition cannot deliver."

Cemex has transformed the industry by combining extensive networking technology with a new leadership approach that taps into the mindpower of everyone in the company. People at Cemex are constantly learning—on the job, in training classes, and through visits to other organizations. As a result, the company has a startling capacity to anticipate customer needs, solve problems, and innovate quickly. As a learning organization, Cemex thrives on constant change in a world of complexity.[1]

Organizations, like biological species, must adapt in order to survive. In a stable environment, many companies developed into highly structured systems with strong vertical hierarchies, specialized jobs, and formal information and control systems. However, these organizations do not work in today's fast-shifting environment, and many leaders are struggling to transform their organizations into more flexible systems capable of continuous learning and adaptation. This requires a new approach to leadership. This chapter will first trace the evolution of leadership thought and action, culminating in a discussion of leadership for learning organizations. In learning organizations, leaders treat the organization as a living system and find ways to encourage adaptive learning. We will examine the adaptive learning cycle and then compare traditional organizations that were designed for efficient performance with new organizational forms that emphasize learning, flexibility, and rapid response. We compare five elements of organization design—structure, tasks, systems, strategy, and culture—and then look at some specific mechanisms leaders use to move organizations toward greater learning. Changes in technology and the global environment are driving a need for a new kind of organization and a new way of leading.

The Evolution of Leadership

Many of our concepts of leadership emerged during times of stability, or at least when people believed the world was stable and could be predicted and controlled with logic and rationality. The concepts and organizational forms created during this more stable era still shape the design of many organizations and the training of managers. However, leaders in today's fast-shifting world stand at the threshold of a new era, and they are learning to free themselves from outdated practices and patterns to meet new challenges.

Context of Organizational Leadership

Leadership is directly related to the leader's way of thinking about self, followers, organizations, and the environment. The evolution of leadership thought and action has unfolded in four eras, which we will discuss by looking at two dimensions: whether leadership works on a *micro* level or a *macro* level, and whether environmental conditions are *stable* or *chaotic*.[2]

The micro side of leadership concerns specific situations, specific tasks, and specific individuals. The focus is on one person and one task at a time, and on the processes and behaviors needed to reach certain goals. This is a logical, objective approach to leadership. The macro side of leadership transcends individuals, groups, and specific situations to focus on whole communities, whole organizations, and deeply fundamental ideals, values, and strategies. It is concerned with purpose, strategy, meaning, and culture. Rather than relying on rules, directions, or controls, the leader focuses on building relationships.

The stable versus chaotic dimension refers to whether elements in the environment are dynamic. An environment is stable if it remains the same over a number of months or years. People can expect history to repeat itself—what worked yesterday will work again tomorrow. Under chaotic conditions, though, environmental elements shift abruptly and unpredictably. Leaders learn to support risk and learning. Their work involves creating a vision and strategy, inspiring and empowering others, and keeping everyone focused in the same direction.

Framework

These two dimensions are combined into a framework for examining the evolution of leadership, as illustrated in Exhibit 15.1. Each cell in the model summarizes an era of leadership thinking that may have been correct for its time but may be inappropriate for today's world.

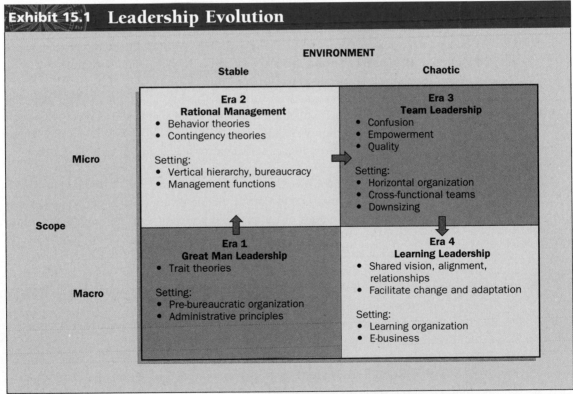

Exhibit 15.1   Leadership Evolution

SOURCE: Thanks to Bob Lengel for creating this model. Adapted with permission of the publisher from Richard L. Daft and Robert H. Lengel, *Fusion Leadership: Unlocking the Subtle Forces that Change People and Organizations*, 1998, Berrett-Koehler Publishers, Inc. San Francisco, CA. All rights reserved.

Macro Leadership in a Stable World *Era 1* may be conceptualized as pre-industrial and pre-bureaucratic. Most organizations were small and were run by a single individual who many times hired workers because they were friends or relatives, not necessarily because of their skills or qualifications. The size and simplicity of organizations and the stable nature of the environment made it easy for a single person to understand the big picture, coordinate and control all activities, and keep things on track. This is the era of Great Man leadership and the emphasis on personal traits of leaders, which we described in Chapter 2 of this book. A leader was conceptualized as a single hero who saw the big picture and how everything fit into a whole.

Micro Leadership in a Stable World In *Era 2*, we have the emergence of hierarchy and bureaucracy. Although the world remains stable, organizations have begun to grow so large that they require rules and standard procedures to ensure that activities are performed efficiently and effectively. Hierarchy of authority provides a sensible mechanism for supervision and control of workers, and decisions once based on rules of thumb or tradition are replaced with precise procedures. This era sees the rise of the "rational manager" who directs and controls others using an impersonal approach. Employees aren't expected to think for themselves; they are expected to do as they're told, follow rules and procedures, and accomplish specific tasks. The focus is on details rather than the big picture.

The rational manager was well-suited to a stable environment. The idea that leaders could analyze their situation, develop careful plans, and control what happened with the organization was quite compelling, but, as we discussed in Chapter 1, rational management is no longer sufficient for leadership in today's world.

Micro Leadership in a Chaotic World *Era 3* represented a tremendous shock to managers in North America and Europe. Suddenly, the world was no longer stable, and the prized techniques of rational management were no longer successful. Beginning with the OPEC oil embargo of 1972 to 1973 and continuing with the severe global competition of the 1980s and early 1990s, many managers saw that environmental conditions had become chaotic. The Japanese began to dominate world commerce with their ideas of team leadership and superb quality. This became an era of great confusion for leaders. They tried team-based approaches, downsizing, reengineering, quality programs, and empowerment as ways to improve performance and get more motivation and commitment from employees.

This is the era of the team leader. Many of today's leaders have become comfortable with ideas of team leadership, empowerment, diversity, and open communication. However, some are still trapped in old ways of thinking, trying to use rational management for a stable world when their organizations and the environment have already moved on.

Macro Leadership in a Chaotic World Enter the digital information age. It seems that everything is changing, and changing fast. *Era 4* represents the learning leader who has made the leap to giving up control in the traditional sense. Leaders influence others through vision, values, and relationships rather than power and control. They are constantly experimenting, learning, and changing, both in their personal and professional lives, and they encourage the development and growth of others. Learning leaders need resilience to flourish in an environment of chaos and uncertainty. Answer the questions in Leader's Self-Insight 15.1 to understand your current level of resilience to life's ups and downs.

Era 4 leaders also strive to create *learning organizations*, in which each person is intimately involved in identifying and solving problems so that the organization continues to grow and change to meet new challenges. This requires the full scope of leadership that goes far beyond rational management or even team leadership. Era 3 and Era 4 leadership is what much of this book is about. Specifically in this final section, we focus on the "big picture" skills that leaders need to be successful in this emerging era. Leaders can learn to stop managing details and instead focus on creating a vision and shaping the culture and values that can help achieve it. They develop relationships rather than relying on hierarchical control, building whole organizations as communities of shared purpose and information.

Learning leader
a leader who is open to learning and change and encourages the growth and development of others

Implications

The flow from Great Man leadership to rational management to team leadership to learning leadership illustrates trends in the larger world. The implication is that leadership reflects the era or context of the organization and society. Most of today's organizations and leaders are still struggling with the transition from a stable to a chaotic environment and the new skills and qualities needed in this circumstance. Thus, issues of diversity, team leadership, empowerment, and horizontal relationships are increasingly relevant. In addition, many leaders are rapidly shifting into Era 4 leadership, focusing on change management and facilitating a vision and values to transform their companies into learning organizations.

The Adaptive Learning Cycle

Learning is not just something students do in response to teachers in a classroom. Many of us remember learning something that was particularly interesting or challenging for us—how to ride a horse, drive a straight shift automobile, or play the guitar. However, we don't consciously realize the subtle learning that goes on every day. What is learning? And why do some individuals and organizations learn faster and better than others?

LEADER'S SELF-INSIGHT 15.1

How Resilient Are You?

Rate yourself from 1 to 5 on the following: (1 = Very little, 5 = Very strong)

	Very little				Very strong
1. Very resilient. Adapt quickly. Good at bouncing back from difficulties.	1	2	3	4	5
2. Optimistic, see difficulties as temporary, expect to overcome them and have things turn out well.	1	2	3	4	5
3. In a crisis I calm myself and focus on taking useful actions.	1	2	3	4	5
4. Good at solving problems logically.	1	2	3	4	5
5. Can think up creative solutions to challenges. Trust intuition.	1	2	3	4	5
6. Playful, find the humor, laugh at self, chuckle.	1	2	3	4	5
7. Curious, ask questions, want to know how things work, experiment.	1	2	3	4	5
8. Constantly learn from experience and from the experiences of others.	1	2	3	4	5
9. Very flexible. Feel comfortable with inner complexity (trusting and cautious, unselfish and selfish, optimistic and pessimistic, etc.).	1	2	3	4	5
10. Anticipate problems to avoid them and expect the unexpected.	1	2	3	4	5
11. Able to tolerate ambiguity and uncertainty about situations.	1	2	3	4	5
12. Feel self-confident, enjoy healthy self-esteem, and have an attitude of professionalism about work.	1	2	3	4	5
13. Good listener. Good empathy skills. "Read" people well. Can adapt to various personality styles. Nonjudgmental (even with difficult people).	1	2	3	4	5
14. Able to recover emotionally from losses and setbacks. Can express feelings to others, let go of anger, overcome discouragement, and ask for help.	1	2	3	4	5
15. Very durable, keep on going during tough times. Independent spirit.	1	2	3	4	5
16. Have been made stronger and better by difficult experiences.	1	2	3	4	5
17. Convert misfortune into good fortune. Discover the unexpected benefit.	1	2	3	4	5

Scoring and Interpretation

Add up your scores from the 17 questions: _____
70 or higher—very resilient!
60–70—better than most
50–60—slow, but adequate
40–50—you're struggling
40 or under—seek help!

In a world that is changing faster than ever, one of the most important qualities a person or organization can have is *resilience*—the ability to bounce back, to thrive in the face of chaos and uncertainty. Some companies offer their employees resilience training. Resilience is an important characteristic for leaders in learning organizations, because they have to become comfortable with constant questioning and change. You can improve your resilience by practicing the qualities described in this list.

SOURCE: Developed by Al Siebert. Adapted from *The Survivor Personality* by Al Siebert, Ph.D. An explanation of the items can be found at Al Siebert's THRIVEnet Web site: http://www.thrivenet.com/ © Copyright 2001, Al Siebert, Ph.D.

Learning is a change in behavior or performance that occurs as a result of experience. Today's leaders look for ways to build and enhance learning capabilities in individuals and the entire organization. Exhibit 15.2 illustrates the adaptive learning cycle, a cycle of action, feedback, and synthesis that all living organisms share.[3] Every living thing survives by sensing the environment around it, responding with action, and correcting itself if feedback and synthesis indicate that previous actions were inappropriate. For a person, sensing the environment might include observing others, reading, or listening to sources of information. The individual then acts based on what he or she has observed, read, or heard. Feedback can be either positive or negative; by evaluating feedback and the consequences of his or her actions, the individual determines whether the actions led to the desired effect. When feedback causes a plant, animal, person, or organization to change its behavior, learning takes place. In simple terms, a puppy might learn not to use the bathroom in the house because it gets reprimanded or a child might learn not to touch a hot stove by being burned touching one.

Learning organizations "live" the adaptive learning cycle every day. Leaders encourage ongoing experimentation, taking risks, making mistakes, and changing. Adaptive learning can lead to new products, new services, and better ways of doing business that would be unlikely to emerge in companies that emphasize maintaining

Learning
a change in behavior or performance that occurs as a result of experience

Adaptive learning cycle
a cycle of action, feedback, and synthesis that all living organisms share

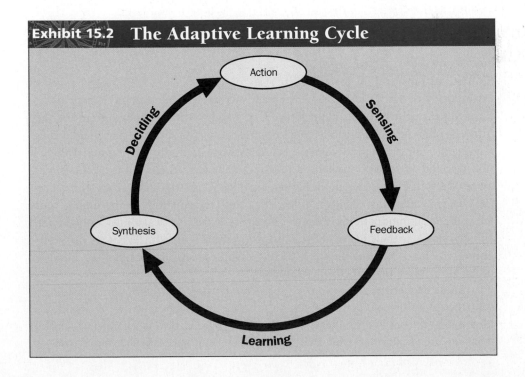

Exhibit 15.2   The Adaptive Learning Cycle

Action

Sensing

Feedback

Learning

Synthesis

Deciding

the status quo and avoiding risks. For example, SRC Holdings Corp., based in Springfield, Missouri, encourages adaptive learning through an educational mechanism called *The Great Game of Business*. Every year, leaders and employees together focus on a specific area of the business and look for changes and adaptations that eliminate weaknesses and make the company stronger. People are encouraged to experiment and take risks because that's where real learning occurs. Bonuses are awarded based on the outcome of the game. President and CEO Jack Stack and other leaders formulated the Great Game as a fun way to integrate learning into everyone's day-to-day activities.[4]

Arie de Geus, who studied companies that have survived more than a century, found that adaptive learning is a key to long-term organizational survival. De Geus argues that the reason the average life span of *Fortune* 500 companies is only about 50 years is because they focus so strongly on turning a profit that they shut down the feedback mechanisms that encourage learning and change.[5] Learning organizations keep feedback mechanisms open so they can evolve, adapt, learn, and grow. The Living Leadership box lists a few basic principles for leaders who want to encourage adaptive learning. Later in this chapter, we will examine some specific mechanisms leaders can use to encourage feedback and learning. First, let's see what a learning organization looks like by comparing its characteristics to those of organizations designed for efficient performance.

From Efficient Performance to the Learning Organization

Shifting an organization toward greater learning and change requires changes in organization design. When the environment was stable, leaders could effectively use rational management to maintain control and stability within the organization. They directed and controlled organizational resources toward following plans and achieving specific goals. At a time when the economy was based primarily on mass-production technology, routine specialized jobs and standardized control procedures were quite effective. Today, though, designing organizations strictly for efficient performance is generally not effective. Knowledge and information are becoming more important than production machinery. Some organizations deal almost entirely with "intangibles." As the CEO of software company Intuit, puts it, "What we do is pure mind. . . . There's nothing physical."[6] Thus, organizations need employees' minds as much as, or more than, their physical labor.

In this new environment, many leaders are redesigning their companies toward something called the learning organization, one in which everyone is engaged in identifying and solving problems. The learning organization is a model or ideal of what an organization can become when people put aside their habitual ways of

Learning organization

one in which everyone is engaged in identifying and solving problems

LIVING LEADERSHIP

Five Beliefs for Learning Leaders

Here are five beliefs that leaders who want to encourage adaptive learning can live by:

1. Failure is the opportunity to begin again with more experience.
2. Go out on a limb; that is where the fruit is.

3. Those who say it can't be done should not interfere with those doing it.
4. Opportunities come from knocking on doors until they open.
5. It is better to attempt great things and fail than to attempt nothing and succeed.

SOURCE: From Irwin W. Kabak, "Beliefs for Management: #10," *IM*, January–February 1995, 5.

thinking and remain open to new ideas and methods—when everyone throughout the organization is continuously learning. Learning organizations are skilled at acquiring, transferring, and building knowledge that enables the organization to continuously experiment, improve, and increase its capability. The learning organization is based on equality, open information, little hierarchy, and a shared culture that encourages adaptability and enables the organization to seize opportunities and handle crises. In the learning organization, leaders emphasize employee empowerment and encourage collaboration across departments and with other organizations. The essential value is problem solving, in contrast to the traditional organization designed for efficient performance.

Exhibit 15.3 compares organizations designed for efficient performance with those designed for learning by looking at five elements of organization design: structure, tasks, systems, strategy, and culture. Each of these five elements will be discussed in detail in the following sections.[7] The efficient performance organization is based on a hard, rational model and is characterized by a vertical structure, routine tasks, formalized systems, competitive strategy, and a rigid culture. The learning organization, on the other hand, emerges from a soft, intuitive perspective of organizations. Structures are more horizontal than vertical and employees are empowered to act independently and creatively rather than performing routine standardized jobs. Systems are fluid, based on networks of shared information. Strategy emerges from collaborative links within and among organizations, and the culture encourages experimentation and adaptability.

Organization Structure

The traditional organization structure, shaped like a pyramid with the CEO at the top and everyone else in layers down below, is a legacy that dates back nearly a century.[8] These vertical structures work well during stable times. However, they become

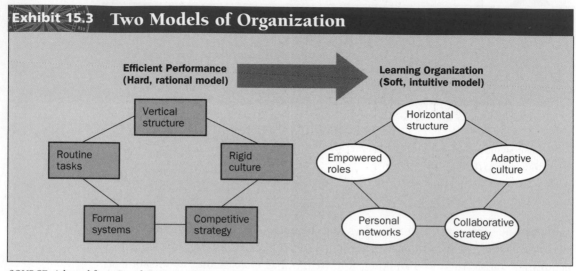

Exhibit 15.3   **Two Models of Organization**

SOURCE: Adapted from David K. Hurst, *Crisis and Renewal: Meeting the Challenge of Organizational Change* (Boston, MA: Harvard Business School Press, 1995).

a liability in a fast-changing environment. Hierarchical, vertical structures create distance between managers and workers and build walls between departments; they do not allow for the fast, coordinated response often needed in today's world. Many of today's organizations are shifting toward horizontal structures based on work processes rather than departmental functions. Exhibit 15.4 shows a simple illustration of the

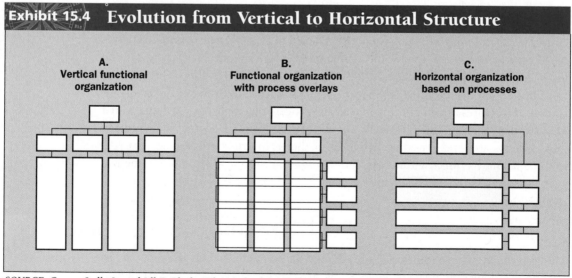

Exhibit 15.4   **Evolution from Vertical to Horizontal Structure**

SOURCE: George Stalk, Jr. and Jill E. Black, "The Myth of the Horizontal Organization, " *Canadian Business Review* (Winter 1994), 26–31.

change from the vertical to the horizontal organization. Most companies are somewhere in the middle of the evolutionary scale; few companies have shifted to an organization structure based entirely on horizontal processes.[9]

Vertical Structure

Traditionally, the most common organizational structure has been one in which activities are grouped together by common function from the bottom to the top of the organization, as shown in part A of Exhibit 15.4. For example, all engineers are located in one department, and the vice president of engineering is responsible for all engineering activities. The same is true for manufacturing, accounting, and research and development. Generally little collaboration occurs across departments, and employees are committed to achieving the goals of their own functional units. The whole organization is coordinated and controlled through the vertical hierarchy, with decision-making authority residing with upper-level managers.

The vertical, functionally organized structure can be quite effective. It promotes efficient production and in-depth skill development of employees. Hierarchy of authority provides a sensible mechanism for supervision and control in a large, complex organization. However, in a rapidly changing environment, the vertical hierarchy becomes overloaded. Decisions pile up and top executives cannot respond quickly enough to threats or opportunities. Poor coordination among departments inhibits innovation. Today, the vertical hierarchy and boundaries between departments are beginning to break down in many organizations.

Most companies maintain elements of a traditional structure but have found ways to increase horizontal communication and collaboration across departments. One popular trend is the use of project managers who coordinate the work of several departments in relation to specific projects, programs, or brands. Organizations are also increasingly using various types of teams, as described in Chapter 10.

Horizontal Structure

In learning organizations, the vertical structure that created distance between the top and the bottom of the organization is disbanded. Structure is created around workflows or core processes rather than departmental functions.[10] All the people who work on a particular process have access to each other so that they can easily communicate and coordinate their efforts, share knowledge, and provide value directly to customers. The claims process at Progressive Insurance provides an example. In the past, a customer would report an accident to an agent, who would pass the information to a customer service representative, who, in turn, would pass it to a claims manager. The claims manager would batch the claim with others from the same territory and assign it to an adjuster, who would schedule a time to inspect the vehicle damage. Today, adjusters are organized into teams that handle the entire claims process from beginning to end. One member handles claimant calls to the office while others are stationed in the field. When an adjuster takes a call, he or she does whatever is possible over the phone. If an inspection is needed, the adjuster contacts a team member in the field and schedules an appointment immediately. Progressive now measures the time from call to inspection in hours rather than the 7 to 10 days it once took.[11]

Self-directed team
___
team made up of employees with different skills who share or rotate jobs to produce an entire product or service

Self-directed teams, as described in Chapter 10, are the fundamental unit of the horizontal structure. Recall that self-directed teams are made up of employees with different skills who share or rotate jobs to produce an entire product or service. Boundaries between departments are reduced or eliminated. In a horizontal structure, the vertical hierarchy is flattened, with perhaps only a few senior executives in traditional support functions such as finance or human resources, as illustrated in part C of Exhibit 15.4. Traditional management tasks are pushed down to lower levels of the organization, with teams and process owners often taking responsibility for training, safety, scheduling, and decisions about work methods, pay and reward systems, and coordination with other teams. People on the team are given the skills, information, tools, motivation, and authority to make decisions central to the team's performance and are empowered to respond creatively and flexibly to new challenges that arise. In a horizontal learning organization, effectiveness is measured by end-of-process performance objectives (based on the goal of bringing value to the customer), as well as customer satisfaction, employee satisfaction, and financial contribution.

Experimentation with teams and horizontal organizing often begins at lower levels of the organization. Today, however, a few companies are structuring plants, divisions, or even the entire organization horizontally. For example, General Electric's Salisbury, North Carolina, plant shifted to a horizontal structure to improve flexibility and customer service.

In the Lead   GE Salisbury

General Electric's plant in Salisbury, North Carolina, which manufactures electrical lighting panel boards for industrial and commercial purposes, used to be organized functionally and vertically. Because no two GE customers have identical needs, each panel board has to be configured and built to order, which frequently created bottlenecks in the standard production process. In the mid-1980s, faced with high product line costs, inconsistent customer service, and a declining market share, leaders began exploring new ways of organizing that would emphasize teamwork, responsibility, continuous improvement, empowerment, and commitment to the customer.

By the early 1990s, GE Salisbury had made the transition to a horizontal structure that links sets of multiskilled teams who are responsible for the entire build-to-order process. The process consists of four linked teams, each made up of 10 to 15 members representing a range of skills and functions. A production control team serves as process owner and is responsible for order receipt, planning, coordination of production, purchasing, working with suppliers and customers, tracking inventory, and keeping all the teams focused on meeting objectives. The fabrication team cuts, builds, welds, and paints the various parts that make up the steel box that will house the electrical components panel, which is assembled and tested by the electrical components team. The electrical components team also handles shipping. A maintenance team takes care of heavy equipment maintenance that cannot be performed as part of the regular production process. Managers have become *associate advisors* who serve as guides and coaches and bring their expertise to the teams as needed.

The key to success of the horizontal structure is that all the operating teams work in concert with each other and have access to the information they need to meet team and process goals. Teams are given information about sales, backlogs, inventory, staffing needs, productivity, costs, quality, and other data, and each team regularly shares information about its part of the build-to-order process with the other teams. Joint production meetings, job rotation, and cross-training of employees are some of the mechanisms that help ensure smooth integration. The linked teams assume responsibility for setting their own production targets, determining production schedules, assigning duties, and identifying and solving problems.[12]

Action Memo

As a leader: Create a learning organization that can succeed in a turbulent environment by using the design elements of horizontal structure, shared information, empowered roles, collaborative strategy, and adaptive culture. In a stable environment, achieve efficiency by using a vertical structure, formal systems, routine tasks, competitive strategy, and a rigid culture.

Productivity and performance at GE Salisbury dramatically improved with the horizontal structure. Bottlenecks in the workflow, which once wreaked havoc with production schedules, were virtually eliminated. A six-week lead time was cut to two and a half days. More subtle but just as important are the increases in employee and customer satisfaction that GE Salisbury has realized since implementing its new structure. Breaking down boundaries between departments and hierarchical levels has enabled the plant to be faster and more flexible in meeting customer needs.

Learning organizations also strive to break down boundaries with other companies. Companies are collaborating in unprecedented ways to share resources and exploit opportunities. Emerging organizational forms, such as the network organization and virtual organization, are horizontal teams of companies rather than teams of individuals. Much like building blocks, parts can be added or taken away to meet changing needs.[13] In a network structure, a company keeps key activities in-house and then outsources other functions, such as sales, accounting, and manufacturing, to partner organizations or individuals. An example is Cunningham Motors, founded by former Chrysler executive Bob Lutz and Briggs S. Cunningham III, the son of racing legend Briggs S. Cunningham Jr. The partners wanted to create a luxury American sports car with a company of only 20 people. To accomplish that,

Cunningham Motors maintains control over the design of the cars, while everything else is outsourced to a vast network of chassis developers, parts makers, fabricators, manufacturers, transportation companies, advertising firms, and so forth. The company's plans call for producing only about 600 cars a year, so building a factory and staffing a huge organization didn't make sense.[14]

 # Tasks versus Roles

Task

a narrowly defined work assignment

Role

a part in a social system

Another response to today's rapidly changing environment is the amount of formal structure and control placed on employees in the performance of their work. A task is a narrowly defined piece of work assigned to a person. In a stable environment, tasks tend to be rigidly defined and employees generally have little say over how they do their jobs. A role is a part in a social system. A role has discretion and responsibility, such as the role of mother in a family or manager in an organization. An organizational role is an opportunity to use one's discretion and ability to achieve an outcome. In chaotic environments, employees need more freedom and responsibility to make decisions and react quickly to changing conditions. One way of considering the distinction between organizations designed for task performance and those designed for learning is through the concept of mechanistic versus organic work processes.

Mechanistic and Organic Processes

Tom Burns and G. M. Stalker use the terms *mechanistic* and *organic* to explain organizational responses to the external environment.[15] When the external environment is stable, the tasks tend to be mechanistic—that is, characterized by rigid rules, formal procedures, and a clear hierarchy of authority with decisions made at the top. Tasks are rigidly defined and are broken down into specialized, separate parts, as in a machine. Knowledge and control of tasks are centralized at the top of the organization, and employees are expected to do as they are told, not to make decisions about how to do it. In rapidly changing environments, on the other hand, tasks tend to be much looser, free flowing, and adaptive. Burns and Stalker use the term *organic* to characterize this type of organization. Leaders push authority and responsibility down to lower-level employees, encouraging them to take care of problems by working with one another and with customers. Teamwork is highly valued and there are few rules and procedures for how things should be done. Thus, the organization is more fluid and able to adapt to changes in the environment.[16]

Mechanistic tasks are characteristic of the efficient performance organization. The clearest example is a mass-production assembly line, where jobs are structured by standardization and division of labor into small, specialized tasks that are governed by formal rules and procedures. At a factory making blue jeans for example, one worker would cut the fabric, another would sew the seams, another fashion pockets, another would add rivets, another put in zippers, and so forth. Workers perform the same small job repetitively, thus little education or experience is needed. Employees are not expected to think for themselves or make any decisions about how they do their jobs. Routine tasks provide little satisfaction for employees, but structuring work into small, specialized tasks made sense in an era of mass-production manufacturing. It was an efficient way of getting the work done, and specialized techniques and procedures ensured reliable performance.

From Routine Tasks to Empowered Roles

Learning organizations use an organic form, an organizational architecture that is fluid and adaptable, with less clear job responsibilities and authority pushed down to the lowest level.[17] Employees play a role in the department or team, and roles are adjusted or redefined through employee interaction within and among teams. There are few rules and procedures, and knowledge and control of tasks are located with workers rather than top executives. Each individual is encouraged to experiment, learn, and solve problems within the team.

The idea of encouraging employees to participate fully in the organization is called empowerment. Empowerment means sharing power with everyone in the organization so they can act more freely to accomplish their jobs. As discussed in the Leader's Bookshelf, giving all employees freedom and responsibility spurs organizational learning and plays an important part in building successful companies. The trend today is clearly toward moving power out of the executive suite and into the hands of lower-level workers. Many of today's organizations are knowledge- and information-based rather than machine-based. Knowledge work relies on project teams and cross-functional collaboration that is inherently resistant to formal authority. Employees are also better educated and more willing to question their leaders. In the emerging learning organization, the leader's role is to give workers the information they need and the right to act on it.[18] Many companies have also shifted their production factories to a team-based system where employees have access to current information about order flows, output, productivity, and quality. Consider how Lucent Technologies plant manager Lynn Mercer did away with the traditional machine-based assembly line in favor of a system of teamwork, empowerment, and shared information.

Empowerment
sharing power with everyone in the organization so they can act more freely to accomplish their jobs

In the Lead   Lynn Mercer, Lucent Technologies

Phillip Dailey strings cables inside a steel box the size of a refrigerator—a digital transmitting station for cellular phone systems. Studying a bottleneck along the assembly line one day, Dailey realized a way to increase output by 33 percent. He didn't have to talk to his bosses about his insight; he simply recruited temporary workers from other teams and made it happen.

LEADER'S BOOKSHELF

Good to Great: Why Some Companies Make the Leap... And Others Don't
by Jim Collins

How and why do some companies move from merely good to truly great long-term perform-ance, while others can't make the leap—or if they do, can't sustain it? This is the question Jim Collins set out to answer in a six-year study that culminated in the book *Good to Great: Why Some Companies Make the Leap . . . And Others Don't*. Collins identifies 11 great companies—those that averaged returns 6.9 times the general stock market over a 15 year period—and compares them to a group of companies that had similar resources but failed to either make the leap or sustain it.

Great Leaders Build Great Companies
Collins identified a number of characteristics that distinguish great companies, but the pri-mary factor in establishing those characteris-tics is great leadership. Here are some of the key factors:

* *Level 5 Leadership.* All good-to-great com-panies begin with a top leader who exem-plifies what Collins calls Level 5 Leadership. Level 5 leaders are character-ized by an almost complete lack of per-sonal ego, coupled with a strong will and ambition for the success of the organiza-tion. They develop a strong corps of lead-ers throughout the organization so that when they leave, the company can grow even more successful. Values of selfish-ness, greed, and arrogance have no place in a great company.
* *The right values.* Leaders build a culture based on values of individual freedom and responsibility, but within a frame-work of organizational purpose, goals, and systems. People have the autonomy to do whatever it takes—within well-defined boundaries and clear, consistent guidelines—to move the organization toward achieving its goals and vision.
* *The right people in the right jobs.* Leaders of good-to-great organizations look for self-disciplined people who embody val-ues that fit the culture. These people are described using terms such as determined, diligent, precise, systematic, consistent, focused, accountable, and responsible. They are willing to go the extra mile to become the best they can be and help the organization continuously improve.
* *Knowing where to go.* Good to great com-panies base their success on a deep under-standing throughout the organization of three essential ideas, conceptualized as three intersecting circles: what they can be the best in the world at, what they are deeply passionate about, and what makes economic sense for the organization. This understanding is translated into a vision and strategy that guides all actions.

The Flywheel Concept
No company makes the leap from good to great in one fell swoop. The process is one of build-up followed by breakthrough, similar to pushing a giant flywheel in one direction, turn after turn, building momentum until a breakthrough is reached. Once leaders get the right people in the right jobs, support the right values, and focus on activities that fit within the three intersecting circles, people begin to see positive results, which pushes the flywheel to full momentum. As success builds upon success, the organization makes the move from good to great.

From Good to Great: Why Some Companies Make the Leap . . . And Others Don't, by Jim Collins, is published by HarperBusiness.

Lynn Mercer, plant manager at Lucent Technologies' factory in Mount Olive, New Jersey, distributes authority three levels down because she believes those people know the job better than she does. In two years, the factory's self-directed workforce of 480 employees hasn't missed a single delivery deadline, and total labor costs represent an exceedingly low 3 percent of product cost. Teams elect their own leaders to oversee quality, training, scheduling, and coordination with other teams. They all follow a one-page list of "working principles," but teams are continually altering the manufacturing process and even the product design itself. The process is so fluid that none of the manufacturing equipment is bolted to the floor. Engineers and assemblers bat around ideas, and the professional staff cubicles sit right next to the assembly cells to promote interaction. According to production manager Steve Sherman, "We solve problems in hallways rather than conference rooms."

The factory is flooded with information because Mercer believes that's how any complex system balances itself. Every single procedure is written down, but procedures are always changing—any worker can propose changing any procedure in the plant, subject to ratification by those whose work it affects. Operating statistics are displayed everywhere. Anyone with a few spare minutes consults an "urgents board" listing orders that are behind schedule, so they can jump in where they're most needed. Assemblers also work directly with customers by attending trade shows and installation sites as well as giving tours of the plant.

Yearly bonuses, based equally on individual achievement and team performance, can be equivalent to 15 percent of regular pay. However, for workers, the greatest motivator is that they have a role in shaping the organization. "This business has been handed to us," says technician Tom Guggiari. "This business is ours."[19]

Although many companies, like Lucent Technologies, are implementing empowerment programs, they are empowering workers to varying degrees, as we discussed in Chapter 8 on motivation.[20] When employees are fully empowered, they are given larger roles with decision-making authority and control over how they do their own jobs, as well as the power to influence and change such areas as organizational goals, structures, and reward systems.

Systems versus Networks

In young, small organizations, communication is generally informal and face-to-face. There are few formal control and information systems because leaders of the company work closely with employees in the day-to-day operation of the business.

Action Memo

As a leader: Network. Build a web of relationships with people inside and outside the organization. Openly share information and encourage others to do so.

Because the organization is small, it is easy for everyone to know what is going on. As organizations grow larger, they establish formal systems to manage the growing amount of complex information. In addition, information is increasingly used for control purposes, to detect deviations from established standards and goals.[21] Extensive formal reporting systems allow leaders to monitor operations on an ongoing basis and help them make decisions and maintain steady performance.

The danger is that formal systems become so entrenched that information no longer filters down to the people on the front lines who can use it to do their jobs better and serve customers. The informal grapevine often survives as a remnant of the days when information was freely shared among all employees, but its functioning is hampered by the lack of opportunity for personal interaction.[22] The learning organization strives to return to the condition of a young, entrepreneurial company in which all employees have complete information about the company so that they can identify needs and act quickly. In learning organizations, formal systems and structures play a much smaller part in how work gets accomplished. Instead, informal personal networks are the basis for sharing information and getting things done.[23] Rather than having most information controlled by managers, information is dispersed throughout the organization. People serve on teams and talk to whoever has the information they need. Everyone is responsible for networking, sharing information across boundaries, and reaching out to those who can further the goals of the team and organization. People who thrive in learning organizations are those who build extensive networks of personal and organizational relationships. You can evaluate your networking skills by completing the questionnaire in Leader's Self-Insight 15.2.

Leaders not only spend time networking with others inside and outside the company, but they understand and nourish the personal networks of other people throughout the organization. Exhibit 15.5 illustrates an informal communication network. Some people are central to the network while others play only a peripheral role. The key is that information flows freely across hierarchical and functional boundaries. For example, in the exhibit, David might be a manager and Sharon a shop foreman, but the network shows that people turn more frequently to Sharon for information or assistance because she has the skills and knowledge they need to solve problems.

Learning organizations encourage open communication, as described in Chapter 9. Knowledge is shared rather than hoarded, and ideas may be implemented anywhere in the company to improve the organization. People are valued and rewarded not just for what they know but for how much knowledge they share with others. Learning organizations also maintain open lines of communication with customers, suppliers, and competitors. Bringing outside people and organizations into communication networks enhances learning capability and the potential to better serve customers. A good example is Australia's Lend Lease Corporation, which is the country's leading real estate company and also involved in financial

Are You Networked?

Think about your current life as an employee or as a student. Please answer the questions below on the 1–5 scale based on the extent to which you agree that each statement applies to you: 5 = Strongly agree; 4 = Agree; 3 = Neutral; 2 = Disagree; 1 = Strongly disagree

	Strongly disagree				Strongly agree
1. I learn early on about changes going on in the organization and how they might affect me or my job.	1	2	3	4	5
2. I maintain personal contacts that keep me informed about industry trends.	1	2	3	4	5
3. I have clear beliefs about the positive value of active networking.	1	2	3	4	5
4. I am good at staying in touch with others.	1	2	3	4	5
5. I network as much to help other people solve problems as to help myself.	1	2	3	4	5
6. I am fascinated by other people and what they do.	1	2	3	4	5
7. I frequently use lunches to meet and network with new people.	1	2	3	4	5
8. I act as a bridge from my work group to other groups.	1	2	3	4	5
9. I regularly participate in charitable causes.	1	2	3	4	5
10. I maintain a list of friends and colleagues to whom I send Christmas cards.	1	2	3	4	5
11. I build relationships with people of different gender, race, and nationality than myself.	1	2	3	4	5
12. I maintain contact with people from previous organizations and school groups.	1	2	3	4	5
13. I actively give information to subordinates, peers, and my boss.	1	2	3	4	5
14. I make it a point to attend trade shows and company events.	1	2	3	4	5
15. I know and talk with peers in other organizations.	1	2	3	4	5

Scoring and Interpretation

Add the numbers circled for the 15 items above and divide by 15 for your average score: _____. An average score above 4 indicates that you are excellent at networking and will fit well in a rapidly changing learning organization. A score below 2 would suggest that you need to focus more on building networks or perhaps work in a slow moving occupation or organization.

Networking is the active process of building and managing productive relationships—a vast web of personal and organizational relationships. Networking builds social, work, and career relationships that facilitate mutual understanding and mutual benefit. Learning organizations accomplish much of their work through networks rather than formal hierarchies. People with active networks tend to be more effective change managers and have broader impact on the organization.

SOURCE: The ideas for this Self-Insight questionnaire were drawn primarily from Wayne E. Baker, *Networking Smart: How to Build Relationships for Personal and Organizational Success* (McGraw-Hill, 1994).

Exhibit 15.5   An Organizational Communication Network

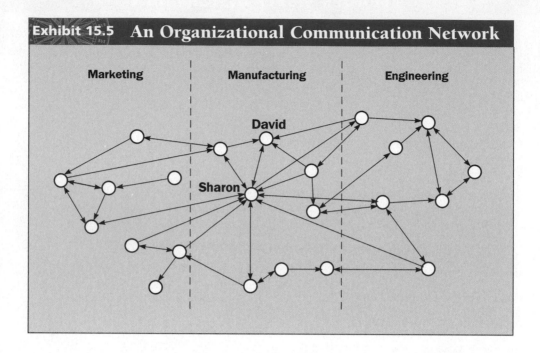

services, computer services, and other businesses. The goal at the beginning of any new project is to put together the best possible mix of mind-sets, skills, ideas, and experiences, which means bringing people not only from different functional areas and hierarchical levels but also representatives of outside stakeholders. The Bluewater shopping complex project in Kent, England, for example, involved a revolving collection of architects, engineers, managers, manufacturers, community advocates, local planning authorities, outside construction experts, retail-delivery specialists, financial analysts, and potential customers.[24] Even after a project is completed, many of these outside people continue to be a part of the informal networks that keep Lend Lease learning, growing, and adapting.

To promote the widespread sharing of information, learning organizations practice open-book management, which means that data about budgets, profits, expenses, and other financial matters are freely available to anyone. At Semco, for example, all employees regularly receive the company's financial statements and learn how to read them in classes organized in collaboration with the labor union. Board meetings are open to any employee who wants to attend. Ricardo Semler, head of the Brazilian firm, believes that when people are given complete information and freedom from strict rules and tight top-down control, they begin to think like business owners and act in the company's best interests.[25]

Open-book
management

sharing data
about budgets,
profits,
expenses, and
other financial
matters with
everyone in the
organization

Competitive versus Collaborative Strategy

In traditional organizations, top executives are responsible for strategy. Strategy is seen as something that is formulated and imposed on the organization. Leaders think about how the organization can best respond to competitors, cope with difficult environmental changes, and effectively use available resources. Research has shown that strategic planning positively affects an organization's performance.[26] Therefore, top executives often engage in formal strategic planning exercises or hire strategic planning experts to help keep the organization performing well.

In learning organizations, however, strategy emerges bottom up as well as top down. Chapter 13 discussed many of the elements of strategy in detail. A strong shared vision is the basis for the emergence of strategy in a learning organization. When all employees are linked with the vision, their accumulated actions contribute to strategy development. Since many employees are in touch with customers, suppliers, and new technologies, they identify needs and solutions and participate in strategy making.

Strategy can also emerge from collaborative partnerships with suppliers, customers, and even competitors. Learning organizations have permeable boundaries and are often linked with other companies, giving each organization greater access to information about new strategic needs and directions.[27] Grupo M, the largest private employer in the Dominican Republic, maintains open lines of communication with customers and suppliers, as well as employees, so the organization can stay on the cutting edge in the garment industry. Employee knowledge and the company's close ties with customers and suppliers helped Grupo M set a new strategic direction that is now spreading throughout the industry. Whereas garment manufacturers typically assemble garments from patterns, cut cloth, and designs provided by manufacturers, Grupo M takes a manufacturer's sketch and does whatever is necessary to transform the sketch into finished products that meet the customer's needs. The next step is "collaborative design." Rather than waiting for customers to provide sketches, a Grupo M team will offer top customers suggestions of styles, colors, and fabric samples for inspiration.[28]

Some learning organizations, like Cemex, described in the opening example, Springfield Remanufacturing, and Andersen Windows, also openly share information with competitors or allow competitors to visit and observe their "best practices." These leading companies believe the best way to keep their organizations competitive is through a mutual sharing of ideas.[29] Other companies go even further in forming strategy together. For example, the CEO of Advanced Circuit Technologies in Nashua, New Hampshire, formed a coalition of 10 electronics firms to jointly package and market noncompeting products. Member companies still conduct their own business, but they now can adopt a strategy of bidding on projects larger than they could deliver individually, and ask partners for services they can't do themselves. The coalition landed a job to design and build a specialized computer board that none of the companies could have handled alone.[30]

 # Rigid versus Adaptive Culture

As we discussed in the previous chapter, for an organization to stay healthy, its culture should encourage adaptation to the external environment. When organizations are successful, the values, ideas, and practices that helped attain the success become institutionalized. However, as the environment changes, those values may become detrimental to future performance. Many organizations become victims of their own success, clinging to outdated and even destructive values and behaviors because of rigid cultures that do not encourage adaptability and change.

One of the most important qualities for a learning organization to have is a strong, adaptive organizational culture. The learning organization reflects the values of adaptive cultures discussed in Chapter 14. In addition, a learning organization culture often incorporates the following values.

1. *The whole is more important than the part, and boundaries between parts are minimized.*[31] People in a learning organization are aware of the whole system, how everything fits together, and the relationships among various organizational parts. Therefore, everyone considers how their actions affect other elements of the organization. The emphasis on the whole reduces boundaries both within the organization and with other companies. The free flow of people, ideas, and information allows coordinated action and continuous learning.

2. *Equality is a primary value.* The culture of a learning organization creates a sense of community, compassion, and caring for one another. Each person is valued and the organization becomes a place for creating a web of relationships that allows people to develop to their full potential. Activities or executive perks that create status differences, such as reserved parking spaces or private dining rooms, are eliminated. At the Igus Inc. manufacturing company in Cologne, Germany, the walls separating the office area from the factory floor are transparent, to eliminate perceived barriers. There are no designated parking spaces for managers, and everyone comes in the same entrance, uses the same restrooms, and eats in the same cafeteria. Igus's factory was designed specifically with a goal of creating an open and egalitarian work environment.[32] The orientation toward equality and treating everyone with respect creates a climate of safety and trust that allows experimentation, frequent mistakes, and failures that enable learning.

3. *The culture encourages change, risk-taking, and improvement.* A basic value is to question the status quo, the current way of doing things. Constant questioning of assumptions opens the gates to creativity and improvement. The culture rewards and celebrates the creators of new ideas, products, and work processes, as well as sometimes rewarding those who fail in order to symbolize the importance of taking risks.[33]

In a learning organization, the culture encourages openness, boundarylessness, equality, continuous improvement, and change. No company represents a perfect example of a learning organization, but one excellent example of an organization that incorporates many of the elements of a fluid, adaptable learning system is Medtronic, Inc.

In the Lead   Bill George, Medtronic, Inc.

When Bill George took over as CEO of Medtronic, Inc. in 1989, it was a $1 billion company that primarily made and sold pacemakers. Twelve years later, it had grown to a value of $63 billion, with worldwide sales of $5 billion from a variety of cardiovascular, neurological, and drug-delivery products. Part of the reason is that George and his top leadership team focused everyone on the company's mission and created a structure, culture, and management system that encourage learning, innovation, and adaptability.

Rather than focusing on shareholder value, leaders at Medtronic align everyone's actions toward the mission of "restoring people to full life and health." To fulfil the mission, they have built an adaptable organization that empowers everyone to contribute, learn, and grow. The structure is based on teamwork rather than a rigid hierarchy. When George came to Medtronic, he felt that employees were too inward-looking and out of touch with customers. He broke down boundaries within the company and with customers by creating small, nonhierarchical teams of employees who work directly with customers and are empowered to come up with new ideas and bring them to fruition. Everyone is considered a "knowledge worker," with production teams doing their own quality control and helping to solve production problems. Physicians and other health care providers, as well as organizational partners, are an important part of Medtronic's communication networks and have an opportunity to contribute directly to the company' creative process and strategic direction.

Another key to learning at Medtronic is the egalitarian culture, which George believes is essential for innovation in a high-tech business. To build a culture where every idea—no matter where it comes from—is treated as equally worthy, George did away with executive perks and status symbols such as corporate cars, reserved parking spaces, and company-paid club memberships. Everyone at Medtronic is treated as an important member of a community. People are encouraged to network across boundaries, communicating with anyone inside or outside the organization who can help the company meet goals and fulfill its mission. Top leaders wander the research labs and production floors, talking with people and learning about creative ideas before they get unintentionally squelched by middle managers faced with budget constraints or lost in the rules and procedures that are needed for control of such a large organization. The company's Quest Program funds individuals with up to $50,000 to pursue creative ideas outside their basic job responsibility.

People at Medtronic are encouraged to tap into their passions for ideas that may lead to new products or administrative innovations. Risk-taking is rewarded, and failure is seen as a route to learning and adaptability. Rather than being fearful of change, Medtronic employees have learned to thrive on it because they see continuing change as the way to serve ill people with a broader range of health care needs. Even though George left as CEO in 2001, the learning environment he helped to create at Medtronic has remained strong and continues to help the company adapt in a volatile industry.[34]

The Leader's Dual Challenge

Ambidextrous organizations
flexible organizations in which leaders incorporate structures and management processes that are appropriate to innovation and learning, as well as to the efficient implementation of ideas

Leaders in learning organizations face a mighty challenge: to *maintain efficient performance* and *become a learning organization* at the same time. Companies must maintain an efficient performance remnant of traditional vertical organizations because they have a responsibility to both shareholders and employees to be competitive and profitable. Learning organization leaders find ways to meet this dual challenge, to support both efficiency and learning, order and change, competition and collaboration. This is achieved by balancing the soft and hard aspects of organizational design. Three leader approaches are to embrace both efficiency and learning in organization design elements, to embrace new technology, and to use a mechanism called the *after-action review*. These approaches facilitate the adaptive learning cycle described earlier in this chapter and enable leaders to foster learning and change at the same time they maintain discipline and efficiency.

Embracing Efficiency and Learning

One approach, called the **ambidextrous organization**, means that leaders incorporate structures and management processes that are appropriate to innovation and learning, as well as to the efficient implementation of ideas. The organization can behave in an organic, flexible way when the situation calls for creativity and the initiation of new ideas and a more mechanistic way to put those ideas to use. For example, Boeing Company purposely staffs its "moonshine shops" with mavericks who aren't afraid to break the rules. The moonshine shops work outside of the traditional factory structure and come up with unconventional approaches to help Boeing build planes faster, better, and less expensively.[35] Other companies set up separate *creative departments* that are organically structured but coexist in the organization with departments structured for discipline and control. One type of creative department is called a *skunkworks*. A skunkworks is a separate, small, informal group where talented people have the time and freedom to be creative and focus on developing breakthrough ideas for the organization. Establishing *venture teams* is another tactic. A venture team is like a small company within a large company. The team is given a separate location and facilities so they are not constrained by traditional organizational procedures as they work on a new project or idea.

The problem for traditional organizations is that rigid boundaries limit learning and change. Learning organization leaders work to replace the sense of concrete walls with permeable boundaries, both horizontally and vertically. All organizations need ways to control and direct resources, but leaders can build processes that also allow for collaboration, teamwork, and innovation.

Embracing New Technology

Even though the technology bubble of the 1990s has burst, the information technology revolution is alive and well. The number of Internet users and online sales continue to grow, and some remaining dot-com companies, such as Amazon and eBay, have become models of successful Internet organizations. Leaders in traditional companies are also using e-business to improve internal coordination, collaborate with partners, cut costs, increase productivity, and serve customers better. Nearly 90 percent of companies surveyed by Forrester Research Inc. in 2002 were involved in some kind of e-business activities, such as the use of intranets for keeping people in the organization connected, extranets for supply chain management and coordinating with partners, or Web sites and customer relationship management systems to improve service and expand markets.[36]

Technology can keep people all across the organization in touch. Networks of computers and the use of *intranets*—internal communication systems that use the Internet but are available only to people within the organization—rapidly get information to the right people at the right time. These systems play a key role in the emphasis learning organization leaders put on knowledge management. Knowledge management refers to the efforts to systematically gather knowledge, make it widely available throughout the organization, and foster a culture of collaboration and learning. At Boston's CareGroup Inc., a cluster of six hospitals and 3,000 doctors,

Action Memo

As a leader: Embrace both efficiency and learning in organization design. Incorporate mechanisms and departments that help the organization behave in an organic, flexible way for creativity and the initiation of new ideas, and a more mechanistic way to efficiently implement ideas.

Knowledge management

the efforts to systematically gather knowledge, make it widely available, and foster a culture of collaboration and learning

Action Memo

As a leader:
Use intranets,
extranets,
Web pages,
knowledge
management
systems, and
other new
technologies
to support
collaboration,
teamwork, and
information
sharing. Apply
technology to
create a sense
of community
among far-flung
employees,
customers, and
partners.

chief information officer Dr. John Halamka developed a knowledge management system that allows caregivers across the system to access complete information about every patient from birth to death. In addition, doctors can brainstorm with colleagues and get access to outside medical knowledge to solve a tough problem or confirm a diagnosis.[37]

Another way in which information technology contributes to learning is by creating a sense of community among far-flung people in today's global economy. One reason Amazon and eBay have been so successful is that they have created an interactive community of customers that gives people a chance to share information about their common interests. Amazon encourages buyers or browsers to write online reviews. At eBay, members rate their buying and selling experiences and participate in chat rooms, message boards, and a customer newsletter to share their passion for trading or their various hobbies.[38] Technology can bring suppliers, partners, customers, and perhaps even competitors into communication networks, expanding the company's potential for learning. Smart leaders also use the community-building potential of technology to foster collaborative, open, and inclusive relationships within the organization.[39] EBay, for example, emphasizes community as a core cultural value and leaders speak about the importance of trust, respect, and collaboration at orientations, staff meetings, and in their daily work with employees. The eBay Foundation, which donates to charitable causes that employees care about, is one way leaders build stronger connections among employees and between employees and the larger community.[40]

There are two main reasons that embracing technology spurs adaptive learning. For one thing, sharing information shares power. New technology enables leaders to share all information, not just part of it, so that people have access to whatever they need, whenever they need it. When employees are limited to certain areas of information, they are constrained in their thinking and decision making. Technology supports the extraordinary openness needed in a fast-changing environment, where advantage comes from seeing first and moving fastest.[41] A related advantage is that technology breaks down the rigid boundaries of a hierarchical pyramid to create a web of relationships—the organization becomes "a flat, intricately woven form that links partners, employees, external contractors, suppliers, and customers in various collaborations."[42] Open, web-like systems allow for ideas, decisions, and strategies to emerge from anywhere within or outside the organization.

Using After-Action Reviews

An essential element of the learning process is that people have time to reflect on what happened or did not happen in response to a particular action and why. When people review the experiences of the past, they learn valuable lessons for how to do things better in the future. Sometimes, with the emphasis on efficiency and productivity, there doesn't seem to be time for reflection. One approach leaders are using to solve this problem is the **after-action review** (AAR), a disciplined procedure whereby leaders invest time to help people review their events and activities on a regular basis and continually learn from them.[43]

An after-action review is held at the end of any identifiable event, with participants exploring the following questions: What was the intended outcome? What was the actual outcome? Why was the actual outcome different from that planned? What have we learned? An event can be something as small as a routine sales presentation or as big as a major construction project. For a small event, an AAR might last only a few minutes, while the AAR of a major five-year project could last a day or so. The key is that leaders invest the time on a regular daily basis and instill a spirit of inquiry, openness and learning. When leaders enlist the whole organization in reviewing the outcomes of activities and events, they can quickly learn what works and what doesn't and use that information to improve the organization. After-action reviews and the "lessons learned" system were originally developed by the U.S. Army, as illustrated by the following example.

After-action review (AAR)
a disciplined procedure whereby leaders invest time to help people review their events and activities on a regular basis and continually learn from them.

In the Lead   U.S. Army

At the National Training Center just south of Death Valley, U. S. Army troops engage in a simulated battle: the "enemy" has sent unmanned aerial vehicles (UAVs) to gather targeting data. When the troops fire upon the UAVs, they reveal their location to attack helicopters hovering just behind a nearby ridge. After the exercise, unit members and their superiors hold an after-action review to review battle plans, discuss what worked and what didn't, and talk about how to do things better. General William Hertzog suggests that such inexpensive decoy UAVs might be just the thing to make a distracted enemy reveal his location. The observation amounts to a "lesson learned" for the entire army.

In the U.S. Army, after-action reviews take just 15 minutes, and they occur after every event—large or small, simulated or real. The review involves asking four simple questions: What was supposed to happen? What actually happened? What accounts for any difference? What can we learn? It is a process of identifying mistakes, of innovating, and of continuously learning from experience. The lessons are based not only on simulated battles, but also on real-life experiences of soldiers in the field. The Center for Army Lessons Learned (CALL) sends experts into the field to observe after-action reviews, interview soldiers, and compile intelligence reports. The lessons learned are stockpiled and disseminated throughout the combat force in places like Bosnia, Afghanistan, and Iraq.[44]

Action Memo

As a leader: Conduct after-action reviews to accelerate adaptive learning. Compare actual to expected outcomes, consider what accounts for the difference, and think about what you can learn from the experience.

In this example, the organization is learning by applying feedback and synthesis to understand and learn from the consequences of field operations and simulated battles. Compiling what is learned creates an improved organization. As an organizational learning method, AARs are an ongoing practice rather than a special procedure."[45] The discipline has become a part of the Army's culture and an integral part of how the organization does business. Many business organizations are beginning to use after-action reviews as well. Steelcase Inc., an office furniture manufacturer, Harley-Davidson, and BP are among the companies adapting the system to create a process of continuous learning and improvement. BP credits the AAR system for ideas that led to $700 million in cost savings and other gains.[46] After-action reviews can spur greater learning for all types of organizations when they are integrated into the daily life of the organization as part of a culture that encourages people to continually ask questions, learn, and change.

 # Summary and Interpretation

This chapter traced the evolution of leadership thought and action, which reflects a shift from stable to chaotic environments. Early leadership perspectives emphasized great men and the traits that enabled them to succeed in government, commerce, the military, or social movements. The next era was rational management that fit the organizational context of vertical hierarchies and bureaucracies. Because of the world's transition to a more chaotic environment in recent years, team leadership became important, with its potential for enabling horizontal organizations and open communication. And finally, the most recent era is about learning leadership, in which leaders use the skills of vision, alignment, and relationships to unlock personal qualities of followers in adaptive, learning organizations.

Leaders can use an understanding of the adaptive learning cycle to encourage ongoing learning. The cycle of action, feedback, and synthesis means that people sense the environment and act on what they observe, then evaluate feedback to see whether actions led to the desired effect. Learning leaders encourage experimentation, taking risks, making mistakes, and reflecting because these activities lead to learning and change. To design learning organizations, leaders look at the five elements of structure, tasks, systems, strategy, and culture. For many of today's companies, these elements developed during a time when environments were stable and organizations were based primarily on mass-production technology. Characteristics such as a strong vertical hierarchy, specialized routine jobs, formal information and control systems, a directed competitive strategy, and a strong internal culture helped organizations perform efficiently and consistently. However, these organizations may no longer work in today's chaotic world.

Many leaders are transforming their organizations into something called the learning organization, a fluid, flexible system almost like a biological entity, capable of continuous learning and adaptability. Vertical structures and functional boundaries are replaced by self-directed teams organized around work processes. Boundaries between organizations are also becoming permeable, as even competitors collaborate to share resources and exploit new opportunities. In a learning organization, responsibility and authority are pushed down to the lowest level, and informal communication networks are the basis for sharing information and getting things done. Strategy, rather than being directed top-down as in a traditional organization, can emerge from anywhere in the learning organization. In addition, learning organizations develop cultural values that emphasize adaptation and change.

Today's leaders face a dual challenge to maintain efficient performance and become a learning organization at the same time. Leaders meet the challenge by building ambidextrous organizations that incorporate structures and processes appropriate to innovation and learning as well as to the efficient implementation of ideas. Other ways to support both efficiency and learning are to embrace new technology and use after-action reviews. Both of these approaches facilitate the adaptive learning cycle and provide ways for leaders to support learning and change at the same time they enhance the organization's efficiency and productivity.

Discussion Questions

1. Do you agree that the world of organizations and leadership is shifting to a new era? How do you feel about being a leader during this time of transition?
2. Think of a recent personal experience that illustrates the adaptive learning cycle. Do you think adaptive learning might affect some parts of an organization more than others? Discuss.
3. What are the primary differences between an organization designed for efficient performance and one designed for learning?
4. Discuss the primary reasons so many of today's organizations are empowering lower-level workers.
5. Discuss how bringing other organizations into a company's information network might contribute to strategy.
6. Why are cultural values of minimal boundaries and equality important in a learning organization compared to an efficient performance organization?
7. What is the difference between a task and a role? Between formal systems and personal networks? Discuss.
8. How can new technology be used to support and accelerate the adaptive learning cycle?
9. Do you think it is reasonable for a leader to conduct an after-action review for every identifiable event, large or small? Have you participated on a work, school, or sports team that used a process similar to that of the after-action review? How did it affect your learning?

Leadership at Work

In Which Era Are You?

To complete this exercise, first review the four leadership eras in Exhibit 15.1. Each era represents a distinctive leadership style for a distinct type of organization. The great man organization reflects a dominant leader's personality and values. The rational manager fits an organization that is designed for efficiency through vertical hierarchy, systems, and procedures. The team leader is suited to an organization that values horizontal teams and networks. The learning leader fits an organization that emphasizes learning and change over rules or efficiency.

Part A. Leaders and organizations today reflect all four eras. Your assignment is to categorize organizations and leaders you have known into the four eras. Write below the era in which you would place the following *organizations* and explain why:

Your family (in which you grew up): Era _____. Why?

_____

_____

_____

The organization in which you have the longest work experience: Era _____. Why?

_____

_____

_____

The university you attend(ed): Era _____. Why?

_____

_____

_____

A numbers-oriented (e.g., finance, statistics) course you have taken: Era _____. Why?

_____

_____

_____

A nonquantitative course (organizational behavior, sociology) you have taken: Era _____. Why?

_____

_____

_____

Part B. Your next assignment is to categorize people who have been in a leadership position over you. Write below the era in which you would place the following *leaders* in your life and explain why.

You: Era _____. Why?

_____

_____

_____

Your parents (individually if they used different styles): Era(s) _____. Why?

_____

_____

_____

The leader or leaders in the organization for which you worked longest: Era(s) _____. Why?

_____

_____

_____

The official (e.g., dean, department head, president) you were most aware of in a university you attended: Era _____. Why?

_____

_____

_____

The instructor in a numbers-oriented course: Era _____. Why?

_____

_____

_____

The instructor in a nonquantitative course: Era_____. Why?

_____

_____

_____

Review your answers. What did you learn about your family's leadership and organization? To what extent did your university, courses, and leaders reflect a learning leadership style? Why would that be?

In Class: The instructor can divide students into small groups to discuss their categorizations, particularly with respect to their families and work experiences. The instructor can ask for a show of hands and record the number of students who worked in an organization of each era, and the number of students who categorized their families in each era. The student groups often share similar university experiences so the group can rate the era for a common university, administrators, and courses. Some key questions for discussion: What is your insight from your group's discussion and categorization? What would happen when a leader's style is different from the organization in which the leader works (i.e., learning leader in a rational organization, or vice versa)? Why would universities or schools not operate in Era 4? What would it be like to work in an Era 4 learning organization? What would be required to move an Era 2 organization to Era 3 or 4? What would be required to move an organization from Era 1 to Era 4?

Leadership Development: Cases for Analysis

The Fairfax County Social Welfare Agency

The Fairfax County Social Welfare Agency was created in 1965 to administer services under six federally funded social service grants:

- The Senior Citizens' Development Grant (SCD)
- The Delinquent Juvenile Act Grant (DJA)
- The Abused Children's Support Grant (ACS)
- The Job Development and Vocational Training Grant (JDVT)
- The Food Stamp Program (Food)
- The Psychological Counseling and Family Therapy Fund (Counseling)

The agency's organizational structure evolved as new grants were received and as new programs were created. Staff members—generally

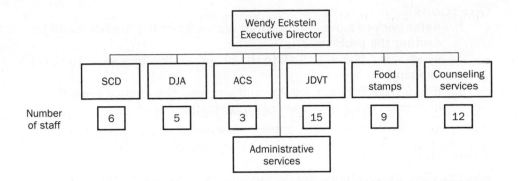

the individuals who had written the original grants—were assigned to coordinate the activities required to implement the programs. All program directors reported to the agency's executive director, Wendy Eckstein, and had a strong commitment to the success and growth of their respective programs. The organizational structure was relatively simple, with a comprehensive administrative department handling client records, financial records, and personnel matters. (See organizational chart above.)

The sense of program "ownership" was intense. Program directors jealously guarded their resources and only reluctantly allowed their subordinates to assist on other projects. Consequently, there was a great deal of conflict among program directors and their subordinates.

The executive director of the agency was concerned about increasing client complaints regarding poor service and inattention. Investigating the matter, Eckstein discovered the following.

1. Staff members tended to "protect" their clients and not refer them to other programs, even if another program could provide better services.
2. There was a total absence of integration and cooperation among program directors.
3. Programs exhibited a great deal of duplication and redundancy; program directors acquired administrative support for their individual programs.

Eckstein concluded that the client or program-based structure no longer met the agency's needs. A major reorganization of this county social welfare agency is being considered.

SOURCE: "The Fairfax County Social Welfare Agency," in 1998–99 *Annual Editions: Management*, Fred Maidment, ed. (Guilford, CT: Dushkin/McGraw-Hill, 1998), 78. Used with permission.

Questions
1. Refer back to Exhibit 15.3. What elements of the agency could be causing the problems?
2. In what era (Exhibit 15.1) do the program directors seem to be? Explain.
3. If you were Eckstein, how would you lead the agency toward becoming more of a learning organization? Discuss.

Acworth Systems

Richard Acworth feels his company slipping away. "How could something that was going so great suddenly turn into such a mess?" he mused. Acworth Systems helps companies design, install, and implement complex back-office software systems. Richard and his brother Tom started the company on a shoestring and within two years had 20 employees and nearly $5 million in revenues.

The brothers made a conscious choice to run the company with as few formal rules and procedures as possible. Richard and Tom both remembered what it was like to have to ask permission "every time you wanted to go to the bathroom," as Tom put it. They had a strong vision of a collaborative organization in which everyone shared the mission and goals of the company and put the good of the whole above individual interests. They spent long hours talking with one another and with trusted advisors to develop a corporate mission statement that outlined their philosophy of an organization built on mutual trust and respect. One thing they were intent on was that people shouldn't be constrained by rigid boundaries. Thus, Acworth had no formal organization chart, no job titles or descriptions, no close supervision, and very few rules. People were expected to decide for themselves, based on widely shared company information, how best to contribute to the mission and goals.

In the early days, everyone in the office would work on a project, but after the firm started getting more business, work was handled by shifting teams of employees. Although Richard and Tom participated in the hands-on work, each team made its own decisions about what it needed to get the job done—whether that meant buying more equipment, bringing in other team members, or consulting with another company. Everyone knew what everyone else was working on, so people could easily pitch in to help if a team ran into problems. Acworth employees were a close-knit group. Not only did they spend long hours in the office and working together at customer sites, but many employees also socialized together. Every once in a while, the Acworths would throw a party or cookout to reward everyone for a job well done.

But all that was before the growth explosion. Within 18 months, sales grew from $5 million to nearly $20 million and the staff grew from 20 to 100. Consultants who were constantly on the go began working out of their homes and keeping in touch with headquarters via phone and e-mail. Teams rarely called on one another for help any more. Everyone was so busy handling their own projects that they had little interest in anyone else's problems. The Acworths scheduled a few "all-hands" meetings to try to keep everyone focused on a common goal. The meetings seemed to bring people together for a while, but eventually, communication and collaboration between teams would decline again.

Richard and Tom have discussed the situation several times and both feel they're out of their league now that the company has grown so large. They miss the camaraderie of the early days and being able to pitch in with the hands-on work. Today, it seems like they spend most of their time trying to find out where the teams are and whether projects are on schedule. Richard finally contacted one of his former professors, who now runs a management consulting firm. Dr. Tyler told Richard and Tom that the first thing they needed to do was create some structure for the organization. Richard is confused. He thought all that stuff about organizational structure was for grandpa's company. "Today's organizations are supposed to be open and flexible, just like Acworth," he thought. "So why do I feel like the company is starting to come apart at the seams?"

Questions

1. What do you think is the primary problem at Acworth Systems?
2. What elements of a learning organization are evident at Acworth? What elements seem to be missing?
3. Do you agree that the Acworths need to create "some structure" for the organization? Discuss how they might do so.

References

1. Thomas Petzinger Jr., "In Search of the New World (of Work)," *Fast Company* (April 1999): 214–220+; Peter Katel, "Bordering on Chaos," *Wired* (July 1997): 98–107; and Oren Harari, "The Concrete Intangibles," *Management Review* (May 1999): 30–33.

2. The discussion of micro and macro is based on Ed Kur, "Developing Leadership in Organizations: A Continuum of Choices," *Journal of Management Inquiry* 4, no. 2 (June 1995): 198–206.

3. This discussion is based on Thomas Petzinger, Jr., *The New Pioneers: The Men and Women Who Are Transforming the Workplace and Marketplace* (New York: Simon & Schuster, 1999): 34–42; and Stephan H. Haeckel, *Adaptive Enterprise: Creating and Leading Sense and Respond Organizations* (Boston: Harvard Business School Press, 1999): 75–92.

4. Jack Stack, "A Stake in the Outcome," *Leader to Leader* (Summer 2001): 20–26.

5. Arie de Geus, *The Living Company* (Boston: Harvard Business School Press, 1997).

6. Geoffrey Colvin, "How To Be a Great eCEO," *Fortune* (May 24, 1999): 104–110.

7. Based on David K. Hurst, "Of Boxes, Bubbles, and Effective Management," *Harvard Business Review* (May–June 1984): 78–88; and *Crisis and Renewal: Meeting the Challenge of Organizational Change* (Boston: Harvard Business School Press, 1995): 32–52.

8. Alan Webber, "The Best Organization Is No Organization," *USA Today* (March 6, 1997), 13A.

9. George Stalk, Jr. and Jill E. Black, "The Myth of the Horizontal Organization," *Canadian Business Review* (Winter 1994): 26–31.

10. The discussion of the horizontal organization is based on Frank Ostroff, *The Horizontal Organization: What the Organization of the Future Looks Like and How It Delivers Value to Customers* (New York: Oxford University Press, 1999).

11. Michael Hammer, "Process Management and the Future of Six Sigma," *Sloan Management Review* (Winter 2002): 26–32.

12. Based on information in Ostroff, *The Horizontal Organization*, 102–114.

13. Kevin Kelly and Otis Port, with James Treece, Gail DeGeorge, and Zachary Schiller, "Learning from Japan," *BusinessWeek* (January 27, 1992): 52–60; and Gregory G. Dess, Abdul M. A. Rasheed, Kevin J. McLaughlin, and Richard L. Priem, "The New Corporate Architecture," *Academy of Management Executive* 9, no. 3 (1995): 7–20.

14. David Welch, "Bob Lutz: The First Virtual Carmaker?" *BusinessWeek* (June 18, 2001): 66–70.

15. Tom Burns and G. M. Stalker, *The Management of Innovation* (London: Tavistock, 1961).

16. John A. Coutright, Gail T. Fairhurst, and L. Edna Rogers, "Interaction Patterns in Organic and Mechanistic Systems," *Academy of Management Journal* 32 (1989): 773–802.

17. Stanley F. Slater, "Learning to Change," *Business Horizons* (November–December 1995): 13–20.

18. Thomas A. Stewart, "Get with the New Power Game," *Fortune* (January 13, 1997): 58–62.

19. Thomas Petzinger, Jr., "How Lynn Mercer Manages a Factory That Manages Itself," *The Wall Street Journal* (March 7, 1997): B11.

20. Robert C. Ford and Myron D. Fottler, "Empowerment: A Matter of Degree," *Academy of Management Executive* 9, no. 3 (1995): 21–31.

21. Hurst, *Crisis and Renewal*, 44.

22. Ibid.

23. For a discussion of informal networks, see Rob Cross, Nitin Nohria, and Andrew Parker, "Six Myths About Informal Networks," *MIT Sloan Management Review* (Spring 2002): 67–75; and Rob Cross and Laurence Prusak, "The People Who Make Organizations Go–or Stop," *Harvard Business Review* (June 2002): 105–112.

24. Polly LaBarre, "Company Without Limits," *Fast Company* (September 1999): 160–184.

25. Geoffrey Colvin, "The Anti-Control Freak," *Fortune* (November 26, 2001): 60, 80; and Ricardo Semler, "How We Went Digital Without a Strategy," *Harvard Business Review* (September–October 2000): 51–58.

26. C. Chet Miller and Laura B. Cardinal, "Strategic Planning and Firm Performance: A Synthesis of More than Two Decades of Research," *Academy of Management Journal* 37, no. 6 (1994): 1649–1665.

27. Marc S. Gerstein and Robert B. Shaw, "Organizational Architectures for the Twenty-First Century," in David A. Nadler, Marc S. Gerstein, Robert B. Shaw, and Associates, eds., *Organizational Architecture: Designs for Changing Organizations* (San Francisco: Jossey-Bass, 1992), 263–274.

28. Cheryl Dahle, "The New Fabric of Success," *Fast Company* (June 2000): 252–270.

29. Justin Martin, "Are You as Good as You Think You Are?" *Fortune* (September 30, 1996): 142–152.

30. Jessica Lipnack and Jefferey Stamps, "One Plus One Equals Three," *Small Business Reports* (August 1993): 49–58.

31. Mary Anne DeVanna and Noel Tichy, "Creating the Competitive Organization of the Twenty-First Century: The Boundaryless Corporation," *Human Resource*

Management 29 (Winter 1990): 455–471; and Fred Kofman and Peter M. Senge, "Communities of Commitment: The Heart of Learning Organizations," *Organizational Dynamics* 22, no. 2 (Autumn 1993): 4–23.

32. Chuck Salter, "This Is One Fast Factory," *Fast Company* (August 2001): 32–33.

33. Bernard M. Bass, "The Future of Leadership in Learning Organizations," *The Journal of Leadership Studies* 7, no. 3 (2000): 18–40.

34. Tim Stevens, "Heart & Soul," *Industry Week* (May 4, 1998): 44+; and Bill George, *Authentic Leadership: Rediscovering the Secrets to Creating Lasting Value* (San Francisco, Calif.: Jossey-Bass, 2003).

35. J. Lynn Lunsford, "Lean Times: With Airbus on Its Tail, Boeing Is Rethinking How It Builds Planes," *The Wall Street Journal* (September 2001): A1, A16.

36. Robert D. Hof with Steve Hamm, "How E-Biz Rose, Fell, and Will Rise Anew," *BusinessWeek* (May 13, 2002), 64–72.

37. Laura Landro, "Both Sides Now," *The Wall Street Journal* (June 10, 2002): R6, R12.

38. Katherine Mieszkowski, "Community Standards," *Fast Company* (September 2000): 368; Rosabeth Moss Kanter, "A More Perfect Union," *Inc.* (February, 2001): 92–98.

39. Kanter, "A More Perfect Union."

40. Ibid.

41. Thomas A. Stewart, "Three Rules for Managing in the Real-Time Economy," *Fortune* (May 1, 2000): 333–334.

42. John A. Byrne, "Management by Web," *BusinessWeek* (August 28, 2000): 84.

43. This discussion is based on David Gurteen, "Introduction to After Action Reviews," *http://www.gurteen.com/gurteen/gurteen.nsf/0/ E380DBA5E0F0CC0E80256836006B18A7/* accessed on March 21, 2003.

44. Thomas E. Ricks, "Army Devises System to Decide What Does, and Does Not, Work," *The Wall Street Journal* (May 23, 1997), A1, A10; Stephanie Watts Sussman, "CALL: A Model for Effective Organizational Learning," *Strategy* (Summer 1999): 14–15; and Thomas A. Stewart, "Listen Up, Maggots! You **Will** Deploy a More Humane and Effective Managerial Style!" *Ecompany* (July 2001): 95.

45. Marilyn J. Darling and Charles S. Parry, "From Post-Mortem to Living Practice: An In-Depth Study of the Evolution of the After Action Review," summary accessed at *http://www.signetconsulting.com/aarsum.html* on March 21, 2003.

46. Stewart, "Listen Up, Maggots!"

Chapter

Your Leadership Challenge

After reading this chapter, you should be able to:

- Recognize social and economic pressures for change in today's organizations.

- Implement the eight-stage model of planned major change and use everyday strategies for gradual change.

- Use techniques of communication, training, and participation to overcome resistance to change.

- Effectively and humanely address the negative impact of change.

- Expand your own and others' creativity and facilitate organizational innovation.

It wasn't easy to entice Bill Zollars to leave his job at Ryder, but the chance to create a new company out of one that had been in business for 70 years was too intriguing to pass up. Yellow Freight System was founded as a small, regional freight-hauling company and grew into a global enterprise with more than 300 terminals and 14 million shipments a year. But by 1996, Yellow was struggling. It had just suffered the worst year in the company's history, with $30 million in losses, a round of major layoffs, and a crippling teamster's strike.

Zollars signed on as CEO with a mandate—not just to revive the company's image in the long-haul transportation business, but to transform Yellow Freight into a completely different company. Today, Yellow is still in the business of hauling big, heavy freight, but how shipments are delivered and the mind-sets of the people doing the work have been totally altered. For years, Yellow was obsessively focused on internal efficiency, but it practically ignored the needs of customers. If someone called wanting a shipment delivered in two days, Yellow's call representative would usually say, "We can probably do it in three." Moreover, the shipment might show up when expected, or it might not. Today, Yellow's mantra is "Yes, we can." The company now offers one-stop shopping for a broad range of transportation needs. Customers, not Yellow's employees, decide when freight will be delivered—in a week, in two days, or in four hours—and Yellow makes sure it is delivered on time. Sophisticated and highly integrated information technology systems speed up order processing, manage customer relationships, monitor thousands of trucks and shipping orders, and facilitate rapid loading and unloading of trailers.

"We've gone from being a company that thought it was in the trucking business to one that realizes it's in the service business," Zollars says. Transforming employee attitudes and behaviors was not easy, however. When Zollars first came to Yellow, employees thought the company was just as good as any in the business. Even looking at hard facts evoked denial and resistance. Zollars spent his first 18 months traveling to terminals all over the country, many more than once, and meeting informally with employees on loading docks and sales offices to reinforce the vision of a customer-centric company. Today, Yellow hosts an annual conference called "Transformation," where employees and customers attend workshops on change. "You have to keep reinventing the company, because the market keeps changing," Zollars says. "If you don't, you end up coasting."[1]

Yellow Freight isn't the only company that has faced a need for dramatic change in recent years. Leaders in many organizations, from small companies to large, non-profit organizations, government agencies, and major corporations have had to reconceptualize almost every aspect of how they do business to meet the changing needs of customers or clients, keep employees motivated and satisfied, and remain competitive in a complex, global environment. Moreover, the rapidity of social, economic, and technological change in today's world means that organizations have to be perpetually changing to keep pace. As we discussed in the previous chapter, some companies are becoming learning organizations that are poised for continual change and adaptation. The pressing need for change management is reflected in the fact that many companies are hiring "transformation officers" who are charged with radically rethinking and remaking either the entire organization or major parts of it.[2]

Recall from our definition used throughout this book that leadership is about change rather than stability. However, in recent years, the pace of change has increased dramatically, presenting significant challenges for leaders. Many leaders today feel as if "they are flying the airplane at the same time they are building it."[3] The patterns of behavior and attitudes that were once successful no longer work, but new patterns are just emerging—and there are no guarantees that the new ways will succeed. Leaders are responsible for guiding people through the discomfort and dislocation brought about by major change.

This chapter explores how leaders guide change and transformation. We will first look briefly at the need for change in today's organizations and examine a step-by-step model for leading major change. We will also explore everyday change strategies, why people resist change, and how leaders can overcome resistance and help people cope with the potentially negative consequences of change. The final sections of the chapter will examine how leaders facilitate change by fostering creative people and organizations.

Change or Perish

Leaders in today's most successful organizations recognize that internal changes must keep pace with what is happening in the external environment. As Jack Welch, the former long-time chairman and CEO of General Electric, put it, "When the rate of change outside exceeds the rate of change inside, the end is in sight."[4] Organizations must poise themselves to change, not only to prosper but to survive in today's world. As illustrated in Exhibit 16.1, rapid technological changes, a globalized economy, changing markets, and the rise of e-business are creating more threats as well as more opportunities for organizational leaders.

A big problem for today's organizations is the failure to adapt to all these changes in the environment. Although there are many reasons for the failure to change and adapt, a primary solution to the problem is better change leadership. Leaders serve

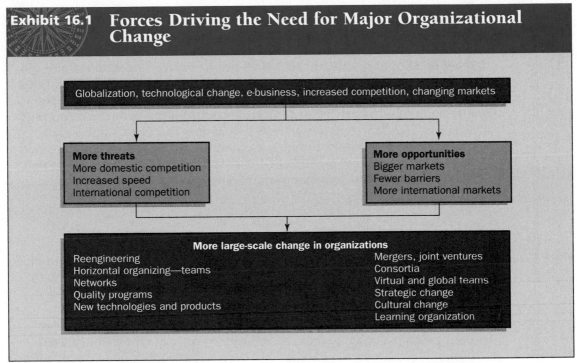

Exhibit 16.1 Forces Driving the Need for Major Organizational Change

Globalization, technological change, e-business, increased competition, changing markets

More threats
More domestic competition
Increased speed
International competition

More opportunities
Bigger markets
Fewer barriers
More international markets

More large-scale change in organizations

Reengineering
Horizontal organizing—teams
Networks
Quality programs
New technologies and products

Mergers, joint ventures
Consortia
Virtual and global teams
Strategic change
Cultural change
Learning organization

SOURCE: Adapted with permission of The Free Press, a division of Simon & Schuster Adult Publishing Group, from *The New Rules: How to Succeed in Today's Post-Corporate World* by John P. Kotter. Copyright © 1995 by John P. Kotter. All rights reserved.

as the main role models for change and provide the motivation and communication to keep change efforts moving forward. Strong, committed leadership is crucial to successful change, and research has identified some key characteristics of leaders who can accomplish successful change projects:[5]

* They define themselves as change leaders rather than people who want to maintain the status quo.
* They demonstrate courage.
* They believe in employees' capacity to assume responsibility.
* They are able to assimilate and articulate values that promote adaptability.
* They recognize and learn from their own mistakes.
* They are capable of managing complexity, uncertainty, and ambiguity.
* They have vision and can describe their vision for the future in vivid terms.

One leader who illustrates many of the characteristics of change leadership is Barbara Waugh of Hewlett-Packard.

In the Lead   Barbara Waugh, Hewlett-Packard

Barbara Waugh began her career at Hewlett-Packard Company in a mid-level personnel position at HP Labs—not the place one would think of for instituting massive change. Yet Waugh always identified herself as an agent for change and looked for opportunities to make things better. She had a vision that the organization could be the "world's best industrial research lab" and she activated dozens of people to talk about what that would mean and how it could be accomplished. She also had the courage to question and challenge senior executives, helping them do their jobs better by serving as a reality check for leaders who had gotten too far away from the day-to-day work of the organization. Waugh believes to be a change leader, "You have to always be willing to lose your job."

Waugh quickly developed a reputation for getting things done, and many people from various parts of the organization would come to her with problems. However, rather than solving the problems herself, Waugh helped each individual assume responsibility and take steps toward accomplishing their own change goals. For example, Tan Ha, a former Vietnamese refugee working at H-P Labs, regularly sent money to a Buddhist orphanage in Bangladesh, only to have the money disappear en route. When he learned about a new H-P project developing low-cost telecommunications and computing services for developing countries around the world, he contacted Waugh and asked her to do something about his money transit problems. Waugh told Ha that she couldn't solve the problem for him, but that she would help him take the steps needed to become personally involved in the project and make sure his concerns were addressed.

During her time in personnel, Waugh contributed directly or indirectly to numerous change projects, including new products, new mentoring relationships among engineers, and a 20 percent reduction in R & D development life cycles. Her passion and ability as a change leader eventually led her to a position as worldwide change manager at HP Labs.[6]

Change does not happen easily, but as illustrated by this example, good leaders throughout the organization can facilitate change and help their organizations adapt to external threats and new opportunities. In the following section, we will examine a model for leading major changes, and later in the chapter we will discuss how to overcome resistance to change.

Leading a Major Change

When leading a major change project, it is important for leaders to recognize that the change process goes through stages, that each stage is important, and that each may require a significant amount of time. Leaders are responsible for guiding employees and the organization through the change process.

Exhibit 16.2 presents an eight-stage model of planned change.[7] To successfully implement change, leaders pay careful attention to each stage. Skipping stages or making critical mistakes at any stage can cause the change process to fail.

1. At Stage 1, leaders *establish a sense of urgency* that change is really needed. Crises or threats will thaw resistance to change. At American Airlines, for example, employees are more receptive to leaders' transformation efforts because the airline has lost billions since 2001 and may not survive without significant changes in how it does business.[8] In many cases, however, there is no obvious crisis and leaders have to make others aware of the need for change. Leaders carefully scan the external and internal environment— looking at competitive conditions; market position; social, technological, and demographic trends; profit and loss; operations; and other factors. After identifying potential crises or problems, they find ways to communicate the information broadly and dramatically.

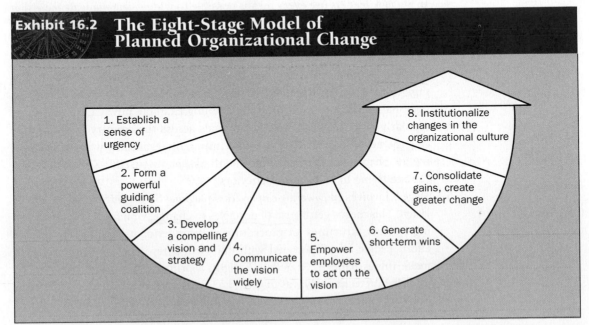

Exhibit 16.2   The Eight-Stage Model of Planned Organizational Change

1. Establish a sense of urgency
2. Form a powerful guiding coalition
3. Develop a compelling vision and strategy
4. Communicate the vision widely
5. Empower employees to act on the vision
6. Generate short-term wins
7. Consolidate gains, create greater change
8. Institutionalize changes in the organizational culture

SOURCE: John P. Kotter, *Leading Change* (Boston: Harvard Business School Press, 1996), 21.

2. Stage 2 involves *establishing a coalition* with enough power to guide the change process and then developing a sense of teamwork among the group. For the change process to succeed, there must be a shared commitment to the need and possibilities for organizational transformation. Middle management change will seek top leader support in the coalition. It is also essential that lower-level executives become involved. Mechanisms such as off-site retreats can get people together and help them develop a shared assessment of problems and how to approach them. At MasterBrand Industries, transformation began with an off-site meeting of some 75 key managers who examined the need for change and discussed ways to remake MasterBrand into a team-based organization.[9]

3. Stage 3 requires *developing a vision and strategy*. Leaders are responsible for formulating and articulating a compelling vision that will guide the change effort, and developing the strategies for achieving that vision. A "picture" of a highly desirable future motivates people to change. At SEI Investments, which started as a business making software for bank trust departments, CEO Al West had a vision of a new kind of financial services company that could quickly respond to customers' changing needs with new products and services. His vision included doing away with the old hierarchical organization chart and assigning all work to self-directed teams that work directly with customers.[10]

4. In Stage 4, leaders use every means possible to widely *communicate the vision and strategy*. At this stage, the coalition of change agents should set an example by modeling the new behaviors needed from employees. They must communicate about the change at least 10 times more than they think necessary. Transformation is impossible unless a majority of people in the organization are involved and willing to help, often to the point of making personal sacrifices. Recall from the opening example how CEO Bill Zollars regularly visited Yellow Freight terminals across the country to communicate the new direction. "Repetition is important, especially when you're trying to change the way a company thinks about itself," Zollars advises. "You're trying to create new behaviors."[11]

5. Stage 5 involves *empowering employees throughout the organization to act on the vision*. This means getting rid of obstacles to change, which may require revising systems, structures, or procedures that hinder or undermine the change effort. People are empowered with knowledge, resources, and discretion to make things happen. At Yellow Freight, a primary purpose of investing in information technology was to give employees on the front lines the information they needed to solve customer problems quickly. The management system was also changed to give employees freedom to make decisions themselves without waiting for a supervisor to review the problem.

6. At Stage 6, leaders *generate short-term wins*. Leaders plan for visible performance improvements, enable them to happen, and celebrate employees who were involved in the improvements. Major change takes time, and a transformation effort loses momentum if there are no short-term accomplishments that employees can recognize and celebrate. Philip Diehl of the U.S. Mint wanted to transform the clumsy, slow-moving government bureaucracy into a fast, energetic organization that was passionate about serving customers, particularly coin collectors. Diehl publicly set an early goal of processing 95 percent of orders within six weeks. Even though that sounds agonizingly slow in today's fast-paced business world, it was a tremendous improvement for the Mint. Achieving the goal energized employees and kept the transformation efforts moving.[12] A highly visible and successful short-term accomplishment boosts the credibility of the change process and renews the commitment and enthusiasm of employees.[13]

7. Stage 7 builds on the credibility achieved by short-term wins to *consolidate improvements, tackle bigger problems, and create greater change*. Leaders change systems, structures, and policies that do not fit the vision but have not yet been confronted. They hire, promote, and develop employees who can implement the vision for change. In addition, leaders revitalize the process with a new round of projects, themes, or change agents. At this stage, Philip Diehl of the U.S. Mint charged his top leadership team with reorganizing the agency to better fit the new vision and strategy. The process resulted in the decision to break the Mint into three strategic business units that can better respond to different sets of customers: one division for circulating coins, one for collectibles, and the third for protection services.

8. Stage 8 involves *institutionalizing the new approaches in the organizational culture*. This is the follow-through stage that makes the changes stick. Old habits, values, traditions, and mind-sets are permanently replaced. New values and beliefs are instilled in the culture so that employees view the changes not as something new but as a normal and integral part of how the organization operates. This stage also requires developing a means to ensure leadership development and succession so that the new values and behaviors are carried forward to the next generation of leadership.

Stages in the change process generally overlap, but each is important for successful change to occur. When dealing with a major change effort, leaders can use the eight-stage change process to provide a strong foundation for success. Sometimes, leaders initiate profound changes in all parts of the organization simultaneously, but leaders also initiate change more gradually.

Action Memo

As a leader: Follow the eight-stage model for leading a major change. Devote appropriate time and energy to each stage. Don't sabotage the change process by skipping stages in an attempt to save time.

Strategies for Everyday Change

Sometimes, leaders see that significant changes need to be made but they are constrained by various circumstances from initiating bold changes or they recognize that aggressive moves would provoke strong resistance. Good leaders work on a daily basis to gradually shift attitudes, assumptions, and behaviors toward a desired future. When individual leaders throughout the organization are involved in daily change efforts, they have a powerful cumulative effect.[14] Answer the questions in Leader's Self-Insight 16.1 to see if you are a change leader.

Leaders can learn strategies for everyday change that will have significant constructive impact as everyday conversations and small actions spread to others throughout the organization. Exhibit 16.3 illustrates a range of incremental change strategies that leaders can use. The strategies range from the individual leader working alone to effect gradual change to working directly with others in a more directed and extensive change effort.[15] Each of the strategies is described below:

❋   *Disruptive self-expression.* This is the least conspicuous way to promote change and involves a single leader acting in a way that others will notice and that reflects the values or behaviors he or she wishes to instill in followers. Disruptive self-expression quietly unsettles others' expectations and routines, whether it be a leader who wears casual pants and sweaters in an organization where most people wear suits or a leader who shifts working hours to balance work and family life. One manager, for example, shifted his work hours so he could always be home by 6:00 P.M. and refused to take calls during the evening

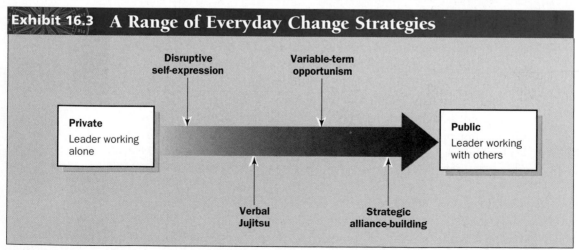

Exhibit 16.3   A Range of Everyday Change Strategies

SOURCE: Adapted from Debra E. Meyerson, "Radical Change the Quiet Way," *Harvard Business Review* (October 2001): 92–100.

Are You a Change Leader?

Instructions: Think specifically of your current or a recent full-time job. Please answer the 10 questions below according to *your perspective and behaviors in that job.* Please circle your response on the 1 to 5 scale to indicate the extent of your agreement with that statement: 1 = Strongly disagree; 2 = Somewhat disagree; 3 = Neither agree nor disagree; 4 = Somewhat agree; 5 = Strongly agree.

	Strongly disagree				Strongly agree
1. I often tried to adopt improved procedures for doing my job.	1	2	3	4	5
2. I often tried to change how my job was executed in order to be more effective.	1	2	3	4	5
3. I often tried to bring about improved procedures for the work unit or department.	1	2	3	4	5
4. I often tried to institute new work methods that were more effective for the company	1	2	3	4	5
5. I often tried to change organizational rules or policies that were nonproductive or counterproductive.	1	2	3	4	5
6. I often made constructive suggestions for improving how things operate within the organization.	1	2	3	4	5
7. I often tried to correct a faulty procedure or practice.	1	2	3	4	5
8. I often tried to eliminate redundant or unnecessary procedures.	1	2	3	4	5
9. I often tried to implement solutions to pressing organizational problems.	1	2	3	4	5
10. I often tried to introduce new structures, technologies, or approaches to improve efficiency.	1	2	3	4	5

Scoring and Interpretation

Please add the circled numbers for your ten answers and divide by 10, for your average score: _____.

This instrument measures the extent to which people take charge of change in the workplace. Change leaders are seen as change initiators. In the original research using this questionnaire, the change leaders were rated by co-workers and received an average score of 3.84. A score above 4.0 indicates a strong take-charge attitude toward change. A score below 2.0 indicates an attitude of letting someone else worry about change.

Before change leaders can champion large planned change projects via the model in Exhibit 16.2, they often begin by taking charge of change in their workplace area of responsibility. To what extent do you take charge of change in your work or personal life? Compare your score with other students' scores. How do you compare? Do you see yourself being a change leader?

between 6:30 and 9:00. In the hard-charging, fast-paced organization, his behavior raised eyebrows, but gradually, as colleagues saw that he actually became more rather than less productive, they also began leading more balanced lives.

⁂ *Verbal jujitsu.* With this strategy, a leader turns an opponent's negative attitudes, expressions, or behaviors into opportunities for change that others in the organization will notice. One good example relates to diversity and the challenges that minorities face in organizations, as described in Chapter 11. A sales executive was disturbed by the fact that the few minority managers in his organization had a hard time getting noticed and listened to. At a staff meeting, Carol, a new female marketing director, raised several concerns and questions but was routinely ignored. Later in the meeting, a white male manager raised similar concerns, and everyone directed their attention toward him. The sales executive quickly jumped in, saying, "That's a really important point and I'm glad you picked up on Carol's comments. Carol, did he correctly capture your thinking on this issue?" By casually calling attention to the fact that Carol had been ignored and her ideas co-opted, the executive made an important point without accusing or embarrassing anyone. In addition, he raised Carol's visibility and drew her directly into the discussion.

⁂ *Variable-term opportunism.* A more public approach is for leaders to look for, create, and capitalize on opportunities for motivating others to change. One woman who was hired as a division president at a technology company was opposed to the company's prevailing command-and-control leadership style but knew she would make enemies by attacking it directly. She focused on leading her own division in a participative way and sharing as much power and authority with followers as she could. Moreover, when she was asked to make presentations to the company's executive staff, she passed the opportunity to those who had worked directly on the project. The employees gained greater skills and experience and other executives were able to see and recognize their abilities and contributions.

⁂ *Strategic alliance building.* With strategic alliance building, the leader works closely with others to move issues to the forefront more quickly and directly that would be possible working alone. This is the most public and most political approach to everyday change. Recall the discussion of coalitions and allies from Chapter 12. The leader enlists the support and assistance of people who agree with his or her ideas for change. In addition, smart leaders look at everyone, even those who may be opposed to their ideas or projects, as a potential ally, as illustrated by the following example.

In the Lead   Paul Wielgus, Allied Domecq

Paul Wielgus doesn't consider himself a revolutionary, but he sparked a transformation at the global company Allied Domecq, whose brands include Courvoisier and Beefeater, by effectively persuading people who were originally opposed to his plans. Wielgus headed a new learning and training department designed to help people throughout the company break out of outdated thinking and be more creative and adaptable. The problem was, even though the department had the support of top management, many executives thought it was a waste of time and money.

One senior executive from Allied Domecq's internal audit department took aim at the learning and training unit when he was asked to identify areas of unnecessary expense. He soundly berated Wielgus and criticized the department's activities. However, rather than becoming defensive and treating the audit executive as an enemy, Wielgus used the meeting as an opportunity to sell him on the benefits of the program. His strategy was to treat the opposition as a friend and potential ally. Wielgus began excitedly telling him about how the workshops functioned and the dramatic changes he had seen in people who'd been through the training program. He enthusiastically explained how people left the workshops feeling more excited about their work and with a renewed commitment to the organization and its goals.

Before long, the senior executive was scheduling training for the internal audit department itself, and he became one of Wielgus's most enthusiastic supporters. The image of the Audit Services Department gradually changed from that of a policing unit to that of a partner helping people do their jobs better.[16]

Paul Wielgus understood the importance of building strategic alliances by reaching out to the opposition as well as to those who already agreed with and supported his ideas.

Leaders use a variety of everyday change strategies depending on the organization, the circumstances, and their own personalities. There are many ways to bring about change, and one of the most important ways is through individual leaders working every day—quietly and alone or publicly in connection with others—to effect small changes that ultimately have a powerful impact on the organization and its members.

Dealing with Resistance

Most changes, whether large or small, will encounter at least some degree of resistance. Leaders frequently see change as a way to strengthen the organization, but many people view change only as painful and disruptive. A critical aspect of leading people through change is understanding that resistance to change is natural—and that there are often legitimate reasons for it. This chapter's Living Leadership box takes a lighthearted look at why employees may resist changes in some overly bureaucratic organizations.

Why Do People Resist Change?

Personal compact

the reciprocal obligations and commitments that define the relationship between employees and the organization

The underlying reason why employees resist change is that it violates the personal compact between workers and the organization.[17] Personal compacts are the reciprocal obligations and commitments that define the relationship between employees and organizations. They include such things as job tasks, performance requirements, evaluation procedures, and compensation packages. These aspects of the compact are generally clearly defined and may be in written form. Other aspects are less clearcut. The personal compact incorporates elements such as mutual trust and dependence, as well as shared values. Employees perceive that change violates the personal compact for several reasons.

※ *Self-interest.* People typically resist a change they believe will take away something of value. Changes in job design, structure, or technology may lead to a perceived loss of power, prestige, pay, company benefits, or even an employee's job. For middle managers and lower-level supervisors, for example, a shift to empowered teams of workers can be quite threatening. Fear of personal loss may be the biggest obstacle to organizational change.[18]

※ *Uncertainty.* Uncertainty is the lack of information about future events. It represents a fear of the unknown. Individuals often do not understand how a proposed change may affect them and find it more reassuring to stay with the known, even if it is disagreeable and certain to lead to failure. Consider the difficulty that public-housing officials are having in getting residents of crumbling, pest-infested public housing projects to leave. For example, at the Robert Taylor Homes in Chicago, one of the nation's worst public housing projects, some residents resisted moving to cleaner, safer housing even as the wrecking ball knocked down building after building. Residents are comfortable there because they know what to expect, whereas the move to a new place brings uncertainty and feelings of dislocation.[19] In organizations, people may worry about how a change will affect their daily routine or friendships in the organization. They might fear that they will be unable to meet the demands of a new task, procedure, or technology.

※ *Different assessments and goals.* Another reason for resistance to change is that people who will be affected by the innovation may assess the situation differently from

LIVING LEADERSHIP

Dealing with a Dead Horse

Ancient wisdom says that when you discover you are astride a dead horse, the best strategy is to dismount. In government and other overly bureaucratic organizations, many different approaches are tried. Here are some of our favorite strategies for dealing with the "dead horse" scenario:

1. Change the rider.

2. Buy a stronger whip.

3. Beat the horse harder.

4. Shout at and threaten the horse.

5. Appoint a committee to study the horse.

6. Arrange a visit to other sites to see how they ride dead horses.

7. Increase the standards for riding dead horses.

8. Appoint a committee to revive the dead horse.

9. Create a training session to improve riding skills.

10. Explore the state of dead horses in today's environment.

11. Change the requirements so that the horse no longer meets the standards of death.

12. Hire an external consultant to show how a dead horse can be ridden.

13. Harness several dead horses together to increase speed.

14. Increase funding to improve the horse's performance.

15. Declare that no horse is too dead to ride.

16. Fund a study to determine if outsourcing will reduce the cost of riding a dead horse.

17. Buy a computer program to enhance the dead horse's performance.

18. Declare a dead horse less costly to maintain than a live one.

19. Form a work group to find uses for dead horses.

And . . . if all else fails . . .

20. Promote the dead horse to a supervisory position. Or, in a large corporation, make it a Vice President.

SOURCE: Author unknown. Another version of this story may be found at http://www.abcsmallbiz.com/funny/deadhorse.html

those who propose the change. Sometimes critics voice legitimate disagreements over the proposed benefits of a change. Employees in different departments pursue different goals, and a change may detract from performance and goal achievement for some departments.

These reasons for resistance are legitimate and real. Leaders cannot ignore resistance to change, but can diagnose the reasons and come up with ways to gain acceptance of the change by employees.

Overcoming Resistance

Leaders can improve the chances for a successful outcome by following the eight-stage model discussed earlier in this chapter and using the strategies just discussed for incremental everyday change. Effective leaders use elements such as storytelling, metaphor, humor, and a personal touch to reach employees on an emotional level and sell them on proposed changes. As discussed in Chapter 9, emotional elements are essential for persuading and influencing others; thus, leaders should not overlook the importance of emotional elements to overcome resistance to change.[20] The Leader's Bookshelf further describes how leaders can use emotion in following the eight-stage change process discussed earlier. Leaders also use a number of specific implementation techniques to smooth the change process.

✳ *Communication and training.* Open and honest communication is perhaps the single most effective way to overcome resistance to change because it reduces uncertainty, gives people a sense of control, clarifies the benefits of the change, and builds trust. In one study of change efforts, the most commonly cited reason for failure was that employees learned of the change from outsiders.[21] Top leaders concentrated on communicating with the public and shareholders, but failed to communicate with the people who would be most intimately affected by the changes—their own employees It is important that leaders communicate with people face-to-face rather than relying solely on newsletters, memos, or electronic communication.

Employees frequently also need training to acquire skills for their role in the change process or their new responsibilities. Good change leaders make sure people get the training they need to feel comfortable with new tasks, such as when Canadian Airlines International spent a year and a half training employees in new procedures before changing its entire reservations, airport, cargo, and financial systems.[22]

✳ *Participation and involvement.* Participation involves followers in helping to design the change. Although this approach is time-consuming, it pays off by giving people a sense of control over the change activity. They come to understand the change better and become committed to its successful implementation. A study of the implementation and adoption of new computer technology at two companies, for example, showed a much smoother implementation process at the company that introduced the change using a participatory approach.[23]

LEADER'S BOOKSHELF

The Heart of Change: Real-Life Stories of How People Change Their Organizations
by John P. Kotter and Dan S. Cohen

In his 1996 book, *Leading Change*, John Kotter, professor emeritus at Harvard Business School, outlined an eight-stage process that leaders should follow in leading major change. With his new book, *The Heart of Change*, Kotter has teamed up with consultant Dan Cohen to look at the typical problems leaders face at each of the eight stages. The authors' main finding is that the biggest barriers to change involve people's attitudes and behaviors.

How People Change
Change comes easier, the authors argue, when people see potent reasons for change that touch their emotions rather than being presented with rational analysis that attempts to change their thinking. Consider these examples connected to three of the eight change stages:

※ *Stage 1: Establish a sense of urgency.* One leader at a company struggling to cut costs was curious about what his company was spending on gloves in its manufacturing plants. His summer intern found that the plants purchased 424 different types of gloves that were roughly equal in quality but varied widely in cost. The two gathered a sample of each type of glove, tagged it with a price on it, and made a pile in the executive boardroom. When division managers saw the display, they were astounded. The gloves became a traveling road show that managers used to show people how bad things had gotten.

※ *Stage 4: Widely communicate the vision and strategy.* At a company in the United Kingdom, leaders personally communicated a new vision with people all around the company, but they wanted to keep the vision fresh in everyone's mind. One morning, when employees turned on their computers, the first thing they saw was a multicolored map of the United Kingdom surrounded by a bright blue circle. As the image moved around the screen, the words "We will be #1 in the UK market by 2001" appeared. The screen saver technique took everyone by surprise and got people talking about the vision.

※ *Stage 5: Empowering employees.* One manufacturing plant's early efforts at empowerment were total chaos. Employee involvement meetings deteriorated into gripe sessions, and morale declined rather than improved. Leaders decided to try a different approach. With the approval of some of their best teams, they began videotaping what they did on the factory floor—everything from grabbing the raw material off the shelf to taking the finished product off the line. When people later viewed the tape, ideas for improvement started flowing immediately—such as reorganizing the machines to cut down on how far people had to walk or setting up a rack with all the tools needed for a process right at hand. Teams now have "before and after" tapes and feel a sense of pride as they show the quality, safety, and cost improvements they have made.

Real-Life Stories; Practical Guidelines
The Heart of Change is based on interviews with about 400 leaders at 130 organizations in the midst of major changes. The numerous personal anecdotes include both successes and fumbles, and each chapter ends with a "What Works/What Does Not Work" guide for each of the eight change stages. With *The Heart of Change*, Kotter and Cohen have combined a lively, highly readable story with a practical, nonsense guide to leading successful change.

The Heart of Change, by John P. Kotter and Dan S. Cohen, is published by Harvard Business School Press.

❋ *Coercion*. As a last resort, leaders overcome resistance by threatening employees with the loss of jobs or promotions or by firing or transferring them. Coercion may be necessary in crisis situations when a rapid response is needed. Coercion may also be needed for administrative changes that flow from the top down, such as downsizing the workforce. However, as a general rule, this approach to change is not advisable because it leaves people angry at leaders, and the change may be sabotaged.

Jack W. ←

The Negative Impact of Change

Leaders can use the techniques just described to overcome resistance in any part of the organization or the company as a whole. Large, organizationwide changes are particularly likely to be met with resistance. Leaders are responsible for smoothly implementing both small and large changes that can help the organization survive and prosper. However, it is essential for leaders to recognize that change can have negative as well as positive consequences.

The Two Faces of Change

Effectively and humanely leading change is one of the greatest challenges for leaders. The nature and pace of change in today's environment can be exhilarating and even fun. But it can also be inconvenient, painful, and downright scary. Even when a change appears to be good for individual employees as well as the organization, it can lead to decreased morale, lower commitment, and diminished trust if not handled carefully.

In addition, some changes that may be necessary for the good of the organization can cause real, negative consequences for individual employees, who may experience high levels of stress, be compelled to quickly learn entirely new tasks and ways of working, or possibly lose their jobs. Some of the most difficult changes are those related to structure, such as redefining positions and responsibilities, reengineering the company, redesigning jobs, departments, or divisions, or downsizing the organization. In many cases, these types of changes mean that some people will be seriously hurt because they will lose their jobs.

Leadership and Downsizing

When Greg Dyke took over at the BBC, he knew the organization needed to increase expenditures on programming to compete with commercial stations, and that meant cuts would need to be made in other areas. Dyke initiated a complete restructuring and cost-cutting program that had highly positive results for the organization. Unfortunately, the changes led to layoffs for many employees.[24] Dyke and other top managers confronted one of the most difficult situations leaders may face—how to handle downsizing in a way that eases pain and tension for departing employees and maintains the trust and morale of employees who remain with the organization.

Downsizing refers to intentionally reducing the size of a company's workforce. During the boom years of the 1990s, few leaders had to be concerned with the need for laying off employees, but the economic downturn of the early 2000s made massive downsizing a common practice in American corporations. In addition, downsizing is a part of many change initiatives in today's organizations.[25] Reengineering projects, mergers and acquisitions, global competition, the trend toward outsourcing, and the transition from an industrial to an information economy have all led to job reductions.[26]

Some researchers have found that massive downsizing has often not achieved the intended benefits, and in some cases has significantly harmed the organization.[27] Nevertheless, there are times when downsizing is a necessary part of a thoughtful restructuring of assets or other important change initiatives. Leaders need to understand that downsizing not only hurts those who lose their jobs but can also have many negative consequences on the morale, commitment, and performance of "survivors," those who remain with the organization. If downsizing is not carefully handled, it can have a detrimental impact.

When job cuts are necessary, leaders should be prepared for increased conflict and stress, even greater resistance to change, and a decrease in morale, trust, and employee commitment.[28] A number of techniques can help leaders smooth the downsizing process and ease tensions for employees who leave as well as those who remain.[29]

❋ *Involve employees.* One important way to cut jobs and keep morale high among remaining employees is to let lower-level employees assist with shaping the criteria for which jobs will be cut or which employees will leave the company. Naturally, this requires that employees be trained to understand the goals leaders hope to achieve through the downsizing. Another option is to offer incentive packages for employees to leave voluntarily. One drawback is that there's no way to predict which employees will take the offer, and the company may lose key employees with critical knowledge and skills. Leaders can offer options, such as job-sharing and part-time work, which may suit some employees well, enabling them to remain employed part-time and allowing the company to retain their talents.

❋ *Communicate more, not less.* Some leaders seem to think the less that's said about a pending layoff, the better. Not so. Leaders should provide advance notice with as much information as possible. Even when they're not certain about exactly what is going to happen, leaders should be as open and honest with employees as possible. Leaders at 3Com Corp. used a three-stage plan as they prepared for layoffs. First, they warned employees several months in advance that layoffs were inevitable. Soon thereafter, they held on-site presentations at all locations to explain why the layoffs were needed and to provide as much information as they could about what employees should expect. Employees being cut were given a full 60 days' notice (now required by a federal regulation called the

Action Memo
As a leader: Be compassionate when making changes such as downsizing that will hurt some people in the organization. Communicate as much as possible about the change and involve employees in making decisions. Provide assistance to displaced workers. Address the emotional needs of remaining employees to help them stay motivated and productive.

Worker Adjustment and Retraining Notification Act).[30] Leaders should remember that it's impossible to "overcommunicate" during turbulent times. Remaining employees need to know what is expected of them, whether future layoffs are a possibility, and what the organization is doing to help co-workers who have lost their jobs.

❋ *Provide assistance to displaced workers.* Leaders have a responsibility to help displaced workers cope with the loss of their jobs and get reestablished in the job market. The organization can provide training, severance packages, extended benefits, and outplacement assistance. In addition, counseling services for both employees and their families can ease the trauma associated with a job loss.

❋ *Help the survivors thrive.* Leaders should remember the emotional needs of survivors, as well. Many people experience guilt, anger, confusion, and sadness after the loss of colleagues, and these feelings should be acknowledged. People may also be concerned about their own jobs and have difficulty adapting to the changes in job duties, responsibilities, and so forth. The state of Oregon hired consultant Al Siebert to help employees adapt following the elimination of more than 1,000 jobs. Most people "just aren't emotionally prepared to handle major disruptions," Siebert says. Through a series of workshops, Siebert helped people acknowledge their anger and unhappiness, then helped them become "change-resilient" by developing coping skills such as flexibility, curiosity, and optimism.[31]

Even the best-led organizations may sometimes need to lay off employees in a turbulent environment. Leaders can attain positive results if they handle downsizing in a way that enables remaining organization members to be motivated, productive, and committed to a better future.

 # Leading for Innovation

In response to the question, "What must one do to survive in the twenty-first century?" the top answer among 500 CEOs surveyed by the American Management Association was "practice creativity and innovation." However, only 6 percent of the respondents felt that their companies were successfully accomplishing this goal.[32] There's an innovation deficit in many of today's organizations, but leaders are beginning to respond by adopting structures and systems that promote rather than squelch the creation and implementation of new ideas. Effective leaders find ways to promote creativity in the departments where it is most needed. For example, some organizations, such as hospitals, government agencies, and nonprofit organizations, may need frequent changes in policies and procedures, and leaders can promote creativity among administrative workers. For companies that rely on new products, leaders need to promote the generation and sharing of ideas across departments. In learning organizations, leaders want everyone to come up with new ideas for solving problems and meeting customer needs. One of the best ways for leaders to facilitate continuous change is to create an environment that nourishes creativity. Creativity is the generation of new ideas that result in improved efficiency and effectiveness of the organization.[33] Creative people come up with ideas that may meet perceived needs, solve problems, or respond to opportunities and are therefore adopted by the organization. However, creativity itself is a process rather than an outcome, a journey rather than a destination. One of the most important tasks of leaders today is to harness the creative energy of all employees to spur innovation and further the interests of the organization.

The Innovative Organization

Leaders can build an environment that encourages creativity and helps the organization be more innovative. Five elements of innovative organization are listed in the left column of Exhibit 16.4, and each is described below.[34] These elements correspond to the characteristics of creative individuals, listed in the right column of the exhibit.

Alignment For creative acts that benefit the organization to occur consistently, the interests and actions of everyone should be aligned with the organization's purpose, vision, and goals. Leaders make clear what the company stands for, consistently promote the vision, and clarify specific goals. In addition, they make a commitment of time, energy, and resources to activities that focus people on innovation. Many organizations set up separate creative departments or venture teams, as discussed in the previous chapter. One increasingly popular approach is the idea incubator, which is being used at companies such as Boeing, Ziff-Davis, and UPS. An idea incubator provides a safe harbor where ideas from people throughout the organization can be developed without interference from company bureaucracy or politics.[35]

Self-initiated Activity Most people have a natural desire to explore and create, which leads them to want to initiate creative activity on their own. Unfortunately, this desire is sometimes squelched early in life by classroom teachers who insist on strict adherence to the rules. Leaders can unleash deep-seated employee motivation for creativity and innovation. Leaders encourage an entrepreneurial spirit by instilling values of risk-taking and exploration and providing the structures and systems that encourage people to explore new ideas. This corporate entrepreneurship can produce a higher-than-average number of innovations. One important outcome is to facilitate idea champions. Idea champions are people who passionately believe in an idea and fight to overcome natural resistance and convince others of its value. Change does not happen by itself. Personal energy and

Creativity
the generation of new ideas that result in improved efficiency and effectiveness of the organization

Idea incubator
a safe harbor where ideas from employees throughout the organization can be developed without interference from company bureaucracy or politics

Corporate entrepreneurship
internal entrepreneurial spirit that includes values of exploration, experimentation, and risk taking

Idea champions
people who passionately believe in a new idea and actively work to overcome obstacles and resistance

Exhibit 16.4	**Characteristics of Innovative Organizations and Creative People**
The Innovative Organization	**The Creative Individual**
Alignment	Commitment Focused approach
Self-initiated activity	Interdependence Persistence Energy
Unofficial activity	Self-confidence Nonconformity Curiosity
Diverse stimuli	Open-mindedness Conceptual fluency *3m Postits* Enjoys variety
Within-company communication	Social competence Emotionally expressive Loves people

SOURCE: Based on Alan G. Robinson and Sam Stern, *Corporate Creativity: How Innovation and Improvement Actually Happen* (San Francisco: Berrett-Koehler, 1997); Rosabeth Moss Kanter, "The Middle Manager as Innovator," *Harvard Business Review*, (July–August 1982): 104–105; and James Brian Quinn, "Managing Innovation: Controlled Chaos," *Harvard Business Review*, May–June 1985: 73–84.

effort are needed to successfully promote a new idea. Champions make sure valuable ideas get accepted and carried forward for implementation. Nokia Corp. relies on idea champions for its record of new product successes.

In the Lead   Erkki Kuisma and Yrjö Neuvo, Nokia

Erkki Kuisma was conducting radio frequency research at Nokia when he came up with what seemed like a crazy idea—why not hide a cell phone's antenna inside the phone? Kuisma tinkered around with his idea and eventually cut the antenna off an existing phone model and patched the hole by remodeling the plastic casing after melting it with a blow dryer. Then, he devised an antenna from a square piece of copper tape and inserted it inside the phone. It worked.

But Kuisma's idea immediately hit resistance among executives at Nokia, who were afraid customers would doubt the phone's power without a visible antenna. Kuisma's boss, Yrjö Neuvo went to work next, waging daily warfare against the hierarchy to champion the new idea. He'd corner executives in lobbies and meeting rooms, showing them the prototype and talking about its potential. He also coached Kuisma on how to support the idea to doubters, since the inventor's commitment to the project could make a substantial difference within Nokia. Before long, the internal antenna debuted in Nokia's 8800 series and became one of the most profitable products in the company's history. The innovation was quickly copied by competitors.

Many other crazy ideas have bubbled up from employees because of Nokia's corporate entrepreneurship, including user-changeable cell phone covers, the first one-chip phone, the first compact battery with power that would last 100 hours, and the first chat room for text messaging. Yrjö, head of research and development at Nokia, fosters an entrepreneurial spirit by encouraging people to try crazy things and never shrink from making mistakes.[36]

Leaders at Nokia encourage allowing employees to investigate crazy ideas and develop new technologies without company approval. Employees know that no idea is too harebrained to get a hearing from Yrjö, who will do whatever it takes to get higher-ups to pay attention, too.

Unofficial Activity Employees need to be able to experiment and dream outside of their regular job description. Leaders can give employees free time for activities that are not officially sanctioned. One study of creativity found that in almost every case the essence of the creative act came during the "unofficial" time period.[37] Dream time is what makes it possible for companies to go where they never expected to. The best-known example is 3M's Post-it Notes, one of the five most popular 3M products and one that resulted from an engineer's free-time experiments with another worker's "failure"—a not-very-sticky glue. 3M lets employees spend 15 percent of their time on any project of their own choosing, without management approval.[38]

Diverse Stimuli It is impossible to know in advance what stimulus will lead any particular person to come up with a creative idea. The seeds of the idea for Post-it Notes were planted when an engineer's bookmarks kept falling out of his church hymnal. Leaders can help provide the sparks that set off creative ideas. Companies such as Hallmark, Nortel Networks' Broad Band, and Bell Laboratories/Lucent Technologies bring in outside speakers on diverse topics to open people up to different ideas. During a nature talk at Bell Labs/Lucent, a scientist jumped up and ran out of the auditorium—something the presenter said about animal communication helped the scientist see a creative solution to a problem with a new technology he'd been working on. Researchers at the company are currently studying the silicon spicules of deep-sea sponges, which are very similar to modern fiber-optic cables except that they don't crack or break.[39]

Leaders can also provide employees with diverse stimuli by rotating people into different jobs, allowing them time off to participate in volunteer activities, and giving them opportunities to mix with people different from themselves. Organizations can give people opportunities to work with customers, suppliers, and others outside the industry.

Internal Communication Creativity flourishes when there is frequent contact with interdisciplinary networks of people at all levels of the organization.[40] Without adequate internal communication and coordination, ideas from creative departments or idea champions can't be implemented. Leaders foster an environment that encourages people to communicate across boundaries. Novartis, a large life sciences corporation that produces diverse products such as pharmaceuticals, genetically engineered seeds, baby food, contact lenses, and animal health products, holds *knowledge fairs* four times a year to give people a chance to learn about creative activities in other parts of the organization.[41]

Leaders can also make collaboration and information sharing an integral part of the culture and use mechanisms that facilitate coordination for the implementation of change and innovation projects. For example, to encourage innovation at Acordia, a healthcare management firm, leaders established cross-functional teams focused on unique customer needs and revised compensation systems to encourage horizontal collaboration and innovation.[42] At Nissan, CEO Carlos Ghosn used cross-functional teams to help mastermind a transformation plan that saved the company.

In the Lead   Carlos Ghosn, Nissan

When Carlos Ghosn arrived as the new CEO of Nissan, the company had been struggling to turn a profit for eight years. Ghosn knew he was facing a do-or-die situation—it was either turn things around or the business would cease to exist. However, he also knew that simply mandating a series of dramatic and wrenching top-down changes would create resistance, damage morale, and ultimately put the company in even more trouble.

Ghosn decided to mobilize Nissan's line managers through a series of cross-functional teams that would identify and lead the radical changes that needed to be made. He believed the team approach was the best way to get managers to see beyond the functional and regional boundaries that had previously defined their jobs. Thus, he created nine management teams and charged them with creating a plan for transformation in all areas of the business. The teams were organized into these areas: business development; purchasing; manufacturing and logistics; research and development; sales and marketing; general and administrative; finance and costs; phaseout of products and parts complexity management; and organization. Each team was made up of members from various functional areas. For example, the purchasing team consisted of members from purchasing, engineering, manufacturing, and finance. The organization team had members from product planning, sales and marketing, manufacturing, engineering, finance, and purchasing. Each team was appointed two leaders drawn from the executive committee, but these leaders took a back seat in the actual functioning of the team, serving more as sponsors to smooth the process and remove administrative obstacles to the team's work.

Within three months, the nine teams had created a detailed blueprint for Nissan's turnaround. Within three years, implementation of the various aspects of the plan had returned the company to profitability. In addition, because managers throughout the company were involved in creating the plan, morale, cooperation, and company identity have grown stronger.[43]

By improving internal communication and coordination, Carlos Ghosn has put Nissan back on the right road. The cross-functional teams continue to operate as an integral part of Nissan's management structure, continuing to search for new ideas and working together to implement them.

Leaders can use the five characteristics of innovative organizations to ignite creativity in specific departments or the entire organization. Many organizations that want to encourage innovation also strive to hire people who display the characteristics of creative individuals, as listed in the right column of Exhibit 16.4. Creative people are often known for open-mindedness, curiosity, independence, self-confidence, persistence, and a focused approach to problem-solving. Clearly, these characteristics are stronger in some people than in others. Completing the exercise in Leader's Self-Insight 16.2 will help you determine if you have a creative personality. However, it is important to remember that recent research on creativity suggests that everyone has roughly equal creative potential. Leaders can help both individuals and organizations be more creative.

Stages in the Personal Creative Process

An important part of becoming more creative is understanding the stages of the creative process. One model of creativity is illustrated in Exhibit 16.5. Stages do not always occur in the same order and may overlap. In addition, if a person encounters a block at one stage, he or she may cycle back to an earlier stage and try again.[44]

Action Memo

As a leader: Help the organization be more innovative. Focus people on innovation. Encourage curiosity, playfulness, and exploration. Provide people with diverse stimuli that can open their minds to new ideas. Build mechanisms for cross-functional collaboration and information sharing.

Exhibit 16.5   Stages in the Creative Process

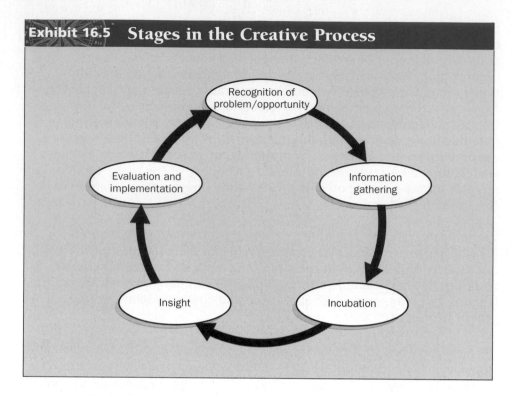

❋   *Stage 1: Recognition of problem/opportunity.* Creativity often begins with the recognition of a problem that needs to be solved or an opportunity to explore. For example, Brian LeGette and Ron Wilson invented the collapsible wrap-around ear warmer after they began talking about how nice it would be if guys could "keep their ears warm without looking like dorks."[45]

❋   *Stage 2: Information gathering.* The next step is to search for background information and knowledge about the problem or opportunity. This may involve reading in a variety of fields; attending professional meetings and seminars; traveling to new places; talking to anyone and everyone about the subject; scanning magazines, newspapers, and journals; and carrying a notebook to jot down useful information and random thoughts. It is also important to set aside time specifically for pursuing ideas and giving curiosity free rein.

❋   *Stage 3: Incubation.* This is the stage where a person allows the subconscious to mull things over. The incubation stage happens while the person is involved in activities totally unrelated to the subject—even during sleep. This is the period that really allows creativity to spring forth. Some helpful ideas for encouraging the incubation period are to engage in routine, "mindless" activities such as cutting the grass; get regular exercise; play and have fun; meditate; and try to relax on a regular basis.

Do You Have a Creative Personality?

In the list below, check each adjective that you believe accurately describes your personality. Be very honest. Check all the words that fit your personality.

1. affected ___
2. capable ___
3. cautious ___
4. clever ___
5. commonplace ___
6. confident ___
7. conservative ___
8. conventional ___
9. egotistical ___
10. dissatisfied ___
11. honest ___
12. humorous ___
13. individualistic ___
14. informal ___
15. insightful ___
16. intelligent ___
17. interests narrow ___
18. interests wide ___
19. inventive ___
20. mannerly ___
21. original ___
22. reflective ___
23. resourceful ___
24. self-confident ___
25. sexy ___
26. snobbish ___
27. sincere ___
28. submissive ___
29. suspicious ___
30. unconventional ___

Scoring and Interpretation

Add one point for checking each of the following words: 2, 4, 6, 9, 12, 13, 14, 15, 16, 18, 19, 21, 22, 23, 24, 25, 26, and 30. Subtract one point for checking each of the following words: 1, 3, 5, 7, 8, 10, 11, 17, 20, 27, 28, and 29. The highest possible score is +18 and the lowest possible score is –12.

The average score for a set of 256 assessed males on this creativity scale was 3.57, and for 126 females was 4.4. A group of 45 male research scientists and a group of 530 male psychology graduate students both had average scores of 6.0, and 124 male architects received an average score of 5.3. A group of 335 female psychology students had an average score of 3.34. If you received a score above 6.0, your personality would be considered above average in creativity.

The adjective checklist above was validated by comparing the respondents' scores to scores on other creativity tests and to creativity assessments of respondents provided by expert judges of creativity. This scale does not provide perfect prediction of creativity, but it is reliable and has moderate validity. Your score probably indicates something about your creative personality compared to other people.

To what extent do you think your score reflects your true creativity? Compare your score to others in your class. What is the range of scores among other students? Which adjectives were most important for your score compared to other students? Can you think of types of creativity this test might not measure? How about situations where the creativity reflected on this test might not be very important?

SOURCE: Harrison G. Gough, "A Creative Personality Scale for the Adjective Check List," *Journal of Personality and Social Psychology* 37, no. 8 (1979): 1398–1405.

❋ *Stage 4: Insight.* This is the stage that most people think of as *creativity.* It is when the person hits upon an idea. The idea may occur while watching television, taking a shower, or reading the newspaper, or it may occur while one is thinking specifically about the problem. In most cases, the idea doesn't come as a bolt out of the blue, but in gradual increments. Ideas to speed up this stage include: daydream and fantasize about the project; practice your hobbies; keep a notebook by your bedside to record late-night or early-morning ideas; take regular breaks from working.

❋ *Stage 5: Evaluation and implementation* This is the most difficult stage and requires courage, tenacity, and self-discipline. Creative people often fail many times before they succeed and have to cycle back through the information gathering and incubation stages. In addition, others may think the "brilliant" idea is crazy. Creative people don't give up when they run into obstacles. Friends thought Brian LeGette and Ron Wilson were nuts when they started talking about reinventing the earmuff, but the two believed in their idea so much that they quit their high-paying jobs to pursue it. Some suggestions during this phase include: increase your energy level with proper diet, rest, and exercise; take note of your intuitive hunches; seek the advice of others; educate yourself in how to sell your ideas; and remember that you are facing challenges rather than problems.

Leaders of today's organizations have powerful reasons to encourage creativity. As we discussed in Chapter 1, many organizations are undergoing fundamental transformations to respond to new challenges. They need employees throughout the organization to contribute new ideas. In addition, creative people are less resistant to change because they are open-minded, curious, and willing to take risks.

Summary and Interpretation

The important point of this chapter is that tools and approaches are available to help leaders manage and create change. Change is inevitable, and the increased pace of change in today's global environment has created even greater problems for leaders struggling to help their organizations adapt. A major factor in the failure of organizations to adapt to changes in the global environment is the lack of effective change leadership. Leaders who can successfully accomplish change typically define themselves as change leaders, describe a vision for the future in vivid terms, and articulate values that promote change and adaptability. Change leaders are courageous, are capable of managing complexity and uncertainty, believe in followers' capacity to assume responsibility for change, and learn from their own mistakes.

Major changes can be particularly difficult to implement, but leaders can help to ensure a successful change effort by following the eight-stage model of planned change—establish a sense of urgency; create a powerful coalition; develop a compelling vision and strategy; communicate the vision; empower employees to act; generate short-term wins; consolidate gains and tackle bigger problems; and institutionalize the change in the organizational culture. Leaders also facilitate change on a daily basis by using several everyday change strategies, including disruptive self-expression, verbal jujitsu, variable-term opportunism, and strategic alliance building.

A critical aspect of leading change is understanding why people resist change and how to overcome resistance. Leaders use communication and training, participation and involvement, and—as a last resort—coercion to overcome resistance. Leaders should recognize that change can have negative as well as positive consequences. One of the most difficult situations leaders may face is downsizing. Leaders can use techniques to help ease the stress and hardship for employees who leave as well as maintain the morale and trust of those who remain.

Leaders are also responsible for moving the organization forward by leading for innovation. One way is by creating an environment that nourishes creativity in particular departments or the entire organization. Five elements of innovative organizations are alignment, self-initiated activity, unofficial activity, diverse stimuli, and within-company communication. These correspond to characteristics of creative individuals. Creative people are less resistant to change. Although some people demonstrate more creativity than others, research suggests that everyone has roughly equal creative potential. Understanding the stages of the creative process can help people be more creative. These stages—recognition of a problem or opportunity, information gathering, incubation, insight, and evaluation and implementation—do not always occur in the same order and may overlap. Leaders can encourage and support creativity to help followers and organizations be more responsive and change-ready.

Discussion Questions

1. Of the eight stages of planned change, which one do you think leaders are most likely to skip? Why?
2. Which of the everyday change strategies (Exhibit 16.3) would you be most comfortable using and why? What are some situations when a passive, private strategy such as disruptive self-expression might be more effective than an active, public strategy such as strategic alliance building?
3. Do you think creative individuals and creative organizations have characteristics in common? Discuss.
4. What advice would you give a leader who wants to increase innovation in her department?

5. Why do employees resist change? What are some ways leaders can overcome this resistance?

6. Why are idea champions considered to be essential to innovation? Do you think these people would be more important in a large organization or a small one? Discuss.

7. Planned change is often considered ideal. Do you think unplanned change could be effective? Discuss. Can you think of an example?

8. Is the world really changing faster today, or do people just assume so?

Leadership at Work

Organizational Change Role Play

You are the new director of the Harpeth Gardens not-for-profit nursing home. Harpeth Gardens is one of 20 elder care centers managed by Franklin Resident Care Centers. Harpeth Gardens has 56 patients and is completely responsible for their proper hygiene, nutrition, and daily recreation. Many of the patients can move about by themselves, but several require physical assistance for eating, dressing, and moving about the nursing home. During daytime hours, the head of nursing is in charge of the four certified nursing assistants (CNAs) who work on the floors. During the night shift, a registered nurse is on duty, along with three CNAs. The same number of CNAs are on duty over the weekend, and either the head of nursing or the registered nurse is on call.

Several other staff also report to you, including the heads of maintenance, bookkeeping/MIS, and the cafeteria. The on-call physician stops by Harpeth Gardens once a week to check on the residents. You have 26 full- and part-time employees who cover the different tasks and shifts.

During your interviews for the director's job, you became aware that the previous director ran a very tight ship, insisting that the best way to care for nursing home patients was though strict rules and procedures. He personally approved almost every decision, including decisions for patient care, despite not having a medical degree. Turnover has been rather high and several beds are empty because of the time required to hire and train new staff. Other elder care facilities in the area have a waiting list of people wanting to be admitted.

At Harpeth Gardens, the non-nursing offices have little interaction with nurses or each other. Back office staff people seem to do their work and go home. Overall, Harpeth Gardens seems to you like a dreary place to work. People seem to have forgotten the compassion that is essential for patients and each other working in a health care environment. You believe that a new strategy and culture are needed to give more responsibility to employees, improve morale, reduce turnover, and fill the empty beds. You have read about the concept of a learning organization (Chapter 15), and would like to implement some of those ideas at Harpeth Gardens. You decide to start with the ideas of increasing empowered roles and personal networks and see how it goes. If those two ideas work, then you will implement other changes.

During your first week as the director, you have met all the employees, and you have confirmed your understanding of the previous director's rigid approach. You call a meeting of all employees for next Friday afternoon.

Your assignment for this exercise is to decide how you will implement the desired changes and what you will tell employees at the employee meeting. Start by deciding how you will accomplish each of the first three steps in the model in Exhibit 16.2. Write your answers to these three questions:

1. How will you get employees to feel a sense of urgency?

_____

_____

_____

2. How will you form a guiding coalition, and who will be in it?

_____

_____

_____

3. What is your compelling vision?

_____

_____

_____

Your next task is to prepare a *vision speech* to employees for the changes you are about to implement. In this speech, explain your dream for Harpeth Gardens and the urgency of this change. Explain exactly what you believe the changes will involve and why the employees should agree to the changes and help implement them. Sketch out the points you will include in your speech:

_____

_____

_____

In Class: The instructor can divide the class into small groups to discuss the answers to questions 1 to 3 above and to brainstorm the key points to cover in the vision speech to employees. After student groups have decided what the director will say, the instructor can ask for volunteers from a few groups to actually give the speech to employees that will start the Harpeth Gardens transition toward a learning organization. The key questions are: Did the speech touch on the key points that inspire employees to help implement changes? Did the speech convey a high purpose and a sense of urgency? Did the speech connect with employees in a personal way, and did it lay out the reality facing Harpeth Gardens?

Leadership Development: Cases for Analysis

Southern Discomfort

Jim Malesckowski remembers the call of two weeks ago as if he just put down the telephone receiver: "I just read your analysis and I want you to get down to Mexico right away," Jack Ripon, his boss and chief executive officer, had blurted in his ear. "You know we can't make the plant in Oconomo work any more—the costs are just too high. So go down there, check out what our operational costs would be if we move, and report back to me in a week."

At that moment, Jim felt as if a shiv had been stuck in his side, just below the rib cage. As president of the Wisconsin Specialty Products Division of Lamprey, Inc., he knew quite well the challenge of dealing with high-cost labor in a third-generation, unionized U.S. manufacturing plant. And although he had done the analysis that led to his boss's knee-jerk response, the call still stunned him. There were 520 people who made a living at Lamprey's Oconomo facility, and if it closed, most of them wouldn't have a journeyman's prayer of finding another job in the town of 9,900 people.

Instead of the $16-per-hour average wage paid at the Oconomo plant, the wages paid to the Mexican workers—who lived in a town without sanitation and with an unbelievably toxic effluent from industrial pollution—would amount to about $1.60 an hour on average. That's a savings of nearly $15 million a year for Lamprey, to be offset in part by increased costs for training, transportation, and other matters.

After two days of talking with Mexican government representatives and managers of other companies in the town, Jim had enough information to develop a set of comparative figures of production and shipping costs.

On the way home, he started to outline the report, knowing full well that unless some miracle occurred, he would be ushering in a blizzard of pink slips for people he had come to appreciate.

The plant in Oconomo had been in operation since 1921, making special apparel for persons suffering injuries and other medical conditions. Jim had often talked with employees who would recount stories about their fathers or grandfathers working in the same Lamprey company plant— the last of the original manufacturing operations in town.

But friendship aside, competitors had already edged past Lamprey in terms of price and were dangerously close to overtaking it in product quality. Although both Jim and the plant manager had tried to convince the union to accept lower wages, union leaders resisted. In fact, on one occasion when Jim and the plant manager tried to discuss a cell manufacturing approach, which would cross-train employees to perform up to three different jobs, local union leaders could barely restrain their anger. Yet probing beyond the fray, Jim sensed the fear that lurked under the union reps' gruff exterior. He sensed their vulnerability, but could not break through the reactionary bark that protected it.

A week has passed and Jim just submitted his report to his boss. Although he didn't specifically bring up the point, it was apparent that Lamprey could put its investment dollars in a bank and receive a better return than what its Oconomo operation is currently producing.

Tomorrow, he'll discuss the report with the CEO. Jim doesn't want to be responsible for the plant's dismantling, an act he personally believes would be wrong as long as there's a chance its costs can be lowered. "But Ripon's right," he says to himself. "The costs are too high, the union's unwilling to cooperate, and the company needs to make a better return on its investment if it's to continue at all. It sounds right but feels wrong. What should I do?"

SOURCE: Doug Wallace, "What Would You Do?" *Business Ethics* (March/April 1996): 52–53. Reprinted with permission from *Business Ethics*, P.O. Box 8439, Minneapolis, MN 55408. 612/879-0695.

Questions

1. If you were Jim Malesckowski, would you fight to save the plant? Why?
2. Assume you want to lead the change to save the plant. Describe how you would enact the eight stages outlined in Exhibit 16.2.
3. How would you overcome union leader resistance?

MediScribe Corporation

MediScribe provides medical transcription, insurance claims, and billing and collection services for doctors, clinics, and hospitals in south Florida. As a production supervisor, Ramona Fossett is responsible for the work of approximately 40 employees, 25 of whom are classified as data entry clerks. Fossett recently agreed to allow a team of outside consultants to come to her production area and make time and systems-analysis studies in an effort to improve efficiency and output. She had little choice but to do so—the president of the company had personally issued instructions that supervisors should cooperate with the consultants.

The consultants spent three days studying job descriptions, observing employees' daily tasks, and recording each detail of the work of the data entry clerks. After this period of observation, they told Fossett that they would begin more detailed studies and interviews on the following day.

The next morning, four data entry clerks were absent. On the following day, 10 failed to show up for work. The leader of the systems analysis team explained to Fossett that, if there were as many absences the next day, his team would have to drop the study and move on to another department, as a valid analysis would be impossible with 10 out of 25 workers absent.

Fossett, who had only recently been promoted to the supervisor's position, knew that she'd be held responsible for the failure of the systems analysis. Concerned both for her employees and her own job, she telephoned several of the absent workers to find out what was going on. Each told approximately the same story, saying they were stressed out and exhausted after being treated like "guinea pigs" for three days.

One employee said she was planning to ask for a leave of absence if working conditions didn't improve.

At the end of the day, Fossett sat at her desk considering what could be done to provide the necessary conditions for completion of the study. In addition, she was greatly concerned about implementing the changes that she knew would be mandated after the consultants finished their work and presented their findings to the president. Considering how her employees had reacted to the study, Fosset doubted they would instantly comply with orders issued from the top as a result of the findings—and, again, she would be held responsible for the failure.

SOURCE: Adapted from "Resistance to Change" in John M. Champion and John H. James, *Critical Incidents in Management: Decision and Policy Issues*, 6th ed. (Homewood, IL: Irwin, 1989), 230–231.

Questions

1. Why do you think employees are reacting in this way to the study?
2. How could leaders have handled this situation to get greater cooperation from employees?
3. If you were Ramona Fossett, what would you do now? What would you do to implement any changes recommended by the study?

References

1. Chuck Salter, "On the Road Again," *Fast Company* (January 2002): 50–58.
2. Marlene Piturro, "The Transformation Officer," *Management Review* (February 2000): 21–25.
3. Nicholas Imparato and Oren Harari, "When New Worlds Stir," *Management Review* (October 1994): 22–28.
4. Quoted in *Inc.* (March 1995), 13.
5. Alain Vas, "Top Management Skills In a Context of Endemic Organizational Change: The Case of Belgacom," *Journal of General Management* 27, no. 1 (Autumn 2001): 71–89.
6. Art Kleiner, "Diary of a Change Agent," *Strategy & Business*, Issue 28 (Third Quarter 2002): 18–21
7. The following discussion is based heavily on John P. Kotter, *Leading Change* (Boston: Harvard Business School Press, 1996): 20–25; and "Leading Change: Why Transformation Efforts Fail," *Harvard Business Review* (March–April 1995): 59–67.
8. Scott McCartney, "Clipped Wings: American Airlines to Retrench in Bid to Beat Discount Carriers," *The Wall Street Journal* (August 13, 2002), A1, A8; and Christine Y. Chen, "American Airlines: Blastoff or Bust?" *Fortune* (October 28, 2002), 37.
9. Patrick Flanagan, "The ABCs of Changing Corporate Culture," *Management Review* (July 1995): 57–61.
10. Jeremy Main, "The Shape of the New Corporation," *Working Woman* (October 1998): 60–63.
11. Salter, "On the Road Again."
12. Anna Muoio, "Mint Condition," *Fast Company* (December 1999): 330–348.
13. Kotter, "Leading Change: Why Transformation Efforts Fail," 65.
14. Debra Meyerson, *Tempered Radicals: How People Use Difference to Inspire Change at Work* (Boston: Harvard Business School Press, 2001).
15. These strategies and examples are from Debra E. Meyerson, "Radical Change the Quiet Way," *Harvard Business Review* (October 2001): 92–100.
16. Meyerson, "Radical Change the Quiet Way."
17. Based on Paul Stebel, "Why Do Employees Resist Change?" *Harvard Business Review* (May–June 1996): 86–92.

18. John P. Kotter and Leonard A. Schlesinger, "Choosing Strategies for Change," *Harvard Business Review* (March–April 1979): 106–114.

19. Jonathan Eig, "Hanging On—A Housing Project Falls But the Poor Resist Orders to Move Out," *The Wall Street Journal* (December 19, 2000), A1.

20. Shaul Fox and Yair Amichai-Hamburger, "The Power of Emotional Appeals in Promoting Organizational Change Programs," *Academy of Management Executive* 15, no. 4 (2001): 84–95.

21. Peter Richardson and D. Keith Denton, "Communicating Change," *Human Resource Management* 35, no. 2 (Summer 1996): 203–216.

22. T. J. Larkin and Sandar Larkin, "Reaching and Changing Frontline Employees," *Harvard Business Review* (May–June 1996): 95–104; and Rob Muller, "Training for Change," *Canadian Business Review* (Spring 1995): 16–19.

23. Phillip H. Mirvis, Amy L. Sales, and Edward J. Hackett, "The Implementation and Adoption of New Technology in Organizations: The Impact of Work, People, and Culture," *Human Resource Management* 30 (Spring 1991): 113–139.

24. Robert Goffee and Gareth Jones, "Why Should Anyone Be Led By You?" *Harvard Business Review* (September–October 2000): 63–70.

25. William McKinley, Carol M. Sanchez, and Allen G. Schick, "Organizational Downsizing: Constraining, Cloning, Learning," *Academy of Management Executive* 9, no. 3 (1995): 32–42.

26. Gregory B. Northcraft and Margaret A. Neale, *Organizational Behavior: A Management Challenge*, 2nd ed. (Fort Worth: The Dryden Press, 1994), 626. "Executive Commentary" on McKinley, Sanchez, and Schick, "Organizational Downsizing: Constraining, Cloning, Learning," *Academy of Management Executive* 9, no. 3 (1995): 43–44.

27. James R. Morris, Wayne F. Cascio, and Clifford E. Young, "Downsizing After All These Years: Questions and Answers About Who Did It, How Many Did It, and Who Benefited from It," *Organizational Dynamics* (Winter 1999): 78–86; McKinley, Sanchez, and Schick, "Organizational Downsizing," Stephen Doerflein and James Atsaides, "Corporate Psychology: Making Downsizing Work," *Electrical World* (September–October 1999): 41–43; and Brett C. Luthans and Steven M. Sommer, "The Impact of Downsizing on Workplace Attitudes," *Group and Organization Management* 2, no. 1 (1999): 46–70.

28. K. S. Cameron, S. J. Freeman, and A. K. Mishra, "Downsizing and Redesigning Organizations," in G. P. Huber and W. H. Glick, eds., *Organizational Change and Redesign* (New York: Oxford University Press, 1993): 19–63.

29. This section is based on Bob Nelson, "The Care of the Un-downsized," *Training and Development* (April 1997): 40–43; Shari Caudron, "Teach Downsizing Survivors How to Thrive," *Personnel Journal*, (January 1996): 38ff; Joel Brockner, "Managing the Effects of Layoffs on Survivors," *California Management Review* (Winter 1992): 9–28; Ronald Henkoff, "Getting Beyond

Downsizing," *Fortune* (January 10, 1994): 58–64; Kim S. Cameron, "Strategies for Successful Organizational Downsizing," *Human Resource Management* 33, no. 2 (Summer 1994): 189–211; and Stephen Doerflein and James Atsaides, "Corporate Psychology: Making Downsizing Work."

30. Matt Murray, "Stress Mounts as More Firms Announce Large Layoffs, But Don't Say Who or When" (Your Career Matters column), *The Wall Street Journal* (March 13, 2001), B1, B12.

31. Caudron, "Teach Downsizing Survivors How to Thrive."

32. Stanley S. Gryskiewicz, "Cashing In On Creativity at Work," *Psychology Today* (September–October 2000): 63–66.

33. Timothy A. Matherly and Ronald E. Goldsmith, "The Two Faces of Creativity," *Business Horizons* (September/October 1985): 8.

34. The elements of creative organizations come from Alan G. Robinson and Sam Stern, *Corporate Creativity: How Innovation and Improvement Actually Happen* (San Francisco: Berrett-Koehler, 1997).

35. Sherry Eng, "Hatching Schemes," *The Industry Standard* (November 27–December 4, 2000): 174–175.

36. Paul Kaihla, "Nokia's Hit Factory," *Business 2.0* (August 2002): 66–70.

37. Robinson and Stern, *Corporate Creativity*, 14.

38. Gail Dutton, "Enhancing Creativity," *Management Review* (November 1996): 44–46.

39. Gryskiewicz, "Cashing In On Creativity," and "This House Comes with Built-In Cable," *Best Friends Magazine* (November–December 2003), 5.

40. Cameron M. Ford, "Creativity Is a Mystery: Clues from the Investigators' Notebooks," in Cameron M. Ford and Dennis A. Gioia, eds., *Creative Action in Organizations: Ivory Tower Visions & Real World Voices* (Thousand Oaks, CA: Sage Publications, 1995): 12–49.

41. Gary Abramson, "Wiring the Corporate Brain," *CIO Enterprise*, Section 2 (March 15, 1999): 30–36.

42. Donald F. Kuratko, R. Duane Ireland, and Jeffrey S. Hornsby, "Improving Firm Performance Through Entrepreneurial Actions: Acordia's Corporate Entrepreneurship Strategy," *Academy of Management Executive*, 15, no. 4 (2001): 60–71.

43. Carlos Ghosn, "Saving the Business Without Losing the Company," *Harvard Business Review* (January 2002): 37–45.

44. This section is based on Donald F. Kuratko and Richard M. Hodgetts, *Entrepreneurship: A Contemporary Approach* (Fort Worth: The Dryden Press, 1998): 125–127.

45. Donna Fenn, "The B-School Boys," segment of "Innovative Minds," *Inc.* (September 2002): 76–85.

Index

Name Index

Company Index

Subject Index